"It is a pleasure to commend this series of homiletical commentaries. They fill an enormous vacuum that exists between the practical needs of the pastor/teacher and the critical exegetical depth of most commentaries. With this series, evangelicalism may now claim its own William Barclay. While remaining true to the text and its original meaning, Dr. Hughes helps us face the personal, ethical, theological, and practical questions that the text wants us to answer in the presence of the living God and his illuminating Holy Spirit."

Walter C. Kaiser Jr., President Emeritus and Colman M. Mockler Distinguished Professor Emeritus of Old Testament, Gordon-Conwell Theological Seminary

"The single best resource for faithful biblical exposition available today. A great boon for genuine reformation!"

Timothy George, Founding Dean, Beeson Divinity School, Samford University; General Editor, Reformation Commentary on Scripture

"Throughout the Christian centuries, from Chrysostom and Augustine through Luther, Calvin, and Matthew Henry, to Martyn Lloyd-Jones and Ray Stedman, working pastors have been proving themselves to be the best of all Bible expositors. Kent Hughes stands in this great tradition, and his exciting expositions uphold it worthily."

J. I. Packer, Board of Governors' Professor of Theology, Regent College

"For this outstanding series of expository commentaries, Kent Hughes has assembled a team of unusually gifted scholar-preachers. The series will be widely used and much sought after."

Eric J. Alexander, Retired Senior Minister, St. George's-Tron Parish Church, Glasgow, Scotland

"There is a long history of informed, edifying biblical expositions that have been mightily used of God to shape and strengthen the church. These volumes admirably fit this tradition."

D. A. Carson, Research Professor of New Testament, Trinity Evangelical Divinity School; Cofounder, The Gospel Coalition

"The Preaching the Word commentary series is one of my favorites. The focus upon explaining a text while preaching it as the goal makes the series resonate with the priorities of the pulpit. No academic aloofness here, but down-to-earth, preacher-to-preacher meat for God's people."

Bryan Chapell, Pastor, Grace Presbyterian Church, Peoria, Illinois

"I'm delighted to endorse the philosophy behind this series. Here sounds out the voice not of the scholar in the study but of the scholar in the pulpit. The authors are all able teachers who regularly expound God's living Word to his people. May this rich material give us 'patterns of preaching' that will not only feed the flock, but, by God's grace, change the church."

R. C. Lucas, Retired Rector, St. Helen's Church, Bishopsgate, London, England

1 KINGS

PREACHING THE WORD
Edited by R. Kent Hughes

Genesis | R. Kent Hughes

Exodus | Philip Graham Ryken

Leviticus | Kenneth A. Mathews

Numbers | Iain M. Duguid

Deuteronomy | Ajith Fernando

Joshua | David Jackman

Judges and Ruth | Barry G. Webb

1 Samuel | John Woodhouse

2 Samuel | John Woodhouse

1 Kings | John Woodhouse

Job | Christopher Ash

Psalms, vol. 1 | James Johnston

Proverbs | Raymond C. Ortlund Jr.

Ecclesiastes | Philip Graham Ryken

Song of Solomon | Douglas Sean O'Donnell

Isaiah | Raymond C. Ortlund Jr.

Jeremiah and Lamentations | R. Kent Hughes

Daniel | Rodney D. Stortz

Matthew | Douglas Sean O'Donnell

Mark | R. Kent Hughes

Luke | R. Kent Hughes

John | R. Kent Hughes

Acts | R. Kent Hughes

Romans | R. Kent Hughes

1 Corinthians | Stephen T. Um

2 Corinthians | R. Kent Hughes

Galatians | Todd Wilson

Ephesians | R. Kent Hughes

Philippians, Colossians, and Philemon | R. Kent Hughes

1–2 Thessalonians | James H. Grant Jr.

1–2 Timothy and Titus | R. Kent Hughes and Bryan Chapell

Hebrews | R. Kent Hughes

James | R. Kent Hughes

1–2 Peter and Jude | David R. Helm

1–3 John | David L. Allen

Revelation | James M. Hamilton Jr.

The Sermon on the Mount | R. Kent Hughes

(((PREACHING *the* WORD)))

1 KINGS

POWER, POLITICS,
and the HOPE *of the* WORLD

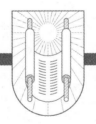

JOHN WOODHOUSE

R. Kent Hughes
Series Editor

WHEATON, ILLINOIS

Library of Congress Cataloging-in-Publication Data

Names: Woodhouse, John, 1949– author.
Title: 1 Kings : power, politics, and the hope of the world / John Woodhouse.
Description: Wheaton : Crossway, 2018. | Series: Preaching the word |
Includes bibliographical references and index.
Identifiers: LCCN 2018021947 (print) | LCCN 2018033743 (ebook) | ISBN 9781433514586 (pdf) |
 ISBN 9781433514593 (mobi) | ISBN 9781433524530 (epub) | ISBN 9781433514579 (hc)
Subjects: LCSH: Bible. Kings,1st—Commentaries.
Classification: LCC BS1335.53 (ebook) | LCC BS1335.53 .W66 2018 (print) | DDC 222/.5307—dc23
LC record available at https://lccn.loc.gov/2018021947

Crossway is a publishing ministry of Good News Publishers.

VP		28	27	26	25	24	23	22	21	20	19	18
13	12	11	10	9	8	7	6	5	4	3	2	1

For
Peter O'Brien
a faithful brother in Christ,
constant friend,
and honored teacher

*Blessed be the L*ORD *your God, who has delighted in you and set you on the throne of Israel! Because the L*ORD *loved Israel forever, he has made you king, that you may execute justice and righteousness.*

1 KINGS 10:9

Behold, something greater than Solomon is here.

MATTHEW 12:42

Contents

A Word to Those Who Preach the Word

There are times when I am preaching that I have especially sensed the pleasure of God. I usually become aware of it through the unnatural silence. The ever-present coughing ceases, and the pews stop creaking, bringing an almost physical quiet to the sanctuary—through which my words sail like arrows. I experience a heightened eloquence, so that the cadence and volume of my voice intensify the truth I am preaching.

There is nothing quite like it—the Holy Spirit filling one's sails, the sense of his pleasure, and the awareness that something is happening among one's hearers. This experience is, of course, not unique, for thousands of preachers have similar experiences, even greater ones.

What has happened when this takes place? How do we account for this sense of his smile? The answer for me has come from the ancient rhetorical categories of *logos*, *ethos*, and *pathos*.

The first reason for his smile is the *logos*—in terms of preaching, God's Word. This means that as we stand before God's people to proclaim his Word, we have done our homework. We have exegeted the passage, mined the significance of its words in their context, and applied sound hermeneutical principles in interpreting the text so that we understand what its words meant to its hearers. And it means that we have labored long until we can express in a sentence what the theme of the text is—so that our outline springs from the text. Then our preparation will be such that as we preach, we will not be preaching our own thoughts about God's Word, but God's actual Word, his logos. This is fundamental to pleasing him in preaching.

The second element in knowing God's smile in preaching is *ethos*—what you are as a person. There is a danger endemic to preaching, which is having your hands and heart cauterized by holy things. Phillips Brooks illustrated it by the analogy of a train conductor who comes to believe that he has been to the places he announces because of his long and loud heralding of them. And that is why Brooks insisted that preaching must be "the bringing of truth through personality." Though we can never perfectly embody the truth we preach, we must be subject to it, long for it, and make it as much a part of our ethos as possible. As the Puritan William Ames said, "Next to the Scriptures, nothing makes a sermon more to pierce, than when it comes out of the inward affection of the heart without any affectation." When a preacher's ethos backs up his logos, there will be the pleasure of God.

Last, there is *pathos*—personal passion and conviction. David Hume, the Scottish philosopher and skeptic, was once challenged as he was seen going to hear George Whitefield preach: "I thought you do not believe in the gospel." Hume replied, "I don't, but he does." Just so! When a preacher believes what he preaches, there will be passion. And this belief and requisite passion will know the smile of God.

The pleasure of God is a matter of *logos* (the Word), *ethos* (what you are), and *pathos* (your passion). As you preach the Word may you experience his smile—the Holy Spirit in your sails!

R. Kent Hughes

Preface

I have often found myself thinking that the book of the Bible I happen to be reading, studying, or teaching at the time is the most important and brilliant book of all. The Bible is like that. Every part makes its own magnificent contribution to the powerful truth given to us in the Scriptures.

It has happened again. The book of 1 Kings has taken my breath away (an experience I am glad to share with the Queen of Sheba, 10:5). It takes us to the highest point of the Old Testament story in the astonishing, glorious kingdom of Solomon and then plunges us to the dismal depths of the reign of King Ahab. In all this our appreciation of the One greater than Solomon is profoundly enriched.

First Kings has its share of drama, but we find a different pace from 1 and 2 Samuel. Those earlier books, which set the scene for 1 Kings, were dominated by the stories of Israel's first two kings, Saul and David. First Kings tells the story of no less than fourteen kings, with most attention given to David's son Solomon at the beginning of the book and Omri's son Ahab at the end.

I have found it helpful to divide the text into eight parts, each of which has a distinct theme (see the Contents pages). Preachers who find the whole book daunting might consider several discreet series of expositions, each based on one part of the book.

Each chapter of this commentary attempts to cover a coherent unit of the text that, in my judgment, would be suitable for a particular exposition. The text considered in each chapter varies in length from a few verses to (in one case) more than a chapter. Of course some preachers in some circumstances will very properly choose to cover the text in larger units.

In this expository commentary I have taken the liberty afforded by the written form of dealing with the text in more detail than would be possible in most sermons. The chapters of the exposition therefore vary in length. There are numerous issues that would not normally appear on the surface of a Sunday sermon, but need to be sorted out to ensure an exposition is following what the text actually says. Some of this detail and some consideration of alternative views on particular points may be found in the endnotes.

I wish to express my heartfelt thanks to Kent Hughes for the kind invitation that has led to my latest discovery of the most important and brilliant book in the Bible. Thanks too to the wonderful staff at Crossway for their support and patient encouragement throughout.

John Woodhouse

Abbreviations

ABD	David Noel Freedman, ed., *The Anchor Bible Dictionary*, 6 volumes (New York: Doubleday, 1992)
BDB	Francis Brown, S. R. Driver and Charles Briggs, eds., *A Hebrew and English Lexicon of the Old Testament* (Oxford: Clarendon Press, 1907)
CBQ	*Catholic Biblical Quarterly*
CHALOT	William L. Holladay, *A Concise Hebrew and Aramaic Lexicon of the Old Testament: Based upon the Lexical Work of Ludwig Koehler and Walter Baumgartner* (Leiden: E. J. Brill, 1971)
Currid, *Atlas*	John D. Currid and David P. Barrett, *Crossway ESV Bible Atlas* (Wheaton, IL: Crossway, 2010)
DOTHB	Bill T. Arnold and H. G. M. Williamson, eds., *Dictionary of the Old Testament: Historical Books* (Downers Grove, IL: InterVarsity Press, 2005)
DOTP	T. Desmond Alexander and David W. Baker, eds., *Dictionary of the Old Testament: Pentateuch* (Downers Grove, IL: InterVarsity Press, 2003)
GKC	A. E. Cowley, *Gesenius' Hebrew Grammar as Edited and Enlarged by the Late E. Kautzsch*, Second English Edition (Oxford: Clarendon Press, 1910)
IBD	J. D. Douglas, ed., *The Illustrated Bible Dictionary*, 3 volumes (Leicester, UK and Wheaton, IL: Inter-Varsity Press and Tyndale House, 1980)
IBH	Thomas O. Lambdin, *Introduction to Biblical Hebrew* (London: Darton, Longman and Todd, 1971)
IDB	George Arthur Buttrick, ed., *The Interpreter's Dictionary of the Bible*, 4 volumes (Nashville and New York: Abingdon, 1962)
IDBSup	Keith Crim, ed., *The Interpreter's Dictionary of the Bible*, Supplementary Volume (Nashville and New York: Abingdon, 1976)
JBL	*Journal of Biblical Literature*
JSOT	*Journal for the Study of the Old Testament*
TB	*Tyndale Bulletin*
TDOT	G. Johannes Botterweck, Helmer Ringgren, and Heinz-Josef Fabry, eds., *Theological Dictionary of the Old Testament*, 15 volumes (Grand Rapids, Michigan: Eerdmans, 1974–2006)
VT	*Vetus Testamentum*

Introduction

FOURTEEN KINGS OF ISRAEL
AND "THE KING OF THE JEWS"

1 Kings and John 19:19

The Old Testament book we know as 1 Kings tells the story of fourteen kings who ruled over all or some of the ancient Israelite people from about 961 to 850 B.C.[1] It is reasonable to ask, as we begin to read this record, why should we bother? Unless you belong to the small group of people these days who have an interest in ancient societies and their political ups and downs, why would you be interested in 1 Kings?

There are several answers to that question. One is that "all Scripture is breathed out by God and profitable . . ." (2 Timothy 3:16). If you believe that (and you should), start reading and expect to profit! More particularly, you can expect to profit because 1 Kings belongs to "the sacred writings, which are able to make you *wise for salvation through faith in Christ Jesus*" (2 Timothy 3:15). Read this book to become wise enough to trust in the Lord Jesus Christ and so be saved.

That raises more questions. Particularly, how can the story of monarchs from the ninth and tenth centuries *before* Christ make us "wise for salvation *through faith in Christ Jesus*"?

My hope and prayer for every reader of this book is that as we listen to the story of these kings, our faith in Christ Jesus will be enriched and strengthened. You see, the kings in 1 Kings are part of the great story that has led to *the* King, who was lifted up on a cross to become the Savior of the world (see John 3:14, 15; 4:42; 12:32, 33; 1 John 4:14).

An excellent vantage point from which to see the importance of the story told in 1 Kings is the day of Jesus Christ's execution.[2] On that day the Roman governor of Judea had an inscription placed on the cross on which Jesus was crucified: "Jesus of Nazareth, the King of the Jews" (John 19:19).

I am sure that Pontius Pilate thought this was a stinging insult to the Jewish people whom he despised. For him the inscription was a cruel joke: this miserable victim was their *king*! We are told that the Jewish chief priests (understandably) repudiated the suggestion (John 19:21). For them the inscription was an offensive lie. However, Pilate had unwittingly proclaimed the truth. The frail and fading man on the cross, about to breathe his last, was indeed "The King of the Jews." Furthermore Pilate had unconsciously intimated the significance of this declaration for the whole world by putting his unintentionally prophetic message in the languages of the known world—Aramaic, Latin, and Greek (John 19:20).

The message of "Jesus Christ and him crucified" (1 Corinthians 2:2) is the greatest paradox in the history of the world. It defies all human wisdom. It is also the most profound, powerful, and important truth in the world: it is "the power of God and the wisdom of God" (1 Corinthians 1:24). The man who died on the cross is the Savior of the world.

The crucified one was obviously unlike any king the world has known. In his own words, "My kingdom is not of [or from] this world" (John 18:36). His reign would certainly impact this world, but not in the usual ways of worldly political power.

Pontius Pilate did not understand this, nor did the Jewish religious leaders who had delivered Jesus to the Roman authority and pressed for his execution. On an earlier occasion, in the context of similar failure to understand him, Jesus had said to the Jews who took offense at him, "You search the Scriptures because you think that in them you have eternal life; and it is they that *bear witness about me . . .*" (John 5:39).

"The Scriptures . . . that bear witness about me" (we call them the Old Testament) also illuminate the inscription that was placed over Jesus as he hung on the cross. These Scriptures "bear witness" to Jesus because they promise a king of the Jews[3] who will be the Savior of the world (cf. John 4:42)![4]

It is difficult to overstate the significance of this promise. According to the promise, this king will bring to fulfillment God's wonderful purposes for his whole creation (see, for example, Isaiah 11:1–9). These purposes are summed up at the beginning of the Old Testament in the word "blessed" (see Genesis 1:22, 28; 2:3). God's promise to Abraham, very early in the Old Testament story, was that "blessing" will reach "all the families of the earth" through Abraham and his "offspring" (see Genesis 12:1–3, 7; 13:15, 16; 15:5; 17:7, 8). The Old Testament then records the history of God's faithfulness to this promise. The "offspring" of Abraham became the nation of Israel—by New Testament times called "the Jews."[5] In the course of this history God's promise was repeatedly reaffirmed in ways that clarified its terms. In particular, the promise came to focus on a king (see Genesis 35:11; 49:10; 1 Samuel 2:10) whose kingdom God will establish "forever" (2 Samuel 7:16).

The notice on the cross of Jesus, if we see it *in the light of these Scriptures*, is breathtaking: "Jesus of Nazareth, the King of the Jews." The one who died on that cross, despised and rejected by his own people (John 1:11), was the one who had been promised in these Scriptures. He is the hope of the world.

The book of 1 Kings tells the story of fourteen kings of the Jews, framed by King Solomon (chapters 1—11), arguably the greatest of them all, and King Ahab (16:29—22:40), certainly the worst of them all (so far). It is a story of power and politics in which we will learn many interesting and important things. By far the most important is the wonder of the extraordinary inscription that Pontius Pilate put on the cross when seen in the light of these Scriptures. The story of these kings will (as Jesus put it) "bear witness about me." Our task is to listen carefully to this testimony.

Part 1

POLITICS OR
PROMISE?

How the Kingdom Was Established

1 Kings 1—2

1

A Frail and Fading King: What Hope Can There Be?

1 KINGS 1:1–4

FIRST KINGS IS A REMARKABLE STORY of power and politics. We will read of the rise and fall of kings, of political intrigue, violence, betrayal, power deployed for good and for evil. We will see an empire established and prospering. We will see the same empire collapse in ruins. It is a story of striking accomplishments and devastating failures. In all this it is much like any slice of human history.

But there is more. This is the story of God's purpose for human history. It is a story intended to teach us to see human power and politics for what they really are, to understand that the world will not be saved by human muscle and planning. There is hope for this troubled world, but we need to know that the best efforts of men and women will achieve little, and even what is accomplished will not last.

The opening scene of 1 Kings is confronting. It is a pathetic picture of weakness and vulnerability:

> Now King David was old and advanced in years. And although they covered him with clothes, he could not get warm. (v. 1)

Great King David—the Sequel (v. 1a)

"Now King David . . ."[1] (v. 1a). The first words of 1 Kings signal that what we are about to read is the continuation of the story of King David's life that has been the subject of the two preceding books, 1 and 2 Samuel. David first appeared in 1 Samuel 16, the youngest son of Jesse of Bethlehem. David's tumultuous journey to become Israel's great king (in 2 Samuel 5:1–5) is told in one of the world's finest pieces of narrative literature. It is not our task here to rehearse that marvelous story, but the reader of 1 Kings is expected to know at least two critical things about King David.

The Man after God's Own Heart

The first is that David had been chosen by God to be king over God's people, Israel. He was the man on whom God set his heart to be a king "for myself," as the Lord said to the prophet Samuel (see 1 Samuel 13:14; 16:1).

Hannah's prophetic prayer at the beginning of 1 Samuel had anticipated this:

> The adversaries of the LORD shall be broken to pieces;
>   against them he will thunder in heaven.
> The LORD will judge the ends of the earth;
>   he will give strength to his king
>   and exalt the horn of his anointed. (1 Samuel 2:10)

It was David who became "his king," "his anointed." The Lord exalted David and his kingdom (2 Samuel 5:10, 12) and by him crushed the enemies of his people (see, for example, 2 Samuel 8). David became a great and good king who did "justice and righteousness for all his people" (2 Samuel 8:15, AT).

However, as Hannah's prayer suggested, God's purpose in choosing David was greater than anything that happened in David's lifetime ("The LORD will judge *the ends of the earth*"). This was made clear in God's momentous promise to David recorded in 2 Samuel 7:

> When your days are fulfilled and you lie down with your fathers, I will raise up your offspring after you, who shall come from your body, and I will establish his kingdom. He shall build a house for my name, and I will establish the throne of his kingdom forever. I will be to him a father, and he shall be to me a son. When he commits iniquity, I will discipline him with the rod of men, with the stripes of the sons of men, but my steadfast love will not depart from him, as I took it from Saul, whom I put away from before you. And your house and your kingdom shall be made sure forever before me. Your throne shall be established forever. (vv. 12–16)

As we begin to read 1 Kings, nothing is more important than keeping in mind this promise. We will see that the words almost provide a Table of Contents for much of 1 Kings.[2] They are a sure guide to the meaning and significance of the history that 1 Kings recounts, as each part of this promise becomes historical reality.

Therefore as we see King David "old and advanced in years" (v. 1), we should remember the promise that began, "When your days are fulfilled . . ." (2 Samuel 7:12).[3] There is more here than a shivering old man huddled under his blankets. This man was God's king, and these were the days spoken of in the promise that his kingdom will be established forever.

The Man Who Sinned against the Lord

The second thing about David that all readers of 1 Kings must remember is the alarming turn his story took when David committed adultery with Bathsheba and arranged for the murder of her husband, Uriah (2 Samuel 11). David, the great and good king, showed himself capable of disastrous foolishness and terrible wickedness. The consequences were dreadful. His family was wracked with violence (see the horror of Amnon's David-like behavior in 2 Samuel 13), and he almost lost the kingdom to his rebellious, fratricidal son Absalom (2 Samuel 15—19). These developments raised serious questions about how God's promise to David could ever be fulfilled. David himself was greatly diminished by his failures, and his sons (certainly if we look at Amnon and Absalom) were no better.

Remarkably the Lord did not withdraw his promise to David. Earlier the Lord had rejected Saul because Saul had rejected the word of the Lord (1 Samuel 15:23, 26). The Lord treated David differently. The difference was made clear in the promise concerning David's son:

> When he commits iniquity, I will discipline him with the rod of men, with the stripes of the sons of men, but my steadfast love will not depart from him, as I took it from Saul, whom I put away from before you. (2 Samuel 7:14b, 15).

While this promise focused on David's future son, it was reflected in David's own experience. Terrible consequences flowed from David's wickedness. He was disciplined with the rod of men (2 Samuel 13—20). However, when he acknowledged his evil deeds ("I have sinned against the Lord," 2 Samuel 12:13a), he heard from Nathan the prophet the astonishing words, "The Lord also has put away your sin" (2 Samuel 12:13b). The Lord's steadfast love did not depart from him.

This meant that David could sing the Lord's praises in these terms:

> Great salvation he brings to his king,
>   and shows steadfast love to his anointed,
>   to David and his offspring forever. (2 Samuel 22:51)

However, 1 Kings begins with a scene that makes us wonder whether, after all, we are near the end of the story of David and his great kingdom. There is little to be seen here of the greatness or goodness of King David.

Great King David—Now Frail and Fading (vv. 1–4)

With these things in mind, let's look more closely at the strange scene with which our book begins.[4] The full royal title ("King David" in v. 1) and the six references to him as "the king" in verses 1–4 remind us of who this man had been. What we now see, however, is his frail and feeble condition.[5]

King David's Frailty (v. 1)

"Now King David was old and advanced in years" (v. 1a). He was now about seventy years old (see 2 Samuel 5:4; 1 Kings 2:11), but rather less sprightly than some seventy-year-olds I know. He was bedridden and appears to have been suffering from advanced arteriosclerosis.[6] "Although they covered him with clothes, he could not get warm" (v. 1b).

It has been suggested (encouraged, no doubt, by the way this scene plays out in vv. 2–4) that the king's inability to "get warm" is really a rather polite way of saying that he was sexually impotent,[7] in a world in which "the authority and even the life of the king depends on his virility."[8] This reads too much into verse 1 and makes the all too common mistake of interpreting the Bible in the light of a supposed background for which the Bible itself gives no evidence.[9] The king's problem here was one that extra blankets[10] should have solved but didn't. The old man was cold! The once great king, now weak and infirm, was a shivering shadow of the mighty ruler he had been.

A Pathetic Plan (vv. 2, 3)

> Therefore his servants said to him, "Let a young woman be sought for my[11] lord the king, and let her wait on the king and be in his service. Let her lie in your[12] arms, that my lord the king may be warm." (v. 2)

The king's servants[13] wanted to help their quivering king. They suggested a rather surprising plan to help raise David's temperature. For three reasons it is difficult to avoid the sexual overtones of their proposal.[14]

First, the Hebrew phrase translated "a young woman" (sometimes rendered "a young virgin"[15]) almost certainly has a sexual nuance here. In Hebrew a word is used that indicates the young woman was to be "sexually mature, of marriageable age."[16]

Second, if the requirement is that this young woman should be sexually mature, the otherwise innocent expression "let her wait on the king and be in his service"[17] sounds like an understatement. She was to be more than his nurse.[18]

Third, the "more" is clarified with the words, "Let her lie in your arms" (literally "in your bosom," ESV margin). While there is still some appropriate indirectness in this expression (it does not *necessarily* mean what it seems to mean here), the proposal of the king's servants is clear enough. Indeed they used exactly the same expression as Nathan in his devastating parable about David and Bathsheba (2 Samuel 12:3; cf. v. 8)![19]

Here was the servants' plan to revitalize their frail old king. They knew David's reputation. A beautiful young woman in his bed would surely "warm my lord the king"![20] I think I can see a nudge and a wink as the idea was put forward.

But it was a pathetic plan. There is more than a hint of denial. Pretending to be young again will not reverse advancing age and diminishing capacities. Aging men (and aging women), take note. Furthermore it was a wicked plan. The idea of the king taking a young woman into his bed for the purpose of arousing his fading vitality should shock us.[21] It is all too reminiscent of the day David took Bathsheba and lay with her for his own selfish purposes (2 Samuel 11:4).[22]

> So they sought for a beautiful young woman throughout all the territory of Israel, and found Abishag the Shunammite, and brought her to the king. (v. 3)

Verse 3 indicates (without saying so) that King David agreed to the plan. At least he did not object. If the plan was pathetic and wicked, what does that tell us about David?

The search was undertaken (presumably in the name of the king) "throughout all the territory of Israel" to find the most "beautiful young woman" in all the land (v. 3a).

It is difficult not to be reminded again that the greatest disaster of David's life had begun when the younger king had spied a "very beautiful" woman from the roof of his palace (2 Samuel 11:2).[23]

The winner of the Miss Israel beauty contest was from the northern town of Shunem.[24] Her name was Abishag.

King David's Frailty (v. 4)

When they brought Abishag to King David's bedroom, we are told that indeed "The young woman was very beautiful" (v. 4a). She did what was expected of

her: "she was of service to the king and attended to him" (v. 4b). This repro-
duces some vocabulary from verse 2, but leaves to the reader's imagination
what she actually did.[25] We are simply told, rather anticlimactically, "but the
king knew her not" (v. 4c)—the well-known Biblical idiom meaning he did
not have sex with her.

Some readers have thought that this last phrase is reassuring, as though
the narrator[26] had said: *Don't get the wrong idea. This was not about sex.
Abishag was just a rather attractive hot water bottle.*[27]

But I don't think so. The last verse of the episode echoes the first. The
bedclothes had failed: "he could not get warm" (v. 1). Now the more audacious
plan had also failed: "the king knew her not" (v. 4). David was too old. He was
too weak. He was too cold. The servants' pathetic plan to arouse the king and
revive his strength had failed. He was simply no longer up to it.[28]

As we prepare to read the story that 1 Kings will tell, think about this
bleak scene: the frail and fading King David, beyond human help, beyond
human hope.

All of us who are permitted to live long enough will experience something
like this. Our strength of body and mind will wane. We will lose our indepen-
dence. Whatever we have been, we will become but a shadow of what we once
were, as David did. And we will know that death is approaching, as it was for
David. Visit a nursing home and spend some time with frail old people. It is
difficult to imagine what they have been and what they have done when they
were young, fit, and healthy. We all find this confronting. None of us likes to
think about this reality, but reality it will be for all of us—unless, of course,
we suffer the even greater tragedy of premature death.

The Bible does not ignore this reality. Looking at King David, near the
end of his life, quivering under his blankets, unresponsive to the beautiful
young woman beside him, we are confronted with human mortality. David
had been one of the greatest and best men to have ever lived. For many years
he had been the one who led Israel to victory over enemies. He had been the
"shepherd of [God's] people Israel" (see 2 Samuel 5:2). But his goodness and
greatness were not only undermined by his wickedness and weakness (as we
have noted)—he grew old, weak, and cold. Human power at its best does not
last long. Nothing human lasts forever. What hope could there be for Israel
when their great king was now so weak that he could not even get warm? What
hope can there be for the world when every human ruler, every human power,
every political system, every scheme to make a better world will sooner or
later fade away—just like King David?

There is more. David had been *God's* king, whose throne, God had promised, "shall be established forever" (2 Samuel 7:16). How is it possible to believe God's promise when we see his chosen king frail and fading away? What would it take for God's promise to be fulfilled?

These are the kind of questions raised by the frail and fading king we see in the opening scene of 1 Kings. Was *this* God's king? Had God really promised that *his* kingdom would be "made sure forever before me" (2 Samuel 7:16)? How can that be?

God's promise to David gives us a clue: "When your days are fulfilled and you lie down with your fathers, I will raise up *your offspring after you* . . . and I will establish *his* kingdom" (2 Samuel 7:12). In our next chapter we will meet one of David's offspring who would very much have liked to be the promised one.

Before we meet Adonijah let us turn our eyes from the day they tried to warm old King David with blankets and a beautiful Shunammite girl to the day, centuries later, when Jesus was hanging on a cross outside the same city in which old David had trembled with cold. Perhaps Jesus was cold. He was thirsty (John 19:28). He was weak. The sign above his head must have seemed like a cruel joke: "JESUS OF NAZARETH, THE KING OF THE JEWS." He was certainly beyond human help. However, even more powerfully than shivering old King David, Jesus on the cross reminds us of the promise of God. Unlike Adonijah, Jesus *was* the promised offspring of David (Matthew 1:1; Romans 1:3; 2 Timothy 2:8). God has now established *his* kingdom forever by raising him from the dead (see Matthew 28:18; Acts 13:32, 33; Romans 1:4; Ephesians 1:19–22). The apparent hopelessness of old King David is like the apparent hopelessness of the crucified Jesus. But in that hopelessness, if we remember God's promise, we see the hope of the world:

> . . . we have seen and testify that the Father has sent his Son to be the Savior of the world. (1 John 4:14)

2

An Up-and-Coming King: "But It Shall Not Be So among You"

1 KINGS 1:5–10

JESUS SAID:

> You know that those who are considered rulers of the Gentiles [nations] lord it over them, and their great ones exercise authority over them. But it shall not be so among you. But whoever would be great among you must be your servant, and whoever would be first among you must be slave of all. For even the Son of Man came not to be served but to serve, and to give his life as a ransom for many. (Mark 10:42–45)

Who do you think he had in mind when he mentioned the "rulers of the nations"? Perhaps it was the Roman authorities of his day. Or was he (as I suspect) thinking of Old Testament Israel's desire to have a king "like all the nations" (1 Samuel 8:5, 20)? He may have had in mind Samuel's devastating critique of the ways of a king like all the nations: "He will take . . . he will take . . . he will take . . ." (1 Samuel 8:10–18).

Jesus said, "But it shall not be so among you."

The ways of God's King are very different from the ways of human politics and power. This is not a lesson that we find easy to learn. Certainly it is very difficult to practice. However, when we see a Christian following Jesus in this regard (seeking not to be served but to serve) we recognize the goodness of it. On the other hand, when we see (as we frequently do) someone behaving like "the rulers of the nations," we can often see the ugliness of it.

As I write these words the newspapers in my part of the world are full of yet another battle between our political leaders. It is ugly. Power plays, arrogance, selfish ambition, dishonesty, manipulation, suspicion, greed, cynicism, malice, anger, self-righteousness can all be seen (compare Colossians 3:5–11). There is not much compassion, kindness, humility, meekness, patience, trust, love, or forgiveness on display (compare Colossians 3:12, 13).

In Christian circles such conflicts are usually (although not always, I regret to say) more refined. But even among us it is all too easy to think that "church politics" (for want of a better expression) can be conducted along the lines of worldly affairs. It is difficult for those engaged in such things to heed Jesus' words, "It shall not be so among you." Those of us who have been involved in the appointment of Christian leaders or the conduct of Christian organizations have probably found ourselves—at least some of the time— playing power games, thinking more highly of ourselves than we ought, ambitious for ourselves, manipulative, showing partiality or even malice, and being less than openly honest. We may justify ourselves with some kind of end-justifying-means thinking, but the words of Jesus call us to account: "It shall not be so among you."

One of the outstanding aspects of the story of King David is that his elevation to the throne of Israel was remarkably Christlike. In the story from 1 Samuel 16 through 2 Samuel 5, David's conduct under severe pressure was exemplary. He did not grasp at power or exalt himself or revile or threaten those who reviled him. He humbly and obediently waited, trusting God (cf. Philippians 2:5–10; 1 Peter 2:23). Many of David's psalms belong to this story (see, for example, Psalms 3, 34, 52, 54, 56, 57, 59, 60, 63, 142, noting the superscriptions[1]). In wonderful ways David foreshadowed the greater Son of David who "came not to be served but to serve."

To appreciate the story of David's life we need to remember two things. The first is that David's goodness and greatness were a consequence of the Lord's kindness toward him. He was the man God had chosen to be his own king (1 Samuel 13:14; 16:1; 2 Samuel 7:21). He was great and good *because* "the LORD was with him" (see 1 Samuel 3:19; 16:18; 18:12, 14; 2 Samuel 5:10). The second thing to remember is that David himself was a flawed human being, capable of shocking wickedness (see 2 Samuel 11, 12). *Only* by the kindness of God could he be the Lord's king (see 2 Samuel 7:14, 15; 12:13; 15:25, 26).

In 1 Kings 1 David had become old. We have seen his frailty and the well-meaning but foolish attempt to rejuvenate the king (1:1–4). The second scene in 1 Kings 1 now takes us out of the old king's bedchamber to see one of David's sons, the vigorous, forceful, assertive, confident Adonijah. He was a complete contrast to his father—in more ways than one.

I have suggested that the key to understanding 1 Kings is the historic promise that the Lord had made concerning David's kingdom:

> "When your days are fulfilled and you lie down with your fathers, I will raise up your offspring after you, who shall come from your body, and I will establish his kingdom." (2 Samuel 7:12)

It is no surprise then that the narrative moves from the fading King David in his final days to one of his sons. Could this be the promised son of David?

The Up-And-Coming King? (v. 5)

Adonijah was David's fourth son (see 2 Samuel 3:2–5). His first, Amnon, had been murdered by his younger half-brother Absalom (2 Samuel 13:23–33). David's second son, Chileab, probably died at a young age, since nothing is recorded about him after the mention of his birth in 2 Samuel 3:3. Absalom was David's third son. He was killed in battle as he attempted to overthrow his father and make himself king (2 Samuel 18:9–15). Adonijah therefore was, at the time of 1 Kings 1, David's oldest surviving son.

These first four of David's sons (and a couple of others) had been born in the early days of David's reign, when he ruled over the tribe of Judah from the town of Hebron (see 2 Samuel 2:1–4; 3:5). Each son had a different mother.[2] They were therefore half-brothers, which contributed to some of the conflicts that arose between them.[3] As Adonijah is reintroduced to the narrative, we are reminded which of David's wives was his mother: "Now Adonijah the son of Haggith . . ." (v. 5a). We know nothing more about Haggith than that she was one of David's wives and the mother of Adonijah. It is more than a little likely, however, that there were tensions between Haggith and other wives of David.[4]

Adonijah has not appeared by name in the story of David's kingdom since his birth notice in 2 Samuel 3:4. However, he was among "all the king's sons" who had witnessed Absalom's murder of Amnon, fled from Absalom in fear for their own lives, and wept with their father at the tragedy (2 Samuel 13:23, 29, 36). He was later among those threatened by Absalom's coup and saved by Joab's execution of Absalom (see 2 Samuel 19:5).

Now he was David's oldest living son, probably about thirty-five years old.[5] The principle of primogeniture had not yet been established in Israel, although it was assumed. Saul had expected his eldest son Jonathan to succeed him (1 Samuel 20:31) unless something exceptional happened, which it did. We are not at all surprised at the narrative turning now to David's oldest surviving son—unless something exceptional happens, which it will.

However, a careful reader of this narrative may have already realized something exceptional about this situation. The promise in 2 Samuel 7:12 spoke of a son who had (at the time of the promise) not yet been born ("who *shall* come from your body"). That cannot be Adonijah. He had been born in Hebron years *before* this promise was given to David in Jerusalem (2 Samuel 3:4).

His Thoughts (v. 5a)

The first thing we are told about this son of David is that he "exalted himself" (v. 5a). Already there is dissonance with the promise, "*I* will raise up your offspring" (2 Samuel 7:12). Furthermore it was *the Lord* who had "exalted" David and his kingdom (2 Samuel 5:12).[6] Adonijah exalted *himself*.

The Hebrew expression suggests that this was Adonijah's habitual disposition.[7] For some time he had had a very high opinion of himself, and he thought that others should share it. We will shortly see a number of factors that contributed to Adonijah's self-esteem problem, but it was a problem of his own making: he exalted *himself*.

These days we hear more about the problem of low self-esteem. Whatever difficulties may arise from a person having a low estimate of himself or herself, that was not Adonijah's problem. Indeed, I wonder whether these days we would recognize that Adonijah had a problem at all. He was self-confident, assertive, assured of his own worth and importance. Aren't those the qualities needed to get on in this world? Indeed, aren't they the qualities we look for in our leaders?

Jesus said, "It shall not be so among you."

His Words (v. 5b)

Adonijah's thoughts about himself were put into words: "I will be king" (v. 5b). Again the Hebrew has an emphasis we can miss in translation: "*I* am the one—I am the only one—who will be king."[8]

We do not know whether these were words spoken to others[9] or only to himself.[10] We will shortly be reminded that Adonijah's expectation to become the next king was apparently reasonable. He was, after all, the oldest son of the old king. He had a right to the throne. He was the obvious candidate. We might say (I'm sure he would say), he was *entitled*.

There was excitement in his words. He was thrilled at the prospect: "I will be king!" Adonijah *so wanted* to be king. The emphasis (again from a subtlety of the Hebrew) is more on the active exercise of royal power than simply the status of the position.[11] Adonijah was elated at the prospect of being the one who wielded the power of the king.

Once again I wonder whether these days we would recognize any problem in Adonijah's ambition. It is generally seen as a virtue when an aspirant for high office has a hunger for the job.[12] Whatever wisdom there may be in that perception, do you think that the words of Jesus might suggest a better way? "It shall not be so among you."

Adonijah's eagerness to *become* king should remind us of that day many years earlier when the elders of Israel demanded to be *given* a king because they wanted to be "like all the nations," and Samuel warned them about the kind of king that the nations had. I have no doubt that Adonijah wanted to be *that* kind of king. The person who exalts himself and grasps for power will be like "the rulers of the nations" of whom Jesus spoke. However, "It shall not be so among you."

His Conduct (v. 5c)

Adonijah's thoughts and words found expression in his public conduct: "And he prepared for himself chariots and horsemen [horses], and fifty men to run before him" (v. 5c).

If you think you have heard something like this before, it probably means that you have read 1 and 2 Samuel (as I hope you have). Adonijah was doing what his older brother Absalom had done as well as what Samuel had warned a king "like the nations" would do. Indeed there seems to be a deliberate echo of the historian's earlier descriptions of these activities. Compare the three descriptions:

"[Adonijah] prepared for himself	"Absalom prepared for himself	"[a king] will take your sons and appoint them for himself
chariots[13]	a chariot	to his chariot
and horses,[14]	and horses,	and his horses
and fifty men to run before him." (1 Kings 1:5c, AT)	and fifty men to run before him." (2 Samuel 15:1, AT)	and to run before his chariot." (1 Samuel 8:11, AT)

Adonijah (like Absalom before him[15]) adopted the trappings of status and power "like the nations."[16] He made himself *look* powerful and important, and he loved it.

Beware of the trappings of positions of prominence, whether ecclesiastical or secular (see Luke 20:46). Be especially careful of those who love such things. That is what Adonijah was like. Again let the words of Jesus ring in your ears: "It shall not be so among you."

The Persuasiveness of His Self-Portrayal (v. 6)

Mind you, Adonijah's self-promoting behavior was not entirely surprising. In verse 6 we are informed of three factors that must have contributed to his sense of self-importance and to the persuasiveness of his self-portrayal.

His Father's Favor (v. 6a)

The first was something his father did not do: "His father had never at any time displeased him by asking, 'Why have you done thus and so?'" (v. 6a). This rather telling comment on David's indulgent treatment of his son is consistent with the king's dealings with his two older sons. When Amnon raped Tamar we read that David was "very angry" (2 Samuel 13:21), but he did nothing.[17] David's grief over the death of Absalom was seen, at least by Joab, to be excessive and improperly overlooked the boy's violent crimes (2 Samuel 19:5–7). David was a passive father. The problem was not anything he did, but what he did not do.

Parents who love their children (as David certainly did) understand how difficult it can be to deal firmly with unacceptable behavior. Some (like David) try to avoid conflict. They do not set or enforce boundaries for their children. It is hardly surprising when these children grow up without valuing self-control, but rather with a sense of entitlement to whatever they want. Children spared the experience of frustration in their younger days will not be well equipped to deal with reality. This is a failure of parental love.

However, David's passivity toward Adonijah was not just an example of poor parenting, although it was that. The focus here is on David's failure to challenge his son's self-promotion, which could easily be understood as the king's endorsement of the lad's ambition. David's silence would have been an encouragement to Adonijah and to anyone inclined to support him.

His Attractive Presence (v. 6b)

Furthermore, Adonijah "was also[18] a very handsome man" (v. 6b). Israelite society shared with our world an attraction to beautiful people. Absalom had also been a beautiful young man. "Now in all Israel there was no one so much to be praised for his handsome appearance as Absalom" (2 Samuel 14:25). We can be sure that Adonijah, like his older brother, was very conscious of his good looks (see 2 Samuel 14:26). I can imagine him with a regular exercise regime, not so much for fitness, but to *look* good. I am sure his clothes mattered a lot to him: he had to show off his magnificence. Also like Absalom before him, Adonijah's good looks contributed to both his self-confidence and his popularity.

The Bible is generally cautious about the value of such external appearances. It is not that there is any virtue in ugliness. The Bible writer seems positive about the good looks of David (see 1 Samuel 16:12).[19] However, appearances can powerfully deceive. Saul was "a handsome young man. There was not a man among the people of Israel more handsome than he" (1 Samuel 9:2). And yet Saul was a disaster. Absalom's beauty hid a violent, rebellious character (the story is told in 2 Samuel 13—18). The mention of Adonijah's appearance (literally "very good of form"[20]) at this point, with its reminders of Absalom and Saul, is not encouraging.

His Privileged Place (v. 6c)

The third factor contributing to Adonijah's sense of importance was his privileged position: "he was born next after Absalom" (v. 6c). He was, as we have noted, the oldest surviving son of the king. He had every right (one might think) to say, "I will be king."

These three factors seem to represent Adonijah's perspective on himself. His father approved of him (since he never disapproved). He was stunning to look at. And he was entitled.

There follows a brief account of Adonijah's strategic moves to obtain what he longed for and considered his right. It is a striking instance of the ways human beings typically pursue power. Adonijah could have written the manual for becoming a great one like "the rulers of the nations."

Four Steps to Self-Exaltation (vv. 7–10)

Step 1: Garner Support (v. 7)

Step One involved talking to the right people and getting them on your side. These days we call it networking. Adonijah targeted two key individuals whose support would greatly strengthen him and who, for different reasons, he may have expected to be sympathetic to his cause.

Joab (v. 7a)

"He conferred with Joab the son of Zeruiah" (v. 7a).[21] David's nephew, Joab, had been David's powerful military commander (2 Samuel 8:16). Like his brothers Abishai and Asahel, Joab was fiercely loyal to David and his kingdom, but often considered that he knew better than David, and did not hesitate in such circumstances to take matters into his own hands.[22] After one such incident (when Joab and Abishai had killed Abner, Saul's old commander, although David had wanted to make peace with him), David said, "These men, the sons of Zeruiah, are more severe than I. The LORD repay the evildoer according to his wickedness!" (2 Samuel 3:39; also v. 29). There is little doubt who David regarded as "the evildoer."[23] It was Joab.

More recently Joab had been responsible for the death of Absalom, directly contrary to David's orders (see 2 Samuel 18:5, 14). In an astonishing move David appointed Amasa as commander in place of Joab. Amasa was the man Absalom had made commander of his rebel army (see 2 Samuel 17:25; 19:13). Joab dealt with this difficulty by killing Amasa (2 Samuel 20:1–10) and taking control again. We are given the clear impression that in the end Joab was still loyal to David's kingdom, but the relationship with David himself had become difficult, to say the least (see 2:5–6).

Adonijah was astute in conferring with Joab. Joab was a very powerful man in Jerusalem, and he was unlikely to wait around for David's approval. If Joab was convinced that Adonijah was the right man to succeed David, he could certainly help it happen.

Abiathar (v. 7b, c)

". . . and with Abiathar the priest" (v. 7b). Adonijah was not a fool. He wanted not only the power of Joab on his side, but also the legitimacy of Abiathar the priest.

Abiathar was the son of Ahimelech, grandson of Ahitub (1 Samuel 22:20), great-grandson of Phinehas, and great-great-grandson of Eli (1 Samuel 14:3). This family line will be important in due course because many years earlier "a man of God" had pronounced God's judgment on the household of Eli for the wicked corruption of Eli's sons, Hophni and Phineas (1 Samuel 2:27–36).[24] It is important to remember this prophecy. Events to be recounted shortly must be understood in its light (2:27).

The prophesied judgment had unfolded over time. First, Eli and his sons died on the same day (1 Samuel 2:34; 4:11, 18). Years later in the days of Saul, descendants of Eli, including his great-grandson Ahimelech, were massacred at Nob (1 Samuel 22:1–19). The prophecy had anticipated that there would be one survivor ("the only one of you whom I shall not cut off from my altar," 1 Samuel 2:33). The survivor was Abiathar (1 Samuel 22:20). He found safety with David (1 Samuel 22:23), served David faithfully through the difficult days on the run from Saul (1 Samuel 23:6, 9; 30:7; see 2 Samuel 8:17), and played an important role in saving David from Absalom's attempted coup (2 Samuel 15:24, 29, 35; 17:15; 19:11; 20:25).

Why did Adonijah think that his ambitions would find encouragement from Abiathar? We are not told. Some have suggested that Joab and Abiathar represented the older and more conservative elements in Jerusalem, having been with David since the very early days.[25] Did Adonijah, who had been born in the early days of David's kingship in Hebron and who was after all the oldest son still living, perhaps expect the support of the conservative old guard, especially against any new and unconventional ideas that may have been emerging in Jerusalem (about which we will hear more in due course)?

Furthermore, since the move of David's base from Hebron to Jerusalem a new leading priest had emerged. This was Zadok (2 Samuel 8:17), about whom we will hear more shortly. Was the tension between old and new expressed in some rivalry or resentment between Abiathar and Zadok? Was this something that Adonijah thought he could exploit to his own advantage?

We do not know the answers to these questions, but they point to the complexity of the relationships in Jerusalem. We are left with the fact that for some reason Adonijah chose to approach Joab and Abiathar. It proved to be a masterstroke: "And they followed Adonijah and helped him" (v. 7c).

At least it looked like a masterstroke. The prophecy in the days of Eli had said, "The only one of you whom I shall not cut off from my altar shall be spared *to weep his eyes out to grieve his heart, and all the descendants of your house shall die by the sword of men*" (1 Samuel 2:33). We do not know how widely this prophecy was known. I doubt that it was a factor in Adonijah's thinking, but Abiathar may have known about it. If so I am sure he did not realize that his decision to support Adonijah would become a critical factor in the fulfillment of this devastating prophecy (as we will see).

Step 2: Identify Opposition (v. 8)

Step Two in Adonijah's plan to make himself great involved identifying the opposition. Verse 8 tells us of a number of people who "were not with Adonijah." This must at least mean that they did not approve of his public displays of pomp (v. 5c) and the aspirations they expressed.

Zadok (v. 8a)

The first of these was "Zadok the priest" (v. 8a). While there has been speculation about the identity of Zadok (much of which disregards some Biblical evidence[26]), the available information indicates that he was a descendant of Aaron's third son, Eleazar, while Abiathar was a descendant of Aaron's fourth son, Ithamar (1 Chronicles 24:3).[27]

Zadok came to prominence after David had taken up residence in Jerusalem (he first appears in the history in 2 Samuel 8:17). He became (with Abiathar) one of the two leading priests in David's kingdom.

With the wisdom of hindsight we can see that the old prophecy from the days of Eli pointed to Zadok: "And I will raise up for myself a faithful priest, who shall do according to what is in my heart and in my mind. And I will build him a sure house, and he shall go in and out before my anointed forever" (1 Samuel 2:35). The house of Zadok was to replace the house of Eli.

If Abiathar suspected this, then some tension between the two priests would be understandable. All we are told here is that Zadok was "not with Adonijah." In this he would prove to be on the right side of history.

Benaiah (v. 8b)

"Benaiah the son of Jehoiada" (v. 8b) was also "not with Adonijah." Benaiah was another man who came into the story of David's kingdom after David had taken Jerusalem. He was a commander alongside Joab, with responsibility for "the Cherethites and the Pelethites"[28] (2 Samuel 8:18; 20:23), and apparently David's personal bodyguard (2 Samuel 23:23). He was one of David's mighty men who had won a name for great feats in war (2 Samuel 23:20–23).

NATHAN (v. 8c)

More important than Zadok the priest and Benaiah the soldier was "Nathan the prophet" (v. 8c). He, too, was "not with Adonijah."

The mention of Nathan (for the first time in this story since 2 Samuel 12) reminds us of the three very significant moments in David's story in which Nathan played a crucial role.

The first was the promise of 2 Samuel 7. It was Nathan who spoke those words of the Lord to David (2 Samuel 7:17). According to this promise a son of David, yet to be born at the time of the promise, would become the king whose kingdom would be established forever by the Lord. That is one reason that Nathan may have been "not with Adonijah."

Second, it was Nathan who brought David to his senses after the Bathsheba/Uriah affair. The Lord sent Nathan to David, and Nathan delivered to David the Lord's severe rebuke for what he had done (2 Samuel 12:1–12).

When David confessed his sin, it was Nathan who told him, "The LORD also has put away your sin; you shall not die" (2 Samuel 12:13).

Third, when Bathsheba bore a son to David (after the first son had died), it was Nathan who brought word that this boy was loved by the Lord. For this reason Solomon was also given the name Jedidiah ("beloved of the LORD," 2 Samuel 12:24, 25). In the light of the great 2 Samuel 7 promise, it is difficult to miss the implication that Solomon was the one the Lord had promised to raise up after David. This was almost certainly behind Nathan's being "not with Adonijah."

Shimei and Rei (v. 8d)

Two other nonsupporters of Adonijah are mentioned by name: "Shimei and Rei" (v. 8d). This Shimei was almost certainly not the son of Gera who had appeared in David's story previously (2 Samuel 16:5–14; 19:16–23) and who will tragically appear again (1 Kings 2:8, 9, 36–46).[29] He may have been the son of Ela who would serve as an official in Solomon's kingdom (1 Kings 4:18). Rei is otherwise unknown to us.[30]

David's Mighty Men (v. 8e)

It remains to mention one other significant group who were "not with Adonijah." They were "David's mighty men" (v. 8e). These great heroes of David's many conflicts were celebrated in 2 Samuel 23:8–39. Interestingly in that catalog of names and accomplishments, Joab was not included.

The fact that these great ones, as well as Benaiah, "were not with Adonijah" would have been a significant obstacle to Adonijah's hopes. Something would need to be done to ensure that support for Adonijah somehow counterbalanced the nonsupport.

Step 3: Consolidate Support (v. 9)

This was Step Three in Adonijah's strategy. Strictly speaking verses 5–8 have been background to the action that begins in verse 9.[31]

What He Did (v. 9a)

"Adonijah sacrificed[32] sheep, oxen, and fattened cattle" (v. 9a). Since we have already been clearly reminded of how Adonijah was thinking, acting and even looking like his older brother, this feast should remind us of Absalom's great get-together at Hebron when he arranged to have himself declared king (2 Samuel 15:7–12). We are not told that Adonijah went that far, but we will soon hear that Nathan believed he had (1:11, 12).

Where He Did It (v. 9b)

The location of Adonijah's big event was "by the Serpent's Stone, which is beside En-rogel" (v. 9b). En-rogel was about 300 yards south of Jerusalem, near where the north-south Kidron Valley east of Jerusalem meets the west-east Hinnom Valley south of the city.[33] The somewhat secluded location suggests the clandestine character of this gathering.[34] En-rogel had earlier been chosen for a rather different covert operation (2 Samuel 17:17).

The more particular setting for the meeting sounds ominous (ESV, "by the Serpent's Stone"), but may have been simply a known rockslide in the vicinity (JB, "the Sliding Stone"[35]).

Who He Included (v. 9c)

The guest list for Adonijah's supporters' function included "all his brothers, the king's sons, and all the royal officials of Judah" (v. 9c).

That is not quite accurate. As with much of this passage, the wording tends to give us Adonijah's view of things. Perhaps we could say that he invited all the king's sons whom he regarded as his "brothers." One, as we will see in the next verse, was not included.

Inviting the king's sons to a big feast the purpose of which was not entirely open must remind us again of Absalom. The thought is ominous (see 2 Samuel 13:23–29).

"All the royal officials of Judah" is more literally "all the men of Judah, the servants of the king." Did this include "his servants" (1:2) who had recently witnessed the sorry condition of the old king? If so, what a contrast the vigorous, self-confident Adonijah must have made![36]

No details are given of what happened at the Serpent's Stone/Sliding Rock. Clearly, however, Adonijah was drawing around him those he hoped would support his ambitions. He had "exalted himself" (v. 5). He wanted others to exalt him too.

Step 4: Isolate Opposition (v. 10)

Step Four was to keep those who would not be supportive away. The ambitious man did not want to hear from anyone who was not likely to endorse his aspirations. We may reasonably assume that none of those mentioned in verse 8 were invited. Verse 10 mentions some of those but adds a significant new name.

"But he did not invite Nathan the prophet . . ." (v. 10a). Of course he didn't. What Nathan stood for was not what Adonijah's party was about.

". . . or Benaiah" (v. 10b). Adonijah had Joab on his side. He did not need Benaiah, nor did he want him. Benaiah was not a known supporter. Certainly he did not invite "the mighty men" (v. 10c). It could have been dangerous for Adonijah's unfolding plans to be known to such a powerful group, who were known to be nonsupporters.

Of the nonsupporters of Adonijah listed in verse 8, Zadok, Shimei, and Rei are not mentioned in verse 10. But we can be sure they, too, were not invited. Those who were not expected to back Adonijah were not welcome.

The final excluded name mentioned is explosive: ". . . or Solomon his brother" (v. 10d). There was this one exception to "all his brothers" in verse 9. We are not told in so many words why Solomon was not invited. Possibly some difficulty in the relationship between the two accounted for Adonijah's exclusion of Solomon. However, we, the readers of this history, know that the difference between Solomon and Adonijah was simply that Solomon was the one the Lord had set his heart upon (2 Samuel 12:24, 25), just as he had set his heart on David (1 Samuel 13:14). Consciously or unconsciously, Adonijah's ambitions could only survive if he kept the one chosen by the Lord out of his life.

Adonijah was the very opposite of what his father David had been as the Lord exalted him and made him king. Consider the portrait of Adonijah we have seen: his high opinion of himself; his aspiration to be important; his love of *displaying* his own importance; his gathering of like-minded people around him; his avoidance of those who did not share his view of himself.

Hear Jesus' call: "But it shall not be so among you. For even the Son of Man came not to be served but to serve, and to give his life as a ransom for many." This is as important as anything that a leader among God's people needs to hear.

3

The Right Side of History

1 KINGS 1:11–40

DO YOU SOMETIMES WONDER whether Christians are on the right side of history? Many, of course, are convinced that we are not. There is widespread rejection of the Christian faith in western societies, which in recent times (as I write this) have become emphatically hostile and convinced that Christianity is a thing of the past. Do you sometimes think they might be right? Will everyone soon realize that Christian faith is one of those naïve superstitions rightly discarded by enlightened people? Will a time come when the whole world leaves behind the foolishness and ignorance that once enabled Christianity to be influential? Will we all come to see the goodness of being freed from the restrictions and prohibitions of the Christian religion? Will Richard Dawkins and Christopher Hitchens turn out to have been prophetic in their angry attacks on religion in general and Christianity in particular?[1]

Christian faith includes the conviction that the answer to all these questions is no. Many times it has seemed foolish to bank on Jesus Christ. Indeed that is how it all began. When Jesus was crucified, who would think that he actually was "The King of the Jews" (John 19:19), let alone the Savior of the world (John 4:42; 1 John 4:14)? When the message about the crucified King was proclaimed, most people regarded it as offensive or foolish (1 Corinthians 1:23). And yet from the beginning Christians have believed that history will vindicate their faith in the King who died on a cross. That began with his resurrection from the dead (Acts 17:31; Colossians 1:18).

As we face the particular challenges to this conviction in our own day, it is important to understand the strength and depth of the foundation on which it rests. It is not simply the case that those who expected the Christian faith not to last were proven wrong at the beginning[2] and have been proven wrong for 2,000 years. It is even deeper and more solid than that. It goes back long before Jesus.

In about 961 B.C.[3] in the city of Jerusalem the future was uncertain. The great king God had given his people Israel was old and frail (1:1–4). His eldest surviving son was energetic, ambitious, and a bit of a show-off (1:5). He had the support of several powerful people in Jerusalem in his aspiration to become king (1:7). However, it was not obvious to everyone that Adonijah should replace David when the old man died, much less that he should take the reins of power before that. Other influential people in Jerusalem did not support Adonijah's presumption (1:8). The monarchy in Israel was a relatively new institution. Furthermore, Israel was no ordinary nation. David had become their king in a most unusual way. It was not a matter of ambition, pomp, and power. It was certainly not a matter of entitlement. Rather, "David knew that *the LORD* had established him king over Israel, and that he had exalted his kingdom for the sake of his people Israel" (2 Samuel 5:12).

On one particular day Adonijah invited supporters and potential supporters to a feast a short distance from Jerusalem, in a secluded location by the Serpent's (or Sliding) Stone near En-rogel (1:9). It was a by-invitation-only event. Those known *not* to support Adonijah's ambitions were not invited (1:10). What was the purpose of this clandestine assembly?

Somehow one of those who were not invited knew what was going on. He took action that would decisively shape the future and put Adonijah on the wrong side of history. As we follow the course of events that day, we will see:

(1) The secret of being on the right side of history (vv. 11–14)
(2) The danger of being on the right side of history (vv. 15–27)
(3) The assurance of being on the right side of history (vv. 28–37)
(4) The joy of being on the right side of history (vv. 38–40)

The Secret of Being on the Right Side of History (vv. 11–14)

While the covert festivities were underway near En-rogel, back in Jerusalem the man who seized the initiative was Nathan the prophet.

Nathan the Prophet (v. 11a)

We have been reminded twice (1:8, 10) and will be reminded again seven more times in this chapter (1:22, 23, 32, 34, 38, 44, 45), that Nathan was "the prophet." That is how he was described when he first appeared in this history (2 Samuel 7:2). On three momentous occasions in David's life "Nathan the prophet" had played a crucial role. First, it was he who delivered to David the Lord's great promise concerning David's offspring whose kingdom would be established forever (see 2 Samuel 7:12–17). Later it was Nathan who spoke the Lord's severe words of rebuke to David after the king committed adultery with Bathsheba, murdered her husband, and took her to be his wife (2 Samuel 12:7–12). At the same time it was Nathan who astonishingly told David, "The LORD also has put away your sin; you shall not die" (2 Samuel 12:13). Later again it was Nathan who brought a message concerning the Lord's surprising love for the son born to David and Bathsheba and named him Jedidiah ("beloved of the LORD") (2 Samuel 12:25[4]). This son's other name was Solomon.

On each of these occasions it was the Lord who sent Nathan with his message (2 Samuel 7:5; 12:1, 25). That, of course, is why the narrator calls him "Nathan *the prophet*." "Thus says the LORD . . ." was the hallmark of a prophet (2 Samuel 7:5, 8; 12:7, 11).

Nathan has not been mentioned in the story from the day he gave that special name to Solomon until the two references to him indicating that he was among those who were "not with Adonijah" (1:8, 10). This is one of several ways in which the narrator has undermined the legitimate-looking but superficial hopes of Adonijah. Nathan the prophet not being with him is tantamount to saying that the Lord was not with him.[5]

Somehow Nathan learned of the festivities at En-rogel to which he had not been invited. Indeed we will soon see that he seems to have known more about what was going on at En-rogel than we have yet been told. We do not know whether Nathan learned these things from the Lord (a distinct possibility for a prophet[6]) or by some other means. With so many people invited (1:9b) Adonijah's feast was probably not a very well kept secret. Either way everything we know about Nathan suggests that his response to Adonijah's self-promotion will be worth taking seriously.

On an earlier occasion Nathan had taken great care in his approach to the king, ensuring that he elicited the required response (2 Samuel 12:1–6). This time he prudently[7] approached the one person in Jerusalem who could help him deal with the crisis of the day: "Then Nathan said to Bathsheba the mother of Solomon . . ." (v. 11a).

Nathan's Words to Bathsheba (vv. 11b–14)

Bathsheba was one of David's wives.[8] She had direct access to the king. Just as important on this occasion, she was "the mother of Solomon," the only son of David who had not been invited to the Serpent's Stone (1:10). Like Nathan, Bathsheba has not been mentioned in the story of David since the birth of

Solomon (2 Samuel 12:24). The reappearance of both Nathan and Bathsheba at this point in the story is a strong reminder of those unforgettable days.

Nathan's speech to Bathsheba now is surprising, informative (for us as well as for Bathsheba), and very alarming.

Adonijah Is King (v. 11b)

It is not unusual for Biblical narratives to withhold a vital piece of information in order to keep readers in suspense and then to reveal it at a dramatic moment. We were left wondering what the festivities at En-rogel were all about (1:9). The narrator does not tell us directly, but reports what Nathan said to Bathsheba: "Have you not heard that Adonijah the son of Haggith has become king . . . ?" (v. 11b).

Nathan's dramatic news confirms what we may have suspected.[9] The by-invitation-only function at the Serpent's Stone was more significant than we have been told—at least according to Nathan.[10] It was like that fateful day years earlier when another son of David had been declared king (2 Samuel 15:10[11]). Adonijah's older half-brother Absalom had then led a bloody rebellion against David (2 Samuel 15—18; see Psalm 3).

Nathan brought this news to Bathsheba as a rhetorical question.[12] It sounds as though Nathan thought she *should* have heard, but that she obviously had not: "Have you not heard . . . ?"

It may be that Nathan's identification of Adonijah as "the son of Haggith" was pointed as he spoke to "the mother of Solomon." There are enough stories of rivalry between wives of the same man (see 1 Samuel 1) to allow us to suspect that Bathsheba would not be pleased to see the son of one of David's other wives being elevated above her own son.[13] If she had heard, she would surely have done something about it.

David Does Not Know (v. 11c)

Nathan added tellingly, "and David our lord does not know it" (v. 11c).

On the one hand these words signaled the illegitimacy of Adonijah's coronation. Adonijah had become king behind David's back. Far from being a development endorsed by King David, the old king did not even know about it.

On the other hand, at least for the reader of this account, these words remind us of David's frailty which had been indicated earlier with the words, "but the king *knew* her *not*" (1:4). Now Adonijah had become king, and "our lord David *knew not*" (v. 11c, AT[14]). How different old David had become from the king who had once been praised (admittedly ironically) as having "wisdom

like the angel of God to know everything in the land" (2 Samuel 14:20, AT).
Now the once great king was impotent and ignorant of what was going on in
his land.[15]

Danger for Bathsheba and Solomon (v. 12)

The situation was very serious and urgent, particularly for Bathsheba and her
son. Adonijah's claim to be king, if it were to go unchallenged, put their lives
in danger. We saw a hint of this in Adonijah's exclusion of his brother Solomon from the feast (1:10). Why, of all Adonijah's brothers, was Solomon the
only one not invited? It can only be that Adonijah saw Solomon as a threat to
what he intended to do at the Serpent's Stone. He was right about that (as we
will see).

Nathan's purpose in approaching Bathsheba now becomes clear. He intended to advise her on the action she needed to take to avert the danger: "Now
therefore come, let me give you advice, that you may save your own life and
the life of your son Solomon" (v. 12).

The Secret of the Future (v. 13)

This was Nathan's advice:

> Go in at once to King David, and say to him, "Did you[16] not, my lord the
> king, swear to your servant, saying, 'Solomon your son[17] shall reign after
> me, and he[18] shall sit on my throne'? Why then is Adonijah king?" (v. 13)

Nathan believed that an oath David had sworn to Bathsheba, rather than
the ambitious scheming of Adonijah, was the secret of the future. While the
oath had been sworn privately to Bathsheba ("to your servant"), Nathan knew
about it. Perhaps he had been present. Indeed the oath may have been sworn in
the context of 2 Samuel 12:24, 25. It is also possible that Nathan the prophet
had learned about the oath from the Lord. Either way Nathan knew about this
oath and understood that the future of the kingdom now depended on it.

The problem for readers of this story is that this oath has not been mentioned previously. This has led some commentators to conclude that Nathan
was making it up.[19] According to this understanding, Nathan was enlisting
Bathsheba's help in a plot to dupe the doddery old king into thinking he had
promised to make Solomon the next king. The plan would then be to persuade
the old man to make this intention public, so that Adonijah's premature grab
at the throne could be immediately rendered null and void.[20]

I don't buy it. Do you? We may not have been told about David's promise to Bathsheba, but that is often how Biblical stories work. David's promise to Bathsheba was not previously disclosed to us, just as it had not been made known to the public. But once we hear about it, it fits well with what we have been told.

First, the promise that Nathan had delivered to David years earlier focused on "your offspring after you, who shall come from your body, and I will establish his kingdom" (2 Samuel 7:12). This suggests that a son, at that time yet to be born ("who *shall* come . . ."[21]), would be king after David. This could not be Adonijah who had been born in Hebron years *earlier* than the 2 Samuel 7 promise (2 Samuel 3:4).

Second, when Solomon was subsequently born the account told us that "the LORD loved him" and sent a message to that effect by Nathan the prophet (2 Samuel 12:24, 25). Nothing like that happened with any other son of David (as far as we know). We have not been told in as many words, but we have been led to expect that Solomon was the offspring of David whose kingdom the Lord would establish.[22]

Therefore Nathan's reference to the oath David had sworn to Bathsheba does not sound like a fabrication at all. It seems that in the light of the Lord's declared love for Solomon and the Lord's promise to David concerning the son who would reign after him, David had sworn to Bathsheba that Solomon was the one. David's oath to Bathsheba was really an affirmation of the Lord's promise. Therefore when Nathan reminded Bathsheba of the oath David had sworn to her, he was pointing to the promise that the Lord had made to David.[23]

Here we touch on the heart of the Bible's astonishing message. The God who is really there, the only true God, has made known his purpose for the world he has made. This revelation unfolds gradually through the history the Bible records. It is God's promise. In the days of King David God's promise had been spoken in the particularly clear terms of 2 Samuel 7:12–16. God's promise is the secret of the future. The secret of being on the right side of history is to believe God's promise. On this day in Jerusalem in 961 B.C. Nathan the prophet was banking on God's promise.

The question he suggested that Bathsheba then ask David ("Why then is Adonijah king?"[24] v. 13) highlights the contradiction between the oath and the reality. As readers of the narrative, we may notice that the question Nathan posed echoes the "Why?" question that we have been told David "never at any time" asked Adonijah (1:6).[25] Nathan may have held David responsible to some extent for the situation they now faced. David did not know what was happening, but his indulgence toward his son as well as his lack of attention to developments taking place in his realm had enabled the present crisis.

David's oath concerning Solomon (and behind it, God's promise concerning David's offspring) demanded a response to what Adonijah had done.

Nathan's Help (v. 14)

Nathan's advice to Bathsheba concluded with a promise to support her in her approach to the king: "Then while you are still speaking with the king, I also will come in after you and confirm your words" (v. 14)—literally, "fill your words," meaning that Nathan would fill in whatever Bathsheba left unsaid.

The Danger of Being on the Right Side of History (vv. 15–27)

If the secret of being on the right side of history is banking on the promise of God, we need to understand that being on the right side of history can also be scary. That is because most of the time it is far from obvious that God's promise will determine the future. Other forces seem more powerful. Adonijah clearly had substantial support in Jerusalem (1:7, 9). If he had his way, Bathsheba's life was in danger along with her son's. It was far from *obvious* that banking on David's oath would put Bathsheba on the right side of history.

We can sense all this first as Bathsheba followed Nathan's advice and went to speak to David (vv. 15–21) and then as Nathan kept his word by appearing at just the right time (vv. 22–27).

According to Bathsheba (vv. 15–21)

"So Bathsheba went to the king in his chamber" (v. 15a)—that is, in the king's private quarters. Picture the frail old man, barely able to get out of bed.[26]

The narrator reminds us of his condition: "now the king was very old, and Abishag the Shunammite was attending to the king" (v. 15b). This does not mean that Abishag was actually present during Bathsheba's meeting with the king.[27] Rather it is simply a reminder of 1:1–4 and the weak, dependent, vulnerable condition in which we saw King David there, confirming our fear (and Bathsheba's) that the old king might not be able to do anything about Adonijah.

"Bathsheba bowed and paid homage to the king" (v. 16a). For her part Bathsheba showed honor to the king, his infirmity notwithstanding. As far as she was concerned he was still "the king."

"And the king said, 'What do you desire?'" (v. 16b). In Hebrew this was just two syllables: "What for-you?"[28] Was David's brevity a further indication of his frailty?

Bathsheba proceeded to speak to the king along the lines that Nathan had advised, but with significant variations.[29]

David's Oath (v. 17)

> She said to him, "My lord, you swore to your servant by the LORD your
> God, saying, 'Solomon your son shall reign after me, and he shall sit on
> my throne.'" (v. 17)

Consistent with her position as the king's wife, Bathsheba spoke more directly to David than Nathan had suggested. In place of his rhetorical question
in verse 13, Bathsheba directly asserted the fact of David's oath concerning
Solomon. It was not something that Bathsheba would forget, and she assumed
that neither would David. She did not need to ask Nathan's question.[30]

Furthermore she added (to Nathan's proposed words) that David had
sworn this oath "by the LORD your God." While this was no doubt implied in
Nathan's version in verse 13, Bathsheba makes an even clearer link between
David's oath and the Lord's will. We sense again that behind David's oath was
the 2 Samuel 7 promise.

Adonijah's Action (Which David Does Not Know) (vv. 18, 19)

Bathsheba explained her reason for reminding David of his oath at this time:
"And now, behold, Adonijah is king, although you,[31] my lord the king,[32] do not
know it" (v. 18).

Bathsheba dramatically presented the shocking new development to
David.[33] The new fact was a contradiction of the earlier oath. Bathsheba's
reference to David's ignorance of this matter could be understood as a gentle
acknowledgment that this was not his fault. It was, after all, done behind his
back. I think it was stronger than that. "The king" *should* know when his son
makes a grab for the throne![34] The king's *not knowing* was the problem rather
than a mitigating factor (see v. 11).

Bathsheba proceeded with details:

> He has sacrificed oxen, fattened cattle, and sheep in abundance, and has in-
> vited all the sons of the king, Abiathar the priest, and Joab the commander
> of the army, but Solomon your servant he has not invited. (v. 19)

We need to appreciate that these festivities were going on at the very time
that Bathsheba was reporting them to David (see 1:41). She knew more about
what was happening than we have been told in 1:9.[35] Presumably Nathan had
told her. She emphasized the lavishness of the occasion ("in abundance"). She
wanted David to see that what was happening was big.

Her reference to "all the sons of the king" may well have reminded
David of a disastrous conversation he had once had with Adonijah's older

brother Absalom and some terrible news he heard at that time (2 Samuel 13:27, 30, 33[36]).

She identified two of the many invited guests by name.[37] "Abiathar the priest" may have been a shock to David. Abiathar had been a key supporter of David the last time one of his sons made a grab at the throne (see 2 Samuel 15:24–29, 35; 17:15, 16). The fact that he was now with Adonijah underlined the seriousness of the situation.

The mention of "Joab the commander of the army" may have been less surprising to King David. For all their ferocious loyalty, Joab and his brothers, "the sons of Zeruiah," had been hard for David to handle (see 2 Samuel 3:39; 16:10; 19:22). In particular three times there had been a major falling out between Joab and David when, contrary to the king's wishes, the commander had killed someone he regarded as a threat (2 Samuel 3:27; 18:14, 15; 20:10). One of those Joab had killed was David's son Absalom. The fact that this powerful, competent, and ruthless commander of the army was now with Adonijah was ominous.

Bathsheba mentioned just one of those who were not invited: "Solomon *your servant*" (1:19; cf. 1:10). With treachery in the air, Bathsheba underlined the faithfulness of herself and her son. They were both "your servant" (vv. 17, 19).

Now that we have heard about David's oath concerning Solomon, his exclusion from Adonijah's feast (see 1:10) takes on deeper significance.

What David Must Do (v. 20)

Bathsheba's speech to David reached its point: "And now,[38] my lord the king, the eyes of all Israel are on you, to tell them who shall sit on the throne of my lord the king after him" (v. 20).

The future of the whole nation ("all Israel") depended on King David. The narrator has carefully informed us that Adonijah's support base was essentially from Judah (1:9). There had been tensions between David's tribe of Judah and the rest of the nation (often loosely called "Israel") since the early days of his kingdom (see 2 Samuel 2:10; 19:41–43; 20:2). Adonijah's grasp at power threatened the unity of "all Israel."

If Adonijah's presumptuous claim was to be thwarted, King David must make public what he had already sworn privately to Bathsheba. He must publicly name his successor.

The Danger (v. 21)

The danger, should the king fail to do this, was not only what might become of "all Israel." There was a more immediate danger: "Otherwise it will come to pass, when my lord the king sleeps with [lies down[39] with] his fathers, that I and my son Solomon will be counted offenders" (v. 21).

Characters in Biblical narratives often speak more truly than they realize. Here Bathsheba (presumably unwittingly) echoed the words of the great promise that Nathan had delivered to David: "*When . . . you lie down with your fathers*, I will raise up your offspring after you, who shall come from your body, and I will establish his kingdom" (2 Samuel 7:12). If David failed to act as Bathsheba proposed, then "*when* my lord the king *lies down with his fathers*," instead of being raised up, the promised son (and his mother) "will be counted offenders." In this context the sense of the word "offenders" is not directly moral. It is, rather, that Bathsheba and her son will be on the wrong side.[40]

While Bathsheba's speech was certainly calculated to draw from David the action that was urgently and desperately needed, I do not think she should be criticized for that. She spoke the truth that needed to be spoken.[41]

According to Nathan (vv. 22–27)

Nathan appeared on cue as promised (v. 14):

> While she was still speaking with the king, Nathan the prophet came in. And they told the king, "Here is Nathan the prophet." And when he came in before the king, he bowed before the king, with his face to the ground. (vv. 22, 23)

Unlike Bathsheba, Nathan needed to be announced before coming into the king's presence. Like Bathsheba he bowed before the king.[42] While Nathan the prophet was about to address the king in a considered and forthright manner, we need not doubt the sincerity of his expressions of respect for the king. Indeed, if we have understood his motives correctly, it is because of his high regard for David's kingdom and the promise of God attached to it that he now approached the king with a difficult message.

We are to understand that Bathsheba withdrew at this point (see v. 28). It seems that Nathan was not confident that Bathsheba's words alone would move David to act. The situation was too serious to allow for the possibility of inaction. Nathan took a rather different approach from Bathsheba, giving no hint of their collaboration.[43] His words were carefully, even cunningly, calculated to ensure the required outcome.[44]

What David Must Have Said (v. 24)

And Nathan said, "My lord the king, have you said, 'Adonijah shall reign after me, and he shall sit on my throne'?" (v. 24)

This may have been a question (as the ESV has it). If so, Nathan knew the answer. The king had said no such thing. Nathan knew about the very different oath that David had privately sworn to Bathsheba (v. 13). Nathan's question (if that is what it was) was not really seeking information. David did not answer the question, nor did Nathan expect him to.

However, the emphases in the Hebrew may be better understood as an ironic assertion: "My lord the king, *you* must be the one who has said, '*Adonijah* shall reign after me, and *he* is the one who shall sit on my throne'!" (v. 24, AT[45]). Of course, we know Nathan did not believe this. He probably knew that David knew he did not believe it. Nathan, however, was (tongue firmly in cheek) suggesting that this could be the only possible explanation for what had happened—indeed what was happening even as he spoke.

What Adonijah Has Certainly Done (v. 25)

Nathan explained the basis for his astonishing assertion (or question):

> For[46] he has gone down this day and has sacrificed oxen, fattened cattle, and sheep in abundance, and has invited all the king's sons, the commanders of the army,[47] and Abiathar the priest. And behold, they are eating and drinking before him, and saying, "Long live King Adonijah!" (v. 25)

Nathan not only confirmed what Bathsheba told the king in verse 19, he added his own particular emphases.

First, Nathan alluded to the fact that Adonijah's celebration was outside the city ("he has gone down"). As we have seen, En-rogel was a somewhat secluded spot in the valley about 300 yards south of Jerusalem.

Second, the celebrations were going on "this day." Indeed they were going on as Nathan was speaking. Implication: "It is not too late to do something about this, Your Majesty!"[48]

Third, Nathan reported the all-important words that were being shouted at the feast in the valley: "Long live King Adonijah!" These words have not previously been explicitly mentioned in connection with the En-rogel festivities (but compare 1 Samuel 10:24; 2 Samuel 16:16). We (like David) only have Nathan's word that this is what was happening. However, everything in the account of Adonijah's doings in this chapter supports the credibility of Nathan's claim. Furthermore, the repeated reminders that Nathan is "the prophet" enhance his trustworthiness (see v. 22). In addition the echoes of the story of Absalom contribute to our sense (as readers) that this really is what was happening (see 2 Samuel 15:10; 16:16).[49] The news, as Nathan presented it, would evoke for David all the anguish of the days of Absalom's attempt to overthrow the king.[50]

Nathan was not being entirely straightforward with the king. In this he was adopting the kind of tactic he had used before in quite different circumstances (2 Samuel 12:1–12). As then, he was using a fiction (that David must have authorized this thing) to provoke a response from the king to a real problem.

What Adonijah Has Certainly Not Done (v. 26)

Nathan expanded on Bathsheba's report that Solomon had not been invited to Adonijah's feast (v. 19):

> But me,[51] your servant, and Zadok the priest, and Benaiah the son of Jehoiada, and your servant Solomon he has not invited. (v. 26)

Nathan's list of the uninvited sounds (on the surface) like a complaint: *How could Adonijah fail to invite me of all people? And Zadok? And Benaiah? And also the son in whom the Lord himself has taken a special interest? What's going on, Your Majesty?*

The first and last mentioned in this list are carefully called "your servant." If those who faithfully serve King David have been excluded by Adonijah, *What's going on, Your Majesty?*

It's Unthinkable! (v. 27)

Of course, the real problem from Nathan's point of view was Adonijah's unauthorized, illegitimate promotion of himself and the treasonous proclamation of him as king. Perhaps Nathan had seen enough of David's inability to curb his sons' behavior (see 1:6) to make him cautious about a direct appeal to the king. Instead he made out that what troubled him was his exclusion from the king's circle of trust:

> Has[52] this thing been brought about by my lord the king and you have not told your servants[53] who should sit on the throne of my lord the king after him? (v. 27)

How could you do such a thing, Your Majesty, without informing your faithful servants (particularly me)?

Nathan's speech to the king was brilliant. He knew very well that David had *not* authorized what Adonijah had done. However, by "accusing" David of doing so, he forced the king's hand. If David did nothing, Nathan had made him responsible for Adonijah's act. If David denied that he had anything to do with it, he would thereby acknowledge Adonijah's illegitimacy and have to do something about it. As on his previous difficult encounter with the king (2 Samuel 12), Nathan had successfully cornered David. In this he was doing his job as "the prophet."

The Assurance of Being on the Right Side of History (vv. 28–37)

It took courage for Bathsheba and Nathan to do what they did. They could not know whether the old king had the strength or the will to act as they hoped. The king could die at any time. Where would that leave them? Might Adonijah hear of their approaches to David? What would then become of the prophet and the mother of Solomon?

Nathan and Bathsheba put their hope in the oath that David had made to Solomon's mother. As I have been arguing, that meant their hope was in the promise of God that stood behind David's oath. As Nathan finished what he had to say to the king, the future of the kingdom (and the future of Nathan and Bathsheba) was in the balance.

The King's Promise (vv. 28–31)[54]

It is worth noting that in the whole of 1 Kings 1 we have heard only two syllables (in the original Hebrew) from David's mouth (v. 16). We have been given the impression of a frail old man, almost too weak to speak. However, what he heard from Bathsheba (essentially a reminder of his oath and therefore of God's promise) and Nathan (essentially a forceful account of Adonijah's presumptuous grab at the throne) moved him to decisive and firm action. I do not doubt that everyone who witnessed and heard of what happened next were astonished. Who would have thought the old man still had it in him?

> Then King David answered, "Call Bathsheba to me." So she came into the king's presence and stood before the king. (v. 28)

The full title "King David" has been used only in verses 1 and 13 of this chapter. It strikes a formal note and signals the importance of what we are about to hear.[55] What David was about to do was in response ("answered") to what he had heard from Nathan and Bathsheba.

Bathsheba was summoned back into the king's presence. This time she did not bow, but "stood before the king." She was at his service.[56] At this point we are to understand that Nathan would have withdrawn (see v. 32).

What David said to Bathsheba would change the course of history:

> And the king swore, saying, "As the LORD lives, who has redeemed my soul out of every adversity, as I swore to you by the LORD, the God of Israel, saying, 'Solomon your son shall reign after me, and he[57] shall sit on my throne in my place,' even so will I do this day." (vv. 29, 30)

David swore an oath about the oath that he had earlier sworn. Both oaths were sworn by the name of the Lord. Both affirmed Solomon as King David's successor. Now, however, David added a phrase not used in verses 13 and 17: "in my place."[58] Beside the words "even so will I do this day"[59] we are to understand that Solomon was to be appointed straightaway as co-regent with David. Only such decisive and immediate action would counter Adonijah.

The significance of this moment is further suggested by David's recollection of the Lord's goodness to him: "who has redeemed my soul out of every adversity" (v. 29). This could be a summary of David's whole life.[60] Elsewhere he has eloquently expanded on this brief expression of heartfelt praise (see 2 Samuel 22:2–7, 44–51). In David's oath we hear his faith in his God. By the God who had been his unfailing savior, David swore that Solomon would become king that very day.

Furthermore this oath was important for the nation of Israel as God's people. The Lord by whose name he swore was "the God of Israel" (see also v. 20).

Bathsheba's relief and gratitude were evident:

> Then Bathsheba bowed with her face to the ground and paid homage to the king and said, "May my lord King David live forever!" (v. 31)

Her posture was now even more expressive than in verse 16 ("her face to the ground," like Nathan in v. 23). Her prayer should not be understood as a wish that the old king would linger on forever, nor should it be taken as referring to life beyond the grave. Rather Bathsheba was praying that the *kingdom* of David would last forever. This was what the Lord had promised. In his offspring: "Your throne shall be established forever" (2 Samuel 7:16). Bathsheba's "forever" suggests that she understood Solomon's accession to the throne in accordance with God's promise.

The King's Commands (vv. 32–37)

The newly enlivened old king wasted no time in acting on his oath:

> King David said, "Call to me Zadok the priest, Nathan the prophet, and Benaiah the son of Jehoiada." So they came before the king. (v. 32)

These are the first three men mentioned in 1:8 who "were not with Adonijah." David "called" those whom Adonijah had not "called" (see v. 26).[61] Their respective roles as priest, prophet, and military man were no doubt important in the task they were about to be given. Here was more than a match for Adonijah's Abiathar the priest and Joab the commander.

In remarkable contrast to the frail figure we saw in 1:1, King David now issued a succession of eight firm and confident commands that together would shape the future.

First, the king said to Zadok, Nathan, and Benaiah, "Take with you the servants of your lord"[62] (v. 33a). How would the faithful followers of the old king compare to the supporters and sympathizers Adonijah had gathered? Despite appearances, these are the people who would turn out to be on the right side of history.

Second, ". . . and have Solomon my son ride on my own mule" (v. 33b). This was a stark demonstration that David was publicly handing authority over to Solomon.[63] While the mule seems to have been regarded as a rare beast in Israel, available only for the privileged (see 2 Samuel 13:29; 18:9), there is an obvious contrast between this display of Solomon's promotion and Adonijah's pompous entourage (1:5).[64] Many years later Jesus would ride into Jerusalem like Solomon, not like Adonijah (Matthew 21:1–11; see Zechariah 9:9). Despite appearances, the future belonged to the king riding the mule.

Third, ". . . and bring him down to Gihon" (v. 33c). "Gihon" means something like "Gusher"[65] and was a spring east of the city of Jerusalem, on the western bank of the Kidron Valley. It was much closer to the city than En-rogel, which was about 650 yards to the south.[66] There was no reason for this occasion to be in a secluded place like En-rogel. At the same time perhaps it was deliberately chosen because it was within earshot of Adonijah's celebration (see 1:41).[67] What was about to happen at Gihon would not be done "in a corner" (cf. Acts 26:26).

Fourth, the climactic command is: "And let Zadok the priest and Nathan the prophet there anoint him king over Israel" (v. 34a). Previously it had been Samuel the prophet/priest who had anointed King Saul (1 Samuel 10:1) and King David (1 Samuel 16:13), although the latter was eventually anointed by the men (elders?) of Judah (2 Samuel 2:4) and subsequently by all the elders of the remaining tribes (2 Samuel 5:3). Here the Hebrew indicates that Zadok the priest was to anoint Solomon, joined in some unspecified way by Nathan the prophet.[68]

"Anoint" is an ordinary word in Hebrew, meaning "smear,"[69] but it took on particular importance as the act of appointing God's king. The Hebrew for "anointed one" is *mashiach*, which has come into English as "Messiah." Similarly the Greek equivalent, *christos*, has given us "Christ."

Solomon was to be anointed as king "over Israel," that is, over the whole people of God. This means that he was to be the one promised in 2 Samuel 7:12 and that his kingdom would be the kingdom promised there.

Fifth, "Then blow the trumpet"[70] (v. 34b). This would signal to the whole city that something momentous had occurred. It would take very little time for everyone to learn what it was. How different this loud event would be from the rather more hushed proceedings that were going on out of sight at En-rogel. The happenings at Gihon were not to be kept secret.

Sixth, ". . . and say, 'Long live King Solomon!'" (v. 34c); more literally, "May King Solomon live!" According to Nathan, this is exactly what the crowd at En-rogel had said (with a different name, of course, v. 25).[71] The difference between En-rogel and Gihon was the difference between being on the wrong side or the right side of history. Who will be king?

A further contrast between the acclamations of Adonijah and Solomon at En-rogel and Gihon respectively is the passivity of Solomon versus the "exalting himself" activity of Adonijah. Solomon became king, but not by taking power as Adonijah did. The kingship was *given* to him.

Seventh, "You shall then come up after him" (v. 35a). It was a steep climb back up to the city from Gihon. More subtly we may see here another contrast to Adonijah who went up ("exalted himself," 1:5) before going down (to En-rogel, 1:9; cf. 1:53). Solomon went "down" to Gihon (v. 33) before going "up" to the throne.[72]

Eighth, ". . . and he shall come and sit on my throne, for he[73] shall be king in my place" (v. 35b). Solomon would not displace David but would join him as co-regent. More importantly, David was designating Solomon as the one of whom the Lord had said, "I will raise up your offspring after you, who shall come from your body, and I will establish his kingdom" (2 Samuel 7:12).

David then summed up the significance of his eight-point order: "And I have appointed him to be ruler over Israel and over Judah." (v. 35c). There is a hint here that David remembered that in this kingdom a king was not like the kings of the surrounding nations. David used a word ("ruler") that seems to deliberately avoid some of the connotations of "king."[74]

This ruler would be "over Israel and over Judah." This is the first time in 1 Kings that the term "Israel" refers not to the whole nation (as in vv. 3, 20, 30, 34) but to the northern tribes, excluding the large southern tribe of Judah. "Israel *and* . . . Judah" recognizes the tensions that had existed for a long time (see 2 Samuel 2—5) and would in due course lead to the division of the kingdom (1 Kings 12).[75] Solomon, however, was to rule over Israel *and* Judah—the whole people of God.

Benaiah, the military man, who had been given no explicit role in David's order, led the response to this historic pronouncement from King David:

> And Benaiah the son of Jehoiada answered the king, "Amen! May the LORD, the God of my lord the king, say so. As the LORD has been with my lord the king, even so may he be with Solomon, and make his throne greater than the throne of my lord King David." (vv. 36, 37)

Benaiah got it! His "Amen!" expressed his confidence in David's orders.[76] His prayer[77] indicated that his conviction came from trust in God's promises. Since characters in the Bible often speak more profoundly than they may have consciously understood, we do not need to make claims about what Benaiah may have known. However, his words confirm the connection we have already seen between King David's command and the Lord's promise. Benaiah saw David's words as God's words.[78] Benaiah identified the most important aspect of King David's reign: the Lord had been "with [him]." The prayer for continuity of *this* aspect of David's greatness in Solomon amounts to a prayer that Solomon would be God's king in the terms of the 2 Samuel 7 promise. The idea that Solomon's throne would be greater than David's likewise reflects the great promise that King David's command was enacting.[79]

Benaiah's faith in the promise of God will place him on the right side of history.

The Joy of Being on the Right Side of History (vv. 38–40)

It remains for us to observe the commands of King David being carried out, to the letter, and to witness the joyful response from "all the people":

> So Zadok the priest, Nathan the prophet, and Benaiah the son of Jehoiada, and the Cherethites and the Pelethites[80] went down and had Solomon ride on King David's mule and brought him to Gihon. There Zadok the priest took the horn of oil[81] from the tent[82] and anointed Solomon. Then they blew the trumpet, and all the people said, "Long live King Solomon!" And all the people went up after him, playing on pipes, and rejoicing with great joy, so that the earth was split by their noise. (vv. 38–40)

Down they went from the hill in Jerusalem where King David's palace stood, into the deep Kidron Valley, to Gihon. Once the commands of the king had been carried out, up they came, back into the city.

The joy of the occasion was extraordinary. "All the people" is not quite literally true. There was still the (relatively small) crowd at En-rogel (see 1:41). However, the point is that the nation as a whole was now joyfully acknowledging Solomon as their king. Such a display of rejoicing may remind us of the day that the ark of the covenant was brought into Jerusalem (see 2 Samuel 6:5, 12, 15). The sounds of joy were so great that the earth shook!

The crowds following Solomon into Jerusalem were on the right side of history. Why? Because God's promise will determine the future. Strangely, that does not exclude human activity. Those who believed God's promise (such as Nathan, Bathsheba, and David) did not passively wait around for God's promise to be realized. They acted boldly, carefully, and emphatically for what God had promised. That is what faith is like, and it puts you on the right side of history.

As we watch the joyful crowds accompanying the son of David up into the city of Jerusalem, we may cast our minds forward to the day when another son of David would ride a donkey into Jerusalem (Matthew 21:1–11). It was not long before the earth quaked as this Son of David was about to begin his reign (Matthew 27:51).

Faith in Jesus Christ means believing God's promise. The kingdom of the son of David will be "forever" (2 Samuel 7:16; see Luke 1:33; Hebrews 1:8; Revelation 11:15).

Are you on the right side of history?

4

Sooner or Later . . .

1 KINGS 1:41–53

When the Son of Man comes in his glory, and all the angels with him, then he will sit on his glorious throne. Before him will be gathered all the nations, and he will separate people one from another as a shepherd separates the sheep from the goats. (Matthew 25:31, 32)

. . . he commanded us to preach to the people and to testify that [Jesus Christ] is the one appointed by God to be judge of the living and the dead. (Acts 10:42)

. . . now [God] commands all people everywhere to repent, because he has fixed a day on which he will judge the world in righteousness by a man whom he has appointed; and of this he has given assurance to all by raising him from the dead. (Acts 17:30, 31)

For we must all appear before the judgment seat of Christ, so that each one may receive what is due for what he has done in the body, whether good or evil. (2 Corinthians 5:10)

SOONER OR LATER every human being will encounter the One who really rules the world. Even the most defiant will, sooner or later, have to bow and confess that Jesus Christ is Lord (Philippians 2:10, 11). Because he is.

Adonijah, the son of King David, wanted to be the one who ruled David's kingdom (1:5). He was so eager that he took steps to establish a powerful support base in Jerusalem (1:7). He carefully avoided those he knew to be of a different mind (1:8). The day came for Adonijah to take his cause decisively forward. He gathered the kind of people he hoped would share his aspirations for himself and hosted a lavish (though covert) feast outside the city, away from public attention, near En-rogel (1:9). It seems that the invited crowd was rather carried along with the festivities and went so far as to celebrate Adonijah as king (1:11, 18, 25). This was a little presumptuous, to say the least, since King David was still alive, even if old and frail (1:1–4). Adonijah's deliberate exclusion of Solomon from the party (1:10) suggests that Adonijah was aware that others in Jerusalem had this younger brother of his in mind for the top job.

As always in Old Testament Israel there was more to all this than political intrigue. Among all the nations of the world Israel had been chosen by God to be his people. King David was God's king. David's kingdom was God's kingdom. God had promised that when David's days were over, God would "raise up" a son of David and would establish his kingdom forever (2 Samuel 7:12, 13, 16).

We do not know how widely known this promise was on the day of Adonijah's feast near En-rogel. Even if we were to suppose that all of Adonijah's guests knew about it, the promise did not specify *which* son of David would be the next king.[1] Indeed there were reasons that made Adonijah a probable candidate—including the important fact that King David had never raised any objections to Adonijah's flamboyant displays of self-importance (1:6).

As the festivities went on by the En-rogel spring, there was a bustle of activity back in Jerusalem, initiated by Nathan the prophet (1:11–37). The upshot was that David announced that Solomon was to be his successor, and furthermore that he was to be made king immediately (1:30, 34). As we have followed the conversations that led to this point, we have seen that behind this development was the fact, known at least to David, Bathsheba, and Nathan, that the Lord had made known his choice of Solomon at the time of the boy's birth (2 Samuel 12:24, 25). In light of this David had earlier sworn to Bathsheba that Solomon would be king after him (1:13, 17, 30). In response to the news of what was happening at En-rogel, Solomon was made king that very day at the Gihon spring just outside Jerusalem and about 650 yards north of En-rogel (1:38, 39). The joy and excitement as the people made their way back into the city was so loud that the earth shook (1:40).

Sooner or later the crowd in En-rogel would have to face the true king. It happened sooner.

The End of the Party (vv. 41, 42)

In verse 41 there is a sudden shift from the loud, joyous procession making its way up from Gihon in the Kidron Valley back into the city. Abruptly we are taken south to the scene of the other celebration, which was brought to a brusque end.

The Noise That Stopped the Party (v. 41a)

Adonijah and all the guests who were with him heard it as [and[2]] they finished feasting. (v. 41a)

The Hebrew suggests that Adonijah may have been the first to notice the noise coming from the direction of the city.[3] Then the others heard it too. They are described, literally, as "all the called who were with him." These were "all his brothers, the king's sons [except one], and all the royal officials of Judah" whom Adonijah had "called" (esv, "invited") to this feast (1:9). "With him" suggests more than being present: they were *going along with* Adonijah's aspirations, just as certain others were "not with[4] Adonijah" (1:8).

We are given the impression that until the disturbing sound was heard from the north, Adonijah and those he had gathered were carousing, completely unaware of the drama that had been unfolding in the city. It did not cross their mind that there would be any challenge to Adonijah's presumptuous self-confidence. However, his arrogance was about to be his undoing.

The noise from the city brought the party to an end. Everyone stopped eating. They sensed that something momentous had happened. They did not yet understand what it was, but the uproar that reached their ears signaled the collapse of the misguided expectations of those who were "with" Adonijah. Their party was over in every sense![5]

The Question That Must Be Answered (v. 41b)

One of the guests had enough experience to discern important sounds: "And when Joab heard the sound of the trumpet, he said, 'What does this uproar in the city mean?'" (v. 41b).

In all the clamor Joab's military-trained ears heard "the sound of the trumpet" (see 1:34, 39). The sound of the trumpet had been heard in Israel at some very significant times (see Exodus 19:16, 19; 20:18; Leviticus 25:9; Joshua 6; Judges 6:34; 7:18; 1 Samuel 13:3). Joab himself had blown the trumpet on several momentous occasions (2 Samuel 2:28; 18:16; 20:22) and had heard it on others (2 Samuel 6:15; 15:10; 20:1). Joab knew that the sound he recognized in all the din meant something big.

But what? The shrewd soldier knew the importance of that question. He put it curiously: "Why the roaring sound of the city?"[6] (literal translation). He did not refer to the trumpet that he (and no one else?) had heard. That is what he had particularly noticed. It made him anxious about the uproar.[7] What did it all mean?

The Worthy Man Who Brought Good News? (v. 42)

As Joab's question hung in the air over the hushed crowd at En-rogel, a familiar young man arrived, breathless because of his sprint down from the city: "While [Joab] was still speaking, behold, Jonathan the son of Abiathar the priest came" (v. 42a).

The narrator has made this sound just like the earlier arrival of Nathan the prophet: "While [Bathsheba] was still speaking" with King David in his bedchamber . . ." (1:22[8]). This time it was "Jonathan the son of Abiathar the priest" who arrived at just the right instant with a message for that moment.

Readers of the larger story have seen Jonathan before. Indeed we have seen him at En-rogel, and we have seen him running (see 2 Samuel 17:17–20)! On that earlier occasion Jonathan had played his part with courage and skill, carrying vital intelligence from David's undercover men in Jerusalem to the exiled king waiting at the Jordan River. We may be disappointed to see this brave lad, who had served David so well, now arriving at En-rogel. Had he abandoned his earlier faithfulness to King David?

Do not judge him too quickly. Of course, we already know that his father was a supporter of Adonijah's aspirations (1:7, 19, 25). But why did Jonathan arrive only now at the site of the feast? Why wasn't he here earlier? Perhaps he had not been invited, although he obviously knew the location of the secret gathering. Jonathan will surprise us.

Adonijah welcomed his timely arrival. He said, "Come in, for you are a worthy man and bring good news" (v. 42b). Adonijah knew the reputation of this fine young man, presumably including his heroic exploits for Adonijah's father. He was indeed "a worthy man."[9]

We sense that Adonijah was still upbeat. He did not yet share Joab's anxious agitation. He probably thought that the news of his own acclamation at En-rogel may have reached the city and caused a joyous uproar. Vanity is capable of such delusion. He was persuaded that Jonathan must be the bearer of *good* news—good news, that is, for Adonijah.

The irony is that Jonathan's message was indeed "good news," news of something very good indeed, as we will shortly hear. But Adonijah will not think so.

In this Jonathan's message was very much like the gospel of Jesus Christ. Indeed the verb here translated "bring . . . news" is, via its Greek translation, the source of our English word *evangelize*, meaning to preach the gospel. The gospel we proclaim is good news, news of something very good indeed. But that does not mean that it is good news for those who do not want Jesus Christ to be the true King.[10]

Jonathan's Gospel (vv. 43–48)

The young man responded to Adonijah's confident complacency. Unfortunately, there is a difficulty (for us) in the first word of his reply. The ESV and other recent English translations have "No" or words to that effect.[11] This would mean that Jonathan knew full well that the news he brought was *not* "good" for Adonijah. However, I think that in this context, some of the older translations have understood his meaning better: "Yes" (JB) or "Verily" (RV).[12] In more modern idiom, he said, "You bet!"[13] In other words, astonishingly, Jonathan considered that the news he brought was indeed "good"![14]

If this is correct, then for a brief moment Adonijah (and we readers) are held in suspense. What *good* news could the young runner be bringing to En-rogel from Jerusalem?

"Solomon Is King!" (v. 43)

With the exuberance (and naiveté?) of youth, Jonathan responded to Adonijah: "You bet! Our lord King David has made Solomon king!" (v. 43, AT).

This was Jonathan's gospel. Everything else we will hear from him is simply an elaboration of this announcement. "Solomon is king!"

The surprise (for us readers) is the way in which Jonathan referred to David: "our lord King David." This is the way in which Bathsheba (1:17, 18, 20, 21, 31), Nathan (1:24, 27), and Benaiah (1:36) had spoken to David, expressing their faithful devotion to him. The surprise is that Jonathan shared this commitment to the old king—and he seems to assume that Adonijah did too ("*our* lord")![15]

That is why, of course, he considered the news he brought to be "good." His words also reveal something that we have not realized earlier. The parallels between Adonijah's ambition and actions and those of Absalom years earlier may have misled us to think that those who joined Adonijah at the En-rogel feast were *consciously* betraying David, as those who had joined Absalom certainly were. The frank words of young Jonathan now help us to see that those who joined Adonijah at En-rogel (or at least many of them) may have been doing no such thing. Adonijah was, after all, David's son and the most obvious candidate to become king after David (1:6), and David was on his last legs (1:1). Whatever was going on in Adonijah's mind, at least many of those feasting with him that day may well have been like Jonathan and still regarded David as "our lord King David" and felt no contradiction between supporting Adonijah and honoring King David.

Jonathan's striking words should not be judged either sarcastic or naïve.[16] He was right to rejoice in Solomon's kingship. He was right to bring the "good" news to Adonijah and those with him. He was, no doubt, mistaken if he thought that Adonijah would be pleased. But that would be a problem for Adonijah, not for Jonathan.[17]

Solomon's Anointing (vv. 44, 45)

Jonathan filled in the details of what had happened:

> . . . and the king has sent with him Zadok the priest, Nathan the prophet, and Benaiah the son of Jehoiada, and the Cherethites and the Pelethites. And they had him ride on the king's mule. And Zadok the priest and Nathan the prophet have anointed him king at Gihon, and they have gone up from there rejoicing, so that the city is in an uproar. This is the noise that you[18] have heard. (vv. 44, 45)

The three people Jonathan named (Zadok, Nathan, and Benaiah) happen to be those whom we were informed earlier in the story were "not with Adonijah" (1:8). Adonijah knew that (1:9, 10). I doubt that Jonathan did. I suspect that many of those at En-rogel were, like Jonathan, unaware of any inconsistency between being "with" Adonijah and being faithful servants of King David. Exceptions would include Adonijah himself and his inner circle of confidants, Joab and Abiathar (1:7).

Jonathan's description of what had happened at Gihon is the third time we have heard the details of the anointing of Solomon (see David's order in 1:32–35 and the narrator's report in 1:38–40). This is clearly what 1 Kings 1 is all about, and this news was the explanation for "the noise that you have heard."

The Kingdom Is Solomon's (v. 46)

The young man has said what he needed to say. We can sense his excitement (and breathlessness) as he kept speaking: "And also Solomon sits on the throne of the kingdom" (v. 46, AT).

In the Hebrew verses 46, 47, and 48 each begin, "And also . . ."[19] We can almost see Jonathan taking a deep breath before continuing: "And also . . . and also . . . and also . . ." What news he had to tell!

It matters little whether he was reporting that Solomon had literally taken his seat on the throne in Jerusalem or whether he was simply announcing that Solomon had been made the one entitled to do so.[20] The point is that the throne that was now Solomon's was the throne of *the kingdom*.[21]

While the word "kingdom" does not always carry heavy theological overtones, in some contexts it certainly does.[22] Whatever Jonathan may have meant by the word, the reader of this narrative, with its many reminders of God's promise in 2 Samuel 7, cannot but be reminded that the throne on which Solomon now sat was the throne of "the kingdom" that the Lord had promised to establish forever (2 Samuel 7:12, 13, 16).[23] This *was* good news!

Solomon Is God's King! (vv. 47, 48)

Jonathan had not finished. He seemed blissfully unaware of the devastating effect his "good" news must have been having on Adonijah. As though Adonijah would want to know all the details, he continued with glad excitement.

What the Servants Said (v. 47)

Moreover [And also], the king's servants came to congratulate[24] our lord King David, saying, "May your God make the name of Solomon more famous than yours, and make his throne greater than your throne." (v. 47a)

The king's servants (are these the servants we met in 1:2?) had echoed the response of Benaiah in 1:36, 37. They believed (and Jonathan was now proclaiming) that God was in this. Solomon would be—if their prayer was answered—God's promised king!

"And the king bowed himself on the bed" (v. 47b). Just as Bathsheba had "paid homage" to David (1:16) and Nathan had "bowed down" before the king (1:23),[25] so now David, on his bed, acknowledged the great thing that had occurred. We are reminded again of David's frail, bedridden condition (1:1–4). Much more, however, we see the old king gladly acknowledging the prayer of his servants for the new king.

What King David Said (v. 48)

For the third time Jonathan took a deep breath: "And . . . also . . ."

And the king also said, "Blessed be the LORD, the God of Israel, who has granted someone to sit on my throne this day, my own eyes seeing it." (v. 48)

For the sixth time in this chapter we hear the name of God ("the LORD," "Yahweh"). This is the name by which David had sworn that Solomon would be king after him (1:17, 29, 30). It is the name invoked by Benaiah in his wonderful "Amen!" to the prospect of Solomon becoming king (1:36, 37). David now praised God by this same name for what had happened.

He is "the God of Israel." The phrase reminds us of God's gracious purpose for Israel.[26] As Samuel put it many years earlier:

> For the LORD will not forsake his people, for his great name's sake, because it has pleased the LORD to make you a people for himself. (1 Samuel 12:22)

What had happened was understood by David to be the Lord's *gift*. There is perhaps some subtle irony in the Hebrew word for "granted" (*nathan*). It is the same as the name Nathan and is contained in the name Jo-*nathan* (which, indeed, means "The LORD has given"). The names of the messengers in this narrative bore witness to the heart of their message about a *gift* from God. That is what King Solomon was.

"Someone to sit on *my throne*" is yet another reminder of the great 2 Samuel 7 promise: "*Your throne* shall be established forever" (2 Samuel 7:16).[27] It had not happened before in Israel that a king's son took his father's throne (at least it had not happened legitimately; see 2 Samuel 2:8, 9). It had happened now because of God's promise. It was God's gift.

And it had happened "this day, my own eyes seeing it." It had happened "this day" because King David had sworn that it would happen "this day" (1:30) and because "this day" Adonijah had made his presumptuous move (1:25). We see the old king now in a rather different light. In his frailty we have been told several times what he did not know (1:4, 11, 18). What the king *did* know was the promise of God, and now his own eyes had seen God's promise come to pass. The future depended on God's promise, not on King David's vitality.

These two brief speeches (by David's servants and by David himself) convey the profound theological dimensions of Jonathan's news. Solomon was king, and the kingdom was his. This was the gift of the God of Israel, and the best was yet to come. Good news indeed!

Responses to Jonathan's Gospel (vv. 49–53)

The news (like the sound that had accompanied it, 1:40) was earth-shattering. In this it was again like the gospel of Jesus Christ. It is certainly good news. But it is devastating news as well. Follow what happened to those who heard Jonathan's gospel.

The Guests (v. 49)

Jonathan's news had an immediate impact on Adonijah's guests at the En-rogel festivities: "Then all the guests of Adonijah trembled and rose, and each went his own way" (v. 49). All at once they recognized that what had been going on at En-rogel had been a big mistake. If (as the evidence suggests) they had thought that the whole Adonijah thing was legitimate, the news that Solomon was the true king was shattering. They had been wrong.

It is easy to be sincere but wrong. The seriousness of being wrong about the big questions of life is not assuaged by honestly believing that you are right. If I sincerely believe that I am healthy when I am dying of cancer, my sincerity will not save me. If I genuinely trust a con man selling a phony cure, my trust is misplaced no matter how deeply it is felt. The sincerity can make the realization that I was wrong even more devastating.

The immediacy of the response by the guests at En-rogel, with no suggestion of defying King David's will by sticking with Adonijah, shows that King David still had their allegiance.[28] For them, like Jonathan, David was still "our lord King David" (vv. 43, 47). Their problem had been that King David had not made his will known before this, and in the absence of a word from their king they had mistakenly thought that Adonijah's aspirations were legitimate.[29] The news of King David making *Solomon* king made them tremble with fear.[30] They had made a big mistake. It is striking how quickly they abandoned Adonijah: "each went his own way."

Adonijah (v. 50)

Adonijah suddenly found himself alone. What impact did the new situation brought about by Jonathan's news have on Adonijah? "Adonijah[31] feared Solomon" (v. 50a). The Hebrew is a little more explicit, indicating that Adonijah was afraid to *face* Solomon.[32] The bravado dissolved. No surprise there. If things had worked out differently, Adonijah knew how he would have dealt with Solomon (see Nathan's warning to Bathsheba, 1:12, and Bathsheba's fear, 1:21). Now he expected the same from his younger brother. He was very afraid.

He sought refuge in a rather surprising place: "So he arose and went and took hold of the horns of the altar" (v. 50b). Our writer gives no further details of this desperate action. On the reasonable assumption that the altar concerned was in the tabernacle, Adonijah would have had to travel some distance, to Gibeon.[33]

The horns of the altar were protrusions from the four corners of the top of the altar (Exodus 27:2) that were smeared with blood at the time of sacrifice (Exodus 29:12; Leviticus 4:7, 18, 25, 30, 34; 8:15; 9:9; Ezekiel 43:20) and had a particular role in making atonement (Exodus 30:10; Leviticus 16:18; cf. Amos 3:14). To grasp the horns of the altar seems to have become a way of seeking asylum. While this particular action is not prescribed in Old Testament law, it is consistent with provisions there for temporary protection of individuals who may have a defense against the death penalty (see Exodus 21:12–14; Numbers 35:9–34; Deuteronomy 4:41–43; 19:1–13).[34]

Adonijah pitifully clinging to the horns of the altar makes a striking contrast to the man who had "exalted himself" and paraded through the Jerusalem streets boasting, "I will be king" (see 1:5). What a difference a day can make![35]

Solomon's Mercy (vv. 51–53)

Solomon was told about Adonijah's plea, now put into words:

> Then it was told Solomon, "Behold, Adonijah fears King Solomon, for behold, he has laid hold of the horns of the altar, saying, 'Let King Solomon swear to me first[36] that he will not put his servant to death with the sword.'" (v. 51)

Adonijah could not escape the reality. His younger brother was king. He addressed him as such ("King Solomon"[37]) and acknowledged his subordination ("his servant"). He had no alternative but to beg for mercy. He dared to ask for an unconditional guarantee that he would not be put to death for his presumptuous defiance of King David.

Solomon did not swear an oath, as Adonijah had asked. Nor did he give an unconditional guarantee. Instead he promised safety for Adonijah on strict conditions:

> And Solomon said, "If he will show himself a worthy man, not one of his hairs shall fall to the earth, but if wickedness is found in him, he shall die." (v. 52)

On the one hand, this was mercy. Adonijah need not die. Solomon was prepared to spare his life. In context this must be seen as a gracious act. Solomon began his reign not by seeking vengeance, but in showing mercy.[38]

On the other hand, Solomon's promise of mercy was not unconditional. Adonijah must "show himself a worthy man."[39] In other words he must display the kind of integrity and valor that Adonijah himself had recognized in young Jonathan ("a worthy man," v. 42[40]). However, "if wickedness is found in him" he would find no mercy from Solomon. These conditions were essentially political. Adonijah's safety depended on no more treachery (as his grab for the throne must now be understood).

The mercy was no doubt welcome, but the condition would have been discomforting. King Solomon would be the one to judge whether Adonijah showed himself "worthy" or "wicked." Adonijah's future was in the king's hands. "So King Solomon sent, and they brought him down from the altar.[41] And he came and paid homage to King Solomon . . ." (v. 53a).

Adonijah had no choice ("they brought him"). This was the meeting he feared. He "paid homage," that is, he prostrated himself or bowed (as the same Hebrew word is rendered earlier, 1:16, 23, 31, 47). In other words, he took the posture of Bathsheba and Nathan before King David earlier in this story. His humiliation had little in common, however, with their humble submission.

The episode (and the opening chapter of 1 Kings) concludes with Solomon's royal word to the one who wanted so much to be king: "Go to your house" (v. 53b). This was clearly a massive humiliation for the once arrogant young man who had "exalted himself" (1:5). There is a note of warning in King Solomon's words: "Go home!"[42]

Consider the inevitability of all this. If Solomon was the rightful king, according to God's promise, then sooner or later those who had put themselves under another king would have to face reality. *Solomon* is king!

What we have seen is a shadow of things to come (cf. Colossians 2:17). If Jesus Christ is Lord, then sooner or later every human being will bow before God's King (see Philippians 2:9–11). It is inevitable.

5

Good Government—What Would It Be Like?

1 KINGS 2:1–12

IN A WORLD WITH SO MANY kinds of wickedness, cruelty, injustice, and violence, it is difficult for us to imagine a government wise and good enough to always do what is right. What would that be like? We can be sure that such a government would not be well-liked by everyone all of the time. Doing what is right is not the same as doing what is popular.

In Western democracies today many feel that there is a crisis of good government. At least part of the problem is that citizens seem to think that *what we would like* our governments to do is what they *ought* to do all of the time. Consequently many of our politicians respond to this thinking, governing by opinion polls and focus groups rather than by clear convictions about what is right. The result is government for the short-term, self-interest of various groups (always with an eye to the next election) rather than government that is wise and good.

It is easy to criticize and complain. Those of us who do not bear the responsibilities of government rarely appreciate the difficulties involved. It is easy to be cynical without understanding the complexity of determining, let alone accomplishing, what is right. The best intentions do not necessarily lead to good government. Indeed, history has taught us to be wary of governments with clear ideas about what they think is right. We call their viewpoint ideological—a term with thoroughly negative connotations in modern politics. It is far from obvious what good government would look like in communities that have long lost the ability to agree about what is right.

Our disappointment with human governments should help us see the wonder of God's promise of a kingdom of righteousness, peace, and joy (Romans 14:17). The failure of human rulers helps us see our need for One who is not only good and powerful but also wise enough to know and to do what is right.

The Bible teaches us that God has promised such a king and such a kingdom. While this promise has roots that go back to the dawn of time, it came to clear expression during the reign of King David: a son of David will reign over a kingdom that God will establish "forever" (2 Samuel 7:12–16). The New Testament teaches us that Jesus Christ is the promised son of David (Matthew 1:1), declared to be such by his resurrection from the dead (Romans 1:3, 4). The Bible calls this astonishing news "the gospel of God" (see, for example, Mark 1:14; Romans 1:1; 1 Thessalonians 2:2, 8, 9).

In the book of 1 Kings we are looking back to the early days of this promise. The first chapter has taken us to the latter days of King David's life, where we have seen that God's great promise (although not explicitly mentioned) was behind the course of events. We have deduced that at least the prophet Nathan and King David remembered the promise and understood that the son of David who was to inherit David's throne (in keeping with the promise of 2 Samuel 7:12) was Solomon.

Accordingly, prompted by Nathan (with a little help from Bathsheba), King David ensured that the expectations and self-promotion of his eldest son, Adonijah, were thwarted. Solomon was made king (at this stage co-regent with his old father). That much has been the story of 1 Kings 1.

In 1 Kings 2 "David's time [literally, days] to die drew near" (v. 1a). God's promise was still on David's mind. Indeed, how could he forget those words, especially as he faced the end of his life?

> *When your days are fulfilled and you lie down with your fathers*, I will raise up your offspring after you, who shall come from your body, and I will establish his kingdom. (2 Samuel 7:12)

For David the hope formed by this promise focused on Solomon. Just as Benaiah and David's servants had prayed that Solomon's kingdom would be even greater than King David's (1:37, 47), David understood that the kingdom of his son would be no ordinary kingdom. It was the kingdom of that promise!

So it was that King David "commanded Solomon his son" (v. 1b). This would be his final charge to his son and heir, David's last will and testament.[1]

We do not know how old Solomon was at this time. Since he would reign for forty years (11:42), it is reasonable to assume he was still a youth.[2]

"I am about to go the way of all the earth," David began (v. 2a). The solemnity of the moment is clear. David's words echo those of Joshua (Joshua 23:14a) near the end of his life. These words are more than a euphemism. The road David was about to tread was the path "all the earth" must take (Ecclesiastes 3:20). The horror of this thought—one's own death in the context of the universality of death—is surely the darkest, most despairing thing the human mind can contemplate. And yet for David (as for Joshua many years earlier), the reality of God's promise filled the moment and drove out despair (see Joshua 23:14b). God's promise has that extraordinary power.

What follows are the last recorded words of King David.[3] They focus on the kind of king Solomon, the king of God's promise, must be. What kind of king does the promised kingdom need?

David spoke first of the character Solomon must display (vv. 2b–4) and then of certain actions he must take (vv. 5–9). In this way David's final words to Solomon give us a picture of at least King David's understanding of the promised kingdom. This is David's vision of good government—inspired by God's promise.[4] It contains some surprises.

The Character of the King (vv. 2b–4)

His Strength (v. 2)

"Be strong, and show yourself a man [or be a man]" (v. 2b). These are words that could be spoken to soldiers facing a fearsome enemy (as in 1 Samuel 4:9[5]). But it was not courage for battle that David had in mind here. Nor was it a call to bear the grief of his father's approaching death bravely. Rather young Solomon must have the strength, courage, and manliness to walk in the ways of the Lord his God, as David will spell out in what follows.

Have you ever been hoodwinked by the nonsensical idea that following God's ways is weak and feeble? On the one hand every believer knows that it takes real courage to stand firm against temptation and the godless ways of the world. On the other hand God's ways are the greatest source of strength. David's son must be strong with the strength that comes from the ways of the Lord.

His Ways (v. 3a)

What are those ways?

> . . . and keep the charge of the LORD your God, walking in his ways and keeping his statutes, his commandments, his rules, and his testimonies, as it is written in the Law of Moses . . . (v. 3a)

"Keep the charge of the LORD" means "keep your obligation to the LORD" (HCSB).[6] This obligation is summed up as "walking in his ways," which is further defined as keeping all that is "written in the Law of Moses."

In a word, the ways of the Lord are the ways of *obedience* to the Lord. This had always been the fundamental requirement for a king over God's people. It had been made clear to Saul (see 1 Samuel 12:14; 15:1). Saul's failure as king was his failure to obey (1 Samuel 13:13, 14; 15:19, 22, 23, 26). This requirement had been spelled out much earlier by Moses (Deuteronomy 17:18–20).

There is poignancy in these words of David to his son because David himself had famously done what was "evil in the eyes of the LORD" (2 Samuel 11:27, literal translation). This would have destroyed his kingdom (as Saul's disobedience had destroyed his), but for the astonishing grace of God's promise to David (see 2 Samuel 7:14, 15; 12:13).

The emphasis in David's words is on the laws given by God to the people of Israel at Mount Sinai and written down for them by Moses (see Deuteronomy 31:9, 24). The terms "statutes," "commandments," "rules," and "testimonies" do not need to be defined precisely and distinguished from each other. Together they refer to the vast and varied body of law that the people of Israel had been given (cf. Deuteronomy 4:1; 6:2; 8:11; 10:13). *Keep them all, Solomon. Be man enough and strong enough to keep them all.*

To our ears this may sound like an impossible and terrible burden. Indeed we will eventually see that Solomon did not live up to his father's charge (see 11:9). However, we ought not to overlook two things.

First, the law God had given Israel was an extraordinarily good gift. Listen to what Moses said about it:

> See, I have taught you statutes and rules, as the LORD my God commanded me, that you should do them in the land that you are entering to take possession of it. Keep them and do them, for that will be your wisdom and your understanding in the sight of the peoples, who, when they hear all these statutes, will say, "Surely this great nation is a wise and understanding people." For what great nation is there that has a god so near to it as the LORD our God is to us, whenever we call upon him? And what great nation is there, that has statutes and rules so righteous as all this law that I set before you today? (Deuteronomy 4:5–8)

David understood this. In his own words:

> The law of the LORD is perfect,
>   reviving the soul;

the testimony of the LORD is sure,
    making wise the simple;
the precepts of the LORD are right,
    rejoicing the heart;
the commandment of the LORD is pure,
    enlightening the eyes;
the fear of the LORD is clean,
    enduring forever;
the rules of the LORD are true,
    and righteous altogether.
More to be desired are they than gold,
    even much fine gold;
sweeter also than honey
    and drippings of the honeycomb.
Moreover, by them is your servant warned;
    in keeping them there is great reward. (Psalm 19:7–11)[7]

David's words to Solomon were certainly solemn, but they were good. It was a call to Solomon to gladly embrace the privilege and blessing of obedience to such wise and good statutes.

Second, while the emphasis is on obedience to God's good laws, "the Law of Moses" was more than laws. Indeed "Law" is an unfortunately narrow translation of the Hebrew term *torah*.[8] *Torah* means "teaching" or "instruction," which can, of course, include laws, but in the Bible it includes much more. Indeed the whole of Genesis through Deuteronomy became known as the Torah. The Torah then includes God's promise (Genesis 12:1–3) and his great acts of grace toward Israel (particularly their redemption from slavery in Egypt). The Torah of Moses sets the laws of God in the context of his promises and grace (see the logic of Exodus 20:2, 3).

All this means that the obedience to which David called his son was not merely obedience to rules. It was obedience to God in the context of knowing God's goodness. It was what we might call "the obedience of faith" (cf. Romans 1:5; 16:26).

His Success (vv. 3b, 4)

The purpose and promised outcome[9] of such obedience would be "that you may prosper [or succeed[10]] in all that you do and wherever you turn" (v. 3b). Such a comprehensive promise is astonishing. The same thing had been said to the people of Israel, and to Joshua (Deuteronomy 29:9; Joshua 1:7). Indeed such "success" was a characteristic of David's early life (1 Samuel 18:5, 14, 15, 30).[11]

Without diminishing the power of this promise, we should clearly understand that the "prosperity" or "success" that will flow from Solomon's obedience to God is in accordance with God's will, not Solomon's. David had been successful in defeating the Philistines because that was God's will for him. Solomon's obedience would result in his "successful" reign as God's king over God's kingdom.

That is why this kind of statement must not be used to support the so-called "prosperity gospel." The obedience of faith looks forward to "prosperity" or "success" only in terms of what God has promised, which for us is not health, wealth, and power in this world. The New Testament is very clear about this (see, for example, John 15:20; 16:33; Acts 14:22; Romans 8:17; 1 Thessalonians 3:3; 2 Timothy 3:12; Titus 2:11–13). We look forward to greater riches by far (see Romans 8:18; Colossians 1:5; 1 Peter 1:4).

In Solomon's case the connection between his "success" and God's promise is clear as David elaborates:

> . . . that the LORD may establish his word that he spoke concerning me, saying, "If your sons pay close attention to their way, to walk before me in faithfulness with all their heart and with all their soul, you shall not lack a man on the throne of Israel." (v. 4)

Solomon's obedience will lead to this "success": God will fulfill his word.

There is a puzzle here. "His word that he spoke concerning me" almost certainly refers to the promise in 2 Samuel 7:12–16. But that promise was expressed *unconditionally*. Indeed "when he [David's son] commits iniquity . . . my steadfast love will *not* depart from him, as I took it from Saul . . ." (2 Samuel 7:14, 15). In other words the promise in 2 Samuel 7 was *not* dependent on the obedience of David's son, as the promise to Saul had been (1 Samuel 12:14). Now, however, David cites a version of that promise that is very definitely *conditional*: "*If* your sons pay close attention to their way . . . [then] you shall not lack a man on the throne of Israel." What is the relationship between the *unconditional* promise in 2 Samuel 7 and the *conditional* promise in 1 Kings 2:4b?

David's version of the promise is not a quotation of the actual words Nathan had spoken to him.[12] It is, however, a valid statement of the promise, as subsequent history will show. Our perplexity here is profoundly theological and has to do with the relationship between human obedience and God's faithfulness.[13] On the one hand, we must not think that God's faithfulness *depends* on our obedience. When we receive God's promised blessings, we must understand that it is all of grace. It is not a reward earned by our obedience. On the other hand, we must not think that God's promised blessings can be enjoyed *without* obedience. In other words, God's grace cannot be received *in disobedience*.

While our minds may struggle to hold these things together, the Bible's message confirms the reality. On the one hand, despite the disobedience of Solomon and every other descendant of David (with one notable exception), God has kept his promise. The kingdom of God's Christ has come, and he will reign forever and ever (Revelation 11:15). On the other hand, the disobedience of David's sons did result in the destruction of the historical kingdom of David (that is the story that the books of Kings recount). Disobedience did not nullify God's faithfulness but did result in the Old Testament form of the kingdom being lost.[14] In the end God himself provided the obedient king, by whose obedience "many will be made righteous" (Romans 5:19).

It is fitting that David's charge to Solomon—his vision for the promised king—has led us to think of Jesus. Consider his strength. Ponder his obedience. Rejoice in his "success." Where Solomon fell short of the kind of king God's kingdom needed (as we will see), Jesus did not.

The Actions of the King (vv. 5–9)

In verse 5 David's final address to his son Solomon takes a sudden and surprising turn. What did King David think Solomon should do?

David's answer to that question in verses 5–9 is often considered far less worthy than his description of the promised king's character in verses 2–4.[15] While I suppose it is possible that David's darker side (which we know he certainly had) emerged in his last recorded words, we should be careful with our judgments. I may not be comfortable with what David said, but I am inclined to think that these last words of King David were true to God's purpose. In other words, what David was calling on Solomon to do *was right*, even if not popular with modern Bible commentators and others.

There were three matters on which David charged his son Solomon to act.

Justice for Joab (vv. 5, 6)

The first was Joab:

> Moreover,[16] you also know what Joab the son of Zeruiah did to me, how he dealt with the two commanders of the armies of Israel, Abner the son of Ner, and Amasa the son of Jether, whom he killed, avenging in time of peace for blood that had been shed in war,[17] and putting the blood of war on the belt around his waist and on the sandals on his feet.[18] (v. 5)

Joab's role in more recent events was not mentioned (1:7, 19, 41). It is true that Solomon would have a problem on his hands if the wily old general continued to back forces unhappy with the younger son's elevation to the throne. David himself had found Joab difficult.

That is an understatement. Joab was impossible. Three times he had defied King David and murdered someone to whom David wanted to show kindness (in different ways). Two of these are mentioned here: Abner and Amasa (for the stories see 2 Samuel 3:20–39; 19:13; 20:4–13). At different times they had been commanders of Israelite forces hostile to David, the former under King Saul, the latter under the usurper Absalom. Both had made peace with David but were subsequently killed by Joab.

The memory of a third unauthorized slaughter by Joab was perhaps too painful for David to put into words here. That was David's loved but rebellious son Absalom (2 Samuel 18).

David had taken these murders personally: "what Joab the son of Zeruiah did *to me*." We should remember that the "me" here was the king. Joab had acted treacherously. On the occasion of the first of Joab's murders (Abner), David had unambiguously condemned the atrocity (see 2 Samuel 3:29, 38, 39), but took no action against Joab. When Joab killed Absalom, we are given a graphic account of David's grief, but again he took no immediate action against Joab, although in due course he replaced Joab with Amasa (2 Samuel 19:13). When Joab then slaughtered Amasa, as far as we know David did nothing.

Was David too weak to stand up to his strong general? That was probably part of it (see 2 Samuel 3:39a, b).[19] Was it also that David deliberately did not take vengeance into his own hands, leaving it to "the LORD [to] repay the evil-doer according to his wickedness" (2 Samuel 3:39c)?[20] Was David's inaction against Joab weakness or patience? Perhaps it was a bit of both.

Be that as it may, David now believed Joab's time had come:

> Act therefore according to your wisdom, but do not let his gray head go down to Sheol[21] in peace. (v. 6)

Whatever we think about David not having taken action himself against Joab, the son of David was to "act." There is no ambiguity about what Solomon was to do, according to the old king. "Do not let his gray hair go down to Sheol in peace" meant "Do not let him die naturally of old age." There is a touch of bitter irony here. "Peace" had characterized David's dealings with those Joab had murdered.[22] It had been "in time of peace" (v. 5) that both Abner and Amasa had been killed. In each case Joab had robbed his victims of this "peace." Therefore he himself must not be allowed to die "in peace."

As the promised king, Solomon was to deliver *justice* to Joab. This aspect of David's charge to his son has too often been evaluated by various opinions about David's failure to have done what he now commanded Solomon to do.[23] I'm not sure that is relevant. The point is that David's vision for the promised king is that he will deliver justice. We may *imagine* ulterior motives, but I do not think they are suggested by the text before us.[24]

David was right to expect God's promised king to bring judgment. He also understood (perhaps from bitter experience) that justice is not straightforward. In this messy world it is always complicated. It was certainly complicated with Joab. Solomon would need to act according to his "wisdom." This is the first mention of the quality for which Solomon would be famous and about which we will hear much more in due course. Here we should simply note that to do what is right, the promised king would need wisdom.[25]

It may not be the most popular aspect of the gospel of God, but Jesus Christ is the One who will bring just judgment to the whole world. As the Apostle Peter explained to Cornelius:

> And [Jesus] commanded us to preach to the people and to testify that he is the one appointed by God to be judge of the living and the dead. (Acts 10:42; cf. 17:31)

Of the promised King Isaiah prophesied:

> He shall not judge by what his eyes see,
>   or decide disputes by what his ears hear,
> but with righteousness he shall judge the poor,
>   and decide with equity for the meek of the earth;
> and he shall strike the earth with the rod of his mouth,
>   and with the breath of his lips he shall kill the wicked. (Isaiah 11:3, 4)

"The Spirit of wisdom and understanding" would rest upon him (Isaiah 11:2). Jesus is the one "in whom are hidden all the treasures of wisdom and knowledge" (Colossians 2:3), who will therefore "judge the world in righteousness" (Acts 17:31; cf. Romans 11:33).

Kindness for Barzillai (v. 7)

The second matter with which David charged Solomon to deal was rather different:

> But deal loyally with [or show kindness to] the sons of Barzillai the Gileadite, and let them be among those who eat at your table,[26] for with such

loyalty [literally, for thus] they met[27] me when I fled from Absalom your brother. (v. 7)

Barzillai was a wealthy old man from the region east of the Jordan River (Gilead). He had shown generous kindness to David in his darkest hour, at Mahanaim when the king had been forced by Absalom's rebellion to flee from Jerusalem. Aware of his old age, this faithful servant of the king later declined David's invitation to join him on his return to Jerusalem. He was content to rejoice in the king's return, but entrusted Chimham (probably a son) to David's care. (For the full story see 2 Samuel 17:27–29; 19:31–39.)

Now it seems there were a number of sons of Barzillai in Jerusalem under David's patronage. Solomon must show "kindness" to these sons of Barzillai. The Hebrew term here (*khesed*) has described King David at his best and has characterized the Lord's dealings with David.[28] Indeed David has been spoken of as the agent of *God's* kindness on more than one occasion.[29] In this King David displayed an essential aspect of God's kingdom and of God's king: kindness.

The kindness we glimpse here in David's vision of the promised king should remind us of the kindness we have experienced from God's King:

> But when the goodness and loving kindness of God our Savior appeared, he saved us, not because of works done by us in righteousness, but according to his own mercy, by the washing of regeneration and renewal of the Holy Spirit, whom he poured out on us richly through Jesus Christ our Savior, so that being justified by his grace we might become heirs according to the hope of eternal life. (Titus 3:4–7)

Justice for Shimei (vv. 8, 9)

There was a third thing David expected Solomon to do:

> And there is also with you Shimei the son of Gera, the Benjaminite from Bahurim, who[30] cursed me with a grievous curse on the day when I went to Mahanaim. But when he came down to meet me at the Jordan, I swore to him by the LORD, saying, "I will not put you to death with the sword." (v. 8)

Shimei,[31] a kinsman and loyalist to the former King Saul, had at one time tormented David. As the king was fleeing from Jerusalem during Absalom's rebellion, Shimei had bitterly cursed him and hurled rocks at him. Joab's brother, Abishai (in the manner of the sons of Zeruiah), was keen to silence Shimei then and there. However, David refused to allow it and entrusted the matter to the Lord. (See 2 Samuel 16:5–13.)

Later when David was returning to Jerusalem to take his place again as king, Shimei hurried to make amends. He had miscalculated. It is one thing to curse a deposed king. It becomes a problem when that king returns. Abishai was again eager to deal with Shimei the only way the sons of Zeruiah knew.[32] Again David intervened and protected Shimei. Shimei's "repentance," whatever its motive, found grace from King David (see 2 Samuel 19:16–23).

We now learn that Shimei was living (or possibly just temporarily present) in Jerusalem ("with you"). David recalled his "grievous curse" on the day that David had fled from Jerusalem. The emphasis seems to be on the hurt and harm that Shimei's curse intended.[33]

David also recalled the mercy that he had extended to Shimei as he was returning to Jerusalem. The earlier account reported that David had given his oath to Shimei that "You shall not die" (2 Samuel 19:23). In context, however, this declaration was tied to "this day" on which David returned as king over Israel: "Shall anyone be put to death in Israel *this day*?" (2 Samuel 19:22). David's recollection of his oath is consistent with this. "I will not put you to death with the sword" was mercy, but it was not an unconditional or absolute pardon.[34]

We do not know anything about Shimei's behavior subsequent to his apparent change of mind when faced with the returning king. Was he thankful for mercy shown? Or did he slip back into his seditious ways? We do not know. Was his presence in Jerusalem a sign of his loyalty to King David, or had he been required to live there where he could be watched? Our lack of answers to such questions should make us cautious in our evaluation of what David told Solomon to do about Shimei.

> Now therefore do not hold him guiltless, for you are a wise man. You will know what you ought to do to him, and you shall bring his gray head down with blood to Sheol. (v. 9)

These are David's very last recorded words in the epic history of his life that began in 1 Samuel 16—surely one of the greatest stories ever told. Are you disappointed? Do you feel that it would have been nicer if David's last words were more generous, less severe?

Since David was far from perfect, it is possible that any disappointment we may have with these last words is justified. But I don't think so. This is like the word about Joab. David expected God's promised king to be a just judge.[35]

Shimei was not, according to David, to be held "guiltless." The long story of David's relationship with Saul and his house has repeatedly emphasized that David *was* "guiltless" (see 1 Samuel 19:5 where ESV has "innocent"; 26:9; and especially 2 Samuel 3:28).[36] This is what Shimei had denied in his curses, falsely accusing David of being "a man of blood" (2 Samuel 16:7, 8). By insisting that Shimei not be held "guiltless," David was reasserting his own guiltlessness with regard to all the violence that had been inflicted on the house of Saul.

Once again, however, doing what was right with Shimei would be complicated. For the second time David mentioned that Solomon was "wise." He would need to be if he was going to judge rightly.[37]

The punishment Shimei deserved was death. He was apparently now an old man ("gray head"), but like Joab he had no right to die in peace. He would die violently ("with blood").

However uncomfortable we may feel with this, it should remind us that God's promised king will bring justice.[38] David was right to see this. We too must see that "the Lord Jesus [will be] revealed from heaven with his mighty angels in flaming fire, inflicting vengeance on those who do not know God and on those who do not obey the gospel of our Lord Jesus. They will suffer the punishment of eternal destruction, away from the presence of the Lord and from the glory of his might" (2 Thessalonians 1:7–9). Praise God, there is more to the glorious gospel of God than this, but there is not less.[39]

The Death of David (vv. 10–12)

"Then David slept with his fathers and was buried in the city of David"[40] (v. 10). David went "the way of all the earth" (v. 2). It was the way his "fathers" had also gone. It would be the way in which his sons would go.

Many years later the cycle was broken:

> For David, after he had served the purpose of God in his own generation, fell asleep and was laid with his fathers and saw corruption, but he whom God raised up did not see corruption. Let it be known to you therefore, brothers, that through this man forgiveness of sins is proclaimed to you. (Acts 13:36–38)

This man was Jesus, the son in whom the promise to David was finally and perfectly fulfilled.

The notice of David's death ("David *slept with his fathers*") reminds us of this promise: "When your days are fulfilled and you *lie down* [or *sleep*[41]] *with your fathers*, I will raise up your offspring after you, who shall come from your body, and I will establish his kingdom" (2 Samuel 7:12).

There is a brief formal notice about David's reign:

> And the time that David reigned over Israel was forty years. He reigned
> seven years in Hebron and thirty-three years in Jerusalem. (v. 11)

There is some shorthand here[42] and rounding of numbers (see 2 Samuel 2:11;
5:4, 5), but that is unimportant. These forty years[43] had seen one of the greatest men the world has known reigning over God's people. He had been great
because the Lord had been with him (2 Samuel 5:10). Even when he failed
(and his failure was spectacular, 2 Samuel 11), the Lord restored his kingdom
and remained faithful to his promise.

That is why:

> So Solomon sat on the throne of David his father, and his kingdom was
> firmly established. (v. 12)

We will see the story of how his kingdom was "established" in 2:13–
46 (see especially v. 46),[44] but here we must be reminded that we are reading
about *what had been promised to David*: "I will *establish* his kingdom . . .
I will *establish* the throne of his kingdom forever . . . Your throne shall be
established forever" (2 Samuel 7:12, 13, 16).

Solomon's kingdom, as we will see, was a taste of the promised kingdom.
More accurately it *was* the promised kingdom, although not yet all that the
kingdom would one day be. David's expectation for the promised king was
only partially realized in Solomon.

In due course it will become clear that God's promised King will be righteous, truthful, wise, and good beyond anything Solomon became (see, for
example, Isaiah 11:1–9). He will rule wisely and judge rightly. It is difficult for
us to imagine such a thing. The Bible's astonishing message, however, is that
this King has now come and has begun to reign. All authority in Heaven and
earth has been given to the risen and ascended Jesus Christ (Matthew 28:18;
John 17:2; Acts 2:36; Romans 1:4; 1 Corinthians 15:27; Ephesians 1:20–22;
Philippians 2:9, 10; Colossians 2:10; Hebrews 2:8; 1 Peter 3:22). Those of
us who submit to his rule now taste the goodness of his kingdom as we look
forward to the day when his reign will be revealed in all its glory and goodness
(Colossians 3:4). Good government at last!

6

The Bible's Disturbing News

1 KINGS 2:12–46

THERE IS NOTHING SENTIMENTAL about the Bible's message. Only by taking random texts out of their proper contexts can the Bible be made into a collection of sweet thoughts. The Bible is about the kingdom God has promised—a kingdom of righteousness, peace, and joy (Romans 14:17)—and the wise, good King who will reign forever and ever (Revelation 11:15). The promised King is Jesus Christ. The establishment of his kingdom has involved his bloody execution on a cross (see Colossians 1:20) and his bodily resurrection from the dead (see Romans 1:4) and also his future coming again to judge the whole world (see Acts 17:31). This is solemn and serious. Indeed, it is disturbing.

We can sense the seriousness of God's coming kingdom in the Bible's account of the establishment of the kingdom of David's son, Solomon. The story is disturbing in a way that—admittedly imperfectly—foreshadows the kingdom of the great Son of David, Jesus. In due course we will see that Solomon's kingdom, unlike that of Jesus Christ, had serious flaws deriving from major failings in Solomon himself (see particularly 11:1–11). Therefore it is possible (as many think) that the story of the establishment of Solomon's kingdom in 2:13–46 displays Solomon's faults more than it reflects the realities of God's kingdom of righteousness, peace, and joy.[1] That would be a more comfortable understanding of our passage, but I am convinced it is mistaken.

We are going to follow the experiences of six men as Solomon's kingdom came to be firmly established. They were Adonijah (vv. 13–25), Abiathar (vv. 26, 27), Joab (vv. 28–34), Benaiah and Zadok (v. 35), and Shimei (vv. 36–46a). The unsettling stories of these men confront us with the solemn seriousness of God's promised kingdom.

The theme of our passage is indicated by two strikingly similar statements that stand at the beginning and the end of the narrative:[2]

> So Solomon sat on the throne of David his father, and his kingdom was firmly established. (v. 12)

> So the kingdom was established in the hand of Solomon. (v. 46b)

This seems to be a way of clearly indicating that the events recounted between this pair of statements must be understood in the light of the promise so strikingly echoed. "Throne," "father," "his kingdom,"[3] "establish" are all key terms in the promise of 2 Samuel 7:12–16. Our passage recounts what it took for that promise to be fulfilled in the establishment of Solomon's kingdom. What it took is deeply disturbing.

We will see:

(1) Adonijah: the man who wanted more (vv. 13–25)
(2) Abiathar: the man who lost his way (vv. 26, 27)
(3) Joab: the man who defied the king (vv. 28–34)
(4) Benaiah and Zadok: the men who served the king (v. 35)
(5) Shimei: the man who forfeited mercy (vv. 36–46a)
(6) The kingdom established (v. 46b).

Adonijah: The Man Who Wanted More (vv. 13–25)

First we hear about what happened to Adonijah as Solomon's kingdom was established. We might have thought we had heard the last of this self-promoting young man when King Solomon had told him to "Go home" (1:53, AT). It would have been better for him if he had accepted the mercy of the king then, been content with his lot, and proven himself to be a "worthy" servant of Solomon (see 1:52).

Adonijah's Foolish Discontentment (vv. 13–18)

However, contentment with obscurity was not Adonijah's way (remember 1:5). He formed a plan. Somehow he managed to get himself into the presence of the king's mother: "Then[4] Adonijah the son of Haggith came to Bathsheba the mother of Solomon" (v. 13a).

The narrator reminds us that Haggith, not Bathsheba, was Adonijah's mother—and that Solomon, not Adonijah, was Bathsheba's son. The names of the rival wives of David highlight the tension in this scene.[5] Their sons were rivals.

There may also be a silent hint of awkwardness in the absence of any reference to Adonijah bowing before Bathsheba. Even her own son, the king, showed this courtesy to the queen mother (see v. 19).[6] There is something brusque and presumptuous in the description of Adonijah simply walking into Bathsheba's presence, uninvited and without appropriate expressions of respect.[7]

Bathsheba was uneasy. She did not trust Adonijah—with good reason. After all, she had been instrumental in crushing his bid for the throne. So she said, "Do you come peacefully?" (v. 13b). In Hebrew there is a curious echo of Solomon's name. The mother of *shelomah* asked Adonijah whether he came "in *shalom*." Had Adonijah come to disturb the "peace" implied by Solomon's name?[8]

Adonijah reassured Bathsheba, saying, "Peacefully" (v. 13c).

Do you believe him? After all we have seen of Adonijah, it is far from obvious that he was a straightforward man whose intentions were always open and honest.

At the very least the matter he wanted to raise with Bathsheba was delicate. He was nervous. He proceeded cautiously: "I have something to say to you" (v. 14a). He wanted Bathsheba's permission to continue. That was clever. If he could make his request *with Bathsheba's permission*, he would shrewdly involve her in the matter.

To his relief she said, "Speak" (v. 14b).

The rather elaborate to-ing and fro-ing with which this meeting began heightens the tension for us as readers, but also draws Bathsheba into Adonijah's scheme. We do not yet have any idea why Adonijah had come to Bathsheba or what he wanted to say to her—any more than she did. Was his "peaceful" assurance genuine? Or had he come to give her a piece of his mind about her role in thwarting his ambitions? Whatever he was about to say, he now had Bathsheba's consent to say it.

He began with what sounded like a complaint: "You know that the kingdom[9] was mine, and that all Israel fully expected me to reign" (v. 15a). *You, Bathsheba, of all people know what was almost mine.*[10]

Adonijah's earlier delusions of grandeur had not subsided. If "all Israel" had really expected him to reign (which is possible, but only in the sense that he was the eldest living son of David), they were very quick to switch those expectations to Solomon (see 1:39, 40). Even at the height of his apparent popularity, Adonijah's support base seems to have been restricted to the tribe of Judah (see 1:9), not "all Israel." It is far from clear that "all Israel" would have been happy with Adonijah's accession. The young man was deceived by his own dreams.

He continued: "However, the kingdom has turned about and become my brother's, for it was his from the LORD" (v. 15b). What a remarkable thing for him to say! It was true: the reason that the kingdom had come to Solomon was not ultimately Nathan's doing, nor Bathsheba's, nor even David's. It was "his from the LORD." But we do not get the impression that Adonijah was pleased with this turn of events. From his lips the words "for it was his from the LORD" sound more like resentment than praise.

If only Adonijah had now expressed his glad acceptance of the Lord's will in this matter, even uttered some remorse for his earlier presumption, things would have worked out very differently for him. Instead it was his discontent with the way in which things had turned out that drove him.

There is an important lesson for us here. True faith in God not only recognizes that the Lord is sovereign over all the circumstances of life, but learns to be content because God is not only the Lord over all, he is good and wise (cf. Philippians 4:11–13). Adonijah had not learned such contentment. He wanted more than the Lord had given him.

It was not going to be easy to make the proposal he had in mind sound good, but he was determined to try. He said to Bathsheba, "And now I have one request to make of you;[11] do not refuse me" (v. 16a). *One little request is all I ask—I hope you will be so kind.* Carefully he concealed what that request would be in order to make it sound small and trivial. It was anything but small and trivial. However, it was essential to his plan that Bathsheba should be deceived into thinking that his request was innocent and insignificant.

Bathsheba seems to have been taken in by this performance. She said to him, "Speak" (v. 16b). Bathsheba invited Adonijah to make his trifling request, whatever it might be. Adonijah had succeeded in drawing Bathsheba further into his scheme.

He said, "Please ask King Solomon—he will not refuse you—to give me Abishag the Shunammite as my wife"[12] (v. 17). With his elaborate preparations, Adonijah had made his request sound almost unremarkable. *Considering what has happened, couldn't I just be given one small compensation for all I have lost?* The very beautiful Abishag would be a comfort. After all, David had no need of her now! It would be a kindness to Abishag to keep her within the family. Perhaps that would be a fitting way to acknowledge Adonijah's good grace in accepting his losses. Perhaps it would signal to everyone that there was no ongoing enmity between Solomon and his older brother.

Some of these thoughts were probably in Bathsheba's mind as she said, "Very well; I will speak for you[13] to the king" (v. 18).[14] I cannot help imagining a secret smirk on Adonijah's face as he realized he had succeeded in the first stage of his audacious secret plan. The queen mother had been duped.

However, thoughtful readers have the luxury of stepping back from the situation and reflecting more objectively than Bathsheba could. We cannot yet be sure exactly what was going on in Adonijah's mind, but we can draw some reasonable inferences.

First, if Adonijah thought he was entitled to Abishag as compensation for his loss, this confirms our impression that he was not content with the outcome of events—despite his fine words, "for it was his [Solomon's] from the LORD" (v. 15).

Second, this sense of entitlement shows that there was no true repentance for his earlier presumptuous grasping for the throne. Certainly he expressed no remorse (look again at v. 15a).

Third, to ask for Abishag (of all the beautiful women in all Israel) was unavoidably political. This is not a romantic story. Don't imagine that Adonijah had happened to spot the gorgeous Abishag across a crowded room, fallen in love with her, and come to Bathsheba with his heart all aflutter. Perhaps Bathsheba was deceived into thinking something like this. But the only real love in Adonijah's life was Adonijah.

Abishag had shared King David's bed (1:1–4, 15). Whatever Bathsheba thought, we cannot regard Adonijah's request for this woman as politically innocent.[15] Whether or not she was strictly speaking a "concubine" of the king,[16] her position and status would have been similar. There have been two occasions in this history when ambitious men sought to advance their positions (or were perceived to have done so) by having sexual relations with the king's concubine. Saul's son Ishbosheth accused General Abner of doing so with Rizpah who had been a concubine of King Saul (2 Samuel 3:7). The political fallout from that accusation (whether or not it was true) saw the end of Ishbosheth's royal pretentions (2 Samuel 3, 4). Later Absalom made his treacherous political intensions unambiguous and irrevocable by publicly having sex with King David's concubines (2 Samuel 16:22).[17]

Adonijah's request did not come from a man who had come to terms with the situation his mouth acknowledged in verse 15b. We might still wonder what Adonijah was up to, but it was certainly not a small matter.

Bathsheba's Unwise Indulgence (vv. 19–22)

Bathsheba was good to her word:

> So Bathsheba went to King Solomon to speak to him on behalf of Adonijah. And the king rose to meet her and bowed down to her. Then he sat on his throne and had a seat [or throne[18]] brought for the king's mother, and

she sat on his right. Then she said, "I have one small request to make of
you; do not refuse me." And the king said to her, "Make your request, my
mother, for I will not refuse you." (vv. 19, 20)

The respect with which Solomon treated Bathsheba highlights the absence
of such formalities in the earlier meeting with Adonijah. This may strengthen
our suspicions that Adonijah had been less honorable than he tried to sound
as he smooth-talked Bathsheba. The meeting with Solomon began in a much
more relaxed, respectful, and trusting way.

The king honored his mother, rising as she entered the room, bowing
down to her, seating her on a throne at his right hand,[19] and assuring her that,
of course, she was welcome to make "one small request."[20]

But did Bathsheba really think that what she was about to ask was
"one small request"? I suspect she did. Adonijah had called it "one request"
(v. 16) and made it sound small. Bathsheba believed him. She had been
hoodwinked.

She made her "one small request." She said, "Let Abishag the Shunammite be given[21] to Adonijah your brother as his wife" (v. 21). Of all the things
she could have said about Adonijah, she called him "your brother," adding to
the reasonableness of her little suggestion. *He is your brother, after all.*

In this family I am not sure that an appeal to brotherly affection carried
much weight. Who could forget Amnon and Absalom (see 2 Samuel 13)? It
certainly did not carry any weight on this occasion for Solomon.

King Solomon answered his mother, "And why do you ask Abishag the
Shunammite for Adonijah? Ask for him the kingdom also, for he is my older
brother, and on his side are Abiathar the priest and Joab the son of Zeruiah."
(v. 22)

Already showing something of the "wisdom" for which he would become
famous (see 2:6, 9), Solomon was not deceived for a moment. Immediately he
saw the political dimensions of this "small request." He saw through Adonijah's pretensions.

As far as Solomon was concerned, to ask for Abishag amounted to a
bid for the kingdom. After all, Adonijah was still the *older* brother. He also
had powerful supporters in Abiathar and Joab. If he were to add to all this a
legitimacy-enhancing marriage to King David's "concubine," he just might
achieve his ambition. This "small request" was taken by Solomon as a clear
sign that Adonijah had not given up his aspirations.

Was Solomon paranoid? Was he eager to rid himself of a possible rival at
any cost? Was he keen to grasp any excuse to take revenge on Adonijah for his

earlier attempted coup? Was he so insecure that he saw a threat to his power where there was none? Was King Solomon jumping at shadows?

I don't think so. Earlier he had shown mercy to Adonijah (1:52) when he could reasonably have acted against him. Solomon, unlike his mother, had seen through Adonijah's devious plans. Solomon *was* "wise," you see.[22]

Solomon's Solemn Verdict (vv. 23–25)

Indeed wise Solomon saw what he had not been told, namely that this request had originated with Adonijah.

> Then King Solomon swore by the LORD, saying, "God do so to me and more also if this word does not cost Adonijah his life! Now therefore as the LORD lives, who has established me and placed me on the throne of David my father, and who has made me a house, as he promised, Adonijah shall be put to death today." (vv. 23, 24)

Are you shocked? I am.[23] Solomon's first recorded act after the death of his father, King David—therefore his first act as king in his own right—was to command the immediate ("today") execution of his brother! And this is the king whose name means "peace"!

Furthermore, he invoked the name of God in this startling act. He "swore by the LORD." This involved not only the solemn claim that in this matter he was doing God's will ("God do so to me and more also if this word does not cost Adonijah his life!") and that the very life of God guaranteed it ("as the LORD lives"), but was also a clear reference to God's hand in placing Solomon on the throne of his father, establishing him there and giving him "a house."[24] All of this was "as he promised." In other words, according to Solomon, Adonijah's death sentence was consistent with the promised kingdom in which Solomon was God's king.

Should we regard this as a terrible example of a wicked tyrant using religion to justify a brutal action designed to protect his own interests?[25] It is tempting to do so. Solomon would then be as culpable as Adonijah in using the truth as an excuse for self-serving ambition (see v. 15b).

The narrator puts the facts (including Solomon's words) before us without explicitly telling us that Solomon was right or wrong—just as he has done with Adonijah. However, Solomon's words so clearly echo the narrator's comments in verses 12 and 46[26]—the frame the narrator has placed around our passage—that Solomon's speech comes to us with the narrator's implicit endorsement. Solomon was fulfilling his father's charge: "Be strong, and show yourself a man, and keep the charge of the LORD your God, walking in his ways . . ."

(2:2, 3). The context leads us to the uncomfortable conclusion that Solomon's terrible words were necessary for and consistent with the establishment of the kingdom God had promised.[27]

The uncomfortable truth is that those who will not have God's king as their king, those who openly or secretly desire to usurp God's king, will be overthrown, whoever they may be. God's king will pronounce judgment on his enemies, whatever high opinion they may have of themselves. That is what we are seeing in King Solomon's treatment of Adonijah. In this way King Solomon foreshadowed the kingdom of our Lord Jesus Christ (compare Luke 19:27).[28] This *is* serious.

This episode concludes with the solemn report, "So King Solomon sent Benaiah the son of Jehoiada, and he struck him down, and he died" (v. 25). Benaiah, the soldier who understood as well as anyone the significance of Solomon's kingdom (see 1:36, 37), had the terrible task of executioner. Look at Adonijah receiving what a rebel against God's kingdom deserves—and tremble.

Abiathar: The Man Who Lost His Way (vv. 26, 27)

The second man whose story is told as part of Solomon's kingdom being "established" was Abiathar the priest. Solomon mentioned him as one of two important supporters of Adonijah (v. 22). We briefly reviewed the earlier record of Abiathar's life when he first appeared in 1 Kings (see 1:7). By this time Abiathar must have been an old man.[29] We have heard that Abiathar "followed Adonijah and helped him" (1:7) and that he was among those invited to Adonijah's supporters' dinner (1:19), where Adonijah was proclaimed king (1:25).

However, we have also heard that it was Abiathar's son, Jonathan, who ended those festivities at the Serpent's Stone by excitedly bringing the "good" news that David had made Solomon king (1:43–48). We noticed then that supporters of Adonijah may not have been *consciously* rebelling against King David. We saw how quickly they abandoned Adonijah as soon as they realized that his aspirations were not legitimate (see 1:49).

How Abiathar Received Mercy (v. 26)

However, King Solomon understood that Abiathar was not among those who abandoned Adonijah (see v. 22). Indeed we may reasonably suppose that the king believed that Abiathar was a supporter of Adonijah's latest outrage in seeking Abishag. So Solomon turned his attention to Abiathar:

> And to Abiathar the priest the king said, "Go to Anathoth, to your estate, for you deserve death. But I will not at this time put you to death, because

you carried the ark of the Lord God before David my father, and because
you shared in all my father's affliction." (v. 26)

It is easy to miss in the English translation, but "the Lord God" is quite
an unusual expression, literally "my Lord Yahweh." The last time God was
referred to with this phrase was when David responded to the historic promise
of 2 Samuel 7. In his prayer David addressed God as "my Lord Yahweh" seven
(or possibly eight) times (2 Samuel 7:18, 19, 20, 22[?], 25[?] 28, 29).[30] The
expression does not occur anywhere else in the books of Samuel and will appear in only one other place (very significantly) in the books of Kings (1 Kings
8:53). In his words to Abiathar, Solomon was speaking as the inheritor of the
2 Samuel 7 promise, from his peculiar relationship to God ("*my* Lord"), as
his servant ("my *Lord*"), according to his promise to his people ("my Lord
Yahweh").[31]

Notice three things in King Solomon's speech to Abiathar. First, what
Abiathar deserved: "you deserve death."[32] The reason he deserved death is
not mentioned here, but has been made clear in the preceding story. Abiathar had supported the rebel (1:7, 19, 25). It appears that he continued to do
so even after Solomon had become king (v. 22). For this, said the king, he
deserved to die.

But did he? Again we ask, are we hearing a paranoid ruler determined to
eliminate any potential threat to his precarious throne? Modern readers may
think so.[33] But that does not seem to be the perspective of the text before us.
Rather, the establishment of God's promised kingdom is a matter of ultimate
seriousness, and King Solomon's pronouncement reflects this. All who set
themselves against God's king (as Adonijah had done) or put themselves on
the side of those opposed to God's king (as Abiathar had done) forfeit the right
to live in God's kingdom. Just so, those "who do not obey the gospel of our
Lord Jesus . . . will suffer the punishment of eternal destruction, away from the
presence of the Lord and from the glory of his might" (2 Thessalonians 1:8, 9).
This is serious. Abiathar deserved death.

But notice, second, what Abiathar received: "Go to Anathoth,[34] to your es-
tate."[35] He was banished from Jerusalem, but he was allowed to live on his own
land in Anathoth. Anathoth was about three miles northeast of Jerusalem and
was one of the cities given "with its pasturelands" to the descendants of Aaron
in the days of Joshua (Joshua 21:18). Some time after the massacre at Nob in
the days of Saul, this city may have been assigned to Abiathar, the only surviving priest (at least in Eli's line).[36] Anathoth's greatest claim to fame will come
much later in the Bible's story, with the appearance of the prophet Jeremiah,

"the son of Hilkiah, one of the priests who were in Anathoth" (Jeremiah 1:1). It has been suggested that Jeremiah may therefore have been a descendant of Abiathar.[37] Whether or not that is the case, King Solomon's sending Abiathar to Anathoth was an act of mercy. The deserved death sentence was commuted: "I will not at this time put you to death."[38] As far as we know he lived out his days in Anathoth.

Third, why did Abiathar receive this mercy? ". . . because you carried the ark of the Lord God before David my father, and because you shared in all my father's affliction." The earlier part of Abiathar's story was remarkable. He had been the only survivor from King Saul's terrible slaughter of the priests at Nob in the days when Saul was desperately seeking to kill David (see 1 Samuel 22:20). David had promised to protect him (1 Samuel 22:23), and Abiathar had then faithfully served David through his years on the run from Saul (see 1 Samuel 23:6; 30:7). When David became king, Abiathar and Zadok served as the priests (2 Samuel 15:24–29, 35, 36; 17:15–20; 19:11; 20:25). His sons Ahimelech (2 Samuel 8:17[39]) and Jonathan (2 Samuel 15:27) also served David with distinction.

Solomon referred to this period of faithful service by mentioning two aspects of it: carrying the ark of God[40] and sharing in David's suffering. The former reminds us of Abiathar's priestly role that also included mediating the word of God to David on occasions (1 Samuel 23:9–12; 30:7, 8). The ark also reminds us of the history of God and his people Israel. The ark originated in the days of Moses after Israel had been rescued from slavery in Egypt by God's mighty power and were given his law at Mount Sinai (see Exodus 25:10–22; Deuteronomy 10:1–8). By means of the ark, the Lord led Israel safely to the promised land (Numbers 10:33–36). The ark went before the people as they entered the promised land (Joshua 3, 4) and was involved in the defeat of their enemies (Joshua 6). The ark had featured in the circumstances that led to Saul's appointment as king (1 Samuel 4—6). Climactically King David had brought the ark into his royal city of Jerusalem, signifying that the Lord, whose promise to Israel was represented by the ark, was the true King in Jerusalem (2 Samuel 6). Abiathar had aligned himself with God's purposes for his king as he had "carried the ark of the Lord God before David."[41]

He also "shared in all [David's] affliction." There were two great periods of affliction for David as first King Saul and later his son Absalom sought his life. These times of "affliction" were the occasion of many of the Psalms,[42] with their frequent references to affliction and suffering. Through all this Abiathar was there, sharing in the hardships of his king (see 1 Samuel 22:22, 23; 23:6–9; 30:7; 2 Samuel 15:24, 29, 35; 17:15; 19:11). We might reasonably suggest that he foreshadowed the experience of those who follow Christ Jesus and share in his sufferings.[43]

All of this makes his recent siding with Adonijah perplexing. It seems that Abiathar had lost his way. His earlier faithfulness was no guarantee that he would end well. Through the darkest days he had remained true, but at the end he was seduced by Adonijah's aspirations. Had he become disillusioned with David? Had he become jealous of the increasing prominence of the relative newcomer, Zadok, his fellow priest? We do not know.

We need to be careful not to draw parallels too closely between Abiathar's particular circumstances and Christian experience today, but servants of the Lord Jesus Christ should note how a lifetime of faithful service through great difficulties did not make Abiathar immune from bitterness, disillusionment, and even rebellion at the end.

However, Abiathar received mercy from the son of David (notice the repeated "my father" in v. 26). Many years later a blind beggar named Bartimaeus understood that Jesus was the Son of David greater than Solomon. He knew what to ask. "Jesus, Son of David, have mercy on me!" he cried (Mark 10:47). He, too, received mercy. Similarly the Apostle Paul, blasphemer, persecutor, and insolent opponent of Jesus, "received mercy" (1 Timothy 1:12–17). In showing mercy to Abiathar, Solomon anticipated the character of the greater Son of David.

How the Word of the Lord Was Fulfilled (v. 27)

However, Solomon's treatment of Abiathar was complicated. Although Abiathar mercifully did not lose his life, sending him from Jerusalem to Anathoth involved stripping him of the responsibilities and privileges of being a priest: "So Solomon expelled Abiathar from being priest to the Lord" (v. 27a).[44] Abiathar's more recent conduct had consequences in the kingdom of Solomon.

The narrator wants us to understand a further and even more important dimension to all this: ". . . thus fulfilling the word of the Lord that he had spoken concerning the house of Eli in Shiloh" (v. 27). Many years earlier, in the days of Abiathar's great-great-grandfather Eli,[45] the Lord had announced the end of the house of Eli serving as priests because of the corruption of Eli's sons and Eli's own ineffectiveness in curbing their ways (1 Samuel 2:27–36). Abiathar was the last surviving descendant of Eli. His banishment by Solomon therefore brought this word of the Lord, spoken four generations earlier, to fulfillment.

Here we meet a theme that we will see again and again throughout the books of Kings. Through the ups and downs of history, by the worthy and unworthy actions of humans, the Lord is accomplishing his purpose, keeping his promise, fulfilling his word. Whatever Abiathar's motives may have been in siding with Adonijah and whatever moved Solomon to spare Abiathar's life, but to dismiss him from the priesthood, the course of history was unfolding under the Lord's faithful and powerful hand. The word of the Lord was fulfilled.

Here, too, we have an anticipation of the great fulfillment of God's promises and purposes in Jesus Christ (see, for example, Matthew 5:17; Luke 4:21; Acts 3:18; 13:27, 33). "For all the promises of God find their Yes in him" (2 Corinthians 1:20).

Joab: The Man Who Defied the King (vv. 28–34)

The third disturbing story underlining the seriousness of the establishment of the kingdom in the hand of Solomon concerns Joab. Like Abiathar, Joab had been mentioned by Solomon in verse 22 as an ongoing supporter of Adonijah. Like Abiathar, Joab may well have had a hand in Adonijah's latest scheme, asking for Abishag. Unlike Abiathar, however, Joab's conduct during David's time as king had been far from admirable.[46] Before his death David had spoken to Solomon about Joab's treachery (2:5) and instructed him, "Act therefore according to your wisdom, but do not let his gray head go down to Sheol in peace" (2:6).

Afraid at Last (v. 28)

> When the news came to Joab—for Joab had supported Adonijah although he had not supported Absalom[47]—Joab fled to the tent of the LORD and caught hold of the horns of the altar. (v. 28)

News of the execution of Adonijah and the banishment of Abiathar reached the old warrior Joab, who was no doubt already nervous about his future. When the narrator tells us that "Joab had supported Adonijah," he probably means in the matter of Adonijah's bid to gain Abishag, since he hardly needs to tell us again about Joab's earlier backing of the ambitious prince.[48]

However, Joab's story is complicated. He had certainly "not supported Absalom," the previous son of David who sought to usurp the throne. We notice, however, that unlike the positive descriptions of Abiathar's faithful service of David (v. 26b), Joab just gets this negative. He did *not* support Absalom. But he had killed Absalom in direct disobedience to David's command (see 2 Samuel 18:5, 14).[49] Joab's relationship with David was fraught with tensions. David could not forget the men Joab had murdered in clear and deliberate defiance of King David's will (see 2:5).

Joab—the man who had never seemed to fear anyone, including King David—was at last afraid. Very afraid. Like Adonijah some time earlier (1:50) he sought refuge in the tabernacle, taking hold of the horns of the altar.[50]

David had shown Joab some leniency. While it is possible that this was a weakness in David, it was more than that.[51] David refrained from vengeance because he trusted God. However, the time had come for Joab to face the son of David, and Joab was rightly afraid.

Condemned Nonetheless (v. 29)

> And when it was told King Solomon, "Joab has fled to the tent of the LORD, and behold, he is beside the altar," Solomon sent Benaiah the son of Jehoiada, saying, "Go, strike him down." (v. 29)

In accordance with his father's word (2:6), Solomon commanded the execution of Joab. For a second time Benaiah was given the executioner's order (see v. 25).

Defiant to the End (v. 30a)

> So Benaiah came to the tent of the LORD and said to him, "The king commands, 'Come out.'" But he said, "No, I will die here." (v. 30a)

Joab was defiant to the end. For one last time he disobeyed his king. As he had lived, so he would die—on his own terms. Notice that Joab did not need to be told that he was facing death.

Justice for Joab: The Cost of Peace (vv. 30b–34)

Benaiah, perhaps intimidated by Joab's defiance (even King David had been intimidated by this man!), reported back to King Solomon: "Thus said Joab, and thus he answered me" (v. 30b). In a tussle of wills between the two soldiers, the domineering Joab had briefly prevailed.

He would not, however, prevail against the son of David. The king replied, "Do as he has said, strike him down and bury him" (v. 31a). There is dignity in the king's words, "and bury him." This showed respect. Joab would die the death he had deserved, but this would not be done with vengeful malice. He would be given a decent burial (contrast 2 Kings 9:10).

Solomon's understanding of the significance of Joab's execution was this: ". . . and thus take away from me and from my father's house the guilt for the blood that Joab shed without cause" (v. 31b). Joab's murders had left a stain. His judicial execution would remove the stain.[52]

Solomon continued:

> The LORD will bring back his bloody deeds[53] on his own head, because, without the knowledge of my father David, he attacked and killed with the sword two men more righteous and better than himself, Abner the son of Ner, commander of the army of Israel, and Amasa the son of Jether, commander of the army of Judah. So shall their blood come back on the head of Joab and on the head of his descendants forever. But for David and for his descendants and for his house and for his throne there shall be peace from the LORD forevermore. (vv. 32, 33)

Notice five points in Solomon's speech. First: "The LORD will bring back his bloody deeds on his own head." According to Solomon what was about to happen to Joab was just: it was the consequence of Joab's own actions. More than this, it was God's justice. Solomon saw himself as God's agent in this judgment of Joab.

Second, Joab's actions were "without the knowledge of my father David." They were acts of treachery.[54]

Third, two men Joab killed were "more righteous and better than himself." This is not simply a moral evaluation of their behavior or character. Both of these men had been enemies of King David, while (at least in his own eyes) Joab had been a devoted servant of King David. The difference was that David had made peace with Abner and Amasa (2 Samuel 3:20, 21; 19:13). Joab refused to accept this. Their right relationship with the king (at the time of their deaths) made them "more righteous and better" than Joab, who was defying his king.

Fourth, "So shall their blood come back on the head of Joab and on the head of his descendants forever." Careful readers of this history may notice that Solomon's words remind us of a prayer of David many years earlier (see 2 Samuel 3:29). In this way there is a sense of fulfillment in the judgment of Joab, as there was with Abiathar.

Fifth, why do you think Solomon spoke of "David" and his "descendants"[55] and his "house" and his "throne"? These were all key words in the great promise to David in 2 Samuel 7, to which Solomon's words here strikingly allude. The downfall of Joab was necessary to the promised establishment of the kingdom. Only then "there shall be peace from the LORD forevermore." This peace is the "rest" of God's promise (2 Samuel 7:10, 11). Peace can be costly. The enemies of peace must be dealt with. While Joab lived, the kingdom of David would not enjoy peace.

This episode concludes:

> Then Benaiah the son of Jehoiada went up and struck him down and put him to death. And he was buried in his own house in the wilderness. (v. 34)

Despite everything, Joab was given a dignified burial (cf. 1 Samuel 25:1; 2 Samuel 2:32). The connotations of "in the wilderness," however, suggest the tragedy of Joab's end.[56]

Benaiah and Zadok: The Men Who Served the King (v. 35)

The fourth and fifth of the men whose stories appear as part of the establishment of the kingdom in Solomon's hands are Benaiah and Zadok. They are mentioned only briefly:

> The king put Benaiah the son of Jehoiada over the army in place of Joab, and the king put Zadok the priest in the place of Abiathar. (v. 35)

Thus two men who had occupied the vital roles of commander of the army and leading priest in David's kingdom but who had in different ways failed regarding faithfulness were replaced. Joab, no doubt, had believed he was indispensable. He was wrong. The spiritually perceptive Benaiah (1:36, 37) took his place, just as Zadok replaced Abiathar.[57]

These two make a sharp contrast to the other men in our passage. They found a place in Solomon's kingdom as faithful servants.

Shimei: The Man Who Forfeited Mercy (vv. 36–46a)

The sixth and last man whose story contributes to this long account of the establishment of the kingdom in the hands of Solomon is Shimei. Solomon's father had given instructions about Shimei, as he had about Joab (2:8, 9). Probably motivated by his father's last recorded words, "the king sent and summoned Shimei" (v. 36a), who was living in Jerusalem at the time.[58]

The Mercy He Received (vv. 36–38)

David had told Solomon to use his wisdom in deciding how to deal with Shimei, the one-time tormentor of King David (see 2 Samuel 16:5–13) who had nonetheless been treated kindly by the restored king (2 Samuel 19:16–23).

In his wisdom, Solomon dealt with Shimei more kindly than we might have expected from David's last words about this matter. He issued a command, a prohibition, and a warning that, if heeded, promised Shimei safety.

The command was: "Build yourself a house in Jerusalem and dwell there" (v. 36b). Shimei was to make his dwelling in Jerusalem permanent. This instruction entailed mercy. Shimei knew he had gravely offended King David (2 Samuel 19:20). Rather than passing the expected sentence (see 2:9), Solomon prescribed Jerusalem as the place where Shimei could live.

The prohibition was, ". . . do not go out from there to any place whatever" (v. 36c). The boundary placed on Shimei's freedom was not severe, but it was real. If he was to enjoy the mercy of the king, his life must be lived within the limits of the city of Jerusalem.

It is possible that Solomon wanted to keep Shimei under observation. Perhaps he had reason to suspect that the troublemaker was still a potential problem. Perhaps he wanted to keep him away from his kinsmen of Benjamin, to ensure he did not stir up trouble there. Was he thinking about what had happened with Shimei's fellow Benjaminite Sheba (2 Samuel 20:1, 2)?

The warning was, "For on the day you go out and cross the brook Kidron, know for certain that you shall die. Your blood shall be on your own head" (v. 37). Scrupulous observance of the boundary set by Solomon would demonstrate Shimei's submission to the king. Only in Jerusalem would Shimei be safe, but there he would be safe.

The brook Kidron was the eastern boundary of the city (see 2 Samuel 15:23), in the direction of Shimei's hometown of Bahurim (2 Samuel 16:5) and therefore the boundary he would be most likely to cross if he decided to leave the city. The prohibition, however, had forbidden Shimei to leave the city in any direction.

Shimei had no complaint about this arrangement. Indeed, he seemed to welcome it, saying to the king, "What you say is good; as my lord the king has said, so will your servant do" (v. 38a). Shimei acknowledged that in this word Solomon was "good" to him, no doubt much better than he had expected. He acknowledged Solomon as "my lord the king" and promised to obey.

"So Shimei lived in Jerusalem many days" (v. 38b). Shimei's story might have ended happily there.

The Boundary He Forgot (vv. 39, 40)

In his earlier conduct with David Shimei had shown himself to be a fickle creature. He tended to change with changing circumstances, cursing David when the king was vulnerable, but begging for mercy as he returned to power.

In due course Shimei's unreliability emerged again. There was another change in his circumstances: "But it happened at the end of three years that two of Shimei's servants ran away to Achish, son of Maacah, king of Gath" (v. 39a).

For three years Shimei lived (happily we presume) under the king's conditions. There is no reason to think that this would have been a hardship or that through these years he had any particular desire to leave Jerusalem. Indeed the fact that he was living with servants (more than two apparently) suggests a reasonably comfortable existence in the capital.

What changed everything was the escape of two of these servants who for some reason found refuge under the protection of the Philistine king Achish in Gath.[59] This was a strange development, particularly for us as readers of the story. In escaping from Shimei and fleeing to Achish in Gath, Shimei's two servants were behaving a little like David when he was on the run from Shimei's kinsman, Saul (see 1 Samuel 21:10; 27:2; 2 Samuel 16:5).[60] If this subtle point reminds us of Shimei's relationship to Saul, we may recall how his ferocious loyalty to Saul once made him deeply hostile to the kingdom of David (see 2 Samuel 16:8).

We may safely presume that at this time Gath was firmly under Israelite control, the Philistines having been subdued by David (2 Samuel 5:17–25; 8:1). Travel between Jerusalem and Gath was no doubt less dangerous than when David sought refuge there. Indeed news soon reached Shimei: "Behold, your servants are in Gath" (v. 39b).

Importantly Gath was *west* of Jerusalem.[61] The brook Kidron was to the *east*. Whether or not Shimei thought this provided a loophole in Solomon's prohibition, his concern for his lost property (as he no doubt regarded his servants) outweighed his concern about the king's command: "Shimei arose and saddled a donkey and went to Gath to Achish to seek his servants. Shimei went and brought his servants from Gath" (v. 40). Twice we are told Shimei "went." His going was in defiance of King Solomon's prohibition.[62]

Mercy Forfeited (vv. 41–46a)

By his disobedience, Shimei forfeited the mercy that Solomon had shown to him:

> And when Solomon was told that Shimei had gone from Jerusalem to Gath and returned, the king sent and summoned Shimei and said to him, "Did I not make you swear by the Lord and solemnly warn you, saying, 'Know for certain that on the day you go out and go to any place whatever, you shall die'? And you said to me, 'What you say is good; I will obey.' Why then have you not kept your oath to the Lord and the commandment with which I commanded you?" (vv. 41–43)

Only now do we learn that three years earlier Solomon had required Shimei to "swear by the Lord." This detail, omitted from the earlier brief account, is added here because it was now crucially relevant.[63] Shimei's disobedience had this added dimension: he had broken his "oath to the Lord" as well as the king's command.

Shimei was not given the opportunity to reply, or (more probably) he had nothing to say in his defense.[64] By his disobedience he had forfeited any claim to mercy. His earlier crime was now therefore held against him, and he would receive his due. The king said to him, "You know in your own heart all the harm [or evil] that you did to David my father. So the LORD will bring back your harm [or evil] on your own head." (v. 44).

Justice for Shimei (now that mercy had been surrendered) meant that the evil he wished upon David and his kingdom would come to Shimei, not to David or his son. Indeed, said the king, "King Solomon shall be blessed, and the throne of David shall be established before the LORD forever" (v. 45). Solomon understood that the justice he was about to administer was consistent with the promise of God that here again he clearly had in mind.

For the third time in this solemn account of the events surrounding the establishment of the kingdom in the hand of Solomon, Benaiah was given the heavy task of executioner (see also vv. 25, 34): "Then the king commanded Benaiah the son of Jehoiada, and he went out and struck him down, and he died" (v. 46a).

The Kingdom Established (v. 46b)

Given all that we have heard, the closing words of 1 Kings 2 are weighty: "So the kingdom was established in [possibly by[65]] the hand of Solomon" (v. 46b). The establishment of this kingdom in the hands of this king involved the death of a prince who could not accept that he would not be king, the banishment of a priest who had lost his first love, the execution of a man who defied the king to the end, and the death penalty for a man who had cursed the king and forfeited the possibility of mercy because he disregarded the king's command. Two are mentioned (although there were many more) who found their place in the new kingdom as servants of the king.

As we turn our thoughts from King Solomon to King Jesus all of this is magnified. This is the Bible's disturbing news. The kingdom of God is at hand. Repent and believe. You will then receive mercy. But be under no illusion: this is serious.

Part 2

THE WISDOM OF GOD

How Things Were Put Right

1 Kings 3—4

7

It's Complicated

1 KINGS 3:1–3

THE WORLD IS COMPLICATED. Now there's an understatement! As I write these words we are reeling and somewhat despairing at a series of terrorist attacks in major world cities.[1] On the one hand these outrageous acts of violence are recognized by almost all people of goodwill as utterly inexcusable; indeed *evil* is an appropriate word. On the other hand, the reactions to these barbarous acts are problematic. Among those who are very clear that what has been done must be condemned there are deep divisions and disagreements about what should be done about it. It is complicated.

At the same time unimaginable numbers of people are fleeing violence and persecution, seeking refuge in some of the countries now fearing terrorist attacks. Should compassion for these people be curbed out of fear that there may be terrorists among them? Or would that be a victory for the terrorists? It is complicated.

As we struggle with these issues, the world seems to be facing a global financial crisis. The now famous global financial crisis of 2008 may have been only the beginning of an economic calamity that some think could bring down the whole capitalist system. Of course, that is only one opinion. Among those who agree that there is at least a massive problem (and that's almost everyone who knows anything about it) there is little agreement about what should be done. It is complicated.

World leaders are about to meet to consider what to do about the widely (but not universally) recognized problem called climate change. Some believe that the future of life on earth is under threat. Some regard that as a gross exaggeration. Some think there is no real problem at all. Some believe drastic action is urgently needed. Some doubt that. Does anyone really know? How far-reaching should actions to combat climate change be? How should economic considerations, particularly effects on poorer nations, shape policies? Agreement is difficult. It is complicated.

As you read these words, the particular crises I have selected may have passed or changed. But they will have been replaced by others. One confident prediction I can make. The world in which you live, dear reader, is complicated.

And, of course, our personal lives are complicated. A few moments reflection will reveal something of the complexity of our lives. Our thoughts and behavior, relationships and pleasures, fears and anxieties, vanities and shames, hopes and dreams are never simple. Who among us has mastered life? It is complicated.

Sometimes unbelievers scoff at "religious" types, saying they are people who need simple, black-and-white answers to life's complexities. There may be some truth in that. But religion should not be confused with Christian faith. Christian faith understands that the world and life are complicated. We do not claim to have simple, black-and-white answers. At least we shouldn't. We understand more deeply than most that the world is in a serious mess, in which our individual lives share. While we want to do what we can and support people of goodwill who offer partial solutions, we do *not* believe in simple, one-size-fits-all answers. For this reason, in my opinion, Christians should not be unquestioningly aligned with any particular political party or philosophy.[2] It is complicated.

What, then, is the hope of the world? How is Christian faith possible? Faith is confidence. Christians are positive about the future while also being more realistic than most about the complexity of the world's problems.

To grasp how this is possible, we will follow the remarkable account of the early days of the kingdom of David's son, Solomon, in 1 Kings 3. In this chapter we will see something of the complexity of King Solomon's world (3:1–3), reflecting in important ways the complexity of our world. In our next chapter we will hear about an unusual event in which we will glimpse the secret of the world's hope (3:4–15). In the chapter after that we will see a remarkable example of a complicated situation properly sorted out (3:16–28). What does a complicated world need?

The first two chapters of 1 Kings have told the story of how the kingdom was "established" (made firm and secure) in the hand of Solomon (see 2:12, 46) over a period of at least three years (2:39). We have seen that this was far from straightforward. It was complicated. Solomon's father had anticipated that he would need "wisdom" (2:6, 9)—and indeed he did. Solomon ordered the execution of three persons who were, in different ways, enemies of this kingdom. Most readers are troubled by these events. Rightly so. Some condemn Solomon's violent acts as tyrannical, but we have seen that it was not as simple as that. The peace and stability of Solomon's kingdom was costly and complicated.

In chapter 3 our historian now begins his description of King Solomon's now "established" reign (3:1—11:43). We will see that Solomon's kingdom was astonishing. Benaiah's prayer (1:37) was answered: Solomon's kingdom was even greater than David's had been at its height.

However, the account of this great kingdom begins with a brief sketch that points to four key factors that made Solomon's kingdom complicated from the beginning in surprising and perplexing ways.

> (1) Egypt: international relations are complicated (v. 1a, b, c)
> (2) Buildings: human undertakings are complicated (v. 1d)
> (3) Religion: The worship of God is complicated (v. 2)
> (4) The Lord: loving God is complicated (v. 3)

Egypt: International Relations Are Complicated (v. 1a, b, c)

The first sentence of this major section of 1 Kings is a surprise: "Solomon made a marriage alliance with [literally, became son-in-law of] Pharaoh king of Egypt"[3] (v. 1a). What are we to make of the fact that the very first thing we are told about Solomon's reign, once it was "established" (2:46), is that he became son-in-law of Pharaoh, king of Egypt?

Solomon's father, David, had entered into a marriage described in similar terms. In his youth David had "become son-in-law of" King Saul.[4] David's marriage to Michal (although it did not work out well) raised none of the questions raised by Solomon becoming son-in-law of *Pharaoh*.[5]

Those with a generally negative view of King Solomon may find here confirmation of their judgment. What was the king of *Israel* thinking, marrying an *Egyptian* princess? Since Abraham arranged for the marriage of Isaac to Rebekah (see Genesis 24:3, 4), it has been unusual for this people to marry foreigners. Indeed, in some cases it was strictly forbidden (Deuteronomy 7:3; Joshua 23:12;[6] cf. Exodus 34:16). In due course we will learn that Solomon breached this prohibition many times over and that this was his undoing (see 11:1–8). Was his marriage to Pharaoh's daughter, noted here at the very beginning of the record of his reign, the seed of his downfall?[7]

Indeed, Solomon already had at least one foreign wife, not yet mentioned in our narrative (Naamah the Ammonite, the mother of Rehoboam; see 11:43; 14:21, 31). Should this color our understanding of his Egyptian marriage? Yet *another* foreign wife!

More particularly we will see that Egypt had an influence on Solomon's kingdom (10:28, 29), played a role in its demise (11:14–22, 40; 12:2), and eventually did great damage (14:25–28). Did this all begin with Solomon becoming son-in-law to Pharaoh, king of Egypt?

Perhaps most puzzling of all, we will be repeatedly reminded in the following pages that the nation over which Solomon now reigned had been rescued *out of* the land of Egypt (6:1; 8:9, 16, 21, 51, 53; 9:9; cf. 12:28). If the account of Solomon's reign begins with this reference to his new association with Egypt, of all places, does this suggest a return, in some sense, to the one from whom they had been redeemed (see Deuteronomy 17:16)?

I am sure there is some truth in all of these considerations.[8] However, I am equally confident that the note our narrator is striking *at this point* in the story of Solomon was not only—or even predominantly—negative. The story of the "establishment" of Solomon's kingdom in 1 Kings 1—2 has reminded us again and again that this was the kingdom that God had promised to David. In due course we will see many indications that Solomon's kingdom was the high point of the history of Israel, a time of fulfillment, when the promises of God were realized more fully than at any other point in the Old Testament. It was not the final, full realization of God's promises (that comes in the New Testament), but it was a very substantial fulfillment of what had been promised.

From a historical and political point of view, Solomon's marriage to Pharaoh's daughter was a sign that his kingdom had become a substantial empire, with a status at least equal to the great power of Egypt.[9] More than that, we should see this as the beginning of a new era in which the nations are not just conquered militarily by God's king (as was the case with David; see 2 Samuel 8), but blessed by God's king. Solomon's marriage to Pharaoh's daughter should be understood in the light of the promise to Abraham that the nations will be blessed through Abraham's seed (Genesis 18:18; 22:18; 26:4). This international relationship is profoundly consistent with the last words of chapter 2 about the "establishment" of Solomon's kingdom. It was a kingdom that extended its peaceful influence to the nations.

It is, then, remarkable that the first-mentioned recipient of this new relationship with the king of Israel should be none other than "Pharaoh king of Egypt." Nothing could demonstrate the astonishing faithfulness of God, realized in the kingdom of David's son, more than this turnaround: Pharaoh king of Egypt now drawn in, as it were, to the sphere of Solomon's reign.

As we have noted, Israel's national history had begun with their deliverance from oppressive slavery to "Pharaoh king of Egypt" (Exodus 6:11, 13, 27, 29; Deuteronomy 7:8). Now, under King Solomon, a positive relationship with "Pharaoh king of Egypt" is brought about.[10]

The wording of verse 1 suggests that Solomon took the initiative in this ("He *took* Pharaoh's daughter . . . ," v. 1b),[11] and our historian does not seem to imply any negative judgment on this act. Indeed his bringing her "into the city of David" (v. 1c) may even suggest that she left behind her Egyptian ways, including the idols of Egypt, as she became a citizen of *David's* city. Indeed, if we are reminded (as we should be) of the story of the exodus we may notice that in both the book of Exodus and in 1 Kings the daughter of Pharaoh plays a positive role, beneficial to Israel.[12] She will be mentioned four more times in 1 Kings (7:8; 9:16, 24; 11:1).

Qualms about this foreign marriage are not shared (in my judgment) by our narrator *at this point*. The prohibition of Deuteronomy 7:3 applied to the peoples of the land of Canaan.[13] Furthermore, when the foreign wives of Solomon who tempted him to idolatry are listed in 1 Kings 11, the daughter of Pharaoh is explicitly distinguished from them (11:1).[14] This marriage was not an act of disobedience on Solomon's part.[15]

If Solomon's becoming son-in-law to Pharaoh reminds us of David's becoming son-in-law to Saul, the contrast we should see is less between the Israelite Michal and the foreign daughter of Pharaoh than between the virtual civil war that followed David's marriage and the international peace signaled by Solomon's marriage.[16]

The negative light in which this marriage is seen by many readers (largely with the benefit of hindsight) and the more positive note that I am sure is being struck at this point by the narrator underline the complexity of this element of Solomon's kingdom. Peace and goodwill between King Solomon and other nations was far from straightforward. It was complicated.

In this respect it was like our world. What would it take to bring the nations of the world together in peace and harmony, trust and mutual respect? *Complicated* is an understatement!

Buildings: Human Undertakings Are Complicated (v. 1d)

We do not know exactly when Solomon took his Egyptian wife, but it was relatively early in his reign, before the completion of his major building projects. We are told that she lived in the city of David (that is, the part of Jerusalem originally conquered by David, otherwise known as "the stronghold of Zion" [2 Samuel 5:7], located on the southeastern ridge of the later city of Jerusalem) until those works were completed (see 9:24): "until he had finished building his own house and the house of the LORD and the wall around Jerusalem" (v. 1d).

The first two of these building projects occupy much of the Bible's record of King Solomon's reign. Chapters 5, 6, and 7:13—8:66 of 1 Kings are concerned with the construction and furnishing of "the house of the LORD." The building of "[Solomon's] own house," is recounted in 7:1–12. The building of "the wall around Jerusalem" (briefly mentioned in 9:15) may be shorthand for Solomon's other considerable constructions in the royal city and elsewhere (see 9:15–28). Solomon was a builder! His ambitious plans and numerous projects were unprecedented in Israel.

Without doubt the most important of all Solomon's undertakings was his building of "the house of the LORD." This was yet another indication that Solomon was the king promised in the Lord's word to David:

> When your days are fulfilled and you lie down with your fathers, I will raise up your offspring after you, who shall come from your body, and I will establish his kingdom. *He shall build a house for my name*, and I will establish the throne of his kingdom forever. (2 Samuel 7:12, 13)

Indeed, we should recall that it was King David's concern about the ark of God dwelling in a mere tent, while he was living in a fine palace (2 Samuel 7:2), that led to the great promise concerning the "house" (dynasty) of David. It was the promised son of David who "shall build a house for my name."[17]

The reference to Solomon's building projects in 1 Kings 3:1 is the first time since 2 Samuel 7:13 that this "house" has been mentioned. After the numerous allusions to the 2 Samuel 7 promise in the previous two chapters, this reference to "the house of the LORD" confirms that Solomon's kingdom was the promised kingdom.

But there was more to it. It was complicated.

First of all, the whole question of building a permanent structure to replace the tabernacle was far from straightforward. David was not permitted to do it (2 Samuel 7:5–7). There even seems to be a reticence to call this "house" a "temple" (as most commentators do). Indeed it is far from clear that Hebrew had a word quite corresponding to "temple," with the clear religious connotations of that term in English. There is a word (*hekal*), often translated "temple" or "palace," depending on the context, but these renderings suggest that the word itself means an important building, perhaps associated with a king (earthly or heavenly). Be that as it may, the word *hekal* was not used in 2 Samuel 7, and it is not used here in 1 Kings 3:1. Indeed it is not used at all in

1 Kings for "the house of the LORD" as such.[18] The preference for the ordinary word "house" (*bayith*) is a little like the reticence we can see in some places to call God's chosen ruler "king."[19] The "house for my name" was to be as different from the temples of the surrounding pagan nations as the promised "king" was to be different from the kings of the nations.[20]

Much later the prophet Jeremiah will condemn his contemporaries who had come to trust in the "temple," by then no doubt understood in terms far too close to the pagan temples: "Do not trust in these deceptive words: 'This is the temple [*hekal*] of the LORD, the temple of the LORD, the temple of the LORD'" (Jeremiah 7:4).

Further complications were associated with Solomon's building projects. There was the problem of priorities. In due course we will learn that Solomon spent thirteen years building his own house (7:1), while the building of the house of the Lord took just seven years (6:38). Is there a hint of confused priorities in the mention of "his own house" *before* "the house of the LORD" in 3:1?[21]

Solomon's building projects were lavish and very expensive. He used forced labor (4:6; 5:13; 9:15). The burden of this (rightly or wrongly) sowed the seeds of discontent that eventually led to the division of the kingdom after his death (see 12:4). There is evidence that at least at one point his kingdom was virtually bankrupt so that he had to cede part of the kingdom to a creditor (but see our discussion of 9:11).

Solomon's undertakings were grand and impressive (as we will see). But did he get it *all* right? Prosperity and the things that wealth enabled Solomon to undertake were complicated.

Again this is familiar to us. What would it take for humans to use the available resources, their ingenuity and skills exclusively and effectively for good ends? It is not straightforward, is it?

Religion: The Worship of God Is Complicated (v. 2)

Religion can be complicated. Everyone has their own ideas about how they would like to worship God (or not worship him). Even among God's own people (today as well as in Old Testament times), people love do-it-yourself religion. Those who love music must have music (*their* kind of music!) in their worship. Those who love traditional ways must have the old forms they know and love. Those who love contemporary informality . . . You get the idea. And it is very difficult—even for Christian people—to learn from the New Testament that worship is now trusting and obeying God in all of our living rather than something we do "in church" (see Romans 12:1; Hebrews 12:28 in the light of what follows in Hebrews 13:1–5).

The difficulty is suggested by the next aspect of Solomon's kingdom: "The people were sacrificing at the high places, however, because no house had yet been built for the name of the LORD" (v. 2). "However" represents a small Hebrew word (*raq*) that signals that what follows is some kind of contrast or limitation to what has just been said.[22] If the comments about Egypt and buildings in verse 1 were, at this stage, more positive than negative, what we are now told is rather more negative than positive. But it, too, was complicated.

Prior to the building of a "house . . . for the name of the LORD," the people of Israel had from time to time gone to a number of "high places" to offer sacrifices. Judging from the very few references prior to this point in the Biblical history, the practice was probably not common. No doubt "high places" were, as the expression suggests, usually located on hills, but the expression itself refers to the setup for religious activities of various kinds there.[23] In Samuel's day there had been a "high place" at or near Ramah, where he built an altar, offered sacrifices, and hosted a very important meal (1 Samuel 7:17; 9:12–25). There was another one at a place called Gibeath-elohim ("the hill of God"), where a band of prophets was based (1 Samuel 10:5, 13). There is no suggestion of any problem with these "high places" at that time.

However, "high places" had a complicated history in Israel. In particular the Canaanite peoples had engaged in their pagan idolatrous religious practices at "high places." The Lord told the Israelites to demolish these "high places" (Numbers 33:52; cf. Deuteronomy 12:2, 3). It was a matter of utmost importance that "You shall not worship the LORD your God in that way" (Deuteronomy 12:4), that is, in the way of the pagan idol worshippers who did their thing at the "high places" in the land.

We do not know how or when or by whom "high places" came to be part of Israel's life.[24] They were not a problem (at first), but neither were they something God had prescribed. However once the "house . . . for the name of the LORD" was built by Solomon, the "high places" were a serious problem. Moses had said:

> . . . when he gives you rest from all your enemies around, so that you live in safety, then to *the place that the LORD your God will choose, to make his name dwell there*, there you shall bring all that I command you: your burnt offerings and your sacrifices, your tithes and the contribution that you present, and all your finest vow offerings that you vow to the LORD. . . . Take care that you do not offer your burnt offerings at any place that

you see, but at *the place that the* LORD *will choose*. . . . (Deuteronomy 12:10, 11, 13, 14)

The time came when it was clear that the house of the Lord in Jerusalem was "the place that the LORD your God [had chosen], to make his name dwell there" (see 8:29; 9:3). Subsequent activities at "high places" were then unambiguous expressions of apostasy (see Psalm 78:58; Hosea 10:8). Our historian will evaluate many of the kings whose stories are told in 1 and 2 Kings by what they did about the "high places" (see, for example, 1 Kings 11:7; 12:31, 32; 13:2, 32, 33; 14:23; 2 Kings 21:3; 23:19, 20).

So what are we to make of the statement in 1 Kings 3:2? It sounds as though the practice of sacrificing at high places, which had very occasionally been mentioned over the previous centuries, had multiplied. While this was not, at this stage, a problem ("because no house had yet been built for the name of the LORD"), it would soon become a problem because the people (and their kings!) will be so attached to their religious practices that they fail to take seriously the new thing that God has done.

In this way the movement from the time before the house of the Lord was built (when "high places" were acceptable) to the time after the house was built (when they were no longer acceptable) is like the movement from the time before the death and resurrection of Jesus (when Old Testament practices were right and proper) to the time after Jesus' resurrection (when a lot of Old Testament practices are no longer okay). The New Testament letter to the Hebrews is the fullest but by no means the only exposition of this. True worship of God must not be do-it-yourself religion. We will hear much more about this in the following pages of 1 Kings.

The Lord: Loving God Is Complicated (v. 3)

Finally, in this brief introductory sketch of Solomon and his kingdom, we come to the wonderful statement, "Solomon loved the LORD" (v. 3a). Perhaps you would like to ask, what could be complicated about that?

We should first appreciate what a striking statement this is. It is not said, in so many words, of any other individual in Israel's history! That is not to say, of course, that Solomon was the first man to have loved God,[25] but he is the first person of whom the Bible writers have chosen to make this simple but profound statement: "He [or she] loved the LORD." Of all the things that could be said about Solomon, this is the testimony placed at the beginning of the history of his reign.

Furthermore, there was nothing superficial about this. Loving the Lord meant, for Solomon, "walking in the statutes of David his father" (v. 3b)—that is, the requirements laid out in David's last words to Solomon, when the old king commanded his son to "Be strong, and show yourself a man, and keep the charge of the LORD your God, walking in his ways and keeping his statutes, his commandments, his rules, and his testimonies, as it is written in the Law of Moses" (2:2, 3).[26]

Love is a powerful word. It is sadly true that the word has been sentimentalized and trivialized in today's world, but we still sense something of the weight of this statement: "Solomon *loved* the LORD." A number of very significant relationships in this history were characterized by "love." In particular "love" is the kind of attachment people had to a king who ruled them well.[27] When applied to God, such love includes a proper "fear" of the Lord and obedience to his law (Deuteronomy 10:12, 13).

However, Solomon's story began with the Lord's love for him: "The LORD *loved* [Solomon]" (2 Samuel 12:24). Solomon knew something of the Christian's experience: "We love because he first loved us" (1 John 4:19). Like the Christian, Solomon's enjoyment of God's blessing depended ultimately on God's love for him, not on his love for God.

The words "Solomon loved the LORD" are indeed wonderful, but it will soon be clear that if everything depended on Solomon's love for the Lord, there would be no hope.

There is more than a hint of this in the tantalizing qualification, "only he sacrificed and made offerings[28] at the high places" (v. 3c). "Only" represents the same Hebrew word (*raq*), rendered "however" in verse 2, suggesting a qualification to what has just been said. The reference here seems to go beyond sacrificing at high places before the building of the house of the Lord mentioned in verse 2. The fact is that *after* the building of that house Solomon will be involved with high places in a disastrous way (see 11:7). Nonetheless we will see that there is a suggestion in the next verse that early in his reign Solomon went to only one "high place." That was before his love for the Lord became compromised.

In due course Solomon's "love" for the Lord was severely compromised by his "love for many foreign women," who turned his heart after their gods (11:1–5).

Solomon's love for God was, as far as it went, wonderful and good. Far more important, however, was God's love for Solomon. Just so, we should love God, but our confidence and joy comes not from our love for God but from his love for us.

In this opening picture of Solomon's world we have seen something of how complicated international relations can be, how confused human undertakings to build a better world can be, how difficult it is for people to worship God rightly, and how we cannot rely even on human love for God to solve the complexities of our difficult world.

The claim of the Christian gospel is therefore immense. It is that in Jesus Christ "all the fullness of God was pleased to dwell, and through him to reconcile to himself all things, whether on earth or in heaven, making peace by the blood of his cross" (Colossians 1:19, 20). We do not believe in simple, black-and-white answers. But we do believe that the answer to the world's complications *is* found in the Lord Jesus Christ. He is the hope of the world.

8

What a Complicated
World Needs

1 KINGS 3:4–15

THE COMPLEXITY OF OUR WORLD and its problems is overwhelming. We are thankful for good people who occasionally make things a little bit better by their selfless efforts. From time to time clever people make some difference by coming up with partial solutions to particular problems. That is welcome. Sometimes power—military or otherwise—is effective in sorting out some difficulties. But just as often good intentions, apparently brilliant plans, and strong responses just make matters worse. The world needs something more than fine ambitions, clever schemes, and powerful interventions. But what?

Another way for Christian people to think about this is to consider, what is it about the Lord Jesus Christ that gives us hope? His goodness surpasses any goodness we have ever seen, but it's more than that. He is certainly clever (so clever that *clever* is an inadequate word), and there is no power greater than his power, by which all things were created. But there is more than his perfect goodness, complete knowledge, and infinite power that makes sense of our utter confidence in him. What is it?

In 3:1–3 we saw something of the complexity of Solomon's world. Our narrator now takes us to a particular occasion in which King Solomon was given what his complicated world needed.[1] The gift he received has become famous. More importantly, it is what makes the Lord Jesus Christ the hope of the world. In wonderful ways we will see in King Solomon a shadow of Jesus Christ.

Solomon at Gibeon (v. 4)

"And the king went to Gibeon to sacrifice there" (v. 4a). Gibeon was about five miles northwest of Jerusalem, in the territory of the tribe of Benjamin (Joshua 18:25), Saul's tribe, and the tribe of one recently deceased trouble-maker, Shimei. It was close to the northern border of Judah and had, a generation earlier, been the location of a disastrous attempt to resolve differences between the tribe of Judah, who had welcomed David as their new king, and the rest of the people of Israel, who had Saul's son Ishbosheth reigning over them. Blood was shed at Gibeon (see 2 Samuel 2:12–32). More recently Gibeon was the place where another recently deceased threat to Solomon's kingdom, Joab, had committed one of his murders in defiance of King David (2 Samuel 20:8–10). Again blood was shed at Gibeon. Much earlier Saul had committed a bloody atrocity against the indigenous inhabitants of Gibeon, which had dreadful consequences years later (see 2 Samuel 21:1–14). In other words, Gibeon was a place of unhappy and violent memories. For a moment we might wonder with foreboding what King Solomon's visit to Gibeon (of all places) might mean.

However, we are immediately informed that Gibeon was now "the great high place" (v. 4b), and that is why ("for" in v. 4b) King Solomon went there. Of all the "high places" (3:2, 3), Gibeon was the most important. Our narrator does not tell us what made Gibeon "great," but a later writer will record that the tabernacle and its altar had been at Gibeon at least since David had brought the ark of the covenant into Jerusalem (1 Chronicles 16:39; 21:29; 2 Chronicles 1:3, 13).

Verse 4 seems to indicate that early in Solomon's reign Gibeon was the only "high place" at which he sacrificed and made offerings. His activities at other "high places" (3:3) came later. Indeed he "used to offer a thousand burnt offerings on that altar" (v. 4c). Whether it was literally a thousand burnt offerings or if "thousand" has a less precise meaning here,[2] it is clear that Solomon was lavish in his practice of offering burnt offerings at Gibeon. Taken with 3:3a, we may reasonably say that this was an expression of his love for the Lord. Burnt offerings, the most frequent kind of sacrifice, were associated with atonement for sin, acceptance by God, and the Lord's favor (see Leviticus 1:3, 4, 9, 13, 17). By the burnt offering "the worshipper bore witness to his faith in God and his willingness to obey his commandments."[3]

Priests may have conducted the sacrifices, under the authority of the king. Be that as it may, Solomon appears here as a king engaged not in war but in priestly activities—like his father, years earlier, when the ark of God was brought into Jerusalem (2 Samuel 6:13, 17). King Solomon's visits to Gibeon were a fitting expression of the new day that had dawned. No longer was Gibeon a place of war, murder, and atrocity. It was a place of peace, worship, and celebration. God was honored by his king at Gibeon!

God's Word to Solomon (v. 5)

On one particular visit, presumably quite early in Solomon's reign, Gibeon was the setting for a momentous experience: "At Gibeon the LORD appeared to Solomon in a dream by night" (v. 5a).

The Bible records a small number of especially significant occasions when a dream conveyed a message from God. On some of these occasions the dream was symbolic, requiring interpretation (like Joseph's dreams in Genesis 37:5–11, Pharaoh's dreams in Genesis 41:1–7, Nebuchadnezzar's dreams in Daniel 2:1–45; 4:4–27, and perhaps Peter's vision in Acts 10:9–17). In other dreams God's message came in words so that no interpretation was needed (as in Abimelech's dream in Genesis 20:3–7 and Joseph's dreams in Matthew 1:20, 21; 2:13, 19, 20). Sometimes a dream contained both symbol and word (for example, Jacob's dream in Genesis 28:10–17). However, there is also a general caution about dreams and warnings not to be deceived by them (Deuteronomy 13:1–5; Jeremiah 23:25–32; 27:9; 29:8; Zechariah 10:2; Ecclesiastes 5:3, 7; Jude 8). Nonetheless it is clear that from time to time God used dreams in various ways (see Judges 7:13–15; cf. 1 Samuel 28:6, 15).

In the Bible there is no clear distinction between a "dream" and a "vision" (see Numbers 12:6; Job 33:15; Isaiah 29:7; Daniel 4:5, 9) because the interest is focused not on the nature of the experience but on the content of the revelation. On this occasion "the LORD appeared" in Solomon's dream. However, we are told nothing about what Solomon "saw."[4] The Lord "appeared" by *speaking*. We do not know whether there was anything visual in the dream. What mattered was not what Solomon saw but what he heard.

Years earlier there had been a night when "the word of the LORD" came to Nathan the prophet. The experience was called "this vision" although the report of it consisted entirely of "these words" (2 Samuel 7:4, 17).[5] We are about to see a deep connection between what Nathan heard on that night and what happened a generation later in Solomon's dream at Gibeon.

It began with words that could hardly be more remarkable: "God said, 'Ask what I shall give you'" (v. 5b). Here is Solomon's astonishing significance. He was the chosen king to whom God said, "Ask what I shall give you."

This is the wonder that God had promised: "I will be to him a father, and he shall be to me a son" (2 Samuel 7:14). In Psalm 2 we hear God's chosen king speaking of this relationship:

> The LORD said to me, "You are my Son;
>   today I have begotten you.
> Ask of me, and I will make [or give] the nations [as] your heritage,
>   and the ends of the earth [as] your possession." (Psalm 2:7–8)[6]

This relationship between God and his chosen king came to its full expression in the Lord Jesus Christ, the Son to whom God has *given* "all authority in heaven and on earth" (Matthew 28:18; cf. John 11:22; 13:3).

Most astonishing of all, those who trust in Jesus are drawn into this relationship with God, so that Jesus says to us, "*Ask*, and it will be *given* to you" (Matthew 7:7; see also Matthew 21:22; John 14:13, 14; 15:7, 16; 16:23, 24).

Solomon's Response (vv. 6–9)

There are many tales about people being granted a wish (or three wishes as many such stories have it). The story of Aladdin's lamp is perhaps the most famous. The account in 1 Kings 3 is different. This was God and his king. How did God's king respond to God's astonishing invitation?

In his response we see Solomon's genuine love for the Lord and his faith in him. There were three dimensions to Solomon's answer.

Solomon Grasped God's Kindness (vv. 6, 7a)

First, he spoke of God's kindness:

> And Solomon said, "You have shown great and steadfast love [or great kindness] to your servant David my father, because [or as[7]] he walked before you in faithfulness, in righteousness, and in uprightness of heart toward you. And you have kept for him this great and steadfast love [or this great kindness] and have given him a son to sit on his throne this day. And now, O LORD my God, you have made your servant king in place of David my father. . . . (vv. 6–7a)

Solomon's response to God's word to him shows how thoroughly his thinking was saturated in God's promise to his father (2 Samuel 7). God's "kindness" (ESV, "steadfast love")[8] had been a feature of David's story. The promise was that God's "kindness" would never be taken away from David's son (2 Samuel 7:15). Indeed the Lord will show this kindness to his chosen king "forever" (2 Samuel 22:51).

At the time of his promise to David, the Lord had pointedly called him "my servant David" (2 Samuel 7:5, 8). In response David had called himself "your servant" (ten times in 2 Samuel 7:18–29). Solomon now calls his father "your servant David"—undoubtedly again under the influence of that earlier occasion.[9]

The "great kindness" God had shown to Solomon's father, David, was to give him "a son to sit on his throne this day," just as he had promised. Solomon saw what had happened to him in the establishment of his kingdom (2:12, 46) in the light of God's promise to his father. Solomon's kingdom *was* the kingdom that God had promised to David.

The jarring note for many in Solomon's words is the suggestion that this kindness of God had something to do with the integrity of King David. Was it really "*because* [David] walked before you in faithfulness, in righteousness, and in uprightness of heart toward you"?

There are two problems here (for many readers). The first is historical and factual. Any reader familiar with the preceding volume in this history (2 Samuel) knows very well that among other things David was an adulterer, deceiver, and murderer (see 2 Samuel 11). How could it honestly be said that "he walked . . . in faithfulness, in righteousness, and in uprightness of heart . . ."? Yet here we have the first of many occasions in which the books of Kings will look back on David's life in unqualified positive terms (see 3:14; 9:4; 11:4, 6, 33, 34, 38; 14:8; 15:3, 11; 2 Kings 16:2; 18:3; 22:2).

The second problem is theological. God's kindness to David, like his kindness to Israel and indeed his kindness to the whole world, is presented in the Bible as a free gift. It is not a deserved reward for the goodness of the recipient. The Bible calls this "grace." The Christian experience of God's grace is classically summed up in a familiar text: "For by grace you have been saved through faith. And this is not your own doing; it is the gift of God, *not a result of works*, so that no one may boast" (Ephesians 2:8, 9). Did Solomon (the son of *Bathsheba*, remember!) really think that his father was so good that God *owed* him the kindness he had shown?

Some solve both of these problems by noting that the speaker here was Solomon. He just got it wrong, they say.[10] That's too easy. There is no suggestion from God (or the narrator for that matter) that Solomon misunderstood. The way in which Solomon's response to God's word is so infused with his confidence in God's promise to David tells against the idea that he was speaking nonsense. Indeed we will shortly see that God was very pleased with Solomon's words.

What Solomon said was deeply true. It was very like David's own remarkable words in 2 Samuel 22:21–25.[11] On the one hand God's kindness to David had included "putting away [David's] sin" (2 Samuel 12:13). This meant that David's considerable wickedness was no longer held against him. This was astonishing grace. It meant that those who shared God's perspective on David (like the Bible writer) saw him as a forgiven, cleansed man. He had been washed clean. That meant that he really was "whiter than snow" (Psalm 51:7)! And that is how Solomon saw him.[12]

On the other hand, this grace of God toward David had a profound impact on him. On many occasions and in various ways his life really did display faithfulness, righteousness, and uprightness of heart.

There was, therefore, a powerful connection between David's integrity and the great kindness of God toward him. It was not, however, that his uprightness *caused* God's grace toward him. It was the other way around.[13]

Solomon Knew His Weakness (vv. 7b, 8)

Second, Solomon recognized his own weakness:

> . . . although I am but a little child [small lad]. I do not know how to go out or come in. And your servant is in the midst of your people whom you have chosen, a great people, too many to be numbered or counted for multitude. (vv. 7b, 8)

Do not miss the fact that Solomon now called himself "your servant," the title he had just applied very significantly to his father (v. 6). Solomon understood that he was now what his father had been, "your servant." Here we see again the defining reality of Solomon's kingship: the relationship of God to this king, just as he had promised his father.

At this time Solomon was probably about twenty years old.[14] He was old enough to have a wife and a son (see 11:42; 14:21). He was more an inexperienced youth than "a little child" (so ESV).[15] To "go out and come in" was an expression for leading military campaigns (see Numbers 27:17; 1 Samuel 18:13, 16). Solomon had no such experience. Here is the very opposite of young Adonijah's bravado (1:5). Solomon was deeply aware of his limited experience and ability.

Furthermore he could see the enormous task before him as the promised son of David. He was the Lord's servant "in the midst of your people whom you have chosen." Here Solomon made the connection between God's promise to David and his choice of Israel. The link is fundamental and important to the Bible's message. In our study of 2 Samuel 7 we have noted how closely the promise to David was related to God's promise to Abraham.[16] Just as David knew that the Lord had established him as king "for the sake of his people Israel" (2 Samuel 5:12), so Solomon now understood that the people he was to rule were the Lord's chosen people. Indeed he saw them with the eyes of faith as "a great[17] people, too many to be numbered or counted for multitude." Solomon was clearly thinking in terms of God's promise to Abraham (see Genesis 13:16; 15:5; 22:17; 26:4; 28:14; 32:12). His understanding of the promise that God had made concerning his chosen people magnified his sense of inadequacy for the task.[18] The Apostle Paul would say many years later, with a similar understanding of God's great promise, "Who is sufficient for these things?" (2 Corinthians 2:16).

Solomon Knew What He Needed (v. 9)

Third, Solomon therefore asked for what he knew he needed:

> Give your servant therefore an understanding mind to govern your people, that I may discern between good and evil, for who is able to govern this your great people? (v. 9)

Understanding himself again as "your servant," Solomon asked the Lord to "give" (see v. 5) him "an understanding mind." The Hebrew expression is richer than that (literally "a hearing [or listening] heart").[19]

What does it tell us about Solomon that, of all the things he could have asked from God, he chose *a listening heart*?

It tells us, first, that Solomon understood that the resources for the task ahead of him would not come from within himself. He did not ask for the realization of his inner potential! There was something he needed to *hear*.

Solomon's request revealed his grasp of the fundamental reality behind all things: God is there, and he is not silent.[20] By his word God created all things (Genesis 1; Psalm 33:9; 148:5, 6; John 1:1–3). By his powerful word he upholds the universe (Hebrews 1:3). Because God has *spoken*, the Bible emphasizes the supreme importance of *hearing*. As God's chosen people, this was Israel's most basic responsibility (see, for example, Deuteronomy 4:1, 12, 33, 36; 5:1, 4, 5, 22). As God's chosen king in the midst of this people Solomon needed, more than anything else, to listen to *the word of God*.[21] It is God's word that brings order to a chaotic world.

Solomon also understood that he needed to hear deeply. He asked for a listening *heart*. In the Bible the heart is the center of a person's consciousness, thought, and will. We tend to think of the heart as the emotional center of a person. In the Bible it is more than that. It is also more than the mind. The word of God needs to be not just heard with the ears and understood with the intellect, but believed, loved, and embraced by the whole person (cf. Proverbs 22:17). Those with a hearing heart will *listen* thoroughly, and their entire being will be shaped by what is heard.

Many years earlier King Saul had been told that he must "listen to the sound of the words of the LORD" (1 Samuel 15:1, AT).[22] This was the fundamental requirement of the Lord's anointed king. Saul's failure consisted in this: he *rejected* the word of the Lord (1 Samuel 15:23, 26; cf. 28:18).[23]

Earlier still, in the days of Moses, there was a king whose hardened heart refused to listen to the Lord's voice. That was Pharaoh, king of Egypt (see Exodus 5:2; 7:13, 22; 8:15, 19; 9:12).

Unlike both Pharaoh and Saul, Solomon asked God for "a listening heart." That was what he needed in order to "govern your people." The Hebrew verb here (*shapat*) is often translated "judge" (1 Samuel 4:18; 7:6, 15–17; 8:5, 6, 20; 1 Kings 8:32) and sometimes "deliver" (2 Samuel 18:19, 31). It has the sense of bringing justice, putting things right, bringing order out of chaos in the life of the people.

Samuel had "judged" Israel in this sense (1 Samuel 7:6, 15–17). Subsequently the elders of Israel had asked for "a king to judge us *like all the nations*" (1 Samuel 8:5, 6, 20; cf. 2 Samuel 15:4). This was tantamount to apostasy. However, at the height of his reign King David "did justice[24] and righteousness for all the people" (2 Samuel 8:15, AT). That is what Solomon wanted to be able to do. If Solomon was to do for his people what God does by his word (put things right, establish order in place of chaos) he needed a hearing heart, a heart that listened to God's word.

Such a listening heart would enable him to "discern between good and evil." This is not an easy thing to do in a complicated world! We could cite numerous examples of complex situations in which it is far from simple to see what is right. Today we need to emphasize that "good" and "evil" are not reflections of community attitudes, nor are they projections of particular people's values. In God's world what is good and what is evil is not something to be *decided* by us; it is to be *discerned* by us. God's king, if his kingdom is to be a kingdom of justice, peace, and joy (Romans 14:17), must be able to discern good and evil. That is why he must have a hearing heart.

What Solomon requested was perfectly present in Jesus, who could say, ". . . he who sent me is true, and I declare to the world *what I have heard from him*" (John 8:26). The gospel of Jesus Christ is a call to *listen*, and the Christian life is a life of *hearing* deeply (see Matthew 7:24–27; 17:5; John 5:24; 8:47; 10:27; Acts 4:4; 13:44; 15:7; 19:10; 28:28; Romans 10:17; Galatians

3:2, 5; Ephesians 1:13; Colossians 1:5, 6, 23; 1 Thessalonians 2:13; Hebrews 3:7, 15; 4:7; 5:11; 1 John 2:24; 4:6; Revelation 1:3; 2:7; 3:20).

Solomon's dilemma ("for who is able to govern [judge] this your great[25] people?") has now been answered. Jesus said, "As I *hear*, I *judge*, and my judgment is just, because I seek not my own will but the will of him who sent me" (John 5:30).

The Lord's Pleasure (vv. 10–14)

"It pleased the Lord that Solomon had asked this" (v. 10). This brief statement is important on several levels.

First, it is the strongest possible affirmation of Solomon's response in verses 6–9. While the Lord's pleasure focused on the request at the end of Solomon's speech (v. 9), that petition followed from his understanding of God's kindness in making him king (vv. 6, 7a) and his own inadequacy for the task (vv. 7b, 8). The whole speech pleased the Lord.

Second, Solomon's speech showed that the Lord had begun to grant his request before it had been spoken. He had asked for a hearing heart so that he could discern between *good* and *evil*. That request was *good*! A literal translation of verse 10 brings this out: "And the thing was *good* in the eyes of the LORD because Solomon asked this thing."

Third, this carefully crafted narrative contains a poignant echo of a statement made much earlier in the story. At the end of the account of David's adultery with Bathsheba and his murder of Uriah, the narrator told us, "And the thing which David did was *evil* in the eyes of the LORD" (2 Samuel 11:27b, AT).[26] Just as David's wickedness had terrible consequences for his kingdom, we are now led to expect great things from this son of David whose response to God's word makes such a contrast to David's self-serving crimes.

How much greater are our expectations of the still greater son of David, of whom a voice from Heaven said, "This is my beloved Son, with whom I am well pleased" (Matthew 3:17).

"And God said to him, 'Because you have asked this, and have not asked for yourself long life[27] or riches or the life of your enemies[28] . . .'" (v. 11a). The goodness of Solomon's response lay as much in what he did not ask for as in what he did request. What was good about not asking for long life, riches, or the life of his enemies? These are the things that a man who does not know God would seek. Jesus said something like this to his disciples:

Therefore do not be anxious, saying, "What shall we eat?" or "What shall we drink?" or "What shall we wear?" For the Gentiles [or nations] seek after all these things, and your heavenly Father knows that you need them all. But seek first the kingdom of God and his righteousness, and all these things will be added to you. (Matthew 6:31–33)

Solomon's request for a hearing heart that can discern between good and evil was his way of seeking first the kingdom of God and his righteousness.

The Lord summarized what Solomon *had* asked for: "but [you] have asked for yourself understanding to discern what is right" (v. 11b). Solomon had asked for "understanding," that is, the ability to "discern between good and evil" (v. 9).[29] "To discern what is right" (literally "to hear justice") echoes Solomon's request for a "hearing heart" to enable him to "judge" God's people. The "justice" (Hebrew, *mishpat*[30]) of Solomon's kingdom was something he needed to "hear." In other words, the "justice" of Solomon's kingdom would be like the creation in Genesis 1: good order shaped by the word of God.

Solomon had not asked for a hearing heart so that he would feel good. It was not like the modern pursuit of spirituality, which is a quest focused on self. Solomon's request was for the good of the Lord's people in whose midst God had made him king.

The Lord granted Solomon's request: ". . . behold, I now do according to your word. Behold, I give you a wise and discerning mind [or heart], so that none like you has been before you and none like you shall arise after you" (v. 12).

It was the Lord who introduced the word "wise" to this conversation. In due course the wisdom of Solomon will be lauded far and wide (see 3:28; 4:29, 30, 34; 5:7, 12; 10:4, 6–8, 23, 24; 11:41). In our next chapter we will see a spectacular example of Solomon's wisdom. At this point we need to understand that what Solomon had requested (a hearing heart that discerns between good and evil and so puts things right for God's people) is what God calls wisdom. In 3:28 it will be called "the wisdom of God . . . to do justice."

While "wisdom" means different things in different contexts, it is important to understand the connection between wisdom and creation. "The LORD by *wisdom* founded the earth" (Proverbs 3:19). "O LORD, how manifold are your works! In *wisdom* have you made them all" (Psalm 104:24). The wisdom God gave Solomon was what was needed to do "justice," that is, to reorder the world according to God's good will.

Curiously David had twice referred to Solomon's "wisdom" (2:6, 9). This is a wonderful example of the Lord answering a prayer even before it was uttered (cf. Matthew 6:8).

Just as Jesus said, "and all these things will be added to you" (Matthew

6:33) if you seek first God's kingdom and his righteousness, so the Lord promised to add to Solomon what he had not asked for, provided that he sought God's kingdom first:

> I give you also what you have not asked, both riches and honor, so that no other king shall compare with you, all your days. And if you will walk in my ways, keeping my statutes and my commandments, as your father David walked, then I will lengthen your days. (vv. 13, 14)

The condition would be fulfilled if Solomon continued to have the listening heart for which he had asked.[31] The tragedy of Solomon's life will be that in due course his heart will turn away (11:4).

Solomon in Jerusalem (v. 15)

> And Solomon awoke, and behold, it was a dream. Then he came to Jerusalem and stood before the ark of the covenant of the LORD, and offered up burnt offerings and peace offerings, and made a feast for all his servants. (v. 15)

"It was a dream" does not, of course, mean that it was *only* a dream.[32] The Lord had appeared to Solomon in this dream (v. 5), and the words heard and spoken were true.

The first effect of Solomon's dream was the shift of his sacrificing activity from the great high place at Gibeon to Jerusalem. There "he *stood* before the ark of the covenant of the LORD." He stood, ready for service.[33] To the burnt offerings that had been made at Gibeon (v. 4), Solomon now added peace offerings, as his father had done when the ark of the covenant had been brought into Jerusalem (2 Samuel 6:17, 18; cf. 24:25). It was time to celebrate the "peace" of Solomon's kingdom in the fullest sense. It was time for "a feast for all [Solomon's] servants."

The movement from Gibeon to Jerusalem anticipated one of the most important changes that will take place in Solomon's kingdom. Solomon will build a "house" in Jerusalem that will (or should) be the end of the "high places" (5:1—6:38).

Solomon's experience at Gibeon was about what his complicated world needed: a *wise* king, whose wisdom came from a listening heart. Many years later the prophet Isaiah will promise a king on whom will rest "the Spirit of wisdom and understanding" (Isaiah 11:2).

The news the world needs to hear is that one "greater than Solomon" has come (Matthew 12:42). Jesus Christ is the hope of the whole world. His contemporaries marveled at his wisdom (Matthew 13:54; cf. Luke 2:40, 52). To us who belong to him he is "wisdom from God" (1 Corinthians 1:30), "in whom are hidden all the treasures of wisdom and knowledge" (Colossians 2:3). The wisdom of Jesus Christ makes sense of our utter confidence in him— the wisdom to mend a shattered world.

In our next chapter we will learn more about this God-given wisdom as we see an amazing example of Solomon's wisdom at work.

9

The Wisdom of God
to Do Justice

1 KINGS 3:16–28

THERE ARE TIMES (I am sure you have known them) when it is difficult to be concerned about the troubles of the world. When the troubles in my little life overwhelm me, I have little energy left to lift my eyes to the "big" problems that have global dimensions. When I can hardly cope with my personal crises, how can I care about the disasters facing the human race? A concern about one of my children (nowadays grandchildren) can drive out all anxiety about the future of the planet.

The Christian life is extraordinary and often difficult for unbelievers to understand. On the one hand Christians are confident that Jesus Christ is the Lord of all things (in the literal sense of *all things*) who has done what is necessary for God's good purpose for the whole creation to be realized. We therefore do not despair at the terrible mess the world is in. We care, but we do not lose heart. We pray to the One who will one day bring peace everywhere by the power of Christ's death and resurrection, and we get to work joyfully serving him with all the energy he gives us (see Colossians 1:15–29). On the other hand, Christians know that the Lord Jesus Christ cares about the ordinary things of our everyday lives. The same power that will heal a broken world is at work healing broken lives (see Colossians 3:1–17). The hope of the world is *my* hope.

That is what the Bible powerfully teaches us and what Christian faith wonderfully experiences. What a privilege it is to learn the scope of the Lord Jesus Christ's concerns—from the words that come out of my mouth (Colossians 3:8) to the harmony of Heaven and earth (Colossians 1:20), from family relationships (Colossians 3:18–21) to the stability of the universe (Colossians 1:17). The secret of the Christian life is the extraordinary and unbounded goodness of our Lord Jesus Christ that touches *everything*.

In a most remarkable way the scope of Jesus' rule was anticipated (in the shadowy way of the Old Testament; see Colossians 2:17) early in the reign of King Solomon. We have seen that Solomon became king in Israel in accordance with God's promise to his father David (1:36, 37; 3:6, 7). The king and the kingdom promised by God were unprecedented. This kingdom would be established by God himself "forever" (2 Samuel 7:12–16). We have seen that there were disturbing aspects to the establishment of Solomon on the throne. Enemies and opponents of various kinds had to be overthrown (2:12–46). Nonetheless the Lord promised to give Solomon the wisdom necessary to bring "justice" (in the big Biblical sense of putting everything right) to the complicated world of God's people Israel (3:9, 12).

The very next scene is a surprise. It is not Solomon's influence over the surrounding nations (as 3:1a might have led us to expect). It is not Solomon embarking on his ambitious and grand building projects (as 3:1b might have suggested). It is not even Solomon taking a lead in sorting out the nation's policy with regard to worship (as 3:2 might have indicated was a priority). It was rather more mundane.

Before we come to the situation faced by Solomon, it is instructive to look briefly at the opening lines of Psalm 72, which appears to be King David's prayer, near the end of his life, for his son and heir.[1] David prayed that Solomon would "have dominion from sea to sea," that "his enemies [would] lick the dust!" and that "all kings [would] fall down before him, all nations serve him!" (Psalm 72:8, 9, 11). But look at how David's prayer for Solomon's kingdom began:

> Give the king your justice, O God,
> and your righteousness to the royal son!
> May he judge your people with righteousness,
> and *your poor* with justice!
> Let the mountains bear prosperity for the people,
> and the hills, in righteousness!
> May he defend *the cause of the poor of the people*,
> give deliverance to *the children of the needy*,
> and crush the oppressor! (Psalm 72:1–4)

The greatness of this king would lie not only in the "big" headline-grabbing issues of the day, but in his dealings with "the cause of the poor" and "the children of the needy." David prayed that Solomon would be a king whose goodness would touch *everything*.

A Situation (vv. 16–22)

The Protagonists (v. 16)

"Then[2] two prostitutes came to the king and stood before him" (v. 16). Two women from the lowest ranks of the community—prostitutes—came and stood before the person of highest standing in the land—the king.[3]

For a reader who has not taken a break between 3:15 and 3:16 the change of scene is a shock. We move from King Solomon offering up burnt offerings and peace offerings "before" the ark in Jerusalem to two prostitutes standing "before" the king. From the sublime to the ridiculous, you might say.

But the scene was serious. To prepare us for what happened, notice three things.

First, consider who these women were.[4] Prostitutes were among the despised and marginalized in Israelite society. God's Law forbade Israelites from allowing their daughters to become prostitutes. This would fill the land with "depravity" (Leviticus 19:29). Indeed it was a capital offense for the daughter of a priest to become a prostitute (Leviticus 21:9). Fees gained from prostitution were not to be brought into the house of the Lord, for "these are an abomination to the LORD your God" (Deuteronomy 23:18[5]). To treat a girl like a prostitute was a serious affront (Genesis 34:2, 7, 31). Having sex with a prostitute brought shame (Genesis 38:23; cf. 1 Corinthians 6:15–20), although prostitutes themselves had a reputation for shamelessness (Jeremiah 3:3). The prophet Amos put the horror of a man's wife becoming a prostitute on a par with the slaughter of his children (Amos 7:17). The despised status of prostitutes is reflected in 1 Kings 22:38 where they are mentioned alongside dogs! All this reflects Israel's calling to be a holy nation (Exodus 19:6; Leviticus 19:2).[6] All sexual relations or practices outside marriage (where sex is a good, powerful, and purposeful gift from God) were serious departures from that vocation. Just as marriage was a potent picture of the relationship between God and his people, so prostitution became a forceful metaphor of unfaithfulness to the Lord and going after "other gods" (Exodus 34:12–16; Leviticus 20:5; Numbers 15:39; Deuteronomy 31:16; Judges 2:17; 8:33; 1 Chronicles 5:25; Jeremiah 2:20–25; 3:1–14; Ezekiel 16; 23; Hosea 1—3[7]).[8]

Despite all this there is ample evidence that there were prostitutes in Israel, as there have probably been in every human society. They were not generally persecuted or punished. In that sense their presence was tolerated.

The prohibition of priests marrying (former) prostitutes (Leviticus 21:7, 14) suggests that such marriages were more generally allowed. Indeed a number of prostitutes played a significant and surprising role in the Bible story. Tamar posed as a prostitute and was judged by her father-in-law, Judah, to be "more righteous than I" (Genesis 38:26). Rahab, the prostitute of Jericho, saved the lives of the Israelite spies and joined the community of God's people, almost certainly having abandoned her old profession (Joshua 2:1–24; 6:25). Rahab is even included in Matthew's genealogy of Jesus (Matthew 1:5)! A prostitute in Gaza was a part of the story of Samson (Judges 16:1).[9]

It is a curious sight, therefore, to see two prostitutes standing before King Solomon. How will the king with a listening heart (3:9, 12) deal with these two outcasts? What will it mean on this occasion for him to walk in God's ways, keeping his statutes and commandments (3:14)?

Second, consider what they were doing in coming to the king. The king's responsibilities included those of the "judge" in an earlier time. Judging meant putting things right for the people at all levels. Defeating external enemies was part of it, but it also involved resolving disputes and conflicts within the community (see 1 Samuel 7:6, 15, 16). Ordinary Israelites could therefore seek access to their king with quite commonplace problems. A woman from Tekoa had taken advantage of this privilege before King David, although her dilemma was fictitious (2 Samuel 14:1–20; cf. 2 Kings 8:3–6). Absalom had stirred up discontent among the people with David's alleged incompetence in the administration of this kind of justice (2 Samuel 15:2–6).

How will Solomon bring "justice" to these two prostitutes?[10]

Third, notice that they "stood" before the king. This is at least unusual. When the woman of Tekoa came to King David "she fell on her face . . . and paid homage" (2 Samuel 14:4). Bathsheba, the king's wife, and Nathan, the prophet of the Lord, showed similar honor when they came before their king (1 Kings 1:16, 23). The two prostitutes adopted a different pose. It is as though they did not have time or energy for the niceties of protocol. Their minds were filled with their personal troubles.

One Version of Events (vv. 17–21)

What then happened is reported, almost entirely, through the words spoken by each of the persons present. First one of the women gave her version of the crisis that had brought the two of them before the king:

> The one woman said, "Oh,[11] my lord, this woman and I live in the same house, and I gave birth to a child while she was in the house. Then on the

third day after I gave birth, this woman also gave birth. And we were alone. There was no one else with us in the house; only we two were in the house. And this woman's son died in the night, because she lay on him. And she arose at midnight [or in the middle of the night] and took my son from beside me, while your servant slept, and laid him at her breast, and laid her dead son at my breast. When I rose in the morning to nurse my child [literally, son], behold, he was dead. But when I looked at him closely in the morning, behold, he was not the child [literally, son] that I had borne." (vv. 17–21)

The house the two prostitutes occupied was presumably a brothel. Their shared accommodation had nothing to do with any friendship between them. Indeed, there seems to be a disparaging tone in the repeated reference to her companion as "this woman."

The two women had each given birth to a child, she said, within three days of each other. The babies (both boys[12]) were, it would seem, born of their prostitution. There is no mention of the fathers. We may guess that they were unknown.

The two mothers and their respective little ones were "alone" in the house. She emphasized this point. "No one else" is, literally "no stranger"—that is, there were no clients of the prostitutes present at the time of the incident about to be described. This meant that there was no independent witness who could be summoned. Furthermore there was no possible suspect for the crime about to be reported other than those who were "alone" in the house.

In the night (it may have been the very night of the second child's birth) there was a tragic accident, she said. The other woman had killed her son by lying on him, presumably rolling onto him in her sleep.

This terrible mishap had been compounded because, she said, the mother of the dead child had swapped the babies while the other mother (the one now reporting these events) slept.

As you listen, are you thinking what I'm thinking? If she was sleeping, how did she know what had happened? We now realize that the woman speaking did not witness the death of the baby, nor the deceitful swap. How, then, did she know this had happened?

Well, she said, when she got up the next morning to feed her baby, she discovered that he was dead, and when she looked more closely[13] in the light of day, she realized that it was not her baby! *And so what I have told you is what must have happened,* she could have said.[14]

Listening to the account it is difficult not to sympathize with this troubled mother who had lost her child in these tragic circumstances either by theft (if she was telling the truth) or something worse. Her measured and polite words are (I find) persuasive[15] and incline us (I think) to believe her version of events, accepting her disparaging view of "this [other] woman."[16] Our sympathy for the other woman's tragic loss is tempered by our horror at her (alleged) crime of baby swapping.

However, this is a fine example of the truth King Solomon will later express:

> The one who states his case first seems right,
>   until the other comes and examines him. (Proverbs 18:17)[17]

Another Version of Events (v. 22a)

On this occasion "the other woman" did not exactly examine anyone, but the effect was the same. "But the other woman said, 'No,[18] the living child is mine, and the dead child is yours'" (v. 22a). The brevity, even sharpness, of the second woman's words may make us somewhat less sympathetic to her. She offered no argument. But what was there to say? She flatly denied that the first woman's story was the truth. She did not claim to know how the child had died. She simply denied that *her* child had been killed and that she had been involved in the alleged baby swap. At least she did not claim to know what she could not have known.

By giving us no more information, the narrator has cleverly put us in the same position as the king. We do not know which woman was telling the truth. Any inclination to one or the other is simply a prejudice.

Irreconcilable (v. 22b, c)

The confusion continued as the first woman stuck to her story: "The first said, 'No, the dead child is yours, and the living child is mine'" (v. 22b).

The situation was escalating. "Thus they spoke before the king" (v. 22c) means that they stopped speaking *to* the king and started shouting (I do not doubt) at each other[19] *before* the king. And they went on and on![20]

It was a classic case of one person's word against another. There was no evidence presented on either side. But the stakes were high. A child was dead. That was not in dispute. But how had it happened? Whose child had died? And whose was the little boy who had survived that terrible night?

There is no way of answering these questions with any confidence on the basis of what we (and the king) have heard. Indeed, even if we had been there, able to observe the body language and hear the tone of the voices, we would be in no better position. This was one of those situations where it is impossible to know what is right from appearances.

We face many, many dilemmas just like that every day. Who is telling the truth? Who knows what they are talking about? Who is holding back relevant information? Every news report contains such perplexities. Courts struggle to solve such puzzles. We resort to the necessary but unsatisfying principle of "innocent until proven guilty" (knowing full well that many who cannot be proven guilty are not innocent). The situation faced by King Solomon that day, like so many situations we come across, simply cannot be judged rightly by what our eyes see and by what our ears hear (see Isaiah 11:3).

The King's Judgment (vv. 23–27)

The king had given his full attention to what the two women had said. He interrupted their squabbling. He did not speak *to* the women (just as they had stopped speaking to him), but as judge he summed up the case before him:[21]

> Then the king said, "The one says, 'This is my son that is alive, and your son is dead'; and the other says, 'No; but your son is dead, and my son is the living one.'" (v. 23)

The king focused on the question that mattered, which was not who did what, nor how the death had occurred, but whose son was each child?[22] That is, who was the mother of each of the boys? The two women made exactly opposite claims (or, more literally, exactly the same claim).[23] At this point the king made no distinction between the women.[24]

Perhaps there was silence as the king considered the impossible case before him.

When he spoke, it was chilling. The king said, "Bring me a sword" (v. 24a).

The sword has featured rather too often for comfort in the story of Solomon's kingdom so far. In the preceding pages each mention of "the sword" has meant death (see 1:51; 2:8, 32; also the unmentioned but deadly sword in 2:6, 9, 25, 34, 46). The king's words were terrifying. No one knew what the king would do with the sword, but there is really only one thing that swords are made for.

"So a sword was brought before the king" (v. 24b)—not actually placed in his hands, but the sword was ready to do whatever the king commanded.[25]

The tension must have been immense. Were these two women about to be executed either for their immorality or for their failure to observe proper royal protocol or for the outrageous way they dared to bring their unseemly bickering before the king or for any number of other possible offenses?

When the king spoke again, it was worse than anyone feared. The king said, "Divide the living child in two, and give half to the one and half to the other" (v. 25).

We now know that others were present.[26] The king commanded a group of officials to perform an unthinkable atrocity. The word he used for "child" is from the verb "gave birth" in verses 17, 18, thus linking the proposed execution with the reported birth.[27] To the women and others witnessing this terrifying scene the king's words must have sounded like: *You want justice? I'll give you justice—both of you shall grieve equally!*

Immediately one of the women interrupted. At this point the narrator plays a little trick on us.[28] He does not tell us whether it was the woman who spoke first (in vv. 17–21) or the second speaker (v. 22a) who now stopped the horrific proceedings. He does tell us, however, that she was "the woman whose son was alive" (v. 26a). The trick is that we are left wondering which of the two women that was.

The difference between the true mother and the deceiver did not lie in any externally observable distinction. However, the true mother's "heart[29] yearned for her son" (v. 26b). Both women wanted the living child. However, the inner love of the true mother had a quality that could not be feigned.

Out of her mother-love she said, "Oh, my lord, give her the living child, and by no means put him to death" (v. 26c). The true mother would suffer the loss of her child rather than see him harmed. She used yet another word for "child," meaning literally, "the borne one,"[30] calling to mind the day she "gave birth" (v. 17 or 18, depending on which woman this was), arousing all her protective instincts. *Please! Do anything, but do not harm my baby!*

The other woman (and, remember, we do not know which is which) was also deeply tormented by profound emotions. She had lost her child. Bitter jealousy over the injustice of her loss and her companion's good fortune gripped her. We are horrified to hear the words that exploded from her mouth: "He shall be neither mine nor yours; divide him" (v. 26d).[31] She spoke first to the other woman ("yours") and then to the officials ("divide," precisely echoing the king's command in v. 25).

Remember, the narrator has told us which of the most recent speakers is the mother of the living child (v. 26a). We have not been left to evaluate the truthfulness of the speeches in verse 26. The king, however, did not have the benefit of the narrator's tip-off. He had to draw his conclusion about the integrity of the women from what they said. He did not hesitate:

> Then the king answered and said, "Give the living child to the first woman, and by no means put him to death; she is his mother." (v. 27)

In the original language the story has a disturbing ambiguity at this point. The king said literally, "Give the living child to *her*."[32] For a moment we wonder whether he made a terrible mistake. In context "her" (see note 32) sounds like the woman who last spoke! Could it be that the king took the true mother at her word and accepted her desperate offer to give her son to the other woman?[33]

This is another little trick played on us by the narrator.[34] It would only have taken a gesture from the king (unseen, of course, by us) to make clear that "her" meant the woman we have been told was the true mother. For us this is indicated indirectly as the king quotes the exact words that this mother had spoken. He used the same intimate word for "child" and echoed her "by no means put him to death."[35] The king pronounced his verdict: "She is his mother."

We are left in no doubt that the king got it right. However, the story has been told in such a way that we are still confused. We simply do not know whether the story we heard from the first woman to speak (vv. 17–21) was true or not. Solomon had the wisdom to sort this out. We do not. Here was a king whose hearing heart gave him an astonishing ability to "discern between good and evil" (3:9).

The King's Reputation (v. 28)

> And all Israel heard of the judgment [or justice] that the king had rendered, and they stood in awe of [or feared] the king, because they perceived that the wisdom of God was in him to do justice. (v. 28)

What a king they had! He had something "better than weapons of war" (see Ecclesiastes 9:18). He had "the wisdom of God . . . to do justice." The important word "justice" appears twice in this summary of Israel's response to their king's dealing with the case of the two prostitutes. Years earlier King David had done "justice and righteousness for all his people" (2 Samuel 8:15, AT).[36] Now all Israel saw and understood that the Lord had indeed given their king a hearing heart to judge (that is, to bring justice in the Biblical sense) to his people (3:9).

The people's first response was to fear the king. No one can hide from the wisdom of God. No one can deceive the wisdom of God. This king would do what is right, and he would put right what is wrong. A healthy fear of him was very sensible![37]

This relatively small and insignificant incident points us to the King in whom we perceive "the power of God and the wisdom of God" (1 Corinthians 1:24; cf. Colossians 2:3). As we learn to trust the heavenly King to bring "justice" not only to the whole creation but to our lives, we are learning to be wise with the very wisdom of God (see Ephesians 1:17; Colossians 1:9, 28; 3:16; James 1:5; 3:13, 17).

10

What a Kingdom!

1 KINGS 4

THE KINGDOM OF OUR LORD Jesus Christ is astonishing. Jesus employed parables to help us understand what this kingdom is like. The kingdom is like a man who sowed good seed in his field where weeds also grew up (Matthew 13:24–30), a grain of mustard seed that becomes a tree (Matthew 13:31, 32; Luke 13:18, 19), leaven hidden in three measures of flour (Matthew 13:33; Luke 13:20, 21), treasure hidden in a field (Matthew 13:44), a pearl of great value (Matthew 13:45, 46), a fishing net gathering fish of every kind (Matthew 13:47–50), a bewilderingly generous master (Matthew 20:1–16), and a marriage feast (Matthew 25:1–13). Each of these pictures provides a wonderful insight into the kingdom that is the hope of the world. We come into this kingdom as we repent and trust the Lord Jesus Christ (Mark 1:15). We pray for the advance of this kingdom as the gospel is proclaimed throughout the world (Matthew 24:14). We look forward to the day when this kingdom will finally bring an end to all that is evil (Revelation 12:10).

To appreciate Jesus' powerful teaching about the kingdom we need to understand that he was not introducing a new idea to his hearers. They knew from their Scriptures (our Old Testament) that a long time ago the kingdom of another "son of David" had been astonishing. Solomon's kingdom was not perfect, as we will see in due course, but it was amazing. And when the weaknesses of Solomon's kingdom eventually brought it to an end, prophets like Isaiah, Hosea, and Amos understood that Solomon's kingdom had been a shadow of things to come (see, for example, Isaiah 11; Hosea 1:10, 11; Amos 9:11–15). Jesus was teaching about the kingdom that was anticipated in Solomon's kingdom.

In 1 Kings 4 we find a description of the wonder of Solomon's kingdom. At first sight you might think that here we have one of the less interesting chapters in the Bible. There are lists with names and numbers, no doubt drawn from the official records of Solomon's government. Not exactly riveting stuff! The story is put on hold while these statistics and details are recorded. It is one of those passages that any Bible reader might be tempted to skip over quickly. That would be a mistake. However we might feel about the details in 1 Kings 4, it is clear that the writer was rather excited! The details are presented in order to give us some idea of the wonder of Solomon's kingdom. The value of this chapter lies in the ways in which we will see foreshadowed here the kingdom of Jesus Christ, greater than the kingdom of Solomon (see Matthew 12:42).

We will see:

(1) The king and his people (vv. 1–20)
(2) The king and the whole world (vv. 21–24)
(3) What a kingdom! (vv. 25–28)
(4) The king and his wisdom (vv. 29–34)

The King and His People (vv. 1–20)

The first verse makes a fitting heading for the whole chapter as well as its first part (vv. 1–20): "King Solomon was king over all Israel" (v. 1). Generally our writer has used the expression "all Israel" to refer to the whole nation (as in 1:20; 2:15; 3:28).[1] In due course this expression will, tragically, refer to just the northern part of that kingdom (as in 12:16, 18, 20). Here, however, we see Solomon established as king over all God's people.

Something similar had been said about King David at the height of his reign: "David reigned over all Israel" (2 Samuel 8:15a).[2] The goodness of David's reign was summed up: "And David did justice and righteousness for all his people" (2 Samuel 8:15b, AT). The form this "justice and righteousness" took was then outlined in terms of the people appointed to administer it (2 Samuel 8:16–18).

A great deal had happened since those glory days of King David. David had been responsible for terrible injustice and unrighteousness (2 Samuel 11). The future of his kingdom seemed uncertain. Indeed the main account of King David's reign in 2 Samuel concluded with another list of officials (20:23–26) similar to the one in 2 Samuel 8. The subtle differences between those two lists signaled the deterioration of David's kingdom.[3]

The problems and uncertainties surrounding the kingdom of David have dominated the opening pages of 1 Kings. However, the outcome of the turbulent days covered in 1 Kings 1—3 was that at last the son of David (the *right* son of David) was now king over all Israel.

Many years later in the very city from which Solomon reigned, Peter announced, "Let *all the house of Israel* therefore know for certain that God has made him both Lord and Christ, this Jesus whom you crucified" (Acts 2:36). "All Israel" again had a king, this time greater than both David and Solomon.

What was Solomon's kingdom like? Some find in the details of 1 Kings 4 a troubling description of an oppressive official bureaucracy.[4] Certainly we will see some indications of problems (or potential problems) in Solomon's kingdom, but the overall mood of the chapter is positive (see especially vv. 20, 29, 34). We will see evidence of continuity with his father's kingdom that should remind us of the "justice and righteousness" of David's reign described in 2 Samuel 8. The general message of 1 Kings 4 is that God kept his promise to David and established the wonderful kingdom of the son of David (see 2 Samuel 7:12–16).

The Good Order of His Kingdom (vv. 2–6)

In verses 2–6 we are given a list of Solomon's "high officials"[5] (v. 2a), along with indications of their responsibilities in the life of his kingdom. The list is an echo of the two similar lists that summarized the administration of Solomon's father (2 Samuel 8:15–18; 20:23–26[6]), but there are differences.

The earlier lists of King David's officials began with the army (2 Samuel 8:16; 20:23). The army commander's chief duty was dealing with enemies. In Solomon's more peaceful kingdom Azariah "the priest" (that is, the head priest, elsewhere called the high priest) is mentioned first (v. 2b). The priest's chief duties concerned the relationship between the people and God.

Azariah was "the son of Zadok"[7] and therefore a brother of Ahimaaz (see v. 15; 2 Samuel 15:27). We may assume that Azariah took up this role after the death of his father and therefore at a later time in Solomon's reign. In this chapter our writer is looking quite comprehensively at Solomon's reign, and the details mentioned are not restricted to any particular moment in time. We hear no more of this Azariah.

In the kingdom of Jesus Christ, the King himself is the priest (Hebrews 7). Our confidence comes from the grace, mercy, and help secured for us by our great high priest (Hebrews 4:14–16).

Next mentioned are Elihoreph and Ahijah who were "secretaries" (v. 3a). David's kingdom needed only one "secretary" at a time (2 Samuel 8:17; 20:25). This role was probably a combination of private secretary to the king and secretary of state, involving responsibility for correspondence and other record keeping.[8] A small measure of Solomon's kingdom being greater than David's (1:37, 47) is the need for this role to be doubled.[9]

In the kingdom of Jesus, books and records will one day be opened (Revelation 20:12).

"Jehoshaphat the son of Ahilud was recorder" (v. 3b), as he had been for David (2 Samuel 8:16; 20:24). The "recorder" may have overseen public records or, as some suggest, he may have been a royal "herald"[10] (the Hebrew suggests "causing remembrance"). Jehoshaphat's long term of service is one of several points of continuity between David's and Solomon's kingdoms.

Without pressing the point (since we are not entirely clear about Jehoshaphat's role), remember that gospel proclamation today is the work of a royal herald, making known the commands of the King.

"Benaiah the son of Jehoiada was in command of the army" (v. 4a; see 2:25). Here was a change from David's days, where Joab had held on to this position (2 Samuel 8:16; 20:23), despite his king's efforts to replace him (2 Samuel 19:13). Benaiah had been commander of David's personal bodyguard (2 Samuel 23:22, 23), a firm believer in Solomon (1:8, 36, 37), and the executioner of the enemies of Solomon's kingdom (2:25, 34, 46). However, this is the last mention of Benaiah in the books of Kings. In Solomon's kingdom the army will have much less to do.

In the kingdom of Jesus Christ, the great and decisive battle against all evil has been fought and won. The Lord Jesus Christ has disarmed the enemies and put them to shame, triumphing over them in the cross (Colossians 2:15). We await the final judgment, but the kingdom of Jesus Christ has no place for an army here on earth. The weapons of our warfare are very different (2 Corinthians 10:4; Ephesians 6:10–20).

"Zadok and Abiathar were priests" (v. 4b). Before his son Azariah took the role, Zadok had been the chief priest, displacing Abiathar (2:35). Abiathar's expulsion from his position in Jerusalem (2:27) may not have meant that he ceased to be a priest in every sense, hence his mention here.[11]

"Azariah the son of Nathan was over the officers" (v. 5a). We cannot be sure whether the father of this second Azariah (see v. 2) was the well-known prophet Nathan or the rather less renowned son of David who bore the same name (2 Samuel 5:14). The former seems more likely in this context.[12] The "officers" under this Azariah's superintendence will be introduced in verse 7.

Azariah had a brother, Zabud, who was "priest and king's friend" (v. 5b). It is possible that "king's friend" was an official position, perhaps a confidential advisor to the king.[13] We are reminded, however, of Hushai, the "friend" of King David (see 2 Samuel 15:37; 16:16, 17), who certainly proved himself to be David's friend in every sense of the word.[14] It is again interesting that the man named as Solomon's "friend" was a "priest." "Priest" should not be understood narrowly, that is, as a consecrated person with prescribed duties in the tabernacle and later in the house of the Lord. In David's kingdom his sons were "priests" (2 Samuel 8:18), and Ira the Jairite was described as "David's priest" (2 Samuel 20:26).[15]

In the kingdom of the Lord Jesus, all who obey him are his "friends" (John 15:14, 15). There is no higher honor.

"Ahishar was in charge of the palace [literally, the house]" (v. 6a). This was a new role, but it will continue through the coming generations (see 16:9; 18:3; 2 Kings 10:5; 15:5; 18:18, 37; 19:2; Isaiah 22:15; 36:3, 22; 37:2). The king's household was now so substantial that official oversight was required.

Jesus spoke of "the faithful and wise servant, whom his master has set over his household, to give them their food at the proper time" (Matthew 24:45)—a profound picture of the faithful pastor feeding the members of Christ's household by healthy teaching of God's Word.

Finally, "Adoniram the son of Abda was in charge of the forced labor" (v. 6b). This is another point of continuity with David's administration, but a more troubling one. Adoniram (also called Adoram, 12:18) had been appointed to this role by King David (2 Samuel 20:24), and therefore Solomon should not be held solely responsible.[16] Furthermore, as we will see in 5:13–14, the policy of compulsory labor may have been reasonable, at least for a time. However, in due course Adoniram will pay with his life for the alleged harshness of the policy he administered for Solomon (with the added aggravation of the stupidity of Solomon's son, Rehoboam, 12:18).

Despite this seed of trouble to come, the picture we are given is of a well-ordered and peaceful kingdom, where priesthood is more important than the army, where records are kept and nothing is forgotten. Turn your mind to the kingdom here foreshadowed. It is a kingdom of perfect peace (Acts 10:36; Romans 14:17; Ephesians 2:17; Colossians 1:20; 2 Thessalonians 3:16), a kingdom with a reliable record of the names of all who belong there (see Philippians 4:3; Revelation 3:5; 21:27), a kingdom in which nothing is forgotten except the sins that have been forgiven (see Colossians 2:13, 14; Revelation 20:12). In Solomon's kingdom we see a shadow of the kingdom of the Lord Jesus Christ.

A Kingdom That Served the King (vv. 7–19)

In verses 7–19 we find that Solomon made arrangements for his great household to be well fed. The territory of Israel was divided into twelve districts, with twelve officials, each responsible to see that his district provided for the palace one month each year. These were the "officers" overseen by Azariah, the son of Nathan (v. 5).

> Solomon had twelve officers over all Israel, who provided food for the king and his household. Each man had to make provision for one month in the year. These were their names: Ben-hur, in the hill country of Ephraim; Ben-deker, in Makaz, Shaalbim, Beth-shemesh, and Elonbeth-hanan; Ben-hesed, in Arubboth (to him belonged Socoh and all the land of Hepher); Ben-abinadab, in all Naphath-dor (he had Taphath the daughter of Solomon as his wife); Baana the son of Ahilud, in Taanach, Megiddo, and all Beth-shean that is beside Zarethan below Jezreel, and from Bethshean to Abel-meholah, as far as the other side of Jokmeam; Ben-geber, in Ramoth-gilead (he had the villages of Jair the son of Manasseh, which are in Gilead, and he had the region of Argob, which is in Bashan, sixty great cities with walls and bronze bars); Ahinadab the son of Iddo, in Mahanaim; Ahimaaz, in Naphtali (he had taken Basemath the daughter of Solomon as his wife); Baana the son of Hushai, in Asher and Bealoth; Jehoshaphat the son of Paruah, in Issachar; Shimei the son of Ela, in Benjamin; Geber the son of Uri, in the land of Gilead, the country of Sihon king of the Amorites and of Og king of Bashan. And there was one governor who was over the land.[17] (vv. 7–19)

This paragraph raises a number of issues. The first is simply whether this is a positive or negative aspect of Solomon's kingdom. Could anyone ever be positive about a taxation system (that's what it was)? As we see these officers Solomon appointed we may be reminded of the tax collectors of Jesus' day, deeply resented and repeatedly linked by the Gospel writers with "sinners" (Matthew 9:10; Luke 15:1). It was shocking and offensive that Jesus became known as "a friend of tax collectors and sinners" (Matthew 11:19). "Why does he eat with tax collectors and sinners?" the Pharisees asked (Mark 2:16). They were perplexed because tax collectors were despised.

Some argue that Solomon was here overriding the traditional tribal system, introducing an oppressive central administration that must have been resented.[18] Was this the fulfillment of Samuel's dire warning of the ways of a king "like the nations" who will take and take and take (1 Samuel 8:5, 11–17)?

It is true that Solomon's regime was in due course deeply resented. However, *at this point* I do not think that the writer is painting a negative picture.[19] Here we have a good and great king served by his subjects. Soon we will hear that they were "happy" (v. 20). That may not be the whole story, but it is the part of the story we are told here.

Consider the joy of serving the Lord Jesus Christ in his kingdom. His subjects gladly serve him and give him the glory (perhaps the richest picture of this wonder is the scene in Revelation 4—5). The description of all Israel gladly giving to provide food for their king and his household should be seen as an anticipation of the day when all God's people will gladly worship King Jesus.

The second matter to note briefly is the identity of the officers responsible for this aspect of the life of Solomon's kingdom. Most of them seem to be identified by their father's name ("Ben-" means "son of"), giving rise to the rather fanciful suggestion that the list comes from a document that may have been damaged down one side, so that the personal names of the officers were not legible.[20] A number of these officers (and their fathers) are otherwise unknown to us (Ben-hur,[21] v. 8; Ben-deker, v. 9; Ben-hesed, v. 10; Ahinadab the son of Iddo,[22] v. 14; Jehoshaphat the son of Paruah, v. 17; Geber the son of Uri, v. 19). One was apparently from Solomon's family circle: Ben-abinadab (v. 11). He was probably Solomon's cousin (assuming his father, Abinadab, to be David's older brother, 1 Samuel 16:8; 17:13). He became the king's son-in-law. Others appear to have been related to other officials in Solomon's administration. Baana (v. 12) may have been the brother of Jehoshaphat the "recorder" (v. 3), both sons of the otherwise unknown Ahilud. Ben-geber (v. 13) may have been the son of another of these twelve officers (Geber in v. 19). Ahimaaz (v. 15) was probably Zadok's son (Zadok had been a faithful servant of David—2 Samuel 15:27, 36; 17:17, 20; 18:19, 22, 23, 27–29) and therefore a brother of Azariah the priest (v. 2). Still others had connections with the recent history of the kingdom. Baana (v. 16) appears to have been the son of David's friend Hushai (2 Samuel 15:37). Shimei, the son of Ela (not to be confused, of course, with Shimei, the son of Gera, 2:8; 2:36–46) was probably among the small group of people noted for their refusal to support the ambitions of Adonijah (1:8)[23] and presumably was therefore a firm and long-time believer in Solomon.

What we know (or surmise) about these men points to a history of faithfulness to Solomon and to his father David. It is not unreasonable to assume something similar for those about whom we know less. The general impression given is that these twelve officers were persons whom Solomon had reasons to trust. It is possible that this aspect of Solomon's kingdom is part of the background to Jesus' parable about the kingdom of God in which the returning king said to his faithful servant, "Well done, good servant! Because you have been faithful in a very little, you shall have authority over ten cities" (Luke 19:17; cf. Matthew 24:47).[24]

The third issue raised by verses 7–19 is what we are to make of the twelve districts and their relationship to the territory of the twelve tribes. The number of districts is based on the number of months in the year for which provisions need to be gathered to support the royal household (v. 7). The officers may be listed in the order in which their responsibilities came up each year, since there is no obvious geographical sense to the sequence. There is a simple and good reason why this task was not simply distributed to the historic twelve tribes. The twelve territories given to the twelve tribes in the days of Joshua (Joshua 13—19) differed in size and productivity. We may suppose that Solomon's twelve officers administered areas of approximately equal economic capacity.[25] These areas are not defined (at least in the text before us) with precise boundaries. Various attempts to map them end up with rather different pictures,[26] but in general terms they look like modifications to the historic tribal boundaries for the sake of equity.[27]

In other words, if we are looking at this picture rightly, here is taxation that was *not* exploitation and oppression. Of course, that is hard to believe. Rarely has any human government achieved such a thing. But that is the point. Solomon's kingdom was greater than any merely human kingdom.

A fourth issue is quite complicated. Solomon's twelve officers were "over all Israel" (v. 7). It is natural to understand this as a reference to the whole nation (as in v. 1). However, the twelve areas for which the officers were responsible seem to cover "Israel" in the narrower sense, excluding Solomon's own tribe of Judah.[28] Those inclined to criticize Solomon's regime can find here another plank for their argument. Did Solomon impose his taxation system on everyone but his own tribe? At the risk of sounding overly positive about Solomon, I think that we should avoid reading too much between the lines. The text says that the scheme covered "all Israel" (v. 7). Just how Judah was involved is not spelled out. There may have been unstated ways in which Judah served King Solomon's household. Once again it seems to go against the grain of the text to find here evidence for cronyism in Solomon's kingdom at this stage of the story.

A Kingdom of Peace and Joy (v. 20)

The generally positive tone we have found in verses 1–19 is confirmed in the summation that concludes these verses:[29] "Judah and Israel[30] were as many as the sand by the sea. They ate and drank[31] and were happy" (v. 20).

The omission of Judah from the areas allocated to the twelve officers in verses 7–19 probably accounts for its explicit mention here. In the blessing and happiness of Solomon's kingdom Judah and Israel (whatever their later history) were together.

Those who read these words with the promises of God in mind (as all readers should) cannot miss the note of fulfillment. Listen to what God had said many years earlier to Abraham:

> I will surely bless you, and I will surely multiply your offspring as the stars of heaven and *as the sand that is on the seashore.* (Genesis 22:17; cf. 32:12)

Our writer is telling us that under King Solomon God's promise to Abraham was fulfilled![32] The innumerable multitude of Solomon's kingdom (see 3:8) anticipated the "great multitude" of Revelation 7:9, the ultimate fulfillment of God's promise to Abraham (cf. Hebrews 11:12).

Life in Solomon's kingdom was (so to speak) an ongoing banquet—and a joyful one. In this kingdom the promised blessing of God was richly enjoyed. The description of Solomon's kingdom may have an element of hyperbole, but what a privilege Judah and Israel enjoyed! How "happy" they were! The Lord Jesus repeatedly likened his kingdom to a banquet (Matthew 22:1–14; 25:1–13; Luke 12:36; 14:12–24; cf. John 7:37; Revelation 19:9). What a privilege and blessing his people enjoy! What joy is ours![33]

The King and the Whole World (vv. 21–24)

God had promised that the blessings enjoyed by the descendants of Abraham would not be limited to that nation (see Genesis 12:3). Solomon's kingdom extended beyond the borders of Israel: "Solomon ruled over all the kingdoms from the Euphrates[34] to the land of the Philistines and to the border of Egypt" (v. 21a).[35]

Again we hear the excitement of the promise fulfilled. God's word to Abraham had been: "To your offspring I give this land, from the river of Egypt to the great river, the river Euphrates . . ." (Genesis 15:18; cf. Exodus 23:31; Joshua 1:4). David's prayer for Solomon[36] had been:

> May he have dominion from sea to sea,
>   and from the River to the ends of the earth!
> May desert tribes bow down before him,
>   and his enemies lick the dust!
> May the kings of Tarshish and of the coastlands
>   render him tribute;
> may the kings of Sheba and Seba
>   bring gifts!
> May all kings fall down before him,
>   all nations serve him! (Psalm 72:8–11)

David's prayer and God's promise (on which the prayer had been based) found fulfillment in Solomon's kingdom. Solomon's kingdom may not have embraced "all the families of the earth" (Genesis 12:3), but for its time it was vast—from the Euphrates River in the far northeast to the border of Egypt in the far southwest, taking in the Mediterranean coast to the west ("the land of the Philistines").

Of course, this great empire was no more than a dim shadow of the kingdom that will take in all the kingdoms of this world (Revelation 11:15), "so that at the name of Jesus every knee [will] bow, in heaven and on earth and under the earth, and every tongue confess that Jesus Christ is Lord, to the glory of God the Father" (Philippians 2:10, 11; cf. 1 Corinthians 15:27; Ephesians 1:20–23). But it is good for us to see in Solomon's extraordinary kingdom a foretaste of the kingdom of our Lord Jesus Christ, to whom "all authority in heaven and on earth has been given" (Matthew 28:18).

The Wealth of the Nations (vv. 21b–24a)

Not every knee that will bow at the name of Jesus will do so willingly. Likewise we may suppose that not every person from the Euphrates to the border of Egypt was glad to submit to King Solomon. Be that as it may, "They brought tribute and served Solomon all the days of his life" (v. 21b). It is worth noting that the "tribute" brought to David in the glory days of his reign (see 2 Samuel 8:2, 6) came after his military victories. The nations appear to have served Solomon without the need for armed force.

For those prepared to see it, Solomon became "a light for the nations" (Isaiah 49:6). To serve this king, if you did so gladly, would be no burden.[37] To bring him "tribute" would be to honor him.[38]

The extent of the nations' submission (glad or otherwise) to King Solomon is reflected in the extraordinary scale of the daily provisions for Solomon's court enabled by their gifts:

> Solomon's provision for one day was thirty cors[39] of fine flour and sixty cors of meal, ten fat oxen, and twenty pasture-fed cattle, a hundred sheep, besides deer, gazelles, roebucks, and fattened fowl. (vv. 22, 23)

From this, estimates of the number of people in Solomon's royal household range from 14,000 to 32,000.[40] Perhaps we should allow for some hyperbole, although comparable examples have been cited from Persia and Egypt.[41]

As we look back at the lavish provision at Solomon's table, consider again the richness given at the banquet of King Jesus. One older commentator put it well:

> Thus Christ fed those whom he taught, five thousand at a time, more than ever Solomon's table would entertain at once: all believers have in him a continual feast. Herein, he far outdoes Solomon, that he feeds all his subjects, not with bread that perishes, but *with that which endures to eternal life.*[42]

We should understand that the rich provision at the tables of Solomon's court were not an oppressive drain on his people. The provisions described in verses 22–23 did not all come from the taxation system outlined in verses 7–19. On the contrary, such lavish provision was possible *because*[43] "he[44] had dominion over all the region west of[45] the Euphrates from Tiphsah to Gaza, over all the kings west of the Euphrates" (v. 24a).

Tiphsah was an important city on the west bank of the Euphrates River and on the trade route west from Mesopotamia.[46] Gaza was where it still is, toward the southwest on the Mediterranean coast.[47] These two significant cities conveniently, though not precisely, signify the extent of Solomon's influence.

The word translated "had dominion" is not particularly common[48] and reminds us of its use in Genesis 1:26, 28. Solomon was a new Adam, exercising in some measure the "dominion" intended for humanity from the beginning.[49] David had subjugated the kings of this region by force (2 Samuel 8; 10). Solomon exercised dominion in peace, as we are about to hear.

The Prince of Peace (v. 24b)

"And he had peace on all sides around him" (v. 24b). This is what God had promised:

> And I will appoint a place for my people Israel and will plant them, so that they may dwell in their own place and be disturbed no more. And violent men shall afflict them no more, as formerly. (2 Samuel 7:10)

Solomon's vast and peaceful empire eventually led to the promise of a king whose reign of peace would never end (see Isaiah 9:6–7). This is the kingdom of Jesus Christ (see, for example, Luke 1:79; 2:14; Acts 10:36; Romans 5:1; 14:17, Ephesians 2:14, 15; Colossians 1:20; 2 Thessalonians 3:16).

What a Kingdom! (vv. 25–28)

In verses 25–28 our attention is drawn back from the wider empire to Solomon's kingdom, that is, "all Israel" (v. 1). What a kingdom it was![50]

Secure (v. 25)

First, it was secure: "And Judah and Israel lived in safety, from Dan even to Beersheba,[51] every man under his vine and under his fig tree, all the days of Solomon" (v. 25).

This second reference to the nation as "Judah and Israel" (cf. v. 20) perhaps hints at the coming days when these two parts of the nation will not be at peace with each other, let alone with the nations around them. The point is, however, that "all the days of Solomon"[52] the south and the north enjoyed "safety." The word suggests a life of security, free from fear (see Deuteronomy 12:10; Jeremiah 23:6).

"Every man under his vine and under his fig tree" is a delightful picture of tranquility and peace, appearing here for the first time in the Old Testament. The image was employed in various ways by the later prophets, particularly to describe the promised fear-free kingdom (Micah 4:4; Zechariah 3:10; cf. Ezekiel 28:26).[53]

That is what Solomon's kingdom was like. As such it was a shadow of the complete and eternal security that is ours in Christ Jesus (see Romans 8:38, 39).

Strong (v. 26)

Second, Solomon's kingdom was strong: "Solomon also had 40,000[54] stalls of horses for his chariots, and 12,000 horsemen [horses]"[55] (v. 26). While Solomon may have had little need to call on military force to keep the peace of his kingdom and empire, it appears that considerable (although not excessive) resources were available to him.[56]

But is that all? I don't think so. Without taking away from the astonishingly positive picture we are being given of Solomon's kingdom, this mention of horses and chariots (a bit like the earlier mention of forced labor in v. 6) strikes a discordant note. Didn't Moses say that a king in Israel "must not acquire many horses for himself" (Deuteronomy 17:16)? Didn't Samuel warn that there would be trouble with a king who had chariots and horsemen (1 Samuel 8:11–18)? Up to this point the only persons in Israel to acquire chariots had been Absalom (2 Samuel 15:1) and Adonijah (1 Kings 1:5)— hardly encouraging precedents.[57] Here is a further hint that Solomon's astonishing kingdom was not without potential problems.

Generous (v. 27a)

However, the positive picture continues for, third, the kingdom of Solomon was generous: "And those officers supplied provisions for King Solomon, and for all who came to King Solomon's table, each one in his month" (v. 27a).

This refers back to the officers of verses 7–19, adding that they supplied provisions "for all who came to King Solomon's table." This suggests generous hospitality. A little later we will see examples of those who came to Solomon from the nations and experienced his generosity (see v. 34; 10:1–5, 13).

Again we see in Solomon's kingdom an anticipation of the kingdom of David's greater son. Jesus said, "And people will come from east and west, and from north and south, and recline at table in the kingdom of God" (Luke 13:29). What a kingdom!

Nothing Lacking! (vv. 27b, 28)

Fourth, there was nothing lacking in Solomon's kingdom: "They let nothing be lacking" (v. 27b). As though to underline "nothing," the writer adds a detail: "Barley also and straw for the horses and swift steeds they brought to the place where it was required, each according to his duty" (v. 28).

In the greater kingdom of Jesus there is no need for anxiety, for "all these things will be added to you" (Matthew 6:33). While it is important not to think that this means health and wealth for Christians in this world (it does *not* mean that), we know that the kingdom of Jesus will not disappoint (see Romans 8:18; 2 Corinthians 4:17; 1 Peter 1:3–9).

The King and His Wisdom (vv. 29–34)

We have followed the lists the writer has so excitedly put before us in verses 1–28. Now we come to the point of it all. What made this astonishing kingdom so good, so glorious? It was not simply the efficient administration and lavish prosperity. There have been many well-organized and opulent regimes in the history of the world that were far from great and good. Why should we admire Solomon's kingdom?

Our chapter concludes by returning to the theme of chapter 3, namely the *wisdom* God gave to Solomon. In this way the writer has set the description of the kingdom in 4:1–28 clearly in the context of Solomon's *wisdom*.[58] Chapter 3 concluded with all Israel in awe of their king "because they perceived that the wisdom of God was with him to do justice" (3:28). Returning to that theme now the writer reminds us:

> And God gave Solomon wisdom and understanding beyond measure, and breadth of mind like the sand on the seashore. (v. 29)

Solomon's wisdom was a gift from God (cf. 3:5, 9, 12; Proverbs 2:6–8). It is described in terms that help us see it as a fulfillment of God's promise to Abraham. Just as the people were "as many as the sand by the sea" (v. 20), so they were ruled by a king with immeasurable wisdom and understanding, "like the sand on the seashore." "Breadth of mind" (literally, "breadth of heart") does not mean that Solomon was broadminded in today's sense. His heart was wide open to hear (the "hearing heart" of 3:9) the word of God (cf. Psalm 119:32).

We have now seen this "wisdom of God . . . to do justice" (3:28) putting things right in the lives of individuals (3:16–28), effectively administrating the nation's life (4:1–20), and touching the nations (4:20–28). It is time to appreciate the glory of this wisdom.

The Glory of the King's Wisdom (vv. 30, 31)

> . . . so that Solomon's wisdom surpassed the wisdom of all the people of the east and all the wisdom of Egypt. For he was wiser than all other men, wiser than Ethan the Ezrahite, and Heman, Calcol, and Darda, the sons of Mahol, and his fame [literally, name] was in all the surrounding nations. (vv. 30, 31)

The world of Solomon's day valued wisdom. In particular there was a reputation for wisdom among "the people of the east" (the peoples east of Canaan; Genesis 29:1; Judges 6:3, 33; 7:12; 8:10; Job 1:3; Isaiah 11:14; cf. Daniel 1:17, 20; Matthew 2:1) and in Egypt (Genesis 41:8; Exodus 7:11; Isaiah 19:11; Acts 7:22). Indeed the world has always valued wisdom. But the wisdom of the world is foolishness when compared with the wisdom of God that was given to Solomon (cf. 1 Corinthians 1:18–25; 3:19, 20).

Solomon's wisdom was far greater than any wisdom the world had seen. It was greater than "all other men [Hebrew, adam]," probably another allusion to Genesis 1—2. Solomon was a new Adam, so to speak. He exercised dominion by his wisdom.

The list of great ones in verse 31, apparently famous for their wisdom, makes the point. Who today has heard of "Ethan the Ezrahite, and Heman, Calcol, and Darda, the sons of Mahol"?[59] But here we are, thousands of years later, thinking about the wisdom of Solomon. The fame of Solomon "in all the surrounding nations" has today spread even to Australia (where I am writing this) where people who know little of the Bible still speak of a difficult decision needing "the wisdom of Solomon."[60]

What was the "wisdom" of Solomon? Why, of all the qualities we might expect in God's king, is *wisdom* so prominent in the Bible's account of Solomon? We will return to these questions shortly.

The Words of the King's Wisdom (vv. 32, 33)

Solomon's wisdom was expressed in words—lots of words:

> He also spoke 3,000 proverbs, and his songs were 1,005. He spoke of trees, from the cedar that is in Lebanon to the hyssop that grows out of the wall. He spoke also of beasts, and of birds, and of reptiles, and of fish. (vv. 32, 33)

These two verses are packed with significance.

First, we learn that Solomon spoke many "proverbs" and "songs." A number of these (but by no means all of them) have found their way into the Old Testament. We have "The proverbs of Solomon, son of David, king of Israel" (Proverbs 1:1); "The Song of Songs which is Solomon's" (Song of Solomon 1:1); "A Song of Ascents. Of Solomon" (superscription to Psalm 127).

From the book of Proverbs we learn that the beginning, the very first, principle of wisdom is "the fear of the LORD" (Proverbs 1:7; 9:10; 15:33), and wisdom is about living well in God's world.

It is more than interesting to note that the Hebrew word for "proverbs" in verse 32 is translated into Greek with the word used in the Gospels of the New Testament for Jesus' "parables." Just as King Solomon spoke many proverbs, the still greater Son of David spoke many parables (see Matthew 13:3, 34; 22:1; Mark 4:33). Those who heard him were astonished and said, "Where did this man get this wisdom?" (Matthew 13:54). He had been filled with wisdom from childhood (Luke 2:40, 52). For those who had eyes to see, in Jesus "something greater than Solomon is here" (Matthew 12:42).

Second, Solomon's wisdom had a great deal to do with understanding God's creation. The range of plants and animals in verse 33 should remind us of Genesis 1.[61] Adam exercised dominion over "every beast of the field and every bird of the heavens" by giving them their names (Genesis 2:19). Solomon mastered the created world with words of wisdom.[62]

This is the extraordinary significance of true "wisdom." God's work of creation is a work of his wisdom. God's wisdom is behind all things he has created (see the remarkable personification of God's wisdom in Proverbs 8:22–31; cf. Psalm 104:24). That is why wisdom is needed to rightly understand and live in the world God has made. Such wisdom begins with rightly acknowledging God ("the fear of the Lord," Job 28:28; Psalm 111:10; Proverbs 1:7; 9:10; 15:33). The wisdom God gave Solomon was the power to put things right ("do justice," 3:28) in God's world.

We are approaching the climax of this remarkable chapter. I hope that by now you can see how rich it has been in illuminating the astonishing wonder of Jesus Christ. He *is* wisdom from God (1 Corinthians 1:30). The *wisdom* that is in Christ Jesus is a major (perhaps neglected) theme of the New Testament. Are you, like those who saw and heard him, astonished not only at his power and authority but at his *wisdom* (Mark 6:2)? Something greater than Solomon *is* here! To know, love, and trust the Lord Jesus Christ is not just right and true, it is *wise* (Colossians 2:3; 2 Timothy 3:15).[63] He is the one who is able to put all things right (see Colossians 1:15–23).

The Wonder of the King's Wisdom (v. 34)

In case we are tempted to think that the wisdom of Solomon (and the greater wisdom of Jesus Christ) is less marvelous than it really is, listen carefully to the last and climactic words of the chapter:

> And people of all nations came to hear the wisdom of Solomon, and from all the kings of the earth, who had heard of his wisdom. (v. 34)

Do not be distracted by the obvious hyperbole here.[64] Solomon's God-given wisdom really was this significant. The nations of the world took notice, as Moses had promised they would take notice of the wisdom of his people Israel who obeyed God's Law (see Deuteronomy 4:6). Here was a king who ruled with the wisdom that human beings, since Adam and Eve were expelled from the Garden of Eden, have found elusive.

When we see the wisdom of God in David's greater Son, Jesus, we understand Paul's exclamation: "Oh, the depth of the riches and wisdom and knowledge of God! How unsearchable are his judgments and how inscrutable his ways!" (Romans 11:33). The manifold wisdom of God is now being "made known to the rulers and authorities in the heavenly places. This was according to the eternal purpose that he [foreshadowed in King Solomon and] has realized in Christ Jesus our Lord" (Ephesians 3:10, 11).

Part 3

THE GOAL OF HISTORY

1 Kings 5—8

The Most Important Building in
the History of the World

1 Kings 5—7

11

A Chosen and Precious Stone

1 KINGS 5

WHAT HAPPENED WHEN YOU BECAME a Christian believer? I never tire of hearing people's honest stories of how things changed when they turned from their former way of life (whatever that may have been) to life with Jesus Christ as their Lord and Savior. It does not normally mean that past problems immediately disappeared. Many Christian believers struggle with the same difficulties they had before becoming Christians. But what a difference it makes to have a great high priest who is able "to sympathize with our weaknesses" (Hebrews 4:15), to have a conscience cleansed by complete forgiveness (Hebrews 9:14), to be delivered from the fear of death (Hebrews 2:15), to know Almighty God as your Father (Romans 8:15, 16; Galatians 4:6), to enjoy fellowship with other believers and with the Father and with his Son Jesus Christ (1 John 1:3)! What would you add to that list? What happened when *you* became a Christian believer?

We need to understand that what happened when we turned to Christ is bigger than the particular changes in our experience of life. One purpose of the Bible is to help us see reality more clearly, more deeply, and more truly than we could otherwise know. This is true of the huge change that occurs when a person becomes a Christian. To grasp something of what has happened to me, I need to learn to "walk by faith [that, is, by believing God's Word], not by sight [that is, only by the appearance of things]" (2 Corinthians 5:7).

I mention this because the section of 1 Kings we will be considering for the next eight chapters (covering 1 Kings 5—8) is an important part of the

Bible's explanation of *what has happened to Christian believers*. It is in fact much more than that. I have given this part of our exposition the title "The Goal of History." We will learn about what has happened to Christian believers by seeing God's purpose for the history of everything. I hope that you will share with me a sense of wonder, praise, and profound thankfulness as we explore the massive significance of King Solomon's most important accomplishment. Its relevance to Christian believers today is far greater than may at first appear.

Solomon's God-given wisdom has been repeatedly emphasized in 1 Kings 2—4 (see 2:6, 9; 3:12, 28; 4:29–34). Indeed the text seems to indicate that behind all the acts and achievements of Solomon described through these chapters was this wisdom. We have begun to see how King Solomon's wisdom helps us appreciate our Lord Jesus Christ, "in whom are hidden all the treasures of wisdom and knowledge" (Colossians 2:3; cf. Luke 11:31; 1 Corinthians 1:24, 30).

We come now to the beginning of the Bible's account of King Solomon's highest achievement, the greatest display of the wisdom given to him by God: the construction of the house of the Lord in Jerusalem. Of the eleven chapters of 1 Kings that cover Solomon's time as king, four are taken up with this one subject: preparations for the project (1 Kings 5), the work itself (1 Kings 6, 7), and theological reflections on the significance of the building (1 Kings 8). There is much for us to explore here. We will see that the greatest accomplishment of Solomon's God-given wisdom anticipated in wonderful ways what God, in his wisdom, has accomplished through Jesus Christ. The house Solomon built in Jerusalem will help us appreciate what happened when we became Christians.

The chapter before us describes the preparations for the building. We will see that it was:

1. An international project (v. 1)
2. A promised project (vv. 2–6)
3. A welcome project (vv. 7–11)
4. A project with more than meets the eye (v. 12)
5. A project with firm foundations (vv. 13–18)

An International Project (v. 1)

The chapter division in our English Bibles obscures the close connection between 4:34 and 5:1.[1] Among "all the kings of the earth" from whom people "came to hear the wisdom of Solomon" (4:34) was Hiram, king of Tyre (5:1)[2]:

> Now Hiram king of Tyre sent his servants to Solomon when he heard that
> they had anointed him[3] king in place of his father, for Hiram always loved
> David. (v. 1)

Tyre was a powerful center on the Phoenician coast, about 100 miles north
of Jerusalem. Much later in Biblical history Tyre and its king will come to
represent human, arrogant defiance of God.[4] However, the first king of Tyre to
appear in Biblical history was not like that.

What Hiram Heard (v. 1b)

The sequence of events about to be recounted began with something King
Hiram of Tyre "heard."[5]

He heard that Solomon was the one who had been anointed king to succeed his father David. Perhaps he had heard about Adonijah's abortive bid for
the throne, but now he heard that Solomon, not Adonijah, had become king of
Israel. This implies, of course, that Hiram had heard of David's death.

Furthermore Hiram was among "all the kings of the earth, who had *heard*
of [Solomon's] wisdom" (4:34). King Solomon's reputation reached the ears
of this neighboring foreign king.

What He Did (v. 1a)

Hiram did what many others did (4:34). He sent servants (I think we would
call them diplomats) to Solomon. Hiram's envoys probably came with good
wishes for the new king. This was not unusual. The death of a king and the
accession of his successor typically created potential tensions and misunderstandings. Good relations with the previous king could not be assumed with
the new king (cf. 2 Samuel 10:1–4). In Hiram's case, we may suppose that access to the trade routes to the south through Solomon's kingdom were a matter
of concern. There may have been other topics of international diplomacy with
which the servants of Hiram were charged. The Biblical account, however,
shows little interest in these matters.

Why? (v. 1c)

Of "all the kings of the earth" (4:34) who sent envoys to the new king in Jerusalem, Hiram is singled out for a reason. Hiram sent his delegation to Solomon
because "Hiram always loved David"[6] (v. 1c). That is a striking thing to say.
Today the word *love* can have an emotional sense and not much more. In the
Bible the term is used in political contexts (like this) where more than emotions
are involved. The story of David includes many who "loved" him (1 Samuel

18:1, 3, 16, 20, 28; 20:17).[7] This generally involved a glad recognition that he was the one chosen by God to be king. They "loved" him *as their (future) king.*

Hiram's attitude to King David (here called "love") has been briefly indicated earlier in this history. He had provided David with materials and craftsmen to build a "house" (in this case, a palace) for David (see 2 Samuel 5:11; 7:2).

All this does not necessarily mean that Hiram "was a worshipper of the true God"[8] in the full sense, but it does mean that he was remarkably positive toward King David. We will shortly hear from his own lips that this did include a glad acknowledgment of David's God (v. 7).

Hiram's delegation joined others from "all nations" who came to Jerusalem "to hear the wisdom of Solomon" (4:34). We are witnessing something of the international impact of the new king.

A Promised Project (vv. 2–6)

King Solomon received the delegation from Hiram. We are told nothing of what they said to him. That was not important. What *was* important was the word that "Solomon sent . . . to Hiram" (v. 2).

Why David Didn't Do It (v. 3)

Solomon's message began:

> You know that David my father could not build a house for the name of the LORD his God because of the warfare with which his enemies surrounded him, until the LORD put them under the soles of his feet. (v. 3)

Apart from the anticipatory references in 3:1, 2, this is the first time that this "house" has been mentioned since the great promise God had made to David in 2 Samuel 7.[9] We have seen that this promise is the key to understanding everything that has happened so far in 1 Kings. The promise was now clearly on Solomon's mind. The heart of God's promise to David was, "I will raise up your offspring after you, who shall come from your body, and I will establish his kingdom" (2 Samuel 7:12). That promise had now been fulfilled: "the kingdom was established in the hands of Solomon" (2:46).[10]

There was, however, a second element in the promise. At the time David had been thinking that perhaps he ought to provide a more appropriate building than a tent in which to house the ark of the covenant. David had "a house of cedar," and "the LORD had given him rest from all his surrounding enemies." Surely (he thought) it was time to do something about the ark of God "dwelling in a [mere] tent" (see 2 Samuel 7:1, 2).

These musings were the occasion for God's great promise to David. In essence the Lord said that David was *not* the one who would "build me a house to dwell in," but the promised son of David, whose kingdom the Lord would establish, would be the one to "build a house for my name" (2 Samuel 7:5, 13). The reason was twofold. First, the "rest" God intended for his people still lay in the future. Until then the tent was appropriate. Second, God intended to build David a "house" (that is, to establish his dynasty) before this other "house" was to be built (2 Samuel 7:11).[11]

Solomon knew this promise of God. I imagine that both his father and the prophet Nathan made sure that he knew it well. He knew that God had said of the promised son of David, "He shall build a house for my name" (2 Samuel 7:13).

The timing was important. David had not been permitted to build this house precisely because of the warfare that surrounded him. The house was to be built only when the Lord gave "rest from all your enemies" (compare 2 Samuel 7:11 with v. 3);[12] in other words, not "until the LORD put [the enemies] under the soles of his feet."[13] This last expression is an echo of God's promise as it was rearticulated by David:

> The LORD says to my Lord:
>   "Sit at my right hand,
> until I make your enemies your footstool." (Psalm 110:1)

While this promise finds its ultimate fulfillment in Jesus Christ,[14] we need to appreciate Solomon's sense of God's promise being fulfilled in him.

Notice that Solomon spoke of "a house for the name of the LORD," echoing "a house for my name" in 2 Samuel 7:13.[15] The "name" of the Lord is both his reputation and the means by which he may be known. But a "house" for the name of the Lord could not be built until God's promise of "rest" had been realized.

Why Solomon Must Do It (vv. 4, 5)

Solomon continued, "But now the LORD my God has given me rest on every side. There is neither adversary nor misfortune" (v. 4).

Here is one of the great "But now" moments of the Bible. Solomon understood that the promised "rest" of 2 Samuel 7:11 was now the reality of his kingdom. There was no "adversary"[16] (as the sons of Zeruiah had been to David, 2 Samuel 19:22).[17] This reminds us of what had happened to the potential adversaries Adonijah, Joab, and Shimei (2:24–26, 33, 34, 44–46). There was no "misfortune," literally no "evil stroke," possibly an allusion to those executions.[18] That was now over.

Solomon's "But now" anticipated the great "But now" of Jesus Christ. *"But now* in Christ Jesus you who once were far off have been brought near by the blood of Christ" (Ephesians 2:13). Our great adversary, Satan himself, has now been defeated (Luke 10:18; cf. John 12:31; 16:11; Colossians 2:15; Hebrews 2:14). The "rest" enjoyed by Solomon was a shadow of the "rest" Jesus gives (Matthew 11:28, 29; Hebrews 4:1–11).

Since Solomon believed God's promise and understood his "But now" circumstances in the light of the promise, he knew that he must act in accordance with the promise. We could call this the "obedience of faith" (cf. Romans 1:5; 16:26).

> And so I intend to build a house for the name of the LORD my God, as the LORD said to David my father, "Your son, whom I will set on your throne in your place, shall build[19] the house for my name." (v. 5)

Notice the most important connection between David and Solomon: "the LORD *his* God" (v. 3) is now "the LORD *my* God" (vv. 4, 5). The time had come. The time of fulfillment was the time for building this house.

What Hiram Must Do (v. 6)

Solomon concluded his word to Hiram:

> Now therefore[20] command that cedars of Lebanon be cut for me. And my servants will join your servants, and I will pay you for your servants such wages as you set, for you know that there is no one among us who knows how to cut timber like the Sidonians. (v. 6)

David's royal house had been built from cedar (2 Samuel 7:2), supplied by Hiram (2 Samuel 5:11). The cedars of Lebanon[21] were famous (see 4:33; also Judges 9:15; 2 Kings 19:23; Psalm 29:5; 92:12; 104:16). Solomon urged Hiram to provide him with the very best materials, cut by the very finest craftsmen.[22]

Solomon's request was neither a command,[23] nor an appeal for a favor. He promised to supply some of the necessary labor and to pay Hiram's workers wages to be set by Hiram.

A Welcome Project (vv. 7–11)

Hiram was delighted: "As soon as Hiram heard the words of Solomon, he rejoiced greatly" (v. 7a). This is remarkable. Why would a foreign king "rejoice greatly" at a request to supply wood to the king in Jerusalem? I do not believe we should put it down to the generous commercial terms of Solomon's proposal. Nor was it simply the importance of good relations with Israel for the sake of Phoenicia's food supply.[24] Hiram's joy is explained by what he understood.

What Hiram Understood (v. 7b)

Hiram said, "Blessed be the LORD this day, who has given to David a wise son to be over this great people" (v. 7b). Remarkably this foreign king used the distinctive name Yahweh ("LORD" in most English versions[25]), by which God was known to his people (see Exodus 3:13–15; 6:2, 3)—the very "name" for which Solomon was proposing to build a "house" (vv. 3, 5). He understood Solomon and his wisdom to be Yahweh's gift. He recognized that Solomon's people were a "great [literally, numerous] people," as our writer has noted in 4:20. Hiram apparently had some understanding of God's promises. And he was delighted![26] Is it too much to suggest that he must have understood something of the fact that God's promise included blessing for the nations (Genesis 12:3; 18:18)? I don't think so.[27]

In due course "the house of the LORD" will cause many to "rejoice" (see Psalm 122:1; also Psalm 43:4; 137:6; Isaiah 30:29; 35:10[28]). The very first of these was Hiram king of Tyre!

What Hiram Said (vv. 8, 9)

The happy king of Tyre sent a surprising message back to Solomon:

> And Hiram sent to Solomon, saying, "I have heard the message that you have sent to me. I am ready to do all you desire in the matter of cedar and cypress timber. My servants shall bring it down to the sea from Lebanon, and I will make it into rafts to go by sea to the place you direct. And I will have them broken up there, and you shall receive it. And you shall meet my wishes by providing food for my household." (vv. 8, 9)

Hiram's generosity exceeded Solomon's request. There was no need for Solomon to supply labor. Hiram's servants would do the job. And he would send "cypress timber"[29] as well as the requested cedar. Furthermore, Hiram worked out an efficient plan for the transportation of the timber. Joining logs together to make rafts would enable them to be floated down the Mediterranean coast to a site convenient for Solomon. As far as payment was concerned, Hiram was happy to accept provisions to feed his household.

Some have suggested that Hiram was in fact rejecting Solomon's terms and renegotiating a deal more favorable to himself.[30] That is not what it sounds like to me—and it is not what it looks like when Hiram matches his words with actions.

What Hiram Did (vv. 10, 11)

So Hiram supplied Solomon with all the timber of cedar and cypress that he desired, while Solomon gave Hiram 20,000 cors of wheat as food for his household, and 20,000 cors of beaten oil.[31] Solomon gave this to Hiram year by year. (vv. 10, 11)

We need to understand that Solomon's building project would take vast amounts of timber. The annual payment was considerable and may have continued through the building project (seven years, 6:38, or twenty years if the building of Solomon's own house was included, 7:1; 9:10). Solomon had not gotten a bargain,[32] but neither had he sought one. Hiram did what was asked of him and Solomon was not stinting toward Tyre's king.

A Project with More Than Meets the Eye (v. 12)

In 3:12 the Lord had promised to give Solomon wisdom. All Israel had "perceived that the wisdom of God was in him to do justice" (3:28). We were told in 4:29 that the Lord gave Solomon wisdom and understanding "beyond measure." His wisdom became internationally famous in 4:34. Now we are told:

And the Lord gave Solomon wisdom, as he promised him. And there was peace between Hiram and Solomon, and the two of them made a treaty. (v. 12)

The Lord kept on giving Solomon wisdom. This can be seen in the "peace" between Hiram and Solomon. This "peace" (Hebrew, *shalom*) was more than the absence of war, since there had never been any prospect of war between these two. This "peace" was a harmonious relationship of trust and goodwill[33] expressed in a treaty (or covenant)—a formalized mutual commitment one to the other.

This commitment, and therefore the peace Hiram and Solomon enjoyed, was expressed in the plans to provide for the building of "a house for the name of the Lord" (v. 3). This building project would be the greatest of all the displays of Solomon's wisdom. It will represent not only the "rest" given to God's people, but "peace" for the nations.

A Project with Firm Foundations (5:13–18)

The strikingly positive tone of verse 12 must be kept in mind as we hear what follows, for some modern readers find it difficult to feel so positive about the description of the final preparations for the building work.

The Workforce (vv. 13–16)

First we have a description of the workforce drafted by Solomon:

> King Solomon drafted forced labor out of all Israel, and the draft numbered 30,000 men. And he sent them to Lebanon, 10,000 a month in shifts. They would be a month in Lebanon and two months at home. Adoniram was in charge of the draft. Solomon also had 70,000 burden-bearers and 80,000 stonecutters in the hill country, besides Solomon's 3,300 chief officers who were over the work, who had charge of the people who carried on the work. (vv. 13–16)

Four categories of workers are mentioned: "forced labor," "burden-bearers," "stonecutters," and "chief officers."

The first of these needs to be clarified. The "forced labor" under Adoniram (see 4:6) was not necessarily slavery.[34] But it was compulsory and certainly had potential for abuse. After Solomon's death there would be complaints that the policy had been too harsh (12:4).[35] There had been "compulsory labor" in the kingdom since David's day (2 Samuel 20:24) and probably earlier. That may have been a kind of slavery involving people from vanquished nations (see Deuteronomy 20:11). Solomon's obligatory draft of workers from "all Israel" was probably a new development, but for a task as important as this one surely defensible.

Did Solomon raise his draft from the whole nation ("*all* Israel")[36] or just from the northern tribes ("all *Israel*")[37]? In due course it will be the northern tribes who complain of the harshness of the policy, but that does not mean that Judah was excluded, and we have no reason to think that it was.

Taking the numbers at face value, the workforce (30,000) was considerable. But so was the project.[38] The arrangement was probably not as generous to the workers as the ESV suggests: "a month in Lebanon and two months *at home*." The Hebrew for the last phrase is more literally rendered "in his house," that is (I suspect), in the "house" Solomon was building in Jerusalem (the only "house" mentioned in this chapter, "the house" in vv. 17, 18).[39]

If Hiram had generously offered to provide all the labor for the work in his region (vv. 8–9), it seems that Solomon insisted on his original proposal (v. 6) and supplied his share of workers.

The additional workers (the "burden-bearers," "stonecutters" and perhaps the "chief officers") were not Israelites (see 9:20, 21; 2 Chronicles 2:17, 18; 8:7, 8).[40] The great army of workers indicates the scale of the enterprise. It was huge.

The Beginning of the Work (vv. 17, 18)

The work began:

> At the king's command they quarried out great, costly stones in order to lay the foundation of the house with dressed stones. So Solomon's builders and Hiram's builders and the men of Gebal[41] did the cutting and prepared the timber and the stone to build the house. (vv. 17, 18)

The work on the building began at the command of the king—the king to whom the Lord had given wisdom. This building will be the work of God's wise king. He ensured that the finest quality stones were obtained and prepared for the foundation of the house.

Before we turn the page to witness the building of this extraordinary house, let us pause to reflect on the subject with which we began this chapter. What could this impressive building project in the days of Solomon have to do with what happened to us when we became Christian believers?

King Solomon said, "I intend to build a house for the name of the LORD my God" (v. 5). The Lord Jesus Christ is building a "house" that is like but unlike the house Solomon built (see Matthew 16:18). It is "a spiritual house" (1 Peter 2:5). In other words, it is not a physical house of wood and stone, but a "house" made up of people. When we come to the Lord Jesus we are the "stones" of this building. The Lord Jesus himself is the precious cornerstone. Peter wonderfully described all this:

> As you come to him, a living stone rejected by men but in the sight of God chosen and precious, you yourselves like living stones are being built up as a spiritual house, to be a holy priesthood, to offer spiritual sacrifices acceptable to God through Jesus Christ. For it stands in Scripture:
>
> > "Behold, I am laying in Zion a stone,
> >   a cornerstone chosen and precious,
> > and whoever believes in him will not be put to shame."
>
> So the honor is for you who believe. . . ." (1 Peter 2:4–7a)

We will be learning more about "the honor" of being a stone in this spiritual house as we hear more about the house Solomon built in Jerusalem. Solomon's building was grand and important. It represented the wisdom of God given to his king, the peace that was now possible with the nations, the rest God gave his people from all their enemies. But the house Solomon built did not last. Jesus' building project is greater. He said, "I will build *my church*, and the gates of hell shall not prevail against it" (Matthew 16:18).

What happened to you when you became a Christian? You came to Jesus and became a living stone in the most important building in the history of everything. That is an honor beyond description.

12

A True Perspective on the History of the Whole World

1 KINGS 6

IT IS DIFFICULT TO KNOW what to make of the times in which we live. Some think we are witnessing the disintegration of western civilization. The exaltation of individual "freedom" above all other values has undermined the foundations (it is thought). The rejection of any truth other than "scientific" truth has robbed us of any basis for moral consensus (many feel). Some see the extraordinary confusion of our time around gender identity as a threat to the fabric of the society we have known. Others are more positive. What we are witnessing (they think) is "progress": liberation from outdated restrictions and taboos, from the constraints of conventional morality, from the intolerance of traditional religion, and from the expectations of old-fashioned gender roles.

What do you make of the times in which we live?

The Bible does not give us a simple answer to that question. That is not surprising. It is not a simple question. But the Bible gives us a perspective on the question that is brilliantly illuminating. Remarkably this perspective comes into sharp focus in 1 Kings 6.

I say "remarkably" because this is a chapter of the Bible that (at first glance) promises little. It is a detailed description of a building—dimensions, materials, layout, and decoration. It is quite technical. Indeed there are a number of terms that are now obscure to us.[1] Unless you have an interest in the architecture of ancient buildings, you might be tempted to skip this tedious material. And yet we are about to see that in 1 Kings 6 we are approaching the high point of the Old Testament—one of the most important moments in the history of the world. We will find ourselves at this high point for the next few chapters of 1 Kings. The chapter before us brings us to this elevated historical moment and will give us a true perspective on the history of the whole world and therefore on our question about the times in which we live.

These are rather grand claims for one of the Bible's apparently more boring chapters. You may suspect that this preacher has been carried away in his desperation to justify his exposition of such material. Not so. There are a number of remarkably important parts of the Bible that may *appear* uninteresting at first sight.[2] This is one of the most important. But the rich lessons of this part of the Bible require patience.

The Most Important Thing Since . . . (v. 1)

We can sense the importance of what we are about to hear from the way the chapter begins:

> In the four hundred and eightieth year after the people of Israel came out of the land of Egypt, in the fourth year of Solomon's reign over Israel, in the month of Ziv, which is the second month, he began to build the house of the LORD. (v. 1)

The reference point from which we are invited to understand what follows in this chapter is the exodus from Egypt in the days of Moses—when "the people of Israel came out of the land of Egypt." That was when the nation of Israel was born. The story is told in the book of Exodus. By mighty acts of judgment against the Egyptian oppressors God rescued his suffering people from terrible bondage. When they reached Mount Sinai he said to them, "You yourselves have seen what I did to the Egyptians, and how I bore you on eagles' wings and brought you to myself" (Exodus 19:4). This historic act of divine grace was the foundation of Israel's knowledge of God: "I am the LORD your God, who brought you out of the land of Egypt, out of the house of slavery. You shall have no other gods before me" (Exodus 20:2, 3). Just as God's grace in his redemption of the people of Israel from Egypt *preceded* the giving of the Law (thus forever excluding the idea that God's grace could be earned by obeying the Law), so we are reminded here that God's grace toward Israel *preceded* and so was independent of the building about to be described in this chapter (thus forever excluding the idea that God's grace could be manipulated through activities—rituals—in a special building).[3]

The implication of 1 Kings 6:1 is that what we are about to hear is the most important thing since the exodus. This is the only event in the Bible that is dated in terms of the number of years from the exodus. The exodus was the beginning of something. We are about to hear the end—that is, the goal or culmination—of that great act of redemption. Much had happened in the centuries since Moses led the Israelites out of Egypt. There had been the conquest of the land in the days of Joshua, the repeated deliverances from enemies through the years of the judges, the reigns of King Saul and King David. It had all been leading to *this*.

The figure 480 may be literal.[4] It is, however, such a suggestive number that it may have symbolic significance and may not need to be taken literally. "In the four hundred and eightieth year" may be a way of saying "in the twelfth generation," a generation being thought of as forty years (cf. Deuteronomy 1:3).[5] "Twelve generations" may convey a sense of completeness (perhaps because Israel consisted of twelve tribes, possibly also because a year has twelve months). Since the actual time between one person's birth and the birth of his or her first offspring would be more like twenty to twenty-five years, "twelve generations" would be about 240 to 300 literal years. The more important point is that the period since the exodus had reached its culmination.[6]

What Solomon was about to do would bring to completion something that had begun 480 years (however understood) earlier. This was anticipated at the time of the exodus. Then Moses and the people of Israel had sung (and no doubt there had been occasions on which Israelites had sung through the centuries since that day):

> "You will bring them in and plant them on your own mountain,
>   the place, O Lord, which you have made for your abode,
>   the sanctuary, O Lord, which your hands have established.
> The Lord will reign forever and ever." (Exodus 15:17, 18)

While the words "mountain," "place," and "sanctuary" probably referred to the promised land,[7] the time had come for God's gift to his people to be completed: a "place" for the Lord's "abode," for him to "reign forever and ever," was about to be built.

Moses had anticipated this day in his address to the Israelites before they entered the promised land:

> But when you go over the Jordan and live in the land that the Lord your God is giving you to inherit, and when he gives you rest from all your enemies around, so that you live in safety, then to *the place that the Lord*

our God will choose, to make his name dwell there, there you shall bring all that I command you: your burnt offerings and your sacrifices, your tithes and the contribution that you present, and all your finest vow offerings that you vow to the LORD. (Deuteronomy 12:10, 11)

The time had at last come to provide the dwelling-place for the name of the Lord because the Lord had given "rest from all your enemies around, so that you live in safety" (see 5:4; 2 Samuel 7:11).

It was the second month of the fourth year of Solomon's reign.[8] The month of Ziv[9] corresponds roughly to our April and May. Then it was that King Solomon "began to build the house of the LORD."

There has never been, in the history of the world, a more significant building than this "house." The world's greatest skyscrapers, most beautiful architecture, and grandest designs pale into insignificance beside the building we are about to see.

Mind you, it would be a great mistake to think that it was the building *itself* that mattered. We will be looking quite closely at the building itself, but that will only be worthwhile if it helps us appreciate what this building *represented*. Indeed the word most commonly used in this chapter for the building itself is "house,"[10] rather than any special religious word like "temple" in English. I am sure that this is one of a number of strategies employed by the writer that should guide us away from focusing on the building itself. It was a "house." In our exposition we will follow the lead of the Biblical text and refrain from calling it a "temple."[11]

Another reason for the prominence of "house" in our chapter is to remind us yet again of the promise of 2 Samuel 7 where "house" was the key word.[12] The building we are about to examine is meant to make us think about God's promise.

The rest of the chapter will take us on a guided tour of "the house of the LORD" that Solomon began to build at the time so carefully indicated in verse 1. The general shape of the building will be clear, and we will be shown a number of detailed features. However, attempts to draw or build a replica of this structure are frustrated by the incompleteness and ambiguity of the information given.[13] We will look at the various features of Solomon's building work pointed out by the text (our tour guide).

Take a Look from the "Outside" (vv. 2–10)

Most Israelites would only ever see this building from the outside. Our guided tour begins with an unusual "outside" perspective. From the outside we will be told about what's inside.

Look at the Size and Shape (v. 2)

First, we see a generally rectangular building with the following dimensions: "The house that King Solomon built for the LORD was sixty cubits long, twenty cubits wide, and thirty cubits high" (v. 2).

It will become clear that these are internal dimensions.[14] This is not what we would see as we looked from the outside, but our guide is informing us that the main internal space of the building we are looking at had these measurements. A cubit[15] was the distance from the elbow to the tip of the fingers. Since precision is not important here, we can roughly translate a number of cubits by dividing the number in half and then multiplying by 3 to get a measurement in feet. The dimensions given here are of a space about 90 feet in length, 30 feet wide, and 45 feet high.[16]

These dimensions are not huge. A larger building will be described in the next chapter (see 7:2). The floor plan of what Solomon built was about double the dimensions of the tent (often called the "tabernacle"[17]) constructed in the days of Moses, and it was about three times as high (see Exodus 26:15–25).[18]

Look at the Front (v. 3)

If we move to the front of the building we see that it had a wide entry porch:

> The vestibule [RV, porch; NIV, portico][19] in front of the nave[20] [main hall] of the house was twenty cubits long, equal to the width of the house, and ten cubits deep in front of the house. (v. 3)

This entry porch was the same width as the main building and about 15 feet deep. This was as far as people who were not priests would be allowed to go. Even the king would go no further than this (as in 2 Kings 11:14; 23:3).

The space beyond the entry porch was the "main hall" of the building. We will hear more about it later.

Look at the Sides (vv. 4–6)

We move from the front of the building to the side and see that there were windows: "And he made for the house windows with recessed frames" (v. 4). We are not told exactly where these windows were, how large they were, or how many. They were probably quite high on the sidewalls and may have been covered with lattice work.[21]

Around the outside of the "house" (but not the front) were three levels of small side-rooms:

> He also built a structure against the wall of the house, running around the walls of the house, both the nave [main hall] and the inner sanctuary [rear room]. And he made side chambers all around. The lowest story was five cubits broad, the middle one was six cubits broad, and the third was seven cubits broad. For around the outside of the house he made offsets on the wall in order that the supporting beams should not be inserted into the walls of the house. (vv. 5, 6)

Again this was more than one could see standing outside the building. We now learn that the house itself (as described in v. 2) had thick walls. The step-like structure of the outside of these walls enabled the side-rooms to be built without actually inserting beams into the main walls. The beams rested on the steps of the wall, each a cubit deep. This meant that the side-rooms were essentially separate from the "house" itself, and they became larger each level up.[22]

Presumably these rooms would be for storage and other practical functions. Although they were an obvious part of the whole structure to an outside observer, our guide carefully distinguishes them from the "house" itself, which is his main interest. We will return to the side-rooms in a moment.

Look at the Stones (v. 7)

Look at the stones from which the building was constructed. Our guide tells us something rather unusual about them:

> When the house was built, it was with stone prepared at the quarry, so that neither hammer nor axe nor any tool of iron was heard in the house while it was being built. (v. 7)

This was no ordinary building site. Care was taken to keep the usual commotion of iron tools far away.[23] Considerable skill would be required in so perfectly preparing the stones at the quarry that no further shaping was needed on location. The relative silence of the building work would have enhanced a sense of order and dignity. The words of a much later prophet seem fitting:

> But the LORD is in his holy temple;
>   let all the earth keep silence before him. (Habakkuk 2:20)

Look More Closely at the Side-Rooms (v. 8)

Look back at the three levels of side-rooms around the main building, and notice how they were accessed:

The entrance for the lowest[24] story was on the south side of the house, and one went up by stairs[25] to the middle story, and from the middle story to the third. (v. 8)

There are a number of difficulties in understanding this sentence,[26] but the gist seems to be that there was an external entrance to the three levels of side-rooms on the "south side" of the building. The rooms, in other words, were not accessible from inside the main building—a further indication that they were not actually connected to the "house."

Step Back and Take It All In (vv. 9, 10)

The first stage of our guided tour is almost complete. We take a step back and see Solomon's finished work:

> So he built the house and finished it, and he made the ceiling of the house of [literally, and he covered the house with] beams and planks of cedar. (v. 9)

Look up. Our guide may be pointing us to the roof[27] or perhaps the ceiling (once again informing us outside observers what was inside the building).[28] Solid cedar beams, supplied by Hiram king of Tyre (5:6, 10), covered the building.

Thus King Solomon "finished" the house. "Finished" is a key word in this chapter (see vv. 14, 38). Now that the Lord had given Solomon "rest" (5:4), the king "finished" his work of building this house.

This is the first of several points where we will see striking connections between this building and the greatest ever "building" project:[29]

> Thus the heavens and the earth were *finished*, and all the host of them. And on the seventh day God *finished* his work that he had done, and he *rested* on the seventh day from all his work that he had done. (Genesis 2:1, 2)

Solomon's work of building this house is presented in terms (and we will see more) that remind us of God's work of creation and indeed his "rest."[30]

As we survey the whole building from the outside one last time we see that the three-story arrangement of side-rooms around the outside of the house ("the structure") went halfway up the thirty-cubit-high sidewalls of the house itself:

> He built the structure against the whole house, [each level[31]] five cubits high, and it was joined to the house with timbers of cedar. (v. 10)

The three levels of rooms around three of the outside walls of the house were, then, fifteen cubits (about twenty-two or twenty-three feet) in height.

More Importantly, Listen to This (vv. 11–13)

We have been given an introductory tour of the building. We have seen its dimensions and general arrangement. Before we see any more, our guide must tell us about something that happened as Solomon was overseeing the construction. It is crucial for understanding this building.

What happened was this: "Now the word of the LORD came to Solomon" (v. 11), just as the word of the Lord had come to Nathan on that historic night years earlier (2 Samuel 7:4).[32]

The subject of the word of the Lord that came on this occasion, as on the earlier one, was "Concerning this house that you are building . . ." (v. 12a). It is a little surprising, therefore, that nothing more is said explicitly about the house itself.

Rather the Lord's word continued:

> . . . if you will walk in my statutes and obey my rules and keep all my commandments and walk in them, then I will establish my word with you, which I spoke to David your father. And I will dwell among the children of Israel and will not forsake my people Israel. (vv. 12b, 13)

This is what "this house that you [Solomon] are building" was really about. It was about the Lord not forsaking the people of Israel but dwelling among them. This was his promise ("word") to Solomon,[33] which had been spoken to his father David. In other words, implicit in the promise that a son of David will build "a house for my name" (2 Samuel 7:13) is the promise that the Lord would "dwell" among his people as they live under this king.

We need to pause and appreciate the wonder of this promise. The Bible teaches us that at the beginning, in the Garden of Eden, the man God created enjoyed the presence of the Lord (see Genesis 2:15–25), but after disobeying him the man and his wife hid "from the presence of the LORD" (Genesis 3:8) and were driven out of the garden, "away from the presence of the LORD" (Genesis 3:24; 4:16).

Since then the alienation of men and women from God has been and is the fundamental problem of the human condition. That is why every effort to put things right among humans and in the world fails in one way or another. Every success is partial and temporary. We ourselves cannot find our way back to God, even if we wanted to.

The extraordinary message of the Bible is that God has promised to restore what we have lost. That is what the promise to Abraham in Genesis 12:1–3 was about. The "blessing" spoken of there is the "blessing" of the beginning (Genesis 1:28; 2:3)—God's presence among his people again. The Bible is the story of God's faithfulness to this promise (see Exodus 25:8; 29:45; Leviticus 26:12; Isaiah 12:6; Ezekiel 37:27; Zechariah 2:10; 8:3; 2 Corinthians 6:16; Revelation 21:3).

However, this can only happen if the people are ruled by a king who is, unlike Adam, thoroughly obedient to the Lord (cf. 1 Samuel 12:14). The word of the Lord that came to Solomon as he was building this house assured him that the promised blessing would be enjoyed by the people of Israel provided that he, King Solomon, "will walk in my statutes and obey my rules and keep all my commandments and walk in them" (v. 12).[34]

That is what this "house" is all about. It is about God's promise to dwell among his people as his people are ruled by an obedient king.

Notice the word "dwell" in verse 13. The Hebrew could be translated, "I will *tabernacle* among the children of Israel." How brilliant is John's description of the coming of Jesus: "And the word became flesh and *tabernacled* among us" (John 1:14, AT[35]).

Take a Look at the Inside (vv. 14–30)

Let's return to our tour of this extraordinary house. Verse 14 takes up the guided tour from where we were in verse 10: "So Solomon built the house and finished it" (v. 14). For the second time Solomon's completed work is described like God's completed work in Genesis 2:1, 2: "finished."

Look at the Lining (v. 15)

Now our guide takes us inside the building. Only priests could actually enter the building, but we are taken there in our imaginations as the interior is described for us.

First we are told that there are no exposed stones inside the building:

> He lined [literally, built] the walls of the house on the inside with boards of cedar. From the floor of the house to the walls of the ceiling,[36] he covered them on the inside with wood, and he covered the floor of the house with boards of cypress. (v. 15)

The two kinds of wood were supplied in quantity by King Hiram (5:10). The more costly (and softer) cedar panels covered the walls. The stronger cypress covered the floor. This was only Stage 1 of the lining of the inside of the house, as we will see shortly.

Come Right Inside! (vv. 16–28)

We have yet to be shown the most important part of the whole structure (although it was mentioned in passing in v. 5).

The "Most Holy Place" (vv. 16, 17)

The rectangular space inside the house proper (ignoring those side-rooms) was 60 cubits long and 20 cubits wide (v. 2). Now we are shown how the back third of this space was made into a very special part of the whole:

> He built twenty cubits of the rear of the house with boards of cedar from the floor to the walls, and he built this within as an inner sanctuary, as the Most Holy Place. (v. 16)

This space, taking up the rear third of the internal floor area of the house, was a perfect cube (see v. 20). It is given two names. On the one hand it is "an inner sanctuary" (ESV). Unfortunately, this translation (like the rendering of a number of terms in this chapter) is probably influenced by traditional church architectural terms. The Hebrew word here means simply "rear room."[37]

On the other hand, and more strikingly, it is called "the Most Holy Place" (literally, "the Holy of Holies"). This is the most explicit indication so far that the house Solomon was building was a new tabernacle. In the days of Moses the tabernacle had a cube-shaped space half the size of this called "the Most Holy Place" (Exodus 26:33, 34).[38] Its purpose was identical to the Most Holy Place in the house that Solomon was building.

"The [rest of the internal space of the] house, that is, the nave [main hall] in front of the inner sanctuary [rear room], was forty cubits long" (v. 17).

Take a Closer Look at Those Walls (v. 18)

It is time to take a closer look at the cedar lining the walls (v. 15):

> The cedar within the house was carved in the form of gourds and open flowers. All was cedar; no stone was seen. (v. 18)

We are now looking at the walls of both rooms within the house. The wooden paneling is covered with carvings of fruit ("gourds"[39]) and opened flowers. The decorations are suggestive of a garden, no doubt *the* garden in which the Lord's presence was once enjoyed (Genesis 2:8).

At the Heart of It All (v. 19)

Our attention is drawn back to the rear cubic room. Since it has been named "the Most Holy Place," we are not surprised to hear:

> The inner sanctuary [rear room] he prepared in the innermost part of the house, to set there the ark of the covenant of the LORD. (v. 19)

Solomon will not actually have the ark of the covenant placed there until chapter 8. At this point we are told his intention.

The ark of the covenant had been placed in the Most Holy Place in the tabernacle in the days of Moses (Exodus 26:34). More recently King David had brought the ark "to the city of David with rejoicing" (2 Samuel 6:12). This had been a profound expression of the character of David's kingship. David was king "before the LORD" (2 Samuel 6:21). The ark of the covenant represented the presence and promises of God. David's kingdom was subordinated to the Lord as King (2 Samuel 6:2).

David had expressed concern that the mere tent in which he placed the ark (which was not the tabernacle itself[40]) was hardly appropriate when he dwelt in a house of cedar (2 Samuel 6:17; 7:2).

Solomon understood all this and prepared to bring the ark of the covenant into the permanent house he was building. To set the ark of *the covenant* in this place would suggest the *fulfillment* of the covenant, the promises of God to his people.

Be Dazzled! (vv. 20–22)

Now take a look at the completed Most Holy Place. First, look at its perfect symmetry: "The inner sanctuary [rear room] was twenty cubits long, twenty cubits wide, and twenty cubits high" (v. 20a). Since the full internal height of the house was thirty cubits (v. 2), either the rear room was elevated up to ten cubits higher than the floor of the main hall[41] or there was a space above the Most Holy Place.[42]

We have been told that the walls, ceiling, and floor were covered with wood. It is just as well we have been told that, because there was no wood to be seen: ". . . he overlaid it [the rear room] with pure gold" (v. 20b). The gold was of high quality. The overlay process probably involved gilding with liquid gold so that the carved forms in the wood were still clearly visible.[43]

"He also overlaid an altar of cedar" (v. 20c). Clearly (since it was made of wood) this was not the altar for burnt offerings (which will be located in the courtyard outside the building, 8:64; 2 Chronicles 4:1), but the altar of incense (cf. Exodus 30:1–10). Our guide is probably assuming that we know that the altar of incense in the tabernacle was not inside the Most Holy Place, but "in front of" that space (Exodus 30:6; 40:5, 26).[44] We may understand that the altar was therefore placed in the main hall, a short distance from the rear room to which it "belonged" (v. 22b). More about this altar in a moment.

First just look at all the gold:

> And Solomon overlaid the inside of the house with pure gold, and he drew chains of gold across,[45] in front of the inner sanctuary [rear room], and overlaid it[46] with gold. And he overlaid the whole house with gold, until all the house was finished. (vv. 21, 22a)

There was plenty of "pure gold" in the tabernacle of Moses' day (see Exodus 25:11–13, 17, 18, 24–31), but this is something else. "The inside of the house" now includes the large main hall. "The whole house" in verse 22 means the Most Holy Place as well as the main hall (but not the entry hall or the side-rooms which were not strictly part of "the house").

"Until all the house was finished" could be translated "until the whole house was perfect."[47]

Just in case we had not guessed, look again at that altar mentioned a moment ago: "Also the whole altar that belonged to the inner sanctuary [rear room] he overlaid with gold" (v. 22b).

Be Afraid! (vv. 23–28)

Just as we are dazzled by the sight of gold covering the entire interior of the house, we are conducted into the special room at the rear: "In the inner sanctuary [rear room] he made two cherubim of olivewood, each ten cubits high" (v. 23).

These two large (fifteen feet high) carved figures were half as high as the room itself and were made of the wood from the wild olive tree, which is hard and durable.[48] They are called "cherubim."[49] Before we think about their significance, look more closely at their shape, size, and arrangement.

> Five cubits was the length of one wing of the cherub, and five cubits the length of the other wing of the cherub; it was ten cubits from the tip of one wing to the tip of the other. The other cherub also measured ten cubits; both cherubim had the same measure and the same form. The height of one cherub was ten cubits, and so was that of the other cherub. He put the cherubim in the innermost part of the house. And the wings of the cherubim were spread out so that a wing of one touched the one wall, and a wing of the other cherub touched the other wall; their other wings touched each other in the middle of the house. (vv. 24–27)

These figures with outstretched wings were placed side-by-side in the middle of the rear room (now called "the innermost part of the house"). One wingtip of each figure touched in the middle of the room. The other wingtip of each touched opposite walls of the room. The carved figures thus dominated the internal space of the room.

"And he overlaid the cherubim with gold" (v. 28). We must dismiss from our minds all images of cherubs from western art. The figures Solomon had made were imposing and impressive, even terrifying. What did they mean?

First, these cherubim were large-scale reproductions of the two gold cherubim that were part of "the mercy seat," that is, the cover of the ark of the covenant (Exodus 25:17–20). They were therefore a further indication that the house Solomon was building would be, on a larger scale in every sense, what the tabernacle had been.

Second, the cherubim represented God's kingship, his sovereignty. The Bible speaks of God enthroned in Heaven (8:27, 30, 32, 34), but on earth the ark of the covenant was his footstool (1 Chronicles 28:2; Psalm 99:5; 132:7; cf. Isaiah 66:1; Lamentations 2:1). He "sits enthroned on [also "above"] the cherubim" (1 Samuel 4:4; 2 Samuel 6:2; 2 Kings 19:15; Psalm 80:1; 99:1; Isaiah 37:16). The cherubim above the ark therefore represented God's throne. The Lord promised to meet and speak with Moses "from between the two cherubim that are on the ark" (Exodus 25:22).

Third, since we have been reminded by Solomon's building work of the early chapters of the book of Genesis, these two cherubim should remind us of the cherubim and the flaming sword the Lord placed to guard the way back to the Garden of Eden (Genesis 3:24).

Take One Last Look Around (vv. 29, 30)

We are invited to take one last look around the interior of the house and notice more details:

> Around all the walls of the house he carved engraved figures of cherubim and palm trees and open flowers, in the inner and outer rooms. (v. 29)

In addition to the carvings of fruit and flowers we noticed in verse 18, we now see engraved cherubim (just as the curtains in the tabernacle had embroidered cherubim, Exodus 26:1, 31; 36:8, 35) and palm trees (just as the Garden of Eden had many trees, Genesis 2:9, 16) covering the walls of the house. "The inner and outer rooms" are the rear room (the "Most Holy Place") and the main hall.

"The floor of the house he overlaid with gold in the inner and outer rooms" (v. 30).[50] There was, therefore, no part of the interior of the house that was not covered with gold.

Check Out the Access (vv. 31–35)

Our guided tour of the house is almost complete. Before we take a brief look around outside the building, our attention is drawn to the means of access to the main hall and to the Most Holy Place (in reverse order).

The Most Holy Place (vv. 31, 32)

> For the entrance to the inner sanctuary [rear room] he made doors of olive-wood; the lintel and the doorposts were five-sided.[51] He covered the two doors of olivewood with carvings of cherubim, palm trees, and open flowers. He overlaid them with gold and spread gold on the cherubim and on the palm trees. (vv. 31, 32)

These doors (made of the harder olivewood) shared the features we have seen on the walls. The symbolism of garden and cherubim (Genesis 2, 3) was everywhere.

To the Main Hall (vv. 33–35)

As for the entrance to the house itself, that is, from the entry porch to the main hall (see v. 3):

> So also he made for the entrance to the nave [main hall] doorposts of olive-wood, in the form of a square,[52] and two doors of cypress wood. The two leaves of the one door were folding, and the two leaves of the other door were folding.[53] On them he carved cherubim and palm trees and open flowers, and he overlaid them with gold evenly applied on the carved work. (vv. 33–35)

The cypress wood was lighter than the olivewood used for the doors of the rear room, but harder than the cedar used on the walls and elsewhere. Again we see the carvings of trees, flowers, and cherubim. If these carvings and the gold covering were on the outside of the doors (as well as inside), this is where a person outside the house would get a glimpse of what was inside.

Look around Outside (v. 36)

To conclude our guided tour, observe the surroundings of the house that Solomon built: "He built the inner court with three courses of cut stone and one course of cedar beams" (v. 36). This inner court (presupposing an outer court not mentioned here) was enclosed with a low wall made of stone and cedar beams (either laid horizontally in the stone wall or placed upright forming a fence[54]).

The Most Important Seven Years Since . . . (vv. 37, 38)

We have been given a careful inspection of the remarkable house Solomon built. The chapter concludes with a reflection on the significance of the event:

> In the fourth year the foundation of the house of the LORD was laid, in the month of Ziv. And in the eleventh year, in the month of Bul, which is the eighth month, the house was finished in all its parts, and according to all its specifications. He was seven years in building it. (vv. 37, 38)

The fourth year (of King Solomon's reign) and the month of Ziv remind us of all we were told in verse 1 about the beginning of the project. In the eleventh year, in the month of Bul,[55] "the house was *finished*" (the third use of the word used for the completion of creation in Genesis 2:1, 2).

"In all its parts, and according to all its specifications" is perhaps more suggestive than the English indicates. The Hebrew terms behind "parts" and "specifications" are words that usually mean "words" and "judgments" or "justices." With what "words" did Solomon's building accord? What "justices"?

On the one hand this building was in accordance with the *word* of the Lord that came to Nathan in 2 Samuel 7:13. Furthermore, a later writer will inform us that the plans for the building had been given to David by the Lord and passed on to Solomon (1 Chronicles 28:19). These may be the "words" referred to here.

On the other hand "justice" is what a king is expected to do—to put things right (see 2 Samuel 8:15; 15:2, 4).[56] "To do justice" was the purpose of the wisdom God had given to Solomon (3:28). The house Solomon built represented the kingdom in which all things will be put right.

The "seven years" Solomon took to build the house is a telling note on which to close the chapter. It must remind us of the seven days of Genesis 1, 2, on the seventh of which the Lord "rested" (Genesis 2:1–3).

It is time for us to think about the importance of what we have heard in 1 Kings 6. At the heart of it is this: In the days of King Solomon, the son of David, God's promise became a visible, tangible, solid reality. This was a climactic moment in the history of the people of Israel. What had begun with their redemption from bondage in Egypt had culminated in the peace and security of Solomon's kingdom, now sealed with the building of "the house of the LORD." The "house" represented Eden restored, where what was lost by the disobedience of Adam and Eve would be enjoyed again as God's people lived under the good rule of an obedient king. God would dwell among his people and not forsake them.

Let us be very clear: the importance of this building lies in what it *represents*. In due course the people will forget this and glory in the magnificent building itself. About four centuries after Solomon, the prophet Jeremiah would proclaim a devastating condemnation of those who trust and glory in the *building*: "Do not trust in these deceptive words: 'This is the temple of the LORD, the temple of the LORD, the temple of the LORD'" (Jeremiah 7:4). Soon afterward God's judgment finally fell on Jerusalem, and the "house" Solomon had built was destroyed (Jeremiah 52:13, 17–23; 2 Kings 25:9, 13–17).

A second but inferior "house" was built when the Jewish people returned from their exile in Babylon about 537 B.C (Ezra 3:8–13; 6:13–18; Haggai 1:12—2:9). It was replaced by a grander structure built by King Herod, beginning in about 20 B.C. It was this third "temple" that was standing in Jerusalem in the days of Jesus' earthly life.

When the disciples of Jesus expressed their admiration for the "house" that had been built in Jerusalem in their own day, he said, "Do you see these great buildings? There will not be left here one stone upon another that will not be thrown down" (Mark 13:2).

Solomon's building was not permanent. It was "a shadow of the things to come, but the substance belongs to Christ" (Colossians 2:17). "The house of the LORD" built by Solomon points us to the meaning and purpose of the history of the whole world—but only when the shadow shows us the substance.

The true "temple" is the Lord Jesus Christ. He "became flesh and tabernacled among us" (John 1:14, AT). Speaking of his own body, he said, "Destroy this *temple*, and in three days I will raise it up" (John 2:19, 21; cf. Hebrews 10:5; Colossians 1:19; 2:9). In Jesus himself, the greater son of David, God's promise became a visible, tangible, solid reality. This was a climactic moment in the history of the whole world. What began with God's creation of the heavens and the earth has culminated in the peace and security of the kingdom of Jesus Christ.

Because of Jesus Christ every person who belongs to him by faith must understand that his or her body is "a *temple* of the Holy Spirit . . . whom you have from God" (1 Corinthians 6:19; cf. 2 Corinthians 6:15, 16).

More than that, the gathering of believers in Jesus Christ is "the church" that he, the greater son of David, is building (Matthew 16:18). This gathering is "built on the foundation of the apostles and prophets, Christ Jesus himself being the cornerstone, in whom the whole structure, being joined together, grows into a holy *temple* in the Lord" (Ephesians 2:20, 21; cf. 1 Corinthians 3:16; 1 Peter 2:4, 5).

Finally, we look forward to a city in which there will be no "temple" because "its *temple* is the Lord God the Almighty and the Lamb" (Revelation 21:22).

What we have seen in this chapter has nothing whatsoever to do with church buildings today. That error keeps creeping into Christian thinking. Whenever we apply "temple" language to our church buildings (like "sanctuary" or "the Lord's house") we are going back to Old Testament times—from the substance to shadows. The *significance* of the house Solomon built points to the "building" work today of the word of God's grace in Jesus Christ (see Acts 20:32). The house of Solomon's day was the most important building the world has known *because* it pointed to the spiritual house that the Lord Jesus Christ is now building by the gospel (1 Peter 2:4, 5).

So what are we to make of the times in which we live? The question is still complicated, but we can see that the times in which we live are the days for building, for the work of the gospel of Jesus. That is the most important building project in all of history. Solomon's building can help us see the outcome of Jesus' building project:

> And I heard a loud voice from the throne saying, "Behold, the dwelling place of God is with man. He will dwell with them, and they will be his people, and God himself will be with them as their God. He will wipe away every tear from their eyes, and death shall be no more, neither shall there be mourning, nor crying, nor pain anymore, for the former things have passed away." (Revelation 21:3, 4)

13

The King Who Will Build

1 KINGS 7:1-12

IN THE BIBLE'S UNFORGETTABLE STORY of great King David one chapter of wars and triumphs is followed by another (see, for example, 2 Samuel 8, 10). In the story of his son, King Solomon, one chapter of building work is followed by another.[1] Solomon's story may appear to be less interesting, but that is only true if you prefer times of war to times of peace. King David fought and defeated the enemies of his people *so that* King Solomon could be the builder of a peaceful kingdom.

Jesus Christ is the fulfillment of what both David and Solomon were. In other words, the purpose of God that lay behind the lives of David and Solomon has been fully realized in Jesus Christ. Or again: the promise of God that explains King David and King Solomon has finally been fulfilled in Jesus.

Therefore we properly understand King David's victories when we see that they were an anticipation of the victory won by Christ Jesus over all the powers of evil. This triumph was won when he died on the cross and rose again from the dead. Jesus Christ, like David, has fought and defeated the enemies of his people (see John 12:31; 16:11; Ephesians 4:8; Colossians 2:15; Hebrews 2:14).

We properly understand King Solomon's building works when we see that they were an anticipation of what Jesus Christ meant when he said, "I will *build* . . ." (Matthew 16:18). Jesus almost certainly had King Solomon in mind when he spoke of "a wise man who *built* his house upon the rock" (Matthew 7:24) and also when he said, "Destroy this temple, and in three days I will raise it up" (John 2:19). Jesus Christ, the Son of David, like Solomon, is engaged in building work.

In chapters 5, 6, and 7 of 1 Kings we have an account of King Solomon's building work. Most attention is given to "a house for the name of the LORD" (5:5). The preparations for building this house were the subject of chapter 5, its construction has been described in chapter 6, and its fitting out will be detailed in 7:13–51. Sandwiched (so to speak) between the construction and the fitting out of the "house of the LORD" is an account of other buildings constructed by King Solomon (7:1–12), collectively called "his own house" or "his entire house" (v. 1). Let's take a look at these buildings, consider their significance, and then turn our mind (as we should) to the greater building project foreshadowed here.

King Solomon's Second Building Project (v. 1)

Our chapter begins with a summary statement of what we are about to read: "Solomon was building his own house thirteen years, and he finished his entire house" (v. 1). "His entire house" was not just his personal residence (which we will come to in v. 8), but a complex of buildings that represented his administration of the kingdom. These buildings are the subject of our passage.

It is fashionable among some commentators these days (as we have noted a number of times) to judge Solomon harshly and to find an implicit criticism of him in the text before us. On this view Solomon's lavish building projects were ostentatious and self-promoting. I am sure this is misguided and more than a little influenced by problems with wealth in the modern world. These problems are real. Much wealth today is acquired by injustices. Too often wealth is used indulgently. For many the acquisition of wealth has become the purpose of life ("Greed is good"). These problems are hardly new (as a glance at Ezekiel 28 or Revelation 18 will confirm). The Bible is powerful in its critique of the love of money (for starters see Psalm 49:6; Proverbs 23:4; Ecclesiastes 5:10; Mark 10:23; 1 Timothy 3:3; 6:10; Hebrews 13:5).

In years to come there would be a king who was severely condemned for the kind of reasons that some want to judge Solomon. This was Shallum, the wicked son of the godly king Josiah. Listen to Jeremiah's assessment of Shallum, and consider whether this is what our writer is saying about Solomon in 1 Kings 6, 7:

> Woe to him who builds his house by unrighteousness,
>   and his upper rooms by injustice,
> who makes his neighbor serve him for nothing
>   and does not give him his wages,
> who says, "I will build myself a great house
>   with spacious upper rooms,"

who cuts out windows for it,
    paneling it with cedar
    and painting it with vermilion.
Do you think you are a king
    because you compete in cedar?
Did not your father eat and drink
    and do justice and righteousness?
    Then it was well with him.
He judged the cause of the poor and needy;
    then it was well.
Is not this to know me?
    declares the LORD.
But you have eyes and heart
    only for your dishonest gain,
for shedding innocent blood,
    and for practicing oppression and violence. (Jeremiah 22:13–17)

In 1 Kings 7:1 the writer turns our attention from "the house of the LORD" (6:37) to "his [Solomon's] own house" (7:1). The two building projects are set side by side. Indeed, when we step back and see chapters 6, 7 as a whole, the account of Solomon's "house" (7:1–12) is enclosed *within* the full description of the house of the Lord (6:1—7: 51). What does this suggest about the writer's perspective on Solomon's second building project?

The first verse of chapter 7 seems to deliberately parallel the last verse of chapter 6. A more literal translation brings this out (excuse the awkward English):

A. *finished* was the *house* [of the LORD] . . .
    B. and he *built* it
        C. seven *years*. (6:38 AT)
    B'. And his [own] house Solomon *built*
        C'. thirteen *years*
A'. and he *finished* his entire *house*. (7:1 AT)

In A and A' the suggestive word "finished," which we saw in 6:9, 14, and 38, is applied not only to the house of the Lord but also to Solomon's "entire house." In B and B' we see that both houses were "built" by Solomon. In C and C' we learn that the houses took seven and thirteen years to build respectively: twenty years in total (9:10).

The effect is this: the two houses *belonged together*.[2] Certainly the house of the Lord had priority. A great deal more detail is given, and a whole lot more space is taken up with the house of the Lord. But the Lord had raised up this son of David and established his kingdom (2 Samuel 7:12; 1 Kings

2:12, 24, 45, 46; 6:12; 9:5). Solomon was *God's* king. Solomon's kingdom was *God's* kingdom. God's glory is not diminished when glory is given to God's king. The opposite is true. This is another aspect of King Solomon that anticipates the gospel of Jesus Christ. "At the name of *Jesus* every knee should bow," and that will be "to the glory of *God the Father*" (Philippians 2:10, 11).[3]

Those who insist on criticizing Solomon for the self-aggrandizement (as it is seen) of his building work, particularly of "his own house," make much of the fact that he spent nearly twice as much time on the buildings that comprise "his entire house" as he spent on the house of the Lord.[4] This is a case of special pleading. The administrative buildings that we are about to see were larger and more complex than the house of the Lord. This did not make them more important, either to Solomon or to our writer. But it did make them a bigger project.[5] Furthermore, the shorter time taken to build the house of the Lord may reflect Solomon's greater commitment and zeal for this task.[6] Whether or not that is the case, the account before us indicates that Solomon did build the house of the Lord *first*.

Bible readers (and teachers) must be careful to listen to what *the text before us* is saying (directly and indirectly) rather than making our own judgments (no matter how enlightened we think we are).

What is called in verse 1 "his entire house" consisted of a number of buildings. We are about to be taken on another guided tour, but this one is rather more rushed than the expedition in the previous chapter. It is as though the writer is in a bit of a hurry to get us back to the other house to explore its contents. The result is that he tells us much less about the buildings we are about to see. We must be content with what he chooses to say and refrain from too much guesswork about what he does not say.

The House of the Forest of Lebanon (vv. 2–5)

The first structure mentioned is the largest:

> He built the House of the Forest of Lebanon. Its length was a hundred cubits and its breadth fifty cubits and its height thirty cubits, and it was built on four rows of cedar pillars, with cedar beams on the pillars. And it was covered with cedar above the chambers that were on the forty-five pillars, fifteen in each row. There were window frames in three rows, and window opposite window in three tiers. All the doorways and windows had square frames, and window was opposite window in three tiers. (vv. 2–5)

The House of the Forest of Lebanon was probably so named because of its many cedar pillars.[7]

This building was considerably larger than the house of the Lord (see 6:2).

It was about the same height (45 feet), but about 150 feet in length (compared with 90), and 75 feet in width (compared with 30). The size of the building was no doubt dictated by its function. It was apparently used as a treasury and armory in which numerous valuable items and weapons were stored (10:17, 21; cf. Isaiah 22:8) and probably also as a place of assembly.

The "four rows of cedar pillars" supporting cedar beams on which the hall was built may have run along the four sides of the building. The structure is not fully explained, but the foundation appears to have also included hewn stones (v. 9).

Verse 3 is difficult. A more literal translation is: "And it was covered with cedar above the chambers that were on the pillars, forty-five, fifteen in each row" (v. 3, AT). This seems to indicate cedar roofing above forty-five chambers[8] or side-rooms built around the hall. These rooms were built in three stories (like those beside the house of the Lord, 6:5, 6), with fifteen rooms on each story ("row").[9]

Verses 4, 5 seem to indicate that the side-rooms had plenty of large windows[10] and that they were arranged opposite one another, so that the hall itself would have been well lit in the daytime.

The Hall of Pillars (v. 6)

The second structure to which we are directed is much smaller:

> And he made the Hall of Pillars; its length was fifty cubits, and its breadth thirty cubits. There was a porch in front with pillars, and a canopy in front of them. (v. 6)

We are not told where this hall stood, but since it is mentioned between the House of the Forest of Lebanon and the Hall of Judgment, it may have stood between these two structures.[11] Since its length corresponds to the width of the House of the Forest of Lebanon, it may have formed a kind of entry porch across the width of the front of that building, perhaps similar to the vestibule to the house of the Lord (6:3).[12]

Once again the verse is far from clear for those who are trying to form a mental picture of these buildings. We may assume that the text is not intended to do that for us and be content with a degree of vagueness.

The Hall of Judgment (v. 7)

Near the center of our passage is the third structure, arguably the most important:[13]

> And he made the Hall of the Throne where he was to pronounce judgment, even the Hall of Judgment. It was finished [or covered] with cedar from floor to rafters.[14] (v. 7)

Even fewer details are given here. We are told nothing about the dimensions of this place and very little about its construction (except that once again there was cedar everywhere).

The significance of this structure displaces such particulars. We are told three things. First, it is called "the Hall of the Throne." The throne will be described in some detail in 10:18–20. "The like of it was never made in any kingdom" (10:20). It was the throne of God's king. This hall therefore represented the sovereign rule of King Solomon, just as the Most Holy Place (6:16, 17, 19) with its cherubim represented the sovereign rule of the Lord.

Second, this was the place where Solomon "was to pronounce judgment" or "would judge" (HCSB). In this context to "judge" (Hebrew *shapat*) means more than to punish wrongdoers. It means to put things right. Many years earlier the elders of Israel had come to the old prophet Samuel and asked him to "appoint for us a king to *judge* us like all the nations" (1 Samuel 8:5, 20). Their request was wrong on several levels. To desire to be "like all the nations" was a rejection of their calling to be God's people. Their request for a "king" was, at that time, a failure to trust the "judges" (like Samuel) whom God had provided as needed. But they were not wrong to long for someone "to judge us." That is what God had done for his people again and again through the preceding centuries as he delivered them from enemies and established justice in the land; he had put things right for them.

King Solomon's throne was the place where he would "judge" in this sense. This is what Solomon had asked God to enable him to do (3:9, where "govern" is the same Hebrew word translated "judge" in Kings 7). We have already seen the wise king putting things right at the level of a personal dispute (3:16–28). King David had been involved in similar "judging" work (although the two examples we have are hardly typical; see 2 Samuel 14:1–20; cf. 15:1–6).

Third, this hall was therefore "the Hall of Judgment" (NIV, "Hall of Justice"). "Judgment" or "justice" represents an important Hebrew word (*mishpat*), derived from the verb "judge." To describe this hall as the "supreme court" building in Israel[15] is inadequate. The "justice" that God's king is to bring, with the wisdom God had given him "to do justice" (see 3:28; 10:9), was something more comprehensive than any legal institution in our world. At his best this is what King David had done. He "did *justice* and righteousness for all his people" (2 Samuel 8:15, AT).

This is the theme of Psalm 72, which I have suggested may be David's prayer for Solomon. Listen carefully to this psalm and consider what *justice*, delivered by God's king, involves:

Give the king your justice, O God,
    and your righteousness to the royal son!
May he judge your people with righteousness,
    and your poor with justice!
Let the mountains bear prosperity for the people,
    and the hills, in righteousness!
May he defend the cause of the poor of the people,
    give deliverance to the children of the needy,
    and crush the oppressor!

May they fear you while the sun endures,
    and as long as the moon, throughout all generations!
May he be like rain that falls on the mown grass,
    like showers that water the earth!
In his days may the righteous flourish,
    and peace abound, till the moon be no more!

May he have dominion from sea to sea,
    and from the River to the ends of the earth!
May desert tribes bow down before him,
    and his enemies lick the dust!
May the kings of Tarshish and of the coastlands
    render him tribute;
may the kings of Sheba and Seba
    bring gifts!
May all kings fall down before him,
    all nations serve him!

For he delivers the needy when he calls,
    the poor and him who has no helper.
He has pity on the weak and the needy,
    and saves the lives of the needy.
From oppression and violence he redeems their life,
    and precious is their blood in his sight.

Long may he live;
    may gold of Sheba be given to him!
May prayer be made for him continually,
    and blessings invoked for him all the day!
May there be abundance of grain in the land;
    on the tops of the mountains may it wave;
    may its fruit be like Lebanon;
and may people blossom in the cities
    like the grass of the field!
May his name endure forever,
    his fame continue as long as the sun!
May people be blessed in him,

all nations call him blessed! (Psalm 72:1–17)

That's what King Solomon's throne in the Hall of *Justice* was all about! "The wisdom of God was in him" for this (3:28).

The Royal Residences (v. 8)

Within the complex of buildings that made up "his entire house" there was the particular house that was the king's dwelling.

> His own house where he was to dwell, in the other court back of the hall, was of like workmanship. (v. 8a)

Once again the wording is not entirely clear, but it seems to indicate that the royal residence was behind the hall (presumably the Hall of the Throne, v. 7) and set in a courtyard, possibly the outer court of the house of the Lord (as suggested by the "inner court" of 6:36).

The high standards of construction we have seen in the other structures (impressive even if the details are imprecise) was matched here: it was "of like workmanship."

Alongside this residence was a second royal abode:

> Solomon also made a house like this hall for Pharaoh's daughter whom he had taken in marriage. (v. 8b)

We met this wife in 3:1, where we learned that she had lived in the old city of David until the present dwelling was completed. The provision of this house for her completes our brief tour of Solomon's "entire house" (v. 1).[16]

The Building Materials (vv. 9–12)

It remains to note that these buildings were constructed, like the house of the Lord, from quality materials:

> All these were made of costly stones, cut according to measure, sawed with saws, back and front, even from the foundation to the coping, and from the outside to the great court. The foundation was of costly stones, huge stones, stones of eight and ten cubits. And above were costly stones, cut according to measurement, and cedar. The great court had three courses of cut stone all around, and a course of cedar beams; so had the inner court of the house of the LORD and the vestibule of the house. (vv. 9–12)

"All these" (that is, the whole complex of buildings described in vv. 2–8) were built with the same kind of great, costly stones as the house of the Lord (5:17). The soft white limestone of the region can be cut with "saws" when freshly quarried and hardens with exposure to the atmosphere.[17]

Impressive as the massive and expensive stones may be, note that there is no sign of the gold that covered almost everything in the house of the Lord. There was a difference between the two kings in Jerusalem, clearly represented in the glory (if not the size) of the two houses!

The arrangement of courts is far from clear, but "the great court" may have surrounded both the house of the Lord and the royal dwelling. If so, this outer court was of comparable construction to the inner court surrounding the former (6:36). "The vestibule of the house" may be the entry hall of the house of the Lord (6:3), which was then also similar.

The effect of these last few verses is to underline similarities between the structures we have seen in 7:1–12 and the house we explored in the previous chapter. Indeed we may now observe a correspondence between the three main parts of the house of the Lord and the three main structures in our present passage:

The House of the Lord

(1) the largest hall (ESV, "nave," 6:3), surrounded by three levels of side-rooms (6:5, 6)
(2) the entry porch for (1) (ESV, "vestibule," 6:3)
(3) the Most Holy Place (ESV, "inner sanctuary," 6:16)

The Royal Residences

(1) the House of the Forest of Lebanon, the largest structure, with three levels of side-rooms (7:2–5)
(2) the Hall of Pillars, which seems to have been an entry porch for (1) (7:6)
(3) the Hall of the Throne (7:7)

Solomon's own "house" was thus close to the house of the Lord and in certain respects modeled on it. This was a fitting expression of the unique status of this king as God's king.[18]

The Greater Building Project

King Solomon's buildings were most remarkable because of what they represented. The structures were a striking picture of the kingdom of God. The house of the Lord comes first. He is the One enthroned on the cherubim (2 Samuel 6:2; cf. 2 Kings 19:15; Psalm 99:1; Isaiah 37:16). But the house of King Solomon comes second. By this king God will bring justice, in the fullest sense of putting things right (Psalm 72). King Solomon's kingdom was the kingdom of God. The buildings we have surveyed in this and in the previous chapter signify no less than this.

However, the picture is not the substance. It is a serious mistake when the account of Solomon's building work is applied to something like a church building project. The same error is often expressed when church buildings, or parts of them, are described with words that suggest they are in some way like the house that Solomon built (for example, we should not call our church buildings, or parts of them, sanctuaries). The physical buildings constructed by Christians are not in any way theologically significant, but Solomon's buildings were. This is not, of course, to deny their practical usefulness.

However, in due course King Solomon, like his father David, proved inadequate for the task represented by his buildings. The buildings were destroyed (see 2 Kings 25:8–17). Prophets began to speak of a new day, a new king, and a new building project. Listen to the prophet Zechariah, long after Solomon's buildings were no more:

> Thus says the LORD of hosts, "Behold, the man whose name is the Branch: for he shall branch out from his place, and *he shall build the temple of the LORD. It is he who shall build the temple of the LORD* and shall bear royal honor, and shall sit and rule on his throne. . . . And those who are far off shall come and help *to build the temple of the LORD.*" (Zechariah 6:12–13, 15; cf. Amos 9:11–15)

Jesus Christ is the promised building king. "I will build my church [or, my assembly[19]]," he said, "and the gates of hell shall not prevail against it" (Matthew 16:18). The greatest building project of all is the calling of people from all nations together into one body:

> . . . members of the household of God, built on the foundation of the apostles and prophets, Christ Jesus himself being the cornerstone, in whom the whole structure, being joined together, grows into a holy temple in the Lord. In him you also are being built together into a dwelling place for God by the Spirit. (Ephesians 2:19–22)

Our wonder at Solomon's buildings now gives way to wonder at the greatest display of God's wisdom (see Ephesians 3:10), where he is at work, through his King, putting *all things* right (see Ephesians 1:7–10).

14

The Truth about Everything

1 KINGS 7:13–51

IT IS VERY IMPORTANT to understand that the Bible's message is about *every-thing*. Of course, the Bible does not tell us everything about everything. Some-times Bible readers have tried to find things in the Bible that are simply not there. That is a mistake and leads to unnecessary confusion and conflict. There is important and exciting, indeed God-given, work of discovery to be done by human beings, through which we learn many things that we cannot learn from the Bible. Indeed so much has been discovered in modern times (I am thinking mainly of the vast scope of human inquiry we call modern science) that it is easy for Bible readers to forget that the Bible teaches us *the truth about everything*. Not *every* truth about everything, but the essential, fundamental, most important truth about everything.

In the simplest possible terms the first sentence of the Bible tells us this truth: "In the beginning, *God created* the heavens and the earth" (Genesis 1:1). "The heavens and the earth" is a Bible way of saying "everything." Just to make sure we understand the meaning of "everything," listen to how another Bible writer puts the same truth: "For by him *all things* were created, in heaven and on earth, visible and invisible, whether thrones or dominions or rulers or authorities—*all things* were created . . ." (Colossians 1:16). "Everything" means *every* thing.

Genesis 1:1 is a kind of heading for the whole Bible. "In the beginning, God created the heavens and the earth," and the Bible explains the conse-quences of that truth.

The consequences are extraordinary and could never have been deduced by human reason—even when we know the fundamental truth that God created

205

everything. The God who created everything has a purpose for it all, a purpose that he will accomplish in his own way and in his own time. His purpose involves humanity, whom he created "in his own image" (Genesis 1:26, 27) and to whom he has made his purpose known through the words and historical events that the Bible records.

In that history there are a number of remarkable high points. The account of the reign of King Solomon over the people of Israel is one of the most important. It is the pinnacle of the Old Testament part of the Bible story. The account of Solomon's reign in 1 Kings focuses on his construction of a building in the city of Jerusalem that was known as "the house of the LORD." We have seen the preparations for building this "house" in 1 Kings 5 and the actual construction in 1 Kings 6, and we have seen how it was set alongside a number of other buildings in 7:1–12. We are about to see how the house built by Solomon tells *the truth about everything*.

Our passage (7:13–51) explains how Solomon had the building we saw constructed in chapter 6 and its surroundings fitted out with various objects. The passage is difficult in many of its details[1] but is nonetheless clear, powerful, and important in its message. As we observe the work that was done, let us be prepared to learn the truth about everything.

The Wise Man Who Served the Wise King (vv. 13, 14)

What Solomon was about to do required unusual skill. For this reason "King Solomon sent[2] and brought Hiram from Tyre" (v. 13). This was not King Hiram, whom we met in 5:1, but another man by the same name.[3] The shared name is fortuitous because both men contributed significantly to the same great project. They shared much more than a name.

His Identity (v. 14a)

This Hiram (unlike his royal namesake) was not exactly a foreigner: "He was the son of a widow of the tribe of Naphtali,[4] and his father was a man of Tyre" (v. 14a). He had a connection with both the people of Israel and the nation of Tyre. This Hiram (along with his namesake) suggests something of the international significance of the project in which he became involved.

His Ability (v. 14b, c, d)

There was also something international about Hiram's expertise. He was "a worker in bronze" (v. 14b). Bronze is an alloy of copper and tin. The addition of a small amount of tin increases the strength and hardness of copper and lowers its melting point. Therefore it was particularly suitable for casting in molds. This process had been discovered many centuries before the time of Solomon.[5]

Plenty of bronze had been used in the tabernacle that had been built in the days of Moses, a point to which we will return. However, bronze was particularly associated with the nations beyond Israel (cf. Genesis 4:22). King David had brought "very much bronze" to Jerusalem from his victories over foreign kings to the north of Israel (2 Samuel 8:8, 10, 11). David's most famous foreign enemy had bronze armor and bronze weapons (1 Samuel 17:5, 6). But apparently Israel lacked the developed skills of metalworking needed for the task that now faced King Solomon (cf. 1 Samuel 13:19), so Solomon sent to Tyre for Hiram.

The reason that Solomon wanted a "worker in bronze" almost certainly lies in his understanding that the house of the Lord was to be a kind of replica of the tabernacle, updated for these times of peace and rest (5:4, 5). This "house" would be like the tabernacle but bigger and better and more permanent. The tabernacle had many articles made of bronze (see Exodus 25:3; 26:11, 37; 27:1–11; etc.). So would "the house of the LORD."

This connection to the tabernacle is further highlighted by the description of Hiram as "full of [or filled with[6]] *wisdom*, *understanding*, and *skill* [or knowledge] for making any *work* in *bronze*" (v. 14c). This is a clear reminder of the craftsmen who worked on the tabernacle. Of one of them, named Bezalel, the Lord had said, "I have *filled* him with the Spirit [or breath] of God,[7] with *wisdom* and *understanding*, with *knowledge* for all *work*, to devise artistic designs, to work in gold, silver, and *bronze* . . ." (Exodus 31:3, 4 AT).[8] Hiram, our writer tells us, had essentially the same gifts God had given those who worked on the tabernacle.

It is difficult to miss the word "wisdom" here. The most striking gift God had given King Solomon was "wisdom" (3:12), for which he had become famous in Israel (3:28) and internationally (4:29–34). It is true that "wisdom" can mean different things in different contexts, but in this context Hiram's "wisdom" and the "wisdom" God had given Solomon came together to work on the house of the Lord. In other words, this building will be the product of God-given "wisdom."

We saw in 4:29–34 that the wisdom God gave Solomon enabled him to master God's creation, just as the creation of everything is the product of God's own wisdom. We will soon see how the wisdom of Hiram and Solomon, as they worked on the house of the Lord, produced a wonderful representation of God's creation. Their work will represent the truth about everything.

So Hiram, filled with wisdom, "came to King Solomon and did all his work" (v. 14d). Hiram's work was King Solomon's work.

This work is now described in some detail. It involved three main projects and a whole lot more. No doubt Hiram headed a team of workmen, but the text attributes to him the work done under him, just as in the end the work will be attributed to King Solomon who oversaw it all (v. 51).

Two Pillars That Tell Us Everything (vv. 15–22)

The first (and I think most important) task was the casting and placing of two large bronze pillars. Before we hear what these pillars were for, take a good look at them.

Look at Their Size (v. 15)

First, look at their size:

> He cast two pillars of bronze. Eighteen cubits was the height of one pillar, and a line of twelve cubits measured its circumference. It was hollow, and its thickness was four fingers.[9] The second pillar was the same. (v. 15)

These two pillars were substantial. The height of each (18 cubits) was about 27 feet. This was a bit more than half the internal height of the main hall of the house (30 cubits); so perhaps they were about half as high as the building itself. A circumference of about 18 feet (12 cubits) means a diameter of about 4 feet. You could not miss them!

Look at Their Tops (vv. 16–20)

But that was just the main part of the pillar. Each was topped with a large bronze "capital," adding a further seven or eight feet (five cubits) to the height:

> He also made two capitals of cast bronze to set on the tops of the pillars. The height of the one capital was five cubits, and the height of the other capital was five cubits. There were lattices of checker work with wreaths of chain work for the capitals on the tops of the pillars, a lattice for the one capital and a lattice for the other capital. Likewise he made pomegranates in two rows around the one latticework to cover the capital that was on the top of the pillar, and he did the same with the other capital. Now the capitals that were on the tops of the pillars in the vestibule were of lily-work, four cubits.[10] The capitals were on the two pillars and also

above the rounded projection[11] which was beside the latticework. There were two hundred pomegranates in two rows all around, and so with the other capital. (vv. 16–20)

What matters is the overall impression rather than the details. The highly decorated capitals on top of the pillars were shaped like bowls (see vv. 41, 42) and were covered with pomegranates and lilies—hundreds of them. Like many parts of the interior we have seen (6:18, 29, 32, 35), the pillars have a stylized garden-like appearance.

Observe Their Position (v. 21a)

"He set up the pillars at the vestibule of the temple[12] [main hall]" (v. 21a). This "vestibule" is the entry porch (as I have called it), mentioned in 6:3. It seems that the pillars had no structural function. They did not support any part of the building. They just stood there in the entrance, impressively reminding all who saw them of the truth about everything.

Listen to Their Names (vv. 21b, 22)

How did they do that? They were given names: "He set up the pillar on the south and called its name Jachin, and he set up the pillar on the north and called its name Boaz" (v. 21b).

It is likely that these names were inscribed on the pillars. To a Hebrew speaker these names were powerful. "Jachin" means "He will establish." "Boaz" means "In him is strength." Let's consider what Jachin and Boaz tell us.

"Jachin" ("He will establish") was a powerful reminder of the Lord's promise to King David, the promise that has been behind all that has happened so far in 1 Kings. "Establish" is a key word of that promise:

> . . . I will raise up your offspring after you, who shall come from your body, and *I will establish* his kingdom. He shall build a house for my name, and *I will establish* the throne of his kingdom forever. . . . Your throne *shall be established* forever. (2 Samuel 7:12, 13, 16; cf. 7:24, 26)

Look back to the story we have been following:

> So Solomon sat on the throne of David his father, and his kingdom was firmly *established*. (2:12)

> Now therefore as the Lord lives, who *has established* me and placed me on the throne of David my father . . . (2:24)

> King Solomon shall be blessed, and the throne of David *shall be established* before the LORD forever. (2:45)

> So the kingdom *was established* in the hand of Solomon. (2:46)

The pillar placed on the south side of the entry to the house of the Lord, bearing the name "He Will Establish," was a powerful testimony to the Lord's promise concerning the kingdom of the chosen son of David. It is possible that "Jachin" was the first word of a longer inscription on the pillar that may have read something like "*He will establish* the kingdom of the son of David."

The pillar on the north side carried a complementary message: "In Him Is Strength." Solomon's kingdom would be *established* only in *the Lord's strength*. It is possible that "Boaz" was also the first word of a longer inscription, perhaps a version of Psalm 21:1: "O LORD, *in your strength* the king rejoices."

Boaz was also the name of David's great-grandfather (Ruth 4:21, 22). This is a further reminder, at the entrance to the house of the Lord, of the house of David. If the house Solomon built represents the kingdom or reign of God "enthroned on the cherubim" in the Most Holy Place (6:16, 23–28; see 1 Samuel 4:4; 2 Samuel 6:2), then these two pillars tie the reign of God closely to the kingdom of the son of David. In other words, these two pillars, standing before the house of the Lord, speak of "the kingdom of our Lord *and* of his Christ [his King]." The Lord will *establish* this kingdom by *his strength*. Therefore "he shall reign forever and ever" (cf. Revelation 11:15).

That is the truth about everything.

The New Testament announces that God's purpose to establish the kingdom of David's Son (that is what the pillars proclaimed) means that in the fullness of time *all things* will be united under Jesus Christ:

> In him we have redemption through his blood, the forgiveness of our trespasses, according to the riches of his grace, which he lavished upon us, in all *wisdom and insight* making known to us the mystery of his will, according to his purpose, which he set forth in Christ as a plan for the fullness of time, *to unite all things in him, things in heaven and things on earth.* (Ephesians 1:7–10)

This is the "wisdom and insight" of God! The wisdom God gave to Solomon and Hiram produced a powerful testimony to this purpose of God, although its fulfillment would remain a mystery (a secret) until Jesus.

A final word (for now) about the pillars: "And on the tops of the pillars was lily-work. Thus the work of the pillars was finished" (v. 22). "Finished" here translates the word we noticed in 6:22. The pillars were "perfect"—exactly what they should be.[13]

The Sea That Was Still (vv. 23–26)

The second project undertaken by Hiram was also impressive: "Then he made the sea of cast metal" (v. 23a).

"He made the sea" is a striking expression. This is what God did. "The LORD *made* . . . the *sea*" (Exodus 20:11; cf. Jonah 1:9; Psalm 146:6; Nehemiah 9:6). Indeed, "The *sea* is his, for he *made* it" (Psalm 95:5). Of course, the sea Hiram made was a pale reflection of the sea God made. The container that held his "sea" was made of cast metal. Nonetheless it was impressive.

Its Size (v. 23b)

"It was round, ten cubits from brim to brim, and five cubits high, and a line of thirty cubits measured its circumference"[14] (v. 23b). A diameter of about 15 feet, a circumference of about 45 feet, and a height of about 7 or 8 feet is a substantial piece of bronze work.

In the tabernacle there had been a relatively small bronze basin for washing (Exodus 30:18). This "sea" appears to have been a huge bowl filled with some 12,000 gallons (22,000 liters) of water (see v. 26). The provision in the house of the Lord for cleansing far exceeded what had been in the tabernacle.

Its Setting (v. 24)

"Under its brim were gourds, for ten cubits [or ten to a cubit[15]], compassing the sea all around. The gourds were in two rows, cast with it when it was cast" (v. 24).

These gourds, molded into the huge bowl at the time it was cast, were like the similar decorations inside the building (6:18). They suggest a garden setting for the "sea." It was like the garden of Eden from which much water flowed, watering the world (see Genesis 2:10–14).

Its Support (v. 25)

The huge structure, which must have been seriously heavy, was supported in an unusual way: "It stood on twelve oxen, three facing north, three facing west, three facing south, and three facing east. The sea was set on them, and all their rear parts were inward" (v. 25).

The number twelve may suggest the twelve tribes of Israel and therefore represents the nation that was symbolically cleansed here.[16] The oxen are powerful representatives of the animate creation as well as prominent representatives of sacrificial offerings (see 4:23). Facing out in the four compass directions, they were pointing to the whole world.

Its Shape (v. 26)

The bowl holding the sea is further described: "Its thickness was a handbreadth, and its brim was made like the brim of a cup, like the flower of a lily. It held two thousand baths" (v. 26). That was a lot of water, as we have already noted.

Just look at this "sea." It is not necessary (indeed it is not helpful) to attempt detailed interpretations of each feature of this large and elaborate structure holding thousands of gallons of water. However, at least two impressions seem appropriate.

First, the "sea" often appears in Biblical poetry about God's work of creation and redemption. God calms the sea and overcomes its waves and billows. He delivers his people from its threatening power. This happened in an unforgettable way at the time of the exodus (Psalm 66:6; 77:19; 78:13, 53), and became a favorite image of God's power over all that threatened his ordered and good creation (see, for example, Psalm 18:13–16; 32:6; 33:6, 7; 65:7; 69:1–3, 14, 15; 74:12–17; 89:9; 130:1). The calm "sea" that stood in the courtyard was therefore a powerful picture of God's reign over all threatening powers. Much later in the Bible there will be a picture of God's throne with "a sea of glass, like crystal" before it (Revelation 4:6; cf. 15:2). It is a powerful picture of the established rule of God and his king, where there is peace and no threat.

Second, the vast quantity of water probably also suggests cleansing on a large scale. This impression is strengthened if we are reminded (as we should be) of the corresponding bronze basin that was in the tabernacle (Exodus 30:17–21). The practical question of how the water in this huge container could have been accessed for any cleansing action need not concern us. Perhaps there were taps fitted. The point is the huge provision for cleansing. Many years later a prophet would speak of a day when there will be a still greater provision: "On that day there shall be a fountain opened for the house of David and the inhabitants of Jerusalem, to cleanse them from sin and uncleanness" (Zechariah 13:1). The Lord Jesus Christ is the one who cleanses us by his blood shed for us:

> Therefore, brothers, since we have confidence to enter the holy places by the blood of Jesus, by the new and living way that he opened for us through the curtain, that is, through his flesh, and since we have a great

priest over the house of God, let us draw near with a true heart in full assurance of faith, with *our hearts sprinkled clean from an evil conscience
and our bodies washed with pure water*. (Hebrews 10:19–22)

The Stands That Carried the Water (vv. 27–39)

Hiram's third project was ten bronze stands that supported ten basins. The passage is particularly detailed and technical. The writer appears to delight in the
fine craftsmanship, which we too can appreciate, even if many of the details
are now obscure.[17]

Their Size (v. 27)

We can observe, first, the size of the stands: "He also made the ten stands of
bronze. Each stand was four cubits long, four cubits wide, and three cubits
high" (v. 27). They were 6-feet-square chests, standing about 4 or 5 feet high.

Their Decoration (vv. 28, 29)

Look more closely at how the stands were made with decorated panels:

> This was the construction of the stands: they had panels, and the panels
> were set in the frames, and on the panels that were set in the frames were
> lions, oxen, and cherubim. On the frames, both above and below the lions
> and oxen, there were wreaths of beveled work. (vv. 28, 29)

Lions and oxen are powerful representatives of the animate creation. Cherubim (see 6:23–29, 32, 35) pointed to the royal presence of the Lord.

Their Wheels (v. 30a)

The ten stands were fitted with wheels: "Moreover, each stand had four bronze
wheels and axles of bronze" (v. 30a). When we see the weight that these
wheels bore, we will not imagine that they were easily movable. The wheels,
however, *represented* mobility. The stands looked rather like small chariots
(v. 33). We will hear more about the wheels in a moment.

Their Function (vv. 30b–37)

The function of these rather elaborate stands now becomes clear: ". . . and at
the four corners were supports for a basin" (v. 30b). The basin supports are
described in some detail:

> The supports were cast with wreaths at the side of each. Its opening was
> within a crown that projected upward one cubit. Its opening was round, as

a pedestal is made, a cubit and a half deep. At its opening there were carvings, and its panels were square, not round. (vv. 30c, 31)

While the language is difficult here, it seems that each stand had a circular
opening in which the basin was held, with carvings and square panels.

Back to the wheels:

And the four wheels were underneath the panels. The axles of the wheels
were of one piece with the stands, and the height of a wheel was a cubit and
a half. The wheels were made like a chariot wheel; their axles, their rims,
their spokes, and their hubs were all cast. (vv. 32, 33)

The wheels were just over two feet in diameter, adding to the height of the
stand. The chariot-like appearance enhances the sense of mobility.

Our attention is taken back to the upper part of the stands:

There were four supports at the four corners of each stand. The supports
were of one piece with the stands. And on the top of the stand there was
a round band half a cubit high; and on the top of the stand its stays and
its panels were of one piece with it. And on the surfaces of its stays and
on its panels, he carved cherubim, lions, and palm trees, according to the
space of each, with wreaths all around. After this manner he made the ten
stands. All of them were cast alike, of the same measure and the same form.
(vv. 34–37)

We do not learn much more here, but the wordy description encourages us to
appreciate the intricacy of this work.

Their Basins (v. 38)

Now we see the basins that these ten remarkable stands were made to hold:
"And he made ten basins of bronze. Each basin held forty baths, each basin
measured four cubits, and there was a basin for each of the ten stands"
(v. 38).

There was again a lot of water. Each of the ten basins held about 240
gallons—almost two and a half thousand gallons in all.

Their Placement (v. 39)

Before we think about the significance of these mobile basins, notice where
they were set: "And he set the stands, five on the south side of the house, and
five on the north side of the house" (v. 39a). They stood in the courtyard, five
on each side of the house of the Lord. They seem to have been extensions (so

to speak) of the "sea," which we now learn was set "at the southeast corner of the house" (v. 39b).

It seems reasonable to say that the house of the Lord was surrounded by mobile provisions for cleansing. Much later the prophet Ezekiel will see a vision of a new temple. He will see water flowing from this point in the temple complex, out into the whole world (Ezekiel 47:1). He will be told:

> This water flows toward the eastern region and goes down into the Arabah, and enters the sea; when the water flows into the sea, the water will become fresh. And wherever the river goes, every living creature that swarms will live, and there will be very many fish. For this water goes there, that the waters of the sea may become fresh; so everything will live where the river goes. Fishermen will stand beside the sea. From Engedi to Eneglaim it will be a place for the spreading of nets. Its fish will be of very many kinds, like the fish of the Great Sea. But its swamps and marshes will not become fresh; they are to be left for salt. And on the banks, on both sides of the river, there will grow all kinds of trees for food. Their leaves will not wither, nor their fruit fail, but they will bear fresh fruit every month, because the water for them flows from the sanctuary. Their fruit will be for food, and their leaves for healing. (Ezekiel 47:8–12)

The fulfillment of all this has come with the Lord Jesus. He now is the new temple (John 2:19–22). He announced the fulfillment of all these things when he stood in the temple of his day and said, "If anyone thirsts, let him come to me and drink. Whoever believes in me, as the Scripture has said, 'Out of his heart will flow rivers of living water'" (John 7:37, 38).

A Summary of All That Hiram Made (vv. 40–47)

These three projects (the two pillars, the sea, and the ten stands supporting their basins) were not everything that Hiram did. There was a whole lot more, and the writer now summarizes all that he did.

The Things (vv. 40–44)

There were many other bits and pieces: "Hiram also made the pots,[18] the shovels,[19] and the basins[20]" (v. 40a).

This brought the work to completion: "So Hiram *finished all* the *work* that he *did* for King Solomon on the house of the LORD" (v. 40b). Here is another echo of Genesis 2:

> Thus the heavens and the earth were *finished*, and all the host of them. And on the seventh day God *finished* his *work* that he had *done*, and he rested on the seventh day from *all* his *work* that he had done. (Genesis 2:1, 2)[21]

The work Hiram and Solomon had now completed was a kind of symbolic reenactment of God's work of creation.

Look again at those pillars and their decorations:

> . . . the two pillars, the two bowls of the capitals that were on the tops of the pillars, and the two latticeworks to cover the two bowls of the capitals that were on the tops of the pillars; and the four hundred pomegranates for the two latticeworks, two rows of pomegranates for each latticework, to cover the two bowls of the capitals that were on the pillars . . . (vv. 41, 42)

Look one more time at "the ten stands, and the ten basins on the stands" (v. 43). I do not think we are going too far to say (particularly once we have heard about Ezekiel's later vision) that here was symbolized life and cleansing for the whole world. That is what God will *establish in his strength.*

Take a last look at "the one sea, and the twelve oxen underneath the sea" (v. 44). He will *establish in his strength* the calm and rest represented by this sea. That is what the reign of the Lord and his king will be like.

How Was All This Work Done? (vv. 45–47)

Hiram's work clearly fascinated our writer. He concludes his account with three reflections.

First, it was high-quality work: "Now the pots, the shovels, and the basins, all these vessels in the house of the Lord, which Hiram made for King Solomon, were of burnished bronze" (v. 45). "Burnished bronze" was smooth and bright. It all looked great!

Second, if you are wondering about the process of producing all this cast bronze work, "In the plain of the Jordan the king cast them, in the clay ground between Succoth and Zarethan" (v. 46). Succoth was on the east side of the Jordan, and Zarethan was on the west.[22] Somewhere between them, in the Jordan valley, there was a location with deep clay soil, suited to making molds for casting the substantial objects Hiram was commissioned to make. There this highly skilled work was done.

Third, our writer is overwhelmed (and wants us to share his amazement) at the sheer quantity of these bronze objects: "And Solomon left all the vessels unweighed, because there were so many of them; the weight of the bronze was not ascertained" (v. 47).

Vessels for the House of the Lord (vv. 48–50)

The account of all these things is not quite finished. Hiram's work in bronze was on display and in use *outside* the house of the Lord. For all its excellence, something finer than the work in bronze was needed for the objects that were to be placed *inside* the house of the Lord.

"So[23] [And] Solomon made all the vessels that were in the house of the Lord" (v. 48a). We may safely assume that Solomon had skilled craftsmen actually doing the work. It was nonetheless his work, just as Hiram's had been.

The first object mentioned is "the golden altar" (v. 48b). This was the altar mentioned in 6:20, 22, which we may deduce from our knowledge of the tabernacle to have been the altar of incense (see Exodus 30:1–10; cf. Numbers 4:16; 16:40; 1 Samuel 2:28).

We do not know a great deal about this altar or the practice of burning incense that took place here. However, it played a role in the events surrounding the birth of Jesus. The old priest Zechariah entered the temple to burn incense, "and there appeared to him an angel of the Lord standing on the right side of the altar of incense" (Luke 1:11). The angel announced to him the birth of a child, who would become John the Baptist. In this passage we see that incense was associated with the prayers of the people (Luke 1:10; cf. Revelation 5:8; 8:3, 4). Furthermore the sacrifice of the Lord Jesus Christ is described as "a fragrant offering and sacrifice to God" (Ephesians 5:2).

The second object mentioned here is "the golden table for the bread of the Presence" (v. 48c). We are once again reminded of a similar furnishing in the tabernacle (Exodus 25:23–30; cf. Hebrews 9:2). The bread was set on the table every Sabbath day and was to be eaten only by priests (Leviticus 24:5–9; see 1 Samuel 21:1–6).

The bread symbolized the covenant between the Lord and Israel (Leviticus 24:8) and should remind us of the One who has now said, "I am the bread of life; whoever comes to me shall not hunger, and whoever believes in me shall never thirst" (John 6:35).

Third, we hear of "the lampstands of pure gold, five on the south side and five on the north, before the inner sanctuary" (v. 49a). The tabernacle had a pure gold[24] lampstand (Exodus 25:31–40). The bigger and better house of the Lord had ten. No doubt these lampstands, and the light they gave out, had the simple practical purpose of illuminating what must have been a rather dark space. In their setting, however, they remind us of the God who said, "Let there be light" (Genesis 1:3) and the One who has now said, "I am the light of the world. Whoever follows me will not walk in darkness, but will have the light of life" (John 8:12).

Finally we hear of other items provided by King Solomon for the house of the Lord: ". . . the flowers, the lamps, and the tongs, of gold; the cups, snuffers, basins, dishes for incense, and fire pans, of pure gold; and the sockets of gold, for the doors of the innermost part of the house, the Most Holy Place, and for the doors of the nave of the temple[25] [or, for the doors to the main hall]" (vv. 49b, 50).

As we saw with the interior of the house of the Lord in 1 Kings 6, gold was everywhere (6:20–22, 28, 30, 32, 35). The bronze objects that Hiram had made to be placed outside the building were impressive. The objects prepared for inside the building were as fine and exquisite as they could be. These were the furnishings of the royal house of the One who rules over everything. It is amazing to see how many of them are applied in various ways to Jesus Christ. All that this house represented finds its fulfillment in him.

The Completion of the House of the Lord (v. 51)

There is a concluding comment to this long and detailed passage. In fact, two comments.

Completion (v. 51a)

First, we need to see the completed work: "Thus all the work that King Solomon did on the house of the LORD was finished" (v. 51a). The English word "finished" has appeared eight times[26] in 1 Kings 6, 7. In five places "finished" represents the Hebrew word (klh) that was used of God "finishing" his work of creation (6:9, 14, 38; 7:1, 40). In two places the Hebrew word (tmm) has a sense of the completeness, the perfection of what has been "finished" (6:22; 7:22). The last verse of the account has a different word (shlm). It has a sense of peace and wholeness. It is the verb form of shalom ("peace") and resonates with Solomon's own name. The completion of this house represented the peace of the kingdom of God and of his king.

King Solomon and King David (v. 51b)

Second, we need to see that the house of peace was the outcome of the reign of King David. Although David had not been permitted to build this house because he was not the king of peace, the victories David won had prepared for this peace and the house that embodied it.

> And Solomon brought in the things that David his father had dedicated, the silver, the gold, and the vessels, and stored them in the treasuries of the house of the LORD. (v. 51b)

"The things that David . . . had dedicated" were largely won in victories over the enemies of his kingdom. King David had "dedicated to the LORD" a great many articles of silver, gold, and bronze (2 Samuel 8:10–12).

This connection between the house Solomon built and furnished, so extravagantly described in these chapters, and King David points us to the deeper connection. The house of the Lord represented the promise God had made to David. Indeed at one level this house is *what was promised* (2 Samuel 7:13). At a deeper level, however, the house represented the promised kingdom of peace, where the One who rules over all things will bring all things under the rule of his King.

The house Solomon built was not the reality to which it pointed. Eventually the king who built this house failed, and to the horror of the people who understood anything of its significance, the house itself was destroyed. The account specifically notes the destruction of the bronze pillars, the stands, and the bronze sea, along with the other objects we have seen (see 2 Kings 25:13–17).

The house of the Lord in Jerusalem represented the truth about everything. God is the Creator of all things who will establish the kingdom of his King forever. In numerous ways this house points us to Jesus Christ who is the truth about everything: "For in him all the fullness of God was pleased to dwell, and through him to reconcile to himself all things, whether on earth or in heaven, making peace by the blood of his cross" (Colossians 1:19, 20).

The Church of the Living God

1 Kings 8

15

King Solomon's "Church"

1 KINGS 8:1–11

I LOVE SUNDAY MORNINGS. Why? Because on Sunday mornings I "go to church." It is a delight to gather in the fellowship of Christian people, brothers and sisters—children of the same heavenly Father, followers of the same Lord Jesus Christ. It is simply wonderful to share in the same Spirit, the same hope, the same faith, the same love. I wonder whether that is how *you* feel about "going to church."

Or could it be that for you going to church has become not much more than a habit, perhaps a duty? You may enjoy going to church, but would you really think of it as the most important, significant, and substantial thing you do all week? That's a big claim. Many churches are relatively small gatherings of people that no one really takes much notice of these days. Indeed many think churches are a relic of the past, with no future—utterly irrelevant to the modern world, or worse—still viable perhaps (for a while, in the conservative pockets of society) but the writing is on the wall.

But what is "church"? *Church* means a gathering of people, an assembly.[1] Is it possible to believe the claim I am making that going to church is hugely significant? Yes, it is. Far from being a relic of the *past, church* is where you can get a glimpse of the *future*! Can you believe that? Or should we accept that going to church is part of a world that is, regrettably, passing away? Like newspapers and bookshops and corner stores.

A Christian church is a gathering of those who have been brought together by the Lord Jesus Christ. As he has opened the way for each of us to come to God the Father, so we are drawn to each other (see Ephesians 2:18–22). That is the spiritual reality expressed when we "go to church." I like to put it like this: *Church is a gathering of people who come together because they have come to Jesus Christ.*

It is easy to lose sight of the spiritual reality because over the centuries institutional structures have become associated with the word *church*. We speak of the Presbyterian Church, the Episcopal Church, the Baptist Church, and so on. The word *church* is also applied to the buildings in which we meet. All this is confusing because the "church" of which the Bible speaks is *the gathering of people* who are drawn into one another's presence by the same gospel that has drawn us to the Lord Jesus Christ. We come together *because* we have come to him. It makes no difference whatsoever to the spiritual reality whether or not we meet in any particular building, whether or not we are associated with any institutional structure.[2]

The spiritual reality of "church" is anticipated, like so much else of the work of the Lord Jesus Christ, through the pages of the Old Testament. In the history of God's great work of redemption there have been a number of "assemblies" or "gatherings" that should never be forgotten. The "church" that Jesus is building (Matthew 16:18) is the fulfillment of this gathering work of God.[3]

In the days of Moses (of which we have been reminded in 1 Kings 6:1), there was a never-to-be-forgotten assembly at Mount Sinai (see Deuteronomy 4:9–10). It was remembered as "the day of the assembly" (Deuteronomy 9:10; 10:4; 18:16). The Hebrew word for "assembly" was rendered into Greek with the word usually translated "church" in the New Testament.[4] It was "the day of the church." The gathered people had "stood before the LORD" (Deuteronomy 4:10) and heard his voice.

Years later Moses reminded them of that day:

> You heard the sound of words, but saw no form; there was only a voice. And he declared to you his covenant, which he commanded you to perform, that is, the Ten Commandments, and he wrote them on two tablets of stone. (Deuteronomy 4:12, 13)

What a gathering that was! God himself had gathered these people, whom he had redeemed from slavery in Egypt and brought to himself (Exodus 19:4).

In 1 Kings 8 we are about to see another never-to-be-forgotten assembly. Solomon's great building works had been completed (7:51). The time had come to see what all the work, described in such detail in the previous three chapters had been for. On this day the wonder of what we do when we "go to church" was anticipated (or foreshadowed). This day was, I believe, the high point of the Old Testament. We will begin by seeing:

(1) A very great assembly (vv. 1, 2)

(2) A very careful procession (vv. 3–5)

(3) A very special word (vv. 6–9)

(4) A very real glory (vv. 10, 11)

A Very Great Assembly (vv. 1, 2)

Chapter 8 of 1 Kings begins with the word "Then." The Hebrew word is not necessarily an indicator of *time* (we will come to the question of exactly *when* this happened in v. 2), but it does signify a *connection* with what precedes. We have heard about the construction of "the house of the LORD" (chapter 6), the surrounding buildings (7:1–12), and the provision of various significant objects that were placed outside and inside the most important building in Jerusalem (7:13–51). The next thing our writer wants us to hear about is connected with that now completed work.

The second word of this chapter (in the Hebrew) means "assembled."[5] It refers to the gathering together of people. While people may be "gathered" or "assembled" for many different reasons (the *word* itself is not particularly important[6]), *this* assembly was far from ordinary.

Who? (v. 1a)

Then Solomon assembled the elders of Israel [and[7]] all the heads of the tribes, the leaders of the fathers' houses of the people of Israel . . . (v. 1a)

The writer seems to be at pains to show that the whole community was represented. It is likely that each phrase ("the elders of Israel," "all the heads of the tribes," and "the leaders of the fathers' houses of the people of Israel") is a different way of describing the same group of people (or perhaps each is a subset of the next). These people represented the families, the tribes, and the whole nation of the people of Israel.

Years earlier "the elders of Israel," representing all the people, had come to David and acknowledged him as their rightful king (2 Samuel 5:1–3).[8] Solomon now assembled the whole people (again representatively) for the climactic moment of Israel's history.

Where? (v. 1b)

They were assembled "before King Solomon in Jerusalem" (v. 1b), into the presence of God's chosen king in the royal city. Picture the scene: God's people gathered to God's king.

This is the first point at which King Solomon's "church" gives us an insight into church as we experience it. We come to church because we are people whom the Lord Jesus has summoned into his presence. This is the essential reality of church. We come together *because* we are those who have been summoned into the presence of the King (see 1 Peter 2:4).

There would have been some excitement in the air that day in Jerusalem, don't you think? Not as much as there should be among those who have been summoned into the presence of the greater Son of David.

Why? (v. 1c)

Why had they been brought together? Had they come to admire the king's building projects? Or to express support for their king? Or to consult with him on government policy?

No. The purpose of this great assembly was "to bring up the ark of the covenant of the LORD out of the city of David, which is Zion" (v. 1c).

The ark last featured in this history in a big way in 2 Samuel 6, when King David had brought it up from Baale-judah to the city of David.[9] What an occasion that was! It would be helpful to turn now to 2 Samuel 6 and read again the dramatic story. The significance of what David did was huge. Bringing "the ark of the covenant of the LORD" into the city of David was David's acknowledgment and proclamation that the true King in David's kingdom was the Lord. David was king "before the LORD" (2 Samuel 6:5, 14, 16, 17, 21), whose presence and promises were represented by the ark. David's kingdom was in reality the Lord's kingdom. That is what David's bringing the ark into his royal city meant.

Now Solomon summoned this great assembly with the purpose of bringing the ark up *from* "the city of David" (see 2:10; 3:1), the Jebusite "stronghold of Zion" that David had taken and occupied early in his reign (2 Samuel 5:7, 9).[10] It was located on a ridge southeast of Jerusalem as it had grown by Solomon's time. The buildings that we have spent so much time on in the last few chapters were on higher ground (hence "to bring *up*") to the north.[11]

The movement of the ark from its situation in David's day had been long anticipated and was packed with significance. David had felt some unease with the existing arrangement. "See now, I dwell in a house of cedar, but the ark of God dwells in a tent," he had said (2 Samuel 7:2). In response to this the word of the Lord had come to David via Nathan that night. It included the promise that once the Lord had given "rest from all your enemies," he would raise up a son of David who "shall build a house for my name, and I will establish the throne of his kingdom forever" (2 Samuel 7:11, 13). The son of David had now built the promised house. It was time for the ark to be brought up from its temporary place in the city of David to the house that had now been built for it.

Bringing the ark up from the city of David signified the fulfillment of God's promise to David. It meant that the promised rest had become a reality and that the kingdom of Solomon was the kingdom of the promised son of David, the kingdom that the Lord promised to establish forever. Solomon had summoned this great assembly for a momentous occasion.

Of course, the people Solomon gathered in Jerusalem did not *themselves* transport the ark. There were too many of them for that. But Solomon had assembled them to join the procession, to be part of this great event.

When? (v. 2)

Verse 2 gives us a curiously obscure indication of when this happened: "And all the men of Israel assembled to King Solomon at the feast in the month Ethanim, which is the seventh month" (v. 2).

We are not told the year in which this "seventh month" fell. The building work on the house of the Lord had been finished in the *eighth* month of the *eleventh* year of Solomon's reign (6:38). If we are talking about the seventh month of the same year, then Solomon summoned the assembly just *before* that house was finished. That seems unlikely. Was it the seventh month of the next year, eleven months *after* the house of the Lord was completed? Perhaps. We cannot be certain, but the arrangement of the account seems to suggest that this assembly was called much later, when *all* the building works described in chapters 6, 7 were completed—that is, thirteen years after the house of the Lord was completed and twenty years after it had begun (6:38; 7:1; cf. 9:1, 10).[12] This would mean that the completion of *both* the house of the Lord (6:1–38) *and* Solomon's own "entire house" (7:1–12) was relevant here. The movement of the ark was not just a matter of religion. It was about the kingdom: Solomon's kingdom was the Lord's kingdom.

The seventh month (roughly September/October) is given the name "Ethanim."[13] This is a Canaanite name for the month, possibly suggesting a significance for this occasion beyond the nation of Israel (see also 8:41–43).[14]

The feast in the seventh month was the Feast of Booths (ESV) (or Tabernacles, NIV) (Leviticus 23:33–43; Deuteronomy 16:13–15). This festival was rich in its associations. First, it commemorated the tent-dwelling days when the people of Israel were in the wilderness (Leviticus 23:43). *This* Feast of Booths would mark the day when the wandering was finally over and the ark itself would no longer dwell in a tent (2 Samuel 7:2), but would be brought at last to "its place" (v. 6). Peace at last.

Second, the Feast of Booths commemorated the harvest as "the blessing of the LORD your God that he has given you" (Deuteronomy 16:13, 17; see Leviticus 23:39). Years later the prophet Zechariah would see this feast as signaling the gathering in of the nations "to worship the King, the LORD of hosts" (Zechariah 14:16). *This* Feast of Booths would celebrate the fulfillment of the Lord's promise (8:15).

Third, the Feast of Booths was the occasion when, every seven years, all the people ("men, women, and little ones, and the sojourner within your towns") were to assemble to hear the Law of God read out, "that they may hear and learn to fear the LORD your God, and be careful to do all the words of this law, and that their children, who have not known it, may hear and learn to fear the LORD your God, as long as you live in the land . . ." (Deuteronomy 31:12, 13). *This* Feast of Booths will celebrate the presence of God promised to his obedient people (6:11–13).

Fourth, the Feast of Booths was a time of great joy (Deuteronomy 16:14, 15). This Feast of Booths will indeed be full of joy (see 8:66).[15]

What a great and important assembly King Solomon's "church" was! It should remind us that we come to church because God's promises have been realized more fully and profoundly than in Solomon's day. We enjoy peace with God and therefore with one another that will never end (Ephesians 2:14–17). The nations are being gathered in (Colossians 3:11). The Lord is with us (Romans 15:33). Our joy is beyond words (1 Peter 1:8). That is why our King calls us together.

A Very Careful Procession (vv. 3–5)

When David had brought the ark into his city, there was enormous excitement. This was tragically interrupted by the perplexing death of Uzzah. However, in due course the joyful, though now very careful, procession recommenced and brought the ark into the city of David (see 2 Samuel 6).

The assembly summoned by King Solomon should be seen as the continuation of David's procession, now that the Lord had given his people rest and peace (5:4). Look carefully at what happened.

The Ark, the Tent, and the Vessels (vv. 3, 4)

"And all the elders of Israel came, and the priests took up the ark" (v. 3). Care was required in carrying the ark. That much was clear from David's experience. Quite properly, the job was done by priests, who were members of the tribe of Levi (see Deuteronomy 10:8).

"And they brought up the ark of the LORD, the tent of meeting, and all the holy vessels that were in the tent; the priests and the Levites brought them up" (v. 4). As the priests brought up the ark, other members of the tribe of Levi assisted in bringing the tabernacle (here called "the tent of meeting"[16]) and the various vessels that had been used in the tabernacle.[17] Just as the portable tabernacle had now been replaced by the permanent house of the Lord, so the vessels of the tabernacle had been replaced by the various objects we have seen in 7:13–50.[18]

We must not miss the historic significance of this moment. Since the ark of the covenant of the Lord with the people of Israel had been captured by the Philistines over a hundred years earlier (1 Samuel 4), the ark had not been in its proper place in the tabernacle. It had lain in obscurity for seventy years[19] or so in the house of Abinadab (1 Samuel 7:1) until David had brought it up from there (2 Samuel 6:3). It had been in the tent David provided for it in the city of David for at least thirty years.[20] For the first time in over a hundred years the ark and the tabernacle were brought together. But the purpose was not to place the ark again in the tabernacle. Something greater than that was about to happen.

Innumerable Sacrifices (v. 5)

> And King Solomon and all the congregation of Israel, who had assembled before him, were with him before the ark, sacrificing so many sheep and oxen that they could not be counted or numbered. (v. 5)

David had been forced to ask, "How can the ark of the LORD come to me?" (2 Samuel 6:9). The answer was: only by atonement being made. The sacrifices he had offered acknowledged this (2 Samuel 6:13).[21] King Solomon did likewise, but like everything else Solomon was doing, it was bigger and better.[22] There were so many sacrifices that they could not be counted.

The ark of the *covenant* represented God's commitment. But they could not presume on this. King Solomon's "church," in this Old Testament way, was *making atonement* for their sins. Only so could they be God's people. God had taught them that. So they made atonement in the only way they knew.

As we assemble as God's people to enjoy the fulfillment of God's promises, we too must be careful. Atonement must be made for our sins. Unlike King Solomon's "church," *we* do not do it. It has been done *for* us by our King. His death on the cross is the full and perfect sacrifice that ends all sacrifices. Only so is it possible for us to gather as the church of Jesus Christ.

A Very Special Word (vv. 6–9)

We have not yet been told (explicitly) where this procession was headed (but see 6:19). Follow the priests carrying the ark to its destination.

The Place (v. 6)

Then the priests brought the ark of the covenant of the LORD to its place in the inner sanctuary [rear room] of the house, in the Most Holy Place, underneath the wings of the cherubim. (v. 6)

The Most Holy Place we saw prepared so carefully in 6:16–28 now received the object for which it had been constructed and decorated. The ark of the covenant of the Lord was brought to "its place," just as David had set it "in its place" earlier (2 Samuel 6:17). There is a sense here, however, that the ark that had moved so often since the days of Moses had now come to its permanent place.[23] This is arguably the high point of the Old Testament story—so far.

The Cherubim (v. 7)

For the cherubim spread out their wings over the place of the ark, so that the cherubim overshadowed the ark and its poles. (v. 7)

The cherubim provided a kind of shelter for the ark. "Overshadowed" in Hebrew is a word that suggests the booths of the Feast of Booths.[24] The ark itself and the poles used to carry it were covered by the huge cherubim (see 6:23–28). They were (again) bigger and better than the cherubim that had overshadowed the mercy seat of the ark in the tabernacle (Exodus 25:20).

The Poles (v. 8)

And the poles were so long that the ends of the poles were seen from the Holy Place before the inner sanctuary [rear room]; but they could not be seen from outside. And they are there to this day. (v. 8)

It had been a requirement from the beginning that the poles for carrying the ark must remain in the rings of the ark and not be removed (Exodus 25:15). Since the poles were a reminder of the portability of the ark, and it had now reached its permanent place, we might have expected the poles now to be removed.[25] It is possible that the poles were left in this conspicuous way (a) in obedience to the command given to Moses, and (b) as an indication that the permanence of this arrangement was not absolute. The ark and all it represented could still be taken away from a rebellious people, as subsequent history would tragically show.[26]

The Contents of the Ark (v. 9)

> There was[27] nothing in the ark except[28] the two tablets of stone that Moses
> put there at Horeb, where the LORD made a covenant with the people of
> Israel, when they came out of the land of Egypt. (v. 9)

The box was empty except for those two stone tablets.[29] The astonishing importance of the ark lay in those tablets. There was *nothing else*. But make no
mistake—those tablets were extraordinary. Moses had cut these tablets at God's
instruction, and God himself had written on the tablets the words of the Ten
Commandments that he had spoken to them on that great day of the assembly
at Mount Horeb (see Deuteronomy 10:1–5). These tablets had been called "the
testimony" (Exodus 25:16; 40:20). The first words on those tablets were:

> I am the LORD your God, who brought you out of the land of Egypt, out
> of the house of slavery. You shall have no other gods before me. (Deuter-
> onomy 5:6–7)

The tablets bore the very words of God that defined his relationship with his
people, that is, the covenant he had made with them in those far-off days when he
had delivered them from slavery in Egypt. The "covenant"[30] was God's gracious
commitment to them ("I am the LORD your God") and their consequent obligation
("You shall have no other gods before me"). That is what the ark represented.[31]

The emphasis on the ark containing *nothing* but these tablets is making
the same point that Moses had made about the assembly at Mount Horeb:
"You heard the sound of words, but saw no form; there was *only* a voice"
(Deuteronomy 4:12). As the people encountered God in his *words* (and nothing else) at Mount Horeb, so the ark contained God's *words* (and nothing else).

King Solomon's "church" recognized and honored God's word that God
had so wonderfully kept ("I *am* the LORD your God") and that they were bound
to obey ("You shall have no *other* gods before me"). That's what the ark contained. *Nothing else.*

Again King Solomon's "church" was a shadowy anticipation of the
Church of the Lord Jesus Christ, where the *word of God* (not now on stone
tablets, but the word of Jesus Christ) is to dwell among us richly (Colossians
3:16). *God's Word* that he has so wonderfully kept and that we are bound to
trust and obey—that's what church is about. *Nothing else.*

A Very Real Glory (vv. 10, 11)

> And when the priests came out of the Holy Place, a[32] [the] cloud filled
> the house of the LORD, so that the priests could not stand to minister

> because of the cloud, for the glory of the Lord filled the house of the Lord. (vv. 10, 11)

It was extraordinary—just as in the days of Moses when "the cloud covered the tent of meeting, and the glory of the Lord filled the tabernacle," so that Moses was unable to enter (Exodus 40:34, 35). As with everything else about Solomon's reign, however, it was now bigger and better. The "house" that was now filled with the glory of the Lord was something greater than the tabernacle.

If you had been there, you would never forget "coming to church" that day, would you?

However, the day would come when the glory of the Lord would depart from this house (Ezekiel 10:18, 19). But that would not be the end of this story. In Jesus Christ "the Word became flesh and tabernacled among us, and we have seen *his* glory" (John 1:14, AT).

Next time you "go to church," it would be good to remember that the assembly in which you participate is even bigger and better than King Solomon's "church." To appreciate this we must see the spiritual reality of the church. Look at King Solomon's "church" and consider how the assembly summoned by our Lord Jesus (that is, your local church) is the *fulfillment* of what was happening on that day.

First, the church is *a very great assembly*. We are the people who have been brought together by our great King. While Solomon's assembly consisted of all the elders of Israel, the church of Jesus Christ assembled into his royal presence draws people from every level, kind, and condition of human beings (Colossians 3:11).

Second, the church *must be careful*. We can belong to this assembly only by atonement being made. In Solomon's assembly numerous sacrifices were made. In the church of Jesus Christ we have been reconciled to God in one body through the death of Jesus himself (Ephesians 2:16).

Third, the church has *a very special word*. "Let the word of Christ dwell in [or among] you richly, teaching and admonishing one another in all wisdom, singing psalms and hymns and spiritual songs, with thankfulness in your hearts to God" (Colossians 3:16).

Fourth, the local church has *a very real glory*. The local church is God's remarkable display of his "manifold wisdom" (Ephesians 3:10). It is where his great work of reconciling all things can now be seen (Colossians 1:15–20, especially v. 18).

The physical place where we meet is no longer special in any way. As we have noted several times now, it is unfortunate and misleading when we use words for the buildings we meet in like "the Lord's house" or "sanctuary." Our "temple" is the Lord Jesus Christ himself (John 2:21, 22). As we come to him we are being built into "a *spiritual* house," of which he is the cornerstone (1 Peter 2:4–8). As we are joined together to him, we are being built into "a holy temple in the Lord" (Ephesians 2:21; cf. 1 Corinthians 3:16; 2 Corinthians 6:16). We meet together as the church in any particular place *because* we are the people in that place who have come to him.

I am so looking forward to next Sunday morning! As I go to church I will experience the hope of the world.

16

Excited about Church?

1 KINGS 8:12–21

DO YOU FIND YOURSELF excited about church? I am not talking about the kind of excitement that can be stirred up in certain churches by music, lighting, oratory, and showmanship. There is little real value in that. I am asking whether you find church itself—people gathered in the name of Jesus Christ—exciting.

It may seem a strange question. Sadly, churches can have a reputation for being anything *but* exciting. *Boring* is the word many people associate with church. I suppose that is why some resort to upbeat music and other tricks of the entertainment industry. We do not want church to be *boring*! But if those things are a *substitute* for the real excitement we should feel about church, they are unhelpful. What is exciting about church?

The assembly (we could call it "church") gathered by King Solomon in Jerusalem (8:1) was certainly exciting. We are about to see how exciting it was and why.

With the benefit of hindsight, we can see that occasion was even more thrilling than anyone then could have realized. The house of the Lord that Solomon had built in Jerusalem anticipated the "spiritual house" that the Lord Jesus is now building. The stones of this "house" are people who come to the Lord Jesus Christ, and Jesus himself is the chosen and precious cornerstone (1 Peter 2:4–6). The gathering of people who come together because they have come to Jesus is the "church" that Jesus is building (see Ephesians 2:19–22). "The gates of hell shall not prevail against it" (Matthew 16:18). The full significance of the house built by King Solomon and the assembly he gathered in Jerusalem can now be seen in the light of its fulfillment: the "house" being built by *the* Son of David, Jesus.

It works the other way too. The full significance of two or three gathered in the *name* of Jesus (Matthew 18:20) is illuminated by the Old Testament accounts from the days of Solomon and the house he built for the *name* of the Lord (5:5). The visible and tangible experience of the Old Testament "church" helps us see the spiritual reality of an otherwise small and unimpressive gathering of Christian believers (Jesus did say "two or three"!).[1]

On the day that King Solomon summoned the great assembly to bring the ark of the covenant up from the city of David to its permanent home in the Most Holy Place (8:1, 6) and the glory of the Lord filled the house of the Lord in the form of a cloud (8:10, 11), Solomon spoke. What he said helped those who heard him understand what was going on. It was thrilling! What Solomon said will help us see what is going on whenever two or three (or more) gather in the name of Jesus.

Three Reasons to Be Excited about Church (vv. 12, 13)

The first words Solomon spoke may not have been heard by many people. I think he was probably standing in the inner court (6:36) facing the house of the Lord, while the great assembly he had summoned was behind him. They could see the miraculous dark cloud that had filled the building (8:10). Solomon's first thought (v. 12) turned into a brief word addressed to the Lord himself (v. 13). Solomon understood the remarkable significance of this moment. Listen to him.

God Has Spoken (v. 12a)

"Then[2] Solomon said, 'The LORD has said . . .'" (v. 12a). It would be easy to pass over this first point, but it is fundamental. Solomon understood that this historic moment was astonishing because *God had spoken*. We will see the connection between God speaking and what was happening on that day in Jerusalem in a moment. First, consider this basic reality: God has spoken.

I fear that Christian people today are sometimes so familiar with this truth that they take it for granted. That is unfortunate, to say the least. Of all the wonders the Bible teaches us, this is central. The God who created all things has *spoken*.[3] That is either true or untrue. If it is untrue, then everything in the Bible, everything Christians have believed, is fanciful. Many today think that is the case and want societies that have been historically influenced by Christianity to change accordingly. But if it is true that *God has spoken*, that has huge implications for the whole human race. It certainly makes church exciting indeed, as we will see. Next time you are in church, think about this: you are there because *God has spoken*.

God Has Promised (v. 12b)

The fact that God has spoken is brilliant, but what matters even more is *what God has said*. The utterly remarkable thing is that what God has said is a *promise*. In summary: God has promised to fulfill his good purpose for all things. This promise has been expressed in different ways, and there are various aspects to what God has promised. Faith (in the Bible's sense) is *believing God's promise*.[4]

As King Solomon looked at the dark cloud filling the house of the Lord, he remembered God's promise. That is what made sense of what was happening. Solomon said (perhaps almost to himself): "The LORD has said that he would dwell in the[5] thick darkness" (v. 12b).

We have no record of God saying, "I will dwell in the thick darkness."[6] Solomon was not *quoting* a promise from God. He was putting what he understood God to have promised in his own words, suited to the occasion.

The two key words he chose were highly significant. The word for "dwell" here is the word used in 2 Samuel 7:10: "I will appoint a place for my people Israel and will plant them, so that they may *dwell* in their own place and be disturbed no more." The fulfillment of this promise was the precondition for the building of the house of the Lord (see 2 Samuel 7:5–13). The people now dwelt undisturbed in their own place (see 5:4). Solomon understood that the Lord had promised to "dwell" with them.

The second key word is "the thick darkness" (one word in Hebrew). Solomon was certainly referring to the dark cloud that had filled the house of the Lord (8:10), but he was also thinking of the day of the much earlier assembly of the people of Israel when "The people stood far off, while Moses drew near to *the thick darkness* where God was" (Exodus 20:21; cf. 19:9). Indeed Moses had later recalled:

> These words the LORD spoke to all your assembly at the mountain out of the midst of the fire, the cloud, and *the thick darkness*, with a loud voice; and he added no more. And he wrote them on two tablets of stone and gave them to me. (Deuteronomy 5:22; cf. 4:11)[7]

God's presence ("where God was") in "the thick darkness" should not be taken as suggesting that God is essentially mysterious.[8] Out of the thick darkness God had *spoken* "with a loud voice." What God said was meant to be *understood*. The point of "the thick darkness" is that God was not *seen*— he was *heard*. "You *heard* the sound of words, but *saw* no form; there was only a voice" (Deuteronomy 4:12).

God's presence in the thick darkness, first encountered at Mount Sinai, had traveled with the people of Israel on their journey from there. In this respect the tabernacle had been a kind of portable Mount Sinai (see Exodus 40:34–38).

Solomon understood that now the people dwelt in their own place, at peace, at rest. God's promise to be with them (see Genesis 26:3; 31:3; Exodus 3:12) had been realized in the Sinai-like cloud that had filled the house of the Lord he had built. How exciting was that!

Christian people know something even more breathtaking. God has promised to dwell with us. This is not now in "the thick darkness," nor does it have anything to do with a physical building. Jesus said, "If anyone loves me, he will keep my word, and my Father will love him, and we will come to him and make our home with him" (John 14:23). Jesus is Emmanuel, "God with us" (Matthew 1:23; cf. 28:20). He has particularly promised to be there among them, "where two or three are gathered in my name" (Matthew 18:20). That makes church exciting indeed. Next time you are in church, think about the spiritual reality: we are "a dwelling place for God by the Spirit" (Ephesians 2:22).

God's King Has Built the House (v. 13)

Solomon's thoughts *about* the Lord (v. 12) became words spoken *to* the Lord: "I have indeed built you an exalted house,[9] a place for you to dwell in forever" (v. 13).

In the light of God's promise and the evident fulfillment of the promise in the cloud that had filled the house of the Lord, Solomon understood the astonishing thing he had done. This house he had built was the "place" where the Lord would now permanently "dwell."

Here the Hebrew word for "dwell" is different from the word we saw in verse 12. It can mean "enthroned" (as in "*enthroned* on the cherubim," 1 Samuel 4:4; 2 Samuel 6:2) and perhaps suggests that the Lord will *reign* from this place.

There are many possible misunderstandings of God's presence in a particular place. Solomon will address the most serious of these in his great prayer in 8:22–53 (especially vv. 27–30). At this point we should appreciate that the presence of God is not a subjective feeling (as in "I felt God's presence"). Our feelings are a poor guide to spiritual reality. God is present where and how he has *promised* to be present. He has not promised to be present in our feelings. In Solomon's day God's king had built the house that God had promised, and the Lord had taken up royal residence there as promised.

The greater Son of David has now said, "I will build my church" (Matthew 16:18). What he is building is greater than anything Solomon built. As you come to him you are being built into his "spiritual house." "The honor is for you who believe" (1 Peter 2:4–7). That really does make church exciting. Don't you agree? Next time you are in church, think about this: we are *the spiritual house that the Lord Jesus Christ is building*.

Understand How Good It Is (vv. 14–21)

King Solomon turned from these relatively private thoughts to address the assembly in the courtyard behind him: "Then the king turned around and blessed all the assembly of Israel, while all the assembly of Israel stood" (v. 14).

The assembly (or "church") stood, presumably in motionless silence. Perhaps they trembled at the sight of the dark cloud billowing from the house of the Lord a few yards in front of them. What was this?

Solomon "blessed" them. This means that he spoke words of goodness and kindness to them.[10] He may have said something like, "Blessed are you . . ." (cf. Luke 6:20–22). More probably he "blessed" them by saying the words that follow in verses 15–21 about the Lord blessing them all.[11]

The Source of the Blessing: The Lord, the God of Israel (v. 15a)

He blessed them by pointing to the source of their blessing: "And he said, 'Blessed be the LORD, the God of Israel . . .'" (v. 15a). How *good* God is![12] What a blessing it was for all the assembly to *know* how good their God had been to them.

The Apostle Paul "blessed" his readers in words that echo Solomon's words to the assembly that day: "Blessed be the God and Father of our Lord Jesus Christ . . ." (Ephesians 1:3). How *good* he is! What a blessing it is for a gathering of believers to *know* how good their God had been to them.

The Nature of the Blessing: Fulfillment of Promise (v. 15b)

". . . who with his hand has fulfilled what he promised [literally, said[13]] with his mouth to David my father . . ." (v. 15b). God's goodness is not an abstract idea or simply an attribute of God. It has been displayed in what he *spoke with his mouth* and what he *did with his hand*.[14]

What made the assembly in Jerusalem that day, when the glory of the Lord filled the house of the Lord (8:11), *so* wonderful was *what God had said* and *what God had done* in fulfillment of what he had said. More about that shortly.

But if that was exciting (and of course it was), what can we say about the Christian experience? "Blessed be the God and Father of our Lord Jesus Christ, *who has blessed us in Christ with every spiritual blessing in the heavenly places*" (Ephesians 1:3). All the promises of God have come together in what God has done in Jesus Christ (cf. 2 Corinthians 1:20; Galatians 3:16).

The Priority of the Blessing: God's King over God's People (v. 16)

What exactly was it that God had said to David?

> Since the day that I brought my people Israel out of Egypt, I chose no city out of all the tribes of Israel in which to build a house, that my name might be there. But I chose David to be over my people Israel. (v. 16)

Solomon was almost certainly thinking of the word of God that had been spoken to David in 2 Samuel 7.[15] That word has been the key to everything that has happened since the opening scene of 1 Kings.

To understand the present situation the assembled people needed to look back to "the day that I brought my people Israel out of Egypt." That was where the story leading to this day began (see 6:1). Since that day the Lord had not chosen a city in which to have a house built (such as Solomon had now done). God had a priority, something that had to be established before such a thing could be done. First he "chose David to be over my people Israel" (see 1 Samuel 13:14; 15:28; 16:1, 12; 2 Samuel 7:8).

Jesus is now God's chosen one (Luke 9:35; cf. 23:35; 1 Peter 2:4, 6). He "has made him both Lord and Christ" (Acts 2:36).

The Hope of the Blessing: A House for the Name of the Lord (vv. 17–19)

However, God's king reigning over God's people was not the end of the story—then or now. Even David had seen that. Solomon continued: "Now it was in the heart of David my father to build a house for the name of the Lord, the God of Israel" (v. 17). David sensed that the ark of the covenant's being in a tent in Jerusalem could not be permanent (see 2 Samuel 7:2).

He was right: "But the Lord said to David my father, 'Whereas it was in your heart to build a house for my name, you did well that it was in your heart'" (v. 18). David's longing was right and good (cf. 2 Corinthians 8:12).

He was just mistaken about the timing: "Nevertheless,[16] you[17] shall not build the house, but your son[18] who shall be born to you shall build the house for my name" (v. 19).

Solomon's building work was, then, the fulfillment of God's promise. The exodus from Egypt had reached its goal. God's good purpose for his people had been accomplished. What a day that was!

But we can now see that it was a shadow of the things to come (cf. Colossians 2:17; Hebrews 10:1). David's greater Son is building a greater house and a greater city. John saw it in a vision:

> And I saw the holy city, new Jerusalem, coming down out of heaven from God, prepared as a bride adorned for her husband. And I heard a loud voice from the throne saying, "Behold, the dwelling place of God is with man. He will dwell with them, and they will be his people, and God himself will be with them as their God. He will wipe away every tear from their eyes, and death shall be no more, neither shall there be mourning, nor crying, nor pain anymore, for the former things have passed away." (Revelation 21:2–4)

That is the building project we are part of. Remember that next time you are in church.

In Summary . . . (vv. 20, 21)

Listen to the closing words of Solomon's address to the assembly, in which he summed up the extraordinary significance of the moment: "Now the LORD has fulfilled his promise that he made [literally, his word that he spoke]" (v. 20a). The time had come for God's people to enjoy the blessing that had been so long promised—peace and rest, with God himself in their midst. Solomon highlighted three aspects of this wonderful circumstance, each of which was a shadow of the even better things to come.

The Son of David on the Throne (v. 20b)

First, "For I have risen in the place of David my father, and sit on the throne of Israel, as the LORD promised" (v. 20b). The promised son of David was now king—God's king.

By now I am sure you can see the pattern of shadow and fulfillment. What happened then has now happened more wonderfully still. Another, greater Son of David has now "risen" and reigns over all things—Jesus Christ our Lord (see Matthew 28:18; Romans 1:3–4).

The House for the Name of the Lord (v. 20c)

Second, "and I have built the house for the name of the LORD, the God of Israel" (v. 20c). God's king had provided the permanent place for God's "name" among his people.

Notice how the "house" has been described similarly five times in as many verses:

a house, that my *name* might be there (v. 16)

a house for the *name* of the LORD, the God of Israel (v. 17)

a house for my *name* (v. 18)

the house for my *name* (v. 19)

the house for the *name* of the LORD, the God of Israel (v. 20)

This is extraordinarily important, as we will explore further in our next chapter. Here is the significance of the ark being placed in this house. The ark was "called by the *name* of the LORD of hosts" (2 Samuel 6:2). The house for *the ark* was the house for the Lord's *name* (cf. 2 Samuel 7:13).

On the one hand, this way of putting it avoids any crude understanding of the house as somehow *containing* God (see 8:27). God's presence in this place is described as the presence of his *name*.

On the other hand, this house was part of an extraordinary wonder. The true and living God has made himself known *by name* (see Exodus 3:13–15; 6:2–3). The Bible is not about a vague, undefined concept of "god," nor is it about the existence of a supreme being in theoretical and abstract terms. Rather the Bible is about knowing God *by name*. Those who know God by name may use a number of different names (Yahweh, God, Father, Lord, and so on), just as any person may be known by several names (John, Dad, and Grandpa come to mind). This is less important than the personal relationship made possible when God has made himself known by "name." Only then we can "call on the *name* of the LORD" (see Genesis 4:26; 12:8; 13:4; 21:33; 26:25; Psalm 79:6; 80:18; 99:6; Joel 2:32; Acts 2:21; Romans 10:13; 1 Corinthians 1:2).

The purpose of the house that Solomon had built (and that God had promised) was closely connected to Israel's great privilege of knowing God by *name*. The "name" by which God may now be known in *every* place is the name of our Lord Jesus Christ (1 Corinthians 1:2). The huge implications of this will become clear in our next chapter.

The Ark in Its Place at Journey's End (v. 21)

Third, "And there I have provided a place for the ark, in which is the covenant of the LORD that he made with our fathers, when he brought them out of the land of Egypt" (v. 21).

The "house for the name of the LORD, the God of Israel" was "a place for the ark." Remember what we heard earlier? "There was nothing in the ark except the two tablets of stone that Moses put there at Horeb" (8:9). The ark was the box containing nothing but *God's word* to his people, the word he spoke to them at the time of the rescue from Egypt, here called "the covenant of the LORD that he made with our fathers." The house for God's name was the house for God's word to his people. They knew him by name; he gave them his word. The house now represented the fulfillment of all that the ark had meant.[19]

As we hear Solomon's speech, and particularly this closing note, let us appreciate the wonder of the gathering assembled by the Lord Jesus Christ, where his word "dwells" richly among us (Colossians 3:16). Here is the fulfillment of all that happened on that day in Jerusalem. As we teach and admonish one another in all wisdom, singing psalms, hymns, and spiritual songs, with thankfulness in our hearts to God (Colossians 3:15–17), remember Solomon's words and you will be excited about church.

17

"Whatever You Ask in My Name"

1 KINGS 8:22–53

I FIND PRAYING DIFFICULT. Do you? Some "praying" is no more than a kind of wishful thinking. I am not talking about that. Real praying is when we speak to God, knowing that he hears us and takes what we say seriously. Is that possible? *How* is it possible?

I think I have some idea of what the Apostle Paul meant when he spoke of his friend Epaphras "struggling" in his prayers (Colossians 4:12), or when he mentioned "striv[ing]" in our praying (Romans 15:30). It really does take an effort. I understand the words, "we do not know what to pray for" (Romans 8:26). Often that is exactly how I feel. I am aware that I need to be told to "continue steadfastly in prayer" (Colossians 4:2). I do not find it easy.

Why is praying difficult for many people? It is not as though it is a difficult thing to do. A child can pray. Perhaps that is part of it. Do you have to be an adult to see the problems with praying?

On the one hand, those who have doubts about God (which is what adults tend to do[1]) will obviously have doubts about praying. Our difficulties in praying can be an expression of our uncertainty, our weak faith, our unbelief.

On the other hand, even those who are clear about the God who is there, confident in their faith in him, may have doubts about whether Almighty God really needs to hear from little old me. Can't we trust God to be good enough, wise enough, and powerful enough to rule the world, including my little part of the world, without interference from my prayers? We can find ourselves believing in *God* (or at least thinking we do) but finding it hard to believe in *praying*.

This is a serious matter. Faith in God that does not lead us to pray is not really faith in God at all. That may be a harsh way to put it, but we need to understand that faith in God is not simply our own thoughts about God. That's make-believe religion, and it is worse than useless. Faith in God is what God himself has made possible. It is what Jesus Christ has opened up for us. And *that* faith will pray.

But just as there can be "faith" that is not really faith at all (see James 2:14, 19), there can be praying that is not really praying. It is no wonder that we have difficulties with praying because true prayer is utterly remarkable. True praying involves words uttered by a mere human being and those words actually being heard—listened to—by Almighty God. Just as the possibility of authentic faith depends on what God has done, so the possibility of genuine praying is a gracious gift from God.

The rather long passage we now have before us records the prayer King Solomon prayed on the day that the ark of the covenant was brought to its place in the "house" Solomon had "built . . . for the name of the LORD, the God of Israel" (8:20, 21). Solomon's prayer on that occasion was about the possibility of praying. Arguably Solomon's prayer is the climactic moment of the whole Old Testament story.

The Person Who Prayed (v. 22)

Before we hear Solomon's prayer, look carefully at the person who prayed:

> Then Solomon stood before the altar of the LORD in the presence of all the assembly of Israel[2] and spread out his hands toward heaven. (v. 22)

King Solomon's greatness is seen at this moment. In the presence of the whole congregation of Israel he stood before the altar of the Lord. He did not delegate this task to one of the priests. He did it himself. This king represented his people to God.

The altar before which he stood has not been mentioned previously in 1 Kings, but was presumably the altar of burnt offering that stood in the inner court (see 8:64).[3] Readers (many years after these events) seem to be expected to know about this altar, possibly because the layout of the house and all that surrounded it was remembered by them, or perhaps because the corresponding arrangement of the tabernacle was assumed (Exodus 27:1–8; 38:1–7).

He "stood" there. His hands were spread out toward the heavens. At some point he fell to his knees (see 8:54). This king was acknowledging the greater King. He understood that the highest service he could render to his people was to pray for them. The people were indeed "blessed" to have such a king (see 8:14).

So are we. "We have an advocate with the Father, Jesus Christ the righteous" (1 John 2:1). As you look at King Solomon standing before the altar in the presence of his people and as you hear his prayer, consider the wonder that our King, Jesus Christ, is interceding for us (Romans 8:34; Hebrews 7:25). This is at the heart of gospel truth: "For there is one God, and there is one mediator between God and men, the man Christ Jesus [or King Jesus]" (1 Timothy 2:5). King Solomon was like that for "all the assembly of Israel."

The God He Addressed (vv. 23, 24)

Solomon knew the One to whom his words were directed. He knew him to be utterly *incomparable* in the way he has proven himself absolutely *faithful*.

Utterly Incomparable (v. 23a)

He began: "O LORD, God of Israel, there is no God like you, in heaven above or on earth beneath . . ." (v. 23a).

Those who know God know that to be true. *No one and nothing* can compare with him. Moses knew this after the experience of the exodus from Egypt (Exodus 15:11; Deuteronomy 4:39). Hannah knew the Lord like this after the birth of Samuel (1 Samuel 2:2). David understood the same truth when he heard God's historic promise to him (2 Samuel 7:22; 22:32; cf. Psalm 86:8).

And we know more deeply still that there is no god (real or imagined) like the God and Father of our Lord Jesus Christ. None is as good, none is as wise, none is as powerful.

Absolutely Faithful (vv. 23b, 24)

This is not simply an idea, a teaching to be believed, a "doctrine." The *incomparability* of God is experienced in his *faithfulness*. This is what impressed God's uniqueness on Solomon:

> . . . keeping covenant and showing steadfast love [or kindness[4]] to your servants[5] who walk before you with all their heart;[6] you have kept with your servant David my father what you declared to him. You spoke with your mouth, and with your hand have fulfilled it this day. (vv. 23b, 24)

It is not just God's goodness, wisdom, and power that make him incomparable. It is God's faithfulness. Solomon knew that God had *done* what he had *said* he would do. That is God's faithfulness, and in this he is utterly without peer.

Solomon was profoundly aware that the establishment of his kingdom and the building of the house for God's name had been God's gift. Behind the political processes (as we might superficially see them in 1 Kings 1—4) and the physical building work (as it has been meticulously described in 1 Kings 5—7) had been the hand of the Lord. Furthermore his *hand* had fulfilled what his *mouth* had spoken years earlier in the great promise to David (cf. 8:15). In his kindness he had kept his covenant or promise.

This is fundamental to authentic knowledge of God. The complete trustworthiness of what God has *said* is displayed in what God has *done*. No god (or imagined god) has promised what God has promised. No god has fulfilled his promises as God has fulfilled his. Solomon was deeply conscious that his present experience was the God-given *fulfillment* of the God-given *word* spoken to his father David.

The same faithfulness of God is central to the news about Jesus. The Lord Jesus knew that he had come to fulfill *all* that God had promised (see Matthew 5:17; 26:54, 56; Mark 14:49; Luke 4:21; 21:22; 24:44; Acts 3:18). Christian believers can be confident that the God who has called us into the fellowship of Jesus Christ will sustain us to the end. He is faithful (see 1 Corinthians 1:8, 9; 10:13; 1 Thessalonians 5:24; 2 Thessalonians 3:3; Hebrews 10:23).

The Prayer Itself (vv. 25–53)

Solomon's knowledge of God's incomparable faithfulness was the basis for the great prayer that followed, which, as we will see, was about the possibility of prayer.

The Possibility of Prayer: Promise (vv. 25, 26)

> Now therefore, O Lᴏʀᴅ, God of Israel, keep for your servant David my father what you have promised him, saying, "You shall not lack a man to sit before me on the throne of Israel, if only your sons pay close attention to their way, to walk before me as you have walked before me." Now therefore, O God of Israel, let your word be confirmed, which you have spoken to your servant David my father. (vv. 25, 26)

The repeated "Now therefore" (vv. 25, 26) marks the transition from what Solomon had said about God (vv. 23, 24) to his request.[7] His request was that the future would be shaped by the faithfulness of God just as his present was—that the God who had kept his promises would continue to keep them.

Solomon's citation of God's promise in verse 25 is very close to what he had heard from his father in 2:4.[8] The "condition" ("if only your sons pay close attention to their way, to walk before me") must be taken with utter seriousness, as subsequent history will show. God's promised king must be obedient.[9] And yet the promise remains certain and *in a sense* unconditional. God himself will provide the obedient King. David's historic kingdom will be lost because of the disobedience of his sons (that is the story that 1 and 2 Kings tells), but the promised kingdom will still be established forever by a greater Son of David (that is central to the message of the books of the prophets from Isaiah to Malachi and then of the New Testament).[10]

Solomon's sense of God's promises fulfilled in his present experience made him confident about the future. His request had this assurance about it. It was a prayer of faith (cf. James 1:6; 5:15). That is what "faith" is: confidence in God's faithfulness to what he has promised.

Prayer (authentic prayer, as described at the beginning of this chapter) is only possible because of God's promises and his faithfulness. "God's promises . . . must be both the guide of our desires, and the ground of our hopes and expectations, in prayer."[11]

The Place of Prayer: A Puzzle (vv. 27–30)

That is all very well (I hear you thinking), but what does it have to do with the house that Solomon had gone to such trouble to build and said so much about? What was the house for?

God Is Uncontainable (v. 27)

On the one hand, Solomon was very clear about what the house was *not* for:

> But will God indeed dwell on the earth? Behold, heaven and the highest heaven[12] cannot contain you; how much less this house that I have built! (v. 27)

The house Solomon had built was not to be a place that confined or "contained" God. He would not be present in this house in any restricted way. Some pagan religions may have had understandings along such lines about their gods and their temples. Solomon understood as clearly as Stephen many years later that "the Most High does not dwell in houses made by hands" (Acts 7:48–50, citing Isaiah 66:1, 2). The house Solomon had built could not make God smaller than he is. It could not limit him.

What, then, was this house for?

The House for His Name (vv. 28–30a)

> Yet have regard to the prayer of your servant and to his plea, O LORD my God, listening to the cry and to the prayer that your servant prays before

you this day, that your eyes may be open night and day toward this house, *the place of which you have said, "My name shall be there,"* that you may listen to the prayer that your servant offers toward this place. And listen to the plea of your servant and of your people Israel, when they pray toward this place. (vv. 28–30a)

The house Solomon had built was God's idea. He had promised, "My name shall be there" (see 2 Samuel 7:13). God promised to make himself accessible by means of this house. It would be the place of his name.

This is a little difficult to grasp, but it is very important. Here is the fundamental difference between religion and what the Bible is about. Religion may be defined as human attempts to relate to the divine (variously understood). Religion consists of human activities, perhaps rituals in special places at special times by special people. Such religion is futile. The God who really is there cannot be reached by human efforts, thoughts, imaginations, or spirituality. Since humanity was expelled from the presence of the Lord (see Genesis 3:24; 4:16), it has simply not been possible for human beings to find their own way back. We cannot do it. The Bible is about something else altogether—namely, what *God* has done to make himself accessible.

The critical point is that God is *only* accessible when, where, and how he has made that possible. Every human attempt to reach God in *other* ways (that is, every religion) is a delusion.

This is the importance of God's "name." God made himself accessible to the people of Israel by giving them his name (Exodus 3:13–15; 6:2, 3). This made it possible for them to "call upon the name of the LORD" (Genesis 4:26; 12:8; 13:4; 21:33; 26:25; 1 Kings 18:24; Psalm 116:4; Joel 2:32; Zephaniah 3:9; Acts 2:21; Romans 10:13; 1 Corinthians 1:2).

The house Solomon had built was the *place* God chose for his name (see Deuteronomy 12:5, 11, 21; 14:23, 24; 16:2, 6, 11; 26:2; Nehemiah 1:9). Strange as this sounds, it meant that it was not for the people to choose how, where, and when they would approach God. Since God chose to set his "name" in this place, the people would call on the Lord's name by praying "toward this place."

Notice that Solomon called himself "your servant," just as he had called David "your servant" in verse 24. His prayer was that God would listen to *this* prayer of the promised son of David *and* the prayers of "your people Israel, when they pray toward this place."

Tragically the people of Israel later came to value the "temple" *itself*, thinking that *the building* gave them security (see Jeremiah 7:4). It did no such thing (2 Kings 25). However, it remains true that people can only approach God—that is, true praying is only possible—when, where, and how *God* chooses. Here is the great importance of the fact that now no physical building functions like the house that Solomon built (and I stress again that church buildings are nothing of that kind, and it is a serious mistake to think so or to encourage people to have such thoughts). *Jesus* is the new "temple" (John 2:21), the fulfillment of all that the house Solomon built meant.[13] People can approach God today only by coming to Jesus (John 14:6). True praying is only possible when our requests are joined to *his* name. We will return to this shortly.

What God Will Do (v. 30b)

What did Solomon believe would happen when the people "pray toward this place"? He continued: "And listen in heaven your dwelling place, and when you hear, forgive" (v. 30b).

This was not wishful thinking on Solomon's part. He was praying to the incomparable and faithful God about what God had promised. In Hebrew "have regard" (v. 28) and "listen" (v. 30) could be rendered "you *will* have regard" (v. 28), "you *will* listen" (v. 30).[14]

He was confident that God would do two things as the people prayed toward this place.

First, God would listen. He would not "listen" because he was located in the building. He would listen "in heaven your dwelling place," perhaps better translated "in heaven, the place where you are enthroned."[15] This is a wonder of grace. When the people approached God in the way that God had provided—that is, praying *in the name* God had given them—then the true and living God who reigns over all things would listen.

Second, when God heard these prayers of the people he would forgive.[16] We are not told, at this point, what the people might pray about. Whatever it was, what Solomon confidently expected God to do was this: forgive. That was the fundamental answer to all prayers: God will *forgive*.

The gulf between God and human beings is bigger than we might imagine. It is not just that he is infinite and we are finite, he is almighty and we are puny, he is omniscient and we know very little. All that is true, and it makes the possibility of true prayer extraordinary. But more than all that, we are sinners (about which we will hear more shortly) and he is the Holy One. Here Solomon's insight was profound (see 3:12). The most important thing that needed to happen between God and praying people was that God would *forgive*.

Prayer for Those Who Will Pray: Seven Situations (vv. 31–51)

The general prayer in verses 28–30 (that God would hear the prayers of Solomon and the people prayed toward this place and that God would forgive) was now elaborated with seven situations in which such praying might take place.

Situation 1: A Dispute between Neighbors

> If a man sins against his neighbor and is made to take an oath and comes and swears his oath before your altar in this house, then hear in heaven and act and judge your servants, condemning the guilty by bringing his conduct on his own head, and vindicating the righteous by rewarding him according to his righteousness. (vv. 31, 32)

Situation 2: A Defeat by an Enemy

> When your people Israel are defeated before the enemy because they have sinned against you, and if they turn again to you and acknowledge your name and pray and plead with you in this house, then hear in heaven and forgive the sin of your people Israel and bring them again to the land that you gave to their fathers. (vv. 33, 34)

Situation 3: A Drought in the Land

> When heaven is shut up and there is no rain because they have sinned against you, if they pray toward this place and acknowledge your name and turn from their sin, when you afflict them, then hear in heaven and forgive the sin of your servants, your people Israel, when you teach them the good way in which they should walk, and grant rain upon your land, which you have given to your people as an inheritance. (vv. 35, 36)

Situation 4: Other Disasters

> If there is famine in the land, if there is pestilence or blight or mildew or locust or caterpillar, if their enemy besieges them in the land at their gates, whatever plague, whatever sickness there is, whatever prayer, whatever plea is made by any man or by all your people Israel, each knowing the affliction of his own heart and stretching out his hands toward this house, then hear in heaven your dwelling place and forgive and act and render to each whose heart you know, according to all his ways (for you, you only, know the hearts of all the children of mankind), that they may fear you all the days that they live in the land that you gave to our fathers. (vv. 37–40)

Situation 5: A Foreigner

Likewise, when a foreigner, who is not of your people Israel, comes from
a far country for your name's sake (for they shall hear of your great name
and your mighty hand, and of your outstretched arm), when he comes and
prays toward this house, hear in heaven your dwelling place and do according to all for which the foreigner calls to you, in order that all the peoples
of the earth may know your name and fear you, as do your people Israel,
and that they may know that this house that I have built is called by your
name. (vv. 41, 43)

Situation 6: A Battle

If your people go out to battle against their enemy, by whatever way you
shall send them, and they pray to the LORD toward the city that you have
chosen and the house that I have built for your name, then hear in heaven
their prayer and their plea, and maintain their cause. (vv. 44, 45)

Situation 7: Captives in a Foreign Land

If they sin against you—for there is no one who does not sin—and you are
angry with them and give them to an enemy, so that they are carried away
captive to the land of the enemy, far off or near, yet if they turn their heart
in the land to which they have been carried captive, and repent and plead
with you in the land of their captors, saying, "We have sinned and have
acted perversely and wickedly," if they repent with all their heart and with
all their soul in the land of their enemies, who carried them captive, and
pray to you toward their land, which you gave to their fathers, the city that
you have chosen, and the house that I have built for your name, then hear
in heaven your dwelling place their prayer and their plea, and maintain
their cause and forgive your people who have sinned against you, and
all their transgressions that they have committed against you, and grant
them compassion in the sight of those who carried them captive, that they
may have compassion on them (for they are your people, and your heritage, which you brought out of Egypt, from the midst of the iron furnace).
(vv. 46, 51)

What Solomon said about each of these seven situations follows a pattern
consisting of some or all of the following five elements:

(a) The situation
(b) Its cause
(c) The possibility of prayer
(d) What will happen in Heaven
(e) What will happen on earth

Let's look at what Solomon prayed under these headings.

The Situations

Solomon contemplates seven situations. The number itself probably suggests that the list is meant to point to all possible situations.[17]

The situations described range from a small-scale dispute between two neighbors (Situation 1: "If a man sins against his neighbor," v. 31) to a major national disaster (Situation 7: the people are given over to an enemy "so that they are carried away captive to the land of the enemy, far off or near," v. 46).

Situations 2, 3, 4 are crises the people may face ("When your people Israel are defeated before the enemy," v. 33; "When heaven is shut up and there is no rain," v. 35; "If there is famine in the land, if there is pestilence or blight or mildew or locust or caterpillar, if their enemy besieges them in the land at their gates, whatever plague, whatever sickness there is," v. 37).

Situation 5 stands out: "Likewise,[18] when a foreigner, who is not of your people Israel, comes from a far country" (v. 41). This is the one entirely positive situation contemplated, and an important reminder that God's purposes for his people were international in their scope (Genesis 12:3).

Situation 6 is also different in that the people are active players rather than passive recipients of what happens ("If your people go out to battle against their enemy," v. 44).

I like to think that Solomon may have been reflecting on Leviticus 26 and Deuteronomy 28, where most of these situations were anticipated.[19] Perhaps these two chapters had been his Bible reading that morning! After all, the king was supposed to have his own copy of God's Law in a book that he read every day (Deuteronomy 17:18, 19). The content of this prayer suggests that Solomon was doing that.

Furthermore most of the situations he described would actually occur in the years ahead, and we will read about them in the pages of 1 and 2 Kings. The dispute between Ahab and Naboth in 1 Kings 21 will have similarities to the first situation mentioned by Solomon. We will see the people defeated by an enemy (see 1 Kings 11:14, 23–25), drought in the land (1 Kings 17:1), famine (1 Kings 18:2; 2 Kings 4:38), siege (2 Kings 6:24–25), a visit from a foreigner (1 Kings 10:1), battles (1 Kings 20:1–30), and finally exile to foreign lands (2 Kings 17:6; 24:14–16).

Solomon's seven situations in fact point to the entire history of the people of Israel to be recounted in the books of 1 and 2 Kings. Solomon was praying about every situation his people would face.

The Causes behind These Situations

Solomon understood that there was more to the situations he described than the observable circumstances. In different ways the purposes of God would impact the life of the people.

Behind the various difficulties the people would face there was the people's sin. The problem between the two neighbors is described as "sin" by one against the other (v. 31).[20] Situations 2 and 3 are "because they have sinned against you" (vv. 33, 35). The same is implied for Situation 4[21] and is elaborated in connection with the final situation of deportation and exile: "If they sin against you—for there is no human (*adam*) who does not sin—and you are angry with them . . ." (v. 46, AT). Sin is *the* human problem and is a factor in any situation involving people. Sin is immensely serious, because God hates sin: he is angry.[22]

This implies that even the foreigner who comes (v. 41) will be a sinner. However, in this case there is something else. The foreigner comes "because of your name" (v. 41, NIV) , "for they shall hear of your great name and your mighty hand, and of your outstretched arm" (v. 42). The "name" of the Lord (so closely associated with the house Solomon had built) will be heard far and wide, and because of this name foreigners can be expected to come. The news of God's great deeds for his people would reach the ends of the earth (cf. Exodus 9:16; 15:14; Joshua 4:24; 5:1).

The immediate cause behind Situation 6 is different again. The people will go out to battle "by whatever way *you shall send them*" (v. 44). Whatever else may be going on, Solomon contemplated the people going out to battle against an enemy in obedience to God's direction.

Behind the various circumstances in which the people would find themselves in the coming days Solomon saw the hand of God. The circumstances were properly understood in relation to God's purposes.

The Possibility of Prayer

Therefore the critical factor in every situation would be the possibility of prayer.[23]

In Situation 1, the alleged offender was "made to take an oath and comes and swears his oath[24] before your altar *in this house*" (v. 31b). The oath was a form of prayer. An accused person could claim to be innocent by swearing his innocence "by the LORD" (see Exodus 22:10, 11; cf. Leviticus 6:1–7), the assumption being that a guilty person would not dare to do so—or that if he did, the Lord would deal with him.[25]

In the other six cases Solomon also speaks of prayer in or toward "this house":

> . . . if they turn again to you and acknowledge your name and pray and plead with you *in this house* . . . (v. 33)

> . . . if they pray *toward this place* and acknowledge your name and turn from their sin, when you afflict them . . . (v. 35)

> . . . whatever prayer, whatever plea is made by any man or by all your people Israel, each knowing the affliction of his own heart and stretching out his hands *toward this house* . . . (v. 38)

> . . . when he comes and prays *toward this house* . . . (v. 42)

> . . . and they pray to the LORD toward the city that you have chosen and *the house that I have built for your name* . . . (v. 44)

> . . . yet if they turn their heart in the land to which they have been carried captive, and repent and plead with you in the land of their captors, saying, "We have sinned and have acted perversely and wickedly," if they repent with all their heart and with all their soul in the land of their enemies, who carried them captive, and pray to you toward their land, which you gave to their fathers, the city that you have chosen, and *the house that I have built for your name* . . . (vv. 47, 48)

In the situations where sin is specifically in view, such praying would involve repentance ("turn again to you," v. 33; "turn from their sin," v. 35). This is elaborated in the climactic final situation. Repentance will involve acknowledging, "We have sinned and have acted perversely and wickedly" (v. 47). Since "there is no one who does not sin" (v. 46), perhaps we should understand that repentance would be at least implicit in all the contemplated prayers.

The specific content of these prayers would vary, but they all had this in common: they were prayed in or toward "this house" or "this place" (vv. 31, 33, 35, 38, 42, 44, 48), which Solomon had "built for your name" (vv. 44, 48). In other words, this praying was *calling on the name of the Lord* where God had promised his name would be.

Of course, praying had been a reality in the life of God's people before Solomon built this house. Clearly God did not need this house in order for praying to be possible. However, this is what the house for God's name represented: the possibility of prayer. God's promise that his name would be there was an invitation to the people to pray in all the circumstances in which they would find themselves.

What Will Happen in Heaven?

The astonishing thing about such praying is that God will "hear in heaven" (vv. 32, 34, 36, 39, 43, 45, 49).[26]

Here is the astonishing thing about true prayer. We should understand that this is what was involved in God's promise, "My name shall be there" (v. 29). Access to God's name on earth meant access to God's ear in Heaven. God, whom Heaven and the highest heavens cannot contain, will hear prayers prayed in his name.

More than that, God will respond to these prayers in ways that will change things here on earth.

What Will Happen on Earth?

In the case of the dispute between neighbors, he will "act and judge your servants, condemning the guilty by bringing his conduct on his own head, and vindicating the righteous by rewarding him according to his righteousness" (v. 32). "The righteous" is the one who is in the right in the particular dispute. The question of how and when God's judgment and vindication would be implemented is not explained. That was God's business.[27]

This first case shows that the access to God provided by the house for his name was a serious matter. To approach God is to come before the just Judge. He will condemn the guilty and vindicate the innocent (see Isaiah 50:8, 9). Do you really want access to this God?

A Christian believer knows God's vindication. The New Testament term is "justification."[28] This is strange because we know that we are sinners. The wonder and mystery of the gospel is that God, the just Judge, justifies (vindicates) the one who has faith in Jesus. We *are* righteous, but only because we are *forgiven*.[29]

In the cases of various disasters that had come because of the people's sin, he will "forgive" (vv. 34, 36, 39, 50). This is huge. It would mean that in each case the cause of the disaster was dealt with. In one case God would "bring them again to the land that you gave to their fathers" (v. 34). In another he will "grant rain upon your land, which you have given to your people as an inheritance" (v. 36). In yet another he will "act and render to each whose heart you know, according to all his ways (for you, you only, know the hearts of all the children of mankind)" (v. 39).[30] For the visiting foreigner, God will "do according to all for which the foreigner calls to you" (v. 43). For those going to battle he will "maintain their cause" (v. 45). "Cause" here is a word (*mishpat*) elsewhere rendered "justice." The idea is that God would act to put things "right" for his people.[31] This is the expectation even when the people are carried away as captives to foreign lands. God will "maintain their cause . . . and grant them compassion in the sight of those who carried them captive, that they may have compassion on them (for they are your people, and your heritage, which you brought out of Egypt, from the midst of the iron furnace)" (vv. 49–51).

In three cases Solomon mentions the effect of God hearing and answering his people's prayers beyond the immediate situations. By the experience of forgiveness and answered prayers God will "teach them the good way in which they should walk" (v. 36). God will *teach* them the right way to live by hearing their prayers, forgiving them, and sending rain. In that experience the people are to *learn* the goodness of God and therefore the goodness of walking in his ways.

Likewise the outcome of God's forgiveness and action on behalf of the praying people will be "that they may fear you all the days that they live in the land that you gave to our fathers" (v. 40). Praise God for this. The way he teaches us to fear him is by forgiveness (see Psalm 130:4; Jeremiah 33:8, 9; Romans 2:4).

Indeed, the experience of the foreigner has this goal: "that all the peoples of the earth may know your name and fear you, as do your people Israel, and that they may know that this house that I have built is called by your name" (v. 43). God's promise, as it was first heard by Abraham, clearly stated that the "blessing" promised to the great nation would "be a blessing" and extend to "all the families of the earth" (Genesis 12:1–3). Solomon would see the fulfillment of this promise in the foreigners who would come and pray toward this house. In the story of God's faithfulness to his promise to Abraham a small number of foreigners in Old Testament times were touched by God's blessing of the people of Israel (examples include Rahab in Joshua 2; 6:22–25, perhaps the Gibeonites in Joshua 9, also Ruth in Ruth 1:16, 17, and Ittai in 2 Samuel 15:19–22). God's Law certainly anticipated that foreigners would join the community of Israel (see Exodus 12:48, 49; Numbers 9:14; 15:14–16). Solomon now saw that the house he had built for the name of the Lord would draw people from the nations.

In due course the prophets would speak of a coming day when what Solomon contemplated would happen on a large scale (Isaiah 2:2, 3), so that the

Lord's house "shall be called a house of prayer for all people" (Isaiah 56:7). This was remembered and reaffirmed by Jesus (Mark 11:17).

Remarkably the prayers of which Solomon spoke and God's gracious answers were intended to advance God's purpose for his people and for the whole world.

The Possibility of Prayer: God's Purpose (vv. 52, 53)

Solomon's prayer concluded by summing up what he was asking:

> Let your eyes be open to the plea of your servant[32] and to the plea of your people Israel, giving ear to them whenever they call to you. For you separated them from among all the peoples of the earth to be your heritage, as you declared through Moses your servant, when you brought our fathers out of Egypt, O Lord God.[33] (vv. 52, 53)

Hear this prayer of mine, and hear the prayers of your people Israel. That is what he had been asking. That is what the house he had built represented— God's people praying and God in Heaven hearing their prayers and acting. That is what Israel had been chosen for.

What does King Solomon's prayer teach Christian people today?

The house Solomon built was the place where God had promised his "name" would be. That house was eventually destroyed (2 Kings 25:9), and Jesus announced the destruction of its replacement (Matthew 24:2). The house of which God said, "My name shall be there" is not now a physical building. Indeed Jesus said, "Destroy this temple, and in three days I will raise it up" (John 2:19). John adds:

> But he was speaking about the temple of his body. When therefore he was raised from the dead, his disciples remembered that he had said this, and they believed the Scripture and the word that Jesus had spoken. (John 2:21, 22)

We need to appreciate that everything the house built by Solomon represented is now fulfilled in Jesus Christ, the new temple.[34] Jesus makes praying possible.[35] The *name* by which we may pray, confident that God will hear, forgive, and act, is the name of Jesus.

On the night before his death Jesus said:

> Whatever you *ask in my name*, this I will do, that the Father may be glorified in the Son. If you *ask me anything in my name*, I will do it. (John 14:13, 14)

> You did not choose me, but I chose you and appointed you that you should go and bear fruit and that your fruit should abide, so that *whatever you ask the Father in my name*, he may give it to you. (John 15:16)

> Truly, truly, I say to you, *whatever you ask of the Father in my name*, he will give it to you. Until now you have asked nothing in my name. Ask, and you will receive, that your joy may be full. (John 16:23, 24)

This is what true praying now is: *asking in the name of Jesus Christ*. This is more than a form of words added to the end of a prayer (*In Jesus' name. Amen*). We come to the Father by coming, not now to the house Solomon built for God's name, but to Jesus (see John 10:7, 9; 14:6; Romans 5:2; Ephesians 2:18; 3:11, 12). We call on the name of the Lord by calling on Jesus (Acts 2:21; Romans 10:13; 1 Corinthians 1:2; Acts 9:21). We receive forgiveness of sins through his name (Acts 10:43; cf. Luke 24:47). We "acknowledge his name" (Hebrews 13:15), "believe in his name" (John 1:12; 3:18; 1 John 3:23; 5:13), are hated, persecuted, dishonored, and insulted on account of his name (Matthew 10:22; 24:9; John 15:21; Acts 5:41; 9:16; 1 Peter 4:14), and yet hold fast to his name (Revelation 2:13), refusing to deny his name (Revelation 3:8). The name of Jesus is now the name above every name (Ephesians 1:21; Philippians 2:9–11).

The remarkable promises we hear from Jesus concerning asking in his name are the fulfillment of what Solomon prayed for. The possibility of this kind of praying is astonishing. We are talking about requests being uttered by mere humans like us, being heard by Almighty God,[36] and being granted.[37] How can that be? Jesus died on the day after he spoke these promises in order to make this astonishing thing possible.

18

The Joy of God's Blessing

1 KINGS 8:54–66

*Blessed be the God and Father of our
Lord Jesus Christ, who has blessed us in Christ
with every spiritual blessing in the heavenly places . . .*

EPHESIANS 1:3

THE WORD THAT SUMS UP God's purpose for the world he has made and for the people he has created is "blessing." On the fifth day in Genesis 1 "God *blessed*" the creatures he had made (Genesis 1:22). On Day Six "God *blessed*" the humans he had created (Genesis 1:28; 5:2). Finally "God *blessed* the seventh day" on which he rested after his work of creation was complete (Genesis 2:3).

Few people would chose the word "blessing" to sum up the state of the world today. Indeed few would choose that word to sum up their own lives. Of course, some of us are aware that we have been very fortunate in life. We have been spared much of the suffering that others endure; we have enjoyed above average prosperity, health, and happiness. We might for these reasons say that we have been "blessed." That is true, but not the whole truth. These "blessings" are fragile, unreliable, and temporary. For all the privileges some of us may enjoy, none of us escape frustration, conflict, sadness, sickness, pain, grief, fear, anxiety. The good things in life are fleeting. None of it lasts. In the end death destroys them all.

The Bible teaches us that this situation has been brought about by human defiance of God. Our disobedience has brought the opposite of blessing.

Genesis 3 tells the story. "Cursed" is the terrible word that now accurately sums up the state of the world (see Genesis 3:14, 17; also 4:11; 5:29; 8:21; 9:25). Much of our experience of life corresponds to that dreadful word, reminding us that we live with the consequences of humanity's rejection of God.

The heart of the Bible's astonishing message is that God has promised that "cursed" will not be the last word. He is committed to his purpose of "blessing." This was made clear in the promise God made to Abram (later called Abraham):

> Now the LORD said to Abram, "Go from your country and your kindred and your father's house to the land that I will show you. And I will make of you a great nation, and I will *bless* you and make your name great, so that you will be a *blessing*. I will *bless* those who bless you, and him who dishonors you I will curse, and in you all the families of the earth shall be *blessed*." (Genesis 12:1–3)

The extraordinary story from this point in the book of Genesis to the end of the book of 2 Kings (repeated more briefly, with particular emphases, in 1 Chronicles to Nehemiah) recounts the history of God's faithfulness to this promise. God gave Abraham's descendants the land mentioned in the promise. He made them a great nation. He blessed them. In small but significant ways they were a blessing to people from other nations (although this fell far short of "all the families of the earth").

In 1 Kings 8 we have come to the high point of that story.[1] Here we see God's promised "blessing" wonderfully experienced by God's people. However, it is obvious that this is not the end point of the Bible's story. That is because, as we will see in due course, the wonders of 1 Kings 8 did not last. The experiences of 1 Kings 8 were not the final and complete fulfillment of God's purpose. They were a shadow of the good things to come (cf. Colossians 2:17; Hebrews 10:1).

As such 1 Kings 8 holds important lessons for us. As God's purpose for the world he has made was foreshadowed in the experience of the people of Israel, we see something of what "blessing" means. It is bigger, better, and more beautiful than the unreliable prosperity, short-lived health, and fleeting happiness many of us seek. We will be helped to see how little those things can really give us, how transitory they actually are, and the downside each certainly brings. As we listen to the final section of 1 Kings 8, let us consider what God's promised blessing is really like as we study verses 54–61 and how very good it is in verses 62–66.

The Blessing (vv. 54–61)

In verses 54–61 King Solomon, having concluded his great prayer about the possibility of praying (8:22–53), addressed the assembled people.[2]

The King Who Blessed Them (vv. 54, 55)

Before we hear what he said, look again at the king himself (as we did at 8:22):

> Now as Solomon finished offering all this prayer and plea to the LORD, he arose from before the altar of the LORD, where he had knelt with hands outstretched toward heaven. And he stood and blessed all the assembly of Israel with a loud voice, saying . . . (vv. 54, 55)

The king had begun his prayer *standing* before the altar of the Lord in the presence of all the assembly of Israel (8:22). At some point he had fallen to his knees, still "with hands outstretched toward heaven." We should once again appreciate the brilliance of this. The people of Israel had a king who knew his place (he humbled himself before the King whom Heaven and the highest heavens cannot contain, 8:27), and yet he had brought his "prayer and plea" to the Lord for his people.

King Solomon here foreshadows what the Lord Jesus Christ is for us. He humbled himself (Matthew 21:5; Philippians 2:8). He is the mediator between God and humanity (1 Timothy 2:5). He intercedes for us with the Father (1 John 2:1; Romans 8:34; Hebrews 7:25). How brilliant is that!

King Solomon stood before "all the assembly of Israel" and "blessed" them. The king who prayed for them *blessed* them. Indeed Solomon's great prayer is bracketed by similar references to how he "blessed all the assembly of Israel" (see 8:14). This great gathering (see 8:1) represented the whole people (see also 8:22). They had a king who "blessed" them. Indeed, we could say that having this king was central to the blessing that was theirs.

Again King Solomon foreshadowed our Lord Jesus Christ. King Jesus brings the blessing promised to Abraham for the nations (Galatians 3:14). Central to this blessing is having Jesus as our King.

King Solomon blessed them "with a loud voice" (or, "out loud"). Solomon's prayer (8:23–53) had probably been spoken more quietly. He now addressed the people audibly. Notice that he *blessed* them by *speaking* to them. The blessing came by what he said.

The God Who Had Blessed Them (v. 56)

What he said began with God:

> Blessed be the LORD who has given rest to his people Israel, according to all
> that he promised. Not one word has failed of all his good promise, which
> he spoke by Moses his servant. (v. 56)

The people needed to understand that the blessing that was theirs had come from
God. King Solomon himself was God's gift to them. This idea has been implied
or stated in various ways through the story so far (see 1:37, 47, 48; 2:4, 12, 15,
24, 33, 45, 46; 3:5–7, 12–14, 28; 4:29; 5:4, 5, 7, 12; 6:12, 13; 8:19, 20, 24).

Verses 54–56 echo 8:14, 15 (also 8:23, 24). Before and after his prayer
for the people (8:22–53) King Solomon "blessed" them, beginning by blessing (that is, praising) God. In 8:15 (and 8:24) he had praised the Lord for
fulfilling with his hand what he had spoken with his mouth to *David*. Now he
praised the Lord for fulfilling what he had said "by his servant *Moses*." What
God said to David (particularly in 2 Samuel 7) and what he had said by Moses
(Solomon probably had Deuteronomy 12 and perhaps Leviticus 26 and Deuteronomy 28 in mind) were different in the details, but essentially the same. It
was the promise that had first been made to Abraham. Moses elaborated the
promised blessing. God's word to David focused on the promised king. But
the stories of Moses and David are about the same promise: the blessing God
had promised Abraham.[3]

What had been promised, and had now been given, is summed up in the
word "rest" (see 5:4).[4] This had been a key idea in God's promise. God himself
had "rested" at the completion of his work of creation (Genesis 2:1–3), suggesting the untroubled enjoyment of the fruit of his work. The people of Israel
had been given a weekly day of "rest" ("Sabbath" means "rest") as a reminder
of God's purpose in creation and an invitation to share in God's "rest" (see
Exodus 20:8–11; Deuteronomy 5:14).[5] The land that God promised them was
to be a place of "rest" (see Exodus 33:14; Deuteronomy 3:20; 12:9, 10; 25:19;
Joshua 1:13, 15; cf. Psalm 95:11). At various points in the history of Israel's
life in the land they had experienced a taste of this "rest" (Joshua 21:44; 22:4;
23:1; 2 Samuel 7:1). And yet God's word to David made clear that the promised rest still lay in the future (2 Samuel 7:11). That is why David was not the
one to build the house for the Lord's name (2 Samuel 7:13).

Solomon understood that the Lord had now given the long-promised rest
to his people. That is why he was able to build the house his father had not
been permitted to build. The people were free from external threat and secure

in the land God had given them, more solidly so than ever before. Centuries earlier Joshua had been deeply conscious that God had been completely and utterly faithful to his word. Not one word had "failed [literally, fallen]" of all his good words (see Joshua 23:14; cf. 21:45). How much more was this the case on the day King Solomon blessed all the assembly of Israel.

Sadly, in just a few more pages we will discover that this "rest" was tragically short-lived. After 1 Kings 8 we will hear no more of "rest" in the books of Kings. This is the high point. The people will eventually lose their resting place (that is, the land; see Lamentations 1:3; cf. Deuteronomy 28:65). In the years to come, as the prophets (particularly Isaiah) reaffirm God's commitment to his purpose for the world, "rest" will become a theme of God's promise once again (see Isaiah 11:10; 14:3; 28:12; 32:18).

The promise points to our Lord Jesus, who gives "rest" to all who come to him (Matthew 11:28, 29). He is Lord of the Sabbath rest (Matthew 12:8). This is the "rest" foreshadowed in Israel's experiences (see Hebrews 4:8–11) and experienced by those who come to Jesus Christ today, and it is the blessing enjoyed for eternity by those who die in the Lord (Revelation 14:13). As we hear King Solomon bless the people by telling them that God had given them rest, turn your mind and heart to the rest that God has given you in Jesus.

The Blessing (vv. 57–61)

Solomon then elaborated five aspects of the blessing of God-given rest under their God-given king.

He Will Be with Them (v. 57)

First, God himself will be "with them":[6]

> The LORD our God be with us, as he was with our fathers. May he not leave us or forsake us . . . (v. 57)

The Lord God had certainly been "with" Solomon's father, David (1 Samuel 16:18; 17:37; 18:12, 14, 28; 20:13; 2 Samuel 5:10; 7:3, 9; cf. Psalm 27:9, 10). This, however, had been the culmination of a long history of God being "with" his people ("our fathers," cf. 8:21).

God's being "with" his people had meant God's active involvement in bringing about what he had promised *for* his people. On the verge of entering the promised land, God had said to Joshua, "Just as I was *with* Moses, so I will be *with* you. I will not leave you or forsake you" (Joshua 1:5). The Lord was "with" them *to give them what he had promised* (Joshua 1:13, 15).

This blessing (God *with* his people) came to its fullest expression in Old Testament times in the house Solomon had built in Jerusalem (see 6:13; Psalm 46, especially vv. 7, 11). Astonishingly, in due course the people would forsake the Lord (9:9; 11:33), and the house Solomon had built would be destroyed. But *God with his people* would become a theme of promise again (Isaiah 7:14; Amos 5:14).

The long and wonderful history of God "with" his people prepared the way for its full expression in Jesus Christ, in whom "all the fullness of God was pleased to dwell" and in whom "the whole fullness of deity dwells bodily" (Colossians 1:19; 2:9). He was given the name Immanuel ("God *with* us," Matthew 1:23; Isaiah 7:14) and promised his disciples, "I am *with* you always, to the end of the age" (Matthew 28:20). This is now the experience of Christian believers as Jesus is "with" us by his Spirit (John 14:16, 17, 23), and we look forward to the day when we will hear:

> Behold, the dwelling place of God is *with* man. He will dwell *with* them, and they will be his people, and God himself will be *with* them as their God. He will wipe away every tear from their eyes, and death shall be no more, neither shall there be mourning, nor crying, nor pain anymore, for the former things have passed away. (Revelation 21:3, 4)

The God who has promised blessing is "with" us: he will do it.

He Will Incline Their Hearts (v. 58)

Second, God's presence with his people will change their hearts:

> . . . that he may incline our hearts to him, to walk in all his ways and to keep his commandments, his statutes, and his rules, which he commanded our fathers. (v. 58)

The human heart (since the Fall) is not inclined to obey God. The opposite is true. Furthermore the human heart is not inclined, by itself, to change. Only God can do that, and it is his purpose to do so. King Solomon looked forward to his heart and the hearts of his people being changed so that they would walk in God's ways. His words here show that the change had already taken place in his heart. This is what his father had charged him to do (2:3).

The tragedy of King Solomon's story is that his heart changed back. It was turned away from the Lord to other gods (see 11:2, 4, 9[7]). It would take a greater work still than what God had done in Solomon's day to permanently change human hearts (see Jeremiah 31:33; Ezekiel 11:19, 20; 36:26, 27). This heart change has been accomplished by Jesus Christ and the work of his Spirit (see Acts 15:9; Romans 2:29; 5:5; 6:17; 2 Corinthians 4:6; Galatians 4:6; Ephesians 1:18; 3:17; Colossians 3:15; 1 Thessalonians 3:13; 1 Timothy 1:5; Hebrews 4:12; 8:10; 10:16; 13:9; 1 Peter 1:22). Now *that's* a blessing, isn't it?

He Will Hear the Prayer of Their King and Make Everything Right (v. 59)

Third, God will hear the prayer of his king for his people:

> Let these words of mine, with which I have pleaded before the LORD, be near to the LORD our God day and night, and may he maintain the cause of his servant and the cause of his people Israel, as each day requires[8] . . . (v. 59)

Solomon's words that he pleaded before the Lord were the prayer we heard in 8:23–53. This prayer, you will recall, was essentially that the Lord would hear the prayers of the people in various circumstances, forgive them, and act to meet their need. This is what Solomon here calls "the cause of his servant [that is, Solomon] and the cause of his people Israel." As we saw in in 8:45, "maintain the cause" [literally, "do justice") means to put things right. Remember that God had given Solomon wisdom "to do justice" (3:28).

Here is yet another way of describing God's promised blessing: everything put right. Only God could do that, and Solomon prayed that he would. The full answer to his prayer has now come in the gospel about Jesus, which is "the power of God for salvation" in which "the righteousness of God is revealed" (Romans 1:16, 17). By this gospel God puts people right ("justifies" them) as they come to faith in Jesus Christ (see, above all, Romans 3:21–26).

He Will Bless the Whole World (v. 60)

Fourth, the whole world will know the truth:

> . . . that all the peoples of the earth may know that the LORD is God; there is no other. (v. 60)

This is what Solomon had prayed for in 8:41–43. There it had been God answering the prayer of a foreigner so that "all the peoples of the earth may know your name and fear you" (8:43). Here God's vindication of his people will result in all people knowing who God is and that there is none like him (cf. 8:23; 1 Samuel 2:2).

In this way the blessing of God's people will impact all the families of the earth, just as God had promised Abraham. There will be those for whom the realization "that the LORD is God" will be devastating (see 18:24, 39, 40). But there will also be those who experience the blessing of gladly bowing before the true and living God (see 10:9, 24).

The international impact of King Solomon's reign was astonishing,[9] as we will see particularly in 1 Kings 10. It was a shadow of the worldwide impact of King Jesus' reign (see Matthew 24:14; 28:18–20; Luke 24:47; Acts 1:8; 13:47; Romans 1:5; Philippians 2:9–11; Colossians 1:23).

They Will Be His People (v. 61)

Fifth, the blessing Solomon outlined (God with them, inclining their hearts to walk in his ways, hearing their prayers and vindicating them, so that the whole world will know who is God) will be enjoyed as the people receive God's gracious kindness by actually walking in his ways:

> Let your heart[10] therefore be wholly true to the LORD our God, walking in his statutes and keeping his commandments, as at this day. (v. 61)

This is an exhortation to the people to receive the blessing that has been spoken to them. Their hearts are to be "wholly true to the LORD." The idea is an undivided heart, entirely at peace with God.[11] This would be expressed in obedience.

"As at this day" is surprising but indicates that Solomon understood that the blessing he had described in verses 57–60 had been received by the people that very day. Their king's words would put their hearts at peace with the Lord and incline them to walk in his ways, as we will see spectacularly in verses 62–66.

But in fact it did not last. We will soon read of King Solomon himself, "his heart was *not* wholly true to the LORD his God" (11:4).[12] What had happened on this day was wonderful, but it was only a shadow of the greater work of God that was needed to establish his purpose of blessing.

The Joy (vv. 62–66)

However, here in 1 Kings 8 we must appreciate the goodness of God's blessing. It may turn out to have been just a shadow of the greater things to come, but (if I may mix the metaphor) the shadow itself was brilliant.

King Solomon had finished speaking. It was time for king and people to respond to God's blessing. They offered an astonishing number of sacrifices, they held a great feast, and they rejoiced at God's goodness to them.

The Sacrifices They Offered (vv. 62–64)

> Then the king, and all Israel with him, offered sacrifice before the LORD. Solomon offered as peace offerings to the LORD 22,000 oxen and 120,000 sheep. So the king and all the people of Israel dedicated the house of the LORD. The same day the king consecrated the middle of the court that was before the house of the LORD, for there he offered the burnt offering and the grain offering and the fat pieces of the peace offerings, because the bronze altar that was before the LORD was too small to receive the burnt offering and the grain offering and the fat pieces of the peace offerings. (vv. 62–64)

Here we see the king and his people together ("the king, and all Israel with him"). This king unified his people in their response to God's goodness.

The sacrifices they offered were huge in number.[13] This was a continuation of their activities earlier in the day (8:5). By their response to God's blessing, the king and all the people "dedicated" the house of the Lord. The Hebrew word has a basic sense of "use for the first time." The translation could be: "So the king and all the people of Israel put the house of the LORD into use."[14]

The sacrifices were so numerous that the king "consecrated"[15] an area in the middle of the courtyard in front of the house of the Lord, because the bronze altar before which Solomon had prayed (8:22, 54) was not big enough for the number of sacrifices being offered.

As we watch their wholehearted Old Testament response to God's blessing, we would do well to hear the New Testament call:

> I appeal to you therefore, brothers, by the mercies of God, to present your bodies as a living sacrifice, holy and acceptable to God, which is your spiritual worship. (Romans 12:1)

Our response to the mercies of God no longer takes the form of animal sacrifices. Rather how we live in our bodies, doing "what is good and acceptable and perfect" (Romans 12:2), is our "living sacrifice," our "spiritual worship."

The Feast They Held (v. 65)

> So Solomon held the feast at that time, and all Israel with him, a great assembly, from Lebo-hamath to the Brook of Egypt, before the LORD our God, seven days and seven days, fourteen days. (v. 65, ESV margin[16])

"The feast" was the Feast of Booths (or Tabernacles) mentioned in 8:2 (see our discussion there). The emphasis is on the whole nation participating. Lebo-hamath[17] and the Brook of Egypt[18] represented the northernmost and southernmost extent of the land promised by God and now ruled by King Solomon (Numbers 13:21; 34:5, 8; Joshua 13:5; 15:4, 47; Judges 3:3; 2 Kings 14:25; 1 Chronicles 13:5; Isaiah 27:12; Ezekiel 47:15, 19, 20; 48:1, 28; Amos 6:14).[19]

The Hebrew text indicates two full weeks of feasting. It probably means that on this occasion the feast of the seventh month (8:2) took fourteen days, seven for the sacrifices just mentioned and seven for the Feast of Booths proper. This was a major celebration! It may appropriately turn our thoughts to the great feast to which we have been invited by the gospel of Jesus Christ (Revelation 19:9; cf. Matthew 22:1–14).

The Joy of Their Hearts (v. 66)

> On the eighth day he sent the people away, and they blessed the king and went to their homes[20] joyful and glad of heart for all the goodness that the LORD had shown to David his servant and to Israel his people. (v. 66)

The "eighth day" would be the day after the second seven days, that is, the day after the Feast of Booths itself (see Numbers 29:35). The king dismissed the people. As the king had "blessed" the people, the people now "blessed" the king. Perhaps they sang something like Psalm 20 or 61:6, 7. There was a lot of "blessing" going on that day!

The joy of the people was palpable. They had been touched by the goodness of God. What promises he had made to David! What goodness he had shown in doing what he had promised.

Try to sense the joy and gladness of the people. What inexpressible joy belongs to those who know that the experience of 1 Kings 8 is just a shadow of the goodness of God that we now know (see Titus 3:4–7; 1 Peter 1:8, 9).

> Blessed be the God and Father of our Lord Jesus Christ! According to his great mercy, he has caused us to be born again to a living hope through the resurrection of Jesus Christ from the dead, to an inheritance that is imperishable, undefiled, and unfading, kept in heaven for you, who by God's power are being guarded through faith for a salvation ready to be revealed in the last time. (1 Peter 1:3–5)

Part 4

NOT YET

1 Kings 9—12

19

What Could Possibly Go Wrong?

1 KINGS 9:1-9

CHRISTIAN ASSURANCE IS A WONDERFUL THING. It is confidence in Jesus Christ as Savior and therefore peace beyond words. It is security in God's complete forgiveness and therefore a clean and yet humble conscience. It is a firm conviction about God's promises and therefore an ultimate optimism. It is being unafraid before God's final judgment and therefore being certain about Heaven.

What could possibly go wrong?

In the reign of King Solomon there were reasons for assurance like that. Under this king the people were at last at peace, just as God had promised long ago (8:24). The house Solomon had built "for the name of the LORD" (5:5) represented the blessing of God that this people could at last enjoy (8:14, 55). It was a time when the people knew that God had done just as he had promised (8:56). They rejoiced in God's kindness and goodness toward them (8:66).

What could possibly go wrong?

With that question in mind, let us return to those exhilarating days and see what happened next.

Solomon's Work Completed (v. 1)

> As soon as[1] Solomon had finished building the house of the LORD and the king's house and all that Solomon desired to build [do] . . . (v. 1)

There is an echo here of Genesis 2:1: "God *finished* his work that he had *done.*" God's work was the creation of the heavens and the earth and all their

273

host. Solomon's work was the building of the house of the Lord, the king's house, and the rest of his building work.

This work is described as "all that Solomon desired to build [do]." The original is a little richer—literally, "all the desire of Solomon which he delighted to do." "Desire" is a strong word that can describe a man's longing for a woman (Genesis 34:8; Deuteronomy 21:11), God's love for his people (Deuteronomy 7:7; 10:15), or human love for God (Psalm 91:14).[2] "Delighted" is a much more common word (Hebrew, *khapats*) with a similar range of meaning. Solomon's desire and delight was to do God's will (see 3:9; cf. Psalm 40:8; Hebrews 10:7, 9).[3] The sense is that the building work was at the heart of King Solomon's reign. The buildings represented the kingdom established (2:12, 24, 45, 46), at peace (2:33; 4:24; 5:12), at rest (5:4; 8:56), and blessed (8:14, 15), as promised (2 Samuel 7:10–12).

It was more than the house of the Lord.[4] Certainly that building was central and most important of all. However, the other buildings that have been described in the preceding chapters are included here, particularly the house of the king. This was not just about religion.[5] It was about the promised kingdom (see our discussion of 7:1).

At the completion of creation in Genesis 2:1–3 and the blessing of the seventh day, we could well ask, what could possibly go wrong? The situation at the completion of King Solomon's work and his blessing of the people (8:55) was similar: What could possibly go wrong?

The Lord Appeared (Again) (v. 2)

God was in this. Just as the Lord had appeared to Solomon at the beginning of his reign (3:5–14), so now that his fundamental work was done he appeared again: ". . . the LORD appeared to Solomon a second time, as he had appeared to him at Gibeon" (v. 2).

The reference to the earlier appearance of the Lord at Gibeon encourages us to see these two appearances as connected. They stand in the record like bookends enclosing the account of Solomon's early reign. The first appearance had been about God's gift of wisdom to Solomon. Solomon's wisdom has been displayed in various ways, but supremely in his building work. Just as God's wisdom shaped creation (Psalm 104:24; Proverbs 3:19), the wisdom of God was in Solomon (3:28) as he built the house of the Lord, the king's house, and the rest.

So what could possibly go wrong?

As at Gibeon earlier what Solomon *saw* when the Lord "appeared" is of no interest to the writer. What mattered was what Solomon *heard*. What he heard falls into two parts. In verses 3–5 the Lord spoke to Solomon himself. In verses 6–9 the Lord's words have a wider reference to all the people of Israel.[6]

The Lord's Assuring Word to Solomon (vv. 3–5)

What Solomon heard that day confirmed just how good things were.

The Lord Heard (v. 3a)

First, "the Lord said to him, 'I have heard your prayer and your plea, which you have made before me'" (v. 3a).

Do not miss the wonder of this. Solomon understood that it was no small thing to ask the God whom Heaven and the highest heavens cannot contain (8:27) to hear the prayer and plea of a man like him. And yet that is what he dared to ask for (8:28). He dared because of God's kindness and faithfulness toward this son of David and the promise God had spoken to David (8:23–26).

Now we learn unambiguously that King Solomon was a king whose prayer and plea was heard by the Lord his God!

The Lord Answered (v. 3b)

Second, the Lord God did not only hear King Solomon's plea, he granted it: "I have consecrated this house that you have built, by putting my name there forever. My eyes and my heart will be there for all time" (v. 3b).

Solomon's prayer and plea had been that God would hear prayers uttered in or toward the house he had built, not only by King Solomon himself, but by the people (including the visiting foreigner) in various situations that they would face—that the Lord would hear, forgive, and put things right (see 8:31–53).

The Lord's answer was that he had "consecrated" the house, that is, he had made it "holy." He had done this "by putting my name there forever." That is the most important thing about the house Solomon had built. Its architecture and lavish decoration may have been impressive, but these were merely trappings. The astonishing wonder was that God had put his name there permanently.

We have discussed this strange-to-our-ears idea before (see our discussion of 8:20 and 8:29). This is the confirmation by God himself that there people would be able to call on the name of the Lord. God had made himself accessible, just as King Solomon had prayed.

God would take such prayers with utmost seriousness, just as King Solomon had prayed. What a promise that was! The house Solomon had built represented God's promise to never miss a word of any prayer brought in his name and to take every such prayer to heart: "My eyes and my heart[7] will be there for all time" (cf. 8:29).

"Forever" and "for all time" (literally "all the days") underlines the sense of fulfillment. Such permanence was an aspect of the promise (2 Samuel 7:13, 16; see 1 Kings 2:45).

What could possibly go wrong?

The Lord Required (v. 4)

Third, God required King Solomon to continue as he had begun: "And as for you, if you will walk before me, as David your father walked, with integrity of heart and uprightness, doing according to all that I have commanded you, and keeping my statutes and my rules . . ." (v. 4).

Of course, the Lord required his king to be obedient. King David had understood that (2:2–4). The Lord himself has said as much at his earlier appearance at Gibeon (3:14).

What we have seen of King Solomon up to this point in his story seems to fulfill the Lord's requirement here admirably. He understood about walking "before the Lord" (3:6; 8:23, 25). He looked to the example of his father David's integrity and uprightness (3:3, 6).[8] He had prayed for the very thing God here required (8:58).

What could possibly go wrong?

Careful readers may remember that Solomon had acknowledged "there is no one who does not sin" (8:46). But we also recall that God can "put away" sin, as he did for David (2 Samuel 12:13). Solomon's prayer had been that God would "forgive" (8:30, 34, 36, 50). If that happens, then what could possibly go wrong?

The Lord Promised (v. 5)

Fourth, the Lord confirmed the promise that stood behind everything that had happened to this point in the book of 1 Kings: ". . . then I will establish your royal throne [or, the throne of your kingdom] over Israel forever, as I promised David your father, saying, 'You shall not lack a man on the throne of Israel'" (v. 5).

The connection between God's requirement (in a word, obedience) and God's promise (in a word, blessing) is fundamental. In the garden of Eden God's blessing ("You may surely eat of every tree of the garden," Genesis 2:16) was closely connected with God's requirement ("but of the tree of the knowledge of good and evil you shall not eat," Genesis 2:17). The blessing was God's free and unmerited gift. The gift could only be enjoyed in obedience to God's requirement.

It was the same at the beginning of Israel's life in the promised land. The land had been God's free and unmerited gift (Deuteronomy 26:9). The blessings of life in the land could only be enjoyed in obedience (Deuteronomy 28:1, 2).

It is easy for us to get this backwards, thinking that God's gifts are *earned* by our obedience. Not so. In the garden of Eden blessing came *first*. Furthermore Israel was rescued from Egypt *before* being called to a life of obedience (Exodus 19:4–6; 20:2, 3). The land was God's gift to them where they could then live in obedience to him (Deuteronomy 4:1, 5–8). Obedience is the *necessary response* to God's grace. No one can receive God's grace by refusing to be obedient to him. In Christian terms, Jesus is our Savior *by* being our Lord.

Back to King Solomon. As God's king, of course he must be obedient to God (see 2:4; 3:14; 6:12; cf. Psalm 132:12). And that is what we have come to expect of this king to whom God had given a "hearing heart" (3:9, literal translation).

The Lord's words to Solomon in verses 3–5 are profoundly assuring.

The LORD's Warning to King and People (vv. 6–9)

In verse 6 there is a shift. In modern English this is partly obscured since we do not distinguish between "you" (singular) and "you" (plural). In verse 6 the "you"s become plural.[9] The Lord was still speaking to Solomon, but was thinking now of the king and his people.

What Could Possibly Go Wrong? (v. 6)

And now the Lord clearly stated what could possibly go wrong:

> But if you turn aside[10] from following me, you or your children,[11] and do not keep my commandments and my statutes that I have set before you, but go and serve other gods and worship them . . . (v. 6)

In the garden of Eden the possibility of disobedience may have seemed remote. Why would the man and the woman God had so wonderfully blessed choose to disobey him? What possible reason could there be for doing so? And yet it was acknowledged as a real possibility ("for in the day that you eat of it . . . ," Genesis 2:17), a possibility that was tragically realized.

Here with King Solomon the possibility contemplated does not seem remote. Too much has happened. The people of Israel had repeatedly done what Adam and Eve so foolishly did. Read Samuel's indictment of the people in 1 Samuel 12:8–17. Consider the failure of King Saul (1 Samuel 13:13; 15:18,

19; 28:18). Consider the wickedness of King David (2 Samuel 11). The possibility of disobedience is no longer remote. It was the possibility that Moses had set before the people before they had entered the promised land (see Leviticus 26:14; Deuteronomy 28:15).

This possibility is described here in three ways: turning aside from following the Lord, not keeping his commandments and statutes, and going and serving other gods and bowing down to them.[12] These are three aspects of abandoning the life of obedience to God that was required of those who had been so blessed by him.

How Wrong It Could Be! (vv. 7–9)

This possibility would be disastrous. It would mean the withdrawal of blessing. In the garden of Eden the seriousness of the possibility of disobedience was clearly stated: "in the day that you eat of it you shall surely die" (Genesis 2:17). That is, the gift of life (Genesis 2:7) would be lost. More recently Moses had set out the devastating consequences of disobedience for the people of Israel (Leviticus 26:14–39; Deuteronomy 28:15–68).

What would happen to the blessings enjoyed by the people of Israel under King Solomon if they should turn away from the God who had so blessed them?

Israel Cut Off from the Land (v. 7a)

First, said the Lord, "then I will cut off Israel from the land that I have given them" (v. 7a). This fundamental aspect of God's promised blessing, basic to the promise made to Abraham (Genesis 12:1; 15:7, 18–21; Exodus 23:31; Joshua 1:2–6), would be taken away.

At the risk of spoiling a great story, we need to know that this is where the history we are reading will end (2 Kings 24, 25).

The House Cast Out of God's Sight (v. 7b)

Second, "the house that I have consecrated for my name I will cast out of my sight" (v. 7b). All that this house had represented would be lost, just as the man and the woman were cast out of the garden of Eden (Genesis 3:23, 24). "This house was designed to protect them in their allegiance to God, but not in their rebellion or disobedience."[13] No longer would the Lord's "eyes and . . . heart be there" (v. 3).

Again the story we are reading will end with the destruction of this house, along with all that King Solomon had built (2 Kings 25:9). The house that

Solomon had built for the Lord's name would be sent away into exile (so to speak) with the people (2 Kings 25:13–17).

Israel a Proverb and a Byword (v. 7c)

The kingdom of Solomon had become famous among the nations (4:34). Solomon expected foreigners to come to the house he had built because they had heard of God's great name (8:41, 42). The disasters that would follow Israel's turning aside from the Lord would be likewise famous: "Israel will become a proverb and a byword among all peoples" (v. 7c).

This is a terrible irony. It was Solomon's proverbs that contributed to the international reputation of his wisdom (4:29–34). In the horrors that would follow from Israel's turning to other gods Israel itself would become "a proverb and a byword among all peoples." This is just what Moses had warned about (Deuteronomy 28:37). The admiration of the nations (4:34; 8:42) would turn to mockery.[14]

Why? (v. 8)

People would be astonished and puzzled by the disaster:

> And this house will become a heap of ruins.[15] Everyone passing by it will be astonished and will hiss,[16] and they will say, "Why has the LORD done thus to this land and to this house?" (v. 8)

"This land" was the land that the Lord had given to his people Israel. "This house" was the place he had consecrated by putting his name there. When the people are cut off from the land (v. 7) and the house is cast out of God's sight (v. 7), the question that cries out to be answered is not just "Why?" but "Why has *the LORD* done thus?"—for no one else could have taken away the blessing God had given.

Because . . . (v. 9)

The answer will be clear:

> Then they will say, "Because they abandoned the LORD their God who brought their fathers out of the land of Egypt and laid hold on other gods and worshiped them and served them. Therefore the LORD has brought all this disaster on them." (v. 9)

Make no mistake. The Lord will bring disaster on those he has blessed, should they abandon him and lay hold on and worship and serve other gods.

This had not yet happened in Solomon's kingdom. However, at the height of the joy and gladness for all the goodness the Lord had shown to this people (8:66), the Lord gave this warning. What could possibly go wrong? Turning away from the God who had so blessed them—that is what could go wrong.

How kind of the Lord to issue this warning. The purpose of the warning, of course, was to prevent the disaster. This is what could *possibly* go wrong, spelled out so that it might *not* go wrong.

But it did (as we will see), just as it went wrong in the garden at the beginning, accounting for all the troubles of the world ever since.

The warning given to King Solomon and his people is echoed in the New Testament. As we enjoy the blessings God has given us in our mighty King, we are warned to take heed lest we fall (1 Corinthians 10:12; cf. Romans 11:20–22). Such warnings to Christian believers are a major theme of the letter to the Hebrews:

> Therefore we must pay much closer attention to what we have heard, *lest we drift away from it*. (Hebrews 2:1)

> . . . how shall we escape *if we neglect such a great salvation*? (Hebrews 2:3)

> Take care, brothers, *lest there be in any of you an evil, unbelieving heart*, leading you to fall away from the living God. (Hebrews 3:12)

> For it is impossible, in the case of those who have once been enlightened, who have tasted the heavenly gift, and have shared in the Holy Spirit, and have tasted the goodness of the word of God and the powers of the age to come, and *then have fallen away*, to restore them again to repentance, since they are crucifying once again the Son of God to their own harm and holding him up to contempt. (Hebrews 6:4–6)

> For *if we go on sinning deliberately* after receiving the knowledge of the truth, there no longer remains a sacrifice for sins, but a fearful expectation of judgment, and a fury of fire that will consume the adversaries. (Hebrews 10:26, 27)

> See that you do not *refuse him who is speaking*. For if they did not escape when they refused him who warned them on earth, much less will we escape *if we reject him who warns from heaven*. (Hebrews 12:25)

Such warnings must be taken seriously. Christian assurance does not mean denying these warnings. The warnings are the very way in which the Lord keeps his own from the terrible consequences of refusing him. The believer will hear and heed the warnings, and so will not fall. "My sheep hear my voice," says Jesus. That is why "they will never perish, and no one will snatch them out of my hand" (John 10:27, 28).[17]

20

Are We There Yet?

1 KINGS 9:10-28

IF WE HAD BEEN THERE, among the people of Israel in the days of King Solomon, enjoying the happiness of his kingdom (4:20) and rejoicing in the goodness of God (8:66), we would probably have had a deep sense that we had, by God's kindness, *arrived*. We may have looked back over the centuries to the promises God had made to Abraham, Moses, and David and wondered at the fact that at last God had given us all that he had promised. And we would have been right (see 5:4; 8:15, 20, 23, 24, 56). But not completely right.

The experience of Christian believers is like that, but more so. We too have (or should have) a profound sense of having, by God's grace, *arrived*. We look back at the promises of God from the dawn of time and know that all the promises of God find their Yes in Jesus Christ (2 Corinthians 1:20). In him God has blessed us with every spiritual blessing (Ephesians 1:3). We have been reconciled to God by Jesus' death (Colossians 1:22). We have died with Christ and have been raised with Christ, and our life is now hidden with Christ in God (Colossians 3:1–3). We know that if anyone is in Christ, he is a new creation (2 Corinthians 5:17). We have peace with God, and God's love has been poured into our hearts through the Holy Spirit who has been given to us (Romans 5:1, 5). In Christ Jesus we consider ourselves dead to sin and alive to God (Romans 6:11). Our cry is, "Blessed be the God and Father of our Lord Jesus Christ!" (2 Corinthians 1:3; Ephesians 1:3; 1 Peter 1:3).

It is all too possible for us as Christian believers to be less aware than we should be of having *arrived*, less conscious of all that Christ has done for us and all that God has given us in him. The old *has* passed away, and the new *has* come (2 Corinthians 5:17). Some New Testament letters seem to have been written to believers who did not adequately appreciate the fullness of what we have been given in Jesus Christ.[1]

Yet it is also possible to *over*state our present experience. We are still waiting for the day when Christ will appear in glory and we will appear with him (Colossians 3:4). All things are not yet subjected to Jesus Christ (1 Corinthians 15:28). Jesus' death and resurrection was the beginning (Colossians 1:18), but the end is yet to come (Hebrews 3:14; 1 Peter 4:7).[2]

There is a tension in the Christian life that has been expressed as *now* and *not yet*. The "now" of the Christian life is magnificent, and we must pray that the Lord will give us "the Spirit of wisdom and of revelation in the knowledge of him" (Ephesians 1:17) so that we will live in its light. The "not yet" is wonderful beyond words, and we pray that the Lord will enlighten the eyes of our hearts so that we may know what is "the hope to which he has called [us,] what are the riches of his glorious inheritance in the saints" (Ephesians 1:18).

Are we there yet? The true answer is, yes *and* no. Both are important.

I can easily imagine an Israelite in King Solomon's day answering the question, "Are we there yet?" with a simple, excited "Yes!" But as we listen to the description of various aspects of Solomon's kingdom in 1 Kings 9:10–28, we begin to see that things were not quite so straightforward. "Yes" *and* "Not yet" is a better answer.

We will be looking at:

(1) Prosperity and its cost (vv. 10–14)
(2) Security and its means (vv. 15–23)
(3) Egypt and its role (v. 24)
(4) The house and its completion (v. 25)
(5) The world and its opportunities (vv. 26–28)

At each point our passage picks up themes from earlier in the story and looks at them again, usually showing us that what we have seen so far of Solomon's astonishing kingdom was not the whole picture. "Yes" was not the whole truth.

Prosperity and Its Cost (vv. 10–14)

In 1 Kings 5 we heard how Hiram, king of Tyre, had been very friendly to Solomon (as he had been to David), supplying materials and expertise for the building of the house of the Lord. This was a commercial transaction. Solomon paid for Hiram's help with considerable annual payments of grain and oil (5:11).

Let's see how that arrangement was going now that the major building works in Jerusalem had been completed.

Are We There? (v. 10)

> At the end of twenty years, in which Solomon had built the two houses, the house of the Lord and the king's house . . . (v. 10)

The house of the Lord had taken seven years to build (6:38), and the complex of buildings called the king's "entire house" had taken thirteen years (7:1). The completion of all this work had been followed by the bringing of the ark of the covenant into the house of the Lord (8:1–11), King Solomon blessing all the assembly of Israel (8:12–21), his prayer about prayer (8:22–53), his blessing the people again (8:54–66), and the Lord's appearance to Solomon for the second time (9:1–9). All of this has made clear what an extraordinary moment this was in the history of Israel, indeed in the history of the world. God had put his name "forever" (9:3) in the house that Solomon had built.

So are we there yet?

Let's look a little more closely at how the arrangements with Hiram had gone.

Receipts (v. 11a)

> . . . and Hiram king of Tyre had supplied Solomon with cedar and cypress timber and gold, as much as he desired . . . (v. 11a)

As far as Hiram keeping his side of the deal, all appears to have gone according to plan. Actually it was even better than planned. In the agreement outlined in chapter 5 there had been no mention of gold (see 5:10). We have heard much about gold used in decorating the house of the Lord (gold is mentioned eleven times in chapter 6) and also for various objects (7:49, 50). Where had all this gold come from? Solomon's father had dedicated a considerable amount of gold to the Lord (2 Samuel 8:7, 10, 11), but we have been told that this was "stored . . . in the treasuries of the house of the Lord" (7:51). Now we learn that Hiram had supplied Solomon with gold.

"As much as he desired" picks up the language of 9:1 ("all the desire of Solomon which he delighted to do," AT).[3] Up to this point in the story Solomon's "desire" seems to have corresponded with God's will. His desire had resulted in his building work (see 9:1). In this Hiram had been a great and reliable help. But I wonder whether there might be a hint of a problem in the mention of Solomon's "desire" for "gold" (see Proverbs 16:16).

Outgoings (v. 11b)

What comes next is a surprise and a puzzle. "Then[4] King Solomon gave[5] to Hiram twenty cities in the land of Galilee" (v. 11b).

Why did that happen? The agreement had involved a payment for Hiram's services in grain and oil (5:11). What was this gift of "twenty cities" for?

We should not be misled by the word "cities." The Hebrew term can refer to "any group of habitations from a hamlet to a metropolis"[6] and almost certainly here designates mere villages.[7] Nonetheless we have just been reminded (by God!) that the land on which these villages stood was God's gift to the people of Israel, in the context of a warning that being cut off from the land would be the consequence of disobedience (9:7). And now we find Solomon giving land to the king of Tyre! We can readily imagine that the Israelite inhabitants of these villages would not be pleased with their king's action.[8]

These "cities" were "in the land of Galilee." Galilee was a northern region of the land occupied by the people of Israel, close to Tyre.[9] The gift of twenty cities would amount to ceding some of the border territory to King Hiram.

Why would King Solomon do this?[10]

Not Happy! (vv. 12, 13)

The recipient of his gift made the situation even more perplexing: "But when Hiram came from Tyre to see the cities that Solomon had given him, they did not please him" (v. 12). Literally, "they were not *right* in his eyes." In 9:4 the Lord had urged "uprightness" on Solomon. In Hiram's evaluation the gift of twenty cities did not live up to that standard.[11]

Of course, Hiram was not privy to the Lord's words to Solomon in 9:1–9. The reason that he regarded the gift as "not right" was probably that the cities were worth less than he considered Solomon owed him.[12] However, by describing his view like this ("not *right*"), the narrator does raise the question whether Solomon's giving away these cities was indeed "right."

"Therefore [Hiram] said, 'What kind of cities are these[13] that you have given me, my brother?'" (v. 13a). The friendly relations between Hiram and Solomon that we saw in chapter 5 are reflected in the words "my brother." His question, however, suggests that the relationship had been put under strain by Solomon's "not right" gift.

The narrator underlines Hiram's unhappiness with the gift by telling us, "So they are called the land of Cabul to this day" (v. 13b). "Cabul" could mean "mortgaged,"[14] perhaps suggesting that Solomon was still in debt to Hiram.

However, "Cabul" may have sounded a bit like the Hebrew for "as nothing." Hiram's displeasure resulted in the cities Solomon had given to him becoming known as "Good for Nothing."[15] They retained this reputation "to this day," probably a reference to the time when the account of this matter was recorded (perhaps in the Book of the Acts of Solomon, 11:41) rather than the much later time of the writer of the books of Kings.[16]

We are still puzzled. What had happened between Solomon and Hiram that caused Solomon to give away twenty cities and Hiram to regard the gift as "not right"?

How Much Gold? (v. 14)

In a flourish typical of many Biblical narratives, our writer only now drops the bombshell that answers our perplexed question: "Hiram had sent to the king 120 talents of gold" (v. 14).

Here our writer expands on his reference to gold provided by Hiram in verse 11. We do not know exactly what our writer meant by a "talent," but 120 talents of gold was a lot of gold! The talent was the highest unit of weight in the Near East, but varied in its size over time and place. Reasonable estimates have concluded that Hiram had sent about four tons (about 4,200 kilograms)[17] of gold to Solomon!

Our initial questions are answered, only to raise a more pressing one. Solomon had surrendered the cities because he had incurred a huge debt to Hiram that could hardly be repaid in grain and oil. Hiram had not found the cluster of presumably poor villages a just and fair payment of Solomon's enormous debt.

Our new question is, why did Solomon "desire" *so much* gold? It is difficult to imagine that the decoration of the house of the Lord, for all its impressiveness, required as much as this. The debt he incurred meant the loss of Israelite towns. Was this king really walking "with integrity of heart and uprightness" (9:4)? In this loss of land to a foreigner, are we seeing the beginning of Israel being "cut off" from the land (9:7)?[18]

It looks as though the prosperity we have seen in Israel under King Solomon was becoming costly, and we may well wonder whether it was all as secure as it seemed.

Security and Its Means (vv. 15–23)

Solomon's building work required not only materials and expertise, it needed labor. How was this provided?

In 5:13–18 we heard about the labor force King Solomon provided for the building of the house of the Lord. There we noted that "forced labor" was a component, but that this was not necessarily a problem (although, rightly or wrongly, it became a problem in due course, see 12:4). We are now given a more complete account of the "forced labor" raised by Solomon for all of his construction works.

The Labor Issue (v. 15a)

"And this is the account of the forced labor that King Solomon drafted . . ." (v. 15a). The compulsory provision of labor for a period of time to accomplish a project as important as the house of the Lord may have been appropriate (5:13). However, the full account of the forced labor enlisted by Solomon raises new questions.

The Extent of the Work (vv. 15b–19)

King Solomon's building projects were far more extensive than those we have already seen.

The Two Houses (v. 15b)

Certainly there were the projects described in some detail in chapters 6, 7: "the house of the LORD and his own house" (v. 15b). However, this is the first time that we have been explicitly told that the building of "his own house" (which included the various buildings described in 7:1–12) had involved "forced labor." A compulsory contribution of labor for the seven years it took to build the house of the Lord may have been justified. Was it right to use the same arrangement for the king's own house (a much longer project, see 7:1)?

The Security of Jerusalem (v. 15c)

But there was more. The "forced labor" was also used to build "the Millo and the wall of Jerusalem" (v. 15c). We are no longer sure what "the Millo" was, but it may have been a stepped stone structure that provided a retaining wall to support buildings above the steep ridges of the city (see 2 Samuel 5:9).[19]

"The Millo" and the city's wall (see 3:1) were important to the city's defenses (cf. 11:27). Solomon probably extended the city wall to enclose the higher ground on which he had built the house of the Lord and his own house. The use of compulsory labor for such basic requirements raises a further question about this arrangement.

The Security of the Land (vv. 15d–18)

The use of forced labor to shore up King Solomon's defenses extended to the building of "Hazor and Megiddo and Gezer" (v. 15d). These three cities were strategically important for defending the northern approaches to Jerusalem. The cities predated Israelite occupation (see Joshua 10:33; 11:1; 12:21). Solomon's project no doubt consisted of strengthening fortifications.

Hazor was "the most significant fortress in northern Galilee, commanding the routes from the north by the crossing of the Jordan,"[20] north of Lake Galilee. Further south, Megiddo was a city in the valley of Jezreel, where a number of critical battles were fought (see 2 Kings 9:27; 23:29). Further south and closest to Jerusalem was Gezer, about twenty miles west of the capital.

These three cities had in different ways resisted the Israelite occupation.[21] Their subjugation under Solomon signals that it was Solomon who brought the promised kingdom to completion.

Mind you, Gezer had come under Solomon's control in a rather unusual way. Our writer cannot resist briefly noting the story:

> (Pharaoh king of Egypt had gone up and captured Gezer and burned it with fire, and had killed the Canaanites who lived in the city, and had given it as dowry to his daughter, Solomon's wife; so Solomon rebuilt Gezer) . . . (vv. 16, 17a)

The Hebrew emphasizes that Pharaoh, king of Egypt, was the one who took the city of Gezer, which by this time may have been occupied by Philistines (see 2 Samuel 5:25).[22] Pharaoh gave Gezer to his daughter as "dowry." The Hebrew term means a wedding gift, "a present on sending away the bride."[23] The gift was therefore directly and deliberately connected to Pharaoh's daughter becoming Solomon's wife (see 3:1). On the one hand this reminds us that the Israelites had previously been unable to fully take Gezer (Joshua 16:10). On the other hand, what a remarkable reversal this is: Pharaoh, king of Egypt (of all people!), whose predecessor had held the Israelites in oppressive bondage, now served the interests of King Solomon.

Three more strategic sites are mentioned: "Lower Beth-horon and Baalath and Tamar[24] in the wilderness, in the land of Judah[25]" (vv. 17b, 18).

Beth-horon was a twin city located on "the ascent of Beth-horon" (Joshua 10:10, 11) about fifteen miles northwest of Jerusalem, Lower Beth-horon (Joshua 16:3) being to the west of Upper Beth-horon (Joshua 16:5). Baalath was about thirty miles west of Jerusalem, in the coastal plain that the Israelites had initially failed to secure (Judges 1:34). It may only have come under

Israelite control with the establishment of Solomon's kingdom. Tamar was located much further to the south, although the precise location is uncertain.

These cities, fortified by Solomon's efforts, provided strategic defenses from the north (Hazor) to the south (Tamar). Solomon accomplished this too with his "forced labor."

The Security of the Security (v. 19)

That was not all. The "forced labor" provided further infrastructure to support these defenses:

> . . . and all the store cities that Solomon had, and the cities for his chariots, and the cities for his horsemen [horses[26]], and whatever Solomon desired to build in Jerusalem, in Lebanon, and in all the land of his dominion. (v. 19)

The list of building work for which Solomon required "forced labor" becomes more disconcerting. No doubt "store cites" were needed to collect provisions, especially food, for the army. But when did we last hear of a king who needed "store cities"? In Biblical history it was a long time ago. The king was Pharaoh in Egypt, and he employed the slave labor of the Israelites to do it (Exodus 1:11).[27] What are we to make of the fact that King Solomon was now using "forced labor" to build "store cities"?

Furthermore King Solomon needed to build "cities for his chariots." Chariots remind us of Adonijah and Absalom, as well as Samuel's warnings many years earlier about the downside of kingship (see 1 Samuel 8:11; 2 Samuel 15:1; 1 Kings 1:5). Much the same can be said of "cities for his horses."

I am sure our writer expects us to remember what Moses had said long ago about what a king over this people must be like:

> Only he must not acquire many horses for himself or cause the people to return to Egypt in order to acquire many horses, since the LORD has said to you, "You shall never return that way again." (Deuteronomy 17:16)

"All that Solomon desired to build" might have referred to the house of the Lord and the king's house in 9:1. Now "whatever Solomon desired to build in Jerusalem, in Lebanon, and in all the land of his dominion" sounds rather more grandiose and concerning.[28] Solomon's building work went far beyond the work that has been so carefully documented with evident approval in the preceding chapters. Solomon's building projects extended from the city of Jerusalem to Lebanon. Historically this is the first time Israelite rule extended as far as "Lebanon," which marked the northern extent of the land God had promised (Joshua 1:4; Deuteronomy 11:24). "All the land of his dominion" is striking (cf. 4:21). The word translated "dominion" has occurred only once before this in the Old Testament, in Genesis 1:16 to describe the "rule" of the sun and the moon over the day and the night. Solomon's dominion is presented here in grand terms. And throughout it all he was building, using "forced labor."

"One gains the impression of a vast growth economy fueled primarily by state investments,"[29] not to mention cheap labor. Could we even say that "Solomon begins acting like Pharaoh"[30] (that is, the Pharaoh of the book of Exodus)?

The Labor Force (vv. 20–23)

With such a vast amount of building work, our writer documents the labor force King Solomon used (v. 15), now categorized as foreigners and Israelites.

Non-Israelites (vv. 20, 21)

> All the people who were left of the Amorites, the Hittites, the Perizzites, the Hivites, and the Jebusites, who were not of the people of Israel—their descendants who were left after them in the land, whom the people of Israel were unable to devote to destruction—these Solomon drafted to be slaves, and so they are to this day. (vv. 20, 21)

In 5:13 we only heard about the labor force drafted from "all Israel" for the purpose of building the house of the Lord. Now we learn that for his much bigger building program Solomon had raised labor from non-Israelites still living in the land.

As with most of the things we are seeing in this passage, there are two sides to this. On the one hand, the remnants of the original inhabitants of the promised land were at last made subject to the Israelites.[31] No longer would they be a threat. This was yet another aspect of the "rest" God had now given his people under King Solomon (5:4; 8:56).

On the other hand, the presence of these peoples among the Israelites was a reminder that "the people of Israel were unable to devote to destruction" the peoples they had been commanded by God to destroy. This had been because they did not obey God's voice (Judges 2:20). The continued presence of these peoples in Solomon's kingdom, albeit as "slaves," contributes to the "not yet" of the description we are being given.

This involves an aspect of the Old Testament that probably causes more trouble than any other for the modern reader: the divinely sanctioned killing of whole populations and the idea that the failure to do so was a *failure*.

"To devote to destruction" translates a Hebrew verb that, in contexts like this, refers to God's judgment on the wickedness of the peoples concerned.[32]

It is a mistake to think of this as genocide or ethnic cleansing. In a sense it was more terrible than that. God brought his righteous judgment on the original inhabitants of the land because of their wickedness (see Genesis 15:16). The agent of that judgment, the people of Israel, was not immune from falling under the same horror (see Deuteronomy 7:1–4, 10).

It had been Saul's failure to obey God in this matter that had been his undoing (1 Samuel 15; 28:18). Now we find King Solomon dealing with the consequences of Israel's failure, not by doing what the Israelites had failed to do, but by conscripting these foreigners into his labor force to accomplish his vast building program.[33]

We should be careful with the word "slaves" here. I do not want to make the text palatable to us by softening its harshness. However, the terrible connotations of the word "slaves" because of the slave trade of the eighteenth and nineteenth centuries or more recent forms of slavery should not be imported to our text. The Hebrew phrase (*mas-'obed*; literally, "forced-labor serving") occurs only three times in the Old Testament[34] and refers to compulsory labor without *necessarily* implying excessively harsh conditions.

The writer notes that they continued in this forced labor "to this day." This aspect of Solomon's kingdom persisted, an ongoing reminder that the promises of God were "not yet" completely fulfilled.[35]

Israelites (vv. 22, 23)

"But of the people of Israel Solomon made no slaves"[36] (v. 22a). The reason[37] was that the Israelites were used to serve in other ways: "They were the soldiers, they were his officials, his commanders, his captains, his chariot commanders and his horsemen" (v. 22b).

These forms of service were not all limited to Israelites.[38] But Israelites were not included in the "forced labor," except temporarily in connection with the house of the Lord (5:13, 14).

From the Israelites came "the chief officers who were over Solomon's work: 550 who had charge of the people who carried on the work" (v. 23).

There had been 3,300 "chief officers" involved in the construction work on the house of the Lord. Perhaps fewer were needed once that great work was done. Or perhaps these 550 chief officers were higher-level supervisors, each managing six lower "chief officers."[39] Either way "It is clear that organizational genius is at work in the deployment of human resources. . . . The scheme exudes competence and efficiency."[40]

This description of the labor requirements to establish the security of Solomon's kingdom (vv. 15–23) draws our attention to the fact that the description in 4:20 ("Judah and Israel were as many as the sand by the sea. They ate and drank and were happy") was not the full picture.

Egypt and Its Role (v. 24)

The account of the early days of Solomon's reign, once the kingdom was "established," began with a surprising reference to Solomon's marriage to the daughter of Pharaoh, king of Egypt (3:1). There we were told that Solomon "brought her into the city of David until he had finished building his own house and the house of the LORD and the wall around Jerusalem." With these projects completed the time had come for Pharaoh's daughter to be given accommodation more suitable to her place in Solomon's kingdom: "But[41] Pharaoh's daughter went up from the city of David to her own house that Solomon had built for her" (v. 24a). The building of this house was mentioned in 7:8 among the complex of buildings that were referred to as "his entire house" (7:1).

As we considered the earlier reference to this marriage in 3:1 we noted that the narrator did not seem at that point to be implying a negative evaluation of this alliance. In the context of our present passage the inclusion of this daughter of Pharaoh in David's royal household seems to me to be a little more ambiguous. After all, we have seen Solomon's behavior develop in a decidedly Egyptian direction (especially in v. 19).

"Then he built the Millo" (v. 24b). The Millo was the first of Solomon's other projects (after the house of the Lord and his own house) mentioned in verse 15. Was the settling of Pharaoh's daughter in her proper royal quarters (itself entirely appropriate) the point at which Solomon embarked on his more extensive building ambitions (which we have found rather more problematic, even Egyptian-like)?

The House and Its Completion (v. 25)

> Three times a year Solomon used to offer up burnt offerings and peace offerings on the altar that he built to the LORD, making offerings[42] with it before the LORD. So he finished [completed[43]] the house. (v. 25)

In 3:3 we heard that before the building of the house of the Lord, Solomon had "sacrificed and made offerings at the high places." In particular he had offered a great number of burnt offerings at Gibeon (3:4). This practice shifted to Jerusalem, where peace offerings were added (3:15). The building of the house of the Lord had at last provided the proper place for such sacrifices (see 3:2; 8:5, 62, 63).

Now we hear how the altar of the house of the Lord (see 8:22, 64) was put to its proper and regular use. The three occasions each year referred to here would be the Feast of Unleavened Bread held in the first month of the Israelite year and associated with Passover (Exodus 13:3–16), the Feast of Weeks in the third month, associated with the firstfruits of the wheat harvest (Exodus 34:22), and the Feast of Booths in the seventh month (see 8:2; 2 Chronicles 8:13).

Burnt offerings were for the atonement of sin (see 3:4). Peace offerings celebrated peace with God. The house of the Lord, Solomon's greatest accomplishment, had become what it was intended to be. "So he completed the house" brings the long section about Solomon and the house of the Lord to a fitting close.

And yet in the context of our passage we might wonder whether what happened at the house and its altar was as central to Solomon's kingdom as it ought to have been. Was it possible for it to become just one of the many activities that made up Solomon's busy year?

The World and Its Opportunities (vv. 26–28)

It certainly was a busy year:

> King Solomon built a fleet of ships at Ezion-geber, which is near Eloth on the shore of the Red Sea,[44] in the land of Edom. And Hiram sent with the fleet his servants, seamen who were familiar with the sea, together with the servants of Solomon. And they went to Ophir and brought from there gold, 420 talents, and they brought it to King Solomon. (vv. 26–28)

Earlier we heard about the wide reach of Solomon's reputation and influence (4:21, 24, 34). Now we hear how this great king was able to exploit and extend the opportunities of his international influence for considerable commercial gain. In turn his trading activities must have contributed to his far-flung fame.

This really was a remarkable development. Never before (to our knowledge) had an Israelite attempted to conquer the seas. Never before had this nation actively engaged with such faraway places.

Ezion-geber and Eloth (or Elath) featured at a much earlier stage of the history of Israel, at the time of their forty-year wandering in the wilderness (Numbers 33:35, 36; Deuteronomy 2:8). Eloth was located on the north coast of the Gulf of Aqaba, at the southern extremity of Solomon's kingdom, in the land of the Edomites (whom David had decisively subdued, 2 Samuel 8:13, 14). It is possible that Ezion-geber was a small island (known today as Coral Island), which provided a safe anchorage for ships.[45]

There King Solomon made a fleet of ships. It must have been a breathtaking enterprise. It was as daring and radical as anything his father David had done. The bold ingenuity he had inherited from David was now employed in peaceful adventures. These ships were not for war. They were for trade.

His friend Hiram helped. The difficulties over those "Good for Nothing" villages had not destroyed their relationship. Perhaps Hiram saw an opportunity in this joint venture to recoup his losses on the earlier deal. Hiram provided experienced sailors to join with Solomon's men to sail Solomon's fleet. I would not be at all surprised if he was involved with the shipbuilding too.

The destination of King Solomon's fleet was Ophir. Scholars have suggested a bewildering range of possibilities for the location of Ophir, from southern Arabia to the east coast of Africa and even India. Ophir is mentioned in Genesis 10:29 alongside Havilah, the land "where there is gold" according to Genesis 2:11.[46]

From Ophir a great quantity of gold was brought to King Solomon—three and a half times as much as had been supplied to Solomon by Hiram (v. 14). That may have been about fourteen tons (14,700 kilograms)! This was probably the total amount acquired over a period of time. Nonetheless it was an enormous amount of gold and would have enabled Solomon to square off any remaining debts to Hiram and then some.

On this note the sketch of Solomon's kingdom concludes. What are we to make of it? Are we there yet? On the one hand our passage does seem to celebrate this remarkable king and his astonishing achievements. Think back. Only a couple of generations earlier this people had been a loose association of poor and weak tribes with an uncertain future. The change in just a few decades was breathtaking. It was now a wealthy kingdom with an economy fueled by international trade, controlling the major trade routes of the region. Much of this must be seen as a blessing from God, who had fulfilled all that he had promised his people.

And yet . . .

The sketch has been honest enough to cause us to see (more clearly with the benefit of hindsight, of course) that this was not the final and complete fulfillment of all that God had promised.

This will be confirmed in due course. For all the achievements of Solomon's kingdom, King Solomon will prove to be inadequate to rule the kingdom of God. Within a few pages we will see his kingdom fail terribly.

There will need to be a better, greater, wiser king than Solomon. Those of us who have come into *his* kingdom (Colossians 1:13) may ask, are we there yet? The answer is, even more profoundly than in the days of Solomon, "Yes!" *and* "Not yet."

21

"All the Treasures of Wisdom"

1 KINGS 10

IT IS IMPORTANT TO UNDERSTAND that Jesus Christ is worthy of our utter and complete trust, our full and absolute confidence, our steadfast and unwavering faith.

Why is it that much of the time few of us feel like that? Why are we hesitant in our trust, uncertain in our confidence, wobbly in our faith in Jesus Christ? What would change us from foolishly feeble believers to those who are joyfully firm, unafraid, and confident in our Lord and Savior?

The answer is simple but powerful. We need to see Jesus Christ *as he is*. When his riches, wisdom, goodness, and power take our breath away, we learn that he really is the hope of the world and the hope of all who trust in him.

We need, in other words, something like the experience of the queen of Sheba when she came to visit King Solomon. Of course, Jesus is greater than King Solomon (Matthew 12:42), but about 1,000 years before Jesus was born, King Solomon was God's chosen king in Jerusalem. His riches, wisdom, goodness, and power were an astonishing anticipation of the greater Son of David who was yet to come. In 1 Kings 10 we hear about the impact he made on a queen from a faraway land (vv. 1–13) and, indeed, on the whole known world (vv. 14–25). Before the chapter ends, however, we will have to ask some questions that did not occur to the queen of Sheba (vv. 26–29).

The Queen of Sheba's Experience of King Solomon (vv. 1–13)

No one now knows precisely where Sheba was.[1] I suspect that no one in Jerusalem in the days of Solomon had much more of an idea. It is usually assumed that Sheba was in the southwest corner of the Arabian Peninsula, more than 1,000 miles from Jerusalem.[2] Wherever it was, Sheba was a land far, far away.

The monarch who reigned there in Solomon's day is known to history only because of the incident recorded in 1 Kings 10. Although this was sufficient to secure her fame for all time, before she arrived in Jerusalem I doubt that anyone in that city had heard of her.[3]

Our narrative has anticipated Solomon's spreading fame by telling us that "people of all nations . . . and from all the kings of the earth" heard of Solomon's wisdom (4:34). King Solomon himself had spoken of the foreigner from a far country who would hear and come to Jerusalem (8:41, 42). It is likely that the international trading activities of Solomon brought news of the king in Jerusalem to the ears of the queen in faraway Sheba. The joint venture with King Hiram of Tyre had ships sailing at least as far as Ophir, possibly not far from Sheba[4] (9:26–28).

What She Heard (v. 1a)

Now when the queen of Sheba heard of the fame of Solomon[5] concerning the name of the LORD . . . (v. 1a)

What the queen of Sheba heard is very important. She heard about King Solomon *and* "the name of the LORD." This probably means that she heard about the house Solomon had built "for the name of the LORD." She would have heard about the magnificence of the building, but more importantly she heard about the "name" for which it had been built (see 3:2; 5:3, 5; 8:16–20, 29, 33, 35, 42–44, 48; 9:3, 7). Perhaps she heard that Solomon's kingdom was the fulfillment of the promise of the one who bore this name (2:24; 8:15, 20, 25, 56; 9:5). The glory of this kingdom therefore enhanced the reputation ("name") of the Lord. This was an answer to Solomon's prayer: "that all the peoples of the earth may know your *name* and fear you" (8:43).

Much later the prophet Isaiah would look forward to the coming of a future son of David. Under his reign, "the earth shall be full of the knowledge of the LORD as the waters cover the sea" (Isaiah 11:9). In other words, the *name* of the Lord will overwhelm the whole world.

When Jesus spoke of the news of *his* kingdom ("all authority in heaven and on earth") going to "all nations," he said that the nations would be bathed, so to speak,[6] in God's *name*: "the *name* of the Father and of the Son and of the Holy Spirit"[7] (Matthew 28:18–20).

Why She Came (v. 1b)

The queen of Sheba's response to what she was hearing was this: "she came to test him with hard questions" (v. 1b). The news about King Solomon must have been very powerful indeed. It motivated this faraway monarch to undergo a long and no doubt arduous journey to discover whether the news was true. She had her doubts. Of course she did. What she had heard was extraordinary. But she went to a great deal of trouble to learn the truth. She came to Jerusalem to "test" him.[8]

She had heard of Solomon's wisdom (v. 6). He was "wiser than all other men" (4:31). We do not know exactly what "hard questions" (or "riddles"[9]) she had in mind that would "test" him. It may have been a kind of battle of wits. More likely she had genuine questions about life and the world. Her purpose was to ascertain whether what she had heard about Solomon and the name of the Lord was true.

Many years later when Jesus impressed his contemporaries in various ways, there were those who came to "test" him (Matthew 16:1; 22:35). Unlike the queen of Sheba, their motives were hostile. They were not seeking the truth. Jesus compared them unfavorably with the queen of Sheba (Matthew 12:42).

How She Came (v. 2a)

> She came to Jerusalem with a very great retinue,[10] with camels bearing
> spices[11] and very much gold and precious stones. (v. 2a)

This was a serious visit. The long journey with such a large company was a huge undertaking. The arrival of the queen with her entourage must have made quite an impact. She honored the king she had come to see with the "very great retinue" she brought.

Perhaps King Solomon remembered his father's prayer for him:[12] "may the kings *of Sheba* and Seba bring gifts! . . . may *gold of Sheba* be given to him!" (Psalm 72:10, 15).

The queen's visit was remembered for many years to come. A later prophet looked forward to the day when something like this would happen on a greater scale:

> A multitude of camels shall cover you,
> . . . all those *from Sheba* shall come.
> They shall bring gold and frankincense,
> and shall bring good news, the praises of the LORD. (Isaiah 60:6)

Later still, when the wise men from the east traveled far with gifts of gold, frankincense, and myrrh for the newborn Jesus (Matthew 2:1–11), they were fulfilling the prophecy and in a sense reenacting the queen of Sheba's visit to Solomon—now to one greater even than he.

What She Found (vv. 2b–5)

She may have come with a list of prepared "hard questions," but she found herself telling this king much more. "And when she came to Solomon, she told him all that was on her mind [literally, her heart]" (v. 2b). "And Solomon answered all her questions; there was nothing hidden from the king that he could not explain to her" (v. 3). Not only could he answer all her riddles, he could tell her all that was in her heart.

> And when the queen of Sheba had seen all the wisdom of Solomon, the house that he had built, the food of his table, the seating of his officials, and the attendance of his servants, their clothing, his cupbearers, and his burnt offerings that he offered at the house of the LORD, there was no more breath in her. (vv. 4, 5)

The queen not only *heard* Solomon's wisdom, she *saw* it, first and foremost in "the house that he had built," probably meaning the house of the Lord and the king's house considered as a complex.[13] In the buildings that represented this astonishing kingdom she saw Solomon's wisdom.

She also saw the impressive provisions in the royal household—the food as well as the orderliness and richness of his court. "His burnt offerings that he offered at the house of the LORD" seem to have made a particular impression (see 9:25). This king honored another King, for whose name that house had been built.[14] All this showed the queen the extraordinary wisdom of Solomon.

And it took her breath away! She was "overwhelmed" (NIV).[15]

What She Said (vv. 6–9)

Paradoxically her breathlessness was expressed in speech.

It's True! (vv. 6, 7)

First, she said to the king:

> The report was true that I heard in my own land of your words and of your wisdom, but I did not believe the reports until I came and my own eyes had seen it. And behold, the half was not told me. Your wisdom and prosperity [goodness] surpass the report that I heard. (vv. 6, 7)

What she had "heard" (v. 1) was "true."[16] But the truth surpassed all that she had heard. King Solomon's wisdom and goodness overwhelmed her.

Have you seen the wisdom and goodness of Jesus Christ, surpassing by far all that the queen of Sheba saw (cf. 1 Corinthians 2:9, 10)? It *is* breathtaking.

It's Good! (v. 8)

Second, the queen said to Solomon:

> Happy are your men![17] Happy are your servants, who continually stand before you and hear your wisdom! (v. 8)

How good it must be to belong to this king and to serve him! What a privilege to continually hear his wisdom and to know his goodness (cf. 4:20)![18]

Are you astonished at how fortunate you are to belong to the Lord Jesus Christ, to serve him, to benefit continually from his wisdom and goodness?

It's God's Love! (v. 9)

Finally, the queen said,

> Blessed be the LORD your God, who has delighted in you[19] and set you on the throne of Israel! Because the LORD loved Israel forever, he has made you king, that you may execute justice and righteousness. (v. 9)

This foreign queen from a distant land found herself praising the true and living God! The wisdom and goodness of Solomon impressed upon her the wisdom and goodness of God. In this she joined another foreigner, King Hiram of Tyre (see 5:7; cf. 17:12, 24).

Remarkably she spoke of God's love for Israel. This had been fundamental to God's dealings with his people (see Deuteronomy 7:6–8; 10:15; Isaiah 43:4; 63:9; Jeremiah 31:3; Hosea 11:1). The queen saw this love of God in his setting Solomon on Israel's throne. God's loving purpose was that this king would do "justice and righteousness."

That is what King David had done for a time. "David reigned over all Israel, and David *did justice and righteousness* for all the people" (2 Samuel 8:15, AT).[20] The righteous justice of David's kingdom was remarkable. It involved victory over all who opposed his rule and threatened his people, peace with all who welcomed his regime, and the wealth of those nations being turned to the service of the Lord rather than to the glory of men who opposed God's kingdom.[21] Solomon's reign took "justice and righteousness" to another level. "The wisdom of God was in him to do justice" (3:28).[22] There was now peace, prosperity, and lasting security beyond anything King David had accomplished. And it took the queen's breath away.

The kingdom of complete and never-ending righteousness and justice has now been established by the Lord Jesus Christ (see Romans 3:21–26; 14:17). The wisdom and righteousness of our King takes your breath away (see 1 Corinthians 1:30).

What She Gave (vv. 10–12)

> Then she gave the king 120 talents of gold, and a very great quantity of spices and precious stones. Never again came such an abundance of spices as these that the queen of Sheba gave to King Solomon. (v. 10)

The queen gave King Solomon a gift of gold that matched the huge amount (about four tons or 4,200 kilograms) Hiram had provided in the context of a commercial transaction, worth more (in Hiram's opinion) than the twenty towns Solomon gave him (9:11–14). The queen was serious!

The gold was supplemented with "a very great quantity of spices and precious stones." It was the biggest gift of its kind ever received by the king in Jerusalem.

I am sure that the gifts of gold, frankincense, and myrrh brought to Jesus many years later were far less in quantity (Matthew 2:11). Nonetheless they signified the same wonder. Here was a King before whom the nations of the world must bow, in whom their hope is found.

Our writer adds a note at this point, as an aside, indicating that while the queen of Sheba's gifts were impressive, they were only one of many sources from which Solomon's kingdom prospered:

> Moreover, the fleet of Hiram, which brought gold from Ophir, brought from Ophir a very great amount of almug wood and precious stones. And the king made of the almug wood supports for the house of the LORD and for the king's house, also lyres and harps for the singers. No such almug wood has come or been seen to this day.[23] (vv. 11, 12)

"The fleet of Hiram" probably means the fleet largely manned by Hiram's sailors (9:27). In addition to gold (9:28), these ships brought "a very great amount of almug wood and precious stones." We are no longer sure what "almug wood" was,[24] but it was presumably regarded as exotic and valuable. From this wood were made "supports" (probably steps[25]) for the house of the Lord and the king's house, as well as musical instruments.

This note sets the queen of Sheba's gifts in the context of King Solomon's thriving Red Sea trade.

What She Received (v. 13)

On the other hand, the queen did not return to Sheba empty-handed. Far from it:

> And King Solomon gave to the queen of Sheba all that she desired, whatever she asked besides what was given her by the bounty of King Solomon. (v. 13a)

Whatever she asked, she received from this wise, good, and wealthy king. No doubt she received tangible gifts matching her own generosity. More than that this queen, who came with such "hard questions" and so much on her heart, received "all that she desired" from King Solomon. He gave not only from his "bounty [literally, hand]," but from the treasures of his wisdom.[26]

Again we find in King Solomon a shadow of our Lord Jesus. Those who come to him find a King not only greater than Solomon, but wiser and kinder. He is "able to do far more abundantly than all that we ask or think" (Ephesians 3:20). Whatever we ask in his name, he will do (John 14:13, 14).

The queen of Sheba "turned and went back to her own land with her servants" (v. 13b). Whether she had any further dealings with Solomon, we do not know. Whether her acknowledgment of the Lord had lasting consequences for her, history does not record. The visit of the queen of Sheba to Jerusalem stands as an astonishing testimony to the king whom the Lord had put on the throne of Israel and so points us to the one whom God has now made "both Lord and Christ" (Acts 2:36).[27]

The Whole Earth's Experience of King Solomon (vv. 14–25)

The magnificent account of the visit of the queen of Sheba must be seen as one instance of the impact that King Solomon had on the whole known world. Just look at what the world saw.

His Gold (vv. 14–17)

> Now the weight of gold that came to Solomon in one year was 666 talents of gold, besides that which came from the explorers[28] and from the business of the merchants,[29] and from all the kings of the west [or Arabia[30]] and from the governors[31] of the land. King Solomon made 200 large shields[32] of beaten gold; 600 shekels[33] of gold went into each shield. And

he made 300 shields[34] of beaten gold; three minas[35] of gold went into
each shield. And the king put them in the House of the Forest of Lebanon.
(vv. 14–17)

The 666 talents of gold that came to Solomon in "one year" was probably a
particular year's revenue rather than the repeated annual income.[36] Perhaps it
was the year of the queen's visit. That would account for 120 talents (v. 10).
If Hiram had given his 120 talents in the same year (9:14) and the ships from
Ophir had brought 420 talents (9:28), that would account for most of the 666
talents (probably over twenty tons, 20,000 kilograms).

This did not include other income from customs and taxes of various
kinds. King Solomon had apparently gained firm control of the profitable trade
routes passing through the territory under his sway.

The House of the Forest of Lebanon (7:2–5) became the place where some
of the king's wealth was on display. One use to which Solomon's abundance
of gold was put was an impressive array of ceremonial gold shields, hung in
that place.

His Throne (vv. 18–20)

The king also made a great ivory throne and overlaid it with the finest gold.
The throne had six steps, and the throne had a round top,[37] and on each side
of the seat were armrests and two lions standing beside the armrests, while
twelve lions stood there, one on each end of a step on the six steps. The like
of it was never made in any kingdom. (vv. 18–20)

The throne was probably made of wood, inlaid with ivory and plated in places
with gold.[38] The throne itself was a seventh level above the floor (hence six
steps), seven being a number of completion or perfection. The back (top) of
the throne was rounded. On each side was an armrest with a female lion beside
it. All six steps to the throne had a male lion at each end.

This magnificent throne represented great power. There was no other
like it.

His Gold (Again) (v. 21)

All King Solomon's drinking vessels were of gold, and all the vessels of
the House of the Forest of Lebanon were of pure gold. None were of silver;
silver was not considered as anything in the days of Solomon. (v. 21)

Everywhere you looked there was gold, gold, gold! We are being given a
picture of unimaginable prosperity, only to be surpassed by the New Je-

rusalem, where the whole city and its streets are pure gold (Revelation 21:18, 21).

And the Rest! (v. 22)

> For the king had a fleet of ships of Tarshish at sea with the fleet of Hiram. Once every three years the fleet of ships of Tarshish used to come bringing gold, silver, ivory, apes, and peacocks.[39] (v. 22)

Just when you may have thought you had grasped the glory of this kingdom, the narrator expands his description further. As well as "the fleet of Hiram" (see also v. 11; 9:26–28), which traveled south to faraway places, Solomon had "a fleet of ships of Tarshish."[40]

Today the exact location of Tarshish is no more certain than that of Sheba, but it seems to have been another faraway place, this time to the west of the land of Israel (see Jonah 1:3; 4:2), perhaps in the vicinity of Spain. The mention of Tarshish has the effect of expanding the horizon of our image of Solomon's influence.

"Ships of Tarshish" may have been an expression for large oceangoing ships, capable of carrying hefty cargo (cf. Ezekiel 27:25) without any actual link with Tarshish.[41] However, a later writer confirms that these ships actually "went to Tarshish" (2 Chronicles 9:21). The great length of these journeys is indicated by their three-year duration. The cargo they brought back was precious and exotic, tokens of the vast scale of King Solomon's reach.

The Fame of King Solomon (vv. 23–25)

> Thus King Solomon excelled all the kings of the earth in riches and in wisdom. And the whole earth sought the presence of Solomon to hear his wisdom, which God had put into his mind [literally, his heart]. Every one of them brought his present, articles of silver and gold, garments, myrrh, spices, horses, and mules, so much year by year. (vv. 23–25)

So God's promise to King Solomon (3:12, 13) was fulfilled. In treasures and wisdom there was none to match him. The new Adam (see 4:29–34) was having dominion over "the whole earth" with his God-given wisdom. Here was God's king bringing blessing to the world. Surely he was the promised offspring of Abraham (Genesis 22:18; 26:4; 28:14; cf. 12:3; 18:18).

The multitude of gifts brought to Solomon each year seems to have been freely and gladly given. The hyperbole matches that in 4:34 and serves to emphasize the sense of God's promises wonderfully fulfilled in the kingdom of Solomon. The point has been effectively made.

And Yet . . . ? (vv. 26–29)

Now our writer adds four notes that take us by surprise. There was more to the astonishing kingdom of Solomon than the queen of Sheba noticed or "the whole earth" cared about at this stage. These four things begin to cast a shadow on all we have seen.

Those Chariots (v. 26)

First, we see the chariots and their horses:

> And Solomon gathered together chariots and horsemen[42] [horses]. He had 1,400 chariots and 12,000 horsemen [horses], which he stationed in the chariot cities and with the king in Jerusalem. (v. 26)

We heard in 4:26 about the stalls for Solomon's horses and chariots. In 9:19 cities were built for horses and chariots. Now we see the chariots and horses he acquired.[43] We have noted previously that the mention of "chariots" is concerning.[44] Solomon was the first legitimate Israelite leader to acquire chariots. Was this a step toward becoming a king "like all the nations" (see 1 Samuel 8:5, 11)?

That Wealth (v. 27)

Second, we take another look at the wealth on display in Jerusalem:

> And the king made silver as common in Jerusalem as stone, and he made cedar as plentiful as the sycamore of the Shephelah. (v. 27)

This is an extension of what was said in verse 21, but perhaps we should now consider the other side of such extraordinary luxury. What is the point of silver being as common as stone or cedar as plentiful as the sycamore wood growing so abundantly in the Judean foothills (as the ESV renders "the Shephelah")? Do these comparisons perhaps hint at a sense of disproportion in Solomon's wealth? Was it "over the top"?

The Horses from Where? (v. 28)

Third, we are briefly told where he got his horses:

> And Solomon's import of horses was from Egypt and Kue, and the king's traders received them from Kue at a price. (v. 28)

Kue was a land to the north[45] of Solomon's kingdom, and Egypt was to the south. It seems that Solomon opened up international trading opportunities in horses.

Perhaps there is nothing surprising in that. Good relations with Egypt were apparently a feature of Solomon's kingdom (3:1; 7:8; 9:16, 24). However, the fundamental requirement for King Solomon, spelled out by his father on his deathbed, was to keep God's commandments "written in the Law of Moses" (2:3). In the Law of Moses it is written:

> Only [the king] must not acquire many horses for himself or cause the people to return *to Egypt in order to acquire many horses*, since the Lord has said to you, "You shall never return that way again." (Deuteronomy 17:16)

When we remember this, what are we to make of Solomon's horse trading with *Egypt*?

The Trouble with Wealth (v. 29)
Fourth,

> A chariot could be imported from Egypt for 600 shekels of silver and a horse for 150, and so through the king's traders they were exported to all the kings of the Hittites and the kings of Syria [Aram[46]]. (v. 29)

This is beginning to look at least a little "like all the nations." The trouble with wealth is the way in which it generates a desire for more, and wisdom can be compromised by greed. Is that what we are seeing here, as Solomon became an international arms dealer?[47] The kings he supplied with chariots and horses were historical and potential enemies (on the Hittites, see 9:20, 21; on the Arameans [esv, "Syria"], see 11:23–25; 15:18; 20:1; 2 Kings 7:6).

These four notes prepare us for the fact that the glory of King Solomon and his kingdom would not last. Briefly his kingdom provided a glimpse of the kingdom of God. It was extraordinary. But it was not and could not be the end.

We have seen through this chapter that King Solomon, in his wisdom, goodness, and resources, points us to the greater Son of David who has now come and has begun to reign (Revelation 11:15, 17). The questions raised at the end of our passage do not apply to him. In him "are hidden all the treasures of wisdom and knowledge" (Colossians 2:3).

> He is the image of the invisible God, the firstborn of all creation. For by him all things were created, in heaven and on earth, visible and invisible, whether thrones or dominions or rulers or authorities—all things were created through him and for him. And he is before all things, and in him all things hold together. And he is the head of the body, the church. He is the beginning, the firstborn from the dead, that in everything he might be preeminent. For in him all the fullness of God was pleased to dwell, and

through him to reconcile to himself all things, whether on earth or in heaven, making peace by the blood of his cross. (Colossians 1:15–20)

King Solomon took the queen of Sheba's breath away. The Lord Jesus Christ is worthy of our utter and complete trust, our full and absolute confidence, our steadfast and unwavering faith once we see him as clearly as the queen of Sheba saw King Solomon.

22

The Failure of King Solomon

1 KINGS 11:1–8

IT IS TERRIBLE TO THINK that your life has been a failure. It is difficult for us to be honest about this. The truth, for all of us, is that our lives are a mixture of successes and failures. No one succeeds at everything. Likewise no one fails at everything. It is comforting to focus on our successes and to downplay our failures, so that on balance our successes outweigh our failures. So we like to think.

The question we prefer not to think about is, what constitutes success and failure in a human life? Many of us have a sneaking suspicion that we may be mistaken in our self-assessment. Perhaps our failures should be given more weight than our successes. Could it be that the areas in which we have succeeded are much less important than the ones in which we have failed? Is the successful businessman deluded when he thinks that the inheritance he will leave his children outweighs his being a failure as a father? Is the successful athlete mistaken to think that the trophies on her shelf make up for her failures in relationships?

What constitutes success and failure in a human life? Has your life been (on balance) a success or a failure?

The Bible brings us the shattering news that every one of our lives is a failure when measured by the criteria that really matter. This is as true of the person who has been a spectacular success in almost every aspect of life as it is of the person who has horribly failed in the things that matter to most of us. The Bible's perspective is this:

None is righteous, no, not one;
    no one understands;
    no one seeks for God.
All have turned aside; together they have become worthless;
    no one does good,
    not even one. (Romans 3:10–12; citing Psalm 14:1–3)

To fail to be "righteous" and to "understand," to fail to "seek God," to instead "turn aside" is to utterly fail in the great enterprise of human life. Such a life has "become worthless."

Let me hasten to add that this is not all that the Bible teaches, but everything else makes little sense until we have taken this seriously.

In 1 Kings 11 we learn that King Solomon failed. I do not mean that he failed in some aspect of life that can be overlooked because of his amazing success in so much that he did, as we have seen in his story so far. I mean that he failed in such a huge way that all of his astonishing accomplishments really did come to nothing. Or they would have come to nothing, but for something we will see in our next chapter.

Our passage (11:1–8) corresponds to the account of King David's tragic and terrible failure (2 Samuel 11). For all his greatness King David was not up to the task of ruling God's kingdom. Nor, we are about to learn, was his son Solomon. These turning points in the history of David's and Solomon's reigns resonate with the original turning point of human history. For all his greatness, being made in the image and likeness of God, Adam proved to be not up to the task of having dominion over God's creation (Genesis 1—3). King David and now King Solomon failed to overcome the failure of Adam. They failed as he failed. It will require one greater than David and greater than Solomon to turn that failure into success.

The careful description of King Solomon's failure is an opportunity for us to reflect on what constitutes failure in a human life and consequently what would count as success. What was it that made King Solomon a failure?

Intriguingly the paragraph before us picks up elements from the paragraph that introduced the account of Solomon's reign (3:1–3).[1] There the writer mentioned:

(a) Pharaoh's daughter (3:1a)
(b) Solomon's building projects (3:1b)
(c) The high places (3:2)
(d) Solomon's love (3:3a)
(e) Solomon and his father David (3:3b)

We saw that in that context each of these elements was either neutral or positive. Each had at least the potential for success. In the passage before us now each of these matters is mentioned again (though the order is different), but now we will see that each of them takes a decisively negative turn. At each point the potential for good in 3:1–3 has turned to something else. Each of the following had something to do with Solomon's failure:

(a) Solomon's love (11:1a)
(b) Pharaoh's daughter (11:1b)
(c) Solomon and his father David (11:4b, 6b)
(d) Solomon's building projects (11:7)
(e) The high places (11:7)

The paragraph in which we hear again of these five matters has two parts that speak, first, of King Solomon's love (vv. 1–3) and then of King Solomon's heart (vv. 4–8).

King Solomon's Love (vv. 1–3)

At the beginning of the account of Solomon's reign we heard that "Solomon loved *the Lord*" (3:3). Although this "love" is not directly mentioned again, through the ensuing account we have seen Solomon's love for the Lord, particularly in his "desire" to build the house of the Lord (5:8, 10; 9:1, 11).[2] The conclusion to the account of Solomon's reign tells us of another "love."

Solomon's New Love (v. 1)

"Now[3] [But] King Solomon loved many foreign women" (v. 1a). The change of tone as we begin 1 Kings 11 is abrupt and ominous.[4] The Hebrew emphasizes the royal office. It was *the king*, Solomon, who loved "many foreign women." The *man* who had loved the Lord (3:3) as *king* came to love "many foreign women."

God's Law for the king in Deuteronomy 17 included: "He shall *not* acquire *many* wives [or women] for himself" (v. 17). Solomon's father David had a number of wives and concubines (see 2 Samuel 3:2–5; 5:13; 15:16; 1 Chronicles 3:1–9). There is no explicit criticism of this in the Biblical text.[5] Perhaps one could ask whether the number amounted to the "many" of Deuteronomy 17:17. However, in Solomon's case there was no ambiguity: he did love "many" women.

Furthermore they were "foreign" women. This was a problem, but not for racist or xenophobic reasons. Solomon had prayed that the Lord would hear the prayers of a "foreigner." Indeed he prayed that all the peoples of the earth might know the Lord's name and fear him (8:41–43).[6] Solomon's kingdom was remarkably positive toward "foreigners," and this clearly accorded with God's purposes.[7]

The problem was King Solomon's "love" for these many foreign women and the consequences that followed. We tend to see only the emotional (and perhaps sexual) associations in the word "love." The Bible uses the word in political contexts, with political overtones.[8] When you are talking about God's king and God's kingdom, political overtones are weighty. God's Law concerning the king said, "You may not put a *foreigner* over you, who is not your brother" (Deuteronomy 17:15). King Solomon *loved* many *foreign* women. Their foreignness included their foreign gods (v. 2). God's king entered into formal relationships with these foreign women (v. 3).[9] The problem, if you cannot yet see it, will be very clear in a moment.

One of Solomon's wives who might be described as "foreign" has been mentioned repeatedly in the account so far. So our writer adds, "along with the daughter of Pharaoh" (v. 1b; see 3:1; 7:8; 9:16, 24). The Hebrew syntax suggests that the writer was making a *distinction* between Pharaoh's daughter and "many foreign women."[10] We have noted earlier indications that the daughter of Pharaoh may well have ceased to be a "foreigner" in the full sense of the word. It seems likely that she left her Egyptian ways behind. The point now is that Solomon's relationships with foreign women did not stop with Pharaoh's daughter.

The many foreign women now before us were "Moabite, Ammonite, Edomite, Sidonian, and Hittite women" (v. 1c). In Hebrew each of these categories is plural. There were many of each. This prepares us for the extraordinary numbers we will hear in verse 3.[11]

This list has a number of resonances. The Moabites (southeast of Jerusalem on the other side of the Dead Sea), the Ammonites (north of Moab), and the Edomites (south) had ancestral ties with the people of Israel. Most, though not all, interactions between these peoples and Israel had been hostile.[12]

The Sidonians are different. Sidon, along with Tyre, was a leading city of Phoenicia. "Sidonians" had been involved in building the house of the Lord (5:6). Both David and Solomon had extensive constructive dealings with the local king, Hiram (2 Samuel 5:11; 1 Kings 5:1–12; 9:11–14, 27; 10:11, 22). However, what began with Solomon's love for Sidonian women will not end well. In due course another king will make a disastrous liaison with a Sidonian woman named Jezebel (1 Kings 16:31; cf. Revelation 2:20).

The Hittites were among the occupants of the land that had been promised to the descendants of Abraham (Genesis 15:20).[13] By the time of King David the Hittites had been reduced to a number of small states to Israel's north.[14] We know of two particular Hittites who became faithful servants of King David. Ahimelech the Hittite was one, about whom we know very little (1 Samuel 26:6). Uriah the Hittite was the other. He has become famous for terrible reasons. He was the first husband of Solomon's mother. David had him killed to cover up David's adultery with Bathsheba (2 Samuel 11; see 1 Kings 15:5; Matthew 1:6). Among the many foreign women whom Solomon loved were kinfolk of Uriah.

Almost certainly there were political dimensions to these relationships.[15] Royal marriages were a part of international diplomacy. For Israel's king to have entered into so many alliances in this way is evidence of widespread peaceful relations after a long history of much hostility.

However, at this point our writer shows little interest in this aspect. To see the significance of Solomon's love for many foreign women that matters here, he reminds us of what the Lord had said.

What the Lord Said Would Happen (v. 2a)

> . . . from the nations concerning which the LORD had said to the people of Israel, "You shall not enter into marriage with them, neither shall they with you,[16] for surely they will turn away your heart after their gods." (v. 2a)

The writer is clear that what King Solomon did had been forbidden by God[17] for one reason: "for surely they will turn away your heart after their gods." That was the problem.

The words strike an abrupt and alarming note. They remind us of one of the most terrible episodes in Israel's history. When the Israelites had been living in Shittim, Israelite men had sex with Moabite women. The women then invited the men to join in sacrifices to their pagan gods. Suffice to say, it did not go well (read Numbers 25, if you dare). We might think, surely such a thing could not happen in Solomon's kingdom! But God had said that is what would *certainly*[18] result from such liaisons.

Solomon's New Love (vv. 2b, 3a)

Our writer, rather enigmatically and worryingly, says, "Solomon clung to these in love" (v. 2b). The language is evocative. The verb ("clung") applies to marriage as it is meant to be ("a man shall . . . *hold fast* [or cling] to his wife," Genesis 2:24). It also applies to faithfulness to the Lord ("*hold fast* [or cling] to him," Deuteronomy 10:20; cf. 2 Kings 18:6).[19] What or who did Solomon "cling to in love"?

In the Hebrew "to these" is emphasized. In context the obvious referent is the foreign women of verse 1. However, "these" is grammatically masculine, raising the possibility that he clung in love to "the nations" or even to "their gods" of verse 2![20]

What is unambiguous about "these" is its plurality. Plurality suits the context: "He had 700 wives, who were princesses,[21] and 300 concubines"[22] (v. 3a). The numbers are astonishing, like so many things in Solomon's kingdom.[23] Our writer was not exaggerating when he said "many" in verse 1!

What Happened (v. 3b)

What happened is what God said would surely happen: "And his wives [or women] turned away his heart" (v. 3b).

Solomon had asked the Lord to give him a "hearing heart" (3:9, AT). His request was granted (3:12; see 10:24), so that he could say:

> The king's heart is a stream of water in the hand of the LORD;
>   he *turns* it wherever he will. (Proverbs 21:1)

However, King Solomon's love for many foreign women introduced another power that "turned" his heart in a very different direction.

King Solomon's Heart (vv. 4–8)

In the Bible the heart is more than the emotional center of a person. The thoughts, plans, will, and decisions, as well as deep emotions, come from the heart. What happened to King Solomon's heart?

A Heart Turned Away (v. 4a)

> For[24] [And] when Solomon was old his wives turned away his heart after other gods, and his heart was not wholly true to the LORD his God . . . (v. 4a)

It happened in the time of his old age. Decisions and actions taken over many years at last had their effect. It seems that this effect was not immediately apparent. Did each compromise make the next one easier? Did each departure from God's ways contribute to a spiritual hearing loss in the "hearing heart" he once had (3:9) until in old age his heart was turned away *from the Lord*?

His heart was turned "after other gods," just as the Israelites had long ago "yoked [themselves] to Baal of Peor" (Numbers 25:3). We may reasonably imagine that in Solomon's mind he continued to honor the Lord, for whose

name he had built a magnificent house (8:13). He simply gave due reverence
to the "gods" of his many foreign women. It may be that he never thought
of these gods as superior or even equal to the Lord. He was just considerate
enough to give them space, so to speak. He was generous, open-minded, ac-
commodating, flexible, tolerant.

That may have been how he thought about himself. The truth was that
"his heart was not wholly true to the LORD his God." In Hebrew "wholly true"
sounds like Solomon's name. Solomon was no longer "Solomon," the son of
David who "loved the LORD" (3:3).[25] He failed by his own words of blessing
in 8:61.

Here is the heart of Solomon's failure. It was *heart failure*. Moses had said:

> Hear, O Israel: The LORD our God, the LORD is one. You shall *love the
> LORD your God* with *all your heart* and with all your soul and with all your
> might. And these words that I command you today shall be on your *heart*.
> (Deuteronomy 6:4–6)

Those words were no longer on King Solomon's heart.

Our Lord Jesus Christ cited these words as "the great and first commandment" (Matthew 22:37–38). They represent the *first principle* of human life.
To fail here is to fail utterly.

In his old age King Solomon failed to follow the counsel of his father
(2:2–4). He failed to heed God's word to him (3:14; 6:12; 9:4). Though the
Lord had loved him remarkably (2 Samuel 12:24; 1 Kings 10:9), he failed to
love the Lord with all his heart.

Mind you, if the great and first commandment is the measure of success
in a human life, then every one of us fails. Who among us loves the Lord our
God with all that we are? Though he is worthy of our love and has loved us
remarkably (1 John 4:9–10), we fail to love him as we ought. Can there be a
greater failure in life than that?

A Heart Unlike David's Heart (v. 4b)

The writer adds the puzzling words (but by now a familiar idea), "as was
the heart of David his father" (v. 4b; cf. 3:6, 14; 9:4). In 3:3 we were told
that Solomon's love for the Lord was expressed in "walking in the statutes of
David his father." In his old age, however, his heart became *unlike* his father
David's heart.

In one sense Solomon's heart became *like* David's heart. Like his father in
2 Samuel 11, he failed in faithfulness. While it may be that David never turned

to other gods, his heart was certainly less than wholly true to the Lord his God. He "despised the word of the LORD" (2 Samuel 12:9); indeed, in God's own words he "despised me" (2 Samuel 12:10).

However, here as often in the books of Kings, David is viewed in the light of God's grace toward him, his sin "put away," washed thoroughly from his iniquity, cleansed from his sin, now whiter than snow (2 Samuel 12:13; Psalm 51:2, 7). Solomon's heart became *unlike* the cleansed, forgiven heart of his father David.[26]

A Heart Lost (v. 5)

We are given a closer look at Solomon's lost heart: "For[27] [And] Solomon went after Ashtoreth the goddess of the Sidonians, and after Milcom the abomination of the Ammonites" (v. 5).

Two of the "other gods" to which Solomon's wives turned his heart are identified. He "went after" them, which is precisely what the Law of Moses forbade (Deuteronomy 6:14; 8:19; 11:28; 28:14) and what Israel had done in her worst times of failure (Judges 2:12, 19). Precisely what "going after" these gods entailed, we are not told.[28] Solomon built high places for them (v. 7), but whether he attended these himself we do not know.

That his heart was turned away to these gods is a tragedy beyond description. Consider the two "gods" mentioned here. Ashtoreth was a female partner of Baal, the great Canaanite storm god. She is known in many texts outside the Bible as Astarte. She was, among other things, a goddess of war. The Biblical form of the name seems to be a deliberate put-down. The vowels of the Hebrew for "shame" (*bosheth*) have been added to the consonants of the deity's name.[29] She was "the goddess of the Sidonians," although versions of Baal and Ashtoreth were worshipped widely in the region.

The Ashtaroth (plural of Ashtoreth[30]), along with the Baals, had been an enticement to the people of Israel since their early days in the land of Canaan (Judges 2:13; 10:6; 1 Samuel 12:10) and until the days of Samuel (1 Samuel 7:3). The appeal of these male and female gods probably had to do with the fertility of land and livestock.[31] However, under Samuel's influence these had been "put away" (1 Samuel 7:4) and had not appeared in Israel through the reigns of Saul, David, and Solomon—until now, in Solomon's old age. That King Solomon returned to the unfaithfulness of earlier days suggests a massive failure, the undoing of all that had been accomplished through the monarchy.

The second god mentioned here, "Milcom," is probably a variant spelling of the pagan god often called Molech (as in v. 7) and occasionally Malcam.[32] Assuming this to be the case, we are here confronted with something appalling. Molech was a deity to whom children were burned in sacrifice.³³ This so-called god became something of a symbol for all that was terrible and evil in the pagan religions of Canaan (see Leviticus 18:21; 20:1–5; cf. Deuteronomy 12:31; 18:10). When the people of Israel adopted the practices of Molech religion (see Psalm 106:34–39; 2 Kings 16:3; 17:17; 21:6; Isaiah 57:5; Jeremiah 7:31; 19:5; 32:35; Ezekiel 16:20, 21; 20:30, 31; 23:37–39), they had become utterly corrupt (see Jeremiah 32:35). Fundamental to Josiah's reform in future days will be cleaning up this horror (2 Kings 23:10). To think that such debauchery can be traced back to King Solomon "going after" Milcom/Molech underlines the immensity of his failure.

Our writer cannot hide his disgust. Milcom was not, in his view, the *god* of the Ammonites, but the "abomination" of the Ammonites. The word expresses the strongest revulsion and disgust.³⁴

A Heart Gone Astray (v. 6a)

Another way of seeing this is: "So Solomon did what was evil in the sight [or eyes] of the LORD and did not wholly follow the LORD" (v. 6a). Things had been different once: "And the thing was *good in the eyes of the Lord* because Solomon asked this thing" (3:10, AT). Now we find that in his old age King Solomon's conduct is a reminder of the worst days of King David when "the thing David had done was *evil in the eyes of the Lord*" (2 Samuel 11:27, AT) and even Saul (1 Samuel 15:19). Solomon's failure fully matched his father's. He "did not wholly follow the LORD"; that is putting it mildly. He certainly did not.

There will be many more in this history who will, like Solomon, do "what was evil in the eyes of the LORD" (14:22; 15:26, 34; 16:19, 25, 30; 21:20, 25; 22:52). Solomon's failure will not be quickly reversed.

A Heart Unlike David's Heart (v. 6b)

Having (implicitly) reminded us of David's failure, our writer again strikes the discordant note of David as the measure of what Solomon ought to have been: he did not wholly follow the Lord "as David his father had done" (v. 6b). Again (as in v. 4) our writer insists on seeing David in the light of God's forgiving, cleansing grace.

A Heart Lost (vv. 7, 8)

Finally we return to the pagan gods to which Solomon's heart was turned:

> Then Solomon built a high place for Chemosh the abomination of Moab, and for Molech the abomination of the Ammonites, on the mountain east

of Jerusalem. And so he did for all his foreign wives, who made offerings
and sacrificed to their gods. (vv. 7, 8)

Chemosh was the national god (rather, in our writer's view, the "abomination") of the Moabites (see Numbers 21:29; Judges 11:24; 2 Kings 23:13;
Jeremiah 48:7, 13, 46), apparently a god of, among other things, war. Molech
we have discussed, but note here that this form of his name is probably another
linguistic insult, putting the vowels of *bosheth* ("shame") on the consonants
of whatever the proper form of the name was, which probably meant "king"
(*melek*). This god was no king. He was a shame.

Solomon, the builder of so many fine and important buildings, particularly the house for the name of the Lord, in his old age built high places for
these disgusting gods. "High places" were mentioned in 3:2, 3, 4. On the
one hand, however, those were not high places for pagan gods. On the other
hand, it was when "no house had yet been built for the name of the LORD"
(3:2). What Solomon did was astonishing and would turn out to be the beginning of the end for the kingdom that had been so wonderfully established
in his hand.

The mountain east of Jerusalem, where these detestable high places were
built, was the Mount of Olives, "as if to confront the temple which he himself
had built."[35] It will later be called "the mount of corruption" (2 Kings 23:13).

The appalling situation could be summed up in the words of Jeremiah:

> Has a nation changed its gods,
>   even though they are no gods?
> But my people have changed their glory
>   for that which does not profit.
> Be appalled, O heavens, at this;
>   be shocked, be utterly desolate,
>   declares the LORD. (Jeremiah 2:11, 12)

That such a king and such a kingdom as we have seen in the previous
pages should fail so utterly and completely (the scale of the failure will be seen
in the pages that follow) is a most devastating demonstration that the fundamental failure of humanity will not be redeemed unless by one far greater than
even King Solomon.

I hope that you are appalled at what happened in Solomon's old age.
I hope that you are troubled by the fact that the heart of Solomon's terrible
failure as God's king is at the heart of your failure as a human being. The
outward expression of our failure will be different. But it is at heart the same.

I hope that you will now look at Jesus Christ and see this wonder: *he did not fail* as we fail. His wholehearted love and faithfulness to God his Father never faltered. His human life was a success by the only measure that finally matters (Philippians 2:8, 9). He is the King and Savior we failures need.

23

There Are Consequences

1 KINGS 11:9–25

LIFE IS SERIOUS. I do not mean that life is somber. Life is good in so many ways. There are pleasures, delights, and countless happy experiences. But it is also serious, more serious than most people are prepared to accept, because there are consequences.

Young people are sometimes criticized by their elders for not taking life with sufficient seriousness. Often the problem is that a young person fails to think about the consequences of his or her behavior. With the impulsiveness of youth, and lacking the life experience of older folk, it is all too common for a young person to choose immediate pleasure over long-term good. A young driver takes risks for the thrill of it, without regard for the harm he might cause. A young student parties instead of studying, giving no thought to the long-term difference that a bit of hard work at this stage could make. A young person may be much more keen to spend money on desirable things today than to save for future needs. Those who have lived longer can be frustrated at how hard it can be to persuade a young person that life involves consequences.

However, it is not only young people who disregard the seriousness of life's consequences. In our last chapter we saw the failure of King Solomon when he was old (11:4), and we thought about what constitutes failure in life. To fail to "love the LORD your God with all your heart and with all your soul and with all your might" (Deuteronomy 6:5) is to fail the first and most fundamental requirement of human life (see Matthew 22:37, 38). That is what Solomon did. In the passage before us now, we will hear first about the terrible *consequences* of King Solomon's failure (vv. 9–13) and then about the historical experience of the consequences of Solomon's failure (vv. 14–25).

We will find ourselves thinking about life's consequences that all of us need to take seriously.

The Consequences of Solomon's Failure (vv. 9–13)

Verse 9 of 1 Kings 11 is a bombshell. It is important to remember what was said about Solomon when he was born: "And the LORD *loved* him" (2 Samuel 12:24). The Lord's love for Solomon, like the place his father David had in God's heart (see 1 Samuel 13:14; 2 Samuel 7:21), speaks of the Lord's gracious purpose for Solomon. The Lord had chosen Solomon (as he had chosen David) to be king over his people (see 10:9). The Lord *loved* him.

However, we have learned that when he was old Solomon's wives turned away his heart after other gods, and his heart was not wholly true to the Lord his God (11:4). The consequences were terrible.

The Lord's Anger (vv. 9, 10)

Consider these devastating words: "And the LORD was *angry* with Solomon" (v. 9a). The horror of these words is sharpened when we realize that Solomon had prayed about the circumstances in which God might be "angry" with the people of Israel because of their sin against him (8:46). Much later in this history we will read of the time when "the LORD was very *angry* with Israel and removed them out of his sight" (2 Kings 17:18). In the entire history of Israel in the land God had given them (from Joshua to 2 Kings) these are the only three occurrences of the Hebrew verb rendered here "was angry."[1] The same expression had been used to describe the Lord's anger against the exodus generation (Deuteronomy 1:37; 4:21; 9:8, 20). Back then the Lord's anger meant that a whole generation (including Moses) was prevented from entering the promised land (see Psalm 95:8–11).

By the time this history ends the Lord's anger will mean that the whole people will be taken away from the land into exile (2 Kings 17:6; 24:10—25:30). This terrible development began with Solomon: "the LORD was *angry* with Solomon."

What? (v. 9a)

We have seen that the fundamental failure of Solomon was the failure of his heart to be wholly true to the Lord (11:4). Now we must understand that the fundamental consequence of such failure was the Lord's anger.

This is a difficult subject for us to consider, but we must. The anger or (to use the older word) wrath of God is the ultimate reality that makes human life serious. On the one hand it is important to see that God's anger is unlike the anger we experience between human beings. With us anger is often uncontrolled, vindictive, impulsive, and disproportionate. Not so with God's anger, which is absolutely righteous and thoroughly consistent with his perfect goodness. God's wrath is his proper and appropriate reaction to evil. On the other hand, we need to know that God's anger is more terrifying than anything else we could possibly imagine. A proper response is to ask, "Who is able to stand before the Lord, this holy God?" (1 Samuel 6:20). We cannot control God's anger; neither can we necessarily understand it (see 2 Samuel 6:7; 22:8, 9; 24:1). We certainly cannot escape God's anger by ourselves.[2]

Difficult as it may be, we need to understand that it is good news that God is angry about evil. Would you rather that God did not care about violence, hatred, death, destruction, cancer, war, starvation, and cruelty (the list could go on and on)? What is so very hard for us is the fact that it is God, not us, who decides what deserves his anger. And to fail to love the Lord with all our heart and to turn to other gods as Solomon did deserves God's anger. The wisest of men (4:29–34) had become a fool (cf. Romans 1:22).

God's king is meant to be an *agent* of God's wrath, expected to carry out God's severity toward his enemies and the enemies of his people. Years earlier King Saul had failed in this (see 1 Samuel 28:18). The horror of 1 Kings 11:9 is that King Solomon became the *object* of God's wrath: "the Lord was angry with Solomon."

Why? (vv. 9b, 10)

The simple but devastating reason for God's anger with Solomon was this: "because his heart had turned away from the Lord" (v. 9b). This was Solomon's monumental failure, described in detail in the preceding paragraph (11:1–8). The Lord's anger was the terrible consequence.

We are reminded that the Lord from whom Solomon's heart had turned was "the God of *Israel*" (v. 9c). This is the God who had so loved Israel that he had made Solomon king in order that he might bring them justice and righteousness (10:9). From *this* God, Solomon's heart had turned to "*other* gods" (11:4), the gods of the Moabites, Ammonites, Edomites, Sidonians, and Hittites (11:1).

The seriousness of Solomon's apostasy is underlined by the fact that the God of Israel "had appeared to him twice" (v. 9d). The Lord had first appeared to him at Gibeon when he had promised to give him both the wise and hearing heart he had asked for and the riches and honor he had not asked for (3:5–14). The Lord had appeared to Solomon a second time after he had completed his great building work and reaffirmed the promise he had made to David concerning the establishment of Solomon's throne "forever" (9:1–9).[3]

How extraordinary that the king to whom the Lord had appeared on these two occasions (with such a promise) would turn his heart away from this God! It makes you think, doesn't it, how extraordinary it is that so many people today refuse to turn their hearts to the God whose grace, goodness, and loving kindness have "appeared" in this world in the person of Jesus Christ (Titus 2:11; 3:4; cf. 1 Corinthians 15:5–8), with the wonderful promise of the gospel (consider Ephesians 3:6; 2 Timothy 1:1; 2 Peter 3:13; 1 John 2:25).

Furthermore, in his appearances to Solomon the Lord "had commanded him concerning this thing, that he should not go after other gods" (v. 10a). This had happened implicitly at Gibeon when the Lord said "if you will walk in *my* ways, keeping *my* statutes and *my* commandments . . ." (3:14). This was more explicit in God's second appearance to Solomon: "But if you turn aside from following *me*, you or your children, and do not keep *my* commandments and *my* statutes that I have set before you, but go and serve *other* gods and worship *them* . . ." (9:6). This fundamental requirement of faithful obedience to the Lord had been set before Solomon repeatedly (see 2:3, 4; 6:12), although such reminders should hardly have been necessary for a king who read his Bible (see 11:2; Deuteronomy 17:19). It is not as though Solomon could plead ignorance of what the Lord required of him.

"But he did not keep what the LORD commanded" (v. 10b). That is why the Lord was angry with Solomon.

The Lord's Word (vv. 11–13)

The Lord's anger was revealed to Solomon by a solemn word, probably spoken to him by a prophet:[4] "Therefore the LORD said to Solomon . . ." (v. 11a).

It is very important to understand that God's wrath is not a religious idea that has come from the minds of imaginative people. We know of God's wrath in the same way that Solomon came to know it. God has spoken. For us today the wrath of God is revealed from Heaven in the gospel of Jesus Christ (see Romans 1:17, 18). Solomon learned of the Lord's anger because of what the Lord said to him.

Why? (v. 11b)

The word of the Lord to Solomon began with his terrible failure: "Since this has been your practice[5] and you have not kept my covenant and my statutes that I have commanded you . . ." (v. 11b). This is the failure explained in

11:1–8 and mentioned in verses 9, 10, now described as failing to keep "my covenant."

In 1 Kings the Lord's "covenant" has been mentioned frequently in connection with "the ark of the covenant" (3:15; 6:19; 8:1, 6). It was "the covenant" made with the people of Israel at Mount Horeb in the days of Moses (8:9, 21). First and foremost "the covenant" was the Lord's *commitment* to this people (8:23), expressed in the words on the tablets inside the ark: "I am the LORD your God, who brought you out of the land of Egypt, out of the house of slavery" (Deuteronomy 5:6). The Lord's commitment to them put them under a fundamental *obligation* (also written on those tablets): "You shall have no other gods before me" (Deuteronomy 5:7). Solomon's failure was a failure to keep (observe, be careful about) the Lord's covenant. He had turned to "other gods" (11:4).

What? (v. 11c)

The consequence of this failure, described in verse 9 as the Lord's anger, is now given concrete expression: "I will surely tear the kingdom[6] from you and will give it to your servant" (v. 11c).

Another bombshell! The kingdom that the Lord had established (2:12, 46) and that had been promised "forever" (9:5; 2 Samuel 7:13, 16) will be torn from Solomon and given to another.

The word "tear"[7] will become a key word in our passage (see vv. 12, 13, 30, 31). It is an appalling reminder of an earlier day when the prophet Samuel had said almost identical words to Saul: "The LORD has *torn* the kingdom of Israel from you this day and has given it to a neighbor of yours, who is better than you" (1 Samuel 15:28; cf. 28:17).[8] The "neighbor" turned out to be David. Could it be that now David's son had become no better than Saul? Was the Lord about to deal with the disobedient Solomon as he had dealt with the disobedient Saul?

Who could "your servant" be? To the extent that we see a parallel with the Lord's dealing with Saul, "your servant" corresponds to "a neighbor of yours." As in the case of Saul, it means someone other than his son. A subordinate would be given the kingdom! Will this "servant," then, be like David, as Solomon had become like Saul?[9]

But! (vv. 12, 13)

The answer is no. There was a factor in Solomon's situation that was not part of Saul's story, namely the promise that the Lord had made concerning David's son:

> I will be to him a father, and he shall be to me a son. When he commits in-
> iquity, I will discipline him with the rod of men, with the stripes of the sons
> of men, but *my steadfast love will not depart from him, as I took it from
> Saul*, whom I put away from before you. (2 Samuel 7:14, 15)

So Solomon heard the words, "Yet[10] for the sake of David your father . . ."
(v. 12a). This is shorthand for "because of my *promise* made to David your
father." "Your father" reminds us that Solomon was the son of David of whom
the promise spoke (see 3:6; 5:5; 8:19; 2 Samuel 7:12).

Because of this promise the consequences of Solomon's failure would be
mitigated in two ways.

First, it would not be immediate: "I will not do it in your days, but I will
tear it out of the hand of your son" (v. 12b). The *only* reason for this delay was
God's grace expressed in his promise to David. It may not have meant a long
delay since Solomon was already old (11:4). Nonetheless it was undeserved
kindness to Solomon that the kingdom was not torn from him immediately.[11]

Second, it would not be entire: "However,[12] I will not tear away all the
kingdom, but I will give one tribe to your son" (v. 13a). This is a remarkable
and hugely important development. A part of the kingdom ("one tribe"[13]) will
remain in the hands of David's offspring. This, too, was God's grace according
to his promise concerning David's son.

Notice that just as David's kingdom had passed to the son of Bathsheba,
the very woman who was involved in David's monumental failure (2 Samuel 11), "your son" in verses 12, 13 will turn out to be a son of one of the many
foreign women Solomon had loved, an Ammonite (see 11:1; 14:31). God's
grace *is* unfathomable!

The reason that the consequences of Solomon's failure will not be immediate, nor entire is stated again: "for the sake of David my servant and for the
sake of Jerusalem that I have chosen" (v. 13b). With the building of the house
of the Lord, in which the ark of the covenant was now placed, Jerusalem had
become "the place that the LORD your God will choose . . . to put his name and
make his habitation there" (Deuteronomy 12:5). Jerusalem represented the
promise of God, just as the ark, now at rest there, had done. Because of (and
only because of) God's promise to David and his commitment to his purpose
for his people (not two things, but one) there will be a future for the kingdom
ruled by a descendant of David.

The difference between Saul and Solomon (like the difference between
Saul and David) is huge and arises from the promise God made to David but
did not make to Saul. It raises the question whether the Lord's solemn word

to Solomon here, like his word to David (2 Samuel 12:1–12), brought about some kind of restoration of Solomon (like David in 2 Samuel 12:13). Did Solomon repent? Was he forgiven, as his father had been?

We do not know. The Bible does not answer that question directly. However, some have suggested that the book of Ecclesiastes represents the repentant wisdom of Solomon. Could it be that words like the following represent the restored Solomon in his latter days (as Psalm 51 represents the changed David)?:[14]

> I turned my heart to know and to search out and to seek wisdom and the scheme of things, and to know the wickedness of folly and the foolishness that is madness. And I find something more bitter than death: the woman whose heart is snares and nets, and whose hands are fetters. He who pleases God escapes her, but the sinner is taken by her. . . .
>
> The end of the matter; all has been heard. Fear God and keep his commandments, for this is the whole duty of man. For God will bring every deed into judgment, with every secret thing, whether good or evil. (Ecclesiastes 7:25, 26; 12:13, 14)

Whatever happened to Solomon, his turning from the Lord to other gods had consequences, just as David's wickedness had consequences. These consequences are the immediate interest of the Biblical historian.

The Historical Experience (vv. 14–25)

The historical experience of these consequences will occupy the rest of 1 and 2 Kings, but that story begins with three particular individuals who impacted Solomon and his kingdom in Solomon's lifetime. They will prove to be instruments of the Lord's discipline, "the rod of men" that had been mentioned in the promise (2 Samuel 7:14). The third of these is of greatest interest, as we will see in our next chapter. Here we consider the first two.

Hadad the Edomite (vv. 14–22)

The first is introduced with the words, "And[15] the Lord raised up . . ." (v. 14a). The impact of these words is accentuated by the fact that "the Lord raised up" is a phrase that a reader of the Bible would not have heard since the book of Judges. There "the Lord raised up" judges (Judges 2:16, 18) or deliverers (Judges 3:9, 15). Now we are about to hear that "the Lord raised up" something very different. We are at a turning point in Israel's history.

These words (in effect repeated in v. 23) may remind us that God's word to Solomon's father after his terrible failure had included, "I will *raise up* evil against you" (2 Samuel 12:11). Solomon's failure had consequences that echo those of David's disaster. All this is against the background of God's promise to "raise up" David's offspring (2 Samuel 7:12).[16]

"The LORD raised up an adversary [Hebrew, *satan*[17]] against Solomon" (v. 14b). That is the opposite of the deliverers he had raised up in the book of Judges. This adversary (as we will see) was not aware of the Lord's purpose. He was, we may reasonably suppose, driven by thoroughly wicked motives of revenge, hatred, and self-serving ambition. It was a case of the Lord using human evil to accomplish his good purposes (cf. Genesis 50:20; Acts 2:23).

Solomon's failure did not take God by surprise. The Lord's response to Solomon's apostasy had been prepared long before the king had fallen. Solomon, of course, did not know this. He had earlier rejoiced in the "rest" that the Lord had given him on every side, so that there was "neither *adversary* [Hebrew, *satan*] nor misfortune" (5:4). At that time Solomon was not at all troubled by the adversary, although (as we will see) he was already at work.[18]

The adversary was "Hadad the Edomite" (v. 14c). Whatever friendly relations might have been suggested by Solomon's relationship with Edomite women (11:1), the long history of hostility from the Edomites toward the people of Israel should not be forgotten (Numbers 20:14–21; 1 Samuel 14:47).[19] Hadad would be an adversary, perhaps reminding us of another Edomite who had played a terrible role in David's story, Doeg the Edomite (see 1 Samuel 21:7; 22:9, 18, 22).

"Hadad" may have been an abbreviation of a longer name like "Hadadezer" ("Hadad is [my] help," v. 23; 2 Samuel 8:3) because Hadad ("The Thunderer" or "The One Who Smashes") was the name of an "ancient Semitic storm god, the deity of rain, lightning (his weapon), and thunder (his voice)."[20] The Bible writer makes the striking point that this man, bearing the name of a foreign god, was raised up by the Lord, the God of Israel. This God is sovereign over all the earth (cf. 8:23, 43, 60; 10:24). From *this* God Solomon's heart had turned away to *other* gods (like the storm god of Hadad). What could be more foolish?

Hadad "was of the royal house in Edom"[21] (v. 14d). He was an Edomite prince.

Our historian now gives us a brief sketch of Hadad's life showing how he became an adversary to Solomon. We are to see the Lord's purposeful hand in these events. The story tells us *how* "the LORD raised up an adversary."

It began "when David was in Edom, and Joab the commander of the army went up to bury the slain, he struck down every male in Edom (for Joab and all Israel remained there six months, until he had cut off every male in Edom)"

(vv. 15–16). If this was the occasion mentioned in 2 Samuel 8:13, 14[22] (which seems likely), the additional details here underline what a violent episode that was. The slain whom Joab went up to bury may have been the Israelites who had fallen in the Valley of Salt (2 Samuel 8:13).[23] "Every male" (like "all Israel") refers to the army, and even then we should allow for some hyperbole.

This reference to the slaughter of "every male" begins a series of points in this story that remind us of Moses.[24] The story of Moses began with the slaughter of "every son . . . born to the Hebrews" (Exodus 1:22). That was in Egypt.

It is therefore intriguing to read, "But Hadad[25] fled to Egypt, together with certain Edomites of his father's servants, Hadad still being a little child [young lad[26]]" (v. 17). Like Moses, Hadad would grow up in Egypt.

The journey of the young prince with the servants of the Edomite king who accompanied him is described with two more allusions to the life of Moses: "They set out from Midian and came to Paran and took men with them from Paran and came to Egypt, to Pharaoh king of Egypt" (v. 18a). This sounds like a forced march. They pressed on from Midian to Paran, then from Paran to Egypt.[27] The points on the way were significant places in Moses' life. Midian was the land to which Moses fled from Egypt as a young man (Exodus 2:15—4:19). Paran was a desert between the Sinai Peninsula and the southern part of Canaan, an important station in the journey of the Israelites under Moses' leadership (Numbers 10:12; 12:16; 13:3, 26; Deuteronomy 1:1).[28]

In Egypt Hadad and his entourage found surprising favor with Pharaoh, "who gave him a house and assigned him an allowance of food and gave him land" (v. 18b). Hadad even became a member of Pharaoh's household: "And Hadad found great favor in the sight of Pharaoh, so that he gave him in marriage the sister of his own wife, the sister of Tahpenes[29] the queen[30]" (v. 19). We are again reminded of Moses (Exodus 2:10).

We do not know how long after David's conquest of Edom that this Edomite prince came to such a privileged position in Egypt, but we should notice that the Lord's action of raising up "an adversary against Solomon" began well before Solomon came to the throne, even, it seems, before he was born.

Time passed. Hadad and his wife had a son: "And the sister of Tahpenes bore him Genubath[31] his son, whom Tahpenes weaned in Pharaoh's house. And Genubath was in Pharaoh's house among the sons of Pharaoh" (v. 20). Again we are reminded of the story of Moses (Exodus 2:10).

Eventually some welcome news reached Hadad: "Hadad heard in Egypt that David slept with his fathers and that Joab the commander of the army was dead" (v. 21a). Hadad's story is now tied into the story we have been following

(2:10, 34). We can assume that news of David's and Joab's deaths reached Hadad in the early days of Solomon's reign.

Hadad responded to this news with a further Moses-like act. He said to Pharaoh, "Let me depart, that I may go to my own country [or land]" (v. 21b; cf. Exodus 5:1). No doubt the Edomite prince had plans to avenge the defeat his people had suffered years earlier.

In the strange continuing echo of the Moses story, Hadad met resistance from the Egyptian ruler. Pharaoh said to him, "What have you lacked with me that you are now seeking to go to your own country [or land]?" (v. 22a; cf. Exodus 5:2). It is possible that by this time Pharaoh had become Solomon's father-in-law (3:1) and that his attempt to keep Hadad in Egypt was in order to keep a potential aggressor from Solomon.[32]

Hadad persisted. He said to Pharaoh, "Only let me depart" (v. 22b). Soon we will see that Hadad apparently had his way and caused trouble for Solomon (see v. 25). This is how "the LORD raised up an adversary against Solomon."

Hadad's story is profound. It teaches us to see that there are consequences in life and human history beyond our normal understanding of cause and effect. The consequences that really matter do not arise simply from the laws of nature and probability (carelessness is likely to result in an accident). There are consequences because *God is sovereign*. He prepared ("raised up") the consequences of Solomon's unfaithfulness long *before* Solomon's heart was turned away from him. Of course, this is difficult for us to understand. That is because we are not God. But let us understand this: the consequences in our lives and in the history of the world (both for good and for ill) are in God's hands, and he is never taken by surprise.

The echoes of Moses' story in the account of Hadad suggest that we should see that Hadad, like Moses, was an instrument in God's hands for his purposes. I suspect (but do not know) that in Solomon's old age the trouble Hadad caused Solomon may have been used by God to restore him, just as David had been restored through the hard experiences that followed from his unfaithfulness (see particularly 2 Samuel 12:22, 23; 15:25, 26).

Rezon Who Reigned over Aram (vv. 23–25)

In verse 23 we hear of another adversary whom the Lord raised up: "God also raised up as an adversary to him, Rezon the son of Eliada" (v. 23a). The similarity of wording to verse 14 indicates that Rezon will be like Hadad, an instrument of God's purpose toward Solomon.

Rezon's story, more briefly told than Hadad's, reminds us of David, just as Hadad reminded us of Moses.[33] Like David he was the servant of a king, and like David he "had *fled* from his master" (v. 23b; cf. 1 Samuel 19:12, 18; 20:1; 21:10; 27:4).

Rezon's master had been "Hadadezer king of Zobah" (v. 23c). Hadaezer ("Hadad is [my] help") had been defeated by David (2 Samuel 8:3–12). It was in the context of this conflict with David that Rezon fled, escaping from the fate of many of Hadadezer's men (2 Samuel 8:4).

Like David, Rezon "gathered men about him and became leader of a marauding band" (v. 24a; cf. 1 Samuel 22:2; 23:5, 8, 13, 24, 26; 24:2; 25:13). This was, as we have said, "after the killing by David" (v. 24b)—that is, the conflict reported in 2 Samuel 8.

"And they went to Damascus and lived there and made him king in Damascus" (v. 24c). The chronology is unclear, but it seems that at some stage in Solomon's reign[34] Damascus, which had earlier come under David's control (2 Samuel 8:6), broke free from Israelite domination and established an independent, indeed an antagonistic, kingdom. They made Rezon their king, again reminding us of David's spectacular career (2 Samuel 2:4; 5:3).

This was the beginning of a line of powerful rulers in Damascus who would impact this story for years to come (15:18; 19:15; 20:1; 2 Kings 8:7).

The point of Rezon's story here is that "He was an adversary [*satan*] of Israel all the days of Solomon" (v. 25a). "All the days of Solomon" may mean all the days *after* Rezon had become king in Damascus. That was probably after Solomon had celebrated the absence of any "adversary" (5:4), but it was still true that the Lord's raising up of Rezon had begun long before his role in God's purposes became clear.

Rezon was "doing harm as Hadad did"[35] (v. 25b). This doesn't help much, since we don't know exactly what Hadad did. However, they were both trouble for Solomon and Israel.

Indeed Rezon "loathed Israel and reigned over Syria[36] [Aram]" (v. 25c). He reigned, in other words, over territory that had been under Solomon's rule and felt nothing but disgust for the people from whom he had broken free.[37] No doubt King Solomon had reason to regret his arms trafficking with "the kings of Aram"(10:29, HCSB)![38]

The echoes of David's story in the way in which Rezon's life is briefly recounted have the same effect as the similarities between Hadad and Moses. Rezon had a place in the purposes of God, just as David did. The God of Israel was, indeed, the God of all the earth (cf. 8:43, 60; also 1 Samuel 2:2, 10; 17:46). Nothing could be more foolish than Solomon's turning from him.

We have begun to see the consequences of King Solomon's foolishness in turning his heart away from the Lord. The wrath of God was more than a religious idea. The stories of Hadad and Rezon show that the Lord's anger was experienced in particular historical events and that these events were deliberate and purposeful acts of God ("the LORD raised up" these adversaries).

The same God promised that Solomon's foolishness would not destroy God's promise. "For the sake of David my servant and for the sake of Jerusalem that I have chosen" (v. 13) the Lord's anger would not be the end of the matter.

We need to see that all people everywhere have been foolish just as Solomon was foolish, and there are consequences. All people are under God's wrath. As the Apostle Paul begins his majestic exposition of the gospel in which "the righteousness of God is revealed," he emphatically asserts, "the wrath of God is revealed from heaven against all ungodliness and unrighteousness of men, who by their unrighteousness suppress the truth" (Romans 1:17, 18; see 2:5, 8; 3:5; 9:22). "Claiming to be wise, they became fools, and exchanged the glory of the immortal God for images resembling mortal man and birds and animals and creeping things" (Romans 1:22, 23). For us, as for Solomon, the wrath of God is more than a religious idea. We experience consequences of our foolishness (see Romans 1:24, 26, 28).

The wonder of the gospel is that God's promise is not destroyed by our sin and its consequences. In faithfulness to his promise so long ago, a son of David has come who "delivers us from the wrath to come" (1 Thessalonians 1:10).

24

What Hope Can There Possibly Be?

1 KINGS 11:26–43

THE BIBLE TEACHES US that the state of the world is far worse than most people think. The Bible also teaches us that the hope of the world is more certain and wonderful than any of the world's pundits predict. In our last chapter we have seen that the state of the world is serious because human wickedness has consequences—consequences that are in God's hands. So it was for King Solomon: "the LORD was angry with Solomon" (11:9) and raised up adversaries against Solomon (11:14, 23). And yet the hope of the world is assured because God is faithful to his magnificent promise. This, too, was reflected in Solomon's experience: "Yet for the sake of David your father . . ." (11:12, 13).

The gospel of our Lord Jesus Christ amplifies this message. The devastating state of the world—the wars, violence, suffering, injustices, tragedies—are consequences of human wickedness. We are witnessing the outworking of nothing less than the wrath of God (see Romans 1:18–32). And yet, in Jesus Christ, God is reconciling all things to himself (Colossians 1:20), and we therefore look forward to standing before him "holy and blameless and above reproach" (Colossians 1:22). We look forward to the day when there will be no more crying (Revelation 21:4). The hope of the world is the faithfulness of God to his promise that we have now heard in the gospel of Jesus Christ (cf. Ephesians 3:6).

The character who is introduced in 1 Kings 11:26 can only be properly understood in the light of these two realities: the wrath of God against wickedness and the faithfulness of God to his promise.

Meet Jeroboam, the Son of Nebat (v. 26)

The man's name was Jeroboam, a name we will hear many times in the history of the following centuries. He is the third mentioned source of trouble for Solomon (after Hadad and Rezon) and will turn out to be the most significant.

Who He Was (v. 26a)

He is introduced as "Jeroboam the son of Nebat, an Ephraimite [literally, Ephrathite] of Zeredah, a servant of Solomon, whose mother's name was Zeruah, a widow" (v. 26a).

Since there will be another important figure in this history named Jeroboam (2 Kings 14:23), this Jeroboam is consistently identified as "the son of Nebat" (12:2, 15; 15:1; 16:3, 26, 31; 21:22; etc.). Nebat was an Ephrathite, reminding us of another "son of an Ephrathite" (1 Samuel 17:12).[1] We will soon see more reminders of David in Jeroboam's story. The similarities will sharpen the differences. Nebat's (and Jeroboam's) hometown was Zeredah, whose location is now uncertain.[2] No more is known about Nebat.

The shock (for the attentive reader with a good short-term memory) comes with the designation of Jeroboam as "a servant of Solomon."[3] This certainly means a royal "official" of some kind (so NIV) rather than a lowly slave. More importantly, however, we have just read that the Lord had said to Solomon that he would give the kingdom to "your *servant*" (11:11). Could this "*servant* of Solomon" be the one who will receive the kingdom?

There is a hint in the mention of Jeroboam's mother's name. This is a little unusual. Two figures whose mother's names have appeared so far in 1 Kings are Adonijah (son of Haggith, 1:5) and Solomon (son of Bathsheba, 1:11), both in the context of their being aspirants to the throne. In the pages that follow we will regularly hear the mother's name of kings who ascend to David's throne (14:21; 15:2; 22:42; 2 Kings 8:26; etc.).[4] Are we to guess that Jeroboam's mother is mentioned at this point because she will soon be the queen-mother?

Her name, as given here, is Zeruah which means "leper," "one suffering a skin disease." Perhaps this was a derogatory nickname since in due course we will see that Jeroboam became the paradigm of evil in this history.[5] She was a widow. Jeroboam's father, Nebat, may have died before his birth.

Jeroboam's name ("May the People Be Many") also sounds king-like. It may have been a throne name given to him after he did indeed become king, but at this stage it is yet another hint of what was to come.[6]

What He Did (v. 26b)

Jeroboam "also lifted up his hand against the king" (v. 26b). As in the cases of Hadad and Rezon, we are given no details about this rebellion.[7] The fact of it is enough to show that Jeroboam was a third "adversary" against Solomon (cf. 11:14, 23). He had a place in God's anger at Solomon's wickedness (11:9).

Hear God's Word to Jeroboam (vv. 27–39)

"And this was the reason[8] why he lifted up his hand against the king" (v. 27a). The NIV has: "Here is the account of how he rebelled against the king."[9] Either way the sentence is puzzling. What follows does not obviously explain the "reason" for a rebellion by Jeroboam, nor is it an "account" of the same. We are simply not told precisely what Jeroboam did against Solomon, why he did it, or when. The writer has something more important to tell us about Jeroboam.

We are told the circumstances (vv. 27, 28) in which an event that changed Jeroboam's life (vv. 29–39) occurred.

The Circumstances (vv. 27, 28)

> Solomon built the Millo, and closed up the breach of the city of David his father. The man Jeroboam was very able, and when Solomon saw that the young man was industrious he gave him charge over all the forced labor[10] [labor force] of the house of Joseph. (vv. 27b, 28)

The building of the Millo points us back to an earlier time in Solomon's reign (see 9:15, 24) when Solomon had completed his most important projects (the house of the Lord and his own house) and was turning to a wider building program. "The breach of the city of David" (whatever that may have been[11]) was no doubt "closed up" by the completion of the wall around Solomon's Jerusalem (3:1; 9:15). This was at least twenty years into Solomon's reign and the point at which we have found ourselves asking questions about the character of Solomon's later projects (see our discussion of 9:24).

In this context Jeroboam's considerable abilities shone. He was, no doubt, energetic and skillful in whatever responsibilities he had as a servant of the king.[12] Jeroboam's industriousness (literally, he was "a doer of work") was noticed by King Solomon, who promptly promoted him to supervisor "over all the labor force of the house of Joseph." "The house of Joseph" here probably means Jeroboam's own tribe of Ephraim along with their near relatives, Manasseh (as in Joshua 17:17; cf. Genesis 46:20).[13] The labor force managed by Jeroboam was probably not the workers of 9:22 but temporary laborers from those northern tribes required from time to time for the king's work.[14]

It has been suggested that it was Jeroboam's experience of Solomon's harsh policies from the vantage point of one who had to administer them to his people that provoked him to an act of rebellion.[15] That is possible, but only a guess. Our narrator is much more interested in something else that happened to Jeroboam when he was in charge of the northern workers for King Solomon.

The Prophet (v. 29a)

"And at that time, when Jeroboam went out of Jerusalem, the prophet Ahijah the Shilonite found him on the road" (v. 29a). This is the meeting that would change Jeroboam's life.

So far in the story of 1 Kings "the prophet" has been Nathan (1:8, 10, 22, 23, 32, 34, 38, 44, 45). However, since the anointing of Solomon as king in chapter 1 we have heard nothing of Nathan. The prophet Ahijah now appears in the narrative as suddenly as Nathan had in 2 Samuel 7:2. He may have delivered God's word to Solomon earlier (11:11), but now we hear his name for the first time.[16] Ahijah was from Shiloh, reminding us of an even earlier prophet, Samuel (1 Samuel 3:21), and his key role in the lives of King Saul and King David. What does the appearance of this new prophet from Shiloh mean—and his apparently deliberate bumping into Jeroboam one day?[17]

The Sign (vv. 29b–31a)

"Now Ahijah[18] had dressed himself in a new garment, and the two of them were alone in the open country" (v. 29b). The garment (Hebrew, *salmah*) was perhaps a large square cloth.[19] The Hebrew word appears to be a deliberate pun on Solomon's name: the garment represents the king and his kingdom.[20] The newness of the garment may suggest the newness of the kingdom over which Solomon reigned.[21]

"Then Ahijah laid hold of the new garment that was on him, and tore it into twelve pieces" (v. 30). As we witness the prophet carrying out this small but dramatic action there are striking hints as to its significance. Perhaps the first thing we notice is the number of pieces into which the garment was torn. In this history "twelve" readily reminds us of the nation of Israel with its "twelve" tribes (cf. 2 Samuel 2:15; 1 Kings 7:25).[22] The second thing that may catch our attention is the word "tore" that links Ahijah's action to God's word to Solomon: "I will surely *tear* the kingdom from you and will give it to your servant" (11:11). Third, the scene now evokes a longer-term memory. Years earlier another garment had been torn, and Samuel had said to King Saul, "The LORD has *torn* the kingdom of Israel from you this day and has given it to a neighbor of yours" (1 Samuel 15:27, 28). To be reminded of that day is ominous. It was the day that "the LORD regretted that he had made Saul king over Israel" (1 Samuel 15:35). Did the Lord now regret having made Solomon king?

With that question in mind, look at what happened next: "And [Ahijah] said to Jeroboam, 'Take for yourself ten pieces . . .'" (v. 31a). *Ten* pieces? The garment had been torn in *twelve* pieces. This is different from the Samuel and Saul scene in 1 Samuel 15.

The Word (vv. 31b–39)

The giving of ten, not twelve, pieces to Jeroboam reminds us that the Lord had said to Solomon, "I will not tear away *all* the kingdom" (11:13). But Jeroboam had not heard that. Indeed the scene before us may have taken place much earlier than the Lord's word to Solomon.

There was a word for Jeroboam: ". . . for thus says the LORD, the God of Israel" (v. 31b). "The LORD, the God of Israel" is the one from whom Solomon's heart had turned away (11:9). He is the One who had made Solomon king because of his love for Israel (10:9). We are about to hear what was to happen when the king of Israel turned away from the God of Israel.

God's word focused first on Solomon (vv. 31c—34) and then on Solomon's son (vv. 35–39).[23] It is a word about two realities that will shape the course of history: the wrath of God against wickedness and the faithfulness of God to his promise.

What the Lord Said Concerning Solomon (vv. 31c–34)

We will consider four points concerning Solomon:

First: "Behold, I am about to tear the kingdom from the hand of Solomon and will give you ten tribes" (v. 31c).

Here is that word "tear" again, representing the first reality, God's wrath. The torn garment in verse 30 signifies the tearing of the kingdom from Solomon (11:11). Moreover, it points to the division of the kingdom. "Ten tribes" will be given to Jeroboam. It is now clear (to the reader) that the "servant" of 11:11 is indeed the son of Nebat.

Second: "but he shall have one tribe, for the sake of my servant David and for the sake of Jerusalem, the city that I have chosen out of all the tribes of Israel" (v. 32). Here is the second reality.

The difference between this day and the day Samuel confronted Saul in

1 Samuel 15 is the promise that the Lord had made to David, given concrete expression by his choice of Jerusalem (see 11:13). Because of the Lord's faithful commitment to his promise, "one tribe" will remain with Solomon.

For the pedantically minded there is a mathematical problem here. "Ten" tribes (v. 31) plus "one" tribe (v. 32) does not equal "twelve" (v. 30). This suggests that the numbers are rather more symbolic than literal.[24] For the numerically precise, it could be argued that "ten tribes" was actually nine if we count Manasseh and Ephraim as the one tribe of Joseph. The "one tribe" probably embraced not only Judah, but also the small tribes of Benjamin and Simeon. The tribe of Levi, not possessing a territory, is probably not included in this categorization.[25]

Third, the reason for point one (v. 31c) is spelled out:

> . . . because they have[26] forsaken me and worshiped Ashtoreth the goddess of the Sidonians, Chemosh the god of Moab, and Milcom the god of the Ammonites, and they have not walked in my ways, doing what is right in my sight and keeping my statutes and my rules, as David his father did. (v. 33)

The king's unfaithfulness, which we heard about in 11:5, 7, had influenced the people. "They" were led along the path that their king had so tragically taken. The king who had been given to Israel to lead them in "justice [Hebrew, *mishpat*] and righteousness" (10:9) had led them to disobey his "rules" (*mishpatim*). In this King Solomon is contrasted with his father David (see 11:4; also 3:6, 14; 9:4).[27] That is why the kingdom was about to be torn from Solomon's hand—God's wrath at wickedness.

The fourth point is an elaboration of point two (v. 32):

> Nevertheless, I will not take the whole kingdom out of his hand, but I will make him ruler[28] all the days of his life, for the sake of David my servant whom I chose, who kept my commandments and my statutes. (v. 34)

Not only will "one" tribe remain with Solomon, the tearing will not happen in Solomon's lifetime (as we heard in 11:12). This, too, will be because of all that David represented, namely God's faithful commitment to his good purpose for his people, expressed in the promise he had made to David.

What the Lord Said Concerning Solomon's Son (vv. 35–39)

Now that we understand that the announced judgment will not fall in Solomon's lifetime, the same message is reiterated, this time with explicit reference to the one who will experience it, namely Solomon's son. Again there are four points.

First, "But I will take the kingdom out of his son's hand and will give it to you, ten tribes" (v. 35). The point made in verse 31c is now made more precisely. The "tearing" will happen after the kingdom has passed to Solomon's son.

Second:

> Yet to his son I will give one tribe, that David my servant may always have a lamp before me in Jerusalem, the city where I have chosen to put my name. (v. 36)

This particularizes the point in verse 32. It will be Solomon's son who will find himself with just "one" tribe. The reason for this is now supplemented with the image of a "lamp" for David. Many years earlier, in the days when Samuel was a lad, our historian had noted that "The lamp of God had not yet gone out" (1 Samuel 3:3). This suggested that in those dark days there was still a glimmer of hope.[29] Later King David had been called "the lamp of Israel," and the people had feared that this lamp might be snuffed out (2 Samuel 21:17). David himself knew that the Lord his God was the "lamp" who lightened his darkness (2 Samuel 22:29). This image will recur in the subsequent history of the dark days to come (see 15:4; 2 Kings 8:19; cf. Psalm 132:17). Hope rested on God's promise to David, and God himself was committed to keeping this flame alive.[30]

Third, point one (v. 35) is elaborated:

> And I will take you, and you shall reign over all that your soul desires, and you shall be king over Israel. And if you will listen to all that I command you, and will walk in my ways, and do what is right in my eyes by keeping my statutes and my commandments, as David my servant did, I will be with you and will build you a sure house, as I built for David, and I will give Israel to you. (vv. 37, 38).

This is remarkable. Jeroboam receives a promise like the promise that had been given to David. To "reign over all that your soul desires" is exactly what was once promised to David (2 Samuel 3:21).[31] Likewise "you shall be king over Israel" (see 1 Samuel 23:17[32]). The promises "I will be with you" (see Deuteronomy 31:6, 8; Joshua 1:5; 1 Samuel 16:18; 18:12, 14, 28; 2 Samuel 5:10; cf. 1 Samuel 17:37; 20:13) and "will build you a sure house" (see 1 Samuel 25:28; 2 Samuel 7:27) are clear echoes of God's promises particularly in connection with David. The comparison with the promise to David is stated plainly: "as I built for David."

However, the "Israel" of the promise to Jeroboam is not all of the "Israel" in the promise to David. This "Israel" is "ten," not "twelve" tribes.

Furthermore, one key idea in the promise to David is lacking in this word to Jeroboam: "forever" (2 Samuel 7:13, 16, 24, 25, 26, 29; 22:51; 1 Kings 2:45; 9:5). Although the condition in the promise to Jeroboam echoes the language of the Davidic promise as it was passed on to Solomon (3:14; 6:12; 9:4), for Jeroboam the condition is no longer set in the context of a "forever" promise.[33]

The fourth point introduces the missing "forever" in a surprising way: "And I will afflict the offspring of David because of this, but[34] *not* forever [literally, not all the days]" (v. 39). Since the promise to David was "forever," the affliction of David's offspring will be "*not* forever." Since the tearing of the kingdom from Solomon's son was at the heart of this affliction, it follows that whatever God might give Jeroboam, it will be "*not* forever."

Here is a new note. Because of God's faithfulness to his promise, not only will the rending of the kingdom be delayed (11:12, 34) and partial (11:13, 32, 36), it will not be permanent. "Not forever" signals the hope in this severe word of God.[35] Ultimately it is the hope of the world under God's wrath. "Not forever" points to the day when a son of David will reign over all things, and all will be well (see Matthew 1:1; Luke 1:32, 69; Romans 1:3; 2 Timothy 2:8; Revelation 5:5; 22:16).

What Happened to Jeroboam—at This Stage (v. 40)

We have still been told nothing about what Jeroboam did "against the king" (vv. 26, 27). Did he take some rebellious action *before* hearing the word from Ahijah? Or did Ahijah's word prompt some defiant deed? It seems that from our historian's perspective, what Jeroboam actually did was not particularly important.

However, "Solomon sought[36] to kill Jeroboam" (v. 40a). This reminds us of Saul's attempts to kill David (1 Samuel 18:11; 19:1, 2, 10; etc.). Solomon, who (again like Saul) had once looked favorably on the son of an Ephrathite (v. 26; cf. 1 Samuel 16:21, 22), now wanted him dead. Had Solomon, in his old age, become rather more like Saul than his father David?[37]

The narrator has presented the facts out of chronological sequence, with dramatic effect. Solomon's attempt on Jeroboam's life, which we may suppose happened after the Lord's word to Solomon in 11:11–13 and therefore in Solomon's old age (11:4), is reported immediately after the word God spoke to Jeroboam, presumably years earlier. The effect is to link Solomon's threat to

Jeroboam with the reader's realization that Jeroboam is the "servant" who will receive the kingdom (11:11). This strengthens our impression of the Saul-like nature of Solomon's behavior.[38]

"But Jeroboam arose and fled into Egypt, to Shishak king of Egypt, and was in Egypt until the death of Solomon" (v. 40b). As Hadad had done a generation earlier (11:18), Jeroboam found refuge in Egypt. The Pharaoh who had become Solomon's father-in-law (3:1) had been succeeded by Shishak,[39] who became the protector of Solomon's enemy. This is not the last we will hear of Shishak (see 14:25; also 2 Chronicles 12:2–12).

Solomon in Summary (vv. 41–43)

We will hear much more about Jeroboam in the pages that follow. For now the mention of Solomon's death in verse 40 prompts a formal notice about the reign of that remarkable king.[40]

What He Did (v. 41)

"Now the rest of the acts of Solomon, and all that he did, and his wisdom, are they not written in the Book of the Acts of Solomon?" (v. 41). We no longer have the Book of the Acts of Solomon. We can only wonder at what more it told about this king. The inspired writer has selected from that record (and perhaps other sources available to him). He reminds us again of Solomon's "wisdom." It was extraordinary, as we have seen, and yet even King Solomon was not wise enough. In the end he was as foolish as us all, and "his heart was not wholly true to the LORD his God" (11:4). Only with the coming of Jesus Christ can we say without qualification that in *him* "are hidden *all* the treasures of wisdom and knowledge" (Colossians 2:3; cf. 1 Corinthians 1:24, 30; Revelation 5:12).

His Reign (v. 42)

"And the time that Solomon reigned in Jerusalem over all Israel was forty years"[41] (v. 42). Our knowledge of those forty years is fragmentary, but the fragments are what matter. To the frustration of historians chronological precision is difficult. Is "forty" years a round number or to be taken literally and precisely? Does "forty years" include the time of co-regency before David's death? See further our discussion of 15:1.

As we look back over the record before us, the emphases stand out. Solomon became king by *God's choice* and in accordance with *God's promise* to his father David (we saw that implied throughout 1 Kings 1). While Solomon's throne was established by the overthrow of his enemies (1 Kings 2), Solomon's reign was characterized by *God-given wisdom to do justice* (1 Kings 3, 4). This wise king built the long promised *house for the name of the Lord* (1 Kings 5—7), the place that made praying in that name possible (1 Kings 8). That is what we know of the first twenty years or so.[42] The second twenty years were more problematic (1 Kings 9), although Solomon's reputation persisted (1 Kings 10). In the end he failed (1 Kings 11). His reign had brought the Old Testament story to its high point. But if we remember God's promise, it cannot be the end point.

His End (v. 43a)

"And Solomon slept with his fathers and was buried in the city of David his father" (v. 43a), just as his father David had done (2:10). This is hardly a surprise. Of course Solomon died. No matter how wise and good he had been, he was going to die. Even if he had not failed in his old age, he would have died. The wonders of Solomon's reign had to come to an end simply because Solomon had to die.

Now one greater than Solomon has come. "We know that Christ, being raised from the dead, will never die again; death no longer has dominion over him" (Romans 6:9).

And Then? (v. 43b)

What happened after the death of Solomon? "And Rehoboam his son reigned in his place" (v. 43b). Here is the "son" of whom we have heard three times in this chapter:

> I will tear [the kingdom] out of the hand of *your son*. (v. 12)

> I will give one tribe to *your son*. (v. 13)

> Yet to *his son* I will give one tribe. (v. 36)

The fulfillment of these words in the experience of Rehoboam will be the subject of the next chapter of 1 Kings. The two realities we have seen—the wrath of God against wickedness *and* the faithfulness of God to his promise—will shape the course of this history. It is an illuminating picture of the state of our world (under God's wrath, Romans 1:18) and the hope of our world (the faithfulness of God to his promise in the gospel of Jesus Christ; cf. Hebrews 10:23).

25

Power in Unworthy Hands

1 KINGS 12:1–24

WHEN JESUS SAID "I am among you as the one who *serves*" (Luke 22:27), he was beginning a revolution. The idea that a great and powerful person would use his strength not to advance his own welfare but for the good of others was radical in the extreme.

It may not seem so radical today. That is because the revolution Jesus began has had such a powerful influence over many centuries. But it is certain that as that influence recedes (which appears to be the mark of our time), we can expect powerful people to insist on using their resources more and more for the powerful rather than the weak, for themselves rather than others.

From the bully in the schoolyard to the strongman dictator of a nation, we have all seen the ugliness of the self-serving use of power. The horror is less obvious to us when we are the ones with power. But what a different world it would be if those in positions of strength—whether through wealth, status, popularity, or authority—actually used what they have been given to *serve*. Whenever we see a person who is even a little bit like that, we recognize how good it is. We may never be impressed by a billionaire because he has built a mansion. But if he uses his wealth to help needy people, that is impressive. We do not admire a politician who clings to office for his own glory. But if he risks his position in order to do good for others, that is striking.

The hope of the world is the revolution Jesus began. The day will come when *all* glory and honor and power are in the hands of "one who *serves*." That is why he, and he alone, is *worthy* to receive "power and wealth and wisdom and might and honor and glory and blessing" (Revelation 5:12).

The problem of power in unworthy hands is familiar to anyone with the smallest interest in history, politics, or, frankly, life. It was on display in a dramatic way in the days after King Solomon died. We have been told that Solomon's son, Rehoboam, succeeded him (11:43). We are about to hear what a disaster that was. Power passed to unworthy hands.

The story is complicated by the fact that we (the readers) have heard what the Lord had said first to Solomon (11:11–13) and then to a man named Jeroboam (11:31–39). We therefore know that the aftermath of Solomon's reign was not going to be straightforward. However, as far as we know, no one apart from Solomon (now dead), Jeroboam (hiding in Egypt), and the prophet Ahijah knew anything about the word that had come from God on this matter.

We will see:

(1) Power with a problem (vv. 1–5)
(2) The search for wisdom (vv. 6–11)
(3) Power in the hands of a fool (vv. 12–15)
(4) How foolish power fulfilled the word of God (vv. 16–24)

Power with a Problem (vv. 1–5)

In order to understand the situation at the beginning of 1 Kings 12 we need to remember that kingship was still a relatively new arrangement in Israel, and the succession process could not yet be taken for granted. King Saul, though he had been the Lord's anointed, was a disaster and was finally rejected by God (1 Samuel 13:14; 15:23, 26; 28:16–19). This made the transition to the one God had chosen to succeed Saul complicated. Some wanted a son of Saul to become king (2 Samuel 2:8–10). When David became king, at first it was only his own tribe of Judah who accepted him (2 Samuel 2:4, 7). It took some time and confusion (to say the least) before David became king over "all the tribes of Israel" (2 Samuel 5:1–3). The transition from David to Solomon was also far from straightforward, as we have seen. Some expected David's oldest surviving son, Adonijah, to take the throne (1:5–8). But it was a younger son of David, Solomon, who came to power (1:11—2:46). There had not yet been a conventional transition of the throne in Israel from father to eldest son.

It is reasonable to assume that Rehoboam was Solomon's eldest son, although the text of 1 Kings does not explicitly tell us this. There is no hint that any other son of Solomon had a claim, nor did Rehoboam's accession appear to need the kind of divine intervention his father and grandfather had experienced. However, Israel's history hardly teaches us to have high expectations for the sons (particularly eldest sons) of even the greatest leaders.[1]

A Meeting at Shechem (v. 1)

Rehoboam did not simply and automatically become king of all Israel upon the death of his father. Rather, "Rehoboam went to Shechem, for all Israel had come to Shechem to make him king" (v. 1).

So far in Israel's history a king had never been imposed on the people by force. Even for a king who had been chosen by God, his reign began with the willing acceptance of him by the people (see Saul in 1 Samuel 10:24; 11:15; David in 2 Samuel 2:4; 5:3; Solomon in 1 Kings 1:39).[2] It would be an exaggeration to call this "democratic," but it is important to see that the kind of king God gave his people had never been a matter of raw power inflicted on an unwilling people.

Our first impression is that the people were positive about Rehoboam. They "had come . . . to make him king." That was their intention. Or at least that is how it appeared.

Who were they? "All Israel" may refer to the whole nation (as a few lines earlier in 11:42).[3] However, it seems more likely that for our narrator "all Israel" has already come to mean the "ten tribes" of 11:31, 35.[4] That is certainly the meaning that "all Israel" will shortly take (see vv. 16, 18, 20).[5]

No doubt it was representatives of "all Israel" who "had come" (cf. 8:1), just as "all the tribes of Israel," that is, "all the elders of Israel," had come to David many years earlier with a similar purpose (2 Samuel 5:1–4).

Why Shechem?[6]

Shechem held troubling memories. Many years earlier it was where Abimelech was made king (Judges 9:6). If readers are expected to recall this episode (and who could forget it?), we might remember the parable that Jotham (the only brother of Abimelech to survive his fratricidal massacre) had told to the leaders of Shechem (Judges 9:7–21). It was a scathing critique of power acquired by violence and is worth remembering as we witness what was about to happen at Shechem this time.

But Shechem had other associations. It was where Abraham first received the promise, "To your offspring I will give this land," and there he built an altar to the Lord (Genesis 12:6, 7). Jacob, too, had built an altar (called "God, the God of Israel") in Shechem, having purchased a plot of land there (Genesis 33:18–20). Jacob's sons pastured their father's flock near Shechem (Genesis 37:12), and Joseph's bones were buried there (Joshua 24:32). It was the setting for a great assembly in the days of Joshua, recognizing the faithfulness of God in giving the people the land he had promised (Joshua 24:1–28). In Shechem they promised to serve the Lord, "for he is our God" (Joshua 24:18). Shechem was a place to remember God's promises from the beginning and his faithfulness through the generations. Not a bad place for the next offspring of David to be made king.

Rehoboam seems to have had no hesitation in traveling the forty miles north from Jerusalem to Shechem for this purpose.

A Key Player Summoned (vv. 2, 3a)

However, we readers know more than Rehoboam knew. We have heard God's word that Solomon's son will not reign over "all Israel" (in any sense), but only over "one tribe" (11:13, 36). We also know that the one who will reign over the rest of the people was a man named Jeroboam, the son of Nebat (11:31), who had been forced to flee to Egypt (11:40).

News (certainly of Solomon's death, perhaps also of the intended enthronement at Shechem) reached Jeroboam in Egypt:

> And when[7] [ESV, as soon as] Jeroboam the son of Nebat heard [ESV adds, of it] (for he was still in Egypt, where he had fled from King Solomon), then Jeroboam remained in [ESV, returned from[8]] Egypt.[9] (v. 2).

It seems that Jeroboam was not keen to take the initiative. We have already seen strange similarities to David's story in Jeroboam, son of Nebat. Here is another. Like David, he was not inclined to take the throne (that the Lord had promised him) by his own hand. He remained in Egypt.[10]

But not for long. "And they sent and called him" (v. 3a). We are not to suppose that the people who summoned Jeroboam back from Egypt had any idea of the word of the Lord that had been spoken to him (11:31–39). He had previously proven himself an able leader (11:28) and had stood up to King Solomon in some way (11:26). That was enough for them to want this man with them for their meeting with Solomon's son in Shechem. They called him back from Egypt.

A Proposal from the People (vv. 3b, 4)

Without further ado we are brought to the meeting in Shechem. Jeroboam seems to be the spokesman:

> . . . and Jeroboam and all the assembly of Israel came and said to Rehoboam, "Your father made our yoke heavy. Now therefore lighten the hard service of your father and his heavy yoke on us, and we will serve you." (vv. 3b, 4)

For a moment there is the possibility of Rehoboam taking his father's place over "all the assembly [Hebrew *qahal*] of Israel." The expression reminds us of King Solomon's "church" (see 8:14, 22, 55, 65). However this is the last time in the books of Kings that we will hear of "the assembly of Israel." King Solomon's "church" did not outlast King Solomon.

Nonetheless we hear the people's willingness: "we will serve you." This does not sound like defiance. What, then, was the problem?

The people claimed that Solomon had made their "yoke[11] heavy." They were discontent. Should we blame them for this? Perhaps they were right. We have seen indications that, for all its glory, Solomon's reign was not without problems (see 9:10–28). Or was their complaint unwarranted? Have we not seen that King Solomon brought unparalleled prosperity, happiness, justice, and peace to the kingdom (4:20–25; 10:9, 23)? Had the people developed an inflated sense of entitlement?

We do not need to come down on one side or the other with these questions. The fact is that Solomon's reign did not establish lasting happiness and contentment. We have seen hints that Solomon's reign drifted toward Egyptian ways. It is disturbing now to hear in the people's words to Rehoboam an echo of their ancestors long ago in Egypt (see Exodus 1:14; 2:23; 5:9).[12] Did they really feel that in some sense their experience under Solomon could be compared to the situation from which God had redeemed them so long ago (see 6:1; 8:9, 16, 21, 51, 53; 9:9)?

What they wanted from Rehoboam was a lighter load, probably referring to both compulsory labor and taxation (see 4:7–19; 5:13–18; 9:15–23).

Many years later Jesus may have had this very incident in mind when he said:

> Come to me, all who labor and are heavy laden, and I will give you rest. Take my yoke upon you, and learn from me, for I am gentle and lowly in heart, and you will find rest for your souls. For my yoke is easy, and my burden is light. (Matthew 11:28–30)

What the people sought from Rehoboam is promised by Jesus. His yoke is easy, his burden is light *because* he is one who serves (he is "gentle and lowly in heart").

Time to Consider (v. 5)

The young and inexperienced Rehoboam was apparently caught unawares by the terms put to him by Jeroboam and the people. He said to them, "Go away for three days, then come again to me" (v. 5a). He needed time to think. Could he, should he, at the beginning of his reign, accede to such a request? Or was it a demand? How could it be done? What would it cost? What would be the consequent effects?

The people, to their credit, cooperated: "So the people went away" (v. 5b). They were prepared to wait for an answer.

The Search for Wisdom (vv. 6–11)

Rehoboam probably returned to Jerusalem. This is suggested by the title now given to him (for the first time) in verse 6: "King Rehoboam." He may not yet have been king among those who had gathered in Shechem. But back in Jerusalem, and presumably throughout Judah, he was King Rehoboam. Like his grandfather before him, his own people were the first to receive him as their king (cf. 2 Samuel 2:4).

From the Old Men (vv. 6, 7)

The young king sought counsel on the difficult decision before him. "Then King Rehoboam took counsel with the old men, who had stood before Solomon his father while he was yet alive" (v. 6a).

These older men were his seniors in years and experience. More than that, they had served Rehoboam's great and wise father.[13] They, more than anyone, would have understood the policies that were being questioned by Jeroboam and those with him in Shechem. They had heard and seen the wisdom of King Solomon. Could they impart wisdom to Solomon's son?

The Question (v. 6b)

Rehoboam had a simple question for his older advisors: "How do you[14] advise me to answer this people?" (v. 6b). He asked about the manner ("How?") of his response rather than the content.[15]

The Wisdom of Humility (v. 7)

The elders' advice was as follows:

> And they said to him, "If today you will be a servant to this people and serve them, and speak good words to them when you answer[16] them, then they will be your servants forever [all the days]."[17] (v. 7)

Rehoboam's response "today" will have consequences for "all the days." How was Rehoboam to act? The advice of the older men was that he should be among them as a *servant* who *serves*.

What strange advice for a *king*! To be a *servant*? To *serve* them? What kind of advice was this?[18] It was the kind of advice that will one day come to full realization in Jesus Christ, who said:

> . . . whoever would be great among you must be your *servant*, and whoever would be first among you must be slave of all. For even the Son of Man came not to be served but to *serve*, and to give his life as a ransom for many. (Mark 10:43–45)

If Rehoboam could be like *that* today, then (according to the older men) his people would serve him "all the days." There was something of the wisdom of Solomon in this advice (see 3:7–9, 28). Indeed there was something prophetic. The kind of king they described is the kind of King that would eventually come.

From the Youngsters (vv. 8–11)

For the first time we glimpse Rehoboam's character: "But he abandoned the counsel that the old men gave him" (v. 8a). Rejecting the wisdom of the elders, he showed himself to be a fool.

Instead he "took counsel with the young men [the youngsters[19]] who had grown up with him and stood before him" (v. 8b).

Since Rehoboam was forty-one years old (14:21) these contemporaries of his were probably called "youngsters" only relative to the "old men" and by virtue of the immature and irresponsible words they were about to utter. That they had "grown up with him and stood before him" (as the elders had "stood before" Solomon) suggests that they had learned from Rehoboam, just as the elders had learned from Solomon. But we will shortly see that neither he nor they had really grown up at all. And they will give the kind of advice that Rehoboam would give himself!

The descriptions of the "old men" and the "youngsters" suggests that the latter had displaced the former. A new generation had come to power and influence in Jerusalem. Perhaps they "have never known anything but extravagant privilege and a heavy sense of their own entitlement."[20] These are the ones to whom Rehoboam now turned.

The Question (v. 9)

And he said to them, "What do you[21] advise that we answer this people who have said to me, 'Lighten the yoke that your father put on us'?" (v. 9).

He now asks the youngsters "what?" (not "how?") he should respond to "this people." *Write my speech for me.* More precisely he asks about what "we" will say. They will do this together.[22] *It will be our speech.*

Rehoboam's report of what the people had asked of him makes no reference to the perceived hardness of their experience under Solomon but focuses entirely on their request for a lighter "yoke," making it sound like a groundless demand. Had he listened at all?[23]

The Foolishness of Arrogance (vv. 10, 11)

Unlike the older men, for whom the *manner* of Rehoboam's response was crucial, the youngsters draw on their juvenile wit to compose Rehoboam's speech for him. It is coarse, crude, and extremely stupid.

> And the young men [youngsters] who had grown up with him said to him, "Thus shall you speak to this people who said to you, 'Your father made our yoke heavy, but you lighten it for us,' thus shall you say to them, 'My little finger is thicker than my father's thighs [or loins]. And now, whereas my father laid on you a heavy yoke, I will add to your yoke. My father disciplined you with whips, but I will discipline you with scorpions.'" (vv. 10, 11)

Notice four things about this speech.

First, it was crude. This is camouflaged in our English versions, but "my little finger" is literally "my little thing" and in context is almost certainly a coarse reference to the male organ.[24] With gutter humor they suggested Rehoboam flaunt his macho potency.

Second, it was arrogant. The young king, who had accomplished nothing, was to present himself as mightier than his father, whose greatness was internationally acclaimed (4:34; 10:6–9). The conceit is breathtaking.

Third, it was tyrannical. They had learned something of the discontent of the people at the burdens of Solomon's reign. But whether justified or not, under Rehoboam they *would* have something to complain about! The speech is Pharaoh-like.[25] *You thought my father was harsh. I'll show you what harsh is!* "Scorpions" suggests "whips with barbed points like the point of a scorpion's sting,"[26] as well as having associations with the wilderness[27] and thus the loss of God's promised blessing.

Fourth, as we will see, it was utterly foolish.

Power in the Hands of a Fool (vv. 12–15)

When the time for consideration and consultation had passed, the parties met again at Shechem.

Potential for Peace (v. 12)

"So Jeroboam and all the people came[28] to Rehoboam the third day, as the king said, 'Come to me again the third day'" (v. 12). It is clear that Jeroboam and the people were acting in good faith. They were prepared to work with Rehoboam.[29]

Foolish Power (vv. 13, 14)

However, on that third day things did not go well:

> And the king answered the people harshly, and forsaking the counsel that the old men had given him, he spoke to them according to the counsel of the young men [youngsters], saying, "My father made your yoke heavy, but I will add to your yoke. My father disciplined you with whips, but I will discipline you with scorpions." (vv. 13, 14)

At least he dispensed with the crudities. But that is all that can be said for Rehoboam's response to the people. He answered "harshly," mimicking in his response the "hard" service they had spoken of at the beginning (v. 4).[30] Rehoboam would not use his power to serve, as the elders had advised, but to oppress. "Not caring whether they loved him or no, he would make them fear him."[31] What a fool he was!

The King Who Did Not Listen (v. 15a)

"So the king did not listen to the people" (v. 15a). How different from his father who had prayed for "a hearing heart to govern your people, that I may discern between good and evil" (3:9, AT). Rehoboam heard nothing, adding to his Pharaoh-like image (see Exodus 7:13).[32]

The Lord and His Word (v. 15b)

I do hope that you are dismayed. The glorious kingdom of Solomon had come into the hands of a foolish, arrogant thug. This turn of events appears to be the consequence of human failure. Whether or not the people's discontent was justified, Rehoboam's self-serving, insensitive, uncaring belligerence brought the glory days of Solomon's kingdom to an end.

Of course, we are not surprised. Human failure had begun with Solomon in his old age (11:1–8). But there was more to it than that:

> . . . for it was a turn of affairs[33] brought about by the LORD that he might fulfill his word, which the LORD spoke by Ahijah the Shilonite to Jeroboam the son of Nebat. (v. 15b)

The foolishness and wickedness of humans does not thwart the good, wise, and righteous purposes of God. On the contrary, even attempts to defy God's ways are used by him to accomplish his purposes (see Acts 2:23, 24 for the starkest example of this in world history[34]). What was about to happen because of Rehoboam's stupidity was what the Lord had said would happen in his word both to Solomon (11:11–13) and to Jeroboam (11:31–39). Ultimately history unfolds according to God's word (see 2 Samuel 22:31; 1 Kings 2:27; cf. Hebrews 1:3). The ultimate meaning of these (and all other) events lies in the purpose of God made known by his word.

How Foolish Power Fulfilled the Word of God (vv. 16–24)

It remains only to follow the consequences of that Shechem conference and see how they fulfilled the word the Lord had previously spoken—with a few further surprises.

In Israel (vv. 16–20)

First we see what happened in "Israel" (now unambiguously meaning the northern tribes).

Two Kingdoms (vv. 16, 17)

And when all Israel saw that the king did not listen to them, the people answered the king, "What portion do we have in David? We have no inheritance in the son of Jesse. To your tents, O Israel! Look now to your own house, David." So Israel went to their tents. (v. 16)

What may have begun as a reasonable petition made with due respect to the new king had been turned into defiant rebellion by the harsh arrogance of Rehoboam. They took up the mutinous cry that had been heard a generation earlier, when a worthless man named Sheba had led the northern tribes in an attempted secession from King David (2 Samuel 20:1). He, and now they, had repudiated the bond that had been affirmed when all the tribes of Israel had made David their king ("we are your bone and flesh," 2 Samuel 5:1; cf. 19:43). What Sheba had unsuccessfully attempted would now be decisively and permanently accomplished. They repudiated their place in David's kingdom ("What portion do we have in David?"), denying that there was anything in it for them ("no inheritance"). God's gift to Israel (as "inheritance" suggests, Deuteronomy 4:21, 38) was not, for them, to be found "in the son of Jesse"—a derogatory way of speaking of David (see 1 Samuel 20:27, 30, 31; 22:7, 8, 13). They withdrew "to their tents" (probably where they had been camped for the Shechem negotiations[35]). The conference was over. Indeed it seems that the united kingdom was finished. "Look now to your own house, David" sounds threatening. Were they already contemplating not only separation but aggression?[36]

Our narrator adds a note that glances forward to explain that the consequences of this walkout were not neat. "Rehoboam reigned over the people of Israel who lived in the cities of Judah" (v. 17). There had, no doubt, been considerable movement of people across tribal borders over the years. Furthermore Simeon's territory lay within the land of Judah (Joshua 19:1), and Benjamin was very close to Jerusalem (see v. 21; Joshua 18:16).[37] For these and perhaps other reasons, there were Israelites other than the tribe of Judah who remained under the rule of the Davidic king. Some see here a token of hope that one day a son of David would again rule over *all* Israel (don't forget the "not forever" of 11:39!).[38]

Foolish Power (Again) and What It Achieved (vv. 18, 19)

But Rehoboam had not finished with his stupidity. He responded to the people's termination of the conference with a further provocative move: "Then King Rehoboam sent Adoram, who was taskmaster over the forced labor . . ." (v. 18a).

This was almost certainly the Adoniram we met in 4:6, who had been appointed to his role years earlier by David (2 Samuel 20:24). He must have been rather old by this time, but he had been the one largely responsible for the policy at the heart of the people's complaint. If Rehoboam sent Adoram to negotiate with the people on his behalf, he could hardly have made a poorer choice.[39] If he sent Adoram to intimidate them, he seriously misjudged the situation. The people had had enough: "all Israel stoned [Adoram] to death with stones" (v. 18b).

At last Rehoboam understood: "And [But] King Rehoboam hurried to mount his chariot to flee to Jerusalem" (v. 18c). He abandoned poor Adoram to the mob and fled to the safety of his royal city. The bully was, after all, a coward. Like most bullies.

Again our narrator glances forward to the consequences of the momentous events he is reporting: "So Israel has been in rebellion against the house of David to this day" (v. 19). Make no mistake. The events at Shechem had consequences for a very long time.[40] Indeed the rest of 1 and 2 Kings is the record of those consequences. And reunification is not part of that story.

The Word of the Lord Fulfilled (v. 20)

If the word of the Lord that we heard in 1 Kings 11 is still ringing in our ears, we will be waiting to hear about Jeroboam.

And when all Israel heard that Jeroboam had returned, they sent and called him to the assembly and made him king over all Israel. There was none that followed the house of David but the tribe of Judah only. (v. 20)

Word spread to the northern population ("all Israel"[41]) that Jeroboam had returned from Egypt, and presumably they also heard about the disastrous outcome of the Shechem conference. They called him to another assembly[42] and did to him what the delegation at Shechem had originally planned to do to Rehoboam. They made him king over "all Israel" (that is, the northern tribes). The house of David had been reduced to one tribe only. And so the word of the Lord was precisely fulfilled (11:32).[43]

In Judah (vv. 21–24)

Rehoboam *was* a slow learner. Having escaped with his life, he decided to use coercive power to reverse the situation he had brought on himself by the threat of power. We need a better word than *stupid*.

Foolish Power (Yet Again!) (v. 21)

When Rehoboam came to Jerusalem, he assembled all the house of Judah and the tribe of Benjamin, 180,000 chosen warriors, to fight against the house of Israel, to restore the kingdom to Rehoboam the son of Solomon. (v. 21)

"All the house of Judah" was all he could now "assemble" (Hebrew, *qahal*), corresponding to "all the assembly [*qahal*] of Israel" in verse 3 that was no longer his. We have seen that the situation was not quite that neat (v. 17). Now we learn that Rehoboam held sway over at least some of the tribe of Benjamin, whose territory lay to the immediate north of Jerusalem.

There is a paradox here. Benjamin had been Saul's tribe (1 Samuel 9:1, 2, 16, 21; 10:20, 21) and the source of simmering discontent with David (2 Samuel 2:15, 25; 16:5, 11; 19:16, 17; 20:1; 1 Kings 2:8). In this divinely overseen twist of events (v. 15), Benjamin (of all the tribes) did not break away from Judah. The old resentments did not have their way.[44]

The number of "chosen warriors" may remind a very attentive reader[45] of the 30,000 plus 70,000 plus 80,000 workers Solomon drafted out of all Israel to work on building the house of the Lord (5:13, 15). What Solomon employed to *build*, Rehoboam engaged for *war*.[46]

Worse still, it was not war against the enemies of God and his people, but "against the house of Israel." While Rehoboam may have thought that his actions were comparable to his grandfather as he defended the kingdom against the rebellions of Absalom (2 Samuel 18) and Sheba (2 Samuel 20), we (the readers) know that Rehoboam was setting himself against the word that the Lord had spoken. The narrator subtly reminds us of this with the otherwise redundant words "the son of Solomon." Rehoboam was the "son" of whom God had spoken in 11:12, 13, 35, 36.

The Word of the Lord and Foolish Power (vv. 22–24)

The word of God stopped him.

> But the word of God came to Shemaiah the man of God: "Say to Rehoboam the son of Solomon, king of Judah, and to all the house of Judah and Benjamin, and to the rest of the people, 'Thus says the LORD, You shall not go up or [better, and] fight against your relatives [literally, brothers] the people of Israel. Every man return to his home, for this thing is from me.'" (vv. 22–24a)

This is the only appearance of the prophet (that is what "man of God" means[47]) Shemaiah in this history.[48] The word of God he was to speak was addressed to "the son of Solomon" (reminding us again of what we have heard earlier about this "son"), the "king of *Judah*" (the first time we have heard this title, emphasizing that he was king of one tribe only, 11:13, 32, 36), "all the house of Judah and Benjamin" (reminding us that "one tribe" and "Judah" should not be pressed literally), and "the rest of the people" (see v. 17). The last expression probably includes the northerners who had withdrawn from the rule of the son of Solomon. God's word was for *all* God's people.[49]

The message from God had three points.

First, they were not to proceed with the planned aggression. Rehoboam's plans were not God's plans.

Second, this was because the people of Israel (the north) were their "brothers." Contrary to the denial of family ties by the northerners ("What portion do we have in David?," v. 16), the people were still one people (2 Samuel 5:1). The one God laid claim to all the people. This division was "not forever" (11:39).

Third, "this thing is from me." As we (the readers) were told in verse 15, now everyone is to hear that the hand of God himself was behind the unfortunate events of these days—not the wickedness involved, but the outcome. The word that had been spoken privately to Solomon and to Jeroboam before Solomon's death was now made public.

The word of God accomplished what nothing else could: "So they listened to the word of the LORD and went home again, according to the word of the LORD" (v. 24b). God's word is like that (Isaiah 55:10, 11).[50]

What hope was there for the people who had too briefly been the envy of the world (see 10:6–9)? Solomon's failure (11:1–8) and now his son's foolishness had shattered the kingdom that had—so fleetingly—enjoyed unparalleled peace, prosperity, justice, and glory (see 3:28; 4:20; 5:4; 10:23). Power in unworthy hands had destroyed it all. What hope could there be?

The question should be extended. What hope is there for the whole world, where power is so consistently in unworthy hands, as you will see on tonight's TV news? The hope of the world lies in the revolution that answered the hopes of the people of Israel: a king who will be a *servant* and *serve* his people. He has taught us to value, support, and encourage every attempt to use any kind of power to *serve*—not for the benefit of the powerful, but for the good of others. We look forward to the day when the One who came not to be served but to serve and to give his life as a ransom for many will receive all power, wealth, wisdom, might, honor, glory, and blessing (Mark 10:45; Revelation 5:12). He is the hope of the world. Only under him will there be full and complete reunification not only of God's people but of all things (see Ephesians 1:10; 2:15; Colossians 1:19, 20). Then, at last, power will be in *worthy* hands.

26

The Terrifying Prospect of Actually Trusting God

1 KINGS 12:25–33

FAITH IN GOD IS NOT for the fainthearted. Don't misunderstand me. Jesus Christ invites the weak, the troubled, the fearful, the anxious to come to him and find strength, comfort, safety, and peace (see, for example, Matthew 11:28–30). But coming to him takes courage. The prospect of actually trusting God and believing his promises can be terrifying.

We are about to see how terrifying it was for Jeroboam (now *King* Jeroboam). He was in a most unusual situation. On the one hand, he had been made king by those who wanted to have nothing more to do with the kingdom that had been established by David (12:16, 20), the kingdom that had been promised by God and so conspicuously blessed by him (see 8:15–26). The high-handed and harsh arrogance of David's grandson, Rehoboam, had a lot to do with it. But had the people overreacted? If they had believed and trusted God's promise to David, would they have so readily withdrawn from his kingdom?

On the other hand, Jeroboam knew (as we know) that this "turn of affairs" was from the Lord (12:15, 24). It was a consequence of the unfaithfulness of David's son, Solomon (11:11, 33). God had promised that if Jeroboam would listen and obey the Lord's commandments in this new situation, God would be with him and build him a "sure house" (11:38).

What would it mean for Jeroboam to trust God in this situation? It would not be easy. Indeed, as we will see, for Jeroboam it was a terrifying prospect.

Let's hear how Jeroboam began his reign:

(1) The security Jeroboam sought (v. 25)
(2) The insecurity Jeroboam felt (vv. 26, 27)
(3) The strategy Jeroboam chose (vv. 28, 29)
(4) The "success" Jeroboam enjoyed (vv. 30–33)

The Security Jeroboam Sought (v. 25)

The first problem that the new king faced was the lack of any kind of institutional structures to support and protect his reign. Over many years King David and then King Solomon had developed administrative arrangements to support the king's rule (see 4:1–19; cf. 2 Samuel 8:15–18; 20:23–26). That had taken time. Solomon had spent twenty years and more constructing an impressive complex of buildings with a variety of functions enhancing, facilitating, and defending his reign (6:1—7:51; 9:15–28). Jeroboam had a lot to do to make his new kingdom secure and functional.

So it is no surprise that the very first recorded act of King Jeroboam was that "Jeroboam *built*" (v. 25). Was Jeroboam perhaps taking his cue from Solomon, the builder-king? He had a long way to go to catch up with the building work in Jerusalem and the kingdom from which his people had withdrawn. But this was a beginning.

What did he build?

Shechem (v. 25a)

First, "Jeroboam built Shechem in the hill country of Ephraim and lived there" (v. 25a). He needed a royal city. What better place than the location of the conference that had initiated his reign, with its many historical associations (see our discussion of 12:1). Furthermore Shechem was centrally located in the new kingdom.[1] An ideal capital for the new king.

Shechem needed some work. It is likely that this included defenses (NIV says he "fortified" it). A royal residence would have been needed, and perhaps other buildings to give visible and practical support to the new government.

Jeroboam "lived there," making Shechem (for the time being) his royal city—his Jerusalem. This was, perhaps, not a bad start.

Penuel (v. 25b)

"And he went out from there and built Penuel" (v. 25b). More building! Penuel was about thirty miles east of Shechem, on the other side of the Jordan River.[2] Penuel (or Peniel, "the face of God") was the name given to this place by Jacob after the remarkable experience in which God gave him the name Israel (Genesis 32:22–32). This association would be enough to make Penuel important for the new king of the kingdom that will be called "Israel."

However, it is also likely that Jeroboam was strengthening his defenses against threats that may have come from the northeast and east.[3]

So far so good. Jeroboam was doing what we might reasonably expect from the new king. He was securing his throne and his people by building the infrastructure he considered necessary.

The Insecurity Jeroboam Felt (vv. 26, 27)

However, Jeroboam was not feeling secure. Buildings and fortifications did not address a fundamental threat that troubled him in the peculiar circumstances of his kingdom.

Where It Came From (v. 26a)

Our writer indicates the source of Jeroboam's insecurity by telling us that "Jeroboam said *in his heart* . . ." (v. 26a). We have heard more than once that God required the "heart" of the king and his people to be faithful and true (2:4; 3:6; 8:23, 61; 9:4; cf. 8:17, 18). Furthermore, the present troubling situation began with Solomon's "heart" being turned away from the Lord (11:2, 3, 4, 9). The future of Jeroboam's kingdom depended on what was going on in the king's *heart*.

What He Feared (vv. 26, 27)

In his heart Jeroboam was afraid.

> And Jeroboam said in his heart, "Now the kingdom will turn back to the house of David. If this people go up to offer sacrifices in the temple [literally, house[4]] of the Lord at Jerusalem, then the heart of this people will turn again to their lord,[5] to Rehoboam king of Judah, and they will kill me and return to Rehoboam king of Judah." (vv. 26, 27)

The first thing to notice is that Jeroboam's fear was reasonable.[6] The people had become used to the house of the Lord in Jerusalem. No doubt the powerful impression that the *account* of the building of this house, its fitting out, and its early use (particularly Solomon's speech and prayer in 8:12–53) has had on us as readers of 1 Kings is a pale reflection of the effect that the *experience* of these things must have had on the people. They may have opted for a different king, but they were still the Lord's people. Is it not likely that they would want to "go up to offer sacrifices at the house of the LORD at Jerusalem"?

In other words, Jeroboam did not see the people's rejection of the "house" of *David* (12:16) as a rejection of the "house" of *the Lord*. And if they go to Jerusalem, aren't they likely to remember that the house of the Lord and the house of David belonged together? Perhaps they would find themselves singing Psalm 2, about "the LORD and . . . his anointed" (Psalm 2:2)! Is it not likely (we can almost hear Jeroboam thinking) that when the people realize that the choice is not just between Jeroboam and Rehoboam, but between Jeroboam and the son of *David*, they "will turn back to the house of David . . . to their lord, to Rehoboam king of Judah"?

Strikingly even Jeroboam, in his heart, thought of Rehoboam as "their lord," even though Rehoboam was now only "king of Judah."[7] If King Jeroboam did not really believe in the legitimacy of his position, it would not take much, would it, for his people to entertain doubts?

Again it was a matter of the "heart" of this people. Jeroboam feared that if "the heart of this people" turned to the Lord their God (cf. 8:39, 47, 48, 58, 61), then their heart would "turn again to their lord, to Rehoboam king of Judah."

If that were to happen, he was quite sure that they would dispose of the evidence of their temporary unfaithfulness: "they will kill me." That would allow them to "return to Rehoboam king of Judah."

Jeroboam was terrified.

At this point Jeroboam could have recalled God's word to him:

> And if you will listen to all that I command you, and will walk in my ways, and do what is right in my eyes by keeping my statutes and my commandments, as David my servant did, I will be with you and will build you a sure house, as I built for David, and I will give Israel to you. (11:38)

He had God's promise. He could have listened, been careful to do what was right in God's eyes, and trusted God to build him a sure house and give Israel to him. He could have trusted God for his security.

The Strategy Jeroboam Chose (vv. 28, 29)

However, the prospect of actually trusting God did not appeal to Jeroboam. It would have limited his options to what was right in God's sight. Jeroboam was not *that* courageous. He needed a less terrifying strategy, one more under his control.

He Took Counsel (v. 28a)

"So the king took counsel" (v. 28a). We are not told whose counsel he sought, but the recent example of how Rehoboam "took counsel" (12:6, 8) is hardly encouraging.

Did anyone advise Jeroboam to listen to God's word and do what was right in *his* sight? Probably not. If they did, he took no more notice than Rehoboam had taken of the wise counsel he had received (12:8).

He Made Two Calves of Gold (v. 28b)

The strategy he chose took a rather different shape. He "made two calves [perhaps better, young bulls[8]] of gold" (v. 28b). At this point anyone familiar with the history of the people of Israel will gasp. *He did what?*

He did what Aaron had disastrously done a long time earlier, after the Lord had brought the Israelites out of bondage in Egypt (Exodus 32:4a;[9] see Deuteronomy 9:16, 21; Nehemiah 9:18; Psalm 106:19, 20; Acts 7:41; cf. 1 Corinthians 10:7). In fact he doubled up on what Aaron had done. Aaron had made one young bull of gold. Jeroboam made two (for reasons that will shortly be clear).[10]

What was Jeroboam thinking? I suspect that he was not thinking very clearly. He had a practical problem, and he had come up with a strategy to deal with it. The problem was too great to let something like obedience to the Lord's commandments stand in his way.

Although the similarity to Aaron's historic blunder is obvious to later Bible readers, I doubt that it occurred to Jeroboam. He probably thought that these two young bulls made of gold would be substitutes for all that gold in the house of the Lord in Jerusalem. But was he thinking that the images could represent the Lord to the people (thus breaking the second commandment, Exodus 20:4–6)[11] or was he thinking that these images could draw the people away from the Lord to other gods altogether (thus breaking the first commandment, Exodus 20:3)?[12] Either way he was giving no attention to doing what was right in God's eyes.

He Preached a Lie (v. 28c)

"And he said to the people, 'You have gone up to Jerusalem long enough. Behold your gods, O Israel, who brought you up out of the land of Egypt'" (v. 28c).

Going up to Jerusalem was to go up to the house of the Lord, the place of which the Lord had said, "My name shall be there" (8:29). This obedience to

God was a joyful blessing (see Deuteronomy 12:5–7, 11–14). Jeroboam's first lie was to present this privilege as a burden from which he would bring relief: "You have gone up to Jerusalem long enough."[13]

A Christian reader may be reminded that our great privilege is to come to "the heavenly Jerusalem" (Hebrews 12:22) by coming to Jesus Christ (see Matthew 11:28; 19:14; John 6:37; 7:37; Hebrews 12:22; 1 Peter 2:4). Beware of anyone who, like Jeroboam, tries to turn the joy and blessing of God's gracious invitation into a burden to be avoided.

Jeroboam's second lie was subtle in a way that is lost in translation. "Behold your gods, O Israel" could mean, "Behold your God, O Israel."[14] He was not *obviously* calling on the people to abandon the Lord and accept some other gods in his place. The people could have heard him calling on them to see God in a new (and more convenient) way, to see these golden calves as representations of the Lord their God. But it was a lie. Regardless of what he *thought* he was doing, Jeroboam had made "other gods" (14:9).

Christian reader, beware of anyone who invites you to see the Lord in more convenient, less demanding ways—to come to God in some way other than coming to the Lord Jesus Christ (see John 14:6; Colossians 2:6, 7). No matter how attractive the words may sound, such a message is a lie.

Jeroboam's third lie was to pretend that the new way in which he was inviting the people to see God, which would not require them to go up to Jerusalem, had all the power of Israel's true faith: ". . . who brought you up out of the land of Egypt." *You can enjoy your redemption while reinventing your Redeemer.*

Christian reader, beware of anyone who links forgiveness and salvation with their own ideas about God. A domesticated Lord, remade for our convenience, will not deliver us from sin and death. Only the Lord Jesus Christ *as we meet him in the Scriptures* can and will do that.

Again I doubt that Jeroboam had thought the matter through thoroughly. He just wanted to adjust the people's understanding of God so that they would not go up to Jerusalem. He was terrified of what might happen if they continued their visits to the house in Jerusalem. He had come up with a less dangerous way of worshipping the one "who brought you up out of the land of Egypt."

However (probably unwittingly), his message echoed, almost word for word, the message of Aaron years earlier: "These are your gods, O Israel, who brought you up out of the land of Egypt!" (Exodus 32:4).[15] The earlier episode illuminates the present one, as the Biblical writer portrays it. Jeroboam's act, like Aaron's, was "corrupt." It was "turning aside" from the way the Lord had commanded. He had "sinned a great sin" (see Exodus 32:7, 8, 30).

The golden bulls of both Aaron and Jeroboam depended for their impressiveness on the associations of gold (wealth) and the animal (virility and strength). The substitutes for trusting God to which people turn have a depressing consistency. Where do we turn when we lack the courage to trust God? Assertive, aggressive human strength and ostentatious displays of wealth still appeal. Perhaps the most spectacular contemporary example is the pseudoreligious carrying on at the modern Olympic Games. Hopes of world peace, no less, are associated with ostentatious expenditure and displays of extraordinary physical prowess.[16] Today's golden bulls?

He Established the Lie (v. 29)

Jeroboam institutionalized his false gospel. Of his two golden bulls we are told "he set one in Bethel, and the other he put in Dan" (v. 29).

Now we see why he made *two* golden bulls. In order to provide a more convenient religion than one involving going up to Jerusalem, he needed to provide places for the people to go that were much easier to reach.

Bethel was no doubt chosen, at least in part, because of its strategic location for Jeroboam's purpose. It was just eleven miles north of Jerusalem, close to the boundary between the two kingdoms (see Joshua 18:13). Anyone considering going up to Jerusalem would be likely to pass Bethel on the way.[17] Who would not be glad to cut twenty-two miles off the round trip?

Bethel had the further advantage of its historic associations. The place's name ("House of God") served Jeroboam's purpose well. Bethel received this name from Jacob after his extraordinary dream in which God's promise to Abraham was reaffirmed (Genesis 28:19; see also Genesis 35:7, 15). Indeed near this place Abraham had pitched his tent and built an altar to the Lord (Genesis 12:8; 13:3, 4). Much later the ark of the covenant had been kept in Bethel for a time (Judges 20:26–28). All this made Bethel an attractive alternative to Jerusalem.

Dan was located at the opposite end of Jeroboam's kingdom, in the far north.[18] It provided a location that was much more convenient for those who lived furthest from Jerusalem. Dan had been named by the Israelite tribe of Dan after their ancestor (Joshua 19:47). There were rather less positive memories associated with Dan. Dan already had a reputation for idolatry (see Judges 18:27–31).[19] No doubt Jeroboam overlooked this awkward fact.

The "Success" Jeroboam Enjoyed (vv. 30–33)

Jeroboam's plan worked. That is, he accomplished his purpose of keeping his people from going up to Jerusalem. They obeyed their king and went instead to Bethel and Dan. It was more convenient, and it was much more comfortable for Jeroboam.

The Sin (v. 30)

But it was the very opposite of trusting God. The narrator makes the chilling comment: "Then this thing became a sin, for the people went as far as Dan to be before one" (v. 30). If they went as far as the remote and distant Dan, we may assume, of course, that they also went to Bethel.[20]

The point is that "this thing became a *sin*." Jeroboam's strategy "became" a sin because the new king led his people to disobey the second (and therefore, in fact, the first) commandment, as well as the requirement to come to the place of God's choice (see 8:44, 48; 11:13, 32, 36; 14:21 in the light of Deuteronomy 12:5, 11, 14). What may have begun as a strategy to secure his kingdom (and himself) from what his heart feared became a "sin" because Jeroboam did not trust God. He did not think that he would be safe if he and his people did what was right in God's eyes.

The particular word used for "sin" here probably suggests guilt before God, deserving his punishment.[21] *That* was what Jeroboam's strategy achieved!

Verse 30 is the narrator's comment to which we, the readers, are privy. Jeroboam, however, had not yet been made aware of this dimension to his "success." He built on the initial accomplishment, unwittingly (I think) adding sin to sin.

The Houses (v. 31a)

"He also made temples [houses[22]] on high places" (v. 31a). These "high places" were presumably at Dan and Bethel (see 2 Kings 23:15). The "house" he made at each location was Jeroboam's substitute for the "house" of the Lord at Jerusalem (see v. 27).

There was a time when it may have been acceptable for the people to offer sacrifices at "high places" but that was when (and because) "no house had yet been built for the name of the LORD" (3:2; see our discussion of 3:2, 3). Now, however, Jeroboam's "high places" were no more acceptable than those provided by Solomon for the pagan gods of his foreign wives (11:7). We will be hearing more about "high places" in the kingdom Jeroboam now ruled (see 13:2, 32, 33; 2 Kings 17:9, 11; cf. 17:29, 32) and even more about those in its southern neighbor (see 14:23; 15:14; 22:43; 2 Kings 12:3; 14:4; 15:4, 35; 16:4; 18:4, 22; 21:3; 23:5, 8, 9, 13, 15, 19, 20). From this point on "high places" will represent the apostate rejection of the place the Lord had chosen. That is what Jeroboam began.

The Priests (v. 31b)

Furthermore he "appointed priests from among all the people,[23] who were not of the Levites [literally, who were not from the sons of Levi]" (v. 31b).

From the days of Moses when the tabernacle had been built, the tribe of Levi ("the Levites") was designated as having particular responsibility "under the direction of Ithamar the son of Aaron the priest" (Exodus 38:21; see also Numbers 1:47–54; Deuteronomy 18:1–8). Strictly speaking, it was only one branch of the descendants of Levi, namely the descendants of Aaron, who were to be the priests (Numbers 3:10). Levites other than the "sons of Aaron" served the priests in various ways (Numbers 3:5–39).[24]

By appointing priests who were not from the tribe of Levi, let alone from the sons of Aaron, Jeroboam was probably deliberately further distancing his "houses" at Bethel and Dan from the house in Jerusalem, where the Levites would continue to have a key role (see 2 Chronicles 11:13, 14).[25] Jeroboam's "priests" were his own invention.[26]

The Feast (v. 32a)

"And Jeroboam appointed a feast on the fifteenth day of the eighth month like the feast that was in Judah" (v. 32a). In Judah the important Feast of Booths was held in the fifteenth day of the *seventh* month (Leviticus 23:34).[27] Jeroboam was taking great care to construct a religious program that was close enough to the real thing down in Jerusalem to claim that it was a substitute, but different enough to draw his people away from Jerusalem and its ways.

The Sacrifices (v. 32b)

To cap it all: "he offered sacrifices on the altar. So he did in Bethel, sacrificing to the calves that he made" (v. 32b). This was probably at the feast just mentioned. "He celebrates at the wrong time, in the wrong place, on the wrong altar, in honor of the wrong gods."[28]

Bringing It All Together at Bethel (vv. 32c, 33)

Take a look at Jeroboam's accomplishment:

> And he placed in Bethel the priests of the high places that he had made. He went up to the altar that he had made in Bethel on the fifteenth day in the eighth month, in the month that he had devised from his own heart. And he

instituted a feast for the people of Israel and went up to the altar to make offerings.[29] (vv. 32c, 33)

"Devised from his own heart"[30] is a good summary of all that Jeroboam had done. He had faced an existential threat to his kingdom and his own life (vv. 26, 27). He chose a plan "devised from his own heart" rather than the terrifying prospect of trusting God and doing what was right in *his* eyes. He acted, in other words, as we all tend to do. How many of us seek our security in trusting and obeying God rather than making our own plans to make ourselves safe?

History has shown the foolishness of Jeroboam's scheme. Bethel became "the king's sanctuary" (Amos 7:13), and what Jeroboam began became a theme of prophetic condemnation (see Hosea 8:4, 5; 10:5, 6; 13:2; Amos 4:4). Eventually it led to the destruction of the kingdom that had been given to Jeroboam (2 Kings 17:6–18).

History will show the foolishness of all human schemes to find security not in trusting and obeying God but in plans devised in our own hearts. Only one man has ever fully, completely, and consistently trusted God. Only with Jesus Christ as our King can we escape the foolishness of Jeroboam.

Part 5

THE POWER BEHIND EVERYTHING

The Word of the Lord

1 Kings 13

27

The Word of the Lord
versus Human Religion

1 KINGS 13:1–10

IN 1 KINGS 13 WE FIND one of the strangest stories in the Bible. I have no doubt that its peculiarity is intended to catch our attention. The bizarre events narrated here suggest that something extraordinary was happening, as indeed it was. Furthermore we will see that the story is told with an ingenuity that suggests levels of meaning beyond the bare sequence of events. This "enormously enigmatic tale"[1] contains the key to the whole story of the books of 1 and 2 Kings and points us to the key to the history of the world.[2] We will follow the story in three episodes here and in our following three chapters.

There is no chronological break between the end of chapter 12 and the beginning of chapter 13.[3] In chapter 12 we have seen that King Jeroboam was using religion for what he perceived to be political gain. He thought that the old religion threatened his kingdom, even his life. His people going up to Jerusalem and the house of the Lord that had been built there troubled him. Indeed these things terrified him (12:26, 27). So Jeroboam set about modifying the faith and practice of his people, establishing more useful and less dangerous ways. He replaced Jerusalem with two more easily accessible centers, one at Dan in the far north, the other at Bethel near the southern border of his kingdom—both within the territory he controlled (12:29). At each of his new centers, in place of the house of the Lord and the ark of the covenant in Jerusalem, he substituted a new "house" with a golden bull, along with a new priesthood, a new altar, and a new annual festival (12:31–33).

All this, as the Biblical writer tells us, "he had devised from his own heart" (12:33). Jeroboam contrived what would become the archetype for man-made religion in Israel. Successive kings in the north will follow in his steps (15:34; 16:2, 7, 19, 26, 31; 22:52; 2 Kings 3:3; 10:29, 31; 13:2, 6, 11; 14:24; 15:9, 18, 24, 28; 17:21, 22).

What would now become of the people of whom the prophet Samuel had once said, "For the LORD will not forsake his people, for his great name's sake, because it has pleased the LORD to make you a people for himself" (1 Samuel 12:22)?

Jeroboam's man-made religion had turned his people away from the *place* where the Lord had put his name (8:29) and kept them from the *king* in the line of David, God's chosen one (see 11:34, 36). He had taken the temporary political division imposed by God (11:39) to another level. His man-made religion became a substitute for trusting and obeying the true and living God. All man-made religion is like that.

Mind you, Jeroboam's religion had clear points of contact with the centuries-old faith of Israel. It celebrated their exodus from Egypt (12:28). There were priests, sacrifices, and a house with an altar, just like in Jerusalem. The Bible writer's description of these things betrays his disapproval ("not of the Levites," "sacrificing to the calves that he made," 12:31, 32), but should not be taken to reflect what Jeroboam thought he was doing, nor the conscious perspective of the people as they followed him. He simply wanted the worship of God to be more useful to him and less risky. I am pretty sure he did not think he was starting a new religion.

What Jeroboam did is natural to the human heart. People want religion to be useful. Consider what politicians today are prepared to do to win the vote of Christians. Consider what Christians are prepared to do to gain political power. We want religion to be useful.[4]

In more personal terms, how do *you* worship God? The true and living God calls us to trust him and obey him. That is how we honor him. Today we come to Jesus Christ (not the house of the Lord in Jerusalem), thankful for all that God has given us in him, and present our bodies (not animals) as a living (not a dead) sacrifice—doing good, sharing what we have, acknowledging his name (see Romans 12:1, 2; Hebrews 12:22–29; 13:15, 16; 1 Peter 2:4, 5.) But when we want religion to be *useful* (on our terms) we devise *from our own hearts* modifications, variations, adjustments, and embellishments to what God requires (buildings, music, liturgies, ceremonies, and more), often deceiving ourselves into thinking that by *these* things we are worshipping the God who is really there.

It did not take long before Jeroboam's new way of worship was confronted by the most important reality he had disregarded. In 1 Kings 13 we will hear the phrase "the word of the LORD" no less than nine times, more often than in any other chapter of the Bible (vv. 1, 2, 5, 9, 17, 18, 20, 26, 32).[5] The reality that will shatter Jeroboam's man-made religion and expose the sham of all man-made religion is *the word of the Lord.*

Before we begin to follow the strange but vitally important story of 1 Kings 13, let us take a few moments to appreciate the most prominent idea in this chapter: "the word of the LORD."

The phrase has appeared only four times so far in 1 Kings (2:27; 6:11; 12:24 [twice]), but we will hear it another twenty-eight times from 13:1 to the end of the book and a further fifteen times in 2 Kings.[6] But this involves much more than statistics. "The word of the LORD" is arguably the most important idea not only in 1 Kings 13 but in the books of 1 and 2 Kings as a whole.

What does the Bible writer mean by "the word of the LORD"? Notice the definite article ("the") and the singular ("word"). "*The word* of the LORD" is not simply "*a* word of the LORD," nor just any "*words* of the LORD."[7] That is, "*the word* of the LORD" does not suggest the general idea that God speaks or that God has said many things. That is true, but "*the word* of the LORD" points to God's *one* word, his singular message. This message has been expressed in the many different *words* God has spoken, but "*the word* of the LORD" reminds us of God's constant will and purpose. The many *words* of God are all expressions or aspects of his *one word* (we could say, *one message*), applied to different people and different circumstances.

"The word of the LORD" had come to Abraham (Genesis 15:1, 4), Samuel (1 Samuel 15:10), Nathan (2 Samuel 7:4), Gad (2 Samuel 24:11), and Solomon (1 Kings 6:11). Each time it was "*the word* of the LORD," although expressed in different *words*. "The word of the LORD" had been rejected by Saul (1 Samuel 15:23, 26) and despised by David (2 Samuel 12:9). We will soon see that "the word of the LORD" is the key to understanding the course of the history recounted in the books of Kings which will unfold "according to the word of the LORD" (see 2:27; 12:24; 14:18; 15:29; 16:12, 34; 17:5, 16; 22:38; 2 Kings 1:17; 4:44; 7:16; 9:26; 10:10, 17; 14:25; 23:16; 24:2). Indeed "the word of the LORD" is the key to understanding everything.[8]

While "the word of the LORD" may take many forms (promises, commands, teachings, warnings, judgments, and so on), its essence is God's promise. God's promise has been expressed in different ways, but behind them all is God's one promise, his commitment to his purpose for his people and his creation.[9] Among the many expressions of this promise prior to 1 Kings, two stand out: "the word of the LORD" that came to Abraham (Genesis 15:1) and "the word of the LORD" that came to Nathan for King David (2 Samuel 7:4).[10]

All this is important as we come to the remarkable story about "the word of the LORD" in 1 Kings 13. In Episode 1 we will see:

(1) The man of God who came "by the word of the LORD" (v. 1)
(2) What he said "by the word of the LORD" (vv. 2, 3)
(3) What happened "by the word of the LORD" (vv. 4–6)
(4) What did *not* happen "by the word of the LORD" (vv. 7–9)
(5) The man of God who went another way (v. 10)

The Man of God Who Came "by the Word of the Lord" (v. 1)

And behold, a man of God came out of [from[11]] Judah by the word of the LORD to Bethel. Jeroboam was standing by the altar to make offerings.[12] (v. 1)

In 12:33 King Jeroboam was initiating his new religion in Bethel. I suspect he was trying to imitate what Solomon had done in Jerusalem (8:1–66). However, instead of a detailed account of what Jeroboam did, our writer dramatically points us to something else that happened just as "Jeroboam was standing by the altar to make offerings." "And look![13] A man of God was coming."[14] It was a moment of high drama. As Jeroboam was fully engaged in "this thing [that] became a sin" (12:30) another figure approached. He is given no name. He was simply "a man of God"—precisely what, at that moment, Jeroboam was not.

We are told four things about the man.

First, he was "a man of God"—an expression that does not simply mean a godly man but more specifically a prophet, one to whom the word of God came (see 12:22; 17:24; also 1 Samuel 2:27; 9:6–10).[15] A "man of God" is a man *from* God.[16]

Second, he came "from Judah." That is, from the kingdom still ruled by the house of David, the focus of Jeroboam's fears (12:26), from the land of Jerusalem where the house of the Lord stood (12:27). In other words, this man of God represented everything that Jeroboam had repudiated in his recent religious innovations. He came *from* the very place that Jeroboam had feared his people would go up *to* (12:27).

"From Judah" is what characterized this unnamed man of God (13:12, 14, 21). He was coming from the tribe the Lord had *not* torn away "for the sake of David my servant and for the sake of Jerusalem that I have chosen" (11:13, 32, 34, 36). It was as Amos would say many years later: "The LORD roars *from Zion* and utters his voice *from Jerusalem*" (Amos 1:2).[17]

Third, the man of God came "*by* [or perhaps *in*] the word of the LORD."[18]

This unusual expression appears seven times in our chapter (vv. 1, 2, 5, 9, 17, 18, 32).[19] On the one hand "the word of the LORD" was the power that was bringing this man from Judah.[20] On the other hand his coming brought "the word of the LORD" into the situation at Bethel.

Fourth, the man came "to Bethel," the very place where "Jeroboam was standing by the altar to make offerings" (see 12:33).[21]

The scene is jam-packed with significance. Just as Jeroboam was in Bethel sealing his repudiation of everything in Judah, *the word of the Lord* brought a man of God from Judah to Bethel. Jeroboam may have rejected Judah, David, and Jerusalem, but he had not escaped the God of Judah, David, and Jerusalem. *The word of the Lord* burst onto the scene of Jeroboam's man-made religion.

What He Said "by the Word of the Lord" (vv. 2, 3)

Remarkably the man of God seemed to take no notice of the king, but addressed the altar by which he was standing: "And the man cried *against the altar*" (v. 2a). It was as though Jeroboam was unworthy to be addressed "by the word of the LORD" (v. 2b). He had had shown himself to be one who did *not* listen (see 11:38).[22]

The Word (v. 2)

This is what the man of God said:

> O altar, altar, thus says the LORD [thus the LORD has said[23]]: "Behold, a son shall be born to the house of David, Josiah by name, and he shall sacrifice on you the priests of the high places who make offerings on you, and human bones shall be burned on you." (vv. 2c, 3)

So we hear "the word of the LORD" that brought the man of God to Bethel. It announces a future event, but the announcement itself brings the event vividly before its hearers (hence, for the second time in this dramatic chapter, "Behold"[24]).

The future event concerns a son to be born to the house of David. This must remind us of the word of the Lord as it had come to King David years earlier: "I will raise up your offspring after you . . . and I will establish his kingdom" (2 Samuel 7:12). This promise was significantly fulfilled in Solomon and his kingdom, as we have seen. However, Solomon was finally a disappointment. Rehoboam was the next son born to the house of David to become king. But he was a fool. These apparent setbacks could make you wonder about God's promise. Had it come to nothing? The word of the Lord that came to Bethel that day reaffirmed the promise: "A son shall be born to the house of David."

Furthermore this promise of this future son of David probably implies the end of Jeroboam's kingdom. There had been a possibility that Jeroboam's dynasty would last, but that was dependent on Jeroboam's faithful obedience and doing "what is right" in the Lord's eyes (11:38). He had failed. The affliction of the house of David would "not [be] forever" (11:39). "A son shall be born to the house of David."

This is the promise that the later Old Testament prophets never let us forget. "A son shall be born to the house of David."[25] In due course this promise (and its prophetic echoes) will cause the contemporaries of Jesus to ask, "Can *this* be the Son of David?" (Matthew 12:23).

However, in Bethel that day the promised son of David was "Josiah by name." It is unusual (although not unparalleled[26]) for an Old Testament prophecy to contain such a specific detail as this. King Josiah will come to the throne of David about three and a half centuries after the events of 1 Kings 13, and he will do precisely what the man of God then said he would do (2 Kings 23:15–20).

It is, of course, possible that God (who knows the end from the beginning; see Isaiah 41:26; 46:9, 10) included the detail of Josiah's name in the message delivered that day in Bethel. However, it is also possible (I think likely) that the words "Josiah by name" should be put in brackets and understood as an explanation added by the Biblical historian (writing years *after* Josiah) rather than words spoken by the man of God centuries *before* Josiah. The historian would then be simply informing us of the name of the son of David who had, by the time of writing, fulfilled this prophecy.[27]

The terrible thing about Jeroboam's man-made religion was that he had disregarded the word of the Lord, the promise concerning a son of David. Indeed his religion had been devised specifically to keep his people away from the influence of that promise (12:27). But the word of the Lord was not undone by Jeroboam's denials. "A son shall be born to the house of David."

This was devastating news for the religion that had been devised as a *substitute* for believing and obeying the word of the Lord. The promised son of David "shall sacrifice on you [Jeroboam's altar] the priests of the high places." The sacrificers will be sacrificed![28] "The priests" are the priests of Jeroboam's man-made religion; "the high places" are his alternatives to Jerusalem, particularly at Dan and Bethel (12:29, 31, 32). Whatever Jeroboam may have thought, his man-made religion was a *denial* of the word of the Lord and was therefore *condemned* by the word of the Lord.[29]

In due course King Josiah would do just what was predicted that day at Bethel (see 2 Kings 23:15–20). He will be able to do it because by then the northern kingdom of Israel will be no more (see 2 Kings 17:18, 21–23).

The reference to the priests as those "who make offerings on you [the altar]" must have been particularly disturbing to Jeroboam, who is the only one we have seen "make offerings" in this context.[30]

The human bones that were burned on the altar were not, as it turned out, the bones of the priests, but bones taken from nearby tombs. This, according to the account of the later deed, "defiled" the altar (2 Kings 23:16).

The Sign (v. 3)

(And he gave a sign the same day, saying, "This is the sign that the LORD has spoken: 'Behold, the altar shall be torn down, and the ashes that are on it shall be poured out.'") (v. 3, ESV lacks parentheses[31])

Perhaps it was later that day, and I suspect that these words were spoken less publicly than those in verse 2.[32] The man of God "gave a sign" by speaking the words "that the LORD has spoken."[33] The Lord's words are the sign: they point to the reality of the destroyed altar.

For the third time in as many verses we hear the vivid, "Behold!" "Look!" The altar will be "torn down," just as the Lord had said he would "tear" the kingdom from Solomon (11:11–13, 31) and Ahijah "tore" the garment into twelve pieces (11:30). The "tearing" of the altar would be a like act of divine judgment, now on Jeroboam's man-made religion.[34]

Furthermore the "ashes" (from the fat of the sacrificed animals, see Leviticus 6:10, 11) would be "poured out," suggesting God's repudiation of the sacrifices offered here.

But when would this happen? Presumably it will be in connection with what Josiah will do, since verse 2 anticipated that the altar would still be standing in Josiah's day.[35]

What Happened "by the Word of the Lord" (vv. 4–6)

We return to the public spectacle of verse 2: "And when the king heard the saying of the man of God, which he cried against the altar at Bethel . . ." (v. 4a).

The King's Power (v. 4b)

The word of the Lord had confronted the power of the king who was in denial of the word of the Lord. The king responded by asserting his power against the man of God: "Jeroboam stretched out his hand from the altar, saying, 'Seize him'" (v. 4b).

Jeroboam had received the kingdom when it was torn from the "hand" of Solomon's son Rehoboam (11:12, 31, 34, 35). He himself had lifted his "hand" against Solomon (11:26). Now he raised his "hand" against the man of God who had come to him by the word of the Lord. The hallmark of man-made religion is that the word of the Lord is rejected, despised, and, if possible, silenced.

The King's Impotence (v. 4c)

What a fool! Did this man who had become king by the word of the Lord (11:29–39) think that his "hand" now had the power to silence the word of the Lord when that word became uncomfortable?

"And his hand, which he stretched out against [the man of God], dried up, so that he could not draw it back to himself" (v. 4c). His power literally "withered" when raised against the word of the Lord. He became a man with a withered hand (cf. Matthew 12:10).[36]

The Sign Fulfilled (v. 5)

The flow of the story is again interrupted to follow up on the aside in verse 3. The writer informs his readers that by the time of writing (long after King Josiah had done all that was predicted that day in Bethel) the altar had indeed been torn down (see 2 Kings 23:15), just as the man of God had said:

> (The altar also [37] was [has been[38]] torn down, and the ashes poured out from the altar, according to the sign that the man of God had given by the word of the LORD.) (v. 5, ESV lacks parentheses)

Go to Bethel, says the narrator to his readers many years later, *and look for yourselves. The shattered altar is there for all to see, just as the man of God said would happen.*[39] *See for yourselves the power of the word of the Lord.*

The King's Plea (v. 6a)

Returning to the day that the man of God came to Bethel, King Jeroboam was brought to his knees (so to speak) by what had happened to the hand he had dared to raise against the man of God. This is how he responded:

> And the king said [literally, answered[40] and said] to the man of God, "Entreat now the favor of the LORD your God, and pray for me, that my hand may be restored to me." (v. 6a)

His golden bulls could not help him now! What good was his man-made religion now that he needed "the favor of the LORD"[41]?

The contrast between the king's words in verses 4 and 6 is stark. *Seize him!* has given way to *Please*[42] *pray for me.* However, he was also conscious that his man-made religion had taken him away from God, as man-made religion always does. For him the Lord was no longer "*my* God" or "*our* God" but "*your* God."

Jeroboam is sounding like King Saul, the disobedient king who begged the prophet Samuel for help.[43] He, too, spoke to Samuel of "*your* God" (1 Samuel 15:15, 21, 30). He, too, took religious initiatives (involving offering sacrifices!) when simple obedience to the Lord was too terrifying for him (1 Samuel 13:8–14; cf. 15:17–26).[44] Like Saul, Jeroboam had forfeited the promise of God by his disobedience (compare 11:38 and 1 Samuel 13:13).

Jeroboam did not ask for pardon or for the preservation of his kingdom, but simply "that my hand may be restored to me."

Mercy? (v. 6b)

This small mercy was given to him:

> And the man of God entreated the LORD, and the king's hand was restored to him and became as it was before. (v. 6b)

We can only wonder what might have been if Jeroboam had thoroughly repented of his ways, particularly his man-made religion. But neither the stern word of the Lord nor this kind act of the Lord softened his heart. We will have to wait a few more pages before we learn what happened to Jeroboam (see 13:33, 34; 14:1–20).

What Did *Not* Happen "by the Word of the Lord" (vv. 7–9)

The King's Hopeful Invitation (v. 7)

The relieved king, with his hand fully restored, was now keen to sort things out:

> And the king said to the man of God, "Come with me to the house [rather than ESV, Come home with me[45]], and refresh yourself, and I will give you a reward." (v. 7)

What was King Jeroboam proposing? Mutual tolerance. If the man of God from Judah would honor the "house" of the high place in Bethel (12:32) with his presence, then Jeroboam would honor the man of God from Judah with a gift. Jerusalem would respect and accept Bethel and vice versa. Light could fellowship with darkness, obedience with disobedience, truth with lies.

Again we might be reminded of King Saul, who was ever so eager to have Samuel honor him before the people after his disobedience (1 Samuel 15:30), but arguably less serious about repentance.

There was no sign of repentance from Jeroboam. He simply wanted the compromise of agreeing to differ.[46] He wanted man-made religion and the word of the Lord to live *together*.

Did Jeroboam think he might then be able to buy influence with his "reward"? If the man of God could bring about the reversal of his paralysis, could he perhaps be persuaded—at an appropriate fee, of course—to bring about the reversal of the terrible threat he had brought to Bethel?[47]

The Man of God's Obedient Refusal (vv. 8, 9)
It did not work.

> And the man of God said to the king, "If you give me half your house, I will not go in with you. And I will not eat bread or drink water in this place, for so was it commanded me by the word of the LORD, saying, 'You shall neither eat bread nor drink water nor return by the way that you came.'" (vv. 8, 9)

"Half your house" can mean "half your household" and therefore tantamount to "half your kingdom." It is also a play on the "house" to which Jeroboam had invited him. The man of God wanted nothing to do with *that* house. He will not even eat or drink in "*this* place."[48] The word of the Lord by which he had come (v. 1) had prohibited him from sharing in the disobedience of Jeroboam's man-made religion. He might have said:

> For what partnership has righteousness with lawlessness? Or what fellowship has light with darkness? What accord has Christ with Belial? Or what portion does a believer share with an unbeliever? What agreement has the temple of God with idols? (2 Corinthians 6:14–16a)

The further prohibition on the man of God returning by the way he came is intriguing. The prophet *not returning* by the way he came suggests that the word of the Lord he had brought to Bethel would *not be reversed*.[49]

The Man of God Who Went Another Way (v. 10)
The man of God who came to Bethel in verse 1 now went from Bethel, but—in obedience to the word of the Lord—not by the way he had come: "So he went another way and did not return by the way that he came to Bethel" (v. 10).

This would appear to conclude the story. However, as the man went by this other way, the story took a bizarre twist, as we shall see in our next chapter.

Before we turn the page we should consider carefully what the story so far has taught us about what happened when the word of the Lord confronted Jeroboam's man-made religion.

In the original language an important word appears five times in verses 1–10 (and a further eleven times in the rest of the chapter).[50] It is variously translated: "draw back" (v. 4), "be restored" (vv. 6, 7), "return" (vv. 9, 10). Interestingly this is the word that Solomon used repeatedly in his great prayer to speak of Israel's possible future repentance: "turn again to you [the Lord]" (8:33), "turn from their sin" (8:35), "turn their heart" (8:47), "repent" (8:47, 48). It was also used by Jeroboam, referring to the possibility of his people "turning back" to the house of David or to Rehoboam (12:26, 27).

"Repent" is what Jeroboam, confronted with the word of the Lord, should have done. But he didn't (see 13:33). Just as he was unable to "draw back" his withered hand, so he did not "turn back" from his man-made religion. He prayed for his hand to "be restored," but he did not pray for his heart to be "turned back" to the Lord. The God who restored his hand could surely have had the greater mercy on him, but Jeroboam did not ask for that.

Therefore the word of the Lord that promised judgment on Jeroboam's man-made religion would not be withdrawn, just as the man of God was prohibited from "returning" by the way he had come (cf. Isaiah 55:10, 11).

Christian reader, consider this. "The word of the LORD" has now come to us. It is the gospel of our Lord Jesus Christ (see especially 1 Peter 1:25; also Acts 8:25; 13:44, 48, 49; 15:35, 36; 16:32; 19:10, 20; 1 Thessalonians 1:8; 2 Thessalonians 3:1). In an important sense it is the same word that came to Abraham and to David and to Jeroboam. The promise of God now comes to the whole world in the gospel of Jesus Christ.

The word of the Lord confronts all man-made religion and demands repentance. Let us ask the Lord to turn our hearts to him in faith and obedience. Let us pray for what Jeroboam conspicuously did not.

28

The Word of the Lord
versus Human Lies

1 KINGS 13:11–24

HAVE YOU EVER BELIEVED A LIE?

Who hasn't? I hear you say. Who hasn't from time to time been taken in by deceptive advertising? Who hasn't at least occasionally been duped by the empty promises of a politician? And, sadly, some of us have been betrayed by the lies of someone close to us. Lies are a wretched fact of life, and they do immeasurable harm. It is difficult to think of a situation in which we would be happy to have believed a lie.

Of course, we make our own contributions to this problem. We, too, have told lies, and there have been times when others have believed our lies, and our lies have done damage, perhaps more than we know.

Jesus said that lies are the characteristic behavior of the devil: "When he lies, he speaks out of his own character, for he is a liar and the father of lies" (John 8:44). He is the father of lies because he told the first lie (Genesis 3:4), from which all subsequent lies have flowed.[1]

While all lies are serious because God never lies (Titus 1:2; Hebrews 6:18) and always speaks the truth (Isaiah 45:19), the worst lies are those that deny the greatest truths. "Who is the liar but he who denies that Jesus is the Christ?" (1 John 2:22). A lie that denies a truth as great as the gospel of Jesus Christ is dangerous indeed. It is as bad as the gospel is good.

This is the diabolical state of the human race: "they exchanged *the truth about God* for a *lie* and worshiped and served the creature rather than the

Creator" (Romans 1:25). The greatest and most harmful lies (like the devil's first lie) deny the truth of God's word.

That is why Christians are warned again and again in the New Testament to beware of teaching that departs from the truth of the gospel entrusted to the apostles by the Lord Jesus Christ. This is not a matter of pedantic, doctrinal nitpicking. The truth is so good, powerful, and enriching that teaching that wanders from the truth must be stopped (see, for example, 1 Timothy 1:3–7, 18–20; 4:1, 2; 6:3–5).

These concerns may seem a long way from the story in 1 Kings 13 of the man of God from Judah who came to Bethel by the word of the Lord in the early days of King Jeroboam's reign over the northern tribes of the people of Israel. However, the second episode of the story is about a lie. It was a big lie. It proved very powerful, and it did terrible damage. The story will give us an important insight concerning what went wrong in the history of God's Old Testament people Israel and will illuminate the world in which we find ourselves where big lies are all around us.

In the previous study we left the man of God on his way back from Bethel to Judah, but not by the same way he had come (13:10). This was because the word of the Lord, which had brought him to Bethel, had commanded him not to return by the way he had come (13:9). I have suggested that this prohibition was probably symbolic, indicating that the word of the Lord he had brought to Bethel from Judah would not simply be taken back.

In verse 11 we are introduced to a surprising new character: "Now an old prophet lived in Bethel" (v. 11a). Like the "man of God" in verses 1–10, this "prophet" is not named. The anonymity of both these figures highlights the places with which they are associated. Just as the man of God was *from Judah*, the old prophet lived *in Bethel*. The men come to represent their places. We will return to this important point shortly.[2]

Each of the three pieces of information we are given about the old prophet who lived in Bethel is tantalizingly ambiguous.

First, he was a "prophet." In times to come there will not only be "prophets" here in the northern kingdom who served the Lord (like Elijah and Elisha), but also many others who served other gods (see 18:19, 22; cf. Jeremiah 23:13). Whose prophet was this prophet of Bethel?[3]

Second, his home "in Bethel" raises further questions. Was he somehow part of Jeroboam's novel setup in Bethel? Did he support the religious innovations there that had so recently been condemned "by the word of the Lord" (13:2)? Or had he simply held his tongue? There is no hint that he had spoken out against Jeroboam's plans to substitute Bethel for Jerusalem. We might wonder why it had been necessary for the man of God to come from Judah with his message when there was already a prophet living in Bethel.[4]

Third, he was "old." Does this mean that he was part of the "old" ways—that is, the ways of Solomon *before* he was old (see 11:4)? Or does his age suggest that he *should* have known better than to acquiesce in Jeroboam's new deal? But did he?

With these questions in mind about the old prophet who lived in Bethel, let's see:

(1) What the prophet of Bethel heard about the man of God from Judah (vv. 11, 12)

(2) What the prophet of Bethel said to the man of God from Judah (vv. 13–19)

(3) The word that mattered (vv. 20–24)

What the Prophet of Bethel Heard about the Man of God from Judah (vv. 11, 12)

The events of 13:1–10 had probably taken place some distance outside the town itself, where the old prophet lived. The next stage in the story began with the old prophet in Bethel hearing the news.

The Deeds and Words of the Man of God (v. 11b)

And his son[5] came and told him all that the man of God had done that day in Bethel. They also told to their father the words that he had spoken to the king. (v. 11b)

This may have been his son (literally) or a member of a group of prophets whom he led.[6] Either way the lad had apparently been present for the events told in 13:1–10—a further hint that the old prophet and his "sons" may have been somehow involved in Jeroboam's innovations. Why else was this young man there?

"All that the man of God had done" would include the speech against the Bethel altar (13:2) and the restoration of Jeroboam's withered hand (13:6).

Other "sons" (in whichever sense) joined in. It sounds as though they were all present at Jeroboam's inaugural religious feast (12:33). They reported "the words that [the man of God] had spoken to the king." This would include his refusal of Jeroboam's invitation to come to "the house" for refreshment and the reason given, as well as the report that he was prohibited by the word of the Lord from returning to Judah by the same way that he had come (13:8, 9).

The Way of the Man of God (v. 12)

It was this last point that the old prophet took up, asking, "Which way did he go?" (v. 12a).

There is something quite brilliant about the carefully crafted narrative in 1 Kings 13. One of its striking features is the frequent repetition of key words and phrases that serve to highlight major themes. We have already noted the phrase "(by) the word of the LORD" and the word meaning "draw back," "be restored," "return," or "repent." Another such word is "way," which has appeared three times already in 13:9, 10 and will occur nine more times in the chapter.[7]

"Which *way* did he go?" The question may be understood at two levels. In addition to the obvious inquiry about which road the man of God had taken, was the old prophet asking whether he had returned "by the (now forbidden) *way* that he came to Bethel" or by "another *way*"? The narrator has already told us (the readers) the answer to that question (13:10).

"And his sons showed him the way that the man of God who came from Judah had gone" (v. 12b).

For the second time in the chapter we are told that the man of God was *from Judah* (see 13:1).[8] The old prophet of *Bethel* now knew that the man of God *from Judah* had taken the way of obedience to the word of the Lord. He also knew, of course, the actual road on which he had gone.

What was the old prophet planning to do with this information?

What the Prophet of Bethel Said to the Man of God from Judah (vv. 13–19)

> And he said to his sons, "Saddle the donkey for me." So they saddled the donkey for him and he mounted it. And he went after the man of God and found him sitting under an [the[9]] oak. (vv. 13, 14a)

The suspense grows. Why did the old prophet set out, at considerable effort, to find the man of God? Were his intentions hostile or friendly? Had he taken offense at what the man of God had said against his king's altar? Or did he want to express solidarity with the man of God from Judah?

A Question Answered (v. 14b)

> And he said to him, "Are you the man of God who came from Judah?" And he said, "I am." (v. 14b)

For the third time in the chapter we hear "from Judah," now on the lips of the prophet of Bethel. What did this northerner want with the man *from Judah*?

An Invitation Refused (vv. 15–17)

He said to him, "Come home with me [Come with me to the house] and eat bread" (v. 15).

As in 13:7, the Hebrew does not indicate that the "house" of this invitation was the speaker's "home." In the context there was another important "house," namely the house Jeroboam had built in Bethel (see 12:32) as his substitute for the house of the Lord in Jerusalem. Which house did the old prophet mean?

Because the old prophet's invitation sounds like an echo of King Jeroboam's invitation in 13:7, it is natural for us (and for the man of God) to think that he meant the same house, namely the Bethel high place house (12:32).[10]

This would lead us (and the man of God) to surmise that the old prophet was trying to do what the king had failed to achieve: a compromise, a rapprochement, a mutual acceptance between Bethel and Jerusalem.[11] Like his king, he did not see a necessary *contradiction* between Bethel and Jerusalem. If the man of God from Judah and the old prophet of Bethel could eat bread together in the house of the high place in Bethel, surely that would show that the house in Bethel (and all that went with it) was an acceptable modification of what happened in Jerusalem, in the light of new political realities. At last we see the old prophet's true colors (or so we think). He was a supporter of King Jeroboam and his religious novelties (or so it seems).

That is how the old prophet's invitation must have struck the man of God from Judah. But was this assessment right?

The man of God's response shows that he heard the old prophet's invitation as a replay of the king's earlier offer. He answered in almost exactly the same way.

I have set the man of God's reply to the old prophet alongside the words he had spoken previously to the king (identical or very similar words and phrases are italicized):

And he said,	And the man of God *said* to the king,
	"If you give me half your house,
"I may not return with you, or *go in with you*,	I will not *go in with you*.
neither will I eat bread nor drink water with you *in this place,*	And I will not eat bread or drink water in this place,
for it was said to me *by the word of the L*ORD,	for so was it commanded me *by the word of the L*ORD, saying,
'You shall neither eat bread nor drink water there,	'You shall neither eat bread nor drink water
nor return by the way that you came.'" (vv. 16, 17)	nor return by the way that you came.'" (vv. 8, 9)

The man of God refused the old prophet's invitation for precisely the same reason that he had earlier refused the king. However, two slight changes in wording suggest, if anything, an added emphasis.

First, he underlined his reference to "this place" with the additional word "there." The *place* (the house in Bethel) really was the problem, confirming that he had understood the old prophet's invitation with reference to that house.

Second, he emphasized that he was repudiating fellowship with the prophet of Bethel by saying "with you" three times. He had used a similar phrase just once in his words to the king, but the Hebrew expression now suggests more clearly the close association with the old prophet that the man of God was repudiating.[12]

The man of God stood firm. He would not share fellowship with an idolater in a place of idol worship.

A Lie Believed (vv. 18, 19)

The old wily prophet had no intention of giving up as easily as the king had done. He quickly insisted that the man of God had misunderstood his invitation.

He made three crucial points. First, "I also am a prophet as you are [literally, like you]" (v. 18a). *You have misunderstood me. I am not an idolater. I am your kind of prophet. There is no difference between you and me. We are on the same side.*[13]

Second, he claimed to have received a revelation as valid as the one the man of God had mentioned: "an angel spoke to me by the word of the LORD" (v. 18b). The key phrase ("by the word of the LORD") ties the old prophet's claim into the story of this chapter and endorses his assertion that the two of them are the same kind of prophets.

Third, by the message he claimed to have received, he "corrects" the man of God's "misunderstanding" of his initial invitation. The word to the old prophet had been (he said): "Bring him back with you into *your house* that he may eat bread and drink water" (v. 18c).

For a moment we must wonder (as the man of God must have wondered) whether we have seriously misjudged the old prophet. Was he, after all, a prophet of the Lord there in Bethel? Was he eager to show his solidarity with the man of God from Judah by sharing hospitality[14] not in the house of the high place in Bethel as we (and the man of God) have supposed but in *his own home*?

The narrator comes to our aid by at last letting us in on what was actually happening: "But he lied to him" (v. 18d).[15]

It was *all* a lie. He was not the same kind of prophet as the man of God.

No angel had spoken to him by the word of the Lord. There was no word from God authorizing his invitation to eat and drink in his home. It was a *lie*.

This brief comment resolves the various ambiguities around the old prophet. He was a liar of the worst sort because he set his lie against the word of the Lord that *had* come to the man of God from Judah.

What was the old prophet up to? The words "Bring him back" now take on sinister significance. Here we have one of the key words of the chapter we noted earlier (variously translated "draw back," "be restored," "return," "repent"). "Bring him back" suggests "Turn him." We now see that the old prophet's invitation, backed up by his lies, was designed to *turn* the man of God *from the way of obedience*.

Of course, the narrator's helpful word to his readers ("But he lied to him") puts us at a decided advantage not enjoyed by the man of God from Judah. He was not told that the old prophet was lying. And he believed him. "So he went back with him and ate bread in his house and drank water" (v. 19). "He went back." He *turned*. He obeyed the lie. What the king had failed to achieve with all his power and privilege (13:4, 7), the old prophet accomplished with his lie.[16]

The man of God did what he had refused to do in verse 16 ("with him" precisely echoes "with you" in v. 16[17]), presumably thinking that the changed venue ("in his house," not "in this place" of v. 16) made all the difference. The man of God *from Judah* joined the old prophet of *Bethel*.

What a powerful lie it was! Before we start criticizing the man of God for being taken in by it, let us recognize that big lies are not easy to pick out. They can be persuasive. They can be presented by impressive and attractive people who speak with authority. They can be subtle and crafty. Are you sure you would not have been taken in by the old prophet's lie?

The whole story in 1 Kings 13 is a kind of real-life parable. We are witnessing in this local story an anticipation, a foreshadowing, of the history to be told in the rest of the books of Kings. What happened to the man of God from Judah will happen in due course to the people of Judah.[18] The disobedience of the northern kingdom will draw their southern brothers after them. They too will believe the lie. One day it will be said, "Judah also did not keep the commandments of the LORD their God, but walked in the customs that Israel [that is, the northern kingdom] had introduced" (2 Kings 17:19).

The Word That Mattered (vv. 20–24)

The two men were now sitting at the table in the old prophet's house in Bethel, eating and drinking. Suddenly something interrupted their conversation.

The Word That Came (v. 20)

> And as they sat at the table, the word of the LORD came to the prophet who
> had brought him back. (v. 20)

We might render the end of the verse, "the prophet who had turned him." The
word of the Lord now came to the deceiving prophet!

This is extraordinary. The man of God who had carried out his commission bravely and refused to deviate from the word of the Lord he had received
was deceived by a lie from a false prophet. But now the word of the Lord came
to the deceiver! It is clear that neither the man of God from Judah nor the old
prophet from Bethel controlled the word of the Lord. It was, indeed, the word
of the Lord.[19]

The Word That Condemned (vv. 21, 22)

The old prophet now swapped places (so to speak) with the man of God. Just
as the latter had earlier "cried" against the Bethel altar (13:2), so now the old
prophet "*cried* to the man of God who came from Judah" (v. 21a).

This is the fourth and last time in the chapter that we are reminded that
the man of God was "from Judah." The word of the Lord that had come *from*
Judah (13:1) was now addressed *to* this representative of Judah.

The false prophet now spoke as a true prophet, with the distinctive "Thus
says [or has said] the LORD" (v. 21b).[20] He delivered a typical prophetic message of judgment with an indictment followed by a declaration of punishment.

Indictment (vv. 21c, 22a)

> Because you have disobeyed the word of the LORD and have not kept the
> command that the LORD your God commanded you, but have come back
> and have eaten bread and drunk water in the place of which he said to you,
> "Eat no bread and drink no water" . . . (vv. 21c, 22a)

By believing and obeying the lie, the man of God had disobeyed the word of
the Lord. The language is a little stronger, vivid, and evocative. Literally, this
reads, "Because you have rebelled against the mouth of the LORD . . ." Strikingly, this is the expression that was used to describe the people of Israel's
rebellion in the days of Moses (ESV, "rebelled against the command[ment] of
the LORD," Deuteronomy 1:26, 43; 9:23) and was used by Samuel in his severe
warning to the people who had demanded a king like the nations (1 Samuel
12:14–15).[21] The language contributes to the impression that in the experience
of the man of God from Judah we are seeing a reflection of the experience of
the people of God.

He had "come back," that is, "turned" from the way of obedience. And he had eaten in the forbidden "place." If (as I have supposed) the man of God had thought that the prohibition applied only to the house of the high place in Bethel, but not to the home of the old prophet, it is now clear that "this place" must be understood as the whole Bethel region, probably the whole land of Jeroboam's kingdom, tarnished as it now was by the idolatry of Dan and Bethel (12:29–30). What he had done was a disastrous compromise.

The story does not invite us to analyze the thought processes of the man of God from Judah. The issue is not how he should have known that the old prophet was lying. The fact is that he had believed the lie and the consequences would be catastrophic.

Punishment (v. 22b)

> . . . your body [or carcass[22]] shall not come to the tomb of your fathers. (v. 22b)

In other words, he will die far from home. In exile, we might say.

The Word That Proved True (vv. 23, 24)

It remains for us to hear that the word of the Lord came to pass, as it always does:

> And after he had eaten bread and drunk, he saddled the donkey for the prophet whom he had brought back. And as he went away a lion met [found] him on the road and killed him. And his body was thrown in the road, and the donkey stood beside it; the lion also stood beside the body. (vv. 23, 24)

The man of God from Judah is now called "the *prophet* whom he had brought back"—"the prophet he had turned."[23] The man from Judah (previously *not* called a "prophet") had indeed become *like* the disobedient "prophet" of Bethel (v. 18a)—just as the people of Judah would one day become like the disobedient people of Israel.

Just as the old prophet had "found" the man from Judah (v. 14), now a lion "found" him on the road. The parallel is telling. We can now see that the earlier encounter was as hostile and destructive as this one. The prophet of Bethel had destroyed the man from Judah with his lies as surely as the lion killed him with his claws.

The man's body (better, "corpse" or "carcass") was thrown onto the road (or "way"). It was the "way" on which the man of God had been obediently traveling at the beginning of this episode (v. 12; see vv. 9, 10), the "way" from which he had been turned by the lie of the prophet from Bethel (v. 19). Now his corpse was flung down on that road.

It is the strangest scene—the deadly lion now standing quietly beside the donkey, both watching over the corpse of the man from Judah. It is as though they were waiting. For what? That we will see in our next chapter.

First, let us pause and reflect on the strange story of the old prophet's lie. I have been hinting that the story seems to point to something bigger than itself. It is a kind of real-life parable in which the peoples of Judah on the one hand and Bethel/Israel on the other are represented by the unnamed characters linked to these places.

Being turned away from obedience to the word of God by a lie is the story of Judah and Israel told in the books of Kings. We will be as astonished that the people of God—particularly the people of Judah—are deceived as we have been at the deception of the man of God from Judah. We will also be amazed at how the word of the Lord will come to the most disobedient of people.

In our astonishment let us reflect on the way in which the human race has been deceived by the devil's lie since Genesis 3. We have "exchanged the truth about God for a lie" (Romans 1:25). It has been a wretchedly powerful lie. We cannot stand in judgment over those who have been deceived, whether the man of God from Judah or later the people of Judah. How easily we, too, believe lies that deny the word of God. It is not as though we are clever enough to spot the lies and discern the truth.

Only one man has had the strength and wisdom to believe and obey the word of God in the face of all the lies that the devil hurls. He, too, was a man from Judah. Read the Gospels of the New Testament to learn about him, particularly Matthew 4:1–11.

We need him to lead us into the truth and to keep us from the deadly deception of the lies (see John 8:32; 16:13; 17:17, 19; 18:37). To believe and know him is to believe and know the truth (John 14:6; Ephesians 4:21; 1 Timothy 4:3).

29

The Word of the Lord and Human Hope

1 KINGS 13:25–34

IT IS EASY TO BE DEEPLY pessimistic about the world. There is a lot to be pessimistic about! Each evening the TV news feeds our despair with stories of unimaginable violence, rampant greed, abject poverty, and incomprehensible moral decline. The scale and scope of these things is deeply distressing. For Christian believers all this is amplified as we see that behind all the horrors is a widespread denial of the God who is there. How few people honor him as they ought! How many have "exchanged the truth about God for a lie" (Romans 1:25)! How rare it is to see anyone actually trusting and obeying God rather than pleasing themselves! Furthermore, it is difficult to see any sign of things getting better.

It would have been easy to be deeply pessimistic in the days of Jeroboam, king of Israel, the northern part of the once famously great kingdom of David and his son Solomon. There was a lot to be pessimistic about. King Jeroboam himself exchanged authentic, obedient trust in God for idolatry "devised from his own heart" (12:33). When the word of the Lord came onto the scene, it was a message of devastating condemnation. A son of David would one day destroy what King Jeroboam had built (13:2, 3).

What hope could there be in this situation?

We have begun to see that the strange story about the word of the Lord in 1 Kings 13 provides a penetrating though puzzling insight into the world of King Jeroboam. It is like a real-life parable. The dire state of affairs in Israel (and Judah) is reflected in the experiences of the two main characters—the man of God from Judah and the old prophet of Bethel. In our last chapter we saw, on the one hand, that the lie from the old prophet of Bethel in Israel was able to deceive the man of God from Judah and turn him from the way of obedience (13:18–19), with tragic consequences (13:24), just as the people of Judah too would one day follow the disobedient ways of the people of Israel (2 Kings 17:19). On the other hand, the word of the Lord was able to overcome the deceiving prophet of the north and turn him into a true prophet, although the message he delivered only confirmed the tragic consequences of the lie he had earlier told (13:20–22). Does all this suggest something about future possibilities for the people of Israel? Keep that question in mind as we consider the conclusion of 1 Kings 13.

Certainly at this point in the story we find ourselves wondering what hope there could be when lies are powerful enough to deceive even the man of God from Judah and the word of the Lord announces only disaster, now not only for King Jeroboam's apostasy (13:2), but even for the man from Judah (13:20–22).

Before the curtain rises for the last episode of this peculiar narrative, let us notice how key aspects of the story so far reflect not only the Old Testament history of the peoples of Judah and Israel but also our world today. Lies denying the word of God deceive many (see Romans 1:23). When we listen carefully to the word of the Lord (now in the form of the gospel of Jesus Christ), it announces disaster for an unbelieving and disobedient world (see Romans 1:18). A son of David will inflict vengeance on those who do not know God and do not obey the gospel of our Lord Jesus (2 Thessalonians 1:7–8).

The story of 1 Kings 13 concludes with six surprises:

(1) What the old prophet heard (v. 25)
(2) What the old prophet said (v. 26)
(3) What the old prophet found (vv. 27, 28)
(4) What the old prophet did (vv. 29, 30)
(5) What the old prophet now believed (vv. 31, 32)
(6) What about King Jeroboam? (vv. 33, 34)

What the Old Prophet Heard (v. 25)

For the fourth time in the chapter we hear, "Behold!" (see vv. 1, 2, 3):

> And behold, men passed by and saw the body thrown in the road and the lion standing by the body. And they came and told it in the city where the old prophet lived. (v. 25)

We are invited to join the passersby, taking in the astonishing and bizarre scene we first saw in verse 24:[1] "Look!" The carcass[2] of a man was lying on the road where it had been hurled. An apparently docile lion was quietly standing guard. The sight of the lion was no doubt so surprising that the passersby did not notice the donkey that was also standing beside the body (v. 24).

Like the whole story of 1 Kings 13, this spectacle catches everyone's attention. The ominously meek lion certainly suggested something out of the ordinary. The powerful and dangerous animal would not naturally stop with the death of his victim. Nor would it leave a defenseless donkey untouched. What could this possibly mean? Did anyone recognize the body? Perhaps they did, since the earlier words and actions of the man of God from Judah at Jeroboam's Bethel altar had been public (13:1–10). But perhaps the bloody corpse was now unrecognizable. Either way the people passing by would not have known about the more recent interaction between the man from Judah and the old Bethel prophet. That had been more private (13:11–24).

The people who witnessed the peculiar, puzzling scene came into Bethel and reported what they had seen. We can imagine the conversations. *You'll never guess what we have just seen! It was the strangest thing! What could it mean?* Soon the old prophet who lived in Bethel heard their chatter.

What the Old Prophet Said (v. 26)

This was the second time that a report about the man of God from Judah reached the ears of the old prophet. Earlier he had been told all that the man had said and done at Jeroboam's altar in Bethel (13:11). Now he heard about the corpse on the road out of Bethel.

> And when the prophet who had brought him back from the way heard of it, he said, "It is the man of God who disobeyed the word of the LORD; therefore the LORD has given him to the lion, which has torn him and killed him, according to the word that the LORD spoke to him." (v. 26)

The writer reminds us pointedly (just in case we had forgotten) that this was "the prophet who had turned [the man of God] from the way" (AT) of obedience with his lie (see 13:18, 19). This was the lying prophet who was at least substantially responsible for the disobedience of the man of God that had led to his violent death. Remember that, our writer seems to say. *That* was the one who now heard about the uncanny scene on the road outside Bethel.

A big part of our problem with this story is that its morality seems (to us) muddled. The "man of God" had been judged and killed because he believed the rather convincing lie of the old prophet. We sympathize because we are not at all sure that we would have been any wiser. However, the old prophet seems to have escaped any consequences for his lie and appears to have been made into a true prophet by the word of the Lord that came to him earlier (13:20). How can that be right? Surely (we mutter to ourselves) it should have been the other way around. If the lying prophet was the one whose corpse was now sprawled on the road and watched over by the lion, and the "man of God" had been brought to see his error, repent, and be on his way, that would fit better with our moral sensibilities.

Like a number of the parables of Jesus, this story gets under our skin precisely because it does not conform to our expectations. How could it be that the one whose courage and faithfulness we admired at the beginning of the story falls under divine judgment? And how could the one who was so obviously a villain now appear to know, believe, and proclaim the truth?

Let's listen to him carefully. He makes four points.

First, without seeing the body he identified it: "It is the man of God," he said. He understood because of the word of the Lord he had spoken earlier to the man of God. He knew that the "body" now lying in the road from Bethel was the "body" in his message: "Your body shall not come down to the tomb of your fathers" (13:22).

Second, he understood why this had happened to the man of God: he "disobeyed the word of the LORD." *Whose fault was that?* we want to ask. But all we hear is the hard fact of the man of God's disobedience, not some excuse we would like to offer for him. This, too, the old prophet understood because of the word of the Lord that had earlier come to him (see 13:21).

Third, the strange death of the man of God was God's doing: "therefore the LORD has given him to the lion, which has torn him and killed him." That is why this lion was behaving so oddly. He was God's agent, doing God's will. No more, no less.

Fourth, like so much that we have already heard and have yet to hear in this history, these things happened "according to the word of the LORD that he spoke to him" (AT). Events have unfolded (as future events will unfold) "according to the word of the LORD." This phrase (which we will hear repeatedly through the rest of 1 and 2 Kings)[3] means that (a) the events on view have taken place in line with the Lord's purpose; (b) the Lord had made his purpose known prior to the events occurring; and (c) what has happened confirms (yet again) the sure truthfulness of "the word of the LORD."

What the Old Prophet Found (vv. 27, 28)

This episode unfolds with striking parallels to what had happened a little earlier.[4] Once again the old prophet "said to his sons, 'Saddle the donkey for me.'
And they saddled it" (v. 27; cf. 13:13). As before, we wonder what the old
prophet was planning to do. Last time (we now know) he set out to deceive
and trick the man of God into disobeying the word of the Lord. What was he
up to this time?

"And he went and found his body thrown in the road" (v. 28a). This is the
third time that the man of God from Judah was "found" on this road. The first
time was by the old prophet in 13:14 prior to his deception, the second by the
lion in 13:24 prior to his slaughter. This time it was the dead carcass (the result
of the deception and the slaughter) that was found by the old prophet.

More than that, he found the signs that this was no ordinary occurrence:
"and the donkey and the lion standing beside the body" (v. 28b). It was not
simply an unfortunate accident. The donkey and the lion standing quietly
side-by-side was odd enough. That they were both standing beside the human
corpse added to the unnatural scene. For those of us who may be a little slow,
the writer points out exactly what was weird: "The lion had not eaten the body
or torn the donkey" (v. 28c).

Marvel at the obedient lion! He "had not eaten." The disobedience of the
man of God was that he *had* eaten (13:19).[5]

What would the old prophet, who was so substantially responsible for the
tragic situation before his eyes, now do?

What the Old Prophet Did (vv. 29, 30)

> And the prophet took up the body of the man of God and laid it [him[6]]
> on the donkey and brought it [him] back to the city of the old prophet,[7] to
> mourn and to bury him. And he laid the body in his own grave. And they
> mourned over him, saying, "Alas, my brother!" (vv. 29, 30)

The behavior of the old prophet is now in stark contrast to his earlier underhanded conduct. In actions that might remind a Christian reader of the Good
Samaritan (see Luke 10:34) the old prophet lifted the mauled carcass of the
man of God, placed him (literally, "caused him to rest") on the donkey (presumably the one that had been standing there), and "brought him back" to
Bethel in order to properly honor and decently bury the man.

"Brought him back" is striking. Here we have the fourteenth of sixteen occurrences of a key word in 1 Kings 13. It is a story about "turnings." We have
just been reminded that the old prophet was the one who had earlier "brought

him back"/"turned him" by his lie (v. 26). This verb was also used of that earlier "turning" from the way of obedience in 13:16, 18, 19, 20, 22, 23. Now we
hear that the old prophet "turned" the man of God again!

But it was different this time. The man he had "turned" from obedience to
disobedience and death he now "turned" with positive purpose.

First, he laid the body (literally, "caused his body to rest") in his own
grave. It was not the tomb of the man of God's ancestors (13:22), but it was
an honorable burial. Again Christian readers may think of a much later act of
similar kindness and honor (see Matthew 27:57–60; John 19:38–42).

Second, he and those with him ("they") mourned over him. This would
have included his "sons" (see 13:11, 12, 13, 27) and perhaps also a number of
those passersby who had brought the news to him (v. 25). They mourned, as
all Israel had mourned Samuel's death (1 Samuel 25:1; 28:3), as David and his
people had mourned over the deaths of Saul and Jonathan (2 Samuel 1:12), as
David had insisted that Joab and the people mourn Abner's death (2 Samuel
3:31), and as Bathsheba had mourned the death of her husband Uriah (2 Samuel 11:26).[8] Led by the old prophet, people in Bethel recognized the tragedy
in the death of the man of God from Judah.

What a remarkable turn of events! This was the man who had in effect announced the end of Jeroboam's kingdom. "A son shall be born to the house of
David" (13:2). Shouldn't the subjects of King Jeroboam rejoice at the downfall
of this messenger? Shouldn't they see his death as divine judgment on his message against their king? Hadn't the old prophet opened their eyes to a better
perspective?

Third, the old prophet put his grief into words: "Alas, my brother!" Earlier he had deceitfully claimed to be a prophet of the Lord, just like the man
of God (13:18). Now that the word of the Lord *had* come to him (13:20), he
could rightly call the man of God "my brother"[9] and genuinely grieve at his
death ("Alas!"[10]).

We do not know how widely the grief described here was shared in Bethel
that day among Jeroboam's subjects. However, it is clear that the death of the
man of God from Judah had, under the influence of the old prophet, turned a
number of hearts.

What the Old Prophet Now Believed (vv. 31, 32)

The last words we hear from the old prophet, after he had buried the man
from Judah, were addressed to his sons. He began by saying, "When I die,
bury me in the grave in which the man of God is buried; lay my bones
beside his bones" (v. 31).

We must appreciate that this is Old Testament speech, without the full revelation of hope that has now come with Jesus Christ and his resurrection from the dead. Nonetheless, it is remarkable. The old prophet spoke as though the man of God had not been abandoned. Yes, he understood that his death was God's doing because of his disobedience to the word of the Lord. But just as the lion had gone no further than killing him, so the old prophet seemed to think that hope (in some sense) lay with the man of God from Judah. "Lay my bones beside his bones." We should not read into this the full Christian hope of resurrection, but there is something faintly similar. The old prophet understood that the man of God from Judah still represented the word of the Lord he had proclaimed. His hope of escaping the coming judgment (that is, the judgment the man of God had announced in 13:2) lay *with* the man of God from Judah.

He was right—again, in an Old Testament way. Centuries later when the promised son of David, King Josiah, came to do the very things that the man of God from Judah had proclaimed, he came across the burial place in which were the bones of the man of God and the old prophet. This is what happened:

> Then [Josiah] said, "What is that monument that I see?" And the men of the city told him, "It is the tomb of the man of God who came from Judah and predicted these things that you have done against the altar at Bethel." And he said, "Let him be; let no man move his bones." So they let his bones alone, with the bones of the prophet who came out of Samaria. (2 Kings 23:17, 18)

"The prophet who came out of Samaria" refers, of course, to the old prophet of Bethel. By this time the whole region was known as Samaria, after the city that became its capital (1 Kings 16:24, 29).

Returning to the old prophet's last recorded words, he concluded:

> For the saying that he called out by the word of the LORD against the altar in Bethel and against all the houses of the high places that are in the cities of Samaria shall surely come to pass. (v. 32)

Anticipating the likes of Elijah and Hosea, there was now a true prophet in the northern kingdom. Like them, he (or at least his message) was now emphatically opposed to his king. He not only confirmed the earlier word of the man of God from Judah ("surely" represents a strong and emphatic Hebrew construction), he expanded its application to "all the houses of the high places that are in the cities of Samaria." At this point of time the only high places (of which we have been told) were in Bethel and Dan. In due course they would be multiplied in many places in the region that would come to be known as Samaria (see 2 Kings 17:9–12; 23:19).[11]

However, the astonishing truth is that the word of the Lord that the man of God from Judah had brought to Bethel had not been silenced in the kingdom of Jeroboam. The lie (13:18) did not, in the end, prevail. "The God of David has neither forgotten nor abandoned the lost sheep of the house of Israel."[12] We asked what hope there could possibly be in Jeroboam's kingdom. We may not yet see it clearly, but is there not the possibility that the word of the Lord will accomplish more widely what was accomplished for the old prophet of Bethel, turning them from lies to the truth?

And What about King Jeroboam? (vv. 33, 34)

Whatever the future might hold, our chapter closes on a disappointing note:

> After this thing Jeroboam did not turn from his evil way, but made priests for the high places again from among all the people. Any who would, he ordained to be priests of the high places. And this thing became sin to the house of Jeroboam, so as to cut it off and to destroy it from the face of the earth. (vv. 33, 34)

Hebrew has one word meaning "thing" or "word." "After this thing" could mean "After this word"—that is, the word of verse 32, perhaps "the *word* of the LORD" that has been the theme of the whole chapter.

On this occasion the word of the Lord did not bring about the repentance of King Jeroboam. He "did not turn from his evil way." The crucial importance of two repeated key words of the chapter is now clear. There has been much "turning" and various "ways"/"roads." In the end, however, King Jeroboam did *not* "turn," and he remained on the "way" he had taken in 12:25–33, now characterized as "evil."

The "turn" word is used for the last time in the chapter in the expression "but made . . . again" (literally, "but turned and made . . ."). The only "turning" we will see from Jeroboam is a returning to his evil ways.

In this behavior[13] Jeroboam led his "house" (in context referring to his dynasty) to fail,[14] be lost,[15] and destroyed[16] "from the face of the earth." The man who had hoped to make religion more useful failed utterly. His "evil way" ran to ruin.

What hope could there possibly now be?

The conclusion to the strange story of 1 Kings 13 should remind us of Solomon's great prayer. It is worth hearing the last words of that prayer again.

I have italicized key words that have been important in the present chapter, particularly in verses 33, 34.

> If they *sin* against you—for there is no one who does not *sin*—and you are angry with them and give them to an enemy, so that they are carried away captive to the land of the enemy, far off or near, yet if they *turn* their heart in the land to which they have been carried captive, and *repent* and plead with you in the land of their captors, saying, "We have *sinned* and have acted perversely and wickedly," if they *repent* with all their heart and with all their soul in the land of their enemies, who carried them captive, and pray to you toward their land, which you gave to their fathers, the city that you have chosen, and the house that I have built for your name, then hear in heaven your dwelling place their prayer and their plea, and maintain their cause and forgive your people who have *sinned* against you, and all their transgressions that they have committed against you, and grant them compassion in the sight of those who carried them captive, that they may have compassion on them (for they are your people, and your heritage, which you brought out of Egypt, from the midst of the iron furnace). Let your eyes be open to the plea of your servant and to the plea of your people Israel, giving ear to them whenever they call to you. For you separated them from among all the peoples of the earth to be your heritage, as you declared through Moses your servant, when you brought our fathers out of Egypt, O Lord GOD. (8:46–53)

The hope for Israel was that they might do what Jeroboam did *not* do: repent, turn from their evil way. *Then* there would be compassion and forgiveness. The presence of the word of the Lord through every stage of 1 Kings 13 testifies to the fact that the Lord had not abandoned his people. As long as the word of the Lord is heard, there is hope, if only his people will hear and repent.

This possibility, the hope of Israel, has now become the hope of the world. The word of the Lord is now news about a son of David who has been declared Lord of all by his resurrection from the dead (Acts 2:32, 36) "to give repentance to Israel and forgiveness of sins" (Acts 5:31). But now the word of the Lord calls not only Israel to repentance, but "all people everywhere" (Acts 17:30; cf. 11:18; 26:20).

The answer to pessimism today is the possibility of repentance—a possibility because of the word of the Lord.

Part 6

POWER POLITICS
PLAYED OUT

1 Kings 14—16

30

Deceiving God

1 KINGS 14:1-20

HAVE YOU EVER TRIED TO DECEIVE GOD?

Ridiculous as it undoubtedly sounds, trying to deceive Almighty God is a common human pastime. We sin, somehow thinking that God will not notice. We conceal our sin from ourselves and from others, somehow imagining that this means God does not see it. We deny our sin, somehow dreaming that if we do not think about it God won't either. Every refusal to come clean and acknowledge our sin is an attempt (even if we deny this too) to deceive God.

When King David committed adultery with Bathsheba, he attempted to cover up his sin, finally by having her husband murdered. He denied (to himself and to Joab) that any of this was evil. The Bible writer concludes the story with these words: "But the thing that David had done *was* evil *in the eyes of the Lord*" (2 Samuel 11:27, AT). God saw. Of course he did. David had only deceived himself.

In 1 Kings 13 we have seen how the word of the Lord came to King Jeroboam, exposing and condemning his evil ways (13:2). Unlike King David, who was shattered by the word of the Lord and brought to repentance (2 Samuel 12:13; cf. Psalm 51), "Jeroboam did not turn from his evil way" (13:33). Jeroboam did not repent. Did he really think he could deceive God? Indeed he did, as we are about to see.

The drama will unfold in three scenes (vv. 1–3, 4–16, and 17, 18), followed by a closing comment on the life of Jeroboam (vv. 19, 20).

Scene One: In Tirzah (vv. 1–3)

We will learn later in the story that Jeroboam was now living in Tirzah (see v. 17). We do not know when or why he moved his royal residence from

401

Shechem (see 12:25) to Tirzah, probably less than ten miles northeast,[1] but Tirzah will remain the king's city in the northern kingdom for thirty years or so,[2] through the reigns of Nadab, Baasha, Ela, Zimri, and Omri (15:21, 33; 16:6, 8, 9, 15, 17, 23), until Omri shifts the capital to Samaria (16:24, 28).

The opening words of our episode, "At that time" (v. 1a), connect what follows with the strange events of the previous chapter.[3] Particularly we should keep in mind the recent failure of Jeroboam to repent ("did not turn from his evil way," 13:33) after hearing the word of the Lord.

Perhaps there is another, more subtle connection. Precisely the same phrase was used by our writer to introduce the first meeting between Jeroboam and the prophet Ahijah (11:29).[4] We will shortly hear a number of reminders of that encounter.

Jeroboam's Crisis (v. 1)

In the context of Jeroboam's not repenting and the serious danger this had brought to "the house of Jeroboam" (13:34), the king found himself facing a crisis: "Abijah the son of Jeroboam fell sick" (v. 1b). The illness was serious enough to worry Jeroboam (as we are about to see), which suggests that the boy's condition was grave.[5]

We are almost certainly right to guess (from the context, especially 13:34) that this son was Jeroboam's oldest son and therefore the heir apparent to his throne.[6] This was a crisis for Jeroboam the man. What father is untroubled by the suffering of his child? It was also a crisis for Jeroboam the king and his "house."

The son's name (Abijah, "My Father Is Yahweh"[7]) may suggest his status as heir apparent (cf. 2 Samuel 7:14) as well as a time when his human father was more positively disposed to Yahweh.

The situation—a king whose son becomes sick after the king has heard the devastating word of the Lord concerning his evil conduct—should remind us of King David's experience some seventy years or so earlier (see 2 Samuel 12:15). The similarities highlight the very great differences. The word of the Lord had brought David to repentance ("I have sinned against the LORD," 2 Samuel 12:13a), the very thing that had not happened with Jeroboam (13:33). David had consequently heard a word of grace ("The LORD himself has put away your sin," 2 Samuel 12:13b, AT). Jeroboam heard nothing like that.

Jeroboam's Plan (vv. 2, 3)

David's response to the illness of his son had been seven nights of earnest and intense prayer for the child (2 Samuel 12:16–18). His repentance had brought to an end his foolish attempts at cover-up and denial. That is the nature of repentance. He was now open, honest, and transparent before the Lord. That is what God's grace does.

What did Jeroboam do?

First, we notice that he himself did nothing. He certainly did not pray. He had a "better" idea, and he would get his wife to carry it out. "And Jeroboam said to his wife . . ." (v. 2a). She will do what he lacked both the courage and the integrity to do himself. We never learn this woman's name, nor do we hear her speak a word. She is just "the wife of Jeroboam," the one behind whom he hides.

His plan was the opposite of open, honest, and transparent. He said to his wife, "Arise,[8] and disguise[9] yourself" (v. 2b). The contrast with David's behavior is sharpened when we realize that Jeroboam was acting more like Saul who "disguised himself" in order to consult the woman medium of Endor (1 Samuel 28:8).[10]

The purpose of this disguise was "that it not be known that you are the wife of Jeroboam" (v. 2c). He wanted to conceal *his* connection with what she was about to do (at his instruction). The purpose of the disguise was to conceal Jeroboam.

Jeroboam wanted his wife, suitably disguised, to "go to Shiloh" (v. 2d). The last we heard of Shiloh was the reference to the word that the Lord had spoken concerning the house of Eli at Shiloh (2:27). That pointed back to the early chapters of 1 Samuel where Shiloh, for a time, had been (in the Lord's own words) "my place . . . where I made my name to dwell at first" (Jeremiah 7:12). That was a long time ago. Shiloh has played no role in this history since the day of the terrible Philistine victory in 1 Samuel 4.[11] Why would Jeroboam send his wife in disguise to Shiloh?

The importance of Shiloh was this: "Behold, Ahijah the prophet is there" (v. 2e). This does not seem to have been common knowledge. Indeed it is the first we readers have heard of it. Jeroboam had to inform his wife of this important fact ("Behold . . .").

The importance of Ahijah the prophet to Jeroboam was that he was the one "who said of me that I should be king over this people" (v. 2f). Indeed he had (11:31, 35, 37). What Jeroboam did not mention is that Ahijah was also the one who, at the same time, made clear that Jeroboam's reign was conditional on careful, faithful obedience to the Lord. This was God's word, spoken to Jeroboam by Ahijah:

> And if you will listen to all that I command you, and will walk in my
> ways, and do what is right in my eyes by keeping my statutes and my

commandments, as David my servant did, I will be with you and will build you a sure house, as I built for David, and I will give Israel to you. (11:38)

That seems to have slipped his mind.

Since those words were spoken to Jeroboam by Ahijah the prophet, Jeroboam had sinned grievously (12:30), heard the word of the Lord about his sin (13:2), and refused to repent (13:33). The reason for the disguise is now clear. Jeroboam knew very well that he would not have the approval of Ahijah the prophet. He did not think that an open, honest, and transparent approach to the prophet was a good idea.

Jeroboam instructed his wife, "Take with you ten loaves, some cakes, and a jar of honey, and go to him" (v. 3a). It was a modest gift, in keeping with the disguise—hardly a gift of royal proportions. She would appear as an ordinary peasant woman, apparently showing her respect to the prophet.

Finally we learn the point of all this: "He will tell you what shall happen to the child[12] [lad]" (v. 3b).

Jeroboam did not *pray* for his son (as David had for his). He did not even propose asking the prophet to pray for him. Some time earlier, when his hand was crippled, he had at least realized that he needed God's help. To the man of God he had said, "Entreat now the favor of the LORD your God, and pray for me" (13:6). But now the unrepentant king does not mention God at all. That is what happens when a person refuses to repent.

We need not suppose that Jeroboam was thinking clearly. He seems to have had the absurd idea that, provided the prophet was unaware of whose son was ill, a humble gift from an unknown woman might elicit a favorable word about her unidentified son and that would make everything okay. "What a strange notion had Jeroboam of God's prophet."[13]

It is worth pausing and reflecting on the utter stupidity of Jeroboam's plan. True repentance and open honesty before God does not remove all the problems of life, nor all the consequences of our sins. It certainly didn't for David (2 Samuel 12). But refusal to repent and attempts to hide from God are farcical and always make matters worse in the long run (and often in the short run too). Can you imagine Jeroboam's plan doing any good for anyone? Then what about your own hidden sins? Do you really think that cover-up, pretending, and denial is better than honest repentance?

Scene Two: In Shiloh (vv. 4–16)

Jeroboam's wife did as she was told: "Jeroboam's wife did so. She arose and went to Shiloh and came to the house of Ahijah" (v. 4a).

Ahijah's Unimportant Disability (vv. 4b, 5)

As the scene shifts to the prophet's house in Shiloh, the absurdity of Jeroboam's plan is heightened by a piece of information that may at first seem significant: "Now Ahijah could not see, for his eyes were dim because of his age" (v. 4b).

Another "old prophet" (see 13:11)! Many years earlier there had been an old man in Shiloh whose sight had faded (1 Samuel 3:2; 4:15[14]). We have been reminded of him more recently (2:27).

Ahijah's blindness suddenly makes Jeroboam's elaborate concealment of his wife's identity look foolish. Who needs a disguise to hide from a blind man? But it could also make us think that Jeroboam's deceit was bound to succeed. How would a blind man see through a disguise?

The information about Ahijah's disability (given as an aside by the writer to his readers) also allows us to deduce that Jeroboam had had no contact with Ahijah for some time. Jeroboam's efforts at camouflage suggest that he did not know of Ahijah's condition.[15]

However, Ahijah's blindness was less significant than it might seem, and Jeroboam's plan was even more ridiculous, for a simple reason that had not occurred to Jeroboam: the Lord.

> But[16] [ESV, And] the LORD[17] had said [ESV, said] to Ahijah, "Behold, the wife of Jeroboam is coming to inquire of you concerning her son,[18] for he is sick. Thus and thus shall you say to her. When she comes, she will be disguising herself."[19] (v. 5, AT)

Jeroboam's attempt to trick Ahijah had been an attempt to hide the truth from God's prophet, which in fact was an attempt to deceive God. That must be the most foolish thing a human being could ever do. God saw and heard everything that Jeroboam had planned. Of course he did. He is God.

God's word to Ahijah made his blindness irrelevant. He could "see" what God could see. Cleverly our narrator has held back precisely what Ahijah was to say to Jeroboam's wife.[20] On that all-important matter we are kept briefly in suspense.

The End of Jeroboam's Hope (vv. 6–16)

What will become of Jeroboam's preposterous plan?

Deception Disclosed (v. 6)

We follow what happened when Jeroboam's wife arrived. "But [And[21]] when Ahijah heard the sound of her feet, as she came in at the door . . ." (v. 6a). There was nothing wrong with the old man's hearing.

We do not know what lengths Jeroboam's wife had taken to disguise herself. Perhaps she was wearing a heavy veil. She was probably dressed in very plain clothing (matching the humble gift she was carrying). As she took the step that brought her to Ahijah's door, a voice came from inside the house: "Come in, wife of Jeroboam" (v. 6b).

The words must have been startling. Her (and Jeroboam's) elaborate efforts at deception had come to nothing. She must have been shaken. It was clear at that moment that nothing would be hidden from the voice she heard from inside the house.

Before she could get her breath, the voice continued, "Why do you pretend to be another [disguise yourself[22]]?" (v. 6c). Why indeed? *What did you hope to achieve? Did you, or your husband, really think you could deceive the Lord's prophet?*

She was not expected to answer. The seriousness of her (and Jeroboam's) folly was made utterly clear by the next sentence she heard. "For I am charged with unbearable news for you" (v. 6d). Literally this is, "But I[23] am being sent to you (with something) hard."[24] *You thought that you had been sent to me by your husband. The truth is that I have been sent to you, by Someone rather more important. And this is very serious.*

No doubt the poor woman would have liked to turn around and get as far from Shiloh as she could as quickly as possible. But she didn't. The voice had told her to "Come in," and I am sure she did just that.

She was now in the presence of the old prophet. He delivered two devastating messages, the first for her to take to her husband (vv. 7–11) and the second addressed directly to her (vv. 12–16).

God's Word to Jeroboam (vv. 7–11)

He began: "Go, tell Jeroboam, 'Thus says the LORD, the God of Israel . . .'" (v. 7a). The first thing that Jeroboam was to hear was that the Lord was still *the God of Israel*. In this phrase "Israel" means the whole people regardless of the recent division. "The LORD, the God of Israel" is a solemn title that emphasizes God's relationship with the people he had made for himself (see 6:13; 1 Samuel 12:22).[25] In this context, however, Jeroboam (king of *Israel*, 12:20) must understand that his pathetic religious innovations have not diminished the Lord's claim on *Israel* (even in the narrower sense).

God's word to Jeroboam had three parts: first, concerning what the Lord had done (vv. 7b–8a); second, about what Jeroboam had done (vv. 8b–9); and third, what the Lord will therefore do (vv. 10–11).

First, the Lord had done four things:

(1) "I exalted you from among the people" (see 11:37)
(2) "and made you leader[26] over my people Israel"[27] (see 11:38)
(3) "and tore the kingdom away from the house of David" (see 11:31)
(4) "and gave it to you" (see 11:35) (vv. 7b, 8a)

These are four aspects of God's gift to Jeroboam. He was king because the Lord had given him the kingdom. Ahijah had made all this known to Jeroboam at their first meeting (11:31–39).

Second, Jeroboam had utterly failed to heed the word of the Lord that Ahijah had spoken to him on that occasion. The Lord's gifts would be his if he did "as David my servant did" (11:38). Now the Lord says:

> . . . and yet you have not been like my servant David, who kept my commandments and followed me with all his heart, doing only that which was right in my eyes (v. 8b).[28]

On the contrary, Jeroboam had done four things that offended everything the Lord had done for him:

(1) "you have done evil above all who were before you"
(2) "and have gone and made for yourself other gods and metal images"
(3) "provoking me to anger"
(4) "and have cast me behind your back" (v. 9)

"All who were before you" may sound strange, since Jeroboam was the first king over the northern tribes.[29] However, before him Solomon, David, and Saul had ruled over these people (along with their southern cousins). Each had done "evil in the eyes of the LORD" (Saul, 1 Samuel 15:19; David, 2 Samuel 11:27; Solomon, 1 Kings 11:6). Jeroboam's evil topped them all as he *made for himself* "other gods" in the form of "metal images" (see 12:26–31). He may have thought that he was merely updating the worship of the Lord, the God of Israel (12:28). In reality, by his disobedience, he had cast the Lord behind his back!

The terrible novelty of Jeroboam's wickedness is marked by the introduction of an expression that will (with slight variations) dominate the history of the people of Israel for many, many years and eventually the people of Judah as well.[30] "Provoking me to anger" here could be taken to mean "in order to provoke me to anger," suggesting that Jeroboam had deliberately incited the Lord's anger.[31] The expression highlights Jeroboam's responsibility for this anger of God. The particular word for "anger" implies a measure of grief and sorrow.[32] It seems to refer to the emotions aroused by being treated wrongly and unfairly (see 1 Samuel 1:6, 7, 16 referring to human experience [ESV, "provoke . . . grievously," "provoke," "vexation"]). It is striking that this vocabulary, which will be found some twenty times in 1 and 2 Kings, is introduced in connection with Jeroboam's offense and will frequently be associated with the memory of the same sin through the coming years.[33] When his people cast him aside and make for themselves other gods, the Lord is moved to grief, sorrow, and anger.

Third, Jeroboam must hear what the Lord will therefore do: ". . . therefore behold,[34] I will bring[35] harm [or evil[36]] upon the house of Jeroboam" (v. 10a).

The strong divine emotion behind this announcement is conveyed in the coarseness of the language that follows. The statement that the Lord "will cut off from Jeroboam every male" (v. 10b) is a more polite way to put it. The old Authorized Version had fewer qualms and instead of "male" translated this quite literally: "him that pisseth against the wall." The few contexts in which this coarse expression occurs in the Old Testament are always angry and violent (see 1 Samuel 25:22 and the echoes of the present verse in 1 Kings 16:11; 21:21; 2 Kings 9:8).[37]

To "cut off" every son of Jeroboam is a stark and horrifying contrast to the (admittedly conditional) promise that had been made to David: "There shall not be cut off for you a man on the throne of Israel" (2:4, ESV margin; also 8:25; 9:5; but cf. 9:7). What is announced here is nothing less than the end of Jeroboam's dynasty.

The comprehensive nature of this judgment is underlined in the expression "both bond and free in Israel" (v. 10c). The precise meaning of this phrase is unclear,[38] but the sense is the inclusion of every male without exception.[39]

The coarse language continues as the Lord announces that he "will burn up the house of Jeroboam, as a man burns up dung until it is all gone" (v. 10d). The references to urine and dung suggest that Jeroboam's house stinks. It will take a lot to clean it up.

> Anyone belonging to Jeroboam who dies in the city the dogs shall eat,[40]
> and anyone who dies in the open country the birds of the heavens shall eat,
> for the LORD has spoken it. (v. 11)

The utter, shameful, dishonorable, and disgraceful end to the house of Jeroboam could hardly be pictured more graphically. This horrible image will reverberate through the coming pages of this turbulent history (see 16:4; 21:19, 23, 24; 22:38; 2 Kings 9:10, 36).

Ahijah's Word to Jeroboam's Wife (vv. 12–16)

Ahijah had finished the dreadful message that Jeroboam's wife was to take back to her husband. He had not finished speaking, however. He had something to say to the woman herself.

Although she had said nothing, Ahijah knew the true reason for her visit (see v. 5). But the news concerning her ill son was not good. The prophet said to her, "Arise therefore, go to your house. When your feet enter the city, the child[41] shall die" (v. 12).

However, he continued:

> And all Israel shall mourn for him and bury him, for he only of Jeroboam shall come to the grave, because in him there is found something pleasing to the LORD, the God of Israel, in the house of Jeroboam. (v. 13)

In the midst of Jeroboam's apostasy there was "something pleasing [literally, "good," the very opposite of Jeroboam's "evil"] to the LORD." We cannot know whether this means that the lad, Abijah, lived up to his name and loved the Lord as his Father. Perhaps it just means that he did not participate in Jeroboam's idolatry. Whatever it was, we may reasonably say that it was a miracle of divine grace that anything "good" could be found in the house of Jeroboam.

Because of this, we must understand that the child's death was a punishment for Jeroboam, not for the child (like the death of David's son in 2 Samuel 12). Of course, we are troubled and saddened. But we must see that the Lord is perfectly capable of looking after a child beyond the grave. The honorable burial of this boy (in contrast to what was announced for every other male in the family) would be a sign of God's favor resting on him.

The fulfillment of this word will be reported shortly (vv. 17, 18).

The rest of Ahijah's speech to Jeroboam's wife elaborated on the message she had been told to take back to her husband. First, "the LORD will raise up for himself a king over Israel" (v. 14a). The Lord had "raised up" adversaries against King Solomon (11:14, 23); now he will raise up a king "for himself." This underlines this king's place in God's purpose. God had described David as "a king . . . for myself" (1 Samuel 16:1).

However, God's purpose for this king was very different. He "shall cut off the house of Jeroboam today"[42] (v. 14b). This king will turn out to be Baasha (15:27–30), the first of many political assassins who will dominate the history of the northern kingdom from now on.

Since Jeroboam had involved the people of Israel in his sin (12:30, 33), the judgment that would fall on the house of Jeroboam would have consequences for the whole northern kingdom.

> [T]he LORD will strike Israel as a reed is shaken in the water, and root up Israel out of this good land that he gave to their fathers and scatter them beyond the Euphrates[43] [the River]. (v. 15a)

A reed, unstable and quivering in swirling water, is a vivid picture of the instability that the people of the northern kingdom will experience for the rest of their troubled history. The tragic end of that history is anticipated here. They will lose the land that the Lord had given to their forefathers, and they will be "scattered" beyond the River, back where Abraham had come from (Joshua 24:3).

Just as Jeroboam had been the recipient of the Lord's generous "giving" (v. 8), so the Lord had "given" this good land to the people of Israel. Their disobedience, like his, would result in the loss of what they had been given.

The "scattering" will be the undoing of the gathering or "assembly" that had briefly marked the high point of Israel's history in this good land (8:1, 2, 14, 22, 55, 65).[44] It will take some time for this history to unfold, but unfold it will (see 2 Kings 17:21–23).

The reason for this is stated: "because they have made their Asherim, provoking the LORD to anger" (v. 15b). These words may be an aside from the writer to his readers indicating what the people of Israel *eventually* did. The people of Israel appear to have taken Jeroboam's idolatry further (they "made" Asherim), just as we will soon hear the people of Judah had done (they "built" Asherim, 14:23). "Asherim" were wooden poles, representing the pagan Canaanite goddess Asherah. She was, in Canaanite religion, the partner of the highest god and mother of the other gods.[45] The people had aroused the Lord's grief, sorrow, and anger just as Jeroboam had done (see v. 9).

This is a most solemn moment in Biblical history. Listen to Ahijah's last words to Jeroboam's wife: "And he will give Israel up because of the sins of Jeroboam, which he sinned and made Israel to sin" (v. 16). This is a refrain which (with minor variations) we will grow tired of hearing (15:26, 30, 34; 16:2, 13, 19, 26; 21:22; 22:52; 2 Kings 3:3; 10:29, 31; 13:2, 6, 11; 14:24; 15:9, 18, 24, 28; 17:21–23; 23:15). This first hearing, however, is shocking. The text does not exactly say that the Lord will give Israel "up," just that he will "give" Israel. The sense may be that he will give Israel "away" or "over" to her enemies. The Lord who had "given" so much to his people (v. 15) will now "give" them. The consequences of their rejection of the Lord, the God of Israel, would be immense.

Scene Three: Back in Tirzah (vv. 17, 18)

Ahijah had said all he had been told to say (the "thus and thus" of v. 5). The meeting was over. We hear no response from the woman. What could she say?

"Then Jeroboam's wife arose and departed and came to Tirzah" (v. 17a). This is a moment of terrible suspense. The prophet had said that her son would die "when your feet enter the city" (v. 12). Why did she return? Perhaps she did not believe the prophet. Or had she fatalistically resigned herself to the tragedy? We do not know. We do know that she did not plead with God for her son's life, as David had done in similar circumstances (2 Samuel 12:16). She, like her husband, had cast the Lord behind her back. That is what unrepentance is like.

A Death (v. 17b)

I wonder whether we should see the gracious hand of God briefly holding back the announced tragedy. It did not happen the moment she entered the city. There was time, even between her arrival at the city gates and reaching her house, in which she could have humbly begged the Lord for mercy. She did not.

"And as she came to the threshold of the house, the child [lad] died" (v. 17b). In addition to the immediate heartbreak of this, the son's death was a clear sign that the word of the Lord spoken by Ahijah would come to pass. All of it.

A Burial (v. 18a)

"And all Israel buried him" (v. 18a), just as the prophet had said.

A Grief (v. 18b)

". . . and mourned for him" (v. 18b), again just as Ahijah had said.

The Word behind It All (v. 18c)

Indeed the point that must be underlined is that all this happened "according to the word of the LORD, which he spoke by his servant Ahijah the prophet" (v. 18c).

As we will hear many more times in this history, what actually happens is not (in the final analysis) determined by powerful men or political schemes.

Certainly those who imagine that they can shape history and influence events while deceiving God are deluded. The power that shapes the course of history is the word of the Lord (cf. Hebrews 1:3).[46]

The Conclusion to Jeroboam's Story (vv. 19, 20)

There is much more that could have been told about the reign of Jeroboam. Our writer, however, has little interest beyond what he has chosen to record. If you want to know more, our writer says, "Now the rest of the acts of Jeroboam, how he warred and how he reigned, behold, they are written in the Book of the Chronicles[47] of the Kings of Israel" (v. 19). The Book of the Chronicles of the Kings of Israel and another work called the Book of the Chronicles of the Kings of Judah are mentioned thirty-three times in 1 and 2 Kings. The books (like the Book of the Acts of Solomon, 11:41) have not survived, but were apparently accessible to at least some of the original readers of 1 and 2 Kings.[48]

"And the time that Jeroboam reigned was twenty-two years. And he slept with his fathers, and Nadab his son reigned in his place" (v. 20; see 2:10; 11:43).[49] We will return to the northern kingdom to follow the story of Nadab in 15:25–31. In the meantime our writer will take us south to fill in what had been happening there through the twenty-two years of Jeroboam's reign.

Before we move south, we should reflect on the disastrous reign of Jeroboam. The considerable ability shown in his younger days (11:28) sadly came to nothing. Our historian has evaluated his life and reign entirely in terms of his sin—making for himself other gods and casting the Lord behind his back (v. 9). For this, and very little else, he will be remembered. He is a pathetic and tragic figure. His failure to actually trust God and therefore obey him even when it seemed dangerous to do so (12:26–27) led to the delusion that he could deceive God. It was disastrous. "Do not be deceived: God is not mocked, for whatever one sows, that will he also reap" (Galatians 6:7).

We follow a better King. "He committed no sin, neither was deceit found in his mouth" (1 Peter 2:22). Let us not be like Jeroboam.

> This is the message we have heard from him and proclaim to you, that God is light, and in him is no darkness at all. If we say we have fellowship with him while we walk in darkness, we lie and do not practice the truth. But if we walk in the light, as he is in the light, we have fellowship with one another, and the blood of Jesus his Son cleanses us from all sin. If we say we have no sin, we deceive ourselves, and the truth is not in us. If we confess our sins, he is faithful and just to forgive us our sins and to cleanse us from all unrighteousness. If we say we have not sinned, we make him a liar, and his word is not in us. (1 John 1:5–10)

31

Do You Dare to Hope?

1 KINGS 14:21–31

IN DARK TIMES, when the forces of evil, corruption, greed, and oppression seem to have the upper hand, it is difficult to hold much hope for the future of the world. In our own time, for all the brilliant developments and advances in so many areas, the relative peace and prosperity that much of the world has enjoyed for almost a century seems fragile. Perhaps we who have enjoyed the peace and prosperity are at last waking up to the fact that we have cared too little about those for whom these decades have been far less happy. Nonetheless, many of us feel that the measure of stability we once took for granted is crumbling before our eyes. Terrorism terrifies. Wealth evaporates. Political matters frustrate. A sense of foreboding is common. Do we dare to hope?

The Bible teaches us how to have solid, realistic hope. It is realistic because there is no denial of the depth of the problems. The hope we learn is not the deluded optimism of so many who refuse to take the darkness seriously. This hope, once you learn how to have it, is strong and transformative. It is real. In the darkest of times those who have learned the secret find joy (Proverbs 10:28; Romans 15:13).

The history of Israel and Judah in 1 and 2 Kings contributes to this profound dimension of the Bible's teaching by taking us to that people's darkest days and showing us why and how there could still be hope. The Bible teaches us that the hope for Israel and Judah is the hope of the world. That is because this people, the descendants of Abraham, are the people chosen by God to bring blessing to the whole world (Genesis 12:1–3).

We have reached a critical point in this history. The glorious kingdom of Solomon, the son of David, has fragmented. The northern bulk of the kingdom has been torn from Solomon's son and given to Jeroboam (12:16–20). Jeroboam wasted little time in taking the break a drastic step further by preventing his people from going up to Jerusalem and the house of the Lord that was there. Instead he introduced alternatives (12:25–33). Whatever was in *his* mind, the Lord said to him, "You have done evil above all who were before you and have gone and made for yourself other gods and metal images, provoking me to anger, and have cast me behind your back" (14:9). We have seen whatever hope there might have been for the northern kingdom of Israel (see 11:38) destroyed by the sins of Jeroboam (see 14:14–16).

The account of these things concluded with the fact that despite the horrors the future held, when Jeroboam died, after twenty-two years as king of Israel, "Nadab his son reigned in his place" (14:20). In due course we will hear how things went for Nadab (15:25–32). But our expectations cannot be high.

Our writer has focused, since 12:25, on the affairs of the northern kingdom. As they have gone from bad to worse, we have heard nothing about what was happening down south. It is time to wind back the clock and hear what had been going on in Judah through the years of Jeroboam's unhappy reign up north.

What about Rehoboam? (v. 21)

"Now Rehoboam the son of Solomon reigned in Judah" (v. 21a). Of course we already know that (11:43). We have heard the unpleasant story of Rehoboam's youthful foolishness (12:1–15) that led to the northerners repudiating his rule (12:16–20). At the same time we have learned that this turn of events was from the Lord (12:15, 24).

However, the last we heard about Rehoboam and his people was just a little more positive. They "listened to the word of the LORD" and acted "according to the word of the LORD" (12:24). The word of the Lord has featured prominently in the story of Jeroboam's reign in the north, but there has been no hint of an obedient response like that (see 13:33).

Might we, therefore, tentatively hope that things may have gone better in Judah after the unfortunate beginning?

Our writer presents basic details of Rehoboam's reign in a rather formulaic manner that we will hear (with variations) many times through the coming pages.

Chronological Facts (v. 21b)

First, we are given the basic chronological facts: "Rehoboam was forty-one years old when he began to reign, and he reigned seventeen years" (v. 21b).[1]

Since Solomon had reigned for forty years (11:42), Rehoboam was born in the last year of David's life.[2] He would not have known his grandfather, although no doubt he heard a great deal about him. Rehoboam would have been a young man when his father's kingdom was at its height. We may reasonably assume that he was present on the day of the great assembly before the newly constructed house of the Lord and heard his father's prayer and words of blessing (8:1–66). Rehoboam had known the wisdom and glory of Solomon and his kingdom.

Rehoboam's seventeen-year reign was much shorter than that of his father, grandfather, or indeed his grandson, all of whom reigned for some forty years (2:11; 11:42; 15:10). Rehoboam's reign was even shorter than the twenty-two years of his northern rival (14:20).

But what were those seventeen years like? What kind of king was Rehoboam? Does his comparatively brief reign suggest failure? Was he even worse than his disastrous northern counterpart, whose reign lasted five more years? Or did he learn better ways after his bad start (12:1–15)? Was the obedience of 12:24 the beginning of better days?

A Rather More Important Fact (v. 21c)

The answer to these questions begins with the single most important difference between Rehoboam and Jeroboam. Rehoboam reigned "in Jerusalem" (v. 21). You might say, *Of course he did. Where else would he have reigned? Of course he would take up residence in the palatial residence his father had built.* And of course *Jeroboam* could hardly have reigned in Jerusalem!

However, that misses the subtle but all-important point. The crucial difference between Rehoboam and Jeroboam was not what each of *them* did or did not do. It was that *Jerusalem* was "the city that *the* Lord had chosen out of all the tribes of Israel, to put his name there" (v. 21c). That is the difference. In faithfulness to his great promise to King David (2 Samuel 7), the house of the Lord had been built in Jerusalem "for the name of the Lord" (3:2; 5:3, 5; 8:17, 18, 19, 20, 44, 48; see also 8:16, 29, 33, 35, 43; 9:3, 7; 11:36).[3]

We know that Rehoboam was king only because of the Lord's commitment to Jerusalem, that is, because of God's 2 Samuel 7 promise to David that Jerusalem represented (see 11:13, 32, 36). The foolishness and failures of kings and peoples will not—cannot—annul God's promise (see our discussion of 2:4).

This is the fact that Jeroboam had defied by building his alternative houses at Dan and Bethel, with their golden bulls (12:29, 31). We have heard the disastrous consequences of that foolishness (see 12:30; 13:2, 3; 14:7–11,

14–16). The question on which the future depends is: *What will be the conse-quence of the fact that the Lord had chosen Jerusalem as the place where he would put his name?*

A Troubling Fact (v. 21d)

The rather formal notice about Rehoboam's reign has one more fact to record. There was another "name" in Rehoboam's life: "His mother's name was Naa-mah the Ammonite" (v. 21d).[4]

This is a shock. We now learn that Rehoboam was the son of one of the "many foreign women" whom his father Solomon had loved (11:1). She was (we have to assume) among those who "turned away his heart after other gods" when he was old (11:4). In particular Solomon was seduced to follow "Milcom/Molech the abomination of the *Ammonites*" (11:5, 7).[5]

There is bitter irony here. Not only does this fact jar terribly with the just-mentioned divine choice of Jerusalem for the "name" of the Lord, but the mention of Rehoboam's mother is part of a pattern whereby the formal record of almost every descendant of David who reigns in Jerusalem includes the name of his mother. The heightened interest in the parentage of the kings in Jerusalem[6] is almost certainly due to the dynastic promise concerning the descendants of David (2 Samuel 7). It is therefore a shock to find that in Re-hoboam's case his mother was an Ammonite.

A moment's reflection tells us something else. Solomon's liaisons with foreign women had begun before David's death. The seeds that would bear such tragic fruit in his old age (11:4) had been sown in his youth. Perhaps David had a part in it.[7]

Our writer will underline the importance of Rehoboam's Ammonite mother by mentioning her again in verse 31.

We are left with the question, which "name" determined the character of Rehoboam's reign? Was it the "name" that the Lord had chosen to put in Jeru-salem? Or was it the "name" of Rehoboam's Ammonite mother?

What about Judah? (vv. 22–24)

In the brief and generally formulaic records of the reigns of the kings (both of Judah and Israel), at this point there is usually an evaluation of the king and his conduct (see, for example, 15:3, 11, 26). In Rehoboam's case, how-ever, attention focuses on what the people of Judah did on his watch. It was not pretty. In due course we will see that in this they were following Rehoboam's lead (see 15:3).

Evil and Its Consequences (v. 22)

> And Judah did what was evil in the sight [or eyes] of the LORD, and they provoked him to jealousy with their sins that they committed, more than all that their fathers had done. (v. 22)

What Judah did is described in precisely the same terms as King Solomon's old-age apostasy (11:6), reminding us again of King David's evil (2 Samuel 11:27). The decisive assessment of all human behavior is how it is seen by the Lord.

The consequence that mattered more than any other was the Lord's reaction to what he saw. "They provoked him to jealousy." At the beginning of their history as God's people they had been taught that "the LORD your God is a consuming fire, a *jealous* God"—"I the LORD your God am a *jealous* God" (Deuteronomy 4:24; 5:9; see also Exodus 20:5; 34:14; Numbers 25:11; Deuteronomy 6:15; 29:20; 32:16, 21; Joshua 24:19).

This is a remarkable truth about God and, when understood, a precious one. We have seen that Judah's northern neighbors had provoked the Lord to "anger" (14:9, 15) and that the language used indicated a measure of grief and sorrow. The "jealousy" to which the people of Judah incited God speaks even more strongly of an astonishing aspect of God's character.[8]

In human experience "jealousy" (Hebrew, *qn'*) "refers primarily to a violent emotion aroused by fear of losing a person or object."[9] In particular this language is used of a husband's passionate protection of his wife and his emotions when he fears losing her (see, for example, Numbers 5:14; Proverbs 6:34). For mere mortals such emotions can be frightening (Proverbs 27:4; Song of Solomon 8:6) and painful (Proverbs 14:30).

God's "jealousy" speaks of his love and commitment to his people. It belongs with the wonderful picture of God as the husband of his people. Consistently we find the Bible speaking of God's "jealousy" in the context of his people's unfaithfulness, their making *other* gods for themselves (see, for example, Numbers 25:11; Psalm 78:58; Ezekiel 8:3; 16:38; 1 Corinthians 10:22) and in the context of others threatening his people (Ezekiel 36:5, 6).

Properly understood, God's "jealousy" is both terrifying and comforting. It speaks of *both* his anger at all that threatens his people (including themselves) *and* his pity (see Ezekiel 39:25; Joel 2:18). God's "jealousy" is his passionate and loving commitment to his people (cf. 1 Corinthians 10:22; 2 Corinthians 11:2; James 4:5).

The people of Judah provoked the Lord to jealousy "more than all that their fathers had done." Indeed the closest that their ancestors had come to this was when Phinehas (in God's words) "was jealous with my jealousy among them, so that I did not consume the people of Israel in my jealousy" (Numbers 25:11). That day, when thousands died because the people joined themselves to Baal of Peor (Numbers 25:3, 9), was remembered for generations to come (Numbers 31:16; Deuteronomy 4:3; Joshua 22:17; Psalm 106:28–30; Hosea 9:10). What would become of the people of Judah if they had exceeded the wickedness of even that day?

In the greatest of all paradoxes, the "jealousy" of the Lord, which fills us with foreboding about the future of this people, was also their hope. There is only one other reference to the Lord's "jealousy" in the books of Kings. It will be heard by King Hezekiah from the prophet Isaiah:

> For out of Jerusalem shall go a remnant, and out of Mount Zion a band of survivors. The zeal [jealousy] of the LORD will do this. (2 Kings 19:31)

Evil and Its Expression (vv. 23, 24a)

What exactly did the people of Judah do that was so evil in the eyes of the Lord?

High Places

First, "they also[10] [they themselves] built for themselves high places" (v. 23a). These were almost certainly "high places" for pagan gods (as Solomon had built, 11:7). Even if these "high places" had the appearance of honoring the Lord (cf. 12:28), now that the house for the Lord's name had been built in Jerusalem, such "high places" were no better than Jeroboam's abominations at Dan and Bethel (12:31, 32; see 13:2, 32, 33). See our discussion of 3:2.

Pillars

They also built "pillars" (v. 23b). "Pillars" were raised stones. They were not part of any other structure. Such objects were common in the ancient world, with various forms and functions. "Despite all variety, the common element is their erect position, the intentional result of human activity. They can be crude and unhewn, or more or less intentionally worked, with varying height and form, with or without inscriptions and pictures."[11]

Like "high places" these objects could be, at an earlier time, unobjectionable (Genesis 28:18, 22; 31:13, 45, 51, 52; 35:14, 20; Exodus 24:4; cf. Isaiah 19:19). However, "pillars" were also part of the Canaanite pagan religions that were absolutely unacceptable (Exodus 23:24; 34:13; Deuteronomy 7:5). God's Law explicitly forbade making "pillars" (Leviticus 26:1; Deuteronomy 16:22). Certainly now that the Lord had chosen Jerusalem as the place for his name, "pillars" were intolerable (see Deuteronomy 12:3–7). It has been suggested that the repudiation of these objects by God may have been related to their association with the fertility religions of Canaan.[12] If there were sexual associations, this would intensify the sense of "jealousy" in verse 22.[13]

The people of Judah had, it seems, embraced the pagan religion of their world.

Asherim

Furthermore, like their northern cousins, the people of Judah built "Asherim" (v. 23c). See our discussion of 14:15b.

Everywhere!

The extent of these practices throughout the land of Judah is emphasized: "on every high hill and under every green tree" (v. 23d). Perhaps we should allow for a degree of hyperbole, but our writer is clearly horrified. Wherever you might look throughout the land, high or low, you would find evidence of the people's pagan practices.

It is possible that this description of the "sins" of the people of Judah (v. 22, like the similar description in 14:15b) looks forward beyond the days of Rehoboam to what the people *eventually* did. However, it began under Rehoboam.

How Far Did They Go?

If we are not yet shocked, the English translation of the rest of this sentence is bound to get our attention: "and there were also [or even] male cult prostitutes in the land" (v. 24a).

Unfortunately (or rather, fortunately!) this traditional translation, reflected in most modern English versions, is uncertain. In recent times doubt has been cast on both the translation of the Hebrew word *qadesh* as "male cult pros-titute" and the existence of "cult prostitution" in the Old Testament world. It seems more likely that the Hebrew term, which is related to the word for "holy," means someone "consecrated" for foreign religious practices, a pagan priest we might say.[14]

If this understanding is right, then notice that our writer seems horrified that such representatives of paganism were "in the land"—the land that the Lord God had given to his people (8:34, 36, 40, 48; 9:7; 14:15).

Evil and Its Horror (v. 24b)

This brief (and no doubt incomplete) sketch of Judah's "sins" is capped with the most extreme condemnation: "They did according to all the abominations[15] of the nations that the LORD drove out before the people of Israel" (v. 24b).

Perhaps this is the reason that our attention is drawn emphatically to Rehoboam's Ammonite mother (vv. 21, 31). Strictly speaking the Ammonites were not among "the nations that the LORD drove out" (see Deuteronomy 2:19), but perhaps the influence of this Ammonite woman and her detestable religion (11:5, 7) had this toxic effect on her son and his reign.

Since the people of Judah became like these nations, should they not expect to be treated in the same way? As the land once vomited out its vile inhabitants, will it not do likewise to those who have become as vile (see Leviticus 18:25, 28; 20:22)? This verdict is not yet actually pronounced (as it was by Ahijah concerning the northern kingdom, 14:14–16), but you have to wonder what hope there could be.

One Event to Sum Up Rehoboam's Reign (vv. 25–28)

Our historian chooses one event from the seventeen years of Rehoboam's reign. Here we see what King Rehoboam accomplished for his people.

The Enemy (v. 25)

"In the fifth year of King Rehoboam, Shishak king of Egypt came up against Jerusalem" (v. 25).

Shishak was the Egyptian ruler who had provided sanctuary to Jeroboam from the threats of Solomon (see 11:40). We may suppose that he was not favorably disposed to Solomon's son. We not only know about Shishak from other historical sources,[16] but this military campaign is documented in an inscription that lists 154 places he claimed to have taken from one end of Palestine to the other.[17] The interest of our historian is focused on Shishak's assault on Jerusalem.[18]

What would happen to "the city that the LORD had chosen" (v. 21) when its people had sinned so grievously (v. 22)? The Lord's choice of Jerusalem was the culmination of the long history that began with his redemption of this people from Egypt (see 6:1). Was Egypt about to come and take them back? Would *Jerusalem* fall to *Egypt*, of all people?

The End (v. 26)

This is what Shishak did: "He took away the treasures of the house of the LORD and the treasures of the king's house. He took away everything. He also took away all the shields of gold that Solomon had made" (v. 26).

"He took away *everything*"[19] is hyperbole.[20] In due course we will hear about further losses from Jerusalem (see 15:18; 2 Kings 14:14; 16:8; 18:15, 16; 24:13; and finally 25:13–17). But that is what it must have felt like. The immense wealth, wonder, and glory that Solomon had put into Jerusalem (see 10:14–17, 21, 25, 27) was stripped away and given to the King of Egypt. Our writer does not say as much, but it sounds as though all this was an enormous tribute paid to Shishak to induce him to withdraw from Jerusalem.[21]

This is shocking! The glory of Solomon's Jerusalem lost! And lost to *Egypt* (contrast Exodus 3:22)!

The Humiliation (v. 27)

The humiliation was immense. "And King Rehoboam made in their place shields of bronze, and committed them to the hands of the officers of the guard, who kept the door of the king's house" (v. 27). The golden age of King Solomon has given way to Rehoboam's bronze age.[22] Bronze had its place in Solomon's kingdom (7:14, 15, 16, etc.),[23] but it was a very poor substitute for gold.[24]

Going through the Motions? (v. 28)

The writer concludes this episode with an enigmatic comment: "And as often as the king went into the house of the LORD, the guard carried them and brought them back to the guardroom" (v. 28).

On the one hand we observe the humiliated king going through the motions with a procession of fake-gold objects reminding everyone of the lost glory.

On the other hand the king was still in Jerusalem. The house of the Lord was still standing. The king was continuing to go to the house of the Lord. All was not lost. Do we dare to hope that Jerusalem was *still* "the city that the LORD had chosen out of all the tribes of Israel, to put his name there" (v. 21)?

The promise to David concerning his offspring had included this assurance:

> I will be to him a father, and he shall be to me a son. When he commits iniquity, I will discipline him with the rod of men, with the stripes of the sons of men, but my steadfast love will not depart from him, as I took it from Saul, whom I put away from before you. And your house and your

kingdom shall be made sure forever before me. Your throne shall be established forever. (2 Samuel 7:14–16)

Shishak had administered "the rod of men." But we have reason to hope that the Lord's steadfast love was stronger than even the sins of Rehoboam and Judah.

The Conclusion to Rehoboam's Story (vv. 29–31)

We have come to the end of this history's presentation of the reign of Rehoboam. Following a pattern that is becoming familiar (see 2:10–12; 11:41–43; 14:19, 20), we have a formal conclusion.

There Was More (v. 29)

Of course, a lot more happened in Rehoboam's seventeen years than we have been told: "Now the rest of the acts of Rehoboam and all that he did, are they not written in the Book of the Chronicles of the Kings of Judah?" (v. 29). See our discussion of 14:19.

There Was War (v. 30)

In particular, "there was war between Rehoboam and Jeroboam continually" (v. 30). Some suggest, in the light of 12:24, that this was "a state of warfare between the two kingdoms . . . but . . . it is likely that this was rather an armed truce, both sides fortifying frontier fortresses."[25] I think it more likely that our writer is signaling that the obedience noted in 12:24 did not last. If 12:24 had given us a glimmer of hope that Rehoboam may have been a better king than Jeroboam, we now know the truth.

What Next? (v. 31)

However, we are left wondering what hope there might be for the kingdom that was the subject of the Lord's great promise when Rehoboam and his people had failed so badly. What should we make of the last three things we hear about Rehoboam?

Look Where He Was Buried (v. 31a)

First, "Rehoboam slept with his fathers and was buried with his fathers in the city of David" (v. 31a; see 2:10; 11:43; 14:20). Like his "fathers" Rehoboam died. He was buried with his father, Solomon, and his grandfather, David, in the city of David (2:10; 11:43). The wording must remind us of God's promise (see our discussion of 2:10).

Don't Forget His Mother (v. 31b)

And yet, second, we are told again, "His mother's name was Naamah the Ammonite" (v. 31b; see v. 21). Rehoboam's Ammonite mother had her Ammonite influence, and it mattered enough to be mentioned, effectively at the beginning and at the end of this account of Rehoboam's reign.

And Then There Was His Son (v. 31c)

Finally we learn that "Abijam his son reigned in his place" (v. 31c). It is striking that Rehoboam had a son with a name very similar to Abijah, the son of Jeroboam (14:1). Indeed it seems that Abijam is a variant form of Abijah, the latter being used in Chronicles for Rehoboam's son (see 2 Chronicles 12:16; 14:1).[26]

This draws our attention to the obvious and stark difference. Jeroboam's son (even though there was something good about him, 14:13) died young (14:17). Rehoboam's son (even though he "walked in all the sins that his father did," 15:3) lived and reigned in Rehoboam's place.[27]

The difference is this: Jerusalem—that is, the promise of God that Jerusalem represents. If anyone in the days of Rehoboam dared to hope, their confidence could not be placed in Rehoboam and his performance. Under him the people of Judah were worse than ever. The only hope was the Lord's promise. If the Lord could be trusted to be faithful to his promise, there was hope.

The Bible's message is that God *can* be trusted to be faithful to his promise. If we had lived in the dark days of Rehoboam, it might have been difficult to see the signs of his faithfulness. But they were there. There was the house in Jerusalem where the Lord had chosen "to put his name" (v. 21). There was the survival of Jerusalem from Shishak's assault, despite the humiliation that followed. And there was still a son of David reigning in Jerusalem.

Today we will dare to hope if we remember that "he who promised is faithful." Remember the Son of David who has now come, and "set your hope fully on the grace that will be brought to you at the revelation of Jesus Christ." "Let us hold fast the confession of our hope without wavering" (Hebrews 10:23; 1 Peter 1:13).

32

Where Is the Promise?

1 KINGS 15:1–24

AS CHRISTIAN BELIEVERS CONSIDER the depressing monotony of contemporary history, it is not difficult to sympathize with the scoffers of the first century A.D. who said, "Where is the promise of his coming? For ever since the fathers fell asleep, all things are continuing as they were from the beginning of creation" (2 Peter 3:4).

By *monotony* I do not mean that current affairs are boring. They are not. They are terrifying. Who knows what disasters will confront us as this century unfolds? I suspect that in my own lifetime there will be horrors that I cannot now imagine. The dismal dreariness lies in the tedious predictability of more bad things happening.

Do you think this is unrealistically pessimistic? I don't.

As the years roll by, national leaders come and go. Rarely do they make the world a safer, happier, and better place. Occasionally a truly great leader seems to emerge, and under his or her influence we sense the promise of significant change. I find myself thinking of Nelson Mandela. A previous generation may have named Winston Churchill. Looking further back, many would think of Abraham Lincoln. It would be interesting to try to draw up a list of the truly great leaders in world history. There would be disagreement about some proposals. By "truly great," I mean great *and* good. Not perfect, of course, but they would be people to whom significant change for the better can be attributed—injustices put right, evils overthrown, conflicts resolved, poverty alleviated, suffering relieved.

I am sure that our list would show two things very clearly. First, we would notice how few truly great leaders there have been. The problems of humanity have been overwhelmingly complex. Change for the better has never been easy. Only rarely do we find someone with the strength, wisdom, and goodness to address the troubles of any particular time. Frustrated good intentions are far more common than genuine solutions. Second, we would see that the good accomplished under the greatest of leaders is imperfect and usually does not last. South Africa after Nelson Mandela is hardly trouble-free.

"Where is the promise of his coming?" The years roll by, and the state of the world improves so little. Even when we see some advances (say, in overcoming poverty or improving health), they seem to be matched by deterioration in other areas (say, in violence or corruption). *How can we keep on believing the promise of the gospel of Jesus Christ?*

That is a big question, and it is tremendously important. Surprisingly the history of the small kingdoms of Israel and Judah through the tenth to sixth centuries B.C. recorded in the books of Kings helps us understand the answer.

In the coming pages we will see kings of Judah and Israel come and go. Very rarely will they make their world a safer, happier, and better place. Occasionally there will be a great and good leader, but even then the good he achieves will be patchy and will not last.

It would be easy to read these pages as a typical slice of the depressing monotony of human history. We could notice parallels between this account of king after king and the political ups and downs of any other period of history, including our own. Moral judgments could be made about these kings and their use or abuse of power, about the wisdom or foolishness of their policies, and so on, leading to similar judgments about today's political realities.[1] That may not be entirely illegitimate, but it does miss something rather important.

The Biblical history of Israel and Judah in the tenth to the sixth centuries B.C. (I am thinking of the continuation of 1 Kings into 2 Kings) is the story of the people of God's promise. These two kingdoms were the fragments of the kingdom God had promised to establish "forever" (2 Samuel 7:16; 1 Kings 2:45; 9:5). Because of this promise, God had said that the division of the kingdom would be "*not* forever" (11:39). Indeed "a son shall be born to the house of David" who will deal with the most flagrant sins that kept the two kingdoms apart (13:2).

As we read of the rise and fall of kings in Judah and Israel and the monotony of very little changing generation after generation, the all-important questions are: *Where is the promise? Can the promise still be believed? Is it still true? Do we have any reason to think that God will stand by his promise when nothing seems to change?*

The true connection between this ancient record and the world in which we live is to be found in these questions about God's promise, for the promise of God's kingdom has now come to the whole world in the gospel of Jesus Christ (see, for example, Ephesians 3:6). As we watch today's news we reasonably ask, "Where is the promise of his coming? For ever since the fathers fell asleep, all things are continuing as they were from the beginning of creation."

In 1 Kings 15 the pace of our story suddenly takes off. Fourteen chapters have been devoted to the forty years of Solomon's reign and the twenty-two years of Jeroboam, along with his part-contemporary, Rehoboam. The next sixty years will be covered in just two chapters in which we will hear of two southern (15:1–24) and six northern kings (15:25—16:34). The writer creates a sense of the monotony by presenting facts about each king in a formulaic manner. As we follow the record keep the all-important question in mind: *Where is the promise?*

In this chapter we will hear the account of the two southern kings who followed Rehoboam. They were:

(1) Abijam: the king who did not last long (vv. 1–8)
(2) Asa: the better king who was not good enough (vv. 9–24)

Abijam: The King Who Did Not Last Long (vv. 1–8)

The second generation of kings over the divided kingdom began first in Judah, while Jeroboam was still on the throne in Israel. What we were told in the last sentence of chapter 14 ("And Abijam [Rehoboam's] son reigned in his place") is now elaborated.

Chronological Facts (vv. 1, 2a)

The somewhat formulaic presentation begins with chronological facts: "Now in the eighteenth year of King Jeroboam the son of Nebat, Abijam began to reign over Judah. He reigned for three years in Jerusalem" (vv. 1, 2a).[2]

The story continues "in Jerusalem," "the city that the LORD had chosen out of all the tribes of Israel, to put his name there" (14:21).

It will be usual from this point on, when we are told about the accession of a king in the north or the south, to hear this fact linked to the reign of the king in the *other* kingdom (see, for example, 15:9, 25, 33; 16:8, 15, 23, 29). The stories of the two kingdoms will be told in parallel. As we hear about Judah, we are not allowed to forget Israel, and vice versa. This is because the two kingdoms should be one kingdom. Their separation is "not forever" (11:39). Abijam, then, became king over *Judah* in the eighteenth year of Jeroboam's reign over *Israel*. It was about four years before Jeroboam's death (14:20).

The rather formal identification of Jeroboam as "the son of Nebat" has not been used since 12:15, but is a reminder that the king in the north was *not* a son of David. Every time Jeroboam is identified as "the son of Nebat" in the coming pages we will be reminded of his "sins" (that is, the idolatry that resulted from his repudiation of Jerusalem, 12:25–33) and their consequences (16:3, 26, 31; 21:22; 22:52; 2 Kings 3:3; 9:9; 10:29; 13:2, 11; 14:24; 15:9, 18, 24, 28; 17:21; 23:15).

Abijam, however, was David's great-grandson. We should remember the word of the Lord that came to Jeroboam at Bethel: "A son shall be born to the house of David" (13:2). While we readers have been informed that this promise would be fulfilled many years hence in a king named Josiah, Abijam represents "the house of David" to which this son will be born. He belongs to "the offspring of David" who will not be afflicted forever (11:39). Will we see something of God's promise in the reign of Abijam?

His reign was remarkably brief, just "three years," which may mean (as I will explain in a moment) not much more than twelve months. This makes Abijam's reign almost sound like a non-event. Indeed our writer confirms this impression by telling us very little about anything particular that happened during Abijam's brief reign.[3]

Before we hear what he does tell us, we should note that the kind of chronological data presented here and in the coming pages for the kings of Judah and Israel have been a challenge to historians. On a straight reading of the numbers, there seem to be significant inconsistencies. These appear to arise from a combination of at least five factors.[4]

First, there is evidence suggesting that the northern kingdom of Israel and the southern kingdom of Judah may have used different calendars, with the first month of the year being regarded as the month of Tishri (September-October) in the north and Nisan (March-April) in the south.

Second, there were sometimes periods of co-regency (like the period between Solomon's acclamation as king in 1:39 and David's death in 2:10). For any particular king, the stated length of his reign may or may not include years of co-regency.

Third, the reigns of kings usually seem to have been measured as the number of whole or partial years, counting a year as beginning with the new year. If this applied to Abijam, for example, his "three" years could have been a month or two from his accession to the throne to the first new year of his reign, *plus* the full year from then until the next new year, *plus* a few more months until his death. In this way, "three years" may have in fact been as little as one year and a bit.

Fourth, there is evidence that for some reigns (particularly of later kings of Judah) only full calendar years were counted.

Fifth, it is not unusual for there to be a discrepancy between the numbers in the standard Hebrew text and the Greek Septuagint version, raising questions about which numbers are original.

In this commentary we will not attempt to unravel the mathematical puzzles arising from these factors. It is sufficient for our purposes to note that there are various possible solutions to apparent discrepancies, without needing to propose an answer to each problem.

A Curious Family Fact (v. 2b)

The next fact to be recorded, following the pattern that began in 14:21, is the name of Abijam's mother: "His mother's name was Maacah the daughter of Abishalom" (v. 2b).

I am pretty sure this should be a surprise. Abishalom is a variant form of Absalom (see 2 Chronicles 11:20). In the absence of evidence to the contrary, it is reasonable to assume that this is the famous Absalom, the son of David.[5] No other Absalom is mentioned in the Old Testament. As far as we know Absalom had only one daughter, named Tamar (2 Samuel 14:27); so it seems likely that Maacah was the *grand*daughter of Absalom, probably the daughter of Tamar.[6]

On the one hand this is a great contrast to Abijam's father's *Ammonite* mother (14:21). Abijam doubly belonged to the house of David: both his father and his mother were descended from David. On the other hand, the reference to Absalom reminds us of the darkest days of King David, when he was forced to flee from Jerusalem and the kingdom was almost lost. This was Absalom's doing (2 Samuel 13:23—18:33) and a consequence of David's wickedness (2 Samuel 12:11, 12). We will be reminded of these things again shortly.

We noted earlier that the record before us has a particular interest in the mothers of the kings who reigned in Jerusalem (see 14:21). More than that, we will soon see that the queen mother in Judah seems to have had an official position (see v. 13). It is profoundly ironic that the royal household in Jerusalem now included the granddaughter of the treasonous Absalom who came so close to destroying David's kingdom.

The Measure of This King (v. 3)

The reminder of Absalom may have prepared us for the writer's summary evaluation of Abijam: "And he walked in all the sins that his father did before him, and his heart was not wholly true to the LORD his God, as the heart of David his father" (v. 3).

Two "fathers" of Abijam are mentioned. The first was Rehoboam. "All the sins that his father did" points to how under Rehoboam "Judah did what was evil in the sight of the LORD" (14:22). The people had followed their king. His son did likewise. Abijam was a true son of Rehoboam.

But he was not a true son of his other "father," his great-grandfather David, for "his heart was not wholly true to the LORD his God." He did not heed the words of his grandfather: "Let your *heart* therefore be *wholly true to the Lord our God*, walking in his statutes and keeping his commandments, as at this day" (8:61).[7] In fact he went the way of his grandfather in his old age, whose "heart was *not* wholly true to the LORD his God," but "turned away . . . after other gods" (11:4).

From this point on in 1 and 2 Kings, every king in Jerusalem will be evaluated against the touchstone of King David. By now we should have learned that this paradox makes profound *theological* sense. David was "whiter than snow" *because* he was washed clean by God's forgiveness (Psalm 51:7; cf. 2 Samuel 12:13; 22:21–25). This grace really did make David "wholly true to the LORD his God": he kept his commandments, and his heart did not turn after other gods.[8]

But Abijam (and Rehoboam before him) was not like David.

The Hope in the Darkness (vv. 4, 5)

There have now been three generations of kings in Jerusalem who have failed by the measure of King David: Solomon (11:6) and now Rehoboam and Abijam. This is getting monotonous! Will the downward spiral never end? *Where is the promise?*

A Lamp (v. 4)

Having painted this dark picture, our writer shows us the light: "Nevertheless, for David's sake the LORD his God gave him [that is, David] a lamp in Jerusalem, setting up his son after him, and establishing Jerusalem" (v. 4).

"For David's sake" was almost a refrain in chapter 11, pointing to God's promise to David and the difference this made (see 11:12, 13, 32, 34). Because of his promise to David, God provided a "lamp" in Jerusalem (see 11:36). There would be a light in the darkness. There would be hope in the midst of the hopelessness.[9]

If we ask, *Where is the promise?* the answer is that there was still a son of

David reigning in Jerusalem, and Jerusalem is still standing.[10] The *only* reason that these two things were true is God's promise to David.

A Hope (v. 5)

Hope therefore did not rest in anything that Abijam did. It is about what the Lord his God did because of his promise to David: "because [in that[11]] David did what was right in the eyes of the LORD and did not turn aside from anything that he commanded him all the days of his life, except in the matter of Uriah the Hittite" (v. 5).

Here again is David seen in the light of God's amazing grace to him. On this one occasion this grace is emphasized by mentioning the elephant in the room: "except in the matter of Uriah the Hittite."[12] The reference, of course, is to David's adultery with Bathsheba and his attempt at a cover-up by having her husband, Uriah, murdered (2 Samuel 11). It is a rather big "except"! The mention of Absalom in verse 2 may well have prompted this reference because of the deep connection between all these things (see 2 Samuel 12:11, 12).

The fact that "the matter of Uriah" is not mentioned again in Kings, despite many references to David as the model of obedience and a true heart, magnifies the significance of this one reference. This history knows full well that "the thing David did was evil in the eyes of the LORD" (2 Samuel 11:27, AT). It is not forgetfulness, nor an attempt to idealize David that lies behind the remarkable positive picture of him, by which every king in Jerusalem will be evaluated. It is that this history takes with full seriousness the grace of God by which David's sin *really was* put away (2 Samuel 12:13).[13]

The Darkness Persisted (v. 6)

However, Abijam was not like David. He was no better than his father Rehoboam. We are therefore not surprised to read, "Now there was war between Rehoboam and Jeroboam all the days of his [that is, Abijam's] life" (v. 6). The darkness persisted. It is a little curious that the war that continued into the days of Abijam is still called "war between *Rehoboam* and Jeroboam," but perhaps it was known as "the Rehoboam/Jeroboam war" since it was Rehoboam who started it and continued it (14:30). More importantly, identifying it as the same war reminds us that this war was an act of disobedience to the word of God (see 12:24).

Abijam's Epitaph (vv. 7, 8)

The formal notice marking the end of the record of Abijam's reign follows the pattern that is now familiar (see 2:10–12; 11:41–43; 14:19, 20, 29–31) and that we will see many more times.

The Rest of What He Did (v. 7a)

"The rest of the acts of Abijam and all that he did, are they not written in the Book of the Chronicles of the Kings of Judah?" (v. 7a). While this was certainly not the much later Biblical book of Chronicles,[14] there are more details about Abijam's reign in 2 Chronicles 13.[15]

The War (v. 7b)

From our writer's perspective there is only one thing to be remembered about Abijam's reign: "And there was war between Abijam and Jeroboam" (v. 7b). He was the king who continued the War of Disobedience.

Death and Burial (v. 8a)

How he met his end, we do not know (although 2 Chronicles 13 indicates that it was not in the war against Jeroboam). We do know that it was not long after his reign had begun, probably less than two years: "And Abijam slept with his fathers, and they buried him in the city of David" (v. 8a)—alongside Rehoboam (14:31), Solomon (11:43) and David (2:10).

Do you feel the monotony? *Where is the promise?*

The Future? (v. 8b)

"And Asa his son reigned in his place" (v. 8b). Another son of David came to the throne in the city that the Lord had chosen. But recent history has not given us very high expectations.

Asa: The Better King Who Was Not Good Enough (vv. 9–24)

Jeroboam was still in charge in the north, and so the record continues with an account of the reign of Abijam's son, Asa, in Jerusalem.[16]

Chronological Facts (vv. 9, 10a)

We begin, as usual, with the basic chronological facts: "In the twentieth year of Jeroboam king of Israel, Asa began to reign over Judah, and he reigned forty-one years in Jerusalem" (vv. 9, 10a).[17]

This was toward the end of Jeroboam's twenty-two year reign over the northern kingdom (14:20). However, "the twentieth year of Jeroboam" does underline the brevity of Abijam's reign (v. 2). Jeroboam has survived to see *three* kings of Judah. The Jerusalem throne was not looking stable. *Where is the promise?*

Then we hear that Asa reigned for forty-one years! That is longer (just) than David (2:11), Solomon (11:42), not to mention Rehoboam (14:21), and the negligible Abijam (15:2). It was almost twice as long as Jeroboam. Can we hope that stability had returned to Judah and Jerusalem?

A Curious Family Fact (Again) (v. 10b)

We now expect the next fact (for a Judean king) to be his mother's name. But what are we to make of this? "His mother's name was Maacah the daughter of Abishalom" (v. 10b; see v. 2)?

Some have understood this to mean that Abijam's wickedness had included an incestuous relationship with his mother, and *that* is where Asa came from![18] I think that is a lot to read into words that may, quite naturally, bear a less alarming meaning. Just as "father" can mean "great-grandfather" ("David his father," v. 3), so "mother" here may mean "grandmother" (so NIV). Perhaps Asa's mother had died, and so his grandmother, Maacah, continued in the role of queen mother, which she had occupied during her son's brief rule. In such circumstances it is possible, of course that Maacah had been responsible for Asa's upbringing and so was a "mother" to him. It seems to me that if the writer had intended to signal such a shocking fact as some suggest, he would have been more explicit.[19]

In any case the daughter (granddaughter) of Abishalom (Absalom) continued in the Jerusalem royal household. What would that mean for Asa's reign?

The Measure of This King (v. 11)

To our immense relief (and surprise) we read, "And Asa did what was right in the eyes of the LORD, as David his father had done" (v. 11).

For the first time since Solomon's failure we hear that the monotonous cycle of wickedness was not unbreakable. Asa was different. "What was right" echoes the "uprightness" of David's heart according to 3:6 and 9:4 and the "right" he did according to 14:8 and 15:5.[20] The Hebrew word can mean "straight." It suggests behavior that conforms to the will of the watching Lord.

The reference to David's right behavior, so soon after the mention of the matter of Uriah (v. 5), suggests that Asa too was a man affected by God's grace. He was no more perfect (in himself) than David, but like David his heart and conduct were shaped by God's forgiving grace.[21]

We are not directly told what motivated Asa's "right" conduct.[22] However, verse 11 sounds as though David's righteousness had not been forgotten. Had

Asa somehow heard about David's deathbed charge to Solomon (2:1–4)? Or perhaps he read his Bible (see Deuteronomy 17:18–20)!

Light Shines in the Darkness (vv. 12–15)

The lamp in Jerusalem (v. 4) was at last shining. What did Asa, the David-like king, do?

Radical Reforms (vv. 12, 13)

First, "He put away the male cult prostitutes [consecrated ones[23]] out of the land and removed all the idols that his fathers had made" (v. 12). Asa did what the Lord had done with David's sin (see "put away" in 2 Samuel 12:13[24]). The pagan priests (if that is what they were) were no longer "in the land" (14:24). (In due course we will learn that Asa's actions in this matter were either incomplete or temporary in their effect; see 22:46).

The "idols" would include the "pillars and Asherim" constructed in Rehoboam's day (14:23) and also Abijam's atrocities (hence "fathers"). They are here described in the most insulting terms. The word for "idols" has appeared previously only in Leviticus 26:30 and Deuteronomy 29:17,[25] where disgust for these things is clear. It seems likely that the Hebrew term is deliberately mocking and insulting, possibly intended to sound like a word for "dung." The word itself suggests filth.[26]

Doing what was "right" (v. 11) meant, first and foremost, taking action to abolish idolatry.

Second, "He also removed Maacah his mother from being queen mother because she had made an abominable image for Asherah. And Asa cut down her image and burned it at the brook Kidron" (v. 13).

"Queen mother" seems to have been an office of considerable prestige. This may be reflected in the honor that was shown by King Solomon to Bathsheba in 2:19.[27] Maacah used the power of her position to contribute to and advance the idolatry of the people. She made an "abominable image." The Hebrew word occurs only here (and the parallel passage in 2 Chronicles 15:16, where ESV has "detestable image") and may suggest something terrifying.[28] It was evidently a representation of the goddess Asherah, who was being honored by the peoples of both Israel (14:15) and Judah (14:23).

Asa dealt with the offense (he "burned it at the brook Kidron") and the offender (she was removed from office). The brook Kidron was the eastern boundary of the city (see 2:37) and became something like the city's rubbish dump (see 2 Kings 23:4, 6, 12).[29]

Doing what was "right" involved taking action against idolaters, even those in high position.

Incomplete Reforms (v. 14a)

And yet Asa's reforms were not complete: "But the high places were not taken away" (v. 14a; see our discussion of 3:2). This seems to be a careful choice of words. Asa is not blamed. We could translate this: "But the high places did not stop."[30] Perhaps he tried to do away with them but could not. Perhaps they were too popular. Perhaps there were too many. It is possible that these "high places" were thought to be places for the worship of the Lord (as in 3:2, 3, 4)[31] and so apparently less objectionable than the more flagrant forms of paganism. Whatever the reasons, under Asa these unacceptable institutions remained (see 11:7; 14:23).

Deep Reform (vv. 14b, 15)

Our writer wants to emphasize that the incompleteness of Asa's reforms has not diminished his estimate of him: "Nevertheless,[32] the heart of Asa was wholly true to the LORD all his days" (v. 14b). He did not only *do* what was "right" (v. 11), his "heart" was right. And unlike his great-grandfather, that did not change in his old age (cf. 11:4).

Indeed Asa set about making amends for one of the failures of his grandfather, Rehoboam. "And he brought into the house of the LORD the sacred gifts of his father and his own sacred gifts, silver, and gold, and vessels" (v. 15). So Asa began to rebuild the glory that Rehoboam had been forced to surrender to Shishak (14:25, 26).[33]

And the Darkness? (vv. 16–22)

However, King Asa did not restore the glory. The glory of Solomon's kingdom included the peace that was enjoyed (4:24). Each king since Solomon has been at war (14:30; 15:6, 7). Asa, too, found himself embroiled in conflict.

In the parallel accounts of the north and the south, our account of the course of affairs in the south has now advanced beyond the point we had reached in the account of the north. With the death of Jeroboam, his son Nadab had become king (14:20). He lasted only "two years," as we will see (15:25) and was succeeded by Baasha in circumstances we will hear about shortly (15:27–30). That happened in Asa's third year (15:28), and Baasha would be king in Israel for the next twenty-four years (15:33).

At this point we learn that those were years of war between north and south: "And there was war between Asa and Baasha king of Israel all their days" (v. 16).

A Crisis in the War (v. 17)

At some point in this conflict Baasha seemed to gain the upper hand. "Baasha king of Israel went up against Judah and built Ramah, that he might permit no one to go out or come in to Asa king of Judah" (v. 17).

This single sentence points to a major crisis. It is natural for us to identify Ramah as the hometown of Samuel that featured in 1 Samuel (1 Samuel 7:17; 8:4; 15:34; 16:13; 19:18, 22, 23; 25:1).[34] It was a few miles north of Jerusalem, just south of the border between Judah and Israel.[35] It seems that Baasha had encroached into Asa's territory, taken Ramah, and "built" (that is, fortified) the town so as to prevent people movement into or out of Asa's kingdom (at least from or to the north).[36] This may have been an intensification of his predecessor's policy (see 12:27), but it now has the appearance of a more explicit act of aggression. Among other things, it may have been an economic blockade.[37]

The situation was serious. Baasha's next move could have been toward Jerusalem itself, just a few miles down the road.

A Plan That Just Might Work (vv. 18, 19)

King Asa formed a plan to shift the balance back in his favor.

> Then Asa took all the silver and the gold that were left in the treasures of the house of the LORD and the treasures of the king's house and gave them into the hands of his servants. And King Asa sent them to Ben-hadad the son of Tabrimmon, the son of Hezion, king of Syria[38] [Aram], who lived in Damascus, saying, "Let there be [There is[39]] a covenant between me and you, [ESV adds, as there was] between my father and your father. Behold, I am sending to you a present of silver and gold. Go, break your covenant with Baasha king of Israel, that he may withdraw from me." (vv. 18, 19)

A new figure enters the story. Ben-hadad was the first king of Aram of Damascus with that name to appear in Biblical history. There will be others (see 20:1; 2 Kings 6:24; 13:3).[40] His name means "Son of (the god) Hadad."[41] His name points to his paganism. His father Tabrimmon ("Rimmon is good"[42]) is otherwise unknown. His grandfather Hezion may have been the same person as Rezon, who had loathed Israel in the days of Solomon (see 11:23–25).[43]

We know nothing more than we are told here about Ben-hadad's "covenant with Baasha" and the covenant that apparently had existed between Tabrimmon and Abijam and now between their sons Ben-hadad and Asa. In each case it may have been an agreement about trade routes or something similar. No doubt it included or implied peaceful relations between the parties. There is no indication that Ben-hadad had been involved on either side in the conflicts between Israel and Judah that had been simmering for some time (14:30; 15:6).[44]

The surprising turn of events is that Asa, the king whose heart was "wholly true to the LORD all his days" (v. 14), should turn to a pagan power to save him from the threat of his rival in Israel. Why would he do that? I am sure that we are expected to feel at least a little uncomfortable with this development. This was *not* like King David (see 2 Samuel 22:2–4, 51).[45]

Our discomfort increases when we notice that in order to approach the pagan king, Asa raided "all the silver and the gold that were left in the treasures of the house of the LORD," as well as those in his own house. The commendable efforts to replenish these things (v. 15) were undone in this single move. Asa took things back to the embarrassing circumstances Shishak had imposed (14:26).

The troubling nature of Asa's behavior is deepened by the message he sent to Ben-hadad with the silver and gold. After a reference to the existing agreement between them (and between their fathers), he said that he was sending the king of Aram a "present." The translation is a little too polite. The money was not a gift, it was a bribe.[46] It was a payment to secure a morally questionable outcome, benefiting the giver of the bribe.

The outcome Asa wanted from Ben-hadad was that he would break his covenant with Baasha. Again breaking a covenant is generally condemned in the Old Testament (Leviticus 26:15; Deuteronomy 31:16, 20). Although this is usually about the Lord's covenant with Israel (but see Ezekiel 17:15), it is disturbing to see Asa (a) stripping the treasures of the house of the Lord and his palace, (b) in order to pay a bribe, (c) to a pagan king, (d) to persuade him to break a covenant!

The implication is that Ben-hadad would break his covenant with Baasha by siding with Asa in this conflict.

It Did Work! (vv. 20, 21)

The thing about bribes is that they work (Proverbs 17:8)!

> And Ben-hadad listened to King Asa and sent the commanders of his armies against the cities of Israel and conquered Ijon, Dan, Abel-beth-maacah, and all Chinneroth, with all the land of Naphtali. (v. 20)

We may conclude that either Asa's bribe was considerable or that Ben-hadad did not need much encouragement to take advantage of Baasha while the Israelite king was preoccupied on his southern border.

The places named were in the north of Israel. Ijon was a strategic location in gaining control of the routes into Israel from the north (see 2 Kings 15:29). Dan was another northern border town, a few miles southeast of Ijon. Abel-beth-Maacah[47] was not far west of Dan and south of Ijon. "All Chinneroth" (also spelled Chinnereth) probably means an area west of the Sea of Galilee (also known as the Sea of Chinnereth, Numbers 34:11; Joshua 13:27) and therefore well into Israelite territory.[48] "All the land of Naphtali," if taken literally, is a vast area on the western side of the Upper Jordan Valley, north of the Sea of Galilee.[49] There is no mistaking the very considerable loss of territory suffered by Baasha as a result of Asa's scheme.

With this severe assault from the north, Baasha could not persist with his aggression toward his southern neighbor. "And when Baasha heard of it, he stopped building Ramah, and he lived in Tirzah" (v. 21). He withdrew from his incursion into Judah and returned to the city Jeroboam had made his home (14:17), no doubt in order to work out how to respond to the changed situation.

An Enigmatic Outcome (v. 22)

Before we reflect on Asa's behavior with its clear "success," let us notice the immediate outcome in Judah.

> Then King Asa made a proclamation to all Judah, none was exempt, and they carried away the stones of Ramah and its timber, with which Baasha had been building, and with them King Asa built Geba of Benjamin and Mizpah. (v. 22)

Geba and Mizpah were towns even closer to the border with Israel than Ramah.[50] Using the building materials that Baasha had left behind in Ramah, Asa set to work fortifying these towns and thus securing his border.

However, our writer seems to stress that in order to do so Asa had to compel "all Judah, *none was exempt*" to provide the labor force. In the days of Solomon there had been compulsory labor. Then it was for a peaceful, even glorious purpose (see 5:13–18), although perhaps Solomon's policies developed in less attractive directions (see 9:15–23). The fact that the security of the kingdom required compulsory labor from all citizens (*none was exempt*) suggests that these were now precarious days.

What, then, are we to make of Asa's reign? The positive assessment in verses 11–13, 14b, 15 is striking. Clearly the writer presents Asa as a breath of fresh air, a bright light in the darkness (cf. v. 4). He was the kind of king we have been hoping for, in so many ways like David.

And yet (like David) he was not able to deal with all the troubles of his kingdom. The high places were still there, and when he attempted a clever plan to deal with the threats from the king of Israel, he did not put his trust in the Lord but instead emptied the house of the Lord of its treasures to bribe a pagan king to assist him. The result? The king in Jerusalem must be held responsible for Israel's significant loss of their God-given land to a pagan king, and the people of Judah were burdened. It was a long way from the glory days when "Judah and Israel were as many as the sand by the sea. They ate and drank and were happy" (4:20).

Asa was a better king, but he was not good enough.

Asa's Epitaph (vv. 23, 24)

It remains to conclude the account of Asa in the usual way.

The Rest of What He Did (v. 23a)

> Now the rest of all the acts of Asa, all his might, and all that he did, and the cities that he built, are they not written in the Book of the Chronicles of the Kings of Judah? (v. 23a)

Two things stand out about Asa's reign in this formal concluding note. "All his might" indicates that Asa was remembered as a powerful king. But he was not powerful enough. "The cities that he built" suggests that it was more than Geba and Mizpah. Asa was a building king.

Old Feet (v. 23b)

As though to underline that Asa, as we might say, had feet of clay, our writer adds one more note: "But in his old age he was diseased in his feet" (v. 23b). "But" suggests a qualification of what has been said.[51] In the end he was ineffective.[52]

Death and Burial (v. 24a)

After his long reign, the inevitable happened. "And Asa slept with his fathers and was buried with his fathers in the city of David his father" (v. 24a). More than his own father and grandfather, Asa had indeed been a "son of David." But he now lay with Abijam, Rehoboam, Solomon, and David in the city of David.

The Future? (v. 24b)

"And Jehoshaphat his son reigned in his place" (v. 24b). It will be some time before we hear more of this son of Asa (see 1 Kings 22), because for most of the rest of 1 Kings we will be moving north to hear about the course of events in the northern kingdom of Israel.

Before we make that move let's return to the big question. *Where is the promise?* There has been little to encourage us in the first few kings of Judah. Even with Asa, the king who received such a surprisingly positive assessment, there seems to be very little improvement. What was achieved was partial and disappointing. What was lost was substantial. *Where is the promise?*

And yet in the darkest days our writer has gone out of his way to remind us of God's promise to David (see 14:21; 15:4) and that what matters is how the Lord sees things (see 14:22; 15:5). In the brighter days we are reminded that this was still about how the Lord sees things and about David (see v. 11). It seems that our writer wants to ensure that we notice the glimmers of light (such as Asa's David-like conduct), and do not forget them when all is bleak.

If we learn from this, we will take with utmost seriousness that an Asa-like king, with none of the weaknesses of Asa, has now come. He has dealt evil and idolatry a fatal blow (cf. Colossians 2:15). God has now "delivered us from the domain of darkness and transferred us to the kingdom of his beloved Son, in whom we have redemption, the forgiveness of sins" (Colossians 1:13, 14). *Where is the promise?* Look at our Lord Jesus Christ now risen, seated at the right hand of God (Colossians 3:1, 2).

As to the monotony of contemporary events, the Apostle Peter wants those troubled by the words of the scoffers ("Where is the promise of his coming?") to remember the Lord's perspective on all that is happening. Indeed, Peter insists, there is a gracious purpose in the monotony of our times:

> The Lord is not slow to fulfill his promise as some count slowness, but is patient toward you, not wishing that any should perish, but that all should reach repentance. (2 Peter 3:9)

33

Power Politics in Perspective

1 KINGS 15:25—16:34

WHAT WAS HAPPENING in the northern kingdom of Israel through the forty-one years of Asa's reign in Jerusalem (15:9–24)? We have only heard that a couple of years after Asa became king Jeroboam died and that his son Nadab succeeded him (see 14:20; 15:9).

In 15:25—16:34 the narrative takes us back to the northern kingdom to follow the course of events there through these four decades or so. The return to the north (which we left in 14:21 in order to catch up on affairs down south) will turn out to be a major move in the unfolding story, which will now focus on the northern kingdom for many chapters.[1]

The years covered in this passage were tumultuous in the northern kingdom of Israel. A deadly game of power politics was played out with astonishing brutality. As the people of Judah enjoyed the relative stability of Asa's long reign, their northern cousins saw power change hands over and over again. It was just as the prophet Ahijah had said: Israel became like a reed shaking in the water (14:15). The dynasty of Jeroboam came to an end with the second generation. A new self-declared royal family, the house of Baasha, then lasted for about the same length of time before being wiped out in its second generation. Out of the bloodshed the house of Omri emerged the victors, and only with them did a stability of sorts settle on the northern kingdom of Israel. That's a brief version of the story, but there was more to it.

Our passage is challenging for the Bible reader, teacher, and commentator because even bloody violence can become tedious. Our writer seems to have wanted to convey this by telling the story in a most repetitive way. Each episode follows a standard pattern with minor variations. This story of power politics is, at first sight, highly predictable.[2]

And yet this is an unusual story. World history has numerous examples of violent politics and ferocious power struggles. This is different. Although we are no longer focused on "Jerusalem, the city that the LORD has chosen" (14:21), nor on a son of David for whom God had promised to keep a lamp burning (11:36; 15:4), nevertheless in the northern kingdom of Israel we will see:

(1) The word of the Lord was still the power behind everything (see 15:29; 16:1, 7, 12, 34)
(2) The Lord was still "the God of Israel" (15:30; 16:26, 33)
(3) He still called Israel "my people" (16:2)
(4) He was watching all that happened (15:26, 34; 16:7, 19, 25, 30)

This provides a crucial perspective on the politics of power. In Israel there was more going on than winners winning and losers losing. Considering this text carefully and in the light of the gospel of Jesus Christ will help us see the power politics of our own day in proper perspective.

The passage unfolds as follows:

The end of the house of Jeroboam (15:25–32)
    Nadab: the king who fell victim to the power of another (vv. 25–32)

The rise and fall of the house of Baasha (15:33—16:14)
    Baasha: the king whose evil power served God's purpose (15:33—16:7)
    Elah: the king who liked his drink (16:8–14)

The beginning of the house of Omri (16:15–34)
    Zimri: the king who lasted seven days (vv. 15–20)
    Tibni and Omri: the two who vied for power (vv. 21–22)
    Omri: the king who tried to do what David did (vv. 23–28)
    Ahab: the king about whom we will hear a lot more (vv. 29–34)

The episodes of this story generally include the following elements:

(1) The basic chronological facts presented in a standard form (15:25, 33; 16:8, 15a, 23, 29)
(2) A negative assessment of the king, each time in similar or identical terms (15:26, 34; 16:13, 19, 25–26, 30–33)
(3) An account of one event from the reign of the king (15:27–30; 16:1–4, 9–12, 15b–18, 24, 34)

> (4) A formulaic conclusion, sometimes with a small elaboration (15:31, 32;
> 16:5–7, 14, 20, 27–28)

The formulaic conclusion to the story of Ahab is delayed until 22:39–40 because our writer has much more to tell about the days of Ahab.

The End of the House of Jeroboam (15:25–32)

The last we heard about northern affairs was that after Jeroboam died, "Nadab his son reigned in his place" (14:20). We have been prepared for Nadab's unfortunate story by the message the prophet Ahijah had delivered to Jeroboam's wife (14:7–16).

Nadab: The King Who Fell Victim to the Power of Another (vv. 25–32)

The first notable thing about Nadab is his name, which is the same as the name of Aaron's firstborn son (Exodus 6:23; Numbers 3:2). Did Jeroboam deliberately name his son after the son of the original maker of a golden bull? Perhaps not, but the terrible end of the earlier Nadab (Leviticus 10:1, 2; Numbers 3:4) may add to our trepidation as we read of Nadab the Second.

Chronological Facts (v. 25)

Nadab's story turns the clock back to the early years of Asa's reign over Judah (15:9). "Nadab the son of Jeroboam began to reign over Israel in the second year of Asa king of Judah, and he reigned over Israel two years" (v. 25).[3] He was presumably the oldest surviving son of Jeroboam, having lost his elder brother some time earlier (14:17). His brief reign (in real time possibly closer to one year; see our discussion of 15:1, 2a) is hardly unexpected after the Lord's prediction of the imminent end of the house of Jeroboam (14:10, 11).

The Measure of This King (v. 26)

Any lingering hope that things might have improved under the new king are dashed with our writer's evaluation of him: "He did what was evil in the sight of the LORD and walked in the way of his father, and in his sin which he made Israel to sin" (v. 26).

Get used to it. These words, with minor variations and occasional elaborations, will be pronounced over every single king who will reign over the northern kingdom of Israel. Just as David will be the touchstone for measuring every king in Jerusalem, Nadab's father Jeroboam will be the gauge for every northern king. The difference is that David is a positive measure, and some southern kings, such as Asa, did "what was right . . . as David his father had done" (15:11). But Jeroboam is a thoroughly negative measure, and *every* king in the north "did what is evil," just like Jeroboam.

At the heart of this adverse assessment is Jeroboam's famous "sin" (12:30). With what may have seemed to him very reasonable motives (12:26, 27), Jeroboam had rejected Jerusalem (see how we have been reminded of the seriousness of *that* in 14:21) and the son of David who reigned there (consider 15:4). His alternatives, the golden bulls at Dan and Bethel (whatever he may have intended), broke the first and second commandments (see 14:9) and rejected God's chosen place and God's chosen king. In this he not only sinned, he also "made Israel to sin," for the whole purpose of his policy was to keep Israel away from Jerusalem and the son of David (see 12:27, 30; 14:16). In this he succeeded.

Nadab was a realistic politician. How could he unravel the policies of his father, now that they had become popular? Why would he even consider doing so? A state of war continued between the two kingdoms (as we will see in v. 32; cf. 15:6, 7, 16). It would have been political suicide to turn back the clock and acknowledge Jerusalem as the true city of the God of Israel and Asa as Israel's true king. You would have to trust God and believe his promises to do that! You would have to believe that God would answer King Solomon's prayer:

> If they sin against you—for there is no one who does not sin—and you are angry with them . . . yet if they turn their heart . . . and repent and plead with you . . . if they repent with all their heart and with all their soul . . . and pray to you toward . . . *the city that you have chosen*, and *the house that I have built for your name*, then hear in heaven your dwelling place their prayer and their plea, and maintain their cause and forgive your people who have sinned against you, and all their transgressions that they have committed against you . . . (8:46–50)[4]

Nadab did *not* believe that.

What Happened to This King (vv. 27–30)

Our writer chooses one event from the reign of Nadab to record. From his point of view this event puts Nadab's brief reign in perspective.

> Baasha the son of Ahijah, of the house of Issachar, conspired against him. And Baasha struck him down at Gibbethon, which belonged to the Philistines, for Nadab and all Israel were laying siege to Gibbethon. So Baasha killed him in the third year of Asa king of Judah and reigned in his place. And as soon as he was king, he killed all the house of Jeroboam. He left

to the house of Jeroboam not one that breathed, until he had destroyed it. ... (vv. 27–29a)

We met Baasha earlier and learned that he became king of Israel (15:16). It is time to hear how that happened.

Baasha is now introduced properly. He was the son of Ahijah. This was not Ahijah the prophet, who was from Shiloh (14:2), but the mention of this name does remind us of the prophet who had said, "the LORD will raise up for himself a king over Israel who shall cut off the house of Jeroboam" (14:14). Baasha was that king.[5] Baasha was also "of the house of Issachar," that is the tribe of Issachar, whose territory lay west of the Jordan River, just below the Sea of Galilee, including the Jezreel Valley.[6] None of these details suggests that Baasha had any natural claim to the leadership of Israel. We may reasonably think of him as "an upstart with no credentials," "a political schemer and terrorist."[7]

The action took place as Nadab and "all Israel" (that is, the army, representing the whole people) were laying siege to Gibbethon, a town that had belonged to Israel, being one of those allotted to the Levites (Joshua 21:23). It was near the southwest corner of the territory of the northern kingdom, on the coastal plain.[8] At this time it had fallen under Philistine control, perhaps an indication of Jeroboam's weakness. The victories of King David had been overturned (2 Samuel 5:25). To his credit, Nadab was making an effort to regain this Israelite territory. Rather less to his credit, he did not succeed. More than two decades later the Israelite army would still be struggling to win back Gibbethon (see 16:15).

It was during the siege of Gibbethon that Baasha made his move. He had been planning this for some time. The writer calls it a conspiracy. This implies that a number of people were bound together in the plot.[9] The language of conspiracy is a reminder of Absalom's conspiracy against David (2 Samuel 15:12, 31). Earlier it was the language that the paranoid Saul had used to describe the nonexistent plots of his imagined enemies (1 Samuel 22:8, 13). Baasha's conspiracy will turn out to be the first of many in the era of the divided kingdom.[10]

Baasha's motives are of no interest to our writer and so do not concern us. He immediately took Nadab's place as king. There is no suggestion that this was anyone's idea but Baasha's. We may conclude that he was a powerful individual. No one stood in his way.

As soon as he had taken the reins of power he launched a bloody massacre of any potential rivals. It was brutal, as the language of the account makes clear: "He left to the house of Jeroboam not one that breathed, until he had destroyed it." This is shocking, but there is more to the shock when we realize that this is exactly how the conquest of the land by the people of Israel under Joshua had been described: ". . . until they had destroyed them, and they did not leave any who breathed" (Joshua 11:14). Under Baasha's coup the whole family of Jeroboam experienced a reversal of what had happened in the days of Joshua.

The comparison highlights the difference. Joshua and the people of Israel had been acting in obedience to God ("Just as the LORD commanded Moses . . . ," Joshua 11:15; cf. Deuteronomy 20:16). Baasha was doing no such thing. Whether he hated Nadab for some reason or (more likely) just wanted to take power into his own hands for his own ends, there is no suggestion that he had any regard whatsoever for God. He was a violent, self-serving brute. What kind of tyrant will a man who takes power in this manner turn out to be?

Yet our writer has one more thing to tell us about Baasha's murderous atrocity. It was, he says:

> . . . according to the word of the LORD that he spoke by his servant Ahijah the Shilonite. (v. 29b)

Don't misunderstand. This does not mean that Baasha was acting in *obedience* to the word of the Lord, as Joshua had done. We see very clearly in verse 30 that what Baasha did was wicked in every way, and yet it accomplished the Lord's purpose, announced beforehand by Ahijah.[11]

This is astonishing and deeply disturbing. True, we have been prepared because we have heard "the word of the LORD that he spoke by his servant Ahijah the Shilonite" (see 14:7–16). But Ahijah did not say that it would be such an evil man as Baasha who would do this. Ahijah had spoken of a king whom "the LORD will raise up *for himself*" (14:14), making him sound like David (1 Samuel 16:1). Are we to believe that the Lord raised up the bloody assassin Baasha "for himself"?

There is more to be said (and it will be said in 16:2–4, 7), but here we must understand that the Bible teaches that even the most wicked human actions can be taken by God and made to serve his purposes. The dreadful Baasha had no idea that he was serving God, but he was. His actions were inexcusably evil (as we will see), but God accomplished his righteous purposes with Baasha.[12]

God's purpose was his righteous judgment on the house of Jeroboam:

> It was for the sins of Jeroboam that he sinned and that he made Israel to sin, and because of the anger to which he provoked the LORD, the God of Israel. (v. 30)

The terrible deeds of Baasha gave expression to the Lord's grief, sorrow, and anger at the evil deeds of Jeroboam, upheld by his son Nadab (see our discussion of 14:9; also 14:15).

Nadab's Epitaph (vv. 31, 32)

The account of Nadab's reign concludes with the usual formal notice and a footnote. The formal notice is: "Now the rest of the acts of Nadab and all that he did, are they not written in the Book of the Chronicles of the Kings of Israel?" (v. 31). There was no honorable burial for Nadab, unlike his older brother (see 14:11, 13), and of course there was no family member left alive to succeed him.

The footnote is: "And there was war between Asa and Baasha king of Israel all their days" (v. 32). That is not news (see 15:16), but this reminds us that the ongoing war of disobedience is the context of this story (12:22–24; 14:30; 15:6, 7, 16).

The Rise and Fall of the House of Baasha (15:33—16:14)

It is time to hear the story of the new self-declared royal family, starting with the usurper himself.

Baasha: The King Whose Evil Power Served God's Purpose (15:33—16:7)

Chronological Facts (15:33)

"In the third year of Asa king of Judah, Baasha the son of Ahijah began to reign over all Israel at Tirzah, and he reigned twenty-four years" (v. 33).[13]

It seems that Baasha, despite the manner of his coming to the throne, was able to bring the whole northern kingdom ("all Israel") under his rule.[14] This suggests considerable strength. Perhaps he had support among the military. His twenty-four-year reign was slightly longer than Jeroboam's. We may wonder whether the one who toppled Jeroboam's son brought any benefits to the nation.

The Measure of This King (15:34)

If he was better than his predecessors in any way, our writer gives no hint of it. His assessment is familiar: "He did what was evil in the sight of the LORD and walked in the way of Jeroboam and in his sin which he made Israel to sin" (v. 34).

I imagine that the new king from a different background, having wiped out the whole family of Jeroboam, changed many things. Our writer is only interested in one thing that he did not change: Jeroboam's policy of rejecting Jerusalem and the son of David. Dan and Bethel continued to receive the full support of King Baasha.

For that reason our writer has no more to say about his twenty-four years as king than he had to say about Nadab's two! Indeed the little he has to say does not concern anything achieved by Baasha.

The Word of the Lord against This King (16:1–4)

The one event recorded from the reign of Baasha is this: "And the word of the LORD came to Jehu the son of Hanani against Baasha" (16:1). As far as our writer is concerned, all that matters about Baasha's relatively long reign is the word of the Lord that came against him.

The prophet Jehu, the son of Hanani, appears only here in 1 and 2 Kings.[15] The Lord's message on this occasion had three clear but devastating points, not much different from the Lord's word to Jeroboam several decades previously.

First, "Since [Because] I exalted you out of the dust and made you leader over my people Israel . . ." (v. 2a). The Lord had said almost exactly the same thing to Jeroboam: "Because I exalted you from among the people and made you leader over my people Israel . . ." (14:7). The only difference ("out of the dust" rather than "from among the people") perhaps makes the Lord's action on behalf of Baasha even more remarkable (creation-like; cf. Genesis 2:7[16]). Perhaps it is also a put-down of the arrogant Baasha, indicating his lowly origins. Be that as it may, the most striking thing is that this usurper is told that *the Lord* had made him "leader" (not here "king," perhaps another put-down[17]), over not just Israel, but over "*my people* Israel." Observant readers will realize that this is what the prophet Ahijah had said (14:14). Baasha's undoubted ignorance of God's hand in his elevation did not change the fact that what he had and what he was, *the Lord* had given him.

Second, what had Baasha done with "my people Israel"? ". . . you have walked in the way of Jeroboam and have made my people Israel to sin, provoking me to anger with their sins . . ." (v. 2b). This is an abbreviated version of what was said to Jeroboam (see 14:8, 9, 16). In each case the wickedness is amplified because the offender is the beneficiary of God's gift.

Third:

> . . . behold, I will utterly sweep away Baasha and his house, and I will make your house like the house of Jeroboam the son of Nebat. Anyone belonging to Baasha who dies in the city the dogs shall eat, and anyone of his who dies in the field the birds of the heavens shall eat. (vv. 3, 4)

The echo of the Lord's words to Jeroboam (14:10, 11) is clear (although not, of course, to Baasha). What happened to the house of Jeroboam—and who would know about that better than Baasha?—will happen to the house of Baasha *because in the things that matter he was just the same as Jeroboam.*

We are told nothing at all about Baasha's response to these devastating words. I take it there was nothing worth reporting.

Baasha's Epitaph (16:5–7)

That is all our writer chooses to tell us about Baasha's twenty-four years. He closes in the usual formal way and adds a brief but important comment.

> Now the rest of the acts of Baasha and what he did, and his might, are they not written in the Book of the Chronicles of the Kings of Israel? And Baasha slept with his fathers and was buried at Tirzah, and Elah his son reigned in his place. (vv. 5, 6)

"And his might" indicates that Baasha, like Asa, was "someone with whom to reckon."[18] He died, it seems, a natural death and received an honorable burial in what was now clearly the northern royal city of Tirzah (see 14:17; 15:21, 33). He was succeeded by his son, just like Jeroboam (14:20).

The additional comment is:

> Moreover, the word of the LORD came by the prophet Jehu the son of Hanani against [to[19]] Baasha and his house, both because of all the evil that he did in the sight of the LORD, provoking him to anger with the work of his hands, in being like the house of Jeroboam, and also because he destroyed it.[20] (v. 7)

The effect of these words at the conclusion of the account of Baasha's reign is threefold.

First, the importance of the word of the Lord that came to Baasha is emphasized. This word is the legacy of Baasha's reign.

Second, the focus on idolatry is sharpened. "Their sins" that provoked the Lord's anger according to verse 2 becomes "the work of his hands." These words emphasize that Baasha continued the policy of leading his people to gods made by human hands (see Deuteronomy 31:29; cf. Deuteronomy 4:26, 28; 2 Kings 19:18; 22:17; Psalm 115:4; 135:15; Isaiah 2:8; 17:8; 37:19; Jeremiah 25:6, 7; Hosea 14:3; Micah 5:13; Acts 17:25).

Third, Baasha's action in destroying the house of Jeroboam is coupled with his idolatry as a second reason for his condemnation. The astonishing power of God that can make wickedness serve his good purpose in no way diminishes the responsibility of the wicked who will be held accountable for their evil deeds. Many years later (in very different circumstances), the Lord Jesus Christ would die "according to the definite plan and foreknowledge of God," but that will not diminish the wickedness of those who "crucified and killed [him] by the hands of lawless men" (Acts 2:23).

Elah: The King Who Liked His Drink (16:8–14)

Just as Jeroboam, although his house had been condemned through the prophet Ahijah, was succeeded by his son, so it was with Baasha. We come now to the account of Elah's reign.

Chronological Facts (v. 8)

"In the twenty-sixth year of Asa king of Judah, Elah the son of Baasha began to reign over Israel in Tirzah, and he reigned two years" (v. 8).[21] He lasted just as long (as short!) as Jeroboam's son.

What Happened to This King (vv. 9–12)

The similarities between Nadab and the unfortunate Elah went beyond the brevity of their reigns. Once again our writer chooses one event from Elah's time as king, and it is disturbingly like the event he chose for Nadab.

The key player this time was "his servant Zimri" (v. 9). Since no further family connections are noted, we may guess that Zimri's background was even less distinguished than that of Baasha (cf. 15:27). He was a middle-level officer in Elah's army, "commander of half his chariots" (v. 9).

Zimri "conspired against [Elah]" (v. 9). Another conspiracy (see 15:27)! This one seems to have involved a second servant of the king, named Arza, who was in charge of the palace (cf. 4:6). Somehow they got the king into Arza's house, ensuring that the drinks flowed freely. Elah drank too much (v. 9). That was probably predictable for those who knew this king. Once Elah was thoroughly drunk, "Zimri came in and struck him down and killed him" (v. 10a).

Our writer calmly tells us that it was "in the twenty-seventh year of Asa king of Judah," and once the deed was done Zimri "reigned in [Elah's] place" (v. 10b). The matter-of-fact presentation of these facts is beginning to give the impression that this is the kind of thing we should expect in the kingdom of Israel—now like a reed shaking in the water (see 14:15).

Even so, and even if we have been hardened a little by the violence of Baasha, we must draw a breath when we hear what Zimri did next. "When he began to reign, as soon as he had seated himself on his throne, he struck down all the house of Baasha. He did not leave him a single male of his relatives or his friends"[22] (v. 11). The narrator echoes the harshness of God's own words in 14:10 concerning the house of Jeroboam ("male" here is the same coarse expression we saw there). But now it was not just the males of the family of the king who were slaughtered, but every single male "of his relatives or his friends." "Relatives" translates a word that can refer to the avenger of blood that has been shed (as in 2 Samuel 14:11).[23] The plural here seems to refer to all those with any relationship to Elah to whom this duty could have fallen.

This was systematic violence carried out with devastating thoroughness. It was designed to eliminate any possible retaliation for the assassination and probably to terrify into silence any who might object to Israel's latest usurper.

As Baasha had done, so it was done to him. God's hand was behind this too. "Thus Zimri destroyed all the house of Baasha, according to the word of the LORD, which he spoke against [to] Baasha by Jehu the prophet" (v. 12)

The Measure of This King (v. 13)

You may have noticed that we have not yet heard the standard evaluation of King Elah (as in 15:26, 34). It comes a bit later in the account this time. The terrible violence was "for all the sins of Baasha and the sins of Elah his son, which they sinned and which they made Israel to sin, provoking the LORD God of Israel to anger with their idols" (v. 13). Elah had followed in the steps of his father.

Our writer adds a bitterly ironic touch to this now rather too familiar description. The word he uses for "idols" means "breath, vapor" and conveys the notion of "fleetingness, transitoriness, emptiness," in effect denying the existence of "gods" represented by the work of human hands.[24] They are *nothings*.

Elah's Epitaph (v. 14)

The last word about Elah is brief and uninformative: "Now the rest of the acts of Elah and all that he did, are they not written in the Book of the Chronicles of the Kings of Israel?" (v. 14). One suspects that "all that he did" was not much.

The Beginning of the House of Omri (16:15–34)

We have seen two royal houses come and go in Israel in less than three decades. We might now expect to hear the story of the house of Zimri. But that is not quite how things went.

Zimri: The King Who Lasted Seven Days (vv. 15–20)

True to form, our writer now provides an account of the reign of Zimri. It is roughly as long as the accounts we are getting used to, but that hides a surprise.

Chronological Facts (v. 15a)

We begin as usual with the basic chronological facts: "In the twenty-seventh year of Asa king of Judah, Zimri reigned seven days in Tirzah" (v. 15).[25] Seven days!

You might wonder how a man resourceful enough to arrange an assassination managed to hold on to power for no more than a week. Before we hear the story, consider this. In that week Zimri managed to execute every male who had any association with his victim. Although we have no idea how many men that involved, it sounds as though the conspiracy was thoroughly and ingeniously planned.[26]

What Happened to This King (vv. 15b–18)

How was it that this clever murderer was overthrown so quickly? He had made one disastrous miscalculation. He had not ensured that he had the backing of the army for his coup. Big mistake.

> Now the troops were encamped against Gibbethon, which belonged to the Philistines, and the troops who were encamped heard it said, "Zimri has conspired, and he has killed the king." Therefore all Israel[27] made Omri, the commander of the army, king over Israel that day in the camp. (vv. 15b, 16)

Either the struggle against the Philistines for control of Gibbethon had gone on for more than twenty-five years (since 15:27) or this was another attempt years after the earlier one had failed. Either way the army did not welcome the news that while they were fighting Israel's enemies, a relatively junior officer had executed their king and put himself on the throne. They immediately declared their commander, Omri, to be Israel's new king. As commander of the whole army Omri would have been Zimri's superior until the upstart made himself king.[28]

The internal crisis took priority over the struggle for Gibbethon: "So Omri went up from Gibbethon, and all Israel[29] with him, and they besieged Tirzah" (v. 17).

Too late Zimri realized his error. He knew that his cleverness could not defeat the brute force of the entire Israelite army. "And when Zimri saw that the city was taken, he went into the citadel of the king's house[30] and burned the king's house over him with fire and died" (v. 18). Note for future reference that Zimri died by his own hand. He may have been forced by Omri, but Omri did not kill him.

The Measure of This King (v. 19)

Seven days on the throne was time enough to carry out the planned executions and apparently time enough for Zimri to show his true character. In particular, he had time to show his support for Jeroboam's defining policy. Zimri's end was "because of his sins that he committed, doing evil in the sight of the LORD, walking in the way of Jeroboam, and for his sin which he committed, making Israel to sin" (v. 19). We must see God's hand in Zimri's death.

Zimri's Epitaph (v. 20)

The last we hear of Zimri is: "Now the rest of the acts of Zimri, and the conspiracy that he made, are they not written in the Book of the Chronicles of the Kings of Israel?" (v. 20). I suspect that it was not a lengthy entry.

In fact that is not quite the last we hear of Zimri. Years later his name will be heard on the lips of Jezebel (see v. 31). She will call her enemy Jehu, "You Zimri, murderer of your master" (2 Kings 9:31). But that is another story.

Tibni and Omri: The Two Who Vied for Power (vv. 21, 22)

Things now became complicated. It seems that Zimri may have had some support among the people. Certainly the army's action in toppling him and installing Omri was not universally applauded. "Then the people of Israel were divided into two parts. Half of the people followed Tibni the son of Ginath, to make him king, and half followed Omri" (v. 21).

We know very little about Tibni.[31] However, he had enough popular support to maintain a power struggle for four or five years (from the twenty-seventh to the thirty-first year of Asa's reign down south, vv. 15, 23) against the military commander who had the backing of the army. If there was bloodshed in this conflict, our writer does not mention it. Perhaps there was little actual violence.

"But the people who followed Omri overcame the people who followed Tibni the son of Ginath. So[32] [And] Tibni died, and Omri became king" (v. 22). I am inclined to think (but we cannot know) that Tibni died of natural causes and his decline contributed to Omri's gaining the upper hand.

Omri: The King Who Tried to Do What David Did (vv. 23–28)

Although Omri's popularity was limited to "half" the people to start with (and based largely in the army), it is worth noting that he was the first king in the north since Jeroboam to take the throne with expressions of popular support (vv. 16, 21; cf. 12:20). This may have contributed to the relative stability of his throne, which would remain in the hands of the house of Omri for more than thirty years (until Jehu became king in 2 Kings 9). Furthermore, as far as we know, Omri was not directly responsible for the deaths of his rivals. That may have contributed to a popular perception of legitimacy.

Chronological Facts (v. 23)

"In the thirty-first year of Asa king of Judah, Omri began to reign over Israel, and he reigned for twelve years; six years he reigned in Tirzah" (v. 23).[33] The chronology is a little complicated. Omri reigned until the thirty-eighth year of Asa (16:29). He had been made king by the army in the twenty-seventh year of Asa (16:15, 16), although he only had the allegiance of half the people for the next four or five years (16:21). Our writer counts the years of the power struggle with Tibni in the "twelve years" of Omri's reign. They were also included in the "six years" he reigned in Tirzah. However, he only began to reign "over Israel" (as distinct from just half of the people who had followed him from Day One) in the thirty-first year of Asa, with Tibni's demise. His undisputed reign therefore lasted about eight years, the first two in Tirzah.

What Did This King Do? (v. 24)

The event chosen by our writer from Omri's reign will turn out to have historic significance.

> He bought the hill of Samaria from Shemer for two talents of silver, and he fortified [or built] the hill and called the name of the city that he built Samaria, after the name of Shemer, the owner [owners[34]] of the hill. (v. 24)

This was an astute political development. "The hill of Samaria" ("Lookout Mountain"[35]) was central and strategically located.[36] It became the capital of the northern kingdom for the rest of its history (until 2 Kings 18:9). Indeed the kingdom itself became known as Samaria (13:32).

Shemer may have been a Canaanite community, tribe, or clan (note the plural, "owners").[37] Omri's purchase of the site from them made it his personal property, just as Jerusalem had become "the city of David" (2 Samuel 5:9).

The purchase price ("two talents of silver") probably indicates that he paid a proper amount.[38]

The establishment of the new royal city of Samaria should be seen as part of Omri's successful effort to found a lasting dynasty in the northern kingdom. The house of Omri will reign through his son Ahab (16:28) and grandsons Ahaziah (22:40) and Jehoram (2 Kings 3:1). Stability (of sorts) came to the government of Israel. Indeed, Omri may remind us of David, who also fought Philistines (1 Samuel 18:30; etc.), came to the throne after the previous king committed suicide (1 Samuel 31:4), but then only after a period of civil war (2 Samuel 2—4), reigned from two capitals (2 Samuel 5:5), established his personal city (2 Samuel 5:9), and purchased a hill from a non-Israelite (2 Samuel 24:24).[39]

The Measure of This King (vv. 25, 26)

However, we would be mistaken if we thought that Israel had at last found another David. They had not. The Lord's involvement in the life of David (see 2 Samuel 5:10) was conspicuously absent from the life of Omri.

> Omri did what was evil in the sight of the LORD, and did more evil than all who were before him. For he walked in all the way of Jeroboam the son of Nebat, and in the sins that he made Israel to sin, provoking the LORD, the God of Israel, to anger by their idols. (vv. 25, 26)

On the scale of evil our writer puts Omri beyond any of his predecessors. Precisely what that meant is not spelled out, but we will get some idea in the long account of his son's reign. It is likely that Omri introduced a degree of compulsion into his idolatrous policies, which his son would take further. Again our writer mocks the stupidity of idolatry, calling idols "vanity, emptiness" (as we saw in 16:13). Omri's follies would be long remembered (see Micah 6:16).

Omri's Epitaph (vv. 27, 28)

> Now the rest of the acts of Omri that he did, and the might that he showed, are they not written in the Book of the Chronicles of the Kings of Israel? And Omri slept with his fathers and was buried in Samaria, and Ahab his son reigned in his place. (vv. 27, 28)

This time "the might that he showed" is an understatement. Others had a far higher estimate of Omri than the Bible writer. Omri is in fact the first king of Israel who is quite well known from sources outside the Bible. From these we know that he subjugated Moab and occupied Medeba (to the north). Indeed in extra-Biblical sources we find the northern kingdom of Israel referred to as "the land of Omri" even after Jehu displaced the family of Omri. In fact Jehu is called "son of Omri," such was the abiding memory of this powerful king.[40]

The Biblical account puts all this in a fresh perspective. Omri's power is subtly acknowledged ("the might that he showed") but is of little interest. Indeed, it is irrelevant to the true evaluation of this king. He "did what was evil in the sight of the LORD." That's what counts.

However, he apparently died a natural death and was buried in his new capital, and his son Ahab succeeded him.

Ahab: The King about Whom We Will Hear a Lot More (vv. 29–34)

What follows is a fairly standard beginning to the account of the reign of Omri's son Ahab. However, in the days of Ahab something very important happened from the perspective of the Bible writer, so that the account of these things will occupy most of the rest of 1 Kings (until 22:40).

Chronological Facts (v. 29)

"In the thirty-eighth year of Asa king of Judah, Ahab the son of Omri[41] began to reign over Israel, and Ahab the son of Omri reigned over Israel in Samaria twenty-two years" (v. 29)—as long as Jeroboam (14:20).[42] We will hear more about these twenty-two years than we have heard about the reign of any king since Solomon.

The Measure of This King (vv. 30–33)

The writer returns to the earlier pattern of moving straight from the chronological notice to his evaluation of this king (as in 15:11, 26, 34). However, the qualities of King Ahab are described at greater length than those of his predecessors:

> And Ahab the son of Omri did evil in the sight of the LORD, more than all who were before him. And as if it had been a light thing for him to walk in the sins of Jeroboam the son of Nebat, he took for his wife Jezebel the daughter of Ethbaal king of the Sidonians, and went and served Baal and worshiped him. He erected an altar for Baal in[43] the house of Baal, which he built in Samaria. And Ahab made an Asherah. Ahab did more to provoke the LORD, the God of Israel, to anger than all the kings of Israel who were before him. (vv. 30–33)

He did not just maintain Jeroboam's "sins" as all his predecessors had done (12:30; 15:26, 34; 16:13, 19, 26), he took evil in Israel to another level (as his father before him had done, 16:25). What the Bible writer means by this assertion will be explained in detail through the next six chapters of his record. Here we have a summary.

It was as though walking in the sins of Jeroboam was not evil enough for Ahab. So he married Jezebel! We will hear much more about Jezebel in the coming pages, and it will confirm the foolish wickedness of this marriage. She was the daughter of Ethbaal ("With Baal"), who had a reputation (perhaps assumed to be known to informed readers of 1 Kings) as having been a priest of the god Astarte and who took power by assassinating the king of Tyre.[44] He was "king of the Sidonians," that is, of the people in the area around Tyre and Sidon that became known as Sidon.[45]

It has been suggested that Jezebel's name in Hebrew (*'izebel*) may have been a deliberately insulting nickname. Originally spelled *'izebul* ("Where is the Prince [that is, Baal]?"), perhaps the Hebrew version changed the title for Baal (*zebul*) to *zebel* ("dung").[46]

Just as we saw shadows of David in the life of Omri, so his son reminds us of David's son Solomon, whose foreign wives were his downfall (11:1, 4, 5). Jezebel served and bowed down to Baal and did more damage to the people of Israel than all of Solomon's wives combined, as we will see. Furthermore, in a tragic distortion of Solomon's greatest achievement, the house of the Lord he built in Jerusalem, Ahab built "the house of Baal . . . in Samaria."

This is the first mention of Baal ("lord, master," the Canaanite deity of storm and fertility[47]) in 1 Kings. Unfortunately, it will not be the last. Baal will be the main alternative tempting the people of God to turn away from the true and living God for many years to come. We will have reason to think more about Baal in due course.

Ahab followed earlier trends in both kingdoms, making an "Asherah," a wooden pole representing the goddess by that name (see 14:15, 23; 15:13). The male and female deities of Canaan were now prominently represented in Israel.[48]

But the Lord was "the God of Israel"! There seems to be a terrible sadness in this arresting phrase. Ahab moved "the God of Israel" to grief, sorrow, and anger more than any before him (see our discussion of 14:9; also 14:15; 15:30; 16:2, 7, 13, 26). Quite an accomplishment!

What Happened in His Days? (v. 34)

Although the Biblical record will present many more events in the days of Ahab, one event is mentioned here that signals the profound significance of his reign in a surprising way.

> In his days Hiel of Bethel built Jericho. He laid its foundation at the cost
> of Abiram his firstborn, and set up its gates at the cost of his youngest son
> Segub, according to the word of the Lord, which he spoke by Joshua the
> son of Nun. (v. 34)

"In his days" brings the report of this event into the account of Ahab's
reign. This happened on Ahab's watch.

It was not something Ahab himself did. Someone called Hiel here has his
one verse of fame. The man is otherwise unknown, but his hometown is very
well known—Bethel. Bethel was the setting for both Jeroboam's famous "sin"
(12:29) and the word of the Lord that dramatically denounced the idolatry represented there (13:1, 2). Bethel represents the issues that, from the perspective
of the Bible, defined the condition of Israel at that time.

Hiel "built Jericho," which would include the fortification of this strategic
site. We may assume that this was done on the orders of Ahab (cf. 22:39). It is
likely that Ahab had understandable reasons for this project. It may have been
connected with a threat from Moab (cf. 2 Kings 3:5).[49] Since Jericho was close
to the border with Judah, continuing tensions with Israel's southern neighbor
may have had something to do with it.

Whatever the political realities may have been, the building of Jericho has
a deeper significance to the Bible writer. Jericho was the first city taken by the
people of Israel when they entered the promised land. It was given to them
by a mighty and amazing act of God (see Joshua 2:1–24; 5:13—6:27; 24:11).
Joshua's response was this:

> Joshua laid an oath on them at that time, saying, "Cursed before the Lord
> be the man who rises up and rebuilds this city, Jericho.
>
> > At the cost of his firstborn shall he
> > lay its foundation,
> > and at the cost of his youngest son
> > shall he set up its gates." (Joshua 6:26)

Since the days of Joshua, Jericho has only been mentioned once (and that
in passing) in the Biblical history (2 Samuel 10:5). The news that in the days
of Ahab Jericho was rebuilt is stunning. It represents the reversal of what had
happened in the days of Joshua.[50]

That is certainly how our writer sees it. He calls Joshua's words "the word
of the Lord" and sees them fulfilled in the deaths of Hiel's two sons.[51]

In this way the writer has characterized the days of Ahab as days of disregard to "the word of the Lord" and days of suffering the consequences. The

consequences were huge. What began with the destruction of Jericho in the days of Joshua was now coming to an end with the rebuilding of Jericho in the days of Ahab.

Before we hear more about the days of Ahab, let us pause and consider the long passage we have covered in this chapter. What are we to make of the snapshot of the power politics in the kingdom of Israel through these decades—from Nadab to Ahab?

In the introduction to this chapter I listed four key aspects of the perspective given through these pages. As we conclude, let us return to these and consider them in the light of the gospel of Jesus Christ.

First, the word of the Lord is *still* the power behind everything. Kings come and kings go; powers rise and powers fall; the world faces threats and promises, challenges and opportunities. The word of the Lord—now the gospel of Jesus Christ (1 Peter 1:25)—is the one certainty in a world of uncertainty. It is variously described as "the word of his grace" (Acts 20:32), "the word of faith" (Romans 10:8), "the word of the cross" (1 Corinthians 1:18), "the word of truth" (Ephesians 1:13; Colossians 1:5; 2 Timothy 2:15), "the word of life" (Philippians 2:16), "the word of his power" (Hebrews 1:3), and "the word of righteousness" (Hebrews 5:13). The most powerful force in the world, just as it was the most powerful force in the history of the kingdom of Israel, is the word of the Lord.

Second, the Lord who was "the God of Israel" is also "the God of Gentiles" (Romans 3:29). His commitment to and claim on his people is as sure today as ever. The new thing is that through the work of Jesus Christ that commitment and claim is far, far bigger than the kingdom of Israel.

Third, just as he still called Israel "my people," there are now many more who are so called (see Acts 18:10).

Fourth, he is still watching all that happens. He sees it all. Just as all that mattered with the kings of Israel was that each "did what was evil in the sight of the LORD" (15:26, 34; 16:13, 19, 25, 30), so the measure of every life, small or great, will be how the Lord sees it (cf. Hebrews 13:21).

Finally, the parade of kings we have seen in Israel, the horror of their power politics, must make us deeply grateful for the King who did only what is pleasing in the sight of his Father (John 8:29). He is "the King of kings and Lord of lords" (1 Timothy 6:15; Revelation 17:14; 19:16)—the King this world desperately needs.

Part 7

THE ULTIMATE QUESTION

Who Is God?

1 Kings 17—19

How the Drought Began

1 Kings 17

34

Does Your God Rule the Rain?

1 KINGS 17:1–7

WHO IS GOD? On whom does the existence, order, and well-being of everything depend?

In the days of King Ahab of the northern kingdom of Israel, in the mid ninth century B.C., there was an attractive and convincing answer to that question. Baal, a god worshipped by the peoples of the land of Canaan, was the great god of storms. He, it was believed, sent the rain on which the fertility and life of the land depended.[1]

Having married the Sidonian princess Jezebel, a passionate devotee of Baal, King Ahab became a worshipper of Baal and his female consort Asherah (16:31–33). He built "the house of Baal" in his royal city. Perhaps Ahab still claimed to honor the Lord, the God of Israel, as well. But he believed that the existence, order, and well-being of his kingdom depended on Baal.

Every society in every age has developed answers to the question, who is God? Even secular atheists today have answers to the slightly recast question, on what does the existence, order, and well-being of everything depend? Insofar as such a question may be answered, it will be in the language of theoretical physics. In their view everything depends, ultimately, on the ways of matter, energy, and time. In today's world this kind of thinking about ultimate questions has led to a mechanistic approach to the world and its problems. The existence, order, and well-being of everything are seen as ultimately depending on the "laws" of science.

Anyone willing to listen to the teaching of the Bible will learn that this is simply not true. Without denying the real (though limited) accomplishments of modern science, the Bible insists that the ultimate question is *Who?* not *What?* And the answer is: the God of Abraham, Isaac, and Jacob, the God of Moses, the God of David, the God and Father of our Lord Jesus Christ. *He* is God. The existence, order, and well-being of everything depend on him.

The modern embracing of the "god" of science is only one of many ways in which people down the ages have turned away from the true and living God. The alternatives vary enormously, but what they have in common is more serious. God sees them as they really are—evil and harmful (see 16:30).

The Bible is God's message telling us what he has done about this situation. Who is God? In chapters 17—19 of 1 Kings we read the dramatic story of how, in the days of King Ahab, that question was answered.

Introducing Elijah (v. 1a)

It began with the sudden, unexplained appearance of a man in King Ahab's royal city of Samaria, where he had built his "house of Baal" (16:32). The man's name was Elijah. Unlike other great ones in Israel's history (such as Moses and Samuel), the Biblical record provides almost no information about the background of Elijah. He will turn out to be a towering figure in Biblical history, hugely significant far beyond his own lifetime. Indeed our Old Testament[2] closes with the promise, "Behold, I will send you Elijah the prophet before the great and awesome day of the LORD comes" (Malachi 4:5; cf. Matthew 17:10). Jesus applied that promise to John the Baptist (Matthew 11:14; cf. 17:12), although John himself apparently did not understand this (John 1:21).[3] Some thought that Jesus was the promised Elijah (Matthew 16:14). On the Mount of Transfiguration Elijah appeared with Moses and talked with Jesus (Matthew 17:3). The stories about Elijah in 1 Kings are featured in the teaching of Jesus, Paul, and James (Luke 4:25, 26; Romans 11:2–4; James 5:17, 18).

However, his first appearance is as enigmatic as it is dramatic. The writer does not even tell us (at this point) that he was a prophet. He is simply described as "Elijah the Tishbite, of Tishbe [of the settlers[4]] in Gilead" (v. 1a).

His name, in Samaria in the days of Ahab, was dramatic and confronting. "Elijah" means "My God Is Yahweh."[5] Elijah's name was his answer to the question, who is God? Before he uttered a word, his appearance posed the question, *And who is your God, Ahab?*

Our writer calls Elijah "the Tishbite" (as in 21:17, 28; 2 Kings 1:3, 8; 9:36). This may mean that he came from an otherwise unknown, possibly obscure place called Tishbe.[6]

It seems that he lived in Gilead (the Israelite land east of the Jordan River[7]), although his origins were elsewhere. He was among the "settlers"[8] in Gilead.

These vague details contribute to a sense of mystery. Who was this man who suddenly appeared to address King Ahab?

Who Sends the Rain? (v. 1b)

The one whose name meant, "My God Is Yahweh" said to the King of Israel, "As the LORD, the God of Israel, lives, before whom I stand, there shall be neither dew nor rain these years, except by my word" (v. 1b).

It was an extraordinary message. "Dew" and "rain" were vitally important for the land of Palestine. Most rain falls from October to March, and in the summer there can be heavy dew in high parts of the land.[9] If this announcement of years of drought was true, it would be devastating for Ahab's kingdom.

For those who cared to remember, long ago the God of Israel had warned that this could happen, and why:

> Take care lest your heart be deceived, and you *turn aside and serve other gods and worship them*; then the anger of the LORD will be kindled against you, and he will shut up the heavens, so that *there will be no rain*, and the land will yield no fruit, and you will perish quickly off the good land that the LORD is giving you. (Deuteronomy 11:16, 17; cf. 28:23, 24; Leviticus 26:19)

King Solomon had anticipated such circumstances: "When heaven is shut up and *there is no rain* because *they have sinned against you* . . ." (8:35). The announced drought was punishment for the "sins" of King Ahab and his people, chiefly the worship and service of Baal (16:30–33).

The New Testament letter of James tells us that Elijah "*prayed* fervently that it might not rain" (James 5:17). It is possible that this refers to prayers of Elijah not mentioned in 1 Kings 17 (perhaps suggested by "before whom I stand"). I think it more likely that James saw the words of Elijah in verse 1 as (in a sense) a prayer. True, he was actually speaking to Ahab. However, when words are spoken according to God's will, the distinction between prayer and pronouncement may be slight.

The punishment would fit the crime. King Ahab had led his people to turn away from the living God to serve the imagined god of rain. Now there would be no rain.

As the stranger with the name "My God Is Yahweh" delivered this message to King Ahab, he pointed to three realities that guaranteed its truth.

First, *Yahweh* ("the LORD"), not Baal, is "the God of Israel." As the God of Israel, Yahweh had kept his promise to Israel (1:48; 8:15, 23, 25, 26). The house of the Lord in Jerusalem (rejected by Ahab and his predecessors) had been built for the name of Yahweh, the God of Israel (8:17, 20). Despite the efforts of the kings of Israel from Jeroboam to Ahab, Yahweh—not Baal—was still "the God of Israel" (11:31; 14:7, 13; 15:30; 16:13, 26, 33).

Second, Yahweh, the God of Israel, "lives." Baal does not live. The events about to unfold will dramatically demonstrate that it is Yahweh who lives and gives life.

Third, Elijah claimed to be the servant of Yahweh ("before whom I stand"). In other words he claimed to be Yahweh's prophet.

Momentarily the writer puts us in the position of Ahab. All we have is Elijah's word for these things, and Elijah asserts that only "by *my* word" (literally, "by the mouth of my word") will dew and rain fall again.

In 1 Kings 17 we will hear the "word" of a number of persons, related in various ways to the most important word of all.[10] The chapter will lead to the vital conclusion that the word in Elijah's mouth is "the word of the LORD" and it is "truth" (17:24). Looking back on the whole story, James will say that Elijah later "prayed again, and the heaven gave rain" (James 5:18). We will see Elijah praying that prayer in 18:42.

The Word of the Lord (vv. 2–6)

"And the word of the LORD came to him" (v. 2). The narrator vindicates Elijah's claim to "stand before" the Lord. Like the man of God from Judah in 1 Kings 13 (and like other prophets) Elijah was a man to whom the word of the Lord came and who became a bearer of the word of the Lord.[11]

On this occasion, as often, the word of the Lord took the form of a command and a promise.

Command (v. 3)

"Depart from here and turn eastward and hide yourself by the brook Cherith, which is east of the Jordan" (v. 3). The location of the brook Cherith is no longer known. The Hebrew is not even clear that it was "east" of the Jordan,[12] although that is possible and would mean that the hiding place was in Gilead, Elijah's home territory.[13]

Why did the Lord send Elijah into hiding? It may have been to keep him safe for the work he was yet to do.[14] In due course we will see that Ahab (and even more so his wife Jezebel) would have loved to silence the word of the

Lord by killing the prophet (see 18:4, 12–14; 19:2, 10). However, since there has not yet been any sign of such murderous intent, it is probably better to see the hiding of Elijah as part of God's judgment. Since rain will only come at Elijah's word (v. 1), Elijah's hiding away ensured the continuance of the drought. "To the famine of bread, Yahweh adds a famine of the word."[15]

Promise (v. 4)

"You shall drink from the brook, and I have commanded the ravens[16] to feed you there" (v. 4). The living Lord is able to do the most surprising things. Ravens were "unclean" in terms of God's Law (Leviticus 11:15; Deuteronomy 14:14), but a raven had played a role in the days of Noah (Genesis 8:6), and the Lord is the one who provides for the ravens (Psalm 147:9; Job 38:41). At the brook Cherith the Lord promised to provide sustenance for his prophet in this most unlikely way.

Command Obeyed (v. 5)

The proper response to the Lord's command is obedience. That is what Elijah did: "So he went and did according to the word of the LORD. He went and lived by the brook Cherith that is east of the Jordan" (v. 5).

Promise Fulfilled (v. 6)

Elijah's obedience was the obedience of faith. He obeyed the Lord's command, believing the Lord's promise. His faith and obedience were vindicated. The Lord did what he had promised: "And the ravens brought him bread and meat in the morning, and bread and meat in the evening, and he drank from the brook" (v. 6).

Elijah's experience of the Lord's provision is reminiscent of the Lord's provision for his people in the days of Moses when he had fed them with manna in the wilderness. On that occasion the Lord had said, "Then you shall know that I am the LORD [Yahweh] your God" (Exodus 16:12). Elijah's faith (his name means "My God Is Yahweh") was being confirmed in his experience. Soon it would be dramatically demonstrated to King Ahab and his people (see 18:21, 39). This is the first of a number of reminders of the life of Moses that we will see in the story of Elijah.

Who Stopped the Rain? (v. 7)

Elijah's experience in his hiding place by the brook Cherith was, of course, private. How many mornings and evenings he was served by the obedient ravens we do not know. I doubt that King Ahab took much notice of the message Elijah had delivered (v. 1). The mysterious messenger had vanished. I am sure Ahab tried to forget him.

There was one problem. It had become very dry. No rain, not even dew. Did he remember that this was just what "My God Is Yahweh" had said? Did it occur to him that this might suggest that the one whose servant had announced "no rain" might indeed be God? As we will see, that is not how Ahab's mind worked. Not yet.

At this stage the focus of the narrative is on Elijah. As time passed, the effects of the drought were felt in his hiding place. "And after a while the brook dried up, because there was no rain in the land" (v. 7).

This did not, of course, mean that the Lord had abandoned his prophet (glance ahead to 17:8, 9 if you are concerned). The drying up of the brook Cherith vindicated Elijah's message (and his name). But that was just the beginning.

There is an aspect of this episode that is easy to miss because it is not explicitly stated. I am sure that King Ahab missed it. If the drought was the fully deserved punishment for the sins of Israel and her king, why Elijah? That is, why did God not simply withhold the rain without any warning? Why did "My God Is Yahweh" *say* to Ahab, "As the LORD, the God of Israel, lives, before whom I stand, there shall be neither dew nor rain these years, except by my word"?

Unless we feel the force of that question we will find it difficult to see the enormity of the kindness of God. It was because of God's kindness that he warned the king of the impending disaster. The message opened up the possibility of repentance, and the prospect of repentance was the opportunity for forgiveness.

This is what Solomon had prayed:

> When heaven is shut up and there is no rain because they have sinned against you, if they pray toward this place and acknowledge your name and *turn from their sin*, when you afflict them, then [you will] hear in heaven and *forgive the sin* of your servants, your people Israel, when you teach them the good way in which they should walk, and *grant rain upon your land*, which you have given to your people as an inheritance. (8:35, 36)

How kind of God to send his word! If only Ahab had listened and turned from his sin. But Ahab did not see the divine kindness.

However, the kindness of God was experienced by Elijah by the brook Cherith as he believed and obeyed the word of the Lord.

Later in this history the writer will sum up the kindness of God over many years as follows:

> Yet the LORD warned Israel and Judah by every prophet and every seer, saying, "Turn from your evil ways and keep my commandments and my statutes, in accordance with all the Law that I commanded your fathers, and that I sent to you by my servants the prophets." (2 Kings 17:13)

In his kindness God sent prophets. That is, he sent his word. By his word he warned his people. If only they had listened and turned from their sin.

This kindness of God in the history of the people of Israel, sending his word before his judgment fell, has now come to the whole world. The word of the Lord—now the gospel of our Lord Jesus Christ—warns all people everywhere of the coming judgment (see, for example, Acts 17:31), opening the opportunity for repentance and forgiveness (Luke 24:47; Acts 2:38; 5:31; 17:30).

To those who, like Ahab, do not listen and do not repent, the Apostle Paul says:

> [D]o you presume on the riches of his kindness and forbearance and patience, not knowing that God's kindness is meant to lead you to repentance? (Romans 2:4)

35

Is Your God Too Small?

1 KINGS 17:8–16

IN HIS 1950S CLASSIC *Your God Is Too Small* J. B. Phillips observed:

> The trouble with many people today is that they have not found a God big
> enough for modern needs. While their experience of life has grown in a
> score of directions, and their mental horizons have expanded to the point of
> bewilderment by world events and by scientific discoveries, their ideas of
> God have remained largely static. It is obviously impossible for an adult to
> worship the conception of God that exists in the mind of a child of Sunday-
> school age, unless he is prepared to deny his own experience of life. If, by
> a great effort of will, he does do this he will always be secretly afraid lest
> some new truth may expose the juvenility of his faith. And it will always be
> by such an effort that he either worships or serves a God who is really too
> small to command his adult loyalty and cooperation.[1]

The problem is still with us. It is not at all unusual for a young person to
come to a vital (but teenaged) faith in Jesus Christ that persists into the busy,
responsible, pressured world of adult life. They may keep coming to church,
identify themselves as Christians, and long for their children to experience
what they once experienced as teenagers. But sometimes their understanding
of and faith in God has not grown up with them. They do not see the relevance
of their God to all of their *adult* life. So their faith seems to make little difference to their business practices, political opinions, accumulation of wealth,
or decision-making. God is for church, family, and a small circle of Christian
friends, but not for the "real" world of sophisticated, clever, powerful people,
where God seems to have no place.

Is your God too small? If so, it is not *God* who is too small. It is our understanding of him, our confidence in him, our love for him that may not be "big enough for modern needs."

In King Ahab's Israel the God of Israel had become too small. That is, the king and his people were deluded into thinking that they needed Baal and Asherah to meet the needs of their day. The old "God of Israel" was insufficient, too small.

Into this situation came Elijah ("My God Is Yahweh"), announcing a severe drought (17:1). As Ahab embraced Baal, depending on him to send rain and fertility, the living God withheld all moisture from the land. Even the stream by which Elijah was hiding dried up (17:7). Since the Lord had been providing plenty of food for Elijah in a rather unusual way (17:6), we might expect that he would miraculously provide water. He had done that in the days of Moses (Exodus 17:6). Alternatively perhaps Elijah could have moved down the dry creek bed a little way to the Jordan River, which would still have been flowing.[2] However, on this occasion the living God of Israel had other plans.

The Word of the Lord to Elijah (Again) (vv. 8, 9)

"Then the word of the LORD came to [Elijah]" (v. 8). Verse 8 repeats exactly the words of 17:2.[3] As the crisis in Israel deepened, as the land became hard and dry, as crops failed, as food grew scarce, the narrative focuses on "the word of the LORD." The most important events were unfolding "according to the word of the LORD" (see 17:5, 16), though not yet known to King Ahab and his people.

Once again the word of the Lord that came to Elijah was a command and a promise (as in 17:3, 4).

Surprising Command (v. 9a)

"Arise, go to Zarephath, which belongs to Sidon, and dwell there" (v. 9a). Elijah may have wondered whether he had heard correctly. Zarephath was a rather unimportant town on the Mediterranean coast between the major cities of Tyre (about fourteen miles south of Zarephath) and Sidon (about eight miles north).[4] It would have been a journey of close to 100 miles north from Elijah's hiding place by the now dry bed of the brook Cherith to Zarephath. In normal circumstances this would have been a long trek. The severe drought and the scarcity of food and water would have made it very difficult indeed. But he had heard correctly. "Go to Zarephath."

The surprise of this command comes from more than the length of the journey and the difficulty of the harsh circumstances. Zarephath was outside the borders of Israel. Elijah was now not only being sent into hiding (17:3), he was being sent right out of the territory ruled by King Ahab. Since the drought would end only by *Elijah's* word (17:1), the removal of Elijah away from the land was a further removal of hope. The word by which the rain was withheld and by which it would fall again (ultimately the word of the Lord) was to be removed from Israel by the removal of the one whose mouth spoke that word (see 17:24).

This suggests (as the subsequent narrative will confirm, see 18:17) that Elijah's word (17:1) had not been accepted by Ahab and his people. As they rejected the word (with its implicit opportunity for repentance and forgiveness), the word was taken from them. The Lord sent Elijah from Israel to the nations, so to speak. We will take up this point later.

But it was even more than that. Zarephath "belongs to *Sidon*." It was Jezebel's home region, from which she had brought Baal into Ahab's kingdom (16:31). The Lord was sending Elijah into the heart of Baal's own territory. If Baal had invaded the territory of Israel, the God of Israel was now sending his prophet into the territory of Baal. Sooner or later there will be a showdown.

Elijah was to "dwell there" for some time (perhaps a couple of years, see 18:1). While the events in Zarephath will be low-key and hardly noticed by powerful people, either in Israel or in Sidon, the God of Israel was about to demonstrate that he is the God of all the earth. There was nothing small about him. He was as able to act in Zarephath as by the brook Cherith near the Jordan. The demonstration (at this stage) was witnessed by just a few people, but it is now available to all who hear the story.

Unlikely Promise (v. 9b)

The surprising command came with a most unlikely promise: "Behold, I have commanded a widow [or widow-woman[5]] there to feed you" (v. 9b). The promise is vividly presented. As Elijah heard the promise he was expected to "see" what was promised. *Look! The God who "commanded" ravens (17:4) has "commanded" a widow-woman in the land of Baal.*[6]

As in the case of the ravens earlier, the Lord's "command"—unlike the word of the Lord that came to Elijah—was not a verbal communication that the widow-woman was expected to understand and obey. The living God orders affairs in this world in various ways. As this story unfolds we will meet this widow-woman, but she will have no conscious knowledge of this command.

Significantly the Lord did not "command" the king of the region to receive and provide for his servant Elijah. That was not his way (cf. 1 Corinthians 1:27–29). He chose a poor widow-woman, the embodiment of weakness and vulnerability. The God of Israel was "protector of widows" (Psalm 68:5; cf. Deuteronomy 14:29; 24:19; 1 Timothy 5:3–16; James 1:27) because the widows needed protection, support, and provision. A widow-woman was a most unlikely source of sustenance.

Furthermore this widow lived in Zarephath. She was not an Israelite widow. To her Elijah was a foreigner, as she was to him. Of all the possible ways in which Elijah might be cared for between the brook Cherith and Zarephath, a widow-woman in the coastal town was as improbable as any. It was as unlikely as the ravens by the brook Cherith.

But this was the word of the Lord that came to Elijah, a most unreasonable command supported by an extraordinary promise. The word of the Lord is often like that.

Elijah Meets the Widow (vv. 10–12)

Obedience to the Surprising Command (v. 10a)

As previously (17:5), Elijah proved to be unswervingly and exactly obedient to the word of the Lord. He was told, "Arise, go to Zarephath" (v. 9a). "So he arose and went to Zarephath" (v. 10a). The brevity is tantalizing. We are not told anything about the challenging journey or how he was sustained along the way. How long did it take? Were the harsh conditions of the drought in Israel ("no rain in the land," 17:7) felt all the way to Zarephath (we will soon learn that they were, v. 14)? These things are not the writer's concern. What matters is Elijah's obedience to the word of the Lord.

Since the command and the promise are one "word," Elijah's response was again the obedience of faith (as in 17:5). He "arose and went," believing the promise. His obedience was the necessary expression of his faith.

The Serious Unlikelihood of the Promise (vv. 10b–12)

Immediately we are taken to the moment of Elijah's arrival at the city gate of Zarephath. What do you think he saw?

Look at the Widow (v. 10b)

"And when he came to the gate of the city, behold, a widow [widow-woman] was there gathering sticks" (v. 10b). The report is as vividly presented as the promise had been. For a moment the writer puts us in Elijah's sandals. *Look! There! A widow-woman gathering sticks.*[7]

The small detail that she was "gathering sticks" as Elijah spotted her adds to the poignancy of the scene. This woman was destitute enough to need to gather sticks here, near the city gate, and she had no one to do this chore for her or even to help her.

Like Elijah we cannot help seeing the woman in the light of the Lord's promise. There were probably other widows in Zarephath. Was *this* the widow-woman whom the Lord had "commanded"? A less likely source of sustenance and provision would be difficult to imagine.

A Very Small Request (vv. 10c, 11)

Elijah believed the promise he had heard more than what his eyes could see. Faith is like that (2 Corinthians 5:7). So "he called to her and said, 'Bring me a little water in a vessel, that I may drink'" (v. 10c). In Hebrew Elijah's words are more gentle and polite ("Would you please bring me . . ."). Furthermore there is an emphasis on the smallness of what was being asked ("a *little* water").

The woman's immediate and positive response to the stranger's request may be surprising to us, but perhaps accords with the expectations of hospitality at that time. After all, he had only asked for a small amount of water. She could manage that. However, Elijah seems to have concluded (from a smile or a nod of her head?) that this was indeed the widow-woman of the Lord's promise. So "as she was going to bring it, he called to her and said, 'Bring me a morsel of bread in your hand'" (v. 11). As before there was a gentleness to his words not quite captured in the English, and again it was a humble request. A "morsel" was not much.[8]

Not Possible! (v. 12)

The widow's response takes us (and probably Elijah) by surprise. Her situation was even more desperate than it may have seemed.

> And she said, "As the LORD your God lives, I have nothing baked, only a handful of flour in a jar and a little oil in a jug. And now [behold] I am gathering a couple of sticks that I may go in and prepare it for myself and my son, that we may eat it and die." (v. 12)

The first (and greatest) surprise is that the first words we hear from the widow-woman of Zarephath precisely echo the first words we heard from Elijah. Elijah had said to King Ahab, "As the LORD, the God of Israel lives . . ." (17:1). The widow-woman now says to Elijah, "As the LORD *your God* lives . . ."

Some have thought that these words mean that the woman was a worshipper of the God of Israel.[9] Some have taken "*your* God" to suggest otherwise.[10]

Perhaps that is beside the point, which is that here in Baal-land *someone* acknowledged that the living God is Yahweh, the God of Elijah, the God of Israel. *He* is alive.[11] Subsequent events will prove the truth of these words.

Hearing the woman speak to Elijah just as Elijah had spoken to Ahab of the living Lord God has a powerful effect on us hearing this story today. She and Elijah are together at least in this: they acknowledge the living reality of Yahweh. It has been some time since we have met anyone else who did that, even in Israel.

However, the woman's speech has another surprise. In Hebrew her first word is "Alive" (literally, "Alive is Yahweh your God"), but her last word is "die." As we will see shortly (v. 14), the drought that had fallen on the land of Israel had extended as far as Zarephath. These tough conditions had brought the poor woman to the brink of starvation, and now we learn she had a son, a second mouth to feed. The way in which the boy plays no active role in the story suggests that he was young and completely dependent on his mother, as we will clearly see in the next episode.[12]

A widow with a child would be even more desperately needy than a childless widow. In Israel there were provisions for the latter to be cared for, but that was primarily to provide an heir. There were no such arrangements for a widow with a son.[13] We may guess that outside Israel the situation was worse.

The woman informed Elijah that the scene he had encountered as he arrived at the town gate was even more distressing that it appeared. *Look,* she said in essence, *I am gathering these sticks to cook our last meal. Then we will die.*

As we hear this story, we know that the woman was speaking to the prophet whose word (being the word of the Lord) had brought the drought and consequent famine and whose word would bring rain again (17:1). The woman did not know this (not yet, see 17:24). Indeed she does not seem to make any connection between the living God she acknowledged and the death she was facing, even though (as we know) he is the one who sends and withholds rain.

In her desperate situation, the woman explained to Elijah the impossibility of granting his request for a "morsel" of bread. She had "nothing baked,"[14] and she was planning to use the very small quantity of ingredients that remained for the last meal she and her son would eat. A "morsel" for the stranger was just not possible, no matter what the customs of hospitality required.[15]

It was no more possible for Elijah to be fed by this widow-woman than it was for him to be fed sitting by the drying bed of the brook Cherith. As then, so now only the living God could feed him here.

The Word of the Lord to the Widow (vv. 13, 14)

Elijah's response to the moving words of the widow-woman was extraordinary and, literally, life-giving.

"Do Not Fear" (v. 13a)

"And Elijah said to her, 'Do not fear'" (v. 13a). Those are among the most wonderful words a person can ever hear. Have you noticed how often God himself says "Do not fear"? It is a characteristic phrase of God's word, or the word of his spokesperson, in many circumstances (see the various circumstances in which these words were heard in 1 Samuel 12:20; 22:23; 23:17; 2 Samuel 9:7).

There is always something shocking about these words. They are always spoken when there are good and reasonable reasons to be afraid. The widow-woman was facing imminent suffering and death, along with her son. What could make less sense than, "Do not fear"?

The shocking words are made comprehensible because they consistently introduce a promise big enough to take away the terror. On this occasion the promise will come in verse 14.

It is important for us to see that the shape of this word of the Lord from Elijah's mouth is heard again by us as we hear the gospel of Jesus Christ. "*Fear not*, for behold, I bring you good news of great joy that will be for all the people" (Luke 2:10). "*Fear not*, I am the first and the last, and the living one. I died, and behold I am alive forevermore, and I have the keys of Death and Hades" (Revelation 1:17, 18). Jesus said, "*Do not fear*, only believe" (Luke 8:50; cf. Matthew 10:31; Mark 6:50; Luke 12:32; John 6:20).

Frightening Command (v. 13b)

Before the widow-woman heard the promise that would enable her not to be afraid, she heard a command that would have been terrifying—until she learned not to fear. Elijah continued, "[G]o and do as you have said [literally, according to your word]. But first make me a little cake of it and bring it to me, and afterward make something for yourself and your son" (v. 13b).

The widow-woman's "word" in verse 12 had not understood the possibilities of "Alive is Yahweh your God." Elijah's "But[16] first . . ." opened up a new and extraordinary possibility. From her last meager resources she was to make a cake (just a little one!) for Elijah *before* attending to herself and her starving son.[17] Why would she do such a thing? What could possibly motivate such extreme and unreasonable behavior?

Reassuring Promise (v. 14)

These questions were answered. "For," Elijah continued, signaling that he was about to give the reason that she need not be afraid and that she should do according to Elijah's word:

> For thus says the LORD, the God of Israel, "The jar of flour shall not be spent, and the jug of oil shall not be empty, until the day that the LORD sends rain upon the earth." (v. 14)

Here is the word of the Lord, the God of Israel, the living God of Elijah the woman had so surprisingly acknowledged (v. 12). As long as the rain was withheld, the God whose hand was holding it back would provide for the widow, just as he had provided for Elijah by the brook Cherith. She and her son would not die. The promise was not in the least interested in how this might happen. All that mattered was the promised provision. "The jar of flour shall not be spent, and the jug of oil shall not be empty."

The Obedience of Faith (vv. 15, 16)

The similarity we see between the woman and Elijah grows. Like the prophet she believed the promise and obeyed the command:

> And she went and did as Elijah said [literally, according to Elijah's word]. And she and he[18] and her household[19] ate for many[20] days. The jar of flour was not spent, neither did the jug of oil become empty, according to the word of the LORD that he spoke by Elijah." (vv. 15, 16).

Elijah's "word" prevailed over *her* "word," and the narrator now assures us that Elijah's "word" was "the word of the LORD that he spoke by Elijah."

Her believing obedience was vindicated. The Lord did exactly as he had promised by the mouth of his servant Elijah.[21] Her little family (we have no reason to think it was more than herself and her boy) is now called a "household," where life has been restored around regular family meals.

We began this chapter considering whether our God is too small. The story of the widow-woman of Zarephath challenges us to see the bigness of God in a particular way. Obviously the story testifies to God's power to wonderfully provide for the destitute woman and her son in a terrible time of famine. Furthermore it underlines that what the living God *promises*, he *does*. With these important points, however, we have not yet come to the heart of this story's importance.

One Sabbath day when Jesus addressed the people of his hometown in the synagogue in Nazareth, he recalled the story we have just read to make a particularly sharp point.

> And he said, "Truly, I say to you, no prophet is acceptable in his hometown. But in truth, I tell you, there were many widows in Israel in the days of Elijah, when the heavens were shut up three years and six months, and a great famine came over all the land, and Elijah was sent to none of them but only to Zarephath, in the land of Sidon, to a woman who was a widow." (Luke 4:24–26)

Jesus' words so enraged his hearers that they wanted to kill him (Luke 4:29). Why? The immediate cause seems to be his refusal to be owned by them. He did not prioritize his hometown. He more than hinted that his hometown would reject him (as they did). He insisted that in this they were acting like Israel of old who rejected the prophets. It was like our story about Elijah. Of all the widows to whom the Lord could send Elijah and who could be blessed by Elijah, the Lord chose to send him outside Israel (where his word had not been accepted) to the land of Sidon and the widow of Zarephath. God's purposes were not restrained by the smallmindedness of King Ahab and his people. God's purposes would not be restrained by the smallmindedness of the people of Nazareth.

This scene in Luke's Gospel is agenda-setting.[22] The way in which the word of God was sent beyond the borders of Israel in the days of Elijah was a shadowy anticipation of the way in which the gospel of Jesus Christ has been sent to the nations of the world. The day would come when Paul and Barnabas would say to the Jews in Antioch:

> It was necessary that the word of God be spoken first to you. Since you thrust it aside and judge yourselves unworthy of eternal life, behold, *we are turning to the Gentiles* [*nations*]. (Acts 13:46)

Later, in Corinth, Paul would say to the Jews there:

> Your blood be on your own heads! I am innocent. From now on I will go to the Gentiles [nations]. (Acts 18:6)

Paul testified that the Lord had said to him (as, we might say, he had said to Elijah), "Go, for I will send you far away to the Gentiles [nations]" (Acts 22:21).

Indeed in the experience of the widow in Zarephath we can see an early sign of Paul's last words in the book of Acts: "Therefore let it be known to you that *this salvation of God has been sent to the Gentiles* [nations]; they will listen" (Acts 28:28).

Our God is too small when he is not (in our mind, heart, and passions) the God of the nations. When our God (in our deluded imagination) is for church and family, but not for the big world out there, our God *is* too small.

36

Can Your God Beat Death?

1 KINGS 17:17–24

AMONG THE MOST WONDERFUL promises of the gospel of our Lord Jesus Christ is that he is able to "deliver all those who through fear of death were subject to lifelong slavery" (Hebrews 2:15).

Have you noticed how the rise of assertive secularism in many western societies seems to have brought a noticeable increase in anxiety about mortality? Although most of us can reasonably expect to live longer than our parents or grandparents, we are eager to learn of the latest advance in medical research, the newest diet regime, or the state-of-the-art exercise program, all in the hope of prolonging healthy life and delaying death. It looks to me like *lifelong slavery to the fear of death.*

I am not suggesting that such concerns are entirely misplaced. The Bible teaches us that life and health are good gifts from God. Death is a terrible enemy (1 Corinthians 15:26). But what would it take to be delivered from lifelong slavery to the fear of death?

We certainly cannot deliver ourselves. Whatever good may be accomplished by drugs, diets, and discipline, death will not be *defeated* by these things. The astonishing news is that through his own death Jesus Christ has "destroy[ed] the one who has the power of death" (Hebrews 2:14), so that death is no longer victorious; its sting has been taken away through the resurrection of Jesus (1 Corinthians 15:54, 55). Faced with death we can now say, "Thanks be to God, who gives us the *victory* through our Lord Jesus Christ" (1 Corinthians 15:57). Death does not have the last word. Death will not finally beat us. Death has been *defeated* by our Savior.

Do you believe that? The test (and the enormous comfort) comes, of course, not when we and those we love are fit and healthy, but when we face the great enemy. When death touches us, we need to know the truth. Our God has beaten death. We will grieve but not like those who have no hope (1 Thessalonians 4:13).

In the days when King Ahab and his people had put their hopes in the rain and fertility god Baal (16:31–33), the Lord, the true God of Israel, quietly demonstrated that *he* was the one who ruled the rain (17:1–7) and that he was as powerful in Baal-land as he was in Israel (17:8–16). To complete this demonstration there was one more thing to be displayed.

In the Canaanite religion of Jezebel, who had brought the worship of Baal into Israel, Baal's archenemy was Mot ("Death"). In the pagan mythology Mot was a powerful deity who regularly defeated Baal, making the god of life (Baal) the slave of the god of death. Eventually Baal would be rescued by another god, the periodic struggle for supremacy reflecting the agricultural cycle.[1]

How different is the Lord, the God of Israel. He is the *living* One, a point made twice so far in 1 Kings 17 (vv. 1, 12). He is celebrated by those who know him as the Lord of life *and* death.

> The LORD kills and brings to life;
>> he brings down to Sheol and raises up. (1 Samuel 2:6;
>>> cf. Deuteronomy 32:39)

This is the faith that was abandoned by those who went after Baal. A little like those who imagine that medicine, healthy eating, and physical fitness can deliver them from the fear of death, King Ahab and the people who followed his lead were deluded into thinking that in the struggle of life against death it was worth backing Baal.

The Shadow of Death (vv. 17, 18)

It is time to return to Zarephath, the coastal town in the territory of Baal worship. In obedience to the word of the Lord (17:8) Elijah was now living there (17:9). As we will hear shortly, he had taken a room in the widow-woman's house.

Some time earlier death had threatened this household as the famine engulfed the land (17:12). By a wonderful (and obviously effortless) act of Elijah's God, the God of Israel, the God who *lives* (17:1, 12), there was now no shortage of food for Elijah and the widow's small family (17:15, 16). The threat of death had been averted for a time. But notice well, Baal had nothing to do with that.

Death's Supremacy (v. 17)

We do not know how long it was before the now safe and well-nourished household of the widow was shattered by the shadow of death falling again. However, "After this the son of the woman, the mistress of the house, became ill" (v. 17a). This is what had happened to Jeroboam's son Abijah (14:1).[2] And he died (14:17). This was an aspect of God's severe judgment on the house of Jeroboam (14:10). The widow-woman knew nothing of that, but we do. What are we to make of the sudden and threatening illness of the widow's son, who had so recently been delivered from death by the Lord?

The narrator informs us that the widow was "the mistress of the house." When we first encountered her gathering sticks by the town gate (17:10), we may have mistakenly thought she was a poor homeless woman. That was not the case. She had her "house" or "household" (17:15; the Hebrew word can mean either). That had not protected her and her boy from the famine and the threat of starvation. Nor did it now protect the lad from the threat of illness. Death is a crafty enemy with numerous means at its disposal.

But why are we informed that she was the "mistress" of the house? It does confirm that she had no other protector or guardian, but we already knew that. I suspect there is something more suggested here. The Hebrew for "mistress" is the feminine form of the name Baal. "Baal" means "master, lord." So the translation is correct, but it does miss something. In Baal-land and in the context of Baal's invasion of Yahweh's land (16:31–33), this woman had Baal-like power and authority over her house. I do not believe there is anything negative here about the woman. But her weakness and vulnerability is Baal-like. Though she was the "mistress" (*ba'alah*) of her house, she had been unable to do anything about the threat of starvation, and now she was powerless before the illness of her son. How like Baal!

"And his illness was so severe that there was no breath left in him" (v. 17b). It was as though Mot had defeated Baal again. The mistress of the house could not keep death at bay. While the writer does not actually say the boy was "dead,"[3] that is what "there was no breath left in him" means (cf. Genesis 2:7; Deuteronomy 20:16; Joshua 10:40; 11:11, 14; Job 27:3).[4]

The sadness of the scene is intensified by its ordinariness. Too often this is just what death is like. It comes unexpected, without warning. Our defenses are useless. Death wins *again*.

Death's Question (v. 18)

It does not matter how many times we witness or hear of death destroying life yet again—we hate it. We cannot get used to it. It never seems right. We cry out, "Why?"

Through her tears the widow-woman sobbed, "What have you against me [or, What have I to do with you[5]], O man of God? You have come [Have you come] to me to bring my sin to remembrance and to cause the death of my son! [?]"[6] (v. 18).

Death changes everything. At least it seems to. The grieving woman quickly forgot the good that had come to her because of Elijah. She had learned that he was a "man of God" from his "thus says the LORD the God of Israel" in 17:14, but now questioned his intentions toward her.[7]

Her second question connected the death of her son to her "sin" or "guilt" (Hebrew, *'awon*). This may be a general reference to the guilt she may have incurred in the course of her life (see 8:46, but with a different Hebrew word for "sin" [*khata'*]). Is there perhaps an allusion to a former attachment to Baal (cf. 12:30; 13:34; 15:34; 16:26, where serving other gods is "sin," although again the word in these texts is the same as in 8:46)?

Had the man of God come to her in order to bring her "sin" to God's remembrance[8] and so bring about her son's death?

Notice how good this woman's theology was. She was not quite right (cf. John 9:3), but her thinking was not pagan. She understood that the hand of Elijah's God was behind her son's death. She did not think in terms of God being defeated by death (as Mot defeated Baal). On the contrary, death was under his control (1 Samuel 2:6). She saw her son's death as we have been shown the death of Jeroboam's son—the Lord's punishment for sin. Her earlier acknowledgment that Yahweh, Elijah's God, lives (17:12) was more than words.

But hear her despair. *Was God's kindness in sparing us from premature death some kind of joke? Was death his intention all along?*

Elijah's Prayer (vv. 19–21)

Elijah did not answer her questions. He took action.

Preparation (v. 19)

> And he said to her, "Give me your son." And he took him from her arms and carried him up into the upper chamber where he lodged,[9] and laid him on his own bed. (v. 19)

Here is the first clear indication that the woman's son was a small boy. She was nursing him. Perhaps he had died there in her arms.

Notice how she did not hesitate to give the child to Elijah. Whatever questions her sorrow had raised, she trusted the man of God.

"The upper chamber" was probably a shelter of some kind on the flat roof of the house, allowing Elijah to be a house-guest without infringing too much on the family life in the small living space below. We may surmise that this arrangement avoided any hint of impropriety as Elijah lodged on the roof, with his female host inside downstairs.[10]

Death's Question (v. 20)

And he cried to the LORD, "O LORD my God, have you brought calamity even [or also[11]] upon the widow with whom I sojourn, by killing her son?" (v. 20)

Elijah's question was an echo of the widow's questions.[12] He brought her questions to the Lord. This confirms our impression that the woman's questions were (if we may put it like this) questions of faith. Elijah, like the woman, attributed the death of the boy directly to the Lord. Neither he nor she held to any kind of dualism or polytheism. Their question was, Why? Why would the Lord bring this calamity on the woman who was providing the man of God with his home away from home?

"Sojourn" reminds us that Elijah was in a foreign land. The word refers to living apart from one's own people, dependent on the hospitality of those among whom you now live. Elijah was a "sojourner" (cf. 2 Samuel 1:13; 4:3; 2 Kings 8:1, 2).[13] He had enjoyed the welcome of this widow-woman. Is she to be repaid by the death of her boy?

The questions asked by both the woman and Elijah imply, *This is not right!* They are more cries of protest than requests for answers. Since (I am suggesting) both the woman's and Elijah's questions arise from a definite trust in God, the questions implicitly (if only subconsciously) look to God to make things right. In this Elijah reminds us again of Moses (Numbers 11:11).[14]

Striking Actions (v. 21a)

"Then he stretched himself upon the child[15] three times" (v. 21a). We are given no explanation for this, and we should be slow to surmise. We can dismiss proposals that it was an attempt at some kind of magic.[16] Since the child was dead, Elijah's action is hardly comparable with the young woman who sought to warm up old King David (1:2).[17] More helpful is the suggestion that this was a symbolic action, "an 'acted out' way of saying, 'Let this lifeless body be as my lively body.'"[18]

We should not miss the strikingly unorthodox nature of Elijah's act. A dead body was "unclean," and whoever touched a dead body became unclean (see Numbers 5:2; 9:6, 10; 19:11, 16). Even to come into a tent where someone had died made a person unclean (Numbers 19:14). However, in this case the contamination worked the other way: the unclean (dead) became clean (alive).[19] It was like Jesus who touched the unclean, and they were made clean (Matthew 8:2, 3).

The Prayer (v. 21b)

Again Elijah "cried to the LORD" (v. 21b; cf. v. 20). This time it was not a troubled question but an impassioned plea: "O LORD my God, let this child's life[20] [breath] come into him again" (v. 21b). In Hebrew we find the small, polite word Elijah had used in 17:10, 11, softening any demanding tone: "May this child's breath please come into him again."[21]

Nonetheless let us be very clear. Elijah's prayer was extraordinary. While he knew, in principle, that the Lord is the one who gives and takes life, who kills and makes alive (Deuteronomy 32:39), there is usually a definite finality about death. King David had prayed earnestly for his sick son, but as soon as the boy died, David said, "But now he is dead. Why should I fast? Can I bring him back again? I shall go to him, but he will not return to me" (2 Samuel 12:23). There was no precedent in Israel's history for a dead person being made alive again. The boundary between life and death had never been crossed in the reverse direction.

Why, we might ask, was Elijah's prayer so different from David's? Why did Elijah ask the Lord to restore the life of this widow-woman's son but David accepted the death of his own son as God's will? Why this unprecedented request from the man of God?

These questions point to what was at stake at this time. It was not simply the sadness of a grieving mother, although that is undeniable. No doubt there were other heartbroken mothers in Sidon (and Israel too) during the famine. We need to see the bigger picture. Baal had invaded Israel (16:31–33), and now the Lord had sent his servant into Baal's territory (17:9). What was at stake was the ultimate question, Who is God? Baal was the so-called god who was (supposedly) regularly defeated by Death. The time had come for the Lord to display his unchallengeable superiority to Baal. Elijah ("My God Is Yahweh") was true to his name. "Yahweh my God," he prayed, "may this child's breath come into him again."

The Lord's Answer (vv. 22, 23)

We are at the dramatic climax of this short story. Elijah had made his extreme request of the Lord. Such a request, as far as we know, had never before been made.

God Listened (v. 22a)

"And the LORD listened to the voice of Elijah" (v. 22a). He did not just hear. He *listened*. In other contexts the Hebrew expression can mean "obeyed" (as in 20:36). The Lord is the God who heeded the voice of Elijah.

God Gave (v. 22b)

"And the life [breath] of the child came into him again, and he revived [lived]" (v. 22b).

Earlier in the story the narrator had employed a technique often found in Biblical accounts where the actions of a human are described in language that corresponds closely to an earlier divine command (see 17:3 and 5, 9, and 10). The effect is to show that the human action was in exact obedience to God's command. Remarkably the same technique is now used to describe God's answer to a man's prayer. God did *precisely* what Elijah asked.[22]

This was an extraordinary demonstration of the Lord's power, not just to give life in the first place and to take life away, but to overcome death. True, the only witness to this (at this stage) was Elijah. Shortly there would be another, and there are now many more as the story has been told.

Life! (v. 23)

> And Elijah took the child and brought him down from the upper chamber into the house and delivered [or gave] him to his mother. And Elijah said, "See, your son lives." (v. 23)

Imagine the scene as Elijah descended the steps from the roof of the house. He may have held the boy in his arms, or perhaps he was holding the lad's hand as they climbed down together. Can you see the widow-woman's tear-stained face turn to astonished joy as Elijah *gave* her the boy he had *taken* from her a short time earlier (v. 19)? She understood the reality. It was the Lord who had taken away her son, and it was the Lord who had now given him back. Hers was the opposite of Job's experience in Job 1:21.

Elijah urged her to take in the evidence of her own eyes. "See, your son *lives*." He lived because, as the woman had earlier acknowledged, "the LORD, [Elijah's] God, *lives*" (17:12). The living God is the life-giving God and the God who has the power to beat death.

The Light of Life (v. 24)

The woman drew a further conclusion. If we take her acknowledgment in 17:12 seriously (as I am sure we should), she had known all along that the

Lord God of Israel is alive. What had she learned from her experience since Elijah came to Zarephath?

> And the woman said to Elijah, "Now I know that you are a man of God, and that the word of the LORD in your mouth is truth." (v. 24)

She had called him "man of God" in verse 18, but now she knew that this meant that what came from his mouth was "the word of the LORD" and it was Truth with a capital T.

We discussed earlier the importance of "the word of the LORD" in the Bible's message, and particularly in 1 and 2 Kings.[23] "The word of the LORD" is the expression in words of God's purpose. When King David heard "the word of the LORD," he responded: "And now, O Lord GOD, you are God, and your words are true [or truth], and you have promised this good thing to your servant" (2 Samuel 7:4, 28).

Now a non-Israelite widow-woman, living in Zarephath, in the land where Baal was worshipped, had come to recognize that "the word of the LORD" is "truth" and that is what came from Elijah's mouth.

Her words form a fitting conclusion to the chapter that had begun with Elijah's announcement that "there shall be neither dew nor rain these years, except by *the mouth of my word*" (17:1, AT). That now makes complete sense, since the word in Elijah's mouth was "the word of the LORD."

The relatively private events of 1 Kings 17 have prepared us for the massive and very public confrontation that is looming in the next chapter. The man who appeared so suddenly in 17:1 we now know speaks the word of the Lord who can raise the dead, feed the starving, and stop the rain.

Before we turn the page and begin to hear about what happened when he returned from Zarephath to the land of Israel, we should carefully consider how centuries later Jesus must have reminded his contemporaries of Elijah. Indeed there was one occasion when Jesus visited the district of Tyre and Sidon. He was in the vicinity of Zarephath, and there he met a Canaanite woman, just as Elijah had. The encounter ended with Jesus saying, "O woman, great is your faith!" and the immediate healing of her child (Matthew 15:28). On another occasion Jesus raised a widow's son from death to life (Luke 7:11–17). Jesus also raised from the dead the daughter of Jairus (Mark 5:35–43) and his friend Lazarus (John 11:38–44). In other words, what happened in those remarkable days when Elijah stayed in Zarephath was the beginning of something bigger and greater. Now Jesus, by his own death and resurrection, promises life to all who believe in him. He

is not only the one who brings the word of the one who can beat death—
he *is* the one who can beat death.

> I am the resurrection and the life. Whoever believes in me, though he
> die, yet shall he live, and everyone who lives and believes in me shall
> never die. Do you believe this? (John 11:25, 26)

How the Drought Ended

1 Kings 18

37

The Troubler

1 KINGS 18:1-19

WHEN THINGS GO WRONG there seems to be a deep human need to ascribe blame. Whose fault was it? Who can be held responsible for what has happened?

In theory this is reasonable. It takes seriously that humans are responsible moral agents who ought to be held accountable for their actions and, when appropriate, the damaging consequences. The drunk driver who causes an accident should pay for the damage caused. The careless builder should be made to repair the dangerous structure. The drug dealer should be punished for the ruined lives. A civil society must have a system of accountability for irresponsible behavior.

But have you noticed how easily this gets out of hand? No one wants to take responsibility when things go wrong. If it appears that I am in some measure to blame, my instinct is to shift the blame. The drunk driver will have an excuse. The careless builder will accuse his workers. The drug dealer will insist that it was the users who ruined their own lives.

In some cases there will be a pinch of truth in this blame shifting. Responsibility for the troubles of life is usually complicated and often involves several parties. In our litigious age this is wonderful for the legal profession who can make a great deal of money out of the blame game—*Who is to blame?* means *Whom can we sue?*

There is an extreme version of the blame game. It is when we blame God for our troubles and the troubles of the world. For many today this is precisely why they refuse to believe that God is really there. "If there is a God," they say, "and he is all-powerful and all-knowing, then he has an awful lot to answer for." They see it as simply impossible to argue that God is good, for, in their view, God is to blame for the overwhelming suffering, violence, injustices, and misery of the world he supposedly made and allegedly rules. Thus belief in God is seen as responsible for all manner of atrocities.[1]

In the days of King Ahab of Israel, as a terrible drought took its toll so that the whole land suffered a severe famine, there was an encounter between the king and the prophet who had announced the drought some years earlier. Ahab played the blame game. "Is it you," he said to Elijah, "you troubler of Israel?" Elijah responded, "I have not troubled Israel, but you have . . ." (18:17, 18). The confrontation between Ahab and Elijah, concisely expressed in this interchange, was deeply significant. Who was really to blame for the suffering of the people of Israel in those days? Who was the troubler? Does this confrontation shed light on the blame game as it is played today? We will look more closely at this encounter shortly.

Time for a Showdown (vv. 1, 2a)

We left Elijah enjoying the hospitality of the widow-woman of Zarephath. She had been convinced in a most remarkable way that he was "a man of God" and that the true and trustworthy "word of the Lord" came from his mouth (17:24). We are told nothing more about Elijah's stay in Zarephath until a couple of years had passed.

"After many days the word of the Lord came to Elijah, in the third year" (v. 1a). This probably means the third year of his stay in Zarephath. He had therefore been there for over two years. If we suppose that he had stayed by the brook Cherith for about a year, this accords with the statements of both Jesus and James that the drought lasted for three years and six months (Luke 4:25; James 5:17).[2]

Three years of drought in this part of the world would have been devastating.[3] A couple of years earlier in Zarephath the widow and her son had been about to die (17:12). By now there must have been many in the region facing starvation. It was a major disaster.

The word of the Lord had earlier sent Elijah into hiding by the brook Cherith (17:3) and then sent him beyond the border of Israel (17:8, 9). The word of the Lord now directed him back to the land of Israel and toward a climactic confrontation. As before, the word of the Lord took the form of a command and a promise.

The command was, "Go, show yourself to Ahab" (v. 1b). We have heard nothing of Ahab since Elijah announced the drought to him in 17:1. We have not been told how he responded to the catastrophe that had come on his kingdom. Not yet.

The promise was, "and I will send rain upon the earth" (v. 1c). This, of course, was a momentous promise. The Lord would shortly do for the whole region what he had done for Elijah initially by the brook and then for the widow in Zarephath. He would give life. He would save from death. "I will send rain" meant no less than that.

It had been clear from the beginning that the drought would one day end. Elijah had spoken to the widow of "the day that the LORD sends rain upon the earth" (17:14). That would only happen, however, at Elijah's word (17:1). Now the Lord was sending Elijah back with this promise.

There is a subtle but important point here that most English translations miss. The Hebrew syntax behind "and I will send rain" indicates that this was the *purpose* of the preceding command. What the Lord said to Elijah was, "Go, show yourself to Ahab *so that* I may send rain upon the earth."[4]

What did that mean? What was the connection between Elijah going and showing himself to Ahab and the Lord sending rain? How would Elijah's return result in the rain being given? If God had decided to send the rain, why was it necessary to send Elijah?

We need to take a step back and consider the significance of the drought and famine. We have seen that the Lord was demonstrating the emptiness and uselessness of Baal, the supposed god of the rain, in whom Ahab and his people had come to trust. But there was more to it. The crucial clues are in the prayer that King Solomon had prayed years earlier.

Solomon had spoken of the very circumstances that had now fallen on Ahab's kingdom, along with their meaning: "When heaven is shut up and there is no rain *because they have sinned against you . . .*" (8:35a). This is what had now happened. *Because of the sins of Ahab and his people* in serving and worshiping the false god Baal (16:31–33), there had been "neither dew nor rain" during these years (17:1). The drought was punishment from the Lord for the sin.

Solomon had also spoken of what must therefore happen for the drought to end. In essence he said:

> If they . . . *turn from their sin*, then you . . . *will forgive the sin* of your servants, your people Israel . . . and *grant rain* upon your land . . . (8:35b, 36, AT)[5]

The Lord will *grant/send rain*[6] when he has *forgiven their sin*. He will forgive their sin when they *repent*.

We will see (by the time we get to the end of 1 Kings 18) that the Lord was sending Elijah back to Ahab *in order to bring Israel to repentance*. That is how Elijah's return will result in the rain coming. When they repent, the Lord will forgive their sin and send the rain, just as Solomon had prayed.

The word of the Lord that initiated this sequence of events was, "Go, show yourself to Ahab." As we have come to expect of the man of God, he was precisely obedient. "So Elijah went to show himself to Ahab" (v. 2a).

Meanwhile, Back in Samaria (vv. 2b–6)

Showing himself to Ahab was not straightforward (and will not happen until v. 17). The situation in King Ahab's realm had deteriorated considerably since Elijah had gone into hiding some years earlier. The narrator takes us back there (ahead of Elijah) to catch up on what was going on.

The Famine (v. 2b)

"Now the famine was severe in Samaria" (v. 2b). "Samaria" here probably means the royal city (as in 16:24, 28, 29, 32) rather than the whole land that came to be referred to by the same name (as in 13:32). While no doubt conditions were just as serious throughout the land, the focus here is on how things were going particularly for Ahab in his city. Things were tough.

A "Servant of Yahweh" (v. 3)

As Elijah was making his way back to the land of Israel (unknown, of course, to Ahab), the king issued a royal summons: "And Ahab called Obadiah, who was over the household" (v. 3a).

Here we meet one of the Bible's heroic characters (not to be confused with the much later prophet of the same name responsible for the book of Obadiah). We will hear no more of this Obadiah after verse 16, but his brief appearance in Biblical history should make a deep impression. His name means "Servant of Yahweh," and that is exactly what he was. He was also an official in Ahab's palace ("over the household"[7]). This was an important role, probably responsible for managing affairs in the palace, and also perhaps the king's estates and livestock.[8]

It is striking that someone with such a noble name was a high-ranking servant in *Ahab's* household. However, the narrator immediately assures us that Obadiah was nonetheless true to his name: "Now Obadiah feared the LORD greatly" (v. 3b). To "fear the LORD" means that attitude of heart, mind, and will that leads to serving and obeying the Lord (see 1 Samuel 12:14[9]). Obadiah exemplified this quality "greatly." This evaluation of Obadiah's character should be kept in mind as his story unfolds.

Deadly Hostility (v. 4a)

The writer adds some background information about Obadiah (rightly put in parentheses in the ESV) that demonstrates his genuine and courageous faithfulness to the Lord.

It was "when Jezebel cut off the prophets of the LORD" (v. 4a). We may suppose that this was not long after the drought—announced in the name of "the LORD, the God of Israel" (17:1)—began. Jezebel, the Baal-worshipping wife of Ahab (16:31), had actively and violently sought to eliminate those she saw as a threat to her promotion of Baal in Israel. To "cut off" means to "root out, eliminate, destroy."[10] This brief statement points to a reign of terror for those who were the objects of Jezebel's fury.

For the first time in 1 Kings we hear that there were in Israel a considerable number of these "prophets of the LORD." We have, of course, met a few individual prophets, but this was a large number of persons who in the face of Jezebel's and Ahab's promotion of Baal remained followers of the Lord, the God of Israel. The "old prophet" of Bethel and his "sons" may have belonged to such a group (13:11).[11] We do not know much about these "prophets" but can safely assume two things. First, they were followers of the Lord, among whom the Spirit of the Lord was at work in some way (cf. 1 Samuel 10:5, 6, 10; 19:20). Second, the designation "prophets" did not put all of these persons into the same class as the great individuals like Samuel, Nathan, Ahijah, and now Elijah to whom and by whom "the word of the LORD came." The "prophets" were not always reliable (see 13:18).

Jezebel saw these "prophets of the LORD" as a threat to her ambition to establish the worship of Baal in Israel. Perhaps she blamed them for the drought and famine. Did she think that their presence had upset Baal? On whatever pretense, she embarked on a program to eradicate them. The famine was severe in Samaria, but the climate of persecution was just as serious.

Brave Faithfulness (v. 4b)

It was in this context that Obadiah secretly lived out his calling as a "Servant of Yahweh." "Obadiah took a hundred prophets and hid them by fifties in a cave[12] and fed them with bread and water" (v. 4b).

This suggests that the total number of prophets of the Lord in Israel had probably been at least several hundred. Obadiah's clandestine operation must have been hugely risky. But he feared the Lord more than he feared Jezebel, and the faithful, brave servant of Yahweh was somehow able to secretly provide bread and water for a hundred prophets in the midst of the harsh shortages. We do not know how he did this, but we have learned that the Lord is well able to provide for his servants (see 17:4, 9).[13]

Ahab's Attempt to Deal with the Famine (vv. 5, 6)

Ahab had summoned Obadiah (v. 3a) for a desperate attempt to overcome some of the effects of the drought.

> And Ahab said to Obadiah, "Go through the land to all the springs of water and to all the valleys [brooks]. Perhaps we may find grass and save the horses and mules alive, and not lose [have to cut off] some of the animals." (v. 5)

Jezebel was at work "cutting off" the prophets of the Lord. Ahab did nothing to protect them but was worried about having to "cut off" some of his livestock.[14] That was a fair indication of his value system.

His desperate search for fodder appears hopeless. We know of one "brook" that had dried up more than two years earlier (17:7). It seems unlikely that there would by now be many green patches to be found in the land. Ahab's desperation underlines the wonder that Obadiah had been able to covertly provide bread and water for the hidden prophets.

The royal search began:

> So they divided the land between them to pass through it. Ahab went in one direction [or way] by himself, and Obadiah went in another direction [or way] by himself. (v. 6)

Ahab and Obadiah moved off separately in different directions, just as they were in a deeper sense following different ways.[15]

Obadiah Meets Elijah (vv. 7–16a)

The narrator has set two actions in motion: Elijah's movement from Zarephath back to Israel "to show himself to Ahab" (v. 2a) and Obadiah's movement in a direction away from Ahab (v. 6). These two movements now intersect: "And as Obadiah was on the way, behold, Elijah met him" (v. 7a).

It is not immediately clear why (in God's providence) Elijah's path did not cross Ahab's rather than Obadiah's since he had set out "to show himself to Ahab." The encounter with Obadiah must be important. Their conversation is reported in surprising detail.

First we hear Obadiah's astonishment at seeing Elijah: "And Obadiah recognized him and fell on his face and said, 'Is it you, my lord Elijah?'" (v. 7b).

The question is an expression of surprise (since he did "recognize" Elijah). *After all this time is it really you, Elijah?*[16] Obadiah's posture (face to the ground) and words ("my lord") speak of his humble subordination to the man of God.

A Command (v. 8)

It was no time for small talk. Elijah responded to Obadiah, "It is I" and immediately issued a solemn instruction: "Go, tell your lord, 'Behold, Elijah is here'" (v. 8)

Obadiah had two "lords." As a servant of Yahweh, he addressed Elijah as "my lord." As a servant of Ahab, Elijah called the king "your lord." The latter gave Obadiah access and opportunity to obey Elijah. We have already seen that Obadiah's faithfulness to Yahweh took precedence over his loyalty to the royal family. Elijah was calling him to do that again. In obedience to Elijah, he must go and tell his other master, *Behold, "My God Is Yahweh" is here.*[17]

Elijah did not *quite* require Obadiah to side openly with Elijah before King Ahab,[18] but he was asking the undercover "Servant of Yahweh" to take a big risk.

A Problem or Two (vv. 9–14)

That is certainly how Obadiah saw it. In an exceptionally long speech (I am tempted to call it a rant), Obadiah blurted out the problems he could see with Elijah's proposal. There were a few.

> And he said, "How have I sinned, that you would give your servant into the hand of Ahab, to kill me? As the LORD your God lives, there is no nation or kingdom where my lord has not sent to seek you. And when they would say, 'He is not here,' he would take an oath of the kingdom or nation, that they had not found you. And now you say, 'Go, tell your lord, "Behold, Elijah is here."' And as soon as I have gone from you, the Spirit [or breath] of the LORD will carry you I know not where. And so, when I come and tell Ahab and he cannot find you, he will kill me, although I your servant have feared the LORD from my youth. Has it not been told my lord what I did when Jezebel killed the prophets of the LORD, how I hid a hundred men of the LORD's prophets by fifties in a cave and fed them with bread and water? And now you say, 'Go, tell your lord, "Behold, Elijah is here"'; and he will kill me." (vv. 9–14)

The main problem was that to obey Elijah's command would be suicidal. Three times Obadiah declared, "he [Ahab] will kill me."[19] It was one thing to secretly work behind the king's back to save the Lord's prophets. It was another thing altogether to openly announce that he has seen "My God Is Yahweh." *He will kill me!*

Two things fed Obadiah's fear. The first was the determined desperation with which Ahab had searched everywhere for Elijah (v. 10). Obadiah does not have to spell out why Ahab was so keen to find Elijah. Suffice it to say his intentions were unlikely to be any more friendly than Jezebel's toward the prophets Obadiah had hidden (and the others he had not been able to save).

The second factor that made Elijah's instruction seem perilous to Obadiah was a reputation Elijah had apparently earned for being elusive. Over the years there may have been rumors of sightings of the prophet, but never had he been discovered. It all began shortly after the original announcement of the drought. The word of the Lord had commanded him to go into hiding by the brook Cherith (17:3). No one knew where he was. Some time later the word of the Lord had sent him to Zarephath (17:8, 9). So Obadiah anticipated, "as soon as I have gone from you, the Spirit [or breath] of the LORD will carry you I know not where" (v. 12). Since the "breath" and the "word" of the Lord are closely related (the Lord *breathes* his *word*), we need not think here of something new. The *breath* of the Lord had been taking Elijah here and there as the *word* of the Lord sent him.[20]

Obadiah feared that Elijah would do it again. Ahab's fury when Elijah slipped through his fingers yet again would be taken out on Obadiah. *He will slaughter me!*

Obadiah stressed that he did not deserve this. He had not "sinned" like Ahab (v. 9). Indeed he had "feared the LORD" all his life (v. 12), most recently in what he had done for the prophets of the Lord (v. 13). What the narrator has already told us about Obadiah in verses 3, 4 confirms that Obadiah was speaking truthfully.[21] The effect is therefore not to suggest a failure of Obadiah at this point, but to emphasize the terror of Ahab's reign—even a "greatly" faithful servant of Yahweh like Obadiah would fear this king.[22] These were terrifying times in Israel for those who served the Lord.

I suspect that the purpose of this meeting between Elijah and Obadiah was to impress this terrible situation first on Elijah, but then on us, the readers of this account. The effect is that before Elijah meets Ahab we all know what a dangerous encounter this will be.

A Promise (v. 15)

Elijah responded to Obadiah's lengthy outburst with a simple promise. "And Elijah said, 'As the LORD of hosts lives, before whom I stand, I will surely show myself to him today'" (v. 15). *This very day he will see me.*

The oath by which Elijah swore expressed the secret of his fearlessness. Earlier he had sworn to Ahab that there would be no rain, "As the Lord the God of Israel lives" (17:1). Now it was "As *the Lord of hosts* lives." "Hosts" refers to all the mighty power at the Lord's disposal. "The Lord of hosts" is a title that has appeared on a few critical occasions since it was first used in the Old Testament story in 1 Samuel 1:3.[23] Elijah sees the might of Ahab, understandably terrifying to Obadiah, in the light of the living Lord of the heavenly armies!

Furthermore it is *before* this God, Yahweh of the heavenly armies, that Elijah *stands* (cf. 17:1). That is, he is *his* servant.

Obedience (v. 16a)

This was enough for the faithful Obadiah: "So Obadiah went to meet Ahab, and told him" (v. 16a). Elijah's promise was enough to change Obadiah's fear into bold obedience.

Ahab Meets Elijah (vv. 16b–19)

The response of Ahab is described as briefly as could be: "And Ahab went to meet Elijah" (v. 16b). What did he expect would happen?

Ahab's Word to Elijah (v. 17)

At last we come to the encounter anticipated in verse 1. "When Ahab saw Elijah, Ahab said to him, 'Is it you, you troubler of Israel?'" (v. 17).

Ahab seems as surprised as Obadiah had been to see Elijah (v. 7). However, Ahab had a special title to confer on the prophet. *Is it really you, you troubler of Israel?*

This was a serious accusation. "Troubler" means one who frustrates by preventing success and well-being.[24] Jonathan had said of King Saul, "My father has *troubled* the land" when Saul's foolishness had frustrated a defeat of the Philistines from being great (1 Samuel 14:29, 30). Famously in the days of Joshua, Achan had brought "trouble" on Israel by his greedy disobedience to the Lord's command (Joshua 7:25) and became known as "the troubler of Israel" (1 Chronicles 2:7), the very title bestowed here by Ahab on Elijah.[25]

There can be no doubt that the trouble Ahab had in mind was the severe famine now engulfing the land. That there was a connection between Elijah and the drought was clear. The dry had begun on the day that Elijah had announced it. Furthermore he had claimed that the rain would return only at *his* word (17:1). To Ahab's mind this meant that Elijah was to blame for the troubles of his kingdom. He blamed the messenger.

Under Jezebel's influence, it is more than likely that Ahab believed Elijah had provoked the wrath of Baal. The god of rain had withheld the rain. And who was to blame but those who opposed Baal, and Elijah was the chief culprit.

By blaming Elijah Ahab was blaming God, in whose name Elijah spoke and whom he served.

Elijah's Word to Ahab (vv. 18, 19)

The blame game is most dangerous when played by the one who is truly to blame. Shifting blame is then very serious because it undermines the possibility of a resolution.

Elijah replied to Ahab, "I have not troubled Israel, but you have, and your father's house, because you have abandoned the commandments of the LORD and followed the Baals"[26] (v. 18).

In "You have abandoned the commandments," "you" is plural, referring to both Ahab and his father Omri ("your father's house"). In "[you have] followed the Baals," the verb is singular. This had been Ahab's very own contribution to the troubles of Israel (16:31–33).

In Ahab we see a reflection of all sinners who suffer punishment from God for their sin and then blame God for their troubles. The man or woman who shakes a fist at God because of the suffering and misery in the world but refuses to humbly confess his or her own sin and beg for mercy is just like Ahab, the real troubler.

It was time for the blame game to be brought to an end. Elijah took control of the conversation and demanded of the true troubler, "Now therefore send and gather all Israel to me at Mount Carmel, and the 450 prophets of Baal and the 400 prophets of Asherah, who eat at Jezebel's table" (v. 19).

What a remarkable assembly this would be! "All Israel" was to be there.[27] But how different from the "all Israel" who had assembled joyfully with King Solomon years earlier (8:65). They were now to gather with the leading devotees of their apostasy: "the 450 prophets of Baal and the 400 prophets of Asherah."

The prophets of the Lord were not the only "prophets" in Israel. Both Baal and Asherah (16:32, 33; see our discussion of 14:15b) had hundreds of them. We will soon see much more of the prophets of Baal. The prophets of Asherah are not mentioned in the ensuing account. Perhaps the narrator does not bother to mention them. More probably they did not turn up.[28]

The prophets of Asherah, perhaps female "prophets" of the female deity, enjoyed the particular patronage of Queen Jezebel ("who eat at Jezebel's table"[29]).

The gathering was to take place on Mount Carmel, near Israel's border with the land of Tyre, Sidon, and Zarephath—Baal-land.[30] It was a dramatic setting for a confrontation between the God of Israel and the god of the Sidonians.[31]

Before we turn the page to hear the extraordinary story of the looming confrontation, let us take in the massive distortion of reality and goodness that King Ahab had accomplished. He had repudiated the true God for a non-god. When he suffered God's punishment for his sin, he blamed God. This inspired hostility toward the servants of the true God and a reign of terror against them.

King Ahab embodied human sinfulness. Consider how much of Paul's description of "the ungodliness and unrighteousness of men" fits Ahab the troubler:

> And since they *did not see fit to acknowledge God* [see 1 Kings 16:31], God gave them up to a debased mind to do what ought not to be done. They were *filled with all manner of unrighteousness, evil, covetousness, malice* [16:33]. They are full of envy, *murder* [18:4], strife, deceit, maliciousness. They are gossips, slanderers, *haters of God* [18:17], insolent, haughty, boastful, *inventors of evil* [16:30], disobedient to parents, foolish, *faithless*, heartless, ruthless. Though they *know God's righteous decree* [18:18] that those who practice such things deserve to die, they not only do them but give approval to those who practice them. (Romans 1:28–32)

Now wonder at the gospel of Jesus Christ, which is the power of God to *save* from such trouble everyone who believes in him (Romans 1:16).

38

Religion for Dummies

1 KINGS 18:20-29

A FEW DAYS AGO I heard about a recent survey of several thousand Australians. Among the questions asked was this: "Do you think that religion is good for society?" The results surprised me. Some 40 percent said that they thought religion is good for society. Only about 20 percent did not think so. The remaining 40 percent had no definite thoughts on the question.

The 20 percent figure corresponds quite closely to the number of Australians who identify themselves as "atheists." That result is therefore not unexpected. Atheists regard all "religion" as superstition, or worse. Of course, they do not think ridiculous fantasies are "good for society." It was the two 40 percent figures that interested me—that 80 percent of Australians today seem to be either neutral or positive toward "religion."

It would be easy for an Australian Christian believer (like me) to be encouraged by this. Perhaps Australians are more open to the gospel of the Lord Jesus Christ than they seem. But I am sure that would be a mistake. The survey question contains a massive lie that most respondents seem to have swallowed. Only those who do not take religion (in any sense) seriously could generalize about "religion" as the question does. Whoever devised the question probably had in mind a modern secular, thoroughly domesticated, and privatized view of "religion." By "religion" I suspect they meant generally harmless things like going to church, mosque, synagogue, or temple from time to time, occasional private meditation or prayer, reading of sacred texts, and so on. But "religion" can involve (for the sake of argument let me be extreme) child sacrifice. Some "religions" contain very bad stuff. It is simply absurd to suggest that "religion" is necessarily good for society. Some religion may be, but definitely not "religion" as such. And yet 40 percent of Australians said "Yes."

I know what you are thinking. *Well, that's Australians!* Perhaps you are right. But it is more than that. There is a widespread view in today's world that "religion" is simply a matter of taste. It is an aspect of "culture," like music and food. No one should be critical of another person's "religion," any more than we should judge another's musical or culinary preferences. There is no such thing as "good religion" and "bad religion," let alone "true religion" and "false religion." Multicultural societies (like Australia) must welcome and appreciate the many "religions" that belong to the different cultural backgrounds of our people. So it is very widely believed.

All this makes the story of Elijah and the prophets of Baal on Mount Carmel very difficult for us. It also means that this powerful narrative poses a fundamental challenge to a world that could ask such an absurd question as, "Do you think that religion is good for society?" This is not a story about "religious tolerance" or even "freedom of religion." It is much more important than that.

Scene 1: The Ultimate Compulsory Question (vv. 20–24)

In 18:19 Elijah instructed King Ahab to "gather all Israel . . . and the 450 prophets of Baal and the 400 prophets of Asherah" to Mount Carmel. We now learn that Ahab complied with this, sort of: "So Ahab sent to all the people of Israel and gathered the prophets together at Mount Carmel" (v. 20).

It is astonishing that the king seems to have offered no obvious resistance to Elijah's demand. Evidently Elijah's authority was formidable, even to Ahab. Mind you, the writer does not employ his usual technique where the wording of a *command* is repeated verbatim to describe precise *obedience* (see, for example, 17:3 and 5; 17:9 and 10; 18:1 and 2; 18:8 and 16; 18:25 and 26; 18:41 and 42). Ahab's actions were not like that.[1] He was told to "gather all Israel," but he simply "sent to all the people of Israel." And "the prophets" he gathered at Mount Carmel do not appear to have included those of Asherah, as Elijah had required. In the following account we will hear only of "the 450 prophets of Baal." Ahab's actions look grudging and half-hearted.

"Mount Carmel" refers to a northwest-southeast range of hills and mountains that juts into the Mediterranean Sea.[2] Close to the border with Tyre/Sidon, the land from which Jezebel had brought the worship of Baal into Israel (16:31), it was an evocative setting for this meeting between the prophets of Baal and Elijah. There is evidence that Carmel may have been, at various times, a sacred site for the worship of Baal.[3] Furthermore, the lush beauty of Carmel (meaning "garden" or "orchard") in its setting "by the sea" (Jeremiah

46:18) was proverbial (see Song of Solomon 7:5; Isaiah 35:2; Jeremiah 50:19). However, in drought Carmel became desolated (as reflected, for example, in Isaiah 33:9; Amos 1:2; Nahum 1:4). Here, then, on Baal's turf, so to speak, the failure of Baal to send rain for more than three years would have been starkly apparent.[4]

Although King Ahab was certainly present there on Mount Carmel, he will not be mentioned again until 18:41. In the drama about to unfold, the king is just one of "the people." Furthermore, even the drought fades into the background. It will not be mentioned for some time. The drama about to unfold will be about issues even bigger than the devastating drought.

The Question (v. 21a, b)

The action begins: "And Elijah came near to all the people" (v. 21a). This was the first movement in the drama on Mount Carmel. Elijah, the man of God who "stands before" the Lord, the God of Israel, and speaks the truthful word of the Lord (17:1, 24; 18:15), "came near" to all the people. Before this day is out, Elijah will say to the people, "*Come near* to me" (18:30). This will be a story about "coming near" (see also 18:36).

Elijah spoke to the people:

> How long will you go limping between two different opinions? If the Lord is God, follow him; but if Baal, then follow him. (v. 21b)

In these two sentences the spiritual sickness of the people was laid bare, and the one question that could not be avoided was posed with stark clarity. I doubt there has ever been a briefer sermon, nor one more sharply focused on the need of the moment.

In the Hebrew "you" is emphatic, suggesting a contrast between the speaker ("My God Is Yahweh") and the hearers. *How long will you lot go on limping . . . ?* The exact meaning of the phrase translated "limping between two different opinions" is uncertain, although its rhetorical impact is clear enough. "Limping" may indicate a staggering movement, bumping into things.[5] "Between two different opinions" could be translated "upon two crutches"[6] or "at the crossroads."[7]

Whatever the exact metaphor may be, the two "opinions," "crutches," or "crossroads" are clearly identified. They are the Lord (Yahweh) and Baal. In the corrupted thinking of the people, they imagined that they could serve *both* the Lord *and* Baal (see 2 Kings 17:33). In the multicultural world of Ahab's kingdom, it was not a matter of either/or. They welcomed the religion of Queen Jezebel and gave it a respected place *alongside* what they imagined was still the worship of Yahweh. A polytheistic outlook embraced inclusiveness. Indeed this kind of inclusiveness requires a polytheistic outlook.

This is what Elijah described as staggering along, bumping into things right and left. It was no way to live. *How long will you stumble along in this ridiculous, contradictory, and unsustainable manner?*

The situation in Israel was not so different from a world that lumps all "religions" together and wonders whether "religion" is good or bad for society. *How long will you stumble along in this ridiculous, contradictory, and unsustainable manner?*

Elijah pressed the question that the people of Israel (like so many today) did not want to face. Is Yahweh God? Or is Baal God? The either/or question excluded the option the people had embraced. *Can't there be room in a multicultural, polytheistic, tolerant, easygoing world for both Yahweh and Baal?*

No, there can't. The one who actually is God demands your wholehearted, undivided, complete allegiance. Otherwise he would not be God. "If the Lord is God, *follow* him; but if Baal, then follow *him*." The ultimate question, Who is God? cannot be merely theoretical. Once you know who God is, you *must* honor him as God, give thanks to him, worship and serve him. Otherwise you are denying that he is God, exchanging the truth about God for a lie (cf. Romans 1:21, 25).

The question is compulsory. That is, it is not possible to avoid answering this question because the one you *follow* is the one you have decided is God. That is, whatever determines the direction and shape of your life is your God. If you are stumbling along, bashing into things on every side, because at one moment "Baal" is your god, and the next moment "Yahweh," you are heading for a fall. If one moment you are driven by your selfish ambitions, and the next by your passions, and the next by peer pressure, and the next by your greed, and the next by your anger, jealousy, love of pleasure, and occasionally (you imagine) by the Lord Jesus Christ, you are no better off. Listen to Elijah: "If the Lord is God, *follow* him."

First Response (v. 21c)

"And the people did not answer him a word" (v. 21c). They were not prepared to make the decision that Elijah insisted was necessary. They were unwilling to make the choice that he put before them. It was so much easier (as people today foolishly imagine) to put Baal and Yahweh together and call it all "religion" and think that perhaps it is good for society.

No "answer" from the people introduces another thread that runs through this story. It is a story about who does and does not "answer." The people begin (as we will see) like Baal—no answer (see vv. 26, 29; cf. vv. 24, 37).

It Is Not a Matter of Opinion (vv. 22–24a)

Elijah refused to accept the people's *non-answer*. Throughout this story the meaning of Elijah's name (obvious in Hebrew) is eloquent. "Then 'My God Is Yahweh' said to the people, 'I, even I only, am left a prophet[8] of the LORD, but Baal's prophets are 450 men'" (v. 22).

We know that 100 prophets of the Lord had been secretly hidden in caves (possibly here on Mount Carmel[9]). However, they had been driven out of the community, and the people did not know that they were still alive. Other prophets of the Lord (probably several hundreds of them) had been eliminated by Jezebel's pogrom (18:4, 13). Elijah's words were therefore a condemning accusation. *How come I am the only prophet of Yahweh here on Mount Carmel? You might all think that you worship both Yahweh and Baal. What, then, has happened to all the prophets of Yahweh? But I see that you have no shortage of prophets of Baal!*

Have you noticed how tolerant, inclusive, "progressive" societies welcome religions of various kinds and allow them to prosper? In Australia today there are more religions than ever, and many are growing. At the same time such societies do their best to silence the prophets of the Lord. In my lifetime I cannot remember a time of greater hostility in the Australian community toward the gospel of Jesus Christ, and the same thing seems to be happening in the United States of America and many other places.

It was decision time on Mount Carmel. "My God Is Yahweh" continued:

> Let two bulls be given to us [Let them give us two bulls[10]], and let them choose one bull for themselves and cut it in pieces and lay it on the wood, but put no fire to it. And I will prepare the other bull and lay it on the wood and put no fire to it. And you call upon the name of your god, and I will call upon the name of the LORD, and the God who answers by fire, he is God. (vv. 23, 24a)

Elijah—clearly in complete control of the situation—gave instructions for a most extraordinary experiment to decide once and for all who is God.

There will be no room for the Baal prophets to protest that the experiment was rigged. Elijah allowed his adversaries to oversee the setting up of the experiment. They will choose the two bulls. They will select the one for themselves. Elijah will accept the one they leave for him.[11]

Apart from the initiative given to his opponents, the rules Elijah laid down were identical for both sides. Both they and he would prepare their animal. Neither they nor he would put fire to it.

Then "you"—that is, not just the Baal prophets, but "the people" (v. 22a)—will "call upon the name of your god" (v. 24a). *You must decide who "your god" is and call upon his "name."*

I wonder whether they noticed that Elijah left open the possibility that the people *could* call upon the name of Yahweh. That is what they would do if he was their God. The balance of the speech, however, and the contrast implied by his next words leave the impression that he expected them all to call on the name of Baal. Their initial non-answer had put them on the side of Baal.[12]

But there was no ambiguity about the name upon which Elijah would call. "I will call upon the name of Yahweh."

Calling upon (literally, "in") the name of Yahweh reminds us again of King Solomon's prayer and the wonder of the house of the Lord he had built in Jerusalem, where prayer "in the name of the LORD" was possible and would be answered.[13]

Here on Mount Carmel, far from Jerusalem, indeed in a place that might be thought to be more Baal's space than Yahweh's, Elijah anticipated that *one* God would answer. "The God who answers by fire, he is God."[14] The fire would prove the point, but the point is that only the God who *answers* is God.[15]

Second Response (v. 24b)

Elijah's words (which are, of course, the true word of the Lord, 17:24) began to do their work. The no-answer of verse 21 was broken: "And all the people answered, 'It is well spoken'" (v. 24b). Literally they said, "The word is good." This response to "the word" was the beginning of the Lord's victory over Baal and his prophets.[16]

Scene 2: The Inadequacy of Sincerity (vv. 25–29)

Verse 25 probably brings us to the morning of the next day (see v. 26). There are indications that the rest of the narrative through verse 46 filled that day.

By this time the prophets of Baal had chosen two bulls, according to Elijah's instruction (v. 23). It was time for the experiment to begin.

Religion on Trial (v. 25)

Again we see the authority with which Elijah spoke and acted. There is no doubt about who was in charge on Mount Carmel. No one dared to oppose or resist him. Elijah now addressed the prophets of Baal directly.

Then Elijah said to the prophets of Baal, "Choose for yourselves one bull and prepare it first, for you are many, and call upon the name of your god, but put no fire to it" (v. 25)

Was there already a note of sarcasm in Elijah's voice? *What an impressive representation Baal has! There are so many of you! This should take you no time at all. I am all on my own. I might be a bit slow. So you go first.*

As Elijah repeated the instructions already given publicly, the words "call upon the name of your god," now addressed to Baal's prophets, were no longer ambiguous. These devotees of Baal were to put their religion to the test—the test set by Elijah.

There is a subtle indication of the change that had begun in the people. Elijah no longer suggests that *the people* might call upon the name of Baal (see v. 24). Baal's prophets were now on their own.

Sincerity at Work (v. 26a)

The extraordinary authority of Elijah prevailed as the prophets of Baal obeyed him precisely:

And they took the bull that was given [he gave[17]] them, and they prepared it and called upon the name of Baal from morning until noon, saying, "O Baal, answer us!" (v. 26a)

Over and over again they called out. It went on for hours. *O Baal, answer us! O Baal, answer us! O Baal, answer us!*

These prophets of Baal were not charlatans, at least not knowingly. There is no suggestion that they tried to cheat by setting the wood alight with sleight of hand. They followed Elijah's instructions to the letter, presumably because they trusted Baal to "answer" them. The prophets of Baal were sincere followers of their "god." The only question was whether their "god" was "God."

First Result (v. 26b)

"But there was no voice, and there was no answerer"[18] (v. 26b, AT). Indeed there was no voice *because* there was no answerer.[19] As they called out to Baal, "Answer us," no one was listening. The silence spoke eloquently of the absence. There was *no one there*!

How Pathetic! (v. 26c)

The first half of this section describing the efforts of Baal's prophets concludes with a description of their pathetic efforts: "And they limped around the altar that they had made" (v. 26c). They embodied an intense version of Elijah's scathing description of the people in verse 21, staggering around, bumping into the altar they had made.[20] It was ludicrous, if it was not so serious. The effect is not only to mock the farcical stumbling around of the prophets, but also to suggest that the lurching of the people of Israel (v. 21) was no better.

Religion Ridiculed (v. 27)

All morning this went on. At midday Elijah turned up the heat. We are told he "mocked[21] them" (v. 27a). He certainly did. Listen to him:

> Cry aloud, for he is a god. Either he is musing, or he is relieving himself,
> or he is on a journey, or perhaps he is asleep and must be awakened. (v. 27)

If, for the sake of argument Elijah suggests, we suspend the truth that no one is there, what explanation can there be for the silence, the non-answer? It is not possible to pin down the exact meaning of each of Elijah's bitingly sarcastic phrases, but the impact is palpable.[22] *He is a god, isn't he? Your god must be busy thinking about something else. Maybe he is on the toilet or traveling. Perhaps he has dozed off. Shout more loudly, and you might wake him up!*

Elijah would not fit in well in the inclusive society that demands respect for all religions. We need to think this through with care, but there is a place for mocking the ridiculous. All too often religion really is ridiculous when you know the God who is really there.

Sincerity Pushed to the Limits (vv. 28, 29a)

It is almost comical that the prophets *again* did *exactly* what Elijah told them, even in his mockery. He had said, "Cry aloud."

> And they *cried aloud* and cut themselves after their custom with swords
> and lances, until the blood gushed out upon them. And as midday passed,
> they raved on until the time of the offering of the oblation. (vv. 28, 29a)

Whatever you think of this performance, it is difficult to doubt their sincerity. Their "custom"[23] included gashing their bodies with blades until they were bleeding profusely. Such self-mutilation was contrary to Yahweh's Law (Leviticus 19:28; Deuteronomy 14:1), but apparently vital to Baal—that is, they imagined that it would please their imagined god. Although modern readers are no doubt repulsed by this routine, there is no more sense to anything we do to honor God if what we do is just our idea of what may please him. That is the problem with mere religion. If Yahweh is God, we can only follow him by trusting and obeying his word, not by devising our own God-pleasing religion, even if we call it "worship."

They "raved on." The Hebrew is an intensive form of the verb "prophesy."[24] *This* was the "prophesying" of these "prophets." It went on and on until "the time of the offering of the oblation"—a puzzling but very important expression.

A reader familiar with God's Law may think that "the offering of the oblation" could be a reference to the lamb that was to be offered at twilight[25] each day according to Exodus 29:39.[26] Such a reader may then be surprised that the writer is measuring time here on Mount Carmel by the activities at the true house of the Lord down south in Jerusalem, where these sacrifices and offerings were now made. Perhaps such a reader would detect a hint that the activities of this day on Mount Carmel highlighted how much the people needed what was going on at that time in the house of the Lord in Jerusalem— the atonement for their sins that was accomplished in its Old Testament way only by these sacrifices and offerings.

However, the narrator uses an expression that does not refer to any *particular* offering or sacrifice.[27] A literal translation is "until the going up of the offering." "Going up" (Hebrew, *'lh*) is a verb often used for the burning of sacrifices and offerings on an altar.[28] "Offering" (ESV, "oblation") is a word simply meaning "gift," but it can refer to a wide range of sacrifices and offerings,[29] all of which had something to do with dealing with sin.[30] As we listen to the narrative the phrase prompts us to wonder, *What "offering" does he mean? When will it "go up"?*

Keep those questions in mind. They will soon (in our next chapter) be answered in an astonishing way.

Second Result (v. 29b)

The more intense and frantic activity of the prophets of Baal was no more effective at the end of the day than their simpler cries had been through the morning: ". . . but there was no voice, and there was no answerer, and there was no attentiveness" (v. 29b, AT).

To the empty silence at noon (v, 26) the writer now adds, "and there was no attentiveness." This is a potent statement. Bible believers know that the Lord *is* attentive to the cries of those who call on *him* (Psalm 5:2; 17:1; 55:2; 61:1; 66:19; 86:6; 142:6; Daniel 9:19; Malachi 3:16[31]). Those who call out to Baal encounter *no attentiveness*! That is why there was no answerer. No one was even listening!

Before we come to the climactic scene of this drama in our next chapter, let us pause and consider the *no voice, no answerer, no attentiveness* as the prophets of Baal continued their noisy, gory, and exhausting performance that day on Mount Carmel.

The experience of the prophets of Baal is not comparable to a person today who earnestly prays for something but seems to receive no answer. We will soon hear that the challenge laid down by Elijah had come from the Lord ("I have done all these things *at your word*," 18:36). It was not as though *Elijah* had come up with the idea that "the God who answers by fire, he is God." In this "the word of *the Lord*" was "in [his] mouth" (17:24).

Mount Carmel was *the Lord's* demonstration of the emptiness and unreality of the Baal religion. The emphasis was not on the harm this religion caused, although the worship of Baal led to much evil. The point was that Baal was not real. There was *no voice, no answerer, no attentiveness*. That matters because the Lord *is* real. He is attentive, he answers, he speaks, as every one of the people of Israel ought to have known.

Here is the persistent problem with religion, even religion that might have imagined benefits ("it's good for society"). It replaces the reality of trusting and obeying the God who is really there with an unreality in which there is *no voice, no answerer, no attentiveness*. Make-believe religion might seem harmless. We might even imagine it does some good for people who like that kind of thing. But when religion is a substitute (as it always is) for the God who really is there, it is not harmless.

The Apostle Paul put it like this: "See to it that no one takes you captive by philosophy and empty deceit, according to human tradition . . . and *not according to Christ*" (Colossians 2:8). He went on to mention various contemporary examples of "philosophy and empty deceit, according to human tradition"—festivals, Sabbaths, asceticism, angelic worship, visions, regulations—all "according to human precepts and teachings," "self-made religion" (see Colossians 2:8, 16, 18, 21–23).

What was wrong with all this? It is *not the Lord Jesus Christ!* "In *him* the whole fullness of deity dwells bodily" (Colossians 2:9). Empty, unreal, and yet impressive religion is still with us. See that no one takes you captive.

One further point (to be explored further in our next chapter), no nation in today's world is the same as Old Testament Israel. Christians do not have a right or responsibility to impose the truth by force or by law on societies made up of people of many religions or none. The existence of many cultures is an opportunity to pray and to teach the Word of God with grace, kindness, gentleness, and love. But the issue is the same. Who really *is* God?

39

Decision Time

1 KINGS 18:30–40

IT IS ONE THING to see the foolishness and empty unreality of religion. That was on display on Mount Carmel on the day that Elijah challenged the prophets of Baal to put their religion to a test set by the Lord. There was *no voice, no answerer, no attentiveness* (see 18:26, 29). I sometimes have some sympathy for the arguments of atheists. Much of what they find ridiculous in religion, I too find ridiculous.

But should all claims about God be lumped together, labeled religion, and welcomed or dismissed as though all religion is fundamentally the same?

Let us return to Mount Carmel.

Scene 3: The God Who Is Really There (vv. 30–39)

It was time for the second stage of the great experiment. In fact, the second stage began before the first had run its course. Verse 30 takes us back to some time, probably during the afternoon, as the Baal prophets were still "raving on" (18:29).[1]

Preparations (vv. 30–35)

Some short distance from the noise of the pagan prophets, Elijah began his preparations. They are described in some detail and provide a new and profoundly important setting for the coming climactic moment.

The People (v. 30a)

Elijah began by drawing "all the people" into what he was about to do. "Then[2] [And] Elijah said to all the people, 'Come near to me.' And all the people came near to him" (v. 30a), just as he "came near" to them earlier (v. 21).

517

The people were not participating in the antics of the Baal prophets. The prophets of Baal had not thought of asking them. But "all the people" will be deeply involved in Stage 2 of the experiment. They "came near" to the Lord's prophet.

The Altar (vv. 30b, 31a, 32a)

Now for a big surprise:

> And he repaired the altar of the LORD that had been thrown down. Elijah took twelve stones . . . and with the stones he built an altar in the name of the LORD. (vv. 30b, 31a, 32a)

At some time in the past there had been an altar of Yahweh here on Mount Carmel. This was probably one of the "high places" at which the people had offered sacrifices prior to Solomon's construction of the house of the Lord in Jerusalem (see 3:2). This would explain it being regarded here as a (once) legitimate "altar of the LORD." However, it had been "thrown down," that is, destroyed, probably in the Baal-inspired hostility of Ahab and Jezebel (see 19:10).

Elijah "repaired" it. Literally he "healed" it—he brought it back to good health, so to speak. It is now clear, if we had not guessed earlier, that Elijah was preparing not just for a spectacular supernatural fireworks display but for a sacrifice. That is what an "altar" is for.

We are told how Elijah "repaired" the altar. He took twelve stones (more on them in a moment) and with them built (that is, rebuilt) the altar "in the name of the LORD." The name that rightly belonged to the house in Jerusalem was now, on the authority of God's prophet, associated with this altar. The altar was therefore a kind of replica of the house for the name of the Lord that Solomon had built in Jerusalem. Before calling in the name of Yahweh (18:24) he built an altar in the name of Yahweh.

The Promise (v. 31b)

The narrator explains all this by telling us that the twelve stones were "according to the number of the tribes of the sons of Jacob, to whom the word of the LORD came, saying, 'Israel shall be your name'" (v. 31b). Here is yet another reminder of Moses who "built an altar . . . and twelve pillars, according to the twelve tribes of Israel" (Exodus 24:4).[3]

The altar built in the "name" of Yahweh was for the people whose God-given "name" was Israel, and that people numbered *twelve* tribes. The division of this people into two kingdoms was "not forever" (11:39). This temporary northern kingdom still belonged to the people to whom Yahweh had given the name "Israel." What were they doing turning to Baal?

They (all *twelve* tribes) were the people of Yahweh's promise. That is what "to whom the word of the LORD came" means. Not only was turning to Baal a denial of their calling and the One who had named them, but the separation from Jerusalem since the days of Jeroboam was just as serious. The temporary political division (again see 11:39) should never have been taken further, as Jeroboam had done (12:26–33, and now Ahab had gone further still (16:31).

Elijah's action in verse 31, explained to us by the narrator, serves to highlight the seriousness of this people's sin against the Lord who had named (that is, chosen) them. Follow the development of the theme of the people's "sin" in 12:30; 13:34; 14:16; 15:26, 30, 34; 16:2, 13, 19, 26, 31.

King Solomon had prayed about such circumstances, when the Lord's people "sin" against him, and what was then needed—that the Lord would "forgive" the sin of his people (see 8:33–36, 46, 47, 50).

These considerations should help us see the profound importance of the altar that Elijah built in the name of the Lord.

What the People Did to Help (vv. 32b–35)

Elijah's preparations now took a strange turn:

> And he made a trench about the altar, as great as would contain two seahs of seed.[4] And he put the wood in order and cut the bull in pieces and laid it on the wood. And he said, "Fill four jars with water and pour it on the burnt offering and on the wood." And he said, "Do it a second time." And they did it a second time. And he said, "Do it a third time." And they did it a third time. And the water ran around the altar and filled the trench also with water. (vv. 32b–35)

We see the change that was taking place in the people as they obeyed Elijah's word to the letter. The prophets of Baal were still "raving on" some distance away. The people were now clearly and actively on Elijah's side.

I am sure that the more alert among them could do the numbers. Four jars of water three times make *twelve* jars. The people were enacting what the stones of the altar represented. Twelve! The number is much more important than trying to calculate how much water was poured over the dismembered beast and the firewood under it. This was about the people who belonged to Yahweh. That is what *twelve* represented.

Did you notice what Elijah now called the animal on the altar? It was a "burnt offering." The fundamental purpose of a burnt offering was "to make atonement" (Leviticus 1:4), that is to deal with sins.[5] For the second time in this story we hear the language of sacrifice. Indeed the Hebrew word translated "burnt offering" is a clear echo of the verb "going up" (ESV, "offering") that we heard in 18:29. Was *this* "the offering of the oblation" the narrator mentioned there? Hold that question for a moment.

The drenching that the people gave the animal and the wood on the altar obviously contributed to the wonder of what would shortly happen, but it was more than that. The actions of the people contributed positively *nothing whatsoever* to what was about to happen. All they did was, so to speak, make matters worse. All that water they poured over the "burnt offering" is a rather dramatic picture of the sins of the people—only making matters worse. Their contribution to the wonder that was about to occur was to make a very great wonder necessary.[6]

Reality Revealed (vv. 36–39)

The moment of truth had arrived: "And at the time of the offering of the oblation . . ." (v. 36a)—literally, "at the going up of the offering," repeating the unusual phrase we heard in 18:29. Again this could be a time reference to the activities in Jerusalem (as v. 29 could be understood).[7] But I think we can now see that the writer is talking about the "burnt offering" that was about to "go up." The time for *this* offering had arrived, and that is what he was alluding to in 18:29.[8]

Elijah's Prayer (vv. 36b, 37)

> Elijah the prophet came near and said, "O LORD, God of Abraham, Isaac, and Israel, let it be known this day that you are God in Israel, and that I am your servant, and that I have done all these things at your word. Answer me, O LORD, answer me, that this people may know that you[9], O LORD, are God, and that you have turned their hearts back." (vv. 36b, 37)

Earlier Elijah "came near" to all the people (v. 21), and later all the people "came near" to Elijah (v. 30). Now we come to the climactic moment, and Elijah "came near." By implication he *came near* to the One he now addressed: "O LORD, God of Abraham, Isaac, and Israel." We can now see that the stages of "coming near" in the narrative have been moving toward this: coming near *to God*.[10] As Elijah "came near" to the Lord, so he was bringing with him those who had "come near" to him.[11] Again Elijah reminds us of Moses (Exodus 24:2).[12]

Notice six things in Elijah's prayer.

First, he addressed Yahweh as "God of Abraham, Isaac, and Israel." This is a clear reference to the promise of God made to the fathers of this nation (see, for example, Genesis 12:1–3; 26:4; 35:10–12). This is a prayer of faith in the promise of God.

Second, Elijah's use of "Israel" (rather than "Jacob") makes the point already noted by the narrator in verse 31. Yahweh is the God of "Israel," in the full sense of the twelve tribes descended from Jacob. To acknowledge that this God is your God has to involve recognizing all of his people as your people—not cutting yourself off from Jerusalem (the foundational sin of the northern kingdom).

Third, Elijah asked Yahweh to make "known" three things: (a) "that you are God in Israel," (b) "that I am your servant," and (c) "that I have done all these things at your word." The first of these is the matter in dispute (v. 21), although the focus now is who is God *in Israel*, in this context meaning the whole twelve-tribe people of Yahweh. The second had not been openly disputed, but neither had Ahab or the people yet acknowledged Elijah as the servant of Yahweh he had claimed to be (see 17:1; 18:15). The third is rather important. We now understand that the great experiment (as I have been calling it) was God's idea, not Elijah's, and he wanted that to be known. Elijah had not been putting the Lord to the test (Deuteronomy 6:16). He had been obeying the word of the Lord. Everything that had happened (and was about to happen) on Mount Carmel was at Yahweh's word.

Fourth, Elijah called on the Lord to "answer." There was no "answerer" for those who called on the name of Baal (18:26, 29). The point of the great experiment was to show that the one who "answers" is God (18:24).

Fifth, the Lord's answer will make known to the people not only who is God *in Israel*, but who is *God*.

Finally, Elijah asked that the people would then know "that you have turned their hearts back." Behold the grace of God at work on Mount Carmel! The God who was about to answer by fire had already been at work, as we have seen, turning the hearts of the people back to him. First they were moved by Elijah's word to answer and acknowledge that the word was good (18:24). Then they did not, as expected, join the prophets of Baal as they called on their god (18:24, 26). Then they "came near" to Elijah (v. 30). Then they obeyed his word precisely and at length, even as the prophets of Baal were still carrying on (vv. 33–34). The Lord was turning their heart back, and Elijah wanted them to know it.[13]

The God Who Answers by Fire (v. 38)

If we have correctly understood 18:29, some distance away the prophets of Baal continued their wild raving until suddenly they were stopped in their tracks.

> Then the fire of the LORD fell and consumed the burnt offering and the wood and the stones and the dust, and licked up the water that was in the trench. (v. 38)

This was spectacular. By all means allow yourself to be amazed at the power and wonder of it all. Imagine, if you will, how the bleeding, exhausted prophets of Baal must have been struck dumb. But do not stop there. What did this all-consuming fire from Heaven do? It turned the beast on the altar into a "burnt offering." No one "offered up" this offering. It was the Lord himself who turned it into a burnt offering. *The Lord himself made atonement for the sins of his people!*

At the same time the fire consumed the altar itself, the dirt that had come from the trenches, and all the water the people had poured out. This was clearly meant to be a one-off event. There was no possibility of the altar on Mount Carmel taking the place of the altar in Jerusalem. It had done its work.

What the People Said—at Last (v. 39)

The work of God that day on Mount Carmel was almost complete.

> And when all the people saw it, they fell on their faces and said, "The LORD, he is God; the LORD, he is God." (v. 39)

At last they took Elijah's name ("My God Is Yahweh") on their own lips. In their confession "he" is emphatic: "Yahweh, *he* is the one (and no other) who is God!"

Scene 4: The End of Religion (v. 40)

What had happened on Mount Carmel was deeply serious. The consequences for religion were devastating.

> And Elijah said to them, "Seize the prophets of Baal; let not one of them escape." And they seized them. And Elijah brought them down to the brook Kishon[14] and slaughtered them there. (v. 40)

The people now participated in this terrible judgment on those who had brought the worship of Baal into Israel. What had happened to the prophets of Yahweh at the hands of Jezebel (18:4, 13) now happened to the pagan prophets. The difference is that Elijah's actions were "at [Yahweh's] word" (v. 36). This was the capital punishment required by the Law of the Lord (Deuteronomy 13).[15]

Such scenes are never easy to witness, nor should they be. But they must be a powerful reminder that the true and living God will deal with all that opposes him. It is part of what it means to be God.

The day was not yet over. Indeed the most remarkable moment of all was yet to come. But before we read on, we must consider the challenge of Mount Carmel.

The heart of it is simple to state. For us who have heard the account as much as for those who were there, it is decision time. *If Yahweh is God, follow him. But if Baal is God, follow him.*

Two observations should be kept in mind.

First, we are reading the *Old* Testament. What happened on Mount Carmel must be seen in the light of what has happened since. We live on this side of the death and resurrection of Jesus Christ. We do not live in Elijah's Old Testament world. What a difference that makes.

Second, this was Old Testament *Israel*. Neither Australia, nor the United States of America, nor any other nation on earth today is the same as Israel in Old Testament times. Parallels should not be directly drawn between Israel then and any modern nation.

With these two important perspectives I will make just three brief points about the challenge of Mount Carmel in the light of the gospel of the Lord Jesus Christ.

First, the God of Abraham, Isaac, and Israel is the God and Father of our Lord Jesus Christ. The One who proved himself to be God on Mount Carmel is the One who has made himself known to the whole world in Jesus Christ (John 1:18). The answer the true God gave on Mount Carmel has been amplified in his word to the whole world when he raised Jesus from the dead (see Matthew 28:18; Acts 10:39–42; 13:30, 31; 17:31; Romans 1:4).

Second, this is serious. It is so much more than pointing to a miracle that proves that there is a God. The God who is there, who proved himself on Mount Carmel and now in Jesus, has done so purposefully. At the heart of what he did on Mount Carmel and what he has now done in Jesus is making atonement for the sins of his people. The burnt offering on Mount Carmel (like all Old Testament sacrifices) was a shadow of the once-and-for-all sacrifice that was made in the death of Jesus Christ on the cross for the sins of the whole world (John 1:29; 3:16; 4:42; 11:51, 52; 12:32; 1 John 2:2; 4:14).

Third, what happened on Mount Carmel must warn us all that there will be terrible consequences for those who choose to follow Baal—or whatever so-called god human hearts might invent. They will not escape (1 Thessalonians 5:3). The prophets of Baal slaughtered by the brook Kidron provide a terrible picture of the consequences of becoming a fool who exchanges the glory of the immortal God for idols (cf. Romans 1:22, 23). Such religion is a disaster (and cannot possibly be good for society).

If the Lord is God, *follow* him.

But if Baal is God follow *him*—and go to Hell.[16]

40

The God Who Answers

1 KINGS 18:41-46

PRAYER IS POWERFUL.

That is true but often misunderstood. Prayer is only powerful because the God who is really there is powerful and answers prayer. Prayer to Baal was not powerful, as we have seen clearly displayed on that day on Mount Carmel. There was no answerer, no attentiveness (18:29, AT). No one was listening. How different it was when Elijah called on the name of the Lord (18:36–38)!

A common misunderstanding about the power of prayer is to think that prayer can be a means of having *my will* done. Certainly the Scriptures contain remarkable promises to those who pray, and as believers we have been given a gracious invitation to make known to God whatever is on our hearts (see, for example, Psalm 37:5; 55:22; Matthew 7:7; 21:22; Mark 11:24; John 14:13; Philippians 4:6; 1 John 3:22). We can cast all our anxieties on him, knowing that he cares for us (1 Peter 5:7). But we must not think that prayer can be a way of my will *prevailing over* God's will. The perfect prayer of faith is this: "Your will be done . . . not as I will, but as you will" (Matthew 6:10; 26:39).

This is a wonderful relief. We pray trusting the God to whom we pray. We do not understand our deepest needs. We do not know what to pray (Romans 8:26; cf. James 4:3). As we pray, we trust the wisdom and goodness of God "to do far more abundantly than all we ask or think" (Ephesians 3:20).

As we learn to pray like this, the promises of God are precious. In the promises of God's Word we learn God's good and wise will, and we learn to pray accordingly. Prayer is as powerful as the promises of God on which it is based.

At the end of the extraordinary day on Mount Carmel—when those who called on the name of Baal had *no answerer*, but when Elijah called on the name of the Lord, the Lord *answered by fire*—Elijah prayed. The prayer was powerful, and we will see that the Lord did far more abundantly than we might at first think.

It is time for us to recall what the drama on Mount Carmel has been about. It had begun when the word of the Lord came to Elijah, saying "Go, show yourself to Ahab, *so that* I may send rain upon the earth" (18:1, AT).

When we considered 18:1 we looked at what was happening in the light of the prayer King Solomon had prayed years earlier. We saw that the drought had been "because they have sinned against you" (8:35). It was punishment from the Lord for the sin of the king and people of Israel. We also saw that what needed to happen was that they "turn from their sin." *Then* the Lord would "forgive the sin of [his] servants" and "send rain upon [their] land" (8:35, 36).

When "all the people" came to their senses on Mount Carmel, fell on their faces, and said, "The LORD, *he* (and no other) is the one who is God!" (18:39, AT), the first step had been taken. They had *turned from their sin*—their sin being precisely this: turning away from the Lord (see 9:6; 11:2, 4, 9). Indeed the Lord had sent Elijah to Ahab (18:1) for the purpose of "turn[ing] their hearts back" (18:37).

Now that the purpose of Elijah's commission ("Go, show yourself to Ahab," 18:1) had been accomplished, the time had come for the promise ("so that I may send rain upon the earth," 18:1, AT) to be fulfilled.

Through the account of the showdown between Elijah and the prophets of Baal (18:20–40) there has been no mention of the immediately pressing crisis: the drought. On the parched slopes of Mount Carmel, some may have wondered at the Lord's "answer" by *fire*. Who needed fire? And the fire "licked up the water" that had flowed into the trench around the altar (18:38)—the precious and scarce resource was taken away.

But the drought had fallen into the background of the narrative because the even more immediate and pressing issue was being dealt with—namely, who is God? The drought was a sideshow. The *cause* of the drought was the people turning away from the Lord (who is God) to Baal (who isn't). The people's repentance resolved the most pressing issue. What, now, about the drought?

King Ahab Gets It (vv. 41, 42a)

And Elijah said to Ahab, "Go up, eat and drink, for there is a sound of the rushing of rain." So Ahab went up to eat and to drink. (vv. 41, 42a)

King Ahab has not been mentioned since 18:20, and only now do we learn for sure that he was there and witnessed the drama that had taken place on Carmel. Are we to understand that the king was among "all the people" whose heart was turned back to the Lord? Did he, too, fall on his face and say, "The LORD, he is God; the LORD, he is God" (18:39)?

The narrator does not exactly say so, but he drops a number of clues suggesting that the king, like the people, had changed.

First, Elijah said to Ahab, "Go up." This seems to indicate that Ahab had gone down to the brook Kishon and had witnessed, presumably approvingly, the capital punishment of the prophets of Baal (18:40). "Go up" would mean to go back up to the place of the burnt offering.[1]

Second, Elijah told Ahab to "eat and drink." Was this to be a meal with Elijah, expressing the restored relationship between king and prophet, and therefore between Ahab and the Lord?[2] Was it more? Perhaps this was specifically a meal associated with the burnt offering, like the famous meal when Moses and the people "beheld God" on Mount Sinai (Exodus 24:3–11).[3] Whatever it was, it suggests that Ahab was invited to *celebrate* what had happened on Mount Carmel and what would follow.

Third, the reason Elijah gave for Ahab to eat and drink was that the prophet could hear "a sound of the rushing[4] of rain." Elijah had the ears of faith. His hearing was sensitized by the promise he had heard (18:1). He was hearing *what had been promised*, not because the rain was yet falling, but because he believed the promise.[5] Indeed, we might say, the promise *was* the sound (voice) of the rushing of rain. Elijah invited Ahab to share his confidence in God's promise.

Fourth, Ahab did exactly as Elijah told him: "Ahab went up to eat and to drink." Unlike Ahab's earlier half-hearted submission to Elijah (18:20), the writer now employs his usual technique, repeating verbatim the words of a command to describe exact and complete obedience.[6] Ahab was, to all appearances, a changed man.

Ahab's story has a long way to go. It will not all be as positive as this moment. However, at this point we see a remarkable change in Israel's king. It seems that the Lord had turned back the hearts of the king and the people (18:37).

Elijah's Prayer (vv. 42b–44a)

It is reasonable to assume that Ahab and Elijah joined in the proposed meal at or near the site of the altar on which the burnt offering so spectacularly went up. The meal may have taken place between verses 42a and 42b. The narrator, however, seems to be in a hurry to get to what happened next and so says nothing more about that meal.

"And Elijah[7] went up to the top of Mount Carmel" (v. 42b). It seems that the place of the burnt offering (and the meal with Ahab?) was below the summit of the mountain, toward which Elijah now climbed, stopping short of the actual summit (as we will see).[8]

Concentrated Prayer (v. 42c)

There, near the mountaintop, "he bowed himself down on the earth and put his face between his knees" (v. 42c). His awkward posture suggests intense concentration.[9] The prophet who believed God's promise (he could hear the sound of the rushing of rain) now gave himself to earnest prayer.

Just as the real crisis in Israel was deeper than the drought (which fell into the background of the narrative until now), so we can be sure that Elijah's prayer on the mountain was about more than water. As we keep in mind King Solomon's prayer we can see, as Elijah would understand, that the rain, when it came, would signal that the Lord had *forgiven the people's sin* (see 8:35, 36). Elijah's uncomfortable posture bears witness to the weight of his prayer—for rain, yes, but for rain as confirmation of the forgiveness of sins. How earnestly Elijah prayed! He understood the gravity of the moment.

Persistent Prayer (v. 43)

And he said to his servant,[10] "Go up now,[11] look toward the sea." And he went up and looked and said, "There is nothing." And he said, "Go again," seven times. (v. 43)

The lad climbed to the very summit and looked westward to the Mediterranean Sea. "There was nothing" introduces a note of tension. Strangely the Hebrew echoes the first word of the devastating phrases we heard earlier: *"there was no* voice, *there was no* answerer, *there was no* attentiveness" (18:29, AT). But that was Baal.

The "nothing" did not deter Elijah. He persisted in his prayer, and seven times (a number that suggests thoroughness, completeness) he sent the lad to look out to the ocean horizon. Knowing what we know (God's promise, 18:1, and the deeper dimension of forgiveness, 8:36) the sevenfold prayer suggests the magnitude of what was about to happen. Of course, the Lord could have sent rain in an instant, as indeed he had sent fire immediately in 18:38. But this was big. If the rain came, it would mean *sins had been forgiven.* The concentrated, persistent prayer of Elijah should impress on us the immense significance of what was being prayed for.

Answered Prayer (v. 44a)

> And at the seventh time he said, "Behold, a little cloud like a man's hand is rising from the sea." (v. 44a)

As Jesus observed, a cloud rising in the west signals coming rain (Luke 12:54). So it was with the news of this "little cloud," possibly shaped like a human hand or, more likely, small enough to be covered from sight by an outstretched hand. After more than three years of clear skies and the heavens shut up (8:35), the small cloud was a sight to behold. For the praying Elijah, it was the sign for which he had been waiting.

King Ahab and Elijah (vv. 44b–46)

Elijah's Word (v. 44b)

Elijah had no doubt what the little cloud meant. He said to the lad, "Go up,[12] say to Ahab, 'Prepare your chariot [Harness up[13]] and go down, lest the rain stop you'" (v. 44b). If the king was to reach shelter for the night, he would need to hurry. The coming rain, Elijah was confident, would not be a gentle shower.

The Rain (v. 45a)

> And in a little while [meanwhile[14]] the heavens grew black with clouds and wind, and there was a great rain. (v. 45a)

So ended the drought that had begun more than three years earlier at Elijah's word (17:1). The wind (Hebrew, *ruakh*) may remind us of the *ruakh* of God that brought the ordered, blessed creation into being at the beginning (Genesis 1:2).[15] The parched land was watered once again. It was "nothing short of a resurrection."[16]

In the excitement and confusion of the downpour I suspect that no one (except, I presume, Elijah) may have thought about the deeper meaning of the breaking of the drought. The story has been told in such a way that we, too, could miss the profound significance of what happened. This, I take it, is deliberate. Very soon we will see that the new beginning for Israel was short-lived. The grace signified by the flooding rains was not embraced by the nation. Jezebel's fury will shortly touch even Elijah (19:1–3).

But we have not reached that point yet, and as we hear the story of Mount Carmel, we must not forget the spectacular "burnt offering" that was perhaps still sizzling as the rain began to fall (18:38). Atonement had been made. King Solomon's prayer must still ring in our ears ("you will hear in heaven and *forgive the sin* of your servants . . . and send rain upon your land . . . ," 8:36, AT). As the rain poured down, we understand that this was a mighty moment in Israel's history. We are witnessing *the forgiveness of sins.*

King Ahab and Elijah (vv. 45b, 46)

As this episode concludes we witness a very different relationship between the king and the prophet from what we saw at the beginning (18:17, 18). "And Ahab rode and went to Jezreel" (v. 45b)—a ride of about seventeen miles in the pouring rain, over muddy terrain. The king did as the prophet told him.

Jezreel was a curiously fitting place for Ahab to go, considering the circumstances. Jezreel means "May God Make Fruitful."[17] The town was at the eastern (upper) end of the Jezreel Valley (Joshua 17:16; Judges 6:33), through which the brook Kishon (18:40) flowed.[18] Ahab had a palace there (21:1), where (we will soon learn) Jezebel was waiting for him (19:1).

Jezreel had rather solemn memories. It was the setting for the final encounter between King Saul and the Philistines (1 Samuel 29:1, 11), which resulted in Saul's death on nearby Mount Gilboa (1 Samuel 31). In years to come Jezreel would come to represent the guilt of the Israelite kingdom (see 21:1–15, 23; 2 Kings 9:10, 30–37; 10:11; also Hosea 1:4, 5).

On this day, however, Ahab's return to Jezreel through the pouring rain looked like a new beginning.

> And the hand of the LORD was on Elijah, and he gathered up his garment and ran before Ahab to the entrance of Jezreel. (v. 46)

"The hand of the LORD" indicates that what Elijah now did was under the direction of God himself.[19] Running "before Ahab" to the entrance of Jezreel was not necessarily a supernatural feat.[20] No doubt it was strenuous, but the point seems to be that Elijah went *before* Ahab as a herald. Elijah was *supporting* the king (cf. 1:5). On the other hand, it meant that Ahab was *following* Elijah.[21] The hostility between king and prophet (18:17, 18) was at last (momentarily) healed.[22]

Before we turn the page and see how short-lived this happy outcome was, we should pause and reflect on the power of Elijah's prayer. In the New Testament this episode was remembered by James:

> The prayer of a righteous person has great power as it is working. Elijah was a man with a nature like ours, and he prayed fervently that it might not

rain, and for three years and six months it did not rain on the earth. Then
he prayed again, and heaven gave rain, and the earth bore its fruit. (James
5:16b–18)

The power of Elijah's prayer (that is, of course, the power of the One to
whom he prayed) was certainly *seen* in the downpour that followed. It is striking to notice, however, that these words of James come in the context of the
forgiveness of sins (see James 5:15, 16a). I am inclined to think that James
understood what we have seen in 1 Kings 18—namely, that the really powerful
thing that was going on was not seen. It was the forgiveness of sins.

I have no desire to downplay visible miracles, nor should we miss their
significance. However, I do not think that James was promising that every
"righteous person" who prays for no rain or rain will see what Elijah saw.
I am sure that on this side of the death of Jesus (by which full atonement was
made for the sins of the whole world, surpassing the burnt offering on Mount
Carmel, 1 John 2:2) and his resurrection (which tells the whole word who is
God, surpassing the fire from Heaven on Mount Carmel, Romans 1:4) James
teaches us that our prayers can be as powerful as Elijah's because we, like him,
can see *sins forgiven*.[23]

Not Quite What We Had Hoped

1 Kings 19

41

There Is No Plan B

1 KINGS 19

"BUT WE HAD HOPED that he was the one to redeem Israel" (Luke 24:21). The followers of Jesus who uttered those heartrending words had held high hopes of his being "the one to redeem Israel"—the one long promised by God who would save his people from their oppressors and bring them freedom and happiness. They had hoped because they had been with Jesus as he taught about the kingdom of God, healed the sick, and astonished the crowds with his wisdom, authority, and power. But it had ended so badly. "Our chief priests and rulers delivered him up to be condemned to death, and crucified him" (Luke 24:20). And three days later the disappointment, even disillusionment, was setting in. "We *had* hoped . . ."

It is easy for us to be rather condescending toward the disciples of Jesus on the road to Emmaus. We wonder why they did not remember that Jesus had not only repeatedly taught them that he *must* die, but also promised he would rise from the dead (Luke 9:21, 22, 44; 18:31–33). How could they have forgotten? If their hopes were shattered by the execution of Jesus, their hopes were misplaced. They did not understand (Luke 9:45; 18:34). We (rather presumptuously I think) nod in agreement when we hear Jesus say, "O foolish ones, and slow of heart to believe all that the prophets have spoken! Was it not necessary that the Christ should suffer these things and enter into his glory?" (Luke 24:25, 26).

Oh, the wonderful wisdom of hindsight! And yet even on this side of the resurrection of Jesus Christ, his followers often experience disappointment, even disillusionment. We have our expectations for the advance of God's kingdom. We have our plans, strategies, and dreams—to grow a church, to evangelize a nation, to change the world. Such plans, strategies, and dreams are the outworking of our faith. We believe the promise and power of the gospel. We mean it when we pray, "Your kingdom come." So we plan and work and hope. So we should. Christian faith cannot be merely contemplative because the word we believe is a promise. The promise not only gives us the big hope of Christ's return and of the new heaven and new earth. It also drives us to work for the kingdom.

But our plans, strategies, and dreams are often shattered. The church does not grow as we had hoped. The gospel does not change the nation as we had dreamed. The world seems to go from bad to worse. We can find ourselves saying, "We had hoped . . ."

What do we need to hear when our hopes have been shattered, when our labor for the Lord seems to have come to nothing, when our gospel-inspired dreams turn to disillusionment?

In 1 Kings 19 the great prophet Elijah experienced something that looks like disillusionment. He seems to have been devastated by shattered expectations. All that had happened on Mount Carmel (and a lot happened!) seemed to have come to nothing. It looked as though the great victory over Baal and the astonishing repentance of the people was undone in a moment. It was not what he had hoped.

But I am getting ahead of myself. What happened to undo the triumphant scene at the end of 1 Kings 18, with King Ahab following the prophet under God's hand to Jezreel as the rain bucketed down?

A Messenger Who Changed Everything? (vv. 1–5a)

Elijah and King Ahab arrived at the entrance to Jezreel (18:46). Only now do we learn that the queen was there in Ahab's palace, waiting for him. Jezebel was not present for the confrontation on Mount Carmel. She did not belong to "all the people of Israel" whom Ahab had gathered there (18:20). She was certainly not among "all the people" who had cried out, "The LORD, he is God; the LORD, he is God" (18:39). She had been waiting in Jezreel.

It had been Jezebel's marriage to Ahab that introduced the vile worship of Baal to Israel (16:31). She had been the patron of the 450 prophets of Baal and the 400 prophets of Asherah (18:19). She had executed hundreds of the prophets of the Lord (18:4, 13). Queen Jezebel was one terrifying lady. Through the whole drama on Mount Carmel, she had been waiting in the comfort of the Jezreel palace, waiting (I imagine) for news that the "troubler of Israel" (18:17) had been dealt with at last.

What Ahab Told Jezebel (v. 1)

The king gave his queen a full account of what had happened on Mount Carmel: "Ahab told Jezebel all that Elijah had done, and how he had killed all the prophets with the sword" (v. 1). He told her about the efforts of her dear prophets, crying out to Baal all day. He told her about the *no voice, no answerer, no attentiveness*. He told her about the rebuilt altar of Yahweh and all that water. He told her about Elijah's prayer. He told her about the fire from Heaven. He told her about all the people falling on their faces saying, "The LORD, he is God; the LORD, he is God." He told her about what happened to all her precious pagan prophets. He told her *everything*.[1]

This is the first of many points in 1 Kings 19 where we will find ourselves puzzling over what we should read between the lines. Was Ahab informing Jezebel of the terrible thing that Elijah had done to those who had enjoyed the queen's favor so that she could now deal with him? Was Ahab initiating appropriate action to eliminate the troubler of Israel?

I don't think so—if we have correctly understood the scene at the end of the previous chapter. Ahab's hurried ride to Jezreel had been instigated by Elijah; indeed Elijah had gone "before Ahab" (18:44, 46). Although Elijah was not present as Ahab spoke to Jezebel (see v. 2), he was not far away. He must have expected Ahab to inform Jezebel of what had happened. It was not the kind of thing you could keep quiet! But what did Elijah hope would then happen?

Given the decisive and unchallengeable nature of what had happened on Mount Carmel, and the apparent change we have seen in Ahab and all the people, isn't it likely that Ahab (and Elijah too) expected, or at least hoped, that the news of Yahweh's irrefutable victory would change even Jezebel? "*All* the people" who saw it had said, "The LORD, he is God; the LORD, he is God"— apparently including Ahab (18:39). Ahab's report to Jezebel sounds, then, like a word of testimony. *Baal has failed us, my dear. We have all repented. I think you should too.*

If that was too much to expect (and perhaps it was), then surely at least King Ahab would now insist on removing Jezebel's influence from the nation's life. There was the example of King Asa down south who had cleaned up his nation and dealt with a problematic "queen mother" (see 15:11–15). Surely Ahab could now do something similar. After all, *he* was the king.

Then, with Jezebel either converted or constrained, the rebuilding of the nation could begin in earnest. Elijah could lead the king and the people in working out the consequences of their confession. The Lord would be God again *in Israel* (cf. 18:36).

Something like that must have been Elijah's hope.

What Jezebel Told Elijah (v. 2)

It did not quite work out that way.

> Then Jezebel sent a messenger to Elijah, saying, "So may the gods do to me and more also, if I do not make your life as the life of one of them by this time tomorrow." (v. 2)

The gospel from Carmel did *not* bring Jezebel to her knees. It infuriated her, and Ahab did not lift a finger to restrain her. Immediately, without allowing Ahab to say another word, she dispatched a messenger to vent her rage on the "troubler of Israel." *Tell that troublemaker that his days are numbered. To one!*

The Septuagint (the Greek version of the Old Testament) inserts a phrase at the beginning of Jezebel's message that is probably not original, but does capture the mood well: "If you are Elijah, I am Jezebel!" *"My God Is Yahweh," you have met your match in Jezebel.*

Defiantly Jezebel employed an oath, an appropriately paganized version of the very oath used by King Solomon in 2:23. Far from acknowledging that Yahweh is God, she swore by her "gods."

Her threat introduces an important theme to this chapter. She planned to make Elijah's "life" (Hebrew, *nephesh*) as the "life" of one of the prophets of Baal he had killed. We will hear more about life and death in this story.[2]

We know too well that Jezebel was capable of carrying out her threat (see 18:4, 13). Some have suggested that sending a messenger to warn Elijah shows that Jezebel just wanted Elijah to flee so she could be rid of him because she no longer felt she could have him executed after the impact that Mount Carmel had had on both the people and the king.[3] Since Elijah clearly believed that her threat was thoroughly serious (see vv. 3, 10, 14), it seems much more likely that Jezebel dispatched the messenger in her fury (without a lot of thought) and perhaps to make perfectly clear to Ahab that the Lady was not for turning.

From Jezreel to a Lonely Broom Tree (vv. 3, 4a)

This was, to put it mildly, not quite what Elijah (and, I suspect, Ahab) had hoped. There are good reasons to think that "Then he was afraid" (v. 3, ESV) should be "Then he saw."[4] Elijah now "saw" the failure of all that had happened on Mount Carmel to change Jezebel. The powerful pagan queen had not been converted. Nor had the spineless king found the courage to rein her in. Jezebel's reign of terror would continue in Israel.

When Elijah saw this:

> ... he arose and ran[5] [went] for his life and came to Beersheba, which belongs to Judah, and left his servant there. But he himself went a day's journey into the wilderness and came and sat down under a broom tree. (vv. 3, 4a)

This takes us by surprise. In one sentence Elijah covers more than 100 miles, taking himself right out of Ahab's kingdom, all the way to Beersheba, in the southern extremities of the kingdom of *Judah* (as our writer carefully notes).[6] Until now all of Elijah's movements have been in obedience to "the word from the LORD" (to the brook Cherith, 17:2–5; to Zarephath, 17:8–10; back to Ahab, 18:1, 2). Even in the run back to Jezreel "the hand of the LORD was on Elijah" (18:46). Now, with no word from the Lord, Elijah took himself to the deep south.

Although we should resist the temptation to psychoanalyze Elijah,[7] we cannot help wondering what was going on. Beersheba was much further from Jezreel than Elijah needed to go to escape the clutches of Jezebel. And then he left (literally "rested") his lad[8] at Beersheba. But there was no "rest" yet for Elijah. He went on by himself "into the wilderness" and sat down under the shade of a single broom tree.

Some think that Elijah was rebelling against his calling, much like Jonah when he fled to Tarshish "away from the presence of the LORD" (Jonah 1:3).[9] I think that is too specific. The difficulty we have in understanding Elijah's motives more probably reflects his own confusion. However, the writer drops in a vital clue with the words "into the wilderness."

How Elijah Saw Things (vv. 4b, 5a)

In the wilderness the prophet

> ... asked that he might die,[10] saying, "It is enough; now, O LORD, take away my life, for I am no better than my fathers." And he lay down and slept under a broom tree. (vv. 4b, 5a)

"Enough!" he cried.[11] *Enough of a rebellious regime that cannot be changed, even by fire from Heaven! I had hoped . . . But look at Jezebel. Nothing has changed.* "Now, O LORD, take away my life (*nephesh*)." *I would rather you take my life than that woman!* "For I am no better than my fathers." *I have done no better than the prophets before me in bringing the necessary change to Israel.*

Elijah reminds us of Moses who in the wilderness had found the burden of the rebellious, complaining people of Israel too much to bear and asked the Lord to take his life (Numbers 11:15). Elijah was reliving the experience of Moses.

Elijah lay down under the solitary broom tree and fell asleep, no doubt hoping not to wake. This was a particular kind of despair. It was the distress of one who "had hoped," the despondency of one whose expectations for God's glory had been shattered.[12]

Another Messenger Who Made a Difference (vv. 5b–8)

The narrative becomes vivid at this point: "Look at this! A messenger is touching him!" (v. 5b, AT). Let's not call him an "angel" (ESV) yet. The word is exactly the same as in verse 2.[13] Another messenger!

A Messenger with a Different Perspective (vv. 5c, 6)

This messenger said to him, "Arise and eat" (v. 5c). If Elijah had lain down to die, this messenger (unlike the earlier one) had other ideas. Elijah was to get up and be refreshed and strengthened with food.

"And he looked, and behold, there was at his head a cake baked on hot stones and a jar of water" (v. 6a). It was like the miracles at the brook Cherith and in Zarephath again (17:6, 15). "And he ate and drank," but then he "lay down again" (v. 6b). He was still ready to die. The messenger's first intervention had not penetrated Elijah's despair.

The Messenger (Again) with a Plan (v. 7)

The messenger did not give up. Now we are told (as we may have guessed) whose messenger this was.

> And the angel [messenger] of the LORD came again a second time and touched him and said, "Arise and eat, for the journey is too great for you." (v. 7)

There is a journey ahead. You will not make it on an empty stomach, Elijah. "Too great for you" has the word Elijah had used in his despairing prayer ("enough," v. 4). It is as though the messenger was saying, *The journey ahead is too much for you, just as the disappointment you have suffered is too much for you. You need strength beyond yourself. Arise and eat.* Perhaps strength for the journey would lead to strength to carry on through the disappointment.

What a Journey! (v. 8)

> And he arose and ate and drank, and went in the strength of that food forty days and forty nights to Horeb, the mount of God. (v. 8)

This is a surprising journey. "Horeb, the mount of God" is Mount Sinai (see Exodus 3:1), where the people of Israel were constituted as a holy nation, God's own people (see Exodus 19:4–6). What could Elijah's journey, another 200 miles south to Horeb,[14] mean?

Some think that this was "a journey of his own devising,"[15] just as the trek to Beersheba appears to have been. However, the echoes here of the command in verse 7 suggest that just as he "arose" and "ate" in obedience to that command, so the trek to Horeb ("in the strength of that food") corresponded to the "journey" anticipated by the messenger.[16] More than that, the "forty days and forty nights" clearly remind us of Moses at Mount Horeb (see Exodus 24:18; 34:28; Deuteronomy 9:9, 11, 18, 25; 10:10) as well as the forty years it took the Israelites under Moses to journey *from* Mount Horeb to the promised land (Numbers 14:34; 32:13; Deuteronomy 1:3). Elijah's journey to Horeb was deeply significant.[17] He was still, in some sense, reliving Moses' experience.

Elijah at Horeb, the Mount of God (vv. 9–18)

In the Cave (v. 9a)

When he reached Mount Horeb, "he came to a [the] cave and lodged in it" (v. 9a). *The* cave suggests a well-known cave, almost certainly (in my opinion) the "cleft of the rock" in which Moses had once stood (Exodus 33:22).[18]

The Lord's Question (v. 9b, c)

The excitement of the narrative grows. "And look! The word of the LORD is coming to him!" (v. 9b, AT). The word of the Lord that had sent him to Ahab (18:1) came to him here, a long way from Ahab. "God asked him, 'What are you doing here, Elijah?'" (v. 9c).

The question is tantalizingly ambiguous. Where is the emphasis? Is it a rebuke: "What are you doing *here*, Elijah?"—implying that he ought not to be here, he should be somewhere else?[19] That is possible. The Lord had not told Elijah to leave Israel. Why was he *here*? Or is it, "What are *you* doing here, Elijah?"—that is, "What are you here *for*, Elijah?"[20] That, too, is possible. What did Elijah think would happen at Mount Horeb? What was he hoping for?

The trouble with both these understandings of the question is that while Elijah may have headed south to Beersheba on his own initiative, we have been given the impression that the journey from Beersheba to Horeb was, at least implicitly, instigated by the Lord's messenger. The question that *the narrative* has raised is, why has the Lord brought Elijah to Horeb?

The word of the Lord is therefore perplexing, as it must have been to Elijah. I can imagine him replying, *Well, Lord, I was about to ask you the same question. What am I doing here?*

How Elijah Saw Things (v. 10)

Elijah's actual response in verse 10 does not answer the question asked (at least not directly), but puts into words his perspective on the situation in which he found himself.

First he said, "I have been very jealous for the LORD, the God of hosts"[21] (v. 10a). Indeed he had. Particularly since he had met with King Ahab (18:17–19) and then through everything that happened on Mount Carmel (18:20–46), Elijah had been "very jealous" for the Lord. The Hebrew has a very intense form of an intense word. To be "jealous" is the quality of God himself that was the basis for the prohibition of idols in Israel:

> You shall not make for yourself a carved image, or any likeness of anything that is in heaven above, or that is in the earth beneath, or that is in the water under the earth. You shall not bow down to them or serve them, *for I the LORD your God am a jealous God* . . . (Exodus 20:4, 5)

Elijah had stood with the Lord in his jealousy against the idolatry of the people of Israel.[22]

Second, he needed to be like this because "the people of Israel have forsaken your covenant" (v. 10b). This is what Elijah had told Ahab: "you have abandoned [forsaken] the commandments of the LORD and followed the Baals" (18:18). Elijah mentioned two expressions of the people's apostasy. They have "thrown down your altars [see 18:30] and killed your prophets with the sword [see 18:4, 13]" (v. 10c).

This, of course, was the situation that Elijah had hoped the impressive events on Mount Carmel would change. Indeed, for a moment it had looked as though the nation had come to its senses (18:39). But in the end Jezebel prevailed. Idolatry had won. So it seemed to Elijah.

Third, as far as Elijah could see, the purposes of the Lord for his people Israel hung by a thin thread indeed. "I, even I only, am left, and they seek my life, to take it away" (v. 10d).

Again while it is not our task to diagnose Elijah's mental and emotional state, we must consider what his response to the Lord's question meant. Again our difficulty no doubt reflects Elijah's own confusion. I am sure that he did not know with any clarity why he was at Mount Horeb. I doubt that he had definite expectations about what could possibly happen.

Some are surprisingly judgmental toward Elijah. "Elijah has overvalued his own significance."[23] "Elijah thus paints a picture at considerable variance with what seems to be the actual situation. . . . We know, however, that the circumstances are not as Elijah portrays them."[24] "Elijah's memory is selective indeed."[25] "Elijah thus betrays his own cynicism about the people's integrity and reveals that his reasons for despair and for renouncing his prophetic office are precipitate and potentially baseless."[26]

All this is far too harsh. We might agree that his words are not exactly a balanced and complete statement. But they are an honest description of the circumstances that had led to his being here at Horeb, as Elijah saw them.

Particularly poignant are his last words: "I, even I only, am left, and they seek my life, to take it away." We might wonder how he could overlook the 100 prophets hiding in another cave (or caves) back in Israel (18:4, 13; cf. 18:22). For some reason they didn't count. Did he really think that the change in the people on Mount Carmel (18:39) had come to nothing? Apparently so.

However, Elijah's lonely cry to the Lord on Mount Horeb suggests something far more profound. I am not sure whether this was in Elijah's mind (although I suspect it may have been), but it should be in our mind as we read this account thoughtfully. Elijah was standing where Moses had stood (probably, as we have seen, in the very cave or cleft that had once hidden Moses, Exodus 33:22). The idolatrous apostasy of the people of Israel that so distressed Elijah was history repeating itself. When Moses had hidden in this very cave, the people made and worshipped Aaron's golden calf (Exodus 32:1–6). The idolatry of Israel in Elijah's day had begun years earlier with Jeroboam's shocking rerun of the golden calf (or bull) episode (1 Kings 12:25–33).

In this setting, then, Elijah's words to the Lord sound like: *Here we are again! After all these years the people of Israel have returned to the idolatrous rebellion of Moses' day. I find myself reliving Moses' experience rather more fully than I like!*

What did Elijah think might happen? *What are you doing here, Elijah?* In

Moses' day one possibility had been that the Lord would start all over again. Indeed, the Lord had said to Moses:

> Now therefore let me alone, that my wrath may burn hot against them and I may consume them, in order that I may *make a great nation of you* ["you" singular, meaning Moses himself]. (Exodus 32:10)

That was an extraordinary moment. Would the Lord destroy Israel and begin all over again with the promise he had once made to Abraham ("I will make of you a great nation," Genesis 12:2) reapplied now to Moses?

In Elijah's day, when (as he saw it) he was the only truly faithful follower of Yahweh left (like Moses), one possibility may have been that the Lord would start all over again. Might the Lord now destroy Israel and begin all over again with Elijah?

On the earlier occasion Moses had prayed for the people, and the Lord had relented (Exodus 32:11–14). The people of Israel survived. But it has now happened *again*. Isn't it time for the nation of Israel experiment that began at this mountain so long ago to be abandoned? Isn't it time to begin again with the only faithful one left?

Whether Elijah was consciously thinking along these lines (and I think he may have been) or not, his "I, even I only, am left" on Mount Horeb suggests this possibility to anyone who remembers the experience of Moses. Isn't it time for a Plan B?

The Lord's Command (v. 11a)

The Lord's response to Elijah heightens the tension. "And he said, 'Go out and stand on the mount before the LORD'" (v. 11a). The Lord had said something similar to Moses (Exodus 33:21). Did this mean that Elijah was indeed about to experience the new beginning, a new revelation to replace the old revelation at Mount Sinai in Moses' day? Was this the beginning of Plan B (and therefore the end of Plan A)?

What Did and What Did Not Happen (vv. 11b, 12)

Before Elijah managed to obey the Lord's command (he was still in the cave, see v. 13), a spectacle unfolded that brings us to the climax of this chapter.

> And behold, the LORD passed by,[27] and a great and strong wind tore the mountains and broke in pieces the rocks before the LORD, but the LORD was not in the wind. And after the wind an earthquake, but the LORD was not in the earthquake. And after the earthquake a fire, but the LORD was

not in the fire. And after the fire the sound of a low whisper [thin silence].
(vv. 11b, 12)

The striking present tense we have heard a number of times in this story is
here again. "Look! The LORD is passing by, and a great and strong wind is tearing . . ." But what exactly happened? Just as importantly, what did *not* happen?

On the one hand "the LORD passed by." This reminds us once again of
Moses' experience here on this mountain (Exodus 33:22; 34:6) and builds our
expectation that perhaps Elijah *was* about to experience something new that
would match and supersede the old Sinai revelation.

What followed initially fuels that expectation. The mighty wind, earthquake, and fire remind us yet again of Moses' experiences at Mount Sinai/
Horeb (see Exodus 3:2; 19:16–18). Surely this impressive display of power
is the prelude to the fresh start we are expecting, just as the similar display of
power in Exodus 19:16–20 introduced the foundational words that all Israel
heard at Horeb so long ago (Exodus 20:1–21; cf. Deuteronomy 4:9–14). Is
this Plan B?

No, it is not. Three times we are told emphatically, "but the LORD was *not*
in" the wind, the earthquake, or the fire. What exactly does that mean? It is
the narrator's comment, and we may regard it as a reflection after the event.
"The LORD was not in" the powerful phenomena in the sense that they did not
turn out to be like the original Mount Sinai experience. They were not a new
revelation, a new beginning.

As the wind, earthquake, and fire faded away there was "a sound of thin
silence." Silence. The finest silence. That was all you could hear.

Before we reflect on this utter silence that now confronted Elijah, perhaps
I should say a word about the traditional and well-known rendering of the last
phrase of verse 12. The Authorized Version's "a still small voice"[28] has found
a place in some forms of Christian piety, where the believer listens for the
"still small voice" of God. This kind of mysticism, where the voice of God is
sought inside our heads, can lead people to think that ideas that come into our
minds are the voice of God. This, to say the least, is unhelpful and sometimes
dangerous.[29] Importantly that is not what 1 Kings 19:12 says.[30]

The silence was profound. There was not going to be a new beginning, a
fresh revelation, a Plan B to supersede the word of the Lord given in the days
of Moses. It was as though the silence—no new word of the Lord—underlined
that the Lord was not in the wind, earthquake, and fire. Not this time. The Lord
may have "passed by," but he had nothing to add to the foundational revelation
he had given to Moses.

Still in the Cave (v. 13a)

> And when Elijah heard it, he wrapped his face in his cloak and went out and stood at the entrance of the cave. (v. 13a)

Paradoxically he "heard" the sound of the silence. We now learn that Elijah had not yet obeyed the command of verse 11. But in the absolute silence following the wind, earthquake, and fire he wrapped his cloak about his face (perhaps thinking of how the Lord had covered Moses in this very cave, Exodus 33:22) and went out but not right out. He stood at the cave entrance.[31]

The Lord's Question (v. 13b)

The next sentence begins: "Look! A voice[32] coming to him!" (AT). At last! Will we *now* hear the Lord's new word?

We are astonished—as Elijah must have been—when we hear the voice. It said, "What are you doing here, Elijah?" (v. 13b), the same question—exactly the same question—as earlier (v. 9).

The implication seems to be that what had happened since the question was first asked should help Elijah understand the question better this time. *Now that the Lord has passed by, but has not brought a new revelation to replace what was given to Moses, what are you doing here, Elijah?*

How Elijah Saw Things (v. 14)

Listen to Elijah's response:

> He said, "I have been very jealous for the LORD, the God of hosts. For the people of Israel have forsaken your covenant, thrown down your altars, and killed your prophets with the sword, and I, even I only, am left, and they seek my life, to take it away." (v. 14)

Elijah's response was exactly the same as previously (v. 10), word for word. At one level this makes sense. The dramatic display of power on Mount Horeb had not changed anything. The Lord was not in the wind, earthquake, and fire. There was no new beginning. Elijah seems to have understood that. Since nothing had changed, he saw things just as he'd seen them before.

The Lord's Command (vv. 15, 16)

At another level Elijah's response fails to grasp the deeper significance of the sound of thin silence. If there was to be no Plan B, which as we have seen was a real possibility in the light of Moses' experience (and as we have imagined Elijah may have hoped), that means that Plan A stands. That is, what the Lord began at Mount Sinai/Horeb in the days of Moses, he will bring to completion. Elijah may have (with good reason) given up on the people of Israel, but the Lord had not. As Samuel had put it generations earlier, "For the LORD *will not forsake his people*, for his great name's sake, because it has pleased the LORD to make you a people for himself" (1 Samuel 12:22).

The people of Israel had a future, and therefore Elijah had work to do.

> And the LORD said to him, "Go, return on your way to the wilderness of Damascus.[33] And when you arrive, you shall anoint Hazael to be king over Syria [Aram[34]]. And Jehu the son of Nimshi you shall anoint to be king over Israel, and Elisha the son of Shaphat of Abel-meholah you shall anoint to be prophet in your place." (vv. 15, 16)

In other words, "*Go back* to the conflict, *go back* to the trouble, *go back* to the risk."[35]

The first puzzle about this series of commands is that they were not carried out by Elijah, and in a strictly literal sense they were not carried out at all. Elijah did (as we will see shortly) call Elisha to join him, and Elisha will eventually take Elijah's place. But Elijah did not "anoint" Elisha. Eventually Jehu will be anointed to be king over Israel, but not by Elijah. This task will be performed by a servant of Elisha after Elijah's departure from this world (2 Kings 9:6). Hazael will become king of Aram, but it will be by a prophetic word, not by an anointing. Again the prophet will not be Elijah, but Elisha (2 Kings 8:13).

It seems that what the Lord said to Elijah in verses 15, 16 was an outline of key elements of the future prophetic task rather than specific commands for Elijah himself to perform immediately. In this context the word "anoint" should also probably not be pressed literally but taken to mean something like "appoint."[36] In due course, the appointment of Elisha, Hazael, and Jehu to their respective roles, with prophetic endorsement, will be very significant for Israel's future. Indeed the name of the prophet-to-be means "My God Saves."

Notice the international dimension signaled in verse 15. The Lord who remains committed to his purpose for Israel is the Lord of all the earth, and he will send his prophets beyond Israel to accomplish his purpose.

The Lord's Promise (vv. 17, 18)

To his command the Lord added a promise:

> And the one who escapes from the sword of Hazael shall Jehu put to death, and the one who escapes from the sword of Jehu shall Elisha put to

death. Yet I will leave seven thousand in Israel, all the knees that have not
bowed to Baal, and every mouth that has not kissed him. (vv. 17, 18)

There were two promises here. The first was that Hazael, Jehu, and Elisha
will bring judgment on Israel. Verse 17 is again an outline sketch of the shape
of the future rather than a series of literal predictions. As it will turn out Elisha
will not put anyone to death. Hazael will brutally fight against Ahab's son
Joram and his ally Ahaziah of Judah (see 2 Kings 8:12, 28, 29). The outcome
of that will be Jehu's rise in Israel and then the slaughter of Ahab's family
(2 Kings 9, 10). This is not the place to dwell on the details of this future, but
to note that Elijah had been mistaken if he thought that the idolatry of Jezebel
had the last word in Israel.

The second promise is brilliant. Elijah had (perhaps understandably) come
to believe that he was the only faithful servant of the Lord left in Israel. This
was how it seemed as Jezebel reimposed her ferocious supremacy. He was
wrong. Within idolatrous, faithless Israel, the Lord was keeping 7,000[37] who
had never bowed to Baal. Here is the concept of a remnant that will play an
important role in the rest of the Old (and New) Testament story.[38] Reflecting
on these very words, the Apostle Paul will later say, "So too at the present time
there is a remnant, chosen by grace" (Romans 11:5), meaning those Israelites
who trust in Christ Jesus. "Not all who are descended from Israel belong to
Israel" (Romans 9:6). Within national, ethnic Israel there are those who are
the true Israel.

These two promises confirm the unstated but implied message of Elijah's
experience on Mount Horeb. The Lord will not begin again. There will not be
a new foundation. The Lord will deal with the idolatry of Israel, particularly
the house of Ahab, and he will accomplish his purposes through the "remnant,
chosen by grace."

What Happened (vv. 19–21)

We are told nothing about Elijah's thoughts or feelings at this utterly unexpected outcome from his time at Horeb. Our writer is much less interested than
some in Elijah's inner life. He moves quickly to tell us how the future outlined
in the Lord's words began to take shape.

Elijah Found Elisha (v. 19)

> So [Elijah] departed from there and found Elisha the son of Shaphat, who
> was plowing with twelve yoke of oxen in front of him, and he was with the
> twelfth. Elijah passed by him and cast his cloak upon him. (v. 19)

Verse 16 indicated that Elisha's home was in Abel-meholah, located in the Jordan Valley within Ahab's kingdom of Israel.[39] Elijah's journey back north to Ahab's (and Jezebel's!) jurisdiction is passed over in two Hebrew words ("he-departed from-there"). Interest is entirely focused on his encounter with a farm boy in the Jordan Valley.

Our introduction to Elisha has indicated where he lived and his family (we know no more about his father, Shaphat, although the fame of his son rubbed off; see 2 Kings 3:11; 6:31). Now we see him plowing with twelve yoke of oxen; it seems that he belonged to a rather well-to-do farm family.[40]

The cloak that had covered Elijah's face as he encountered the Lord on Mount Horeb was now thrown onto the unsuspecting farm boy. No word was spoken, and Elijah kept walking. This cloak ("a garment of hair") was part of Elijah's well-known and distinctive attire (see 2 Kings 1:8). It will play an important role in due course when Elisha takes Elijah's place (see 2 Kings 2:8, 13, 14). Here, we might say, the story of Elijah's succession begins.

Elisha Left Everything and Followed Him (vv. 20, 21)

Surprisingly Elisha knew what Elijah's enigmatic action meant. Perhaps he recognized that cloak.

> And he left the oxen and ran after Elijah and said, "Let me kiss my father and my mother, and then I will follow you." And he said to him, "Go back again, for what have I done to you?" (v. 20)

Elisha's willingness, even eagerness, to follow Elijah is remarkable. The request to kiss his parents good-bye emphasizes rather than undermines his readiness to leave his home for who knows what.

The mention of kissing, in this innocent context, may remind us of the recent mention of "every mouth that has *not* kissed [Baal]" (19:18).[41] This farm boy was among the faithful remnant that the Lord was keeping in Israel.

Elijah's response (like so much in this story) is enigmatic. He gave permission for Elisha to return. His reason for doing so draws attention to "what have I done to you?" The sense is probably, *Do not forget what I have just done, the significance of which you have indeed grasped.*

When a similar situation arose in the life of Jesus, it was clear that the importance, priority, and urgency of following Jesus was even greater than Elijah's call to Elisha (see Luke 9:57–62).

> And [Elisha] returned from following him and took the yoke of oxen and sacrificed[42] them and boiled their flesh with the yokes of the oxen and gave

it to the people, and they ate. Then he arose and went after Elijah and assisted him. (v. 21)

Elisha's farewell was a decisive break with his past. The tools of his old trade were burnt or eaten. This was a memorable symbolic farewell shared with the people (of his community, I presume).

The last word of the chapter holds the seeds of the future. The echoes of Moses' experience that we have heard throughout this chapter suggest that Elisha was Elijah's Joshua. As Joshua was Moses' "assistant," who succeeded him (Joshua 1:1), so Elisha assisted Elijah and will in due course take his place.

I asked at the beginning of this chapter what people disappointed, even disillusioned, by the apparent failure of God's purposes in their day need to hear. The answer is the sound of thin silence. That is, we do not need to hear anything new. The God of Abraham, Moses, David, Elijah, and Jesus has *one* plan, and he will never give up on it. Never! There is no Plan B. Our disappointment and disillusionment ("We *had* hoped . . .") arise because of our inadequate understanding of God's plan, our small vision of God's ways. Like the disciples on the Emmaus road, we need to learn that what has disappointed us is included in God's Plan A. Like Elijah we need to see that there is work to do because the promises of God are as sure as ever.

Listen to the Apostle Paul responding to the deep disappointment of so many Jewish people rejecting Jesus Christ. His mind turned to Elijah at Mount Horeb.

> I ask, then, has God rejected his people? By no means! For I myself am an Israelite, a descendant of Abraham, a member of the tribe of Benjamin. God has not rejected his people whom he foreknew. Do you not know what the Scripture says of Elijah, how he appeals to God against Israel? "Lord, they have killed your prophets, they have demolished your altars, and I alone am left, and they seek my life." But what is God's reply to him? "I have kept for myself seven thousand men who have not bowed the knee to Baal." So too at the present time there is a remnant, chosen by grace. But if it is by grace, it is no longer on the basis of works; otherwise grace would no longer be grace. (Romans 11:1–6)

That is Plan A.

Part 8

THE FAILURE OF POLITICAL POWER

1 Kings 20—22

42

King Ahab Did Not
Destroy the Enemy

1 KINGS 20

THE FIRST ELEVEN CHAPTERS of 1 Kings presented the reign of the son of David, King Solomon. We saw the wisdom, peace, prosperity, goodness, and international fame of Solomon's kingdom. "Judah and Israel were as many as the sand by the sea. They ate and drank and were happy." "And people of all nations came to hear the wisdom of Solomon, and from all the kings of the earth, who heard of his wisdom." The Queen of Sheba was right when she said to Solomon, "Blessed be the LORD your God, who has delighted in you and set you on the throne of Israel! Because the LORD loved Israel forever, he has made you king, that you may execute justice and righteousness" (4:20, 34; 10:9). Solomon was the king God had promised. Solomon's kingdom was the kingdom of God, at the center of which was the house Solomon built in Jerusalem. The Lord had said, "My name shall be there" (8:29).

We also saw how King Solomon failed. He was, in the end, but a shadow of the good things to come. His greatness and goodness anticipated another son of David, in whom "something greater than Solomon is here" (Matthew 12:42).

The last six chapters of 1 Kings (to be precise, 16:29—22:40) present the reign of the son of Omri, King Ahab. More space is given to Ahab's reign than any other king since Solomon. He was the worst king Israel (or Judah for that matter) had suffered so far (16:30). As such he represents the antithesis of God's promised king—human political power exercised in disregard and defiance of the God who is really there.

The climactic event of Ahab's reign (from the perspective of the Biblical account) was the extraordinary showdown on Mount Carmel (18:20–46). We may fairly compare this occasion with the climactic moment of King Solomon's reign, the great assembly in Jerusalem when the house of the Lord had been built and King Solomon proclaimed, "Blessed be the LORD who has given rest to his people Israel, according to all that he promised. Not one word has failed of all his good promise, which he spoke by Moses his servant" (8:56). On Mount Carmel the Lord had turned back the hearts of "all the people" (including Ahab, we have presumed). "The LORD, he is God; the LORD, he is God," they cried (18:39).

However, the human capacity to suppress the truth and pursue ungodliness and unrighteousness is breathtaking (Romans 1:18). King Ahab's "conversion" was short-lived. His pagan wife Jezebel prevailed over any feeble inclination Ahab may have had to change his ways and his kingdom (19:1, 2). The victory of the Baal-loving Jezebel had seemed to Elijah to be the end for Israel as the people of the living God (19:10, 14). It took a strange journey, and an even stranger experience at Mount Horeb, for Elijah to learn that he was wrong (19:9–18). The Lord had not abandoned his purpose for his people. There was to be no Plan B. The Lord would deal with the wickedness that distressed Elijah (19:17). Furthermore the Lord would preserve "seven thousand in Israel, all the knees that have not bowed to Baal, and every mouth that has not kissed him" (19:18). The original promise of God would be carried by this remnant.

In the meantime Ahab was still king over the northern kingdom of Israel, and the final chapters of 1 Kings focus on the inadequacy of such a king. The account of King Solomon's reign provided a portrait of God's promised king, pointing us to the hope of the world. The closing chapters of this book present the failure of God-denying human political power. It cannot be the hope of the world.

The presentation will unfold in six snapshots from King Ahab's last three years or so (22:1). These will occupy the remaining six chapters of this commentary. Each will remind us of the greater King Solomon and of the One even greater than Solomon. Here is a bird's-eye view of the landscape we will traverse:

Chapter 42: King Ahab Did Not Destroy the Enemy (20)
Chapter 43: King Ahab Did Not Put Things Right (21)
Chapter 44: King Ahab Hated the Truth (22:1–14)
Chapter 45: King Ahab Did Not Have a Listening Heart (22:15–28)

The first of these episodes takes us to a time about three or four years before the end of Ahab's twenty-two year reign (16:29; 22:1). It is possible (since we hear nothing of Elijah in chapter 20, and he reappears in chapter 21) that some or all of the events of 1 Kings 20 took place during Elijah's absence from Israel (chapter 19). It is a story about a powerful enemy in which we will see:

(1) A powerful, menacing enemy (vv. 1–12)
(2) A surprising, astonishing promise (vv. 13, 14)
(3) An unexpected, comprehensive victory (vv. 15–21)
(4) Different reactions (vv. 22–25)
(5) The powerful, menacing enemy (again) (vv. 26, 27)
(6) Another surprising, astonishing promise (v. 28)
(7) Another unexpected, comprehensive victory (vv. 29, 30)
(8) Different reactions (vv. 31–34)
(9) The word of the Lord that puts the politics in perspective (vv. 35–43)

A Powerful, Menacing Enemy (vv. 1–12)

The enemy's name was Ben-hadad. He was the king of Aram (ESV, "Syria" (v. 1). We may safely assume he was not the same Ben-hadad, king of Aram we met in 15:18. That was more than fifty years earlier (see 15:33; 16:8, 23, 29). Perhaps this Ben-hadad was his son.[1] However, *another* Ben-hadad does remind us of that earlier episode and the unfriendly relations between Aram and Israel that had probably continued through the reigns of Omri and Ahab.

Meet Ben-Hadad II (v. 1)

Ben-hadad the king of Syria [Aram[2]] gathered all his army together. Thirty-two kings were with him, and horses and chariots. And he went up and closed in on Samaria and fought against it. (v. 1)

The sudden introduction of this "Ben-hadad the king of Aram" marks a new episode. A few lines earlier we heard that someone called Hazael was to become king of Aram (19:15), something of which we can be quite sure Ben-hadad was blissfully ignorant. But it does help the reader to know from the outset that Ben-hadad was not as almighty as he imagined.[3]

We are taken from the Shaphat farm in the Jordan Valley (19:19–21) to the malevolent maneuvering of the king of Aram against the royal capital of King Ahab. Ben-hadad had gathered his forces ("*all* his army"), along with a very considerable coalition of "thirty-two kings." No doubt "kings" is a rather grand title for what were rulers of cities and their immediate surrounding territories.[4] They were vassals of the more powerful King Ben-hadad and would have been obliged to support him militarily in his foreign excursions.

The "horses and chariots" indicate a well-equipped and formidable fighting force. There is some bitter irony in the memory that it was King Solomon who had facilitated the arms trade that, at an earlier time, had supplied horses and chariots to the kings of Aram (10:29). There were some blind spots in Solomon's wisdom.[5]

It is not clear how close the forces under Ben-hadad came to the city of Samaria at this stage. The expression translated "closed in on" is elsewhere rendered "lay siege to" or "besieged" (15:27; 16:17; also 1 Samuel 23:8; 2 Samuel 11:1; 20:15), but here we do not seem to have a full-on siege. Furthermore "fought against it" may have been more sabre rattling than actual violence at this stage, although it may have involved some preemptory displays of aggressive intentions. Whatever the specifics may have been, Ben-hadad's presence on Israelite soil was extremely menacing. It was meant to be.

Who Said What to Whom (vv. 2–11)

The real hostilities began with words rather than blows. Steadily the tension escalated. This was clearly Ben-hadad's purpose. He was determined to humiliate and subjugate his neighbor.

Ben-hadad's Opening Insult (vv. 2, 3)

The first shot in the war of words was fired by the king of Aram.

> And he sent messengers into the city to Ahab king of Israel and said to him, "Thus says Ben-hadad: 'Your silver and your gold are mine; your best wives [or women] and children also are mine.'" (vv. 2, 3)

Ben-hadad had the upper hand—or at least felt that he did. "Thus says Ben-hadad" (or "Thus Ben-hadad has said"[6]) sounds weighty. *Listen up! Here is a royal decree from the mighty King Ben-hadad!*

The pronouncement was not (yet) a demand for silver, gold, women, and children to be actually handed over to the foreign king. It was a declaration of Ahab's vassal status. It was an insult to an independent king, as Ahab had been until now. It was a demand that the Israelite king acknowledge the rights of Ben-hadad as his overlord: the king of Aram *owned* Ahab and all that was dear to him. The threat posed by the amassed forces under Ben-hadad's command, already within Ahab's kingdom, was no doubt a powerful incentive for Ahab to agree.

Ahab's Meek Compliance (v. 4)

Ahab was intimidated. He could see that the Aramean forces were poised to overrun his kingdom. If he could negotiate peaceful terms now, no matter how humiliating, perhaps he and his kingdom could be spared much loss and bloodshed. "And the king of Israel answered, 'As you say, my lord, O king, I am yours, and all that I have'" (v. 4).

He complied. "My lord" is obsequious. "O king" is fawning. "I am yours, and all that I have" is servile. Ahab was groveling.

Ben-hadad's First Threat (vv. 5, 6)

Ben-hadad was a bully. He had no intention of allowing a small humiliation to satisfy his egomania.

> The messengers came again and said, "Thus says Ben-hadad: '[7]I sent to you, saying, "Deliver to me your silver and your gold, your wives [or women] and your children." Nevertheless [Surely[8]] I will send my servants to you tomorrow about this time, and they shall search your house and the houses of your servants and lay hands on whatever pleases you and take it away.'" (vv. 5, 6)

Listen up again! Here is a further royal decree from the mighty King Ben-hadad! He now insisted (falsely) that his original message had demanded the *handing over* of Ahab's silver, gold, women, and children. *I am not interested in your mealymouthed words, Ahab. Give me all that you say is mine.*

A normal vassal relationship, which Ahab may have thought he was entering by his initial response, could have expected the more powerful party to demand the payment of tribute from what was now, theoretically, all his. Such demands could be harsh. But Ben-hadad wanted to strip Ahab and Israel bare. In order to do this he would send his "servants" (no doubt well-armed and numerous soldiers) to loot Ahab's palace and perhaps the whole city. *Everything you value, Ahab, they will take away. It will happen tomorrow!*

Ahab's Nervous Consultation (vv. 7, 8)

This was getting serious. We have seen enough of Ahab to know that he was not a strong man in any sense. He had very quickly given in to Jezebel and her promotion of Baal worship in Israel (16:31). He had allowed her a free hand in the deadly persecution of the Lord's prophets (18:4, 13). When she was unmoved by the spectacle on Mount Carmel (unmoved for the better, that is), he did not restrain her as she threatened the life of the prophet Elijah (19:2), whose prayers (as Ahab well knew) had brought the rains that broke the drought (18:42, 44). If Ahab did not have the backbone to stand up to Jezebel, how do you think he will go against the bully king, Ben-hadad?

He needed help.[9]

> Then the king of Israel called all the elders of the land and said, "Mark, now,[10] and see how this man is seeking trouble, for he sent to me for my wives [or women] and my children, and for my silver and my gold, and I did not refuse him." And all the elders and all the people said to him, "Do not listen or [literally, and do not] consent." (vv. 7, 8)

"All the elders of the land" suggests a wider consultative body than the city of Samaria and that at this stage movement in and out of the city was still possible. Ahab shared his assessment of Ben-hadad with them: "This man is seeking trouble [literally, evil]." He then summarized his initial exchange with the hostile king: "I did not refuse him."

We are not told what the elders thought of that. Perhaps they were diplomatic enough to keep their thoughts to themselves. But they did not hesitate to insist that Ahab go no further in his bowing to the will of Bully Ben-hadad. "Do not listen and do *not* consent." In Hebrew the second "not" is stronger than the first. *Do not listen to him, and whatever you do, do not give in to him!*

Ahab's Polite Reply (v. 9)

What does a weak king do when he is terrified of an aggressor and under extreme pressure from those around him not to give in? Ahab seems to have tried to please everyone. That was his way. He did not consent to Ben-hadad's most recent announcement. The elders were probably in the room as he spoke to Ben-hadad's messengers. But he was ever so polite to the man who was seeking evil.

> So he said to the messengers of Ben-hadad, "Tell my lord the king, 'All that you first demanded of your servant I will do, but this thing I cannot do.'" (v. 9a)

He was groveling again: "My lord the king." He reaffirmed his earlier acceptance of vassal status. Again I am not sure what the elders thought of that. But he did not dare to say, "I *will* not." He feebly said, "But this thing [the latest demand] I *cannot* do." Perhaps the implication was, *The people won't let me!* Poor Ahab. He would if he could, but he just can't.

"And the messengers departed and brought him [that is, Ben-hadad] word again" (v. 9b). They reported back to the Boss.

Ben-hadad's Second Threat (v. 10)

I doubt that Ben-hadad was surprised. His utterly unreasonable demand had been calculated to be impossible for Ahab to accept. It provided him the perfect pretext to do what he had planned to do all along.

> Ben-hadad sent to him and said, "The gods do so to me and more also, if the dust of Samaria shall suffice for handfuls for all the people who follow me." (v. 10)

Ben-hadad's oath ("The gods do so to me and more also") is very close to a word-for-word echo of Jezebel's ferocious pagan curse in 19:2. Ben-hadad's threat to Ahab and Israel sounds very much like Jezebel's threat to Elijah. Ahab's performance on the former occasion does not fill us with hope that he will stand against Ben-hadad.

The threat itself is extreme, emphasizing on the one hand that Ben-hadad will reduce Samaria to a few handfuls of dust. On the other hand, "all the people who follow me" are so numerous that there will not be enough dust for each to take a handful. *I am going to pulverize Samaria, Ahab!*

Ahab's Cheek (v. 11)

Ahab had the last word in this war of words. Like a weakling shoved and pushed by a bully until at last he feebly lashes out, Ahab sent a defiant answer to Ben-hadad: "Tell him, 'Let not him who straps on his armor boast himself as he who takes it off'" (v. 11). In Hebrew this was just four punchy words: *Don't-let one-who-buckles-up brag like-one-who-loosens.* If we took him seriously, he would be suggesting that Ben-hadad did not know what he was up against. It is easy to crow about what you are *going* to do. Let's see who is bragging at the *end* of the day.

But it is difficult to take Ahab seriously. His outburst sounds pitiful. Can there really be any doubt who will be boasting after Ben-hadad has done his worst?[11]

Ben-hadad Was Not Joking (v. 12)

> When Ben-hadad heard this message as he was drinking with the kings in the booths, he said to his men, "Take your positions." And they took their positions against the city. (v. 12)

Take in the scene. The Bully King was lounging about with his subordinate "kings." "Booths" were the temporary field shelters for an army, made of branches and twigs (cf. exactly the same expression in 2 Samuel 11:11).[12] These particular booths were the senior officers' mess. The booze was flowing freely. The mood was upbeat. I imagine jokes about Ahab, Samaria, and the pulverizing defeat these kings were soon to inflict, with much backslapping and bold, raucous, well-lubricated hilarity.

In came the messengers. *What does the weakling have to say for himself?* "Well, Your Majesty, he said, 'Let not him who straps on his armor boast himself as he who takes it off.'"

The laughter faded. The bully was done with joking. He ordered his forces to prepare to teach the upstart the lesson of his life—which was, of course, what the bully had intended all along.

A Surprising, Astonishing Promise (vv. 13, 14)

Did anyone, in Ben-hadad's camp or in Samaria or in the whole of Ahab's kingdom, doubt that Ben-hadad would carry out his threat? The next few lines of this story (we sense) are not going to be pretty.

A Promise (v. 13a, b)

But suddenly, without warning, something completely unexpected happened. "But look! A solitary prophet came near to Ahab, king of Israel" (v. 13a, AT).

There had been a lot of prophets in Ahab's kingdom. What kind of prophet was this? Had one of the prophets of Baal survived the executions by the brook Kishon (18:40)? Or was this one of the prophets of Asherah who had been clever enough to stay away from Mount Carmel (18:19)? We do not expect that it would be a prophet of the Lord. Most of them had been wiped out by Jezebel, and, as far as we know, the survivors were hiding in caves (18:4, 13). Elijah was somewhere, but this was not Elijah.[13]

As soon as the unexpected prophet opened his mouth, it was clear whose prophet he was. He said, "Thus says the LORD, Have you seen all this great multitude? Behold, I will give it into your hand this day" (v. 13b).

Here was one of the "seven thousand in Israel" about whom the Lord had spoken to Elijah (19:18). Ahab may not have seen many prophets of the Lord recently, but the Lord had his servants ready to do his bidding.

The scene is subtly reminiscent of Mount Carmel, where Elijah "came near" to all the people (18:21), and the people "came near" to him (18:30). Ahab again saw a prophet of the Lord "come near" to him.

Twice Ahab had heard the chilling words, "Thus says Ben-hadad" (vv. 2, 5). Those words were now neutralized by "Thus says the LORD." *Listen up! Here is a royal decree from the mighty God of Israel!*

Ahab was not used to hearing *good* news from a prophet of the Lord (see 17:1; 18:18; but note 18:41). But this was very good news. It was an astonishing promise. It confirmed that the forces arrayed against Ahab were formidable ("all this great multitude"[14]), but promised that this very day Ahab would be victorious over them.

This development is curious at a number of levels. The obvious point is that the promise was astonishing. On any ordinary reading of the situation Ahab and Samaria had no hope against the amassed forces of Ben-hadad and his thirty-two cobelligerents. However, Bible readers know well that the Lord, the God of Israel, had a reputation for giving his people impossible victories.

The more puzzling question is, why? Thoughtful readers of this history must suspect, by the time we get to verse 12 of this chapter, that Ben-hadad was (unwittingly, of course) bringing the Lord's judgment on the king of Israel and his kingdom. Ahab had failed miserably to complete the repentance that had begun on Mount Carmel. We have seen nothing from him since his initial spark of enthusiasm (18:41, 42, 46) to suggest that he had really changed his ways. Indeed, isn't it striking that Ahab did not seek out a prophet of the Lord, nor did he call on the Lord for help when threatened by Ben-hadad? He looked no further for help and direction than the elders of the land. Ahab had not asked for the Lord's help. So why was help promised?

A Purpose (v. 13c)

The prophet continued, "and you shall know that I am the LORD" (v. 13c). "You" here is singular. This was about Ahab, and this confirms our understanding that even after Mount Carmel this king was not yet soundly "converted." He may have joined the chorus on Carmel—"The LORD, he is God" (18:39). But he did not "know" the reality in any deep and lasting way.

The most astonishing thing about the Lord's promise to Ahab is that the Lord was *still* at work to bring the king to "know" him.

The purpose of the promise affirms (for the reader) the message of Elijah's experience at Horeb. The Lord's plan had not changed. The goal of his redemption of Israel from Egypt in the days of Moses was that Pharaoh, the Egyptians, the Israelites, indeed the whole world would "know that I am the LORD" (see Exodus 6:7; 7:5, 17; 9:16). The Lord had come to Ahab with the same purpose. Plan A was still in play.

A Plan (v. 14)

Ahab's response began well (although we have become used to Ahab responding positively to almost every voice he hears). He understood that the prophet's intervention meant that this would be no ordinary battle. The Commander-in-Chief was now the Lord.

The king therefore (at last!) consulted the prophet for strategy. He asked two key tactical questions.

First, "By whom?" That is, who will be instrumental in this promised victory? Who will take the enemy down? Answer: "By the servants [lads] of the governors of the districts" (v. 14a). This phrase is rather opaque to us, although it is repeated in verses 15, 17, and 19.[15] The "lads" were probably young men with some relatively junior role in Ahab's government.[16] In other words, it was hardly the kind of fighting force that you might expect could deal with an enemy like Ben-hadad.[17]

Second question: "Who shall begin the battle?" (v. 14b). It is not clear exactly what Ahab meant by this question. Perhaps he himself was not sure. More literally he said, "Who shall *tie up* the battle?" which could mean "Who will *finish* the battle?,"[18] "Who shall *open* the battle (that is, *join* battle)?,"[19] "Who will *clinch* the fighting?,"[20] or even "Who will *pull together* the plan of battle?"[21]

Whatever he meant, the answer was simple: "You" (v. 14c). *You have the promise of God, Ahab. Now get to work in believing obedience.*

An Unexpected, Comprehensive Victory (vv. 15–21)

Ahab's Unimpressive Force (v. 15)

> Then he mustered the servants [lads] of the governors of the districts, and they were 232. And after them he mustered all the people of Israel, seven thousand. (v. 15)

Two hundred and thirty-two lads from the public service would hardly fill anyone with confidence. Against the massed forces of Ben-hadad and his mates a couple of hundred boys must have looked absurd. Even when Ahab backed them up with an army from "all the people of Israel," 7,000 was hardly imposing, particularly when we remember that "thousand" can refer to a military unit much less than a thousand in number.[22]

However, unlike Ahab we have read 1 Kings 19 and have heard the words "seven thousand" before. We are reminded of God's promise that he will keep a remnant of "seven thousand" faithful Israelites (19:18). This unimpressive force looks a whole lot more impressive when seen in the light of God's promise.[23]

Forward! (vv. 16–19)

Ahab, apparently fortified by the word of the Lord, made the first move. "And they went out at noon" (v. 16a). That is, the 232 young men followed by the army, all under the command of King Ahab, chose the middle of the day to move out of Samaria to face the enemy. It was hardly a strategically sensible move. There was no cover of darkness. There would be no element of surprise. But this was not an ordinary battle.

Meanwhile,[24] Ben-hadad was fortified by something else. "Ben-hadad was drinking himself drunk in the booths, he and the thirty-two kings who helped him" (v. 16b). They were supremely confident. How could anything possibly go wrong?

Back to Samaria: "The servants [lads] of the governors of the districts went out first" (v. 17a). All 232 of them! Teenagers! Were they carrying sticks? The scene is reminiscent of another "lad" who went out against a very impressive enemy (see 1 Samuel 17:33, 42, 55, 58, where David facing Goliath was referred to with the same word).

As the band of boys were making their way out of the city of Samaria, "Ben-hadad sent out scouts, and they reported to him, 'Men are coming out from Samaria'" (v. 17b). They got that wrong. They were not "men"!

Ben-hadad was a little the worse for wear. The drink had done what drink does. Incoherently he slurred, "If they have come out for peace, take them alive. Or if they have come out for war, take them alive" (v. 18)—whatever that might mean. His drinking buddies were probably in much the same state and were not bothered by the confused command.[25]

Back to Samaria: "So these went out of the city, the servants [lads] of the governors of the districts and the army that followed them" (v. 19).

The Battle (vv. 20, 21)

The battle itself was over in three words:[26] "And-each struck-down his-man" (v. 20a). More details about the fighting are unimportant. The outcome is all that matters. "The Syrians [Arameans] fled, and Israel pursued them" (v. 20b). It was indeed like the David and Goliath battle of old (see 1 Samuel 17:51, 52).

Except for one thing that will turn out to be very important: "but Ben-hadad king of Syria [Aram] escaped on a horse with horsemen" (v. 20c). A portion, at least, of the Aramean mounted cavalry managed to get the king away safely.

Nonetheless King Ahab won an unexpected and comprehensive victory: "And the king of Israel went out and struck the horses and chariots, and struck the Syrians [Arameans] with a great blow" (v. 21). This is a summary of the whole battle, rounding off the story that began with Ben-hadad's "horses and chariots" in verse 1.[27]

Different Reactions (vv. 22–25)

But what should we make of Ben-hadad's escape? It meant that the conflict had not been finally resolved. The bully was still around. In the aftermath of the battle at Samaria both Ahab (v. 22) and Ben-hadad (vv. 23–25) received some advice.

Some Advice for Ahab from the Prophet (v. 22)

The advice for Ahab came from the prophet who had spoken to him earlier.

> Then the prophet came near to the king of Israel and said to him, "Come, strengthen yourself, and consider well what you have to do, for in the spring [at the return of the year] the king of Aram [ESV: "Syria"] will come up against you." (v. 22)

Again the anonymous prophet "came near" to King Ahab (as in v. 13). It was not time to rest. The enemy may have suffered a surprising blow, but Ben-hadad was still a threat. *He will be back.* The Lord's promise in verse 13 had a way to go yet.

"The return of the year" (traditionally understood to mean the spring[28]) is almost certainly a reference to "next year about this time."[29] *Do not imagine that Ben-hadad will accept this humiliation. This time next year he will be back. So pull yourself together and prepare.*

"Consider well what you have to do" is literally "know and see what you will do."[30] From a prophet, this could be understood as an invitation to seek again a word from the Lord about how to engage the enemy next time. Note (for future reference) that Ahab did not take up the invitation.

Some Advice for Ben-hadad from His Servants (vv. 23–25)

Perhaps it was back in Damascus, Ben-hadad's royal city, that the king of Aram also received some advice. The most important thing about this counsel was that it confirmed (we might say, fulfilled) the words of the prophet to Ahab.

It involved an insight from Aramean theology, a proposal for reconstituting the command structure of the army, and a logistical recommendation.

> And [But[31]] the servants of the king of Syria [Aram] said to him, "Their gods are gods of the hills, and so they were stronger than we. But let us

fight against them in the plain, and surely we shall be stronger than they. And do this: remove the kings, each from his post, and put commanders in their places, and muster an army like the army that you have lost, horse for horse, and chariot for chariot. Then we will fight against them in the plain, and surely we shall be stronger than they." (vv. 23–25a)

The theological insight is laughable. They understood, correctly, that their unexpected thrashing had been unnatural. Ahab had divine help. However, their pagan view of the God or "gods"[32] of Israel was too small. They had not read 1 Kings 17! The idea that the God of Israel was somehow more able to help his people in the hills than on the plains is a wonderful example of pagan stupidity.

The proposal to rearrange the army's command suggests that the thirty-two kings were either less competent or less committed than they might be. The new "commanders" would be chosen for their loyalty to Ben-hadad and would be directly under his control.[33]

Regarding logistics, Ben-hadad was advised to set about raising his army to its previous strength.

With the army at full strength again, under a more effective command, they would be ready to engage the feeble forces of Ahab again, but this time where the "gods of the hills" could not help. *We will fight them in the plain.*

"And he listened to their voice and did so" (v. 25b). Ben-hadad seems more responsive to the advice of his servants than Ahab was to the prophet.

The Powerful, Menacing Enemy (Again) (vv. 26, 27)

Twelve months passed, during which Ben-hadad was no doubt busy implementing the recommendations of his advisers. We are not told what Ahab did during this time, but about the same time the next year (just as the prophet had said) Ben-hadad was back.

> In the spring [At the return of the year], Ben-hadad mustered the Syrians [Arameans] and went up to Aphek to fight against Israel. And [But[34]] the people of Israel were mustered and were provisioned and went against them. The people of Israel encamped before them like two little flocks of goats, but the Syrians [Arameans] filled the country [or land]. (vv. 26, 27)

This is another scene to take in carefully. Notice that this time the Arameans chose the ground. They were not going to confront the Israelites again in the hills, where their gods could help them.

For a Bible reader with a sharp memory the mention of Aphek is alarming. The last time we heard of Aphek was when the Philistines gathered there for the battle that would end in King Saul's death (1 Samuel 29:1). Before that it was at Aphek that the Philistines camped before the battle that would end in their capture of the ark of the covenant (1 Samuel 4:1). There appear to be a number of different places called Aphek in the Bible, and this Aphek was probably not the same as the site of those earlier conflicts.[35] However, "Aphek" rouses shocking memories.

Ben-hadad's purpose was clear. He had gathered his forces and advanced to Aphek "to fight against Israel."

In contrast to Ben-hadad's deliberate activity in verse 26, in verse 27 Ahab is not mentioned. He was there (v. 28), but the writer keeps him in the background. He uses passive verbs: the people of Israel "were mustered" and "were provisioned." The subtle suggestion is that while the active player in Aram was Ben-hadad, in Israel there was an unseen Commander. Ahab was less relevant.

However, the appearance of things was worrying. The Israelite forces were "like two little flocks of goats."[36] Perhaps they were gathered on a couple of hillsides overlooking the enemy forces below. They looked (and felt) like two miserable herds of goats, while the mighty army of Arameans seemed to fill the land.

Another Surprising, Astonishing Promise (v. 28)

The appearance of things is never the best guide to the reality of things. To see the truth you need to hear the word of God. Look what happened: "And a [the[37]] man of God came near and said to the king of Israel . . ." (v. 28a). For the third time this prophet "came near" (vv. 13, 22). There has still been no hint of Ahab turning to the prophet for help or guidance. The movement was all one way.

A Reason (v. 28b)

The prophet began: "Thus says the LORD, 'Because the Syrians [Arameans] have said, "The LORD is a god of the hills but he is not a god of the valleys . . ."'" (v. 28b). The lie of the Aramean theology must be answered.

For a second time Ahab heard "Thus says the LORD," just as he had twice heard "Thus says Ben-hadad" (vv. 2, 5).

A Promise (v. 28c)

". . . therefore I will give all this great multitude into your hand" (v. 28c). The promise of verse 13 was stated again and more than matched the threat of Ben-hadad.

A Purpose (v. 28d)

The Lord's purpose had not changed: "and you shall know that I am the LORD" (v. 28d). However, now "you" was plural. It was not just about Ahab. It was for all the people. This suggests that the experience on Mount Carmel had failed to bring deep and lasting change in the people just as it was with Ahab. Yet the Lord was still at work to bring the people to true knowledge of the Lord. Plan A.

Another Unexpected, Comprehensive Victory (vv. 29, 30)

> And they encamped opposite one another seven days. Then on the seventh day the battle was joined. And the people of Israel struck down of the Syrians [Arameans] 100,000 foot soldiers in one day. And the rest fled into the city of Aphek, and the wall fell upon 27,000 men who were left. Ben-hadad also fled and entered an inner chamber in the city.[38] (vv. 29, 30)

There are resonances here of a famous and extraordinary victory in Israel's early days. When Jericho fell, there were seven days before the decisive action on the "seventh day," which involved the collapse of the city wall (Joshua 6:12–21).

The victory was comprehensive—except that, as before, Ben-hadad, the one who had started all this, escaped *again*.

Different Reactions (vv. 31–34)

Just as there was a word of advice to both parties following the battle at Samaria, so there were two reactions to the battle of Aphek.

Revised Advice for Ben-hadad from His Servants (vv. 31, 32a)

This time we hear about the reaction among the surviving Arameans first. Listen to the advice Ben-hadad's servants had for him now.

> And his servants said to him, "Behold now, we have heard that the kings of the house of Israel are merciful kings [literally, kings of kindness]. Let us put sackcloth around our waists and ropes on our heads and go out to the king of Israel. Perhaps he will spare your life." (v. 31)

What happened to the Aramean theology? In place of the assertion that Israel's god(s) only worked in the hills (v. 23), they now remembered that the Israelite kings had a reputation for "kindness." "Kindness" had been a characteristic of God's dealings with Israel (3:6; 8:23, ESV "steadfast love" in both verses) and on occasion had characterized both David and Solomon (2 Samuel

2:6; 9:1, 3, 7; 10:2; 1 Kings 2:7).[39] Had some of these stories spread and been remembered in Aram? It seems so. Having found that the "gods" of the Israelites were just as powerful on the plain as in the hills, the only hope the servants of Ben-hadad could see lay in the reputed kindness of the kings of Israel.

They proposed approaching Ahab with signs of sorrow and penitence for what they had done (the sackcloth) and absolute surrender (the ropes, possibly around their necks). Perhaps the king of Israel would spare Ben-hadad's life. That *would* be kindness!

No response from Ben-hadad is noted. His defeat seems to have silenced the bully. The servants took matters into their own hands.

> So they tied sackcloth around their waists and put ropes on their heads and went to the king of Israel and said, "Your servant Ben-hadad says [has said], 'Please, let me live.'" (v. 32a)

As far as we know, Ben-hadad had said no such thing, but it is what the servants thought he ought to say. We hear no more of the pompous "Thus says Ben-hadad." Now it is "Your *servant* Ben-hadad has said . . ." No longer was he Ahab's "lord" (vv. 4, 9). The bully was begging for his life (according to these messengers). Who was groveling now?

Reaction from Ahab All on His Own (vv. 32b–34)

King Ahab was a slow learner. Who had given him victory over Ben-hadad—twice? Who was the true Commander-in-Chief here? Despite the obvious answers to these questions, Ahab did not seek out the prophet to ask for God's direction at this critical moment.

Instead he appears to have been somewhat flattered by Ben-hadad's humble submission (for which, remember, he only had the messengers' word). Ahab's surprise that Ben-hadad had survived turned to delight that he might consider himself an equal to the great king of Aram. He said, "Does he still live? He is my brother" (v. 32b). *Not my servant—my brother!*

"Now the men were watching for a sign" (v. 33a). They were pagans, remember. They were looking for an omen. In other contexts the Hebrew means "to practice divination" (Deuteronomy 18:10; 2 Kings 17:17). They took Ahab's words as a portent, "and they quickly took it up from him and said, 'Yes, *your brother* Ben-hadad'" (v. 33b). This was going better than they could have hoped!

Ahab said, "Go and bring him" (v. 33c). Still the Israelite king acted all on his own, as though he did not have access to a prophet of the Lord.

"Then Ben-hadad came out to him, and he [Ahab] caused him to come up into the chariot" (v. 33d). This was beyond any "kindness" Ben-hadad could have expected. Ahab treated Ben-hadad as an equal. He *honored* him!

Ben-hadad could hardly believe his good fortune. He grasped the initiative and said to Ahab, "The cities that my father took from your father I will restore, and you may establish bazaars for yourself in Damascus, as my father did in Samaria" (v. 34a). Since our knowledge of the history of the tensions and conflicts between Aram and Israel is sketchy, we cannot be sure, but "my father" here was probably Ben-hadad I who conquered Israelite cities in the days of Baasha, Ahab's "father" in the sense of being a predecessor as king (see 15:20).[40] "Bazaars" seems to mean trading opportunities in Samaria, perhaps taken at a later time (since Samaria only became the Israelite capital under Omri, 16:24), but about which we know nothing more. Ben-hadad would now provide similar openings in Damascus for the king of Israel. How generous of the king who, if things had turned out differently, would have looted everything in Samaria and turned it to dust!

Ahab still felt no need to consider God's will in this matter. He said to Ben-hadad,[41] "I will let you go on these terms" (v. 34b). Ahab offered "these terms," literally "the covenant." "So he made a covenant with him and let him go" (v. 34c). The terms of the covenant, note carefully, had been proposed not by Ahab, but by Ben-hadad.

This was not the last that Ahab would have to do with Ben-hadad. He will have reason to regret this deal (see 22:29–36).

The Word of the Lord That Puts the Politics in Perspective (vv. 35–43)

If we had been there, if we can for a moment put ourselves in Ahab's sandals, the deal he had struck must have seemed brilliant. He had secured peace and the prospect of prosperity, as well as gaining a reputation for "kindness." King Ahab the politician had done well—for a politician. What more could be expected of him?

Our chapter closes with a very strange and surprising episode. In a number of ways it will remind us of chapter 13, and therefore bring to bear the message of that key section of 1 Kings on the political accomplishment of Ahab with Ben-hadad. Politics is one thing. The word of the Lord is another.

A Word That Must Be Obeyed (vv. 35–37)

> And a certain man of the sons of the prophets said to his fellow at the command of the LORD [by the word of the LORD], "Strike me, please." But the man refused to strike him. Then he said to him, "Because you have not

> obeyed the voice of the LORD, behold, as soon as you have gone from me, a lion shall strike you down." And as soon as he had departed from him, a lion met [found] him and struck him down. Then he found another man and said, "Strike me, please." And the man struck him—struck him and wounded him. (vv. 35–37)

A new character is introduced. "A certain man of the sons of the prophets" does not sound like the prophet who appeared earlier, although I do not think we should exclude that possibility in this unusual scene. This is the first mention of "the sons of the prophets" (in so many words) in the Old Testament, although there may have been an allusion to such a body in 13:11, and groups of prophets have been around for some time (18:4, 13). "The sons of the prophets" will play a significant role in the life of Elisha.[42]

The unusual phrase "by [or perhaps in] the word of the LORD" is certainly a reminder of chapter 13, where this phrase was almost a refrain.[43] "The word of the LORD" was the power by which Ahab's politics was about to be measured.

However, before that this "certain man" told his fellow prophet *by the word of the Lord* to "strike" him. That is, the companion was to inflict a blow, as the combatants had done in the recent battles (in vv. 20, 21, 29 "struck" is the same word).

The refusal of the colleague to do this (understandable, even commendable, of course, if it were only a matter of human relations) was in fact disobedience to the voice of the Lord. The consequence was the same as it was for the man of God in chapter 13 who "rebelled against the mouth of the LORD" (13:21, AT). A lion "found" him and struck him down (see 13:24).[44] It is the very character of the word of the Lord that it *must* be obeyed. Note carefully that what may appear to be an act of kindness is disastrous if it is in fact disobedience to the voice of the Lord.

The first man "found" another man (just as the lion had "found" the disobedient one) who obeyed, leaving a wounded prophet ready for the next stage of this bizarre sequence of events.

A Hidden Word (vv. 38–40)

It is not unusual to find a prophet with a difficult message for a king hiding the word in a fictitious story that draws the necessary response from the king before the monarch realizes what he has said (see 2 Samuel 12:1–6; 14:1–11).

This time the prophet prepared to play the part of the leading character in his story by disguising himself[45] with a bandage, which presumably also covered his wound. "So the prophet departed and waited for the king by the way, disguising himself with a bandage over his eyes" (v. 38).

The king came along the road, fresh from his brilliant political triumph, no doubt rather pleased with himself. The bandaged man beside the road called out to him:

> Your servant went out into the midst of the battle, and behold, a soldier turned[46] and brought a man to me and said, "Guard this man; if by any means he is missing, your life shall be for his life, or else you shall pay a talent of silver." And as your servant was busy here and there, he was gone. (vv. 39, 40a)

The story concerned the very "battle" that had recently concluded with such satisfying results for King Ahab (the "battle" of v. 29[47]). The storyteller had been entrusted, he said, with a prisoner, whom he was to guard. Should the prisoner escape, then he himself would pay either with his life (probably meaning he would take the prisoner's place as a slave) or an impossible financial penalty. A talent of silver was 100 times the price of a slave (see Exodus 21:32),[48] way beyond the capacity of an ordinary soldier.

Unfortunately "as your servant was busy here and there" (allowing himself to be distracted from his responsibility) the prisoner escaped. The implication was clear. The man was imploring the king to intervene and save him from his punishment. So it seemed.

The king took the story at face value and gave his judgment. "So shall your judgment be; you yourself have decided it" (v. 40b). *There is no excuse for such irresponsible behavior. You have brought the penalty on yourself.*

A Devastating Word for a Disobedient King (vv. 41, 42)

The king had fallen into the trap. "Then he [the prophet] hurried[49] to take the bandage away from his eyes, and the king of Israel recognized him as one of the prophets" (v. 41). How the king recognized him, we are not told. Is this a hint that this was the same prophet as earlier in the chapter? Perhaps.[50]

The now exposed prophet was a sign that it was time for the word of the Lord to be no longer hidden. So the prophet said to King Ahab:

> Thus says the LORD, "Because you have let go out of your hand the man whom I had devoted to destruction, therefore your life shall be for his life, and your people for his people." (v. 42)

Here at last is the word of the Lord by which everything in this chapter can be seen clearly. Now we (and Ahab) learn that Ben-hadad was a man whom the Lord had "devoted to destruction." That is, he was under God's judgment for his wickedness, just as the original inhabitants of the promised land had been (see our discussion of 9:20, 21) and as the Amalekites had been in the days of King Saul (1 Samuel 15).[51]

It may be that King Ahab should have understood this simply because the Lord had taken command, as it were, of the Israelite forces in this conflict. Ben-hadad was *the Lord's* enemy. Ahab's failure to seek guidance from the Lord in this matter (by approaching the prophet) had led him to act against God's will. Ahab's treatment of Ben-hadad may have looked like an act of kindness, but it was an act of disobedience to the word of the Lord that we have now all heard.

Ahab's conduct is frighteningly reminiscent of King Saul with Agag the Amalekite king. When Saul spared Agag, the prophet Samuel said to him, "Because you have rejected the word of the LORD, he has also rejected you from being king" (1 Samuel 15:23).

Likewise there will be terrible consequences for King Ahab and his people. This is not elaborated at this stage, but we will hear more in due course (see 22:29–40).

A Devastated but Unrepentant King (v. 43)

Did Ahab now beg for God's forgiveness? Did he, even at this late stage, ask the prophet what he must now do? No. The episode closes: "And the king of Israel went to his house vexed and sullen and came to Samaria" (v. 43).

Perhaps we can get a feel for Ahab's mood by listening to some of the translations of "vexed and sullen." NIV has "sullen and angry"; HCSB, "resentful and angry"; JB, "gloomy and out of temper." The Hebrew terms may be stronger than these phrases convey. The first word (*sar*) may suggest "not only resentment but willfulness that clings obstinately to its position in the face of pressure to change."[52] The second word (*za'ep*) "refers to a hotter emotion than 'sullen' indicates; it is the stormy rage that characterizes balked kings."[53] We will be seeing more of Ahab's "vexed and sullen" mood (see 21:4).

The problem is that King Ahab was not willing—and perhaps this weak king was not able—to be God's king. God's king must carry out God's judgment on God's enemies. In this Ahab failed, as Saul had failed many years earlier. What seemed like a brilliant political move was a disaster. He did not destroy the enemy.

In this way Ahab in the closing pages of 1 Kings is a stark contrast to Solomon in the opening pages. The establishment of Solomon's kingdom involved the very effective overthrow of enemies (see Chapter 6 of this book).

This is difficult for us. We must be careful. On the one hand the text before us cannot be taken today as a justification for violence of any kind against enemies. We live under a King who commands us to love our enemies and to pray for those who persecute us (Matthew 5:44). We are not the agents of God's wrath. "Beloved, never avenge yourselves, but leave it to the wrath of God, for it is written, "Vengeance is mine, I will repay, says the Lord" (Romans 12:19; cf. Hebrews 10:30).

On the other hand the Old Testament text, as usual, presents a shadowy anticipation of the New Testament reality. We have a King who has done and will do what political power like Ahab's cannot do. He has destroyed and he will destroy the Enemy behind the enemies. The death of Jesus means that "through death he [has destroyed] the one who has the power of death, that is, the devil" (Hebrews 2:14). The resurrection of Jesus means that "he must reign until he has put all his enemies under his feet. The last enemy to be destroyed is death" (1 Corinthians 15:25, 26).

Political power will never overcome all evil. The Lord Jesus Christ has come to do just that. He is the hope of the world.

43

King Ahab Did Not Put Things Right

1 KINGS 21

IN THESE CLOSING CHAPTERS of 1 Kings we are hearing about various ways in which King Ahab failed the people of Israel. In 1 Kings 20 we saw that he failed to destroy the enemy of his people. His failure reflects the consistent failure of God-denying political power to overcome the enemy. The Bible teaches us to see that behind all threats is the Evil One who wields the power of death. The political powers of this world may occasionally defeat a particular malevolent foe, but what about the evil behind the evil? Hitler was (eventually) defeated, but was the wickedness that motivated Nazism eradicated? Human political power is not wise enough, good enough, or strong enough to destroy the Enemy. Thank God for the Lord Jesus Christ who has come to do just that. He is the hope of the world.

In 1 Kings 21 we will see that King Ahab, having failed to destroy the enemy, failed to deal justly with one of his citizens. He did the very opposite of putting things right. His failure is a reflection of the failure of political power in the hands of selfish people.

I have heard it said (and I am sure it is true) that many men and women go into politics with high ideals but find that over time they are disillusioned. They begin with a desire to make the world a better place but often find that the obstacles to accomplishing much are just too great.

It is easy for the rest of us to be cynical and critical of our political leaders. But a big part of the problem of making the world a better place is the selfishness of all of us. How many of us are willing to make sacrifices that would benefit others? When did you last hear people in a prosperous democracy welcome an increase in taxes because the revenue would make some improvement in other people's lives possible? I recognize that any particular policy will be complicated. My simple point is that we should appreciate how difficult it is to make changes for the better in a community when everyone is self-interested, caring only about themselves and their own family.

However, it is also the case that the selfishness (a rough synonym for sinfulness) of those with political power undermines the ability of political power to make the world a better place. King Ahab was like that.

In this chapter we will see:

(1) What King Ahab wanted (vv. 1–4)
(2) What Queen Jezebel promised (vv. 5–7)
(3) How Queen Jezebel did it (vv. 8–14)
(4) What King Ahab got (vv. 15, 16)
(5) How the word of the Lord puts all this in perspective (vv. 17–29)

The story is set in the context of the conflicts with Ben-hadad, king of Aram (chapter 20). Attention turns from this external difficulty (to which we will return in 22:1) to the relationship between King Ahab and one particular Israelite.[1]

What King Ahab Wanted (vv. 1–4)

Meet Naboth (v. 1)

We are introduced to a man who will say very little and do even less in the story before us. However, he is central to this narrative. His name will appear nineteen times (Ahab's name appears just fifteen times and Jezebel's only nine times).

"Now[2] Naboth the Jezreelite had a vineyard in Jezreel, beside the palace[3] of Ahab king of Samaria" (v. 1). Two things we are told about Naboth are important.

First, he was a Jezreelite. That is, he and his family belonged in the town of Jezreel.[4] Naboth had roots in Jezreel.

Second, he owned a vineyard in his hometown. The vineyard happened to be situated alongside the king's palace. The palace may have been a summer[5] or winter[6] residence for King Ahab and Queen Jezebel, since (as this verse reminds us) Ahab reigned over Israel from Samaria, about twenty miles south of Jezreel (16:24, 28, 29; 20:43).[7]

The unusual designation of Ahab as "king of Samaria" (a title found elsewhere only in 2 Kings 1:3) may suggest a contrast between Ahab and Naboth that will shortly become important. Ahab's roots in Samaria were shallow. He may have lived there, but his father had purchased the place only six years or so before Ahab became king (16:23, 24).

Readers of this history will remember that we have been in Jezreel before. It was in this palace that Queen Jezebel had received news of what happened on Mount Carmel. It was from this palace that she defiantly sent her threatening message to Elijah (19:1, 2). The return to Ahab's Jezreel palace stirs troubling memories.

King Ahab's Wish and King Ahab's Way (v. 2)

> And after this[8] Ahab said to Naboth, "Give me your vineyard, that I may have it for a vegetable garden, because it is near my house, and I will give you a better vineyard for it; or, if it seems good to you, I will give you its value in money." (v. 2)

King Ahab decided that he wanted the vineyard next door. He did not need it, nor did he have plans to do good for others with it. He simply decided that he would like to have a vegetable garden on his grounds, and the vineyard, beside the palace, no doubt with a sunny aspect, was the ideal spot.

Notice that his desire was trivial and entirely selfish: "that I may have it for a vegetable garden." We may safely assume that the king of Israel did not have any difficulty acquiring vegetables for his dinner table. Vegetables were not even a luxury (see Proverbs 15:17, where the same word is translated "herbs"). He just wanted a vegetable garden of his own.

It is possible that the writer, expecting readers to be thoroughly familiar with the preceding books, was hinting at something more troubling still. The only other "vegetable garden" mentioned in the Old Testament is in the book of Deuteronomy, where "a garden of vegetables" is an unfavorable image of the land of Egypt, "where you sowed your seed and irrigated it," compared to the promised land, "a land flowing with milk and honey," "a land that the LORD your God cares for" (Deuteronomy 11:9–12). Does Ahab's desire to turn the vineyard into a vegetable garden suggest "a king who wants to make Israel like Egypt"[9]?

Note carefully the way in which King Ahab went about getting what he wanted. He used the power of his position as king and the wealth available to him to make his wish seem reasonable and his terms generous. The request ("Give me your vineyard") may have been spoken politely, but from the king it was more than a request. His offer of a better vineyard or a fair price (hardly difficult for a king) would seem to remove any possible objection to the king having what he wanted.

Naboth's Faithfulness (v. 3)

"But Naboth said to Ahab, 'The LORD forbid that I should give you the inheritance of my fathers'" (v. 3). Naboth was one of those faithful "seven thousand" Israelites who still followed the Lord. He would obey God rather than man (cf. Acts 5:29).

Naboth spoke as a much better man than Ahab had once spoken. David had said, "The LORD forbid" in 1 Samuel 24:6; 26:11.[10] On this occasion the issue was that the vineyard in question was "the inheritance of my fathers." Now we see the importance of Naboth being a Jezreelite and his vineyard being in Jezreel. The vineyard was land understood to belong to the Lord and given to Naboth's "fathers" as an "inheritance" (see 8:36). Naboth was forbidden by God's Law from alienating this land from his family (Leviticus 25:23–28; cf. Numbers 36:7–9). The vineyard was not a tradable commodity (which is how Ahab saw it), but God's gift, entrusted to Naboth's ancestors and their descendants.[11]

Naboth's refusal of Ahab's seemingly generous offer was based on the Lord's will and his law. Once we have heard from Naboth, we can see that Ahab should never have made this request in the first place. He did not share Naboth's regard for the Lord's will and his law.

King Ahab's Unhappiness (v. 4)

> And Ahab went into his house vexed and sullen because of what Naboth the Jezreelite had said to him, for he had said [and he said[12]], "I will not give you the inheritance of my fathers." And he lay down on his bed and turned away his face and would eat no food. (v. 4)

As the story unfolds, it will become apparent that Ahab probably returned to "his house" in Samaria at this point (see v. 8).[13] His mood is described in exactly the same words ("vexed and sullen") as in 20:43 (see our discussion of that verse). That is how this king reacted when the Lord's will crossed his will.[14]

Ahab muttered to himself a twisted version of what Naboth had said. He omitted Naboth's opening reference to the Lord, and he turned Naboth's words into a refusal of his request ("I will not give you" is *not* what Naboth said).[15]

Like a spoiled child, rather too used to getting his own way, Ahab sulked in his bedroom, his face to the wall, refusing to come down to dinner.

We should not give this petulant but weak king credit for refraining from forcing Naboth to submit. He certainly did not gladly accept Naboth's God-honoring reasons for declining the royal offer. Ahab's infantile behavior, like many childhood tantrums, may even have been deliberately manipulative, to get what he wanted when he lacked the backbone to do what was necessary.[16]

What Queen Jezebel Promised (vv. 5–7)

How fortunate sulky King Ahab was to have Queen Jezebel!

Queen Jezebel's Question (v. 5)

She was concerned for her brooding husband. "Why is your spirit so vexed that you eat no food?" she asked (v. 5). She had seen his moodiness before. Did she know too well the kind of thing that brought it on?

King Ahab's Answer (v. 6)

> And he said to her, "Because I spoke to Naboth the Jezreelite and said to him, 'Give me your vineyard for money, or else, if it please you, I will give you another vineyard for it.' And he answered, 'I will not give you my vineyard.'" (v. 6)

Notice how Ahab put his own spin on the earlier conversation. He did not mention the trivial reason for the request. Jezebel did not need to hear about the veggie patch he wanted. Then he mentioned his offer of money *before* his offer of another vineyard (it was the other way around in v. 2). Did this reflect his understanding of Jezebel's values? He left out the fact that he had offered a "better" vineyard to Naboth. There was no need for his wife to hear that he had been so generous. That was not her way. When he reported Naboth's words he made them into a flat refusal to comply with the king's wishes (again "I will not give you"), omitting entirely Naboth's references to the Lord and the Law. He even makes Naboth speak of "*my* vineyard" when in fact he had spoken of "the inheritance of my fathers." To Jezebel Ahab made Naboth sound as selfish as he himself was.[17]

Queen Jezebel's Promise (v. 7)

Jezebel was, as we have seen, a force to be reckoned with. She said to her husband, "Do you now govern Israel?" (v. 7a). It is not clear whether this was a sarcastic question or a mocking assertion (literally, "*You* are the one who does kingship over Israel!"). There is certainly an emphasis on "you," and "govern" is explicitly about being *king*. She used the word that Adonijah had used in 2:15 where what mattered was the position, status, and glory of being king.[18] *Is this how you do kingship over Israel, Ahab?*

"Arise and eat bread and let your heart be cheerful; I will give you the vineyard of Naboth the Jezreelite" (v. 7b). Jezebel put as much emphasis on "I" as she had on "you." *My dear, let me show you how to do kingship!*

It is worth remembering that Jezebel had learned what being king could mean from her father, the pagan king of the Sidonians (16:31). She knew what a king like the nations could be like. What such a king wants, such a king takes (cf. 1 Samuel 8:11–17).[19]

How Queen Jezebel Did It (vv. 8–14)

Like an earlier monarch in Israel, determined to have what he wanted at any cost, Queen Jezebel used the means of written correspondence to put her plan into action. She kept her distance and had others do her dirty work (cf. 2 Samuel 11:14).

The Plan (vv. 8–10)

> So she wrote letters in Ahab's name and sealed them with his seal, and she sent the letters to the elders and the leaders who lived with Naboth in his city. (v. 8)

Clearly, in Jezebel's opinion, Ahab was not doing kingship very well. She took on the role for him, writing "in Ahab's name" and sealing the letters "with his seal."[20] This will be Jezebel's way of doing kingship.

The letters were addressed to "the elders and the leaders"[21] of Jezreel. These were the leading citizens of the town who were responsible for justice (see Deuteronomy 16:18–20; cf. 19:12; 21:2, 3, 4, 6). It is emphasized that they were Naboth's neighbors ("who lived with Naboth in his city").

The sending of letters suggests that Jezebel was some distance from Jezreel at the time, confirming our guess that Ahab had gone back to Samaria to sulk (v. 4).

> And she wrote in the letters, "Proclaim a fast, and set Naboth at the head of the people. And set two worthless men opposite him, and let them bring a charge against him, saying, 'You have cursed God and the king.' Then take him out and stone him to death." (vv. 9, 10)

It was a careful five-step plan.

First, the elders of the town were to declare a fast. They would need to come up with a credible excuse—some troubling circumstances in the town that could be given as a reason to fast and call on the Lord (see 1 Samuel 7:6; 2 Chronicles 20:3; Ezra 8:21; Jeremiah 36:9).

Second, at an assembly of the people, presumably to deal with the supposed troubles of the town, Naboth was to be seated "at the head of the people." If the assembly was some kind of court, this may have been the position of a defendant.[22] Otherwise Naboth may have been given this position as a leading citizen.[23] Either way Naboth was to be put in a prominent place where everyone could see him.

Third, two scoundrels were to be seated opposite him. These were "worthless men" (literally "sons of *belial* [destruction, wickedness, rebellion]"), like the sons of Eli long ago and other troublemakers such as Nabal (1 Samuel 2:12; 10:27; 25:17, 25; 30:22; 2 Samuel 20:1).[24] But who were they? I suspect that they were chosen agents of Jezebel (perhaps sent from her with the letters). I doubt that *she* called them "worthless men" in writing. Remembering that the conventions of quoted words are not as strict in Hebrew writing as English quotation marks imply,[25] "worthless men" was probably inserted here by the narrator, indicating his evaluation of them (as in v. 13). Importantly, as we will see, there were two of them.

Fourth, these lying rogues were to bring a charge against Naboth. That is why there were two of them, to satisfy the Law's requirement that such a charge be supported by at least two witnesses (Numbers 35:30; Deuteronomy 17:6; 19:15).[26] The false charge was that Naboth had cursed[27] God and the king (see Exodus 22:28). It is possible that this charge was linked to Naboth's refusal to give away his vineyard, when he had invoked God's name and rejected the king's wishes (v. 3).

Fifth, for this trumped-up charge Naboth was to be stoned to death, all very conveniently according to the Law (Leviticus 24:16).

It was a clever, if diabolical, plan, leaving nothing to chance and providing an ingenious cover of legality. Even the Law of God can be made into a tool for evil in the hands of the unscrupulous. That was Jezebel.

Many years later two false witnesses would take part in a sham trial with a pretense of legality that would lead to the execution of the innocent man Jesus. Caiaphas did kingship like Jezebel did (see Matthew 26:57–68).

The Execution (vv. 11–13)

Her evil plan worked alarmingly well.

> And the men of his city, the elders and the leaders who lived in his city, did as Jezebel had sent word to them. As it was written in the letters that she had sent to them, they proclaimed a fast and set Naboth at the head of the people. And the two worthless men came in and sat opposite him. And the worthless men brought a charge against Naboth in the presence of the

people, saying, "Naboth cursed God and the king." So they took him outside the city and stoned him to death with stones. (vv. 11–13)

The entirely redundant repetition of the details in Jezebel's letter emphasizes the meticulous obedience of the community leaders in Jezreel. The
wicked regime of Ahab and Jezebel had produced a cowardly subservience in
the people. The repeated emphasis on these leaders as neighbors of Naboth
("of his city," "who lived in his city") underlines the corruption of what they
did. The narrator's assessment of the rogues ("worthless men" twice in v. 13)
adds to the outrage this account stirs in the reader.

Strikingly a straight reading indicates that it was the "worthless men" who
executed Naboth, probably carrying through the orders of their royal mistress
(cf. Deuteronomy 17:7).[28]

The Report (v. 14)

"Then they sent to Jezebel, saying, 'Naboth has been stoned; he is dead'" (v. 14).
There are two surprises here. First, the obvious antecedent of "they" is again "the
worthless men" of the previous verse. Why were they the ones to report back
rather than "the elders and the leaders" to whom the diabolical instructions had
been addressed? Second, why did the report go to Jezebel rather than to Ahab in
whose name and with whose seal the correspondence has come to Jezreel? Both
of these puzzling developments suggest that the worthless men were indeed agents
of Jezebel who knew more than others about the conspiracy and its source.[29] Jezebel's lackeys had served her well. But they certainly were "sons of *belial*."

A sad footnote to this tragic story of wickedness is that much later in this
history we will learn that not only was Naboth killed that day, but his sons
were murdered with him (2 Kings 9:26). That would have served Jezebel's
purpose well (leaving no heir to interfere with the confiscation of the vineyard)
but did not fit well with the sham pretense of legality given to this process. It
may be that the murder of the sons was done more secretly by Jezebel's agents
and that this is reflected by it being out of sight in 1 Kings 20.

What King Ahab Got (vv. 15, 16)

As soon as Jezebel heard that Naboth had been stoned and was dead,
Jezebel said to Ahab, "Arise, take possession of the vineyard of Naboth the
Jezreelite, which he refused to give you for money, for Naboth is not alive,
but dead." (v. 15)

Here was the news Jezebel had been waiting for. She heard from her trusted
scoundrels that all had gone according to plan.

She enacted the final step herself. For this she ignored legal process. There was no provision in Israel's law for what she now proposed.[30] There is some irony in the words of Jezebel to Ahab. "Arise, take possession" sounds like Moses commanding the Israelites to take the promised land (see Deuteronomy 2:13 where the same words are used). Ahab's action would be the undoing of Israel's foundational experience of God's grace. He would take away what God had given to the family of Naboth.

For the third time we hear a convenient twisting of the original conversation between Ahab and Naboth (see vv. 4, 6). Now Jezebel puts it like this: "he refused to give you [the vineyard] for money." That is hardly a fair representation of Naboth.

Perhaps most striking of all, Jezebel simply informed her husband that Naboth was dead. No explanation. How did he die? How did Jezebel know that he was dead? Ahab did not ask. His silence is damning. He could not be innocently ignorant that this was Jezebel's doing.

> And as soon as Ahab heard that Naboth was dead, Ahab arose to go down to the vineyard of Naboth the Jezreelite, to take possession of it. (v. 16)

Notice how verse 16 begins just like verse 15. Here is the news *Ahab* had been waiting for! He did precisely what his trusted queen told him to do. He was learning from her how to do kingship.

How the Word of the Lord Puts All This in Perspective (vv. 17–29)

The second half of our chapter, like the episode at the end of 1 Kings 20, puts the story we have heard into the clear perspective of "the word of the LORD."

"Then the word of the LORD came to Elijah the Tishbite"[31] (v. 17). When we last heard about Elijah he was somewhere in the Jordan Valley having recruited Elisha as his assistant (19:21). Elisha will not be mentioned again until 2 Kings 2:1, although he may have been in the background.

We are about to see Jezebel's way of doing kingship in the light of the power behind everything, "the word of the LORD."

What the Lord Said about What Ahab and Jezebel Did (vv. 18–24)

Elijah's Mission (v. 18)

This is what Elijah heard: "Arise, go down[32] to meet Ahab king of Israel, who is in Samaria; behold, he is in the vineyard of Naboth, where he has gone to take possession."

For the third time in Elijah's experience "the word of the LORD" sent him to Ahab (see 18:1; 17:1, reading between the lines). It had not gone particularly well on those previous occasions.

There is a slight awkwardness with the words "who is in Samaria" alongside "he is in the vineyard of Naboth" (which, of course, was in Jezreel). Ahab *belonged* in Samaria (recalling "king of Samaria" in v. 1). What he was doing in Jezreel was illegitimate: "he has gone to take possession." The illegitimacy of Ahab's action is underlined by the pointed reference to "the vineyard *of Naboth*." In the Lord's eyes the ownership of the vineyard had not changed!

Elijah's Message (v. 19)

> And you shall say to him, "Thus says the LORD, 'Have you killed and also taken possession?'" And you shall say to him, "Thus says the LORD: 'In the place where dogs licked up the blood of Naboth shall dogs lick your own blood.'" (v. 19)

Here are two simple but devastating messages. The first was a question, although it hardly needed Ahab to answer it.[33] The question specified and exposed his guilt. The second was an announcement of the consequences. The Judge passed the sentence.

The word of the Lord uncovered not only Jezebel's clandestine operation, but the fact that *Ahab* was guilty. Whether he had in fact manipulated Jezebel by his sulks or simply allowed her to do kingship her way without interference, Ahab was guilty of Naboth's death and the stealing of his land. "Killed" is the word used in the Sixth Commandment, "You shall not *murder*" (Exodus 20:13; Deuteronomy 5:17). "Taken possession" is a key word in this chapter (vv. 15, 16, 18, 19 [see note 44]), pointing to the deep significance of the offense—to take for oneself what God had given to another.[34]

Whatever Jezebel's theory of kingship might say, according to the word of the Lord what Ahab had done deserved death. He would die an untimely and undignified death, just as Naboth had done. Although there is about to be a surprising change in the implementation of this punishment, it will not be long before we see the dogs doing what the word of the Lord said they would do (see 22:38).[35]

Ahab's "Enemy" (v. 20)

Commissioned with this terrible message, Elijah "found" Ahab.

> Ahab said to Elijah, "Have you found me, O my enemy?" He answered, "I have found you, because you have sold yourself to do what is evil in the sight of the LORD." (v. 20)

Much as the lion had "found" the disobedient prophet (both in 13:24 and 20:36, ESV, "met"), now Elijah had "found" the king, who now saw the prophet as his "enemy." The last time Ahab had been surprised by Elijah, he had accused the prophet of being the "troubler of Israel" (18:17). Ahab was now less concerned about Israel. He had become preoccupied with himself and so saw Elijah as "*my* enemy."

This time Elijah seems to have accepted the designation. They were enemies, but that was not Elijah's doing. It was because "you have sold yourself to do what is evil in the sight of the Lord." The people of this kingdom would one day be accused of the same thing (see 2 Kings 17:17). The image is that of a person selling himself into slavery (see Deuteronomy 28:68).[36] Ahab had so given himself to evil as to have no will of his own (cf. Romans 7:14). He had given himself to conduct like David's at his worst (see 2 Samuel 11:27). He had made an enemy not just of Elijah but of the Lord.

Elijah's (the Lord's) Message (vv. 21–24)

Without warning or formal introduction, Elijah delivered the word of the Lord to Ahab.[37]

> Behold, I will bring disaster [or evil[38]] upon you. I will utterly burn you up, and will cut off from Ahab every male, bond or free, in Israel. And I will make your house like the house of Jeroboam the son of Nebat, and like the house of Baasha the son of Ahijah, for the anger to which you have provoked me, and because you have made Israel to sin. (vv. 21, 22)

The *words* of verses 21, 22 are different from those in verse 19, but it is the same *word*.[39] The punishment fits the crime. As Ahab had given himself over to doing *evil*, the Lord will bring *evil* upon him.

The punishment is described in terms that we have heard before. The word that Ahijah spoke about Jeroboam included: "I will bring harm upon," "burn up," "cut off . . . every male, both bond and free in Israel" (14:10).[40] Ahab stood in the shameful tradition of kings of Israel who had moved the Lord to grief, sorrow, and anger[41] by leading Israel into idolatry. The first of these kings had been Jeroboam (see 14:7–11). Another was Baasha (see 15:34; 16:1–4). Ahab's house will come to ruin like theirs.

Elijah had not finished. He continued, "And of Jezebel the Lord also said [has spoken, saying[42]], 'The dogs shall eat Jezebel within the walls of Jezreel'" (v. 23). The grizzly fulfillment of this word will come in 2 Kings 9:30–37.

The word of the Lord from the mouth of Elijah concluded, "Anyone belonging to Ahab who dies in the city the dogs shall eat, and anyone of his who dies in the open country the birds of the heavens shall eat" (v. 24; cf. 14:11; 16:4). If you have the stomach for it, glance ahead to 2 Kings 10:1–17 to see that once again the word of the Lord in the mouth of Elijah will prove true.

How Bad Was Ahab? (vv. 25, 26)

The narrator seems to sense the despair readers might feel at the unrelenting horror of God's judgment. He now speaks directly to his readers to make sure we understand just how bad Ahab had been.

> (There was none who sold himself to do what was evil in the sight of the LORD like Ahab, whom Jezebel his wife incited. He acted very abominably in going after idols, as the Amorites had done, whom the LORD cast out [dispossessed] before the people of Israel.) (vv. 25, 26)

In terms of evil, King Ahab (ably assisted by his queen) excelled and surpassed all who had gone before him. The heart of his wickedness, from which all other evil flowed, was idolatry. He not only followed the perversions set up by Jeroboam (12:25–33), but allowed, encouraged, and perhaps even enforced the influence of the pagan religions (16:31–33), with Jezebel's energetic patronage (18:4, 13, 19).

The horror of this can only be grasped when we see that Ahab had made Israel like the Amorites,[43] that is, the previous inhabitants of the land, whose wickedness had grown to an intolerable scale (Genesis 15:16). Indeed in a striking and shocking way Ahab had made Naboth like the Amorites. He had "dispossessed" innocent Naboth, just as the Lord had "dispossessed" the wicked Amorites.[44] Ahab's mistreatment of Naboth was an expression of his fundamental perversion of the ways of God.

What the Word of the Lord Did to Ahab (v. 27)

If you have taken in the narrator's extraordinary description of Ahab's abject, unqualified wickedness, you will be astonished to hear what the word of the Lord did to Israel's most evil king.

> And when Ahab heard those words, he tore his clothes and put sackcloth on his flesh and fasted and lay in sackcloth and went about dejectedly. (v. 27)

The words Ahab heard, of course, were not verses 25, 26, but 20–24. The cynics among us may not be impressed. Ahab had allowed himself to be pushed around by Jezebel and Ben-hadad. He was even impacted, briefly, by the events on Mount Carmel (18:41–46). Ahab was so weak, he seemed to be swayed by the most recent voice he had heard. Let us not get too excited about some torn garments, sackcloth, and lost appetite. He "went about dejectedly" may mean that he walked about very slowly, like someone in deep trouble.[45] We have heard enough about Ahab to justify a degree of skepticism about all this.

However, the power of the word of the Lord is impressive. This worst of kings was brought to his knees by the word of the Lord. We may note that he did not cry out to God for mercy, nor did he take steps to make amends for anything that he had done. But the word of the Lord did impact him.

What the Lord Now Said (vv. 28, 29)

Our surprise at what the word of the Lord did to Ahab is eclipsed by the word of the Lord that then came to Elijah.

> And the word of the LORD came to Elijah the Tishbite, saying, "Have you seen how Ahab has humbled himself before me? Because he has humbled himself before me, I will not bring the disaster in his days; but in his son's days I will bring the disaster upon his house." (vv. 28, 29)

Our cynicism is not shared by the Lord! Even about Ahab! This may be difficult for us to appreciate, but we must. Ahab's punishment was not revoked, but the Lord gladly postponed it. This is a magnificent glimpse of God's eagerness to have mercy. What would have happened if Ahab had truly repented and begged God for forgiveness?

We will see in 1 Kings 22 that Ahab's humiliation before the Lord did not last. His own death will come "according to the word of the LORD" we have heard (22:38). The end of his "house" would come in the days of his sons (2 Kings 10:1–17).

King Ahab embodied God-rejecting political power. When humans wield power but do not submit to the God who is there, power is corrupted and is not used to serve others, to do justice and righteousness. King Ahab became the kind of king we may imagine Adonijah would have been (see 1 Kings 2). He was the antithesis of King Solomon who embodied the wisdom of God to do justice and righteousness (3:28; 10:9).

We must pray for our political leaders that they may do much better than Ahab, that their selfishness will not do as much harm as it might. But we know that political power in the hands of selfish (sinful) men and women cannot bring complete justice and perfect righteousness.

Precisely this is the wonder of the gospel of Jesus Christ. In him we have a king whose wisdom is perfect. As we trust in him "we ourselves eagerly wait for the hope of righteousness" (Galatians 5:5).

44

King Ahab Hated the Truth

1 KINGS 22:1–14

WHAT A CONFUSED WORLD we live in! Some call it a post-truth world, meaning that people form opinions with little regard for evidence and with a general disdain for so-called "experts." Have you noticed that those who express alarm at this state of affairs are often remarkably sure that their own views and opinions are based on "fact"? Those who disagree, who question whether the "facts" are actually facts, are accused of being post-truth. In other words, post-truth is a state of affairs in which *others* are caught up. No one thinks that their own views, opinions, beliefs, and values are unrelated to truth.

So ours is not so much a post-truth world as a world in which people profoundly disagree about what is true and how we discern it.

The Bible teaches us—and experience confirms—that there is a further complicating dimension to this. The human heart and mind are not neutral in the matter of understanding what is true. It is not the case that we look out on the world with clear eyes that can see "the truth" without distortion. We are not open to the truth in a straightforward way. In our sinfulness we ourselves twist and distort the truth. We tend to believe what we want to believe. Frequently we form opinions and hold views either to conform to or to react against the opinions and views around us. Often we select "facts" to justify our outlook and ignore other "facts" that are less convenient.

The Bible also teaches us that we do this with the truth about God. Jesus put it like this: "The light has come into the world, and people loved the darkness rather than the light because their works were evil. For everyone who does wicked things hates the light and does not come to the light, lest his works should be exposed" (John 3:19, 20). Mere rational arguments and evidence will not bring people into the light while they love the darkness. The problem is not lack of light. It is that they hate the light! It has been a post-truth world for a very long time.

All this means that disagreements between people can be difficult to resolve. This may not be serious when disagreements are trivial, but many of our differences are hugely important. How should we address the divisions in our communities over what to do, if anything, about changes in the climate, managing the economy, fair treatment of disadvantaged people, taxation policies, health care, poverty, inequality, terrorism, war?

Of course, there is an important place for people of goodwill to think, discuss, argue, and try to work toward agreement. Some will be prepared to change their minds, some will be prepared to compromise, and in some areas we may make a little progress. But our sinfulness will always be there. That is, we cannot fully escape our self-centeredness. We love ourselves more than we love the truth. So our ability to agree about what is true is hindered by what we *want* to be true.

If this brief and admittedly rather too simple analysis has any validity (truth), it means that the problems of our so-called post-truth world are not new. It also means that political power alone will not save us—not when political power is in the hands of those who love darkness rather than light. The stubborn divisions between people, even in prosperous and relatively peaceful democracies, are indications of a much deeper problem. It is a problem we will see in King Ahab and a further indication of why political power repeatedly fails us.

Two Kings Working Together on a Problem (vv. 1–4)

After the story of Ahab's way of getting (that is, taking) a vegetable garden for himself, the horizon of our story returns to the international scene of 1 Kings 20.

A Peace That Could Not Last (v. 1)

"For three years Aram [Syria[1]] and Israel continued without war" (v. 1).[2] King Ahab's political wisdom, such as it was, had brought about a state of peace with King Ben-hadad of Aram (see 20:34). But it lasted just three years—long enough for Ahab to think about things like vegetables.

A High-Level Meeting in Samaria (vv. 2–4)

What happened after these "three years"? There was a problem that will come to light as we witness a rather important meeting apparently called by King Ahab in his headquarters in Samaria.

The Key Players (v. 2)

"But in the third year Jehoshaphat the king of Judah came down to the king of Israel" (v. 2). We were very briefly introduced to Jehoshaphat, the son of King Asa, in 15:24. Since that point our history has focused on events in the northern kingdom of Israel, beginning about three decades before Jehoshaphat became king down south in Jerusalem.[3] Jehoshaphat had come to the southern throne in the early years of Ahab's reign in the north (22:41),[4] but the narrator's focus on northern matters has meant that Jehoshaphat has been ignored until now.

It seems reasonable to suppose that Jehoshaphat "came down" to Samaria at Ahab's invitation. The language probably reflects Jehoshaphat's view of things. To go anywhere from Jerusalem was to "go down," if you had any idea of the importance of Jerusalem (see Psalm 48:1), which I am sure Jehoshaphat did (see 22:42), but Ahab definitely did not.[5]

We are told nothing at this stage about the relationship between Jehoshaphat and Ahab. We will hear in 22:44 that Jehoshaphat "made peace with the king of Israel." Whether this was altogether wise is another question. Jehoshaphat had his son marry into Ahab's family (2 Kings 8:18), to Athaliah (2 Kings 8:26).[6] That will not work out well (see 2 Kings 11). Be that as it may, at this stage the long running hostilities between the north and the south (14:30; 15:6, 7, 16, 32) seem to have settled down, and this meeting in Samaria was an expression of peaceful relations between Israel and Judah.

Through the story told in 22:1–38 the writer avoids using Ahab's name (he will similarly avoid Ben-hadad's name). We hear repeatedly of "the king of Israel" (and "the king of Aram") or just "the king" but "Ahab" only once (22:20). "It is as though the narrator, finally, cannot bear to say his [Ahab's] name."[7] The effect is to make the story less personally about Ahab and more about the characteristic behavior of a "king of Israel."

The Presenting Problem (v. 3)

The meeting opened with a word from the king of Israel to his advisers who were present.

> And the king of Israel said to his servants,[8] "Do you know that Ramoth-gilead belongs to us, and we keep quiet and do not take it out of the hand of the king of Aram [ESV: "Syria"]?" (v. 3)

It was one of those moments in international diplomacy when words were spoken to one group of people but designed for someone else to hear.

The question was rhetorical. Of course, the counselors knew. The purpose was to put Jehoshaphat in the position of listening to a problem that concerned the northerners. The agenda for the meeting was set. *What is to be done about this?*

Ramoth-gilead ("Gilead Heights"[9]) was one of Israel's "cities of refuge" (Deuteronomy 4:43; Joshua 20:8; 21:38), located east of the Jordan River.[10] It had been the base for Ben-geber, one of King Solomon's officers administering his taxation system (4:13). It had certainly belonged to Israel. Somehow it had fallen into the hands of the king of Aram. This may have been in the days of Ben-hadad I[11] when Baasha was king of Israel and Asa was king of Judah (see 15:20) or perhaps at some other time in the history of Aram/Israel tensions. The point, however, is that the terms of the peace of the last three years had included Ben-hadad's promise to restore cities previously taken from Israel (20:34). But he had not returned Ramoth-gilead.

It is not hard to guess why Ben-hadad held on to Ramoth-gilead. It was almost certainly a strategic location, dominating the way to the Israelite heartland from the east.[12] It is equally easy to see why Ahab would be keen to get it back.

Jehoshaphat was essentially saying, *But we are doing nothing[13] about it!* The Hebrew emphasizes "we." *What are we doing? Nothing!* This is another diplomatic ploy. "We" distributes the responsibility. The truth is that *Ahab* was doing nothing.

In particular we note that Ahab had not sought the word of the Lord on this matter. That is striking simply because the word of the Lord has played such a decisive role in Ahab's recent experience (20:35; 21:17, 28). But seeking the word of the Lord was never Ahab's way.

The Agreement (v. 4)

Instead of seeking the word of the Lord, Ahab sought an alliance with Jehoshaphat. Political power would sort this matter out.

> And he said to Jehoshaphat, "Will you go with me to battle at Ramoth-gilead?" And Jehoshaphat said to the king of Israel, "I am as you are, my people as your people, my horses as your horses."[14] (v. 4)

Recent experience had shown that Israel had no difficulty defeating Aram when they fought in obedience to the word of the Lord (chapter 20). Why did Ahab think he needed help from Jehoshaphat? It can only be because he had no intention of seeking help from the Lord.

Jehoshaphat's generous agreement may be judged naive or perhaps a little hasty. But it was brotherly. Behind Jehoshaphat's words we can sense an awareness that his people and Ahab's people were really one people. They were the Lord's people. Jehoshaphat knew that even if Ahab spent most of his life in denial of it. This was not the submission of a vassal (contrast 20:4), nor even the acquiescence of a junior partner.[15] It was (at the risk of overstatement) brotherly love.

Translated into the practicalities of the moment, Jehoshaphat was agreeing to join with Ahab militarily to restore what belonged rightly to Israel.

Two Voices for the Two Kings to Choose From (vv. 5–14)

However, Jehoshaphat was not like Ahab (see 22:43). He insisted on doing what Ahab had so conspicuously not done.

King Jehoshaphat and the Word of the Lord (v. 5)

"And Jehoshaphat said to the king of Israel, 'Inquire[16] first for the word of the LORD'" (v. 5). I doubt that Jehoshaphat had any knowledge about Ahab's recent experience of "the word of the LORD." The word of the Lord had announced a terrible end for both Ahab and his family (21:17–24). This word had humbled Ahab (21:27). The word of the Lord had then announced the postponement of the disaster (21:28, 29). Given Ahab's recent experience, how would he respond to Jehoshaphat's proposal?

King Ahab and His Four Hundred Prophets (v. 6)

> Then the king of Israel gathered the prophets together, about four hundred men, and said to them, "Shall I go to battle against Ramoth-gilead, or shall I refrain?" And they said, "Go up, for the Lord will give [ESV adds "it"] into the hand of the king." (v. 6)

Jehoshaphat must have been impressed. Ahab had no shortage of "prophets." He was quick to "gather" them and consult them. They responded in a way that must have seemed to give clear support to King Ahab's proposal.

But first impressions can mislead. A careful reader (and a careful listener, like Jehoshaphat) would have questions.

The first and most obvious is, who are these "prophets"? The number of them is worrying (to the reader, if not to Jehoshaphat). We have heard about "four hundred prophets" before. They were pagan prophets of Asherah, sponsored by Queen Jezebel (18:19). Furthermore we have seen Ahab "gather" prophets before. Elijah had told him to "gather . . . the 450 prophets of Baal and the 400 prophets of Asherah" (18:19), which he did—sort of (18:20). Who were "the prophets" Ahab now "gathered"?

The second concern (which I am sure Jehoshaphat noticed) is that the name of the Lord, Yahweh ("the LORD"), was not uttered either by Ahab in his question, nor by the prophets in their answer. They spoke of "the Lord" which could be any "lord."[17] This raises the urgent question, *whose* prophets were these?

Once we (and Jehoshaphat) notice these concerns, we should then realize that the prophet's message was like many sham oracles. Like a modern horoscope, the prophets managed such complete ambiguity that their words were meaningless. Not only did they avoid saying which "lord" would deliver victory, they carefully refrained from saying *what* will be delivered (the Hebrew does not have any object after "will give"), or indeed to *which king* it will be delivered! A careful listener would realize that the words of the prophets could be made to fit any course of events. They could be taken to mean that *Ahab* would be given into the hands of *Ben-hadad*![18]

King Jehoshaphat's Persistence (v. 7)

The southern king was not satisfied. "But Jehoshaphat said, 'Is there not here another prophet [Is there no longer here a prophet[19]] of the LORD of whom we may inquire?'" (v. 7). Ever the diplomat, Jehoshaphat gently enquired whether there still was in Ahab's kingdom a prophet *"of the LORD,"* that is, of Yahweh. To inquire for the word *of* Yahweh (v. 5), you need a prophet *of* Yahweh.

Jehoshaphat had deduced, from the kind of observations we have noted, that Ahab's 400 prophets were not Yahweh's prophets. What they said was therefore not Yahweh's word. He seemed to understand that prophets of Yahweh may be in short supply in Ahab's kingdom (remember 18:4, 13). *Isn't there one left?*

Our writer does not satisfy our curiosity by letting us know just whose prophets Ahab had gathered. Perhaps they were the 400 prophets of Asherah who had been smart enough not to show up at Mount Carmel.[20] It seems unlikely that the ranks of the prophets of Baal would have been replenished so quickly after what happened at the brook Kishon (18:40), but perhaps after a few years that was possible. It is also possible that these were prophets who served in the false religion Jeroboam had established, with its centers at Dan and Bethel (12:25–33).[21] It really does not matter. We have been told enough to agree with Jehoshaphat. They were not true prophets of Yahweh. That's all that matters.

King Ahab's Reluctance (vv. 8, 9)

> And the king of Israel said to Jehoshaphat, "There is yet [still] one man[22] by whom we may inquire of the LORD, but I hate him, for he never prophesies good concerning me, but evil: Micaiah the son of Imlah."[23] (v. 8a)

Well, if you must know, there is one of those prophets left. Can you hear Ahab's sulky tone? He had had enough of *those* prophets. Encounters with them had never gone well. We think, of course, of the stories we have heard of Ahab and Elijah. There had been the drought (17:1) that led Ahab to call Elijah "troubler of Israel" (18:17). There had been Mount Carmel that had led to a very angry queen (19:2). There had been that nasty confrontation about the vegetable garden when Ahab called Elijah "my enemy" (21:20).

Ahab seems to have moved on from his brief and what must now be seen as superficial positive responses to the word of the Lord that he had heard from Elijah (see 18:41–46; 21:27). Now he stated his present relationship to the one prophet of the Lord that was still around: "I hate him, for he never prophesies good concerning me, but evil." In this sentence "I" is emphatic. It was all about Ahab. *I hate him because of what he says about me.* Ahab was one of those who "loved the darkness rather than the light because their deeds were evil" (John 3:19).

Ahab had no interest in the truth. He just wanted to hear what he wanted to hear. If the truth was something he did not want to hear, he hated the truth.[24]

It comes as a surprise that the prophet of Yahweh whom Ahab hated was not Elijah but someone we have not previously heard about—Micaiah, the son of Imlah.[25] We will not hear about Micaiah again after the present sequence of events.[26] We can only suppose that the elusive Elijah (remember 18:12) was not at Ahab's beck and call, whereas it seems that Micaiah may already have been imprisoned for his faithfulness (see "take him back" in 22:26, 27) and so was easy to find.[27]

Once again Jehoshaphat was diplomatic but determined. "Let not the king say so," he said (v. 8b). *Let's not be so negative, Your Majesty, about a prophet of Yahweh.*

Ahab had no room left to maneuver. "Then the king of Israel summoned an officer and said, 'Bring quickly Micaiah the son of Imlah'" (v. 9). His words were abrupt. *Hurry! Micaiah the son of Imlah!*[28]

The Voice of King Ahab's Prophets (vv. 10–12)

As we wait for the summoned prophet to appear, we (and Jehoshaphat) are treated to a display from Ahab's 400 prophets. We now see more clearly the setting of the meeting (or perhaps the meeting was moved to a suitable site for these prophets to do their thing). It was an open space near the entrance gate to the city of Samaria:

> Now the king of Israel and Jehoshaphat the king of Judah were sitting on their thrones, arrayed in their robes, at the threshing floor[29] at the entrance of the gate of Samaria, and all the prophets were prophesying before them. (v. 10)

Observe the pomp—the kings, their thrones, their flowing robes. No doubt they were somewhat elevated above the common throng. They were a picture of political power.

Beneath them the throng of prophets were "prophesying" (the word is translated "raved on" in 18:29), reminding us of Mount Carmel. Perhaps they refrained from bloodletting on this occasion (but who knows?). But remember the response to the antics on Mount Carmel: "there was no voice, and there was no answerer, and there was no attentiveness" (18:29, AT).

This time, however, there was a voice—not from Heaven, but from one of the prophets.

> And Zedekiah the son of Chenaanah made for himself horns of iron and said, "Thus says the LORD, 'With these you shall push Aram [ESV: "the Syrians"] until they are destroyed.'" (v. 11)

Lies are only effective if they can take on the appearance of truth. One of the 400 prophets was known by name. Perhaps he was the leader. His name, Zedekiah ("Yahweh Is Righteousness"), is impressive. Perhaps he had adopted this name for this particular occasion? But his father's name, Chenaanah, sounds very like "Canaan."[30] Was this a Canaanite prophet dressed up with an Israelite name?

He spoke *like* a true prophet of Yahweh: "Thus Yahweh has said" (AT).[31] Ahab had heard that signature phrase of Yahweh's prophets many times (20:13, 14, 28, 42; 21:19). Zedekiah put on a performance that may remind us of true prophets of Yahweh who sometimes symbolically acted out their message (11:30; cf. 1 Samuel 15:27, 28). In this case he put two iron spikes on his head, like horns. This may have represented on the one hand the two kings before whom he was performing and on the other hand an ancient Scripture:

> A firstborn bull—he has majesty,
>   and his horns are the horns of a wild ox;

with them he shall gore the peoples,
   all of them, to the ends of the earth. (Deuteronomy 33:17)[32]

Zedekiah supported his street theater with a commentary. Did he see that the earlier dissembling had not fooled Jehoshaphat? He abandoned the ambiguities of the previous message. He now spoke unequivocally in the name of Yahweh. He unmistakably identified the victor ("you," that is, Ahab[33]) and the vanquished (Aram).

The throng of prophets followed Zedekiah's lead. *If it's a word from Yahweh you want, then that's what we will give you.* "And all the prophets prophesied so and said, 'Go up to Ramoth-gilead and triumph; the LORD will give [ESV adds "it"] into the hand of the king'" (v. 12). The prophets tweaked their earlier message (v. 6) just enough to bring it into line with Zedekiah's unambiguous word. Now they, too, named Yahweh and explicitly stated that Ahab will "triumph."[34]

Does this mean that we (and Jehoshaphat) were mistaken in our doubts about these prophets? Or does it mean that they were willing and eager to modify their message—including the god they claimed to speak for—to please their audience?

The Voice of the Prophet of the Lord (vv. 13, 14)
While all this was going on,[35] the messenger (the "officer" of v. 9) had some advice for the prophet he had been sent to fetch.

> And the messenger who went to summon Micaiah said to him, "Behold, the words of the prophets with one accord are favorable [literally, good] to the king. Let your word be like the word of one of them, and speak favorably [good]." (v. 13)

This was more a friendly warning than a command.[36] But note well the view of prophecy reflected here. The prophet was expected to have the freedom to frame his message to please the recipient. The messenger had no doubt noticed Ahab's complaint about Micaiah, that he never had anything "good" to say about him (v. 8). *Take your cue from the other prophets and say something "good" to the king.*

But Micaiah was not that kind of prophet. He said, "As the LORD lives, what the LORD says [will say[37]] to me, *that*[38] I will speak" (v. 14). Micaiah, like Elijah, was a servant of the Lord, from whose mouth the word of the Lord will be faithfully spoken (cf. 17:24). That is exactly why King Ahab hated him.

Before we turn the page and follow the confrontation that took place when this one true prophet of the Lord came before the two kings and the 400 prophets they had been listening to, let us notice this fatal flaw in King Ahab. Because his deeds were evil (21:25, 26), he hated the truth. He particularly hated the word of the Lord.

I suspect that we are too used to this state of affairs in our experience of political power and so are less alarmed than we ought to be. In this confused world, where people profoundly disagree about what is true, and where people in fact "love the darkness rather than the light" and "suppress the truth" (John 3:19; Romans 1:18), what hope can there be that the troubles, tragedies, suffering, and disappointments of the world can ever be resolved?

Here the gospel is as amazing as ever. There is a King who is "full of grace and *truth*" (John 1:14). He has described himself as "the way, and the *truth*, and the life" (John 14:6). A truth-hating, darkness-loving world needs the light of this gospel more than anything else. In this gospel we find hope. The confusion will not last forever.

45

King Ahab Did Not Have a Listening Heart

1 KINGS 22:15–28

AT THE HEART OF King Ahab's failure was the failure of King Ahab's heart. It was now about 100 years since King Solomon had asked God for a "listening heart," receptive to the word of the Lord, so that he would be able to discern between good and evil and so rule God's people rightly (see 3:9).[1] A century later, King Ahab was unable to discern between good and evil because he did not have a listening heart. He did not want to hear the word of the Lord (22:8).

The problem of discerning right from wrong, good from evil, wise from foolish is at the heart of the failure of political power even today. What is the right policy to bring peace to the Middle East? What should be done about terrorism? What actions will be effective in addressing the huge number of problems facing the nations of today's world? We have no shortage of opinions, often held with vehement certainty. But who is right? In the face of the complexity and gravity of the world's problems, the elusiveness of true wisdom is alarming. It is too easy for some leaders to win support by claiming to have all the answers. Disillusionment is inevitable.

We return to the story of King Ahab and King Jehoshaphat, with the proposal of a joint military operation to regain Ramoth-gilead from the king of Aram. What was the right policy? The two kings were seated on their thrones in all their royal regalia, listening to the encouraging counsel of Zedekiah, the son of Chenaanah and a few hundred others urging them to proceed: "Go up to Ramoth-gilead and triumph; the LORD will give it into the hand of the king" (22:12). Was that sound advice or not?

Meanwhile a messenger had gone to fetch another prophet named Micaiah, who swore that he would speak only "what the LORD will say to me" (22:14, AT).

King Ahab: Confused Unbelief (vv. 15–18)

Micaiah arrived at the meeting in the open space near the entrance gate of the city of Samaria. King Ahab was presiding and initiated the exchange with Micaiah.

Ahab's Insincere Question (v. 15a)

The king asked Micaiah, "Micaiah, shall we go to Ramoth-gilead to battle, or shall we refrain?" (v. 15a). Notice three things about this question.

First, it is exactly (almost word for word) the same question the king had asked the 400 prophets earlier (22:6a). He had received an answer then that seemed to satisfy him (22:6b). It was only at Jehoshaphat's insistence (22:7–8) that he had summoned this other prophet.

Second, Ahab had only asked this question in the first place because he was pressed to do so by King Jehoshaphat (22:5). Ahab knew what he wanted to do (see 22:3, 4). He felt no need to "inquire first for the word of the LORD."

Third, there is a slight change in this second version of the question. Originally it had been about Ahab's idea of going up against Ramoth-gilead: "Shall *I* go . . . ?" Now he asked about the *joint* operation: "Shall *we* go . . . ?" Perhaps his past experiences with this prophet (22:8) had led him to think that Micaiah might speak more positively if he included Jehoshaphat in his question.[2] Perhaps he had already decided that *he* would go (supported by *his* prophets), and now he was simply asking the prophet (whom *Jehoshaphat* had insisted on consulting) whether the king of Judah should join him.

All things considered, Ahab's question to Micaiah was not sincere and honest; he was not genuinely ready to hear the answer. He was playing a diplomatic game. There are fairly clear indications that he had made up his mind. Subsequent events will confirm this impression.

Micaiah's Mocking Answer (v. 15b)

Micaiah's answer to Ahab takes us (and Ahab, I suspect) by surprise: "Go up and triumph; the LORD will give [ESV adds "it"] into the hand of the king" (v. 15b). It sounds at first as though Micaiah was taking the advice of the messenger who had fetched him (22:13) because what he said was *exactly* (word for word) what "all the prophets" had said under the influence of Zedekiah, the son of Chenaanah (22:12).[3] For a moment we might suspect that Micaiah was the same kind of prophet as the others. After all, we only have Ahab's word (22:8) and Micaiah's claim (22:14) that he was different. Have we been mistaken to believe them?

The other possibility, of course, is that Micaiah spoke these words mockingly. *You have asked me a question without wanting to hear the answer. Let me give you the answer you already have, and the only answer you are prepared to hear.*

One hint that this was indeed Micaiah's tone is that his answer did not correspond to the question. Ahab had asked about "we"—himself *and* Jehoshaphat. The Hebrew verbs translated "go up" and "triumph" in Micaiah's reply are singular. Micaiah focused his words on Ahab. In effect Ahab had asked, "Shall King Jehoshaphat and I go up to Ramoth-gilead to battle?" Micaiah replied, "*You* go up, Ahab, as you have already decided to do and see how you do at triumphing."

Ahab's Annoyed Rebuke (v. 16)

Our suspicions (that Micaiah's reply was mocking Ahab's question) are supported by Ahab's reaction. With the benefit of hearing Micaiah's tone of voice, he responded, "How many times shall I make you swear that you speak to me nothing but the truth in the name of the LORD?" (v. 16).

Poor Ahab. He hated the truth (22:8), but he did not like being mocked for his love of lies. Being an unbeliever can be very confusing. It sounds as though Ahab had experienced Micaiah's sarcasm many times before.[4] He had had enough![5]

Micaiah's Message for Ahab (v. 17)

Be careful what you ask for, Ahab. If you really want the truth from the prophet of the Lord, here it is. Micaiah said:

> "I saw all Israel scattered on the mountains,
>   as sheep that have no shepherd.
> And the LORD said,
> 'These have no master;
>   let each return to his home in peace.'" (v. 17)[6]

Two lines describe what Micaiah *saw*, and two report what he *heard*. This was a devastating message, its poetic form magnifying its depth. Various words and expressions reverberate with levels of meaning.

What He Saw (v. 17a)

He saw "all Israel." The context suggests that at one level, "all Israel" means the army of Ahab (cf. 15:27; 16:17; 20:15). However, by calling the army "all Israel" we are reminded that the army represented the whole nation. The nation was caught up in what happened to the army. Furthermore, while "all Israel" has often meant the northern kingdom (as in 12:1, 16, 18, 20; 14:13, 18; 15:33; 18:19), here the combined forces of Ahab and Jehoshaphat (remember the "we" of Ahab's question in v. 15) represented "all Israel" in the fullest sense. Micaiah's vision concerned the whole people who had once been called "Israel."

They were "scattered." The vision of all Israel "scattered" is deeply troubling. The high point of this history was the "assembly" of "all Israel" by King Solomon (8:65; cf. 8:1) in Jerusalem. The ominous verb "to scatter" (Hebrew, *pwts*) is a key word in describing God's judgment, actual or anticipated (see Genesis 11:8, 9; Deuteronomy 4:27; 28:64; 30:3).

The image of "sheep that have no shepherd" is particularly pointed. "Shepherd" was a metaphor for "king" or other national leaders (see 2 Samuel 5:2; 7:7; Psalm 78:71, 72; cf. Matthew 2:6). Moses had spoken of the people without a leader as "sheep that have no shepherd" (Numbers 27:17), an image taken up by later prophets (Ezekiel 34:5; Zechariah 13:7) and understood by Jesus (Matthew 9:36).

At one level all Israel scattered on the mountains like sheep without a shepherd suggests that their shepherd has died. That is why they are scattered. Micaiah was predicting the death of Ahab.[7] Perhaps there is the further implication that they would be scattered because even now the sheep did not have a good shepherd. A good shepherd would not take them into this disaster.

What He Heard (v. 17b)

The implications of the vision were made explicit in a word from the Lord: "These have no master."[8] The implication is that their lord and master (Ahab) is dead. This line interprets the vision. The shock comes with the next line: "let each return to his home in peace." The *death* of Ahab will mean *peace* (*shalom*) for the people of Israel![9] He had been such a bad shepherd that the sheep will be better off when he is gone! Having no shepherd would be better than having Ahab as shepherd.

Ahab's Grumpy Sulk (v. 18)

Ahab had now been told "the truth in the name of the LORD" (v. 16). A better man than Ahab might have welcomed this warning and abandoned plans to "go to Ramoth-gilead to battle." But Ahab did not have a listening heart. He responded as he usually did when he heard something he did not like. He sulked. Turning to King Jehoshaphat seated on the throne beside him, he said, "Did I not tell you that he would not prophesy good concerning me, but evil?" (v. 18). That is why Ahab hated Micaiah (22:8).

The Word of the Lord: What Ahab Did Not Want to Hear (vv. 19–23)

It is important to understand the deep seriousness of King Ahab's failure to have a listening heart. It was not just that he chose to accept poor advice when better was available. He chose to ignore and indeed defy the word *of the Lord*. Micaiah launched into a speech that spelled out the gravity of what Ahab had done.

The Power behind Everything (v. 19)

> And Micaiah[10] said, "Therefore hear the word of the LORD: I saw the LORD sitting on his throne, and all the host of heaven standing beside him on his right hand and on his left . . ." (v. 19)

It is possible that Micaiah took no notice of Ahab's grumpy (whispered?) remark to Jehoshaphat and continued with the speech he had begun in verse 17. "Therefore" would then mean, *Because the Lord has shown me that your Ramoth-gilead adventure will be a disaster, Ahab, you had better listen to the word of the Lord.*[11]

Alternatively (and I think preferably) Micaiah heard Ahab's words to Jehoshaphat, and the following speech was his response. "Therefore" then means, *I know you hate hearing unwelcome news, Ahab, but you must listen to the word of the Lord.*[12]

"The word of the LORD" is not just superior advice. It is certainly not one political opinion among many. It is the power behind everything.[13] It is the word of the One Micaiah had seen "sitting on his throne." The contrast between *this* throne and the two thrones on which Ahab and Jehoshaphat were seated by the city gate (22:10) is breathtaking. Here is the throne that rules over all of creation and the history of the nations. *As you sit on your puny throne, Ahab, you would be wise to listen to the word of the One seated on the throne of Heaven.*

Around the heavenly throne, Micaiah saw the heavenly armies standing, ready to carry out the will of their King (cf. Psalm 103:21; Luke 2:13).[14] This does make the scene with Ahab and Jehoshaphat surrounded by Ahab's raving prophets look rather ridiculous. *Would you really choose to listen to their voices, Ahab, rather than the word of the Lord?*

This presents the fundamental reality that the course of history, in matters great and small, is not determined by the wills of human rulers but by the will of the Heavenly King (cf. Psalm 82:1). The utterly amazing thing is that he discloses his plans to his servants, his prophets (see Jeremiah 23:18–22; Amos 3:7). Micaiah had seen the heavenly gathering!

Heaven's Plan (vv. 20–22)

In what seems to me to be a kind of cosmic parody of the negotiations of Ahab and Jehoshaphat, Micaiah described the deliberations of the heavenly assembly.

> . . . and the LORD said, "Who will entice Ahab, that he may go up and fall at[15] Ramoth-gilead?" And one said one thing, and another said another. Then a spirit came forward and stood before the LORD, saying, "I will entice him." And the LORD said to him, "By what means?" And he said, "I will go out, and will be a lying spirit [or a spirit of a lie] in the mouth of all his prophets." And he said, "You are to entice him, and you shall succeed; go out and do so." (vv. 20–22)

Just as Ahab had a plan to take back Ramoth-gilead from the king of Aram (22:3), the Lord of the host of heaven was deliberating on a plan to bring his judgment on Ahab at Ramoth-gilead. He intended to "entice" Ahab. This verb (Hebrew, *pth* piel) conveys the sense of making a fool of Ahab.[16] The fool who would not listen to the word of the Lord will be fooled into his own destruction.

There was a discussion in Heaven ("one said one thing, and another said another"). The picture is of a council of war, with the matter at hand being taken with utmost seriousness by everyone. The judgment of Heaven's King on the king of Israel was not a small matter.

The deliberations concluded with a volunteer coming forward, offering to carry out the plan. "*I* will entice him."[17] The volunteer is called, literally, "*the* spirit" or "*the* breath." It would, I think, be a mistake to probe too specifically into this scene, which must be understood as a vision, not therefore a literal description of the ontological reality. We should not identify "the spirit" here too closely with "the Spirit of the LORD" known from other contexts (see 18:12; 1 Samuel 16:13; 2 Samuel 23:2).[18] Let's accept that this "spirit" (or "breath"; Hebrew, *ruakh*) is somewhat mysterious to mere human observers of the heavenly scene.[19]

The Lord questioned the spirit. How would he lure the foolish king to his destruction? He would do so by being a spirit/breath of a lie in the mouth of all Ahab's prophets.[20] It would be like the "harmful spirit from the LORD" who tormented Saul (1 Samuel 16:14).[21] For the man who hated the truth the spirit would bring the lie he wanted to believe and by that means "entice" him.

The proposal received the Lord's endorsement. The spirit was to do as he had said, and the Lord promised that it would work ("you shall succeed," literally, "you shall be able").

Heaven's Plan Working (v. 23)

Micaiah concluded by explaining plainly that Heaven's plan was already at work. What Ahab had been hearing from his 400 prophets was the lie sent from Heaven to entice him to his own destruction:

> Now therefore behold, the LORD has put a lying spirit [or a breath/spirit of a lie] in the mouth of all these your prophets; the LORD has declared disaster [literally, evil] for you. (v. 23)

The kings sitting on their little thrones by the entrance gate to Samaria, with their flowing robes, needed to know that the King of Heaven was in charge of all that was happening. The focus is on Ahab ("your" and "you" are singular).

Rather than troubling ourselves with questions about whether God tells lies (he doesn't; see 1 Samuel 15:29), let us notice that the Lord's punishment of Ahab took the form of giving him over to what he had chosen. The lie was what he wanted, and the lie was what he got. Furthermore, do not miss the fact that through Micaiah the Lord was now telling Ahab that the lie was a lie. You cannot get fairer than that![22]

Responses to Reality (vv. 24–28)

The stakes had been considerably raised in the gathering by Samaria's gate. According to Micaiah, the King of Heaven was dealing with the king of Israel. The reality was much more than met the eye.

There were two responses to what Micaiah had said, one from the leader of Ahab's prophets, the other from Ahab himself. Each response was firmly answered by Micaiah.

Zedekiah's Opposition (v. 24)

> Then Zedekiah the son of Chenaanah came near and struck Micaiah on the cheek and said, "How did the Spirit of the LORD go from me to speak to you?" (v. 24)

Zedekiah showed his true colors by striking Micaiah on the cheek (just as some other religious pretenders will show their depravity by similarly striking

Jesus, Matthew 26:67; cf. John 18:22; Acts 23:2). I do not think it is worth trying too hard to work out what Zedekiah meant by his odd question.[23] We have no reason to believe that he was a clear theological thinker. Along with the slap he said something like, *How dare you suggest that the Lord has spoken to you! He has already spoken to me!*[24]

Reality (v. 25)

Micaiah did not need to defend himself with words or blows. Reality would prove the truth of his words. He said, "Behold, you shall see on that day when you go into an inner chamber[25] to hide yourself" (v. 25). What Micaiah had "seen" in vision (vv. 17, 19), Zedekiah will "see" in the concrete experience of frantically looking for a hiding place from the disaster the Lord had declared by Micaiah. The historian does not subsequently bother to tell us about the fulfillment of this word. There were more important things to record.

King Ahab's Oppression (vv. 26, 27)

Ahab's response was similar in spirit to Zedekiah.

> And the king of Israel said, "Seize Micaiah, and take him back to Amon the governor of the city and to Joash the king's son, and say, 'Thus says the king, "Put this fellow in prison and feed him meager rations of bread and water, until I come in peace."'" (vv. 26, 27)

We know nothing more than we learn here about the two officials responsible for Micaiah's incarceration. "Governor" renders a common word (*sar*) that can refer to a variety of officials (1:19, "commander"; 4:2, "high officials"; 5:16, "chief officers"; 11:24, "leader"; 14:27, "officers"; 20:14, "governors). "The king's son," Joash, may not have been an actual member of the royal family but an official, perhaps with a direct responsibility to the king.[26]

Micaiah was to be taken *back* to these officials, suggesting that he was being held by them previously. This king imagined (as powerful people often do) that the word of the Lord could be controlled by restraining the messenger (cf. 2 Timothy 2:9).

The prophet was to be returned to harsher conditions than before. "Meager rations of bread and water" is literally, "bread of oppression and water of oppression." He was to be held "until I come in peace." Micaiah had said that only with Ahab's death would the people return "in peace" (v. 17). Defiant to the end, Ahab insisted that the prophet be confined behind bars until he, the king, returned "in peace."

Reality (v. 28a)

Again Micaiah would allow reality to reveal the truth. He said, "If you return[27] in peace, the Lord has not spoken by me" (v. 28a). The unfolding of events will demonstrate that, by the words of Micaiah, King Ahab had been granted to hear the voice of the Heavenly King. If only he had had a listening heart!

Conclusion (v. 28b)

The last words we hear from Micaiah are startling. He said, "Hear, all you peoples!" "Peoples" means "nations."[28] In the first instance Micaiah was calling on the "peoples" of the two kingdoms represented by Ahab and Jehoshaphat to "Hear!" The word of the Lord, delivered that day in Samaria, would determine the future for these peoples. The singular "hear" of verse 19 is now plural. If only the peoples would have a listening heart and hear the word of the Lord!

About a century after Micaiah another prophet with a similar name would begin his message with these very words: "Hear, you peoples, all of you"[29] (Micah 1:2).[30] He meant the "peoples" of all the earth. Micah was announcing the *international* significance of the judgment that the Lord God was about to bring on Samaria and would in due course bring on Jerusalem. It is reasonable to see Micah's message as picking up, so to speak, where Micaiah had left off.[31] The Lord of the heavenly hosts has the nations of the whole world in his hands. *Hear, you peoples, all of you.*

The failure—the refusal—of King Ahab to hear the word of the Lord was a disaster. He could not shepherd God's people when he did not have a listening heart. It is simply not possible for a human ruler to bring peace (in the fullest sense) in this world while defying and opposing the rule of the King of Heaven. We will see the immediate tragic consequences of Ahab's foolish defiance in our next chapter.

At this point let us reflect on the limitations of political power in the hands of sinful men and women to make our world a better place. On the one hand, this does not mean that nothing can be achieved. Let us pray for those with political responsibilities; let us seek people of relative integrity, compassion, and justice to serve in political office. By all means. But let us not be surprised when they accomplish less than we hope for. On the other hand, I am not suggesting that if only our politicians would read their Bibles and listen carefully to God's Word, we would be able to do much better. The problems are deeper than that. The solution is far more radical. It has to be. The news is that "all authority in heaven and on earth" has been given to One who is wise enough, good enough, and powerful enough to do what all human power has failed to achieve (Matthew 28:18). The claim of the gospel is huge. The risen Lord Jesus Christ is the Good Shepherd the world needs (John 10:11), the One who will, in his way and in his time, establish the kingdom of God, a kingdom of righteousness, peace, and joy (Romans 14:17; cf. Isaiah 9:7). He is the hope of the world.

46

King Ahab Died

1 KINGS 22:29–40

IS THERE ANYTHING GOOD about death? That's a tough question. We are all aware that death is a terrible enemy. We hate it. We fear it. We do not want to think about it. Death robs us. Death destroys God's gift of life. Is there anything more wonderful in the gospel of Jesus Christ than the news that death has been defeated in the death of Jesus for us and will be finally destroyed? This news resounds through the pages of the New Testament (taste and wonder at this message in John 5:24; 8:51, 52; 11:25, 26; Romans 5:17; 6:9, 10, 23; 1 Corinthians 15:21, 26, 54, 55; 2 Timothy 1:10; Hebrews 2:9, 14, 15; 1 John 3:14; Revelation 1:18; 21:4).

It is therefore difficult to consider anything *good* about death. However, some of us may have observed how sometimes death can be a relief. It can bring terrible suffering to an end. The sadness, pain, and loss of death are not diminished, but we are glad to see no more pain. Of course, we would be happier if there had been no suffering in the first place, but in the face of terrible suffering, perhaps we can see *something* good about death.

There is more. Death can bring terrible wickedness to an end. I am glad that Hitler did not live forever, aren't you? When God warned Adam that disobedience to the word of God would lead to death (Genesis 2:17), we can see God's justice (sin deserves death). We can also see that God is the source of life (sin is rejecting God and so by its nature is deadly). But we can also see God's grace. In God's world wickedness will be limited. It will not be allowed to do all the damage that it could. Of course, we all feel that it would be better if there was no wickedness in the first place. That's another matter. But given the evil humans can do, there is something good about the fact that sinfulness is limited by death.

I am aware that these are difficult things to think about. But as we come to the last dramatic scene in 1 Kings we are about to see King Ahab's death. In his death there is hope. The God who is really there will not allow wickedness (like Ahab's) to rule in his world forever. In the death of Ahab we glimpse the grace of God who has promised a better King.

But let's not get ahead of ourselves. Ahab's death does not take us by surprise. We have heard about it no less than three times ie recent chapters. So has Ahab. First there was the unnamed prophet who announced, after Ahab had failed to dispose of Ben-hadad:

> Thus says the LORD, "Because you have let go out of your hand the man whom I had devoted to destruction, therefore *your life shall be for his life,*[1] and your people for his people." (20:42)

Second, when Ahab failed to deal with Naboth justly (an understatement!), Elijah was sent to him with this word:

> Thus says the LORD, "Have you killed and also taken possession?" . . . Thus says the LORD: "In the place where dogs licked up the blood of Naboth *shall dogs lick your own blood.*" (21:19)

Third, when Ahab displayed his hatred of the truth and his refusal to heed the word of the Lord, Micaiah had seen the outcome of the battle he was determined to wage:

> I saw all Israel scattered on the mountains, as sheep *that have no shepherd.* And the LORD said, "These *have no master*; let each return to his home in peace." . . . the LORD has declared *disaster for you.* (22:17, 23)

We could add a fourth from Micaiah's last words to Ahab: "*If you return in peace*, the LORD has not spoken by me" (22:28).

It is time for us to hear what happened. The story unfolds in four stages:

(1) Preparations for Ahab's battle (vv. 29–31)
(2) How it became Ahab's last battle (vv. 32–34)
(3) The end of Ahab's last battle (vv. 35–38)
(4) Ahab's epitaph (vv. 39, 40)

Preparations for Ahab's Battle (vv. 29–31)

We know that it was the Lord's purpose to entice with a lie the king who hated the truth and would not listen to the word of the Lord. The lie would persuade him (although he needed little persuading) to go up to Ramoth-gilead, where he would fall (22:20–22). The king had been told all this (including the fact that the lie was a lie), and yet he still followed the lie in the mouth of his prophets (22:12). Ahab did what Ahab had wanted to do all along (22:3, 4).

The Allies (v. 29)

"So [And²] the king of Israel and Jehoshaphat the king of Judah went up to Ramoth-gilead" (v. 29)—just as Ahab had originally proposed (22:4). It was as though he had heard nothing from verse 13 to verse 28 of this chapter. He certainly had not listened to the word of the Lord.

Nonetheless we are surprised to hear that Jehoshaphat joined Ahab in this venture, after his eagerness to seek the word of the Lord (22:7) and having heard it from Micaiah (see 22:18). Since the writer's interest is focused on Ahab, this development receives no attention. However, it is certainly not to Jehoshaphat's credit that he joined Ahab.³

The Allies' Strategy (v. 30)

King Ahab proposed a strange strategy. He said to Jehoshaphat, "I will disguise myself and go⁴ into battle, but you wear your robes" (v. 30a). From all that we have learned about Ahab, it is highly unlikely that this was a matter of humility, allowing his southern ally to take command of the operation and therefore the glory of the hoped-for victory. Nor can we consider it an act of bravery, whereby Ahab was throwing himself into the dangers of the battle, while leaving Jehoshaphat highly visible and therefore highly protected by his army.⁵ In the light of the message Ahab had heard from Micaiah, which focused on disaster for Ahab himself (22:23), we cannot avoid the impression that Ahab's disguise was like the foolish disguises of Jeroboam's wife (14:2) and, earlier still, King Saul (1 Samuel 28:8). Each, in their own way, was trying to deceive God.⁶ Ahab entertained the thought that if he were unrecognizable, perhaps the word of the Lord would not come to pass. Ridiculous? Certainly. That, surely, is the point. The word of the Lord had moved Ahab but not to obedient repentance. His response was fear and absurd measures. Ungodliness is like that.

Ahab was (as usual) preoccupied with himself. There was no need for Jehoshaphat to disguise himself since the word of the Lord that had frightened Ahab had not been directed at Jehoshaphat.⁷

It seems that Jehoshaphat raised no objection to the plan. "And the king of Israel disguised himself and went into battle" (v. 30b).

The Enemy (v. 31a)

Ramoth-gilead was in the hands of Ben-hadad, the king of Aram (22:3). He gathered forces to respond to Ahab's advance on the town. "Now the king of Aram[8] had commanded[9] the thirty-two captains of his chariots . . ." (v. 31a). These thirty-two officers were probably the replacements for the thirty-two kings, as recommended by Ben-hadad's advisers earlier (20:24). This suggests that Ben-hadad still had at his disposal the considerable forces (replenished after the earlier losses, cf. 20:25) with which he had earlier menaced Israel (20:1).

The Enemy's Strategy (v. 31b)

In a rich irony we now learn that as Ahab was busy disguising himself, Ben-hadad was saying to his men, "Fight with neither small nor great, but only with the king of Israel" (v. 31b). Did Ahab have a hunch that this would be Ben-hadad's approach? Possibly. The fact is that Ahab's disguise suddenly seems rather sensible![10]

From another commander in another context Ben-hadad's direction to his officers might be understood as an efficient strategy. The quickest way to win the war would be to bring down the king. The army will not fight on without its supreme commander. But there was more going on with Ben-hadad. This was the man who had experienced the "kindness" of the king of Israel and made a covenant with him (20:31–34). The covenant included a promise to return towns like Ramoth-gilead to Israel. It is clear that these things had had little effect on Ben-hadad. His hostility toward the king of Israel (20:1) was undiminished. Indeed it seems that after the two humiliating defeats Ben-hadad had suffered (20:21, 29, 30), his personal animosity toward Ahab had only grown. All Ben-hadad wanted from this battle was the life of the king of Israel.

Ahab's self-deceived folly in letting Ben-hadad go is now plain (see 20:42). Ben-hadad would never cease to be an enemy. Ahab's failure to destroy the enemy was about to bring his own destruction.

How It Became Ahab's Last Battle (vv. 32–34)

However, as the battle began Ahab's strategy seemed, briefly, to work.

Hope for Ahab? (v. 32a)

"And when the captains of the chariots saw Jehoshaphat, they said, 'It is surely the king of Israel.' So they turned to fight against him" (v. 32a). There was only one figure on the field of battle in royal garb. It *must* be Ahab. When they "turned" to focus their deadly force on the man they thought was King Ahab, it seems that Ahab's strategy had worked—at least for Ahab. Is this what this most selfish of kings had plotted all along? Had he no concern for his ally? Probably not.

Hope for Jehoshaphat (vv. 32b, 33)

But look what happened: "And Jehoshaphat cried out. And when the captains of the chariots saw that it was not the king of Israel, they turned back from pursuing him" (vv. 32b, 33).

Did he cry out to his men for help? Was it a war cry? Did he perhaps cry out to God (as perhaps implied by the later historian in 2 Chronicles 18:31)? It does not matter. The cry revealed to the enemy that he was not Ahab. It may have been what he said, or his dialect, or something else. Again it does not matter. What mattered was that at that moment the danger that Ahab's strategy had wittingly or otherwise brought on Jehoshaphat fell away. "They turned back from pursuing him."

Ahab's "Unlucky" Day (v. 34)

Things were going rather well for Ahab and Jehoshaphat. The enemy forces were under orders to focus all their efforts on bringing down Ahab. Jehoshaphat was safe now that they knew he was not Ahab. Clearly the enemy was unable to identify Ahab, dressed as he was like an ordinary soldier.

But we know (because we have heard the word of the Lord from Micaiah, particularly in 22:19) that there was more going on than the strategies of Ahab and Ben-hadad. The outcome of the battle that day was determined by neither of them.

This is what happened (or at least what *appeared* to happen): "But a certain man drew his bow at random and struck the king of Israel between the scale armor and the breastplate" (v. 34a). Somebody[11]—even our narrator has no idea who it was—drew his bow. The expression behind "at random" is tantalizing. Literally it means "to his wholeness," which could refer to his physical vigor, meaning that the man pulled his bow with all his strength, to its full tension. This would explain how the arrow pierced the king's armor, wounding him fatally. Alternatively the expression could refer to the man's "innocence," that is, that he did not intentionally aim at the king.[12] He was aiming at what he thought was an ordinary soldier.[13] Ahab's disguise was effective, but it did not work out quite as he had intended!

Precisely how the arrow penetrated Ahab's armor is a little unclear. It seems that the arrow found a small gap, perhaps between the breastplate and the protective covering of his lower abdomen.

Would the wound be fatal? Ahab hoped not. He said to the driver of his chariot, "Turn around and carry me out of the battle,[14] for I am wounded" (v. 34b). Perhaps the king would survive, if only they could get him away from the fighting and attend to his wound.

The End of Ahab's Last Battle (vv. 35–38)

It was not to be, for "the battle continued that day" (v. 35a). Literally the battle "went up," that is, it became more and more violent.[15] It seems that so intense was the conflict that Ahab's chariot driver could not withdraw to safety. It may have been physically impossible to turn the chariot around.

The Death (v. 35)

So "the king was propped up in his chariot facing the Syrians [Arameans], until at evening he died. And the blood of the wound flowed into the bottom [literally, bosom] of the chariot" (v. 35). I doubt very much that this was "a bit of royal bravado."[16] Rather the press of the battle was so great that there was no room for the king to collapse.[17] He slowly bled to death, breathing his last at the end of the day.

The blood collected in the hollow of the floor of the chariot. We will hear more about that blood shortly.

The "Peace" (vv. 36, 37)

Micaiah had seen "all Israel scattered on the mountains, as sheep that have no shepherd," and he had heard the Lord say, "Let each return to his home *in peace*" (22:17). We have also heard Ahab promise to "come *in peace*" back to Samaria (22:27).

For the Sheep (v. 36)

The word of the Lord came to pass. "And about sunset a cry went through the army, 'Every man to his city, and every man to his country!'" (v. 36). They were to return home, whether in the northern kingdom of Israel or the southern kingdom of Judah. The war was over. Each would return to his home "*in peace*."

The "cry" that went through the army that evening is evocative. Although the Hebrew word (*rinnah*) can sometimes be used for a cry of distress,[18] it usually refers to a cry of joy.[19] I have a hunch that the cry that went through the army at the news of Ahab's death was more glad than sad. As Micaiah had foretold, only with the death of this king would the people find peace. That is what happened.

Not for the Shepherd (v. 37)

The word of Ahab did not come to pass. "So the king died, and was brought to Samaria. And they buried the king in Samaria" (v. 37). "Was brought to Samaria" is more literally, "*came* to Samaria." He had said he would "*come* in peace" (22:27). He *came* dead,[20] and he was buried.

The Horror and the Shame! (v. 38a)

"And they[21] washed the chariot by the pool of Samaria, and the dogs licked up his blood, and the prostitutes washed [ESV adds, themselves in it]" (v. 38a). This horrible scene is the final impression our writer gives us of King Ahab: dogs licking up his blood as prostitutes washed in the pool.[22]

"The pool of Samaria" was probably a rock-cut reservoir that collected rainwater.[23] Such pools have appeared a number of times in this history (including the "pool of Gibeon" in 2 Samuel 2:13 and the "pool at Hebron" in 2 Samuel 4:12). On this occasion the dogs and the prostitutes signify "the ignominious contempt which was heaped upon [Ahab] at his death."[24] The negative associations of "dogs" can be seen in numerous insulting expressions (see 1 Samuel 17:43; 24:14; 2 Samuel 3:8; 9:8; 16:9).

The only other place in the Old Testament that mentions "dog" and "prostitute" in the same sentence is Deuteronomy 23:18, where "dog" may be a derogatory term for a male prostitute who with his female counterpart is said to be "an abomination to the LORD your God." Ahab's end was shockingly fitting, this king who had acted "very abominably" (21:25, 26).

Since we have found in the story of Ahab at this end of 1 Kings a number of contrasts with the story of King Solomon at the other end, it is interesting to note that prostitutes featured in Solomon's story.[25] But how different are the two stories. King Solomon was the wise king with a listening heart who put things right (did "justice") in a dispute between two prostitutes (3:16–28). Here at the end of Ahab's life, the prostitutes bathing beside Ahab's chariot as his blood is washed away suggest his shameful end. No glory here! No "wisdom of God to do justice" in this king (cf. 3:28).

The Power behind Everything (v. 38b)

All this happened "according to the word of the LORD that he had spoken" (v. 38b). Here is the power that determined the outcome of the battle that day.

What looked like a remarkably unlucky, chance event for the king of Israel was in fact what the Lord who sits on his throne, surrounded by the host of Heaven, had spoken.

Some are troubled by the fact that there seems to be a discrepancy between what actually happened and the Lord's word on the second of the three occasions when he had spoken of Ahab's death. The Lord had said that the dogs would lick up Ahab's blood "in the place where dogs licked up the blood of Naboth" (21:19). That would have been in or near Jezreel, but for Ahab it happened by the pool of Samaria. It seems to me that this was the result of God's mercy, by which the judgment announced in 21:19 did not fall immediately because of Ahab's apparent repentance (see 21:29). Since the change in Ahab did not last, the word of the Lord came to pass, but at a different time and place.[26]

Ahab's Epitaph (vv. 39, 40)

> Now the rest of the acts of Ahab and all that he did, and the ivory house that he built and all the cities that he built, are they not written in the Book of the Chronicles of the Kings of Israel? So Ahab slept with his fathers, and Ahaziah his son reigned in his place. (vv. 39, 40)

The formal notice of Ahab's death follows the pattern of his father and earlier kings of Israel (see 14:19, 20; 15:31, 32; 16:5, 6, 14, 20, 27, 28). In this notice we see a final echo of King Solomon's reign. Ahab, too, was a builder, apparently famous for the lavish palace he built, with paneling and furniture inlaid with ivory (cf. Amos 3:15; 6:4). Presumably this was the palace in Samaria, completed by Ahab. His father had lived there for only six years (16:23) and was probably preoccupied with building the defenses of his new capital.[27] Ahab also "built" (perhaps meaning "fortified") quite a number of cities. Unlike King Solomon, however, our writer has no interest in these accomplishments. They are not important. The best thing about this wicked king (see 16:30–34; 21:25, 26) is that he died.[28]

The long account of King Ahab's reign has shown us a king who did not destroy the enemy of his people, did not deal justly with his people, hated the truth, and did not listen to the word of the Lord. Therefore he died. The very best thing about King Ahab is that his story shows us that the world needs a King who will finally deal with the Enemy, bring justice, and rule according to the good word of God. The world needs a King like that who will live forever.

Thank God for the eternal kingdom of our Lord and Savior Jesus Christ (2 Peter 1:11; cf. Colossians 1:13; Hebrews 1:8; 12:28; Revelation 11:15)!

47

The Hope of the World and the Legacy of King Ahab

1 KINGS 22:41–53

THE BOOK OF 1 KINGS has taken us through more than a century of the ups and downs of the once great nation of Israel, from the heady days of great King Solomon's kingdom (chapters 1—11) to the dreadful years of the weak and wicked King Ahab (chapters 17—22). Solomon's kingdom gave us a glimpse of the glory of the kingdom of God. Ahab's reign over the northern breakaway kingdom has been a litany of the failure of political power in the hands of an unworthy man.

The story has two powerful themes. The first is the decisive certainty of the word of the Lord. This word is the power behind everything and shapes the course of Israel's history. The power behind Solomon's glorious kingdom was the promise of God to establish the kingdom of the son of David (2:12, 46; cf. 2 Samuel 7:12). The demise of the corrupt King Ahab was also according to the word of the Lord (22:37, 38; cf. 21:19). The second theme is a corollary of the first. Human power and political schemes will end in disaster if they refuse to pay close attention to their way, to walk before the Lord God in faithfulness with all their heart and with all their soul (2:4). Tragically that is what happened to Solomon's kingdom (11:9). It also explains the disaster of Ahab's reign (see 16:33; 18:18; 20:42; 21:20–22, 25, 26).

As we reach the end of 1 Kings the obvious question is: What hope can there be for the people whose kings so consistently fail them?

The story will continue in the book of 2 Kings. Indeed the break between the two books of Kings is often thought to be arbitrary. It is supposed that perhaps the size of the original scrolls may have required the material to be divided into roughly two equal parts simply because it would not all fit onto one scroll. That is possible and may be supported by the obvious continuity between the end of 1 Kings and the beginning of 2 Kings. The account of Ahaziah's reign spans the two (1 Kings 22:51—2 Kings 1:18).

However, it seems to me that there is more going on here. The death of Ahab (22:37–40) marks a very significant moment in the story. To end 1 Kings here is not arbitrary. Indeed it has the effect of framing, so to speak, the book with the lives of the two contrasting paradigmatic kings—the one in whom was the wisdom of God to do justice (3:28) and the one who sold himself to do what is evil in the sight of the Lord more than any before him (21:25). Of course 1 Kings is not a complete story, but it contributes a co-herent segment to the bigger story that began in Genesis 1 and will end in 2 Kings 25.[1]

But 1 Kings does not quite end at 22:40 with the death of Ahab. The last words of 1 Kings strike two notes that take us back to the book's main themes, raising the question of what hope there can be. First we will be taken back in time to hear a little about what had been happening in the southern kingdom of Judah through the long years of Ahab's reign in the north that have occupied our attention for many pages (vv. 41–50). Here we will be reminded of Israel's only hope, which is also the hope of the whole world. Then we will return to the aftermath of Ahab's death (vv. 51–53). What was the legacy of King Ahab? Can we learn the lesson?

King Jehoshaphat and the Hope of the World (vv. 41–50)

It has been a long time since we have heard anything about what was going on in the southern kingdom of Judah. From 15:25 we have followed the course of events in the northern kingdom. We have seen the rise and fall of six northern kings (Nadab, Baasha, Elah, Zimri, Omri, and Ahab). Through these pages all we have heard about the southern kingdom has been reports of ongoing conflict with their northern neighbors (15:32) and, toward the end, a surpris-ing but disastrous collaboration between the southern and the northern kings (22:1–40).

King Ahab had reigned in Samaria for twenty-two years (16:29). Those years have filled the last six chapters of 1 Kings. Before we come to the end of the book our writer takes us back to the early years of Ahab's reign to tell us something of what was happening down south while we have been preoc-cupied with the drama of Ahab.

Chronological Facts (vv. 41, 42a)

The basic time frame is sketched in a familiar way (cf. 14:21; 15:1, 2; etc.):

> Jehoshaphat the son of Asa began to reign over Judah in the fourth year of
> Ahab king of Israel. Jehoshaphat was thirty-five years old when he began
> to reign, and he reigned twenty-five years in Jerusalem. (vv. 41, 42a)

For most of Ahab's twenty-two year reign in Samaria, Jehoshaphat had reigned in Jerusalem, and his reign continued beyond Ahab's death.[2] We were told about Jehoshaphat coming to the throne following the death of his father, Asa, in 15:24, but heard nothing more of him until he came to a meeting with King Ahab in Samaria in 22:2.

The most striking word in this formal notice is "Jerusalem." It is striking because although the name of this city appeared twenty-eight times in 1 Kings 1—15 we have not heard it since 15:10. For readers of 1 Kings it is a long time since we have heard "Jerusalem." That is because our attention has been focused on the northern kingdom that had cut itself off from Jerusalem and everything Jerusalem represented. This was Jeroboam's "sin" (see 12:28–30), in which each subsequent king of Israel had followed him (15:26, 34; 16:13, 19, 26, 31). The absence of any mention of *Jerusalem* since 1 Kings 15 is no accident. It reflects Israel's problem: Jerusalem had been forgotten in the northern kingdom (contrast Psalm 137:4–6).

But our writer will not allow his readers to forget Jerusalem. Before this book ends we must go back to Jerusalem. After such a long silence, the mention of "Jerusalem" reminds us of what we heard much earlier in this book. Jerusalem was the city the Lord had chosen (11:13, 32). It was "the city where I have chosen to put my name" (11:36), where Solomon had built the house for the name of the Lord, just as the Lord had promised his father David (5:5; 8:18–20).

To remember Jerusalem is to remember God's promise. Our writer wants us to know, before this book ends, that Jerusalem was still standing and that a son of David was reigning there. It was still true that "for David's sake the Lord his God gave him a lamp in Jerusalem, setting up his son after him, and establishing Jerusalem" (15:4).[3] The Lord's promise was still shaping history.

His Mother's Name (v. 42b)

"His mother's name was Azubah the daughter of Shilhi" (v. 42b). Although we know nothing more about Azubah or her father Shilhi, the mention of Jehoshaphat's mother reminds us of the arrangements in the house of David, where the mother of the king held an honored place. Remember how Bathsheba was seated at Solomon's right hand and was honored by her son in 2:19. Our writer particularly noted that Rehoboam's mother, Naamah, was an Ammonite (14:21). Abijam's mother, Maacah (15:2), had to be deposed from the position of "queen-mother" by Abijah's son, Asa.[4] The interest in the mothers as well as the fathers of the kings in Jerusalem almost certainly arises from the promise that concerned the "offspring" of David (2 Samuel 7:12). Jehoshaphat's mother's name is therefore another subtle reminder of the promise that was at work in Jerusalem.

The Measure of This King (v. 43a)

Like a breath of fresh air or a ray of bright sunshine, after the many pages of gloom and darkness through the story of Ahab, we now read:

> He walked in all the ways of Asa his father. He did not turn aside from it, doing what was right in the sight of the LORD. (v. 43a)

This would be a good time to turn back and read the account of Jehoshaphat's father's reign in 15:9–24. "All the ways of his father" is encouraging, for there was much good in Asa's reign (see 15:11–13, 14b, 15). "Doing what was right in the sight of the LORD" is a wonderful contrast to Ahab (cf. 21:25, 26).

Like his father, Jehoshaphat was the kind of king that those who knew God's promise to David would be hoping for. Well, almost.

His Record (vv. 43b–49)

Like his father, Asa, Jehoshaphat's record was actually mixed. Yes, there was much to celebrate, but problems remained. Certainly his reign fell short of the glory days of King Solomon. Our writer briefly notes several features of Jehoshaphat's record, generally noting qualifications to the positive assessment just given. He was good but not good enough.

The High Places (v. 43b)

Item One: "Yet[5] the high places were not taken away, and the people still sacrificed and made offerings on the high places" (v. 43b; see our discussion of 3:2 and 14:23a). This had been a problem for Asa (see the identical words in 15:14a). Neither Asa nor Jehoshaphat are blamed for this failure (see our discussion of 15:14a), but neither of them was able to do away with these unacceptable institutions that had proliferated under Rehoboam (14:23) after Solomon had started this troubling trend (11:7).

The first entry in Jehoshaphat's record shows that, like his father, though he was a good king (and such an encouraging contrast to Ahab), he was not good enough.

Relations with Ahab (v. 44)

Item Two: "Jehoshaphat also made peace with the king of Israel" (v. 44).

What are we to make of that? There had been hostility between the neighboring kingdoms since the division of Solomon's kingdom in the days of Rehoboam (see 14:30; 15:6, 7, 16, 17, 32). Asa had managed (at a cost) to push back against the northern aggression (see 15:16–22) but had not brought an end to the conflict. Jehoshaphat made "peace"—*shalom*. Should we hear an echo of the name of Solomon, the peaceful king (4:24)? Did Jehoshaphat restore the "peace" of the kingdom of Solomon?

Well, no. Did you notice that our writer still has difficulty uttering the name of Ahab? We have seen the weakness and wickedness of this "king of Israel." We have seen the foolish and disastrous adventure that came out of Jehoshaphat's "peace" with Ahab (22:1–40). Peace with *Ahab*, of all people, cannot be counted to Jehoshaphat's credit.[6] Peace is wonderful but not peace with wickedness.

The Rest of What He Did (v. 45)

> Now the rest of the acts of Jehoshaphat, and his might that he showed, and how he warred, are they not written in the Book of the Chronicles of the Kings of Judah? (v. 45)

With these words our writer returns to the familiar reference to the more detailed royal records (cf. 14:19, 29; 15:7, 23, 31; 16:5, 14, 20, 27; 22:39; see our discussion of 14:19). While the book referred to here is no longer available to us, it so happens that there is a much fuller account of the reign of Jehoshaphat in 2 Chronicles 17—20.

The note about "peace" with the king of Israel in verse 44 is now qualified with reference to "how he warred." Jehoshaphat did not restore the peaceful kingdom of Solomon (4:24).

The Pagan Priests (v. 46)

However, certain shortcomings having been noted, it is important to appreciate that Jehoshaphat *did* do "what was right in the sight of the LORD." In one important area he completed the good work his father had begun:

> And from the land he exterminated the remnant of the male cult prostitutes [the consecrated ones] who remained in the days of his father Asa. (v. 46)

We have noted that this is probably a reference to priests of foreign religions (rather than "male cult prostitutes").[7] They had been practicing "in the land" since the days of Rehoboam (14:24). Asa had got rid of them (15:12), but apparently not completely, or not permanently. Jehoshaphat brought this reform to completion. That was no small achievement. He was good!

A Glimmer of Glory? (vv. 47–49)

There was one episode in Jehoshaphat's reign that receives a little more attention. The background is: "There was no king in Edom; a deputy was king" (v. 47). "Deputy" renders a term[8] that has been used of the "officers" or "chief officers" in Solomon's administration (4:5, 7, 27; 5:16; 9:23). This may suggest that Edom was now under an administrative official appointed by Jehoshaphat (see 2 Kings 8:20).[9]

Edom had been a source of some difficulty for King Solomon (11:14), although he had been able to develop his trading fleet within the land of Edom without opposition (9:26). Jehoshaphat's control over Edom provided him with a similar opportunity.

"Jehoshaphat made ships of Tarshish to go to Ophir for gold" (v. 48a). This is the clearest indication that Jehoshaphat was striving to recover something of the glory of his great-great-grandfather. Like Solomon he made Tarshish-ships (see 10:22) and planned to bring back gold from Ophir (see 9:28; 10:11).

But it did not happen, "for the ships were wrecked at Ezion-geber" (v. 48b), where Solomon (and presumably Jehoshaphat) had built his ships ("in the land of Edom," 9:26). Before the ships had even put to sea, they were destroyed, perhaps by a storm.

The only explanation we are given is this: "Then [probably meaning "That was the time when"[10]] Ahaziah the son of Ahab said to Jehoshaphat, 'Let my servants go with your servants in the ships,' but Jehoshaphat was not willing" (v. 49). This seems to suggest that the ship-building enterprise had involved a partnership with Ahab's son (as Solomon had partnered with Hiram, 9:27; 10:11, 22). However, for unstated reasons Jehoshaphat did not agree to have Ahaziah's servants join his own in manning the ships. Our writer seems to suggest that the involvement of Ahab's son had something to do with the catastrophic end to the project.[11]

While the record of Jehoshaphat's reign has taken some of the shine off the opening statement ("doing what was right in the sight of the LORD," v. 43), we must not forget how different Jehoshaphat was from Ahab. He was *a different kind of king* who reminds us, imperfectly to be sure, of King Solomon.

But he was not good enough. He did not come even close to restoring the glory of Solomon. If we are reminded of the Lord's promise by the mention of Jerusalem (and we should be), we are also reminded that it will take one greater than Jehoshaphat to fulfill the promise.

Death and Burial (v. 50a)

"And Jehoshaphat slept with his fathers and was buried with his fathers in the city of David his father" (v. 50a). Jehoshaphat was buried in Jerusalem with his father Asa (15:24), his grandfather Abijam (15:8), his great-grandfather Rehoboam (14:31), his great-great-grandfather Solomon (11:43), and his great-great-great-grandfather David (2:10).

The writer does not want us to forget "David his father." Whatever we think of Jehoshaphat, he was a son of David. Remember: there is a promise about a son of David. It is the hope of Israel. It is the hope of the world.

The Future? (v. 50b)

Although we may grow weary of the repeated disappointments, when we hear that "Jehoram *his son* reigned in his place" (v. 50b), the right question is, could *this* be the Son of David? The answer will come in 2 Kings 8:16–19. Those who believe the promise (and do notice 2 Kings 8:19) will be asking, "Could *this* be the Son of David?" for some time. But the day will come when the answer is "Yes!" (see Matthew 1:1; 12:23; 21:9).

King Ahaziah: The Legacy of Ahab (vv. 51–53)

But that day had not come at the end of the book of 1 Kings. Our writer has one more note to strike. He takes us back to his notice of Ahab's death in 22:40 to tell us that the death of Ahab was not the end of Ahab's influence.

The New King in Israel: Chronological Facts (v. 51)

> Ahaziah the son of Ahab began to reign over Israel in Samaria in the seventeenth year of Jehoshaphat king of Judah, and he reigned two years over Israel.[12] (v. 51)

In real time it may have been more like one year (see our discussion of 15:1, 2a), and this reminds us of the similarly brief reigns of Nadab (15:25) and Elah (16:8). Those two kings of Israel had also been sons of evil kings who had received the Lord's word of condemnation (Jeroboam in 14:7–11; Baasha in 16:1–4). Their brief reigns were cut short by the fulfillment of the Lord's word (Nadab in 15:27–30; Elah in 16:9–13). We must wonder what the Lord's condemnation of Ahaziah's father will mean for him (see especially 21:29).

The Measure of This King (vv. 52, 53a)

He did what was evil in the sight of the LORD and walked in the way of his
father and in the way of his mother and in the way of Jeroboam the son
of Nebat, who made Israel to sin. He served Baal and worshiped him . . .
(vv. 52, 53a)

Like father, like son. Indeed, like *mother*, like son. On the reasonable assumption that Ahaziah's mother was Jezebel (the only wife of Ahab of whom we have heard), this is bad news. The worship of Baal and all that entailed would prosper in Israel under Ahab's son.

The Legacy of Ahab (v. 53b)

The last line of 1 Kings describes the terrible legacy that Ahab left. Ahaziah, like his father, "provoked the LORD, the God of Israel, to anger in every way that his father had done" (v. 53b).

The book of 1 Kings closes with a reference to the grief, sorrow, and anger (on these connotations of the Hebrew *k's*, see our discussion of 14:9) to which the rebellion of the northern kingdom and her kings had moved the Lord. This has been something of a refrain since we first heard this expression in connection with Jeroboam's offenses (14:9, 15), then those of his son Nadab (15:30), then of Baasha (16:2, 7) and his son Elah (16:13), then of Omri (16:26) and his son Ahab (16:33; 21:22). The expression will not be used again until the summation of the northern kingdom's offenses in 2 Kings 17:11, 17.

It is a somber note on which to close this book, but it must be heard and taken with utmost seriousness. The distressing anger of the Lord, the God of Israel, at the evil of Ahaziah, his father Ahab, and the rest of them must now be seen in the light of the gospel of Jesus Christ as a small-scale reflection of the wrath of God "against all ungodliness and unrighteousness of men, who by their unrighteousness suppress the truth" (Romans 1:18).

The only hope for Israel at the end of 1 Kings is the promised son of David (see 13:2). The hope of Israel and of the world is the Son of David who has now come. By him we are saved from the wrath to come (Romans 5:9; 1 Thessalonians 1:10). In the light of all that we have heard from the book of 1 Kings, pause and wonder at this: "There is therefore now no condemnation for those who are in Christ Jesus" (Romans 8:1).

Soli Deo gloria.

Notes

Introduction: Fourteen Kings of Israel and "The King of the Jews"

1. The fourteen kings, in order of their appearance in 1 Kings, are: David (1:1), Solomon (1:10), Jeroboam (11:26), Rehoboam (11:43), Nadab (14:20), Abijam (14:31), Asa (15:8), Baasha (15:16), Jehoshaphat (15:24), Elah (16:6), Zimri (16:9), Omri (16:16), Ahab (16:28), and Ahaziah (22:40).

In this commentary I will follow the dates proposed by John Bright, *A History of Israel*, Third Edition (London: SCM, 1980), pp. 469, 470. I have assumed that David died (2:10) within the year that Solomon was made his co-regent (the story of 1 Kings 1). Other chronological schemes suggest dates about a decade earlier. So K. A. Kitchen, *On the Reliability of the Old Testament* (Grand Rapids, MI and Cambridge, UK: Eerdmans, 2003), p. 83. There are complex issues here that have little bearing on the exposition of the text before us, and so will be largely left untouched in this commentary. However, see further our discussion of 15:1, 2a.

2. Christian believers read the Old Testament with the enormous privilege of knowing the "end" of the story. "We must never regard the [Christian] gospel as an afterthought because things went wrong in Israel. The gospel was always God's forethought to everything, including creation, for how else can God have chosen us in Christ before the foundation of the world (Eph. 1:4)? It is important, then, to remind ourselves in sermon preparation that the gospel is God's forethought to the entire historical process in the Old Testament." Graeme Goldsworthy, *Preaching the Whole Bible as Christian Scripture: An Application of Biblical Theology to Expository Preaching* (Grand Rapids, MI and Cambridge, UK: Eerdmans, 2000), p. 142.

3. Although the Old Testament never uses the phrase "king of the Jews," the essentially synonymous expression "king over/of Israel" is prominent (1 Samuel 23:17; 2 Samuel 5:3, 12, 17; 12:7; 19:22; 1 Kings 1:34; 4:1; 11:37; 14:14; Proverbs 1:1; Ecclesiastes 1:12; cf. Ezekiel 37:22). Note how God himself is called "the King of Israel" in Isaiah 44:6 (cf. 43:15); Zephaniah 3:15. Jesus was called "the King of Israel" (Matthew 27:42; John 1:49; 12:13) as well as "the King of the Jews" (Matthew 2:2; 27:11, 29; John 19:3).

4. Old Testament passages that contribute to this expectation include 2 Samuel 22:50, 51; Isaiah 2:1–5; 9:1–7; 11:1–11; Jeremiah 3:17; Amos 9:11–15.

5. "The Jews" is an expression that originally referred to the people of Judah (2 Kings 16:6, KJV; Nehemiah 1:2; Jeremiah 32:12, NIV). However, even in Biblical times the term was fluid. In later Old Testament times it could refer to the people of Israel in contrast to Gentiles (Esther 9:15–19; Daniel 3:8; Zechariah 8:23), a sense found also in the New Testament (John 4:9; Acts 14:1). The precise sense of the term must be considered in each context (see Esther 8:17). For a useful summary see J. A. Sanders, "Jew, Jews, Jewess," *IDB* 2, pp. 897, 898.

Chapter One: A Frail and Fading King: What Hope Can There Be?

1. More literally, "And King David . . ." In the books from Genesis to 2 Kings only Genesis and Deuteronomy do *not* begin with the Hebrew conjunction "and," although in other respects 1 Kings 1:1 is an unusual opening sentence for a separate book. Cf. Burke O. Long, *1 Kings with an Introduction to Historical Literature*, The Forms of Old Testament Literature, Vol. 9 (Grand Rapids, MI: Eerdmans, 1984), p. 34. The conjunction signals a connection with what precedes, but does not it-self make the break between the books "arbitrary," as argued by Simon J. DeVries, *1 Kings*, Word Biblical Commentary, Vol. 12 (Waco, TX: Word Books, 1985), p. xix.

2. The contents of the early pages of 1 Kings can be seen to follow quite closely the terms of the 2 Samuel 7 promise: "When your days are fulfilled" (see 1:1–4); "and you lie down with your fathers" (see 2:10); "I will raise up your offspring after you" (see 2:13–46); "and I will establish his kingdom" (2:12, 46); "He shall build a house for my name" (see 5:1—8:66); "I will be to him a father, and he shall be to me a son" (see 3:1–28); "When he commits iniquity . . ." (see 11:1–11); "but my steadfast love will not depart from him" (see 11:12, 13).

3. In the Hebrew of 1 Kings 1:1 we may discern an allusion to "your *days*" in 2 Samuel 7:12, since the Hebrew idiom translated "advanced in years" (1 Kings 1:1) is more literally "he came into the *days*" (see also Genesis 18:11; 24:1; Joshua 13:1; 23:1, 2; 1 Samuel 17:12).

4. It was about the year 961 B.C. See note 1 to the Introduction.

5. Jerome T. Walsh, *1 Kings*, Berit Olam: Studies in Hebrew Narrative & Poetry (Collegeville, MN: The Liturgical Press, 1996), p. 5 proposes the following structure for the passage, which shows how the scene begins and ends with David's frailty:

> A. David's feeble condition (1:1)
> > B. Plan: find a virgin to care for David (1:2a)
> > > C. Her specific duties (1:2b)
> > B'. Abishag is found (1:3)
> > > C'. She carries out her duties (1:4a)
> A'. David is still impotent (1:4b).

6. A common arterial disease, especially in the elderly, that obstructs the flow of blood. So DeVries, *1 Kings*, p. 12, and others.

7. So Walter Brueggemann, *1 & 2 Kings*, Smyth & Helwys Bible Commentary (Macon, GA: Smyth & Helwys, 2000), p. 12.

8. John Gray, *I & II Kings: A Commentary*, Third, Fully Revised, Edition (London: SCM, 1977), p. 77.

9. Nowhere does the Old Testament suggest that a king's authority depends on his sexual prowess.

10. The context indicates that "clothes" here means "bedclothes" (as 1 Samuel 19:13). James A. Montgomery, *A Critical and Exegetical Commentary on the Books of Kings*, The International Critical Commentary (Edinburgh: T. & T. Clark, 1951), p. 81.

11. The first person singular suggests that the words were spoken by one individual, speaking no doubt on behalf of "his servants."

12. The third person references to "the king" accord with formal respectful speech, while this second person pronoun emerges in the most intimate reference in the speech.

13. We are not told exactly who these were, but given the particular conversation that follows, we may reasonably suppose they were personal attendants to the king.

14. Cf. Iain W. Provan, *1 & 2 Kings*, Understanding the Bible Commentary Series (Grand Rapids, MI: Baker, 1995), pp. 27, 28.

15. So RV, REB, HCSB, NIV.

16. The Hebrew text has two words, the first of which (*na'arah*) simply means "young woman" and the second (*bethulah*) "most often denotes a girl who is sexually mature, of marriageable age. The element of chastity may or may not be present (or stressed) depending on the context." H. M. Orlinsky, "Virgin," *IDBSup*, p. 939. The common translation "virgin" probably reads more into the term than it should. It has been argued that *bethulah* signifies "an individual [who] has arrived at the age when he or she is capable of sex relations *but has not yet had this experience*." O. J. Baab, "Virgin," *IDB* 4, p. 787 [emphasis mine]. The last part of this description is doubtful. "Out of the 51 times that *bethulah* occurs in the OT, 3 times it clearly means 'virgin' (Lev. 21:13f; Dt. 22:19; Ezk. 44:22), and once it certainly does not (. . . Joel 1:8)." M. Tsevat, "*bethulah*," *TDOT* 2, p. 341. "From significant passages, one sees that the word's meaning is not that of the modern English word ['virgin'], one who has not experienced sexual intercourse. The Hebrew word is usually qualified by a phrase such as 'who has never known a man' (e.g., Gen 24:16; Num 31:18) when the word is used specifically to mean what the word 'virgin' means today. The Hebrew word designates a young woman who has not yet married, although in Joel 1:8 it seems to refer to a woman who has already had a husband." John J. Schmidt, "Virgin," *ABD* 6, p. 853. See also G. J. Wenham, "Betulah, 'A Girl of Marriageable Age,'" *VT* 22 (1972), pp. 326–48.

17. "Wait on" is, more literally, "stand before." "Be in his service" has a participle of a verb meaning "be of use." Translations such as "be his caregiver" (HCSB) and "become his nurse" (NASB) might be appropriate if the context was not so obviously charged with sexuality.

18. I therefore doubt that "Her duties were confined to nursing the failing king." Mordechai Cogan, *1 Kings: A New Translation with Introduction, Notes & Commentary*, The Anchor Bible, Vol. 10 (New York: Doubleday, 2001), p. 156.

19. Such verbal reminders of an earlier part of the narrative would not have been intentional as far as the servants were concerned (they had not heard Nathan's parable). It is possible, however, that the narrator intended careful readers to detect this echo of the David-Bathsheba episode, of which many more reminders will soon be heard.

20. Although the proposal bristles with sexual overtones, Davis is surely correct to dismiss the view that it is "a virility test that David failed . . . [so that] his loss of sexual prowess was a sign of his inability to rule." Dale Ralph Davis, *The Wisdom and the Folly: An Exposition of the Book of First Kings* (Fearn, Ross-shire, UK: Christian Focus, 2002), p. 15, note 2. Contra Gray, *Kings*, p. 77; Gwilym H. Jones, *1 and 2 Kings*, 2 volumes, New Century Bible Commentary (Grand Rapids, MI and London: Eerdmans and Marshall, Morgan & Scott, 1984), pp. 89, 90. Eugene Peterson has captured the sense if not the indirect wording of the servants' plan, paraphrasing the end of verse 2: "she'll get in bed with you and arouse our master the king." Eugene H. Peterson, *The Message: The Bible in Contemporary Language* (Colorado Springs: NavPress, 2002), p. 562.

21. Contra DeVries, *1 Kings*, p. 13: "In a culture that accepted polygamy and the institution of concubinage, this arrangement had nothing in it that was shocking." Likewise: "the whole affair is to be judged according to the circumstances of the times, when there was nothing offensive in polygamy." C. F. Keil, "1 and 2 Kings," in C. F. Keil and F. Delitzsch, *Commentary on the Old Testament*, Vol. 3 (Peabody, MA: Hendrickson Publishers, 1996), p. 14. Few modern commentators seem troubled by the immorality of the servants' plan. I feel this is more an expression of modern moral insensitivity than an understanding of the different standards of Old Testament times. Compare the older wisdom of Matthew Henry: ". . . they knew what would gratify their own corruptions, and perhaps were too willing to gratify his, under colour of consulting his health." Matthew Henry, *Matthew Henry's Commentary on the Whole Bible*, Vol. 2 (Old Tappan, NJ: Revell, no date), p. 577.

22. While the difference (namely, that Bathsheba had a husband) magnifies the earlier offense, it does not make the present proposal morally acceptable.

23. The Hebrew expression for "beautiful" in 2 Samuel 11:2 is different from the word in 1 Kings 1:3, 4. However, the latter is found in 2 Samuel 13:1; 14:25. The recent history of "beautiful" people has not been a happy one.

24. Shunem was a town in the territory of Issachar (Joshua 19:18), where the Philistines had camped as they prepared for their final battle with King Saul (1 Samuel 28:4). See Map 5–7 in Currid, *Atlas*, p. 124. Later this town was to be the location of a remarkable event that also involved one human body warming another (2 Kings 4:8–37, especially v. 34).

25. It is possible that the last phrase of verse 3 ("brought her to the king") "implies that she was brought into a sexual relation to the king (cf. Judg. 12:9)." Martin J. Mulder, *1 Kings: Volume 1: 1 Kings 1–11*, Historical Commentary on the Old Testament (Leuven, Belgium: Peeters, 1998), p. 36.

26. In this commentary I will from time to time refer to "the narrator" or "the writer." It is generally believed these days that 1 Kings went through a complex process of compilation and editing. Be that as it may, I will be attempting to listen to the text that has resulted from whatever the process may have been. The "narrator" or "writer" is the voice we hear when we attend to the text before us, to be distinguished, of course, from the voices of the various characters reported by the "narrator."

27. This seems to be the view of Montgomery, *Kings*, p. 72: "that she was simply a nurse is emphasized in this v." Similarly: "[verse 4c] is not introduced either to indicate the impotence of David or to show that she did not become David's concubine, but simply to explain how it was that it could possibly occur to Adonijah (ch. 2:17) to ask for her as his wife." Keil, *Kings*, p. 14.

28. In the context it is reasonable to understand what the king *did* not do as an indication of what he *could* not do.

Chapter Two: An Up-and-Coming King: "But It Shall Not Be So among You"

1. I have listed psalms that have an explicit reference in their superscription to relevant events in David's life. Many other psalms (with or without "Of David" in the superscription) almost certainly belong to the same story.

2. For a brief discussion of the issues raised by David's multiple wives, see John Woodhouse, *2 Samuel: Your Kingdom Come*, Preaching the Word (Wheaton, IL: Crossway, 2015), pp. 100, 101.

3. In particular, when Amnon raped his half-sister Tamar, it was her full-brother Absalom who took up her cause (2 Samuel 13).

4. The kind of tensions that must have been almost inevitable when a man had more than one wife had been anticipated in Deuteronomy 21:15–17 and illustrated in a number of particular cases (see, for example, Hannah and Peninnah in 1 Samuel 1).

5. Donald J. Wiseman, *1 and 2 Kings*, Tyndale Old Testament Commentaries (Leicester, UK: Inter-Varsity Press, 1993), p. 68.

6. "Exalted" in 2 Samuel 5:12 and 1 Kings 1:5 translates forms of the same Hebrew verb (*ns'*).

7. The Hebrew participle (ESV, "exalted himself") in verse 5 does not describe an action of Adonijah's that followed *as a consequence* of verses 1–4. Rather, there is simply a shift of scene that is only implicitly connected to what precedes. Adonijah had been like this for some time. Contra Richard D. Patterson and Hermann J. Austel, "1, 2 Kings," in *The Expositor's Bible Commentary*, Revised Edition, eds. Tremper Longman III and David E. Garland, Vol. 3 (Grand Rapids, MI: Zondervan, 2009), p. 641: "David's feebleness and failure to make his choice of his successor public encouraged Adonijah to force David's hand by presenting him and the people with a *fait accompli*." Similarly Iain W. Provan, *1 & 2 Kings*, Understanding the Bible Commentary Series (Grand Rapids, MI: Baker, 1995), p. 24.

8. This paraphrase is an attempt to express the significance of the emphatic use of the pronoun ("I") in the Hebrew. Cf. J. P. Fokkelman, *Narrative Art and Poetry in the Books of Samuel: A Full Interpretation Based on Stylistic and Structural Analyses, Volume 1: King David (II Sam. 9–20 & I Kings 1–2)* (The Netherlands: Van Gorcum, Assen, 1981), p. 349.

9. So Wiseman: "a public claim." Wiseman, *1 and 2 Kings*, p. 68.

10. So Martin J. Mulder, *1 Kings: Volume 1: 1 Kings 1–11*, Historical Commentary on the Old Testament (Leuven, Belgium: Peeters, 1998), p. 42.

11. This is a matter of emphasis only. The two aspects of being king are hardly mutually exclusive. The Hebrew here has a verb (*malak*) meaning "reign," "be(come) king," not the noun (*melek*) "king."

12. Paul House astutely notes, "But what kind of man cannot wait for his father to die before seeking power?" Paul R. House, *1, 2 Kings*, The New American Commentary, Vol. 8 (Nashville: Broadman & Holman, 1995), p. 88.

13. The Hebrew word for "chariot" in 2 Samuel 15:1 and twice in 1 Samuel 8:11 usually refers to a war chariot. The corresponding term in 1 Kings 1:5 is a cognate singular noun usually understood in a collective sense (Genesis 50:9; 1 Kings 9:19), although it occasionally refers to a single chariot (1 Kings 22:35). So Mordechai Cogan, *1 Kings: A New Translation with Introduction, Notes & Commentary*, The Anchor Bible, Vol. 10 (New York: Doubleday, 2001), pp. 485–91.

14. The Hebrew word for "horses" (*parashiym*) in 1 Kings 1:5 and 1 Samuel 8:11 (so REB, NIV; ESV has "horsemen") seems to be a semi-technical term for chariot or cavalry horses. The corresponding term in 2 Samuel 15:1 is the more usual word (*susiym*) meaning "horses." Similarly James A. Montgomery, *A Critical and Exegetical Commentary on the Books of Kings*, The International Critical Commentary

(Edinburgh: T. & T. Clark, 1951), p. 83; Jerome T. Walsh, *1 Kings,* Berit Olam: Studies in Hebrew Narrative & Poetry (Collegeville, MN: The Liturgical Press, 1996), p. 7. See H. Niehr, *"parash," TDOT* 12, pp. 124–28.

15. It is just possible that the slight differences in wording in 1 Kings 1:5 compared to 2 Samuel 15:1 suggest that Adonijah "had made the decisive step toward rebellion by gathering a military force." So T. Ishida, "Adonijah the Son of Haggith and His Supporters: An Enquiry into Problems about History and Historiography," in R. E. Friedman and H. G. M. Williamson, eds., *The Future of Biblical Studies: The Hebrew Scriptures* (Atlanta: Scholars Press, 1987), p. 173.

16. The mention of "chariots" is itself rather telling. Chariots were typically used by Israel's enemies, and in due course "trust in chariots" became a sign in Israel of failure to trust in the Lord (Psalm 20:7). For a fuller discussion of the significance of chariots in the Bible, see Woodhouse, *2 Samuel*, pp. 239, 240.

17. The Septuagint makes this point explicit by adding, "But he would not punish his son Amnon, because he loved him, since he was his firstborn" (2 Samuel 13:21, esv margin).

18. "Also" signals that this is a series of items. In verse 6 we have three things about Adonijah that sum up the case for his importance, probably presented from his point of view. Similarly Fokkelman, *David*, p. 350; also Walsh, *1 Kings*, p. 7.

19. Although, to be fair, the comments in 1 Samuel 16:12 suggest a cute lad and may be a little ironic. John Woodhouse, *1 Samuel: Looking for a Leader*, Preaching the Word (Wheaton, IL: Crossway, 2008), p. 289.

20. "The emphasis here falls on Adonijah's exceptionally fine figure." Mulder, *1 Kings 1–11*, p. 44.

21. Zeruiah was David's sister (1 Chronicles 2:16).

22. For events that display the character of the sons of Zeruiah see 1 Samuel 26:6–12; 2 Samuel 2:12–32; 3:22–39.

23. In 2 Samuel Joab is certainly a complex character, sometimes judged more positively than I have suggested here. One writer describes him as "a complex figure, a man of shrewd judgment, ruthless energy, and potentially great treachery, who nonetheless sought no more than to look out for his own interests in the context of his greater service to his king." D. G. Schley, "Joab," *ABD* 6, p. 853. See also Michael A. Eschelbach, *Has Joab Foiled David? A Literary Study of the Importance of Joab's Character in Relation to David*, Studies in Biblical Literature, Vol. 76 (New York: Peter Lang, 2005), a thorough and stimulating study that nonetheless comes to a more positive view of Joab than I think is warranted.

24. This complex message of judgment is considered in some detail in Woodhouse, *1 Samuel*, pp. 63–72.

25. So Montgomery, *Kings*, p. 73; John Gray, *I & II Kings: A Commentary*, Third, Fully Revised, Edition (London: SCM, 1977), p. 79; Gwilym H. Jones, *1 and 2 Kings*, 2 volumes, New Century Bible Commentary (Grand Rapids, MI and London: Eerdmans and Marshall, Morgan & Scott, 1984), p. 91; Walter Brueggemann, *1 & 2 Kings*, Smyth & Helwys Bible Commentary (Macon, GA: Smyth & Helwys, 2000), p. 14; Peter J. Leithart, *1 & 2 Kings*, Brazos Theological Commentary on the Bible (Grand Rapids, MI: Brazos Press, 2006), p. 31. Similarly Provan, *Kings*, pp. 24, 25.

26. Influential studies of this kind include H. H. Rowley, "Zadok and Nehushtan," *JBL* 58 (1939), pp. 113–41 (Zadok was the hereditary priest of the local pre-Israelite cult of Jerusalem); F. M. Cross, "The Priestly Houses of Early Israel," in *Canaanite Myth and Hebrew Epic: Essays in the History of the Religion of Israel* (Cambridge, MA and London: Harvard University Press, 1973), pp. 195–215 (Zadok's origins were among the priests of Hebron.) See Roland de Vaux, *Ancient Israel: Its Life and Institutions*, trans. John McHugh (London: Darton, Longman & Todd, 1973), pp. 372–74.

27. I have attempted to clarify the complex of available data in Woodhouse, *1 Samuel*, pp. 65, 66 and Woodhouse, *2 Samuel*, pp. 251, 252.

28. The Cherethites and the Pelethites were probably foreigners (perhaps of Cretan and Philistine origins respectively) who had joined David's personal service. For more, see Woodhouse, *2 Samuel*, p. 252.

29. Contra John W. Olley, *The Message of Kings: God Is Present*, The Bible Speaks Today (Nottingham, UK: Inter-Varsity Press, 2011), p. 53 and Lissa M. Wray Beal, *1 & 2 Kings*, Apollos Old Testament Commentary, Vol. 9 (Nottingham, UK and Downers Grove, IL: Apollos, 2014), pp. 70, 75 who think that Shimei in 1:8 and 2:8 are most likely the same person. More emphatically Provan, *Kings*, p. 28.

30. The obscurity (to us) of the names Shimei and Rei have led some to suspect a textual difficulty here. See Gray, *Kings*, p. 79, note a.

31. Walsh, *1 Kings*, p. 9. This could be brought out more clearly in English translation by the use of pluperfect tenses throughout our passage, except in verse 9a. So Fokkelman, *David*, p. 348.

32. Walsh, *1 Kings*, p. 9 argues that the Hebrew verb (*zabakh*) translated "sacrificed" here "usually occurs in cultic contexts." However, it can refer to the slaughter of animals for the purposes of providing food, without any implication of "sacrifice" as such (cf. 1 Samuel 28:24). So RV ("slew"); also Gray, *Kings*, p. 82. However, Mulder argues that this "slaughter" was performed "ritually," and the meal was not a common meal but a cultic or ritual ceremony (at least in many cases). Mulder, *1 Kings 1–11*, p. 48.

33. See Map 5–15 in Currid, *Atlas*, p. 133.

34. Similarly Patterson and Austel, "Kings," p. 643; Beal, *Kings*, p. 71.

35. So Simon J. DeVries, *1 Kings*, Word Biblical Commentary, Vol. 12 (Waco, TX: Word Books, 1985), p. 14. The phrase "might signify some rock mass detached from the overhanging cliffs by an earthquake . . ." Gray, *Kings*, p. 83.

36. The restriction of the guest list to men of Judah is significant. It hints at tensions between Judah and Israel (the northern tribes) that will come catastrophically to the surface in 1 Kings 12. Similarly Provan, *Kings*, p. 25.

Chapter Three: The Right Side of History

1. Dawkins and Hitchens have been leading voices among the angry atheists of the early twenty-first century. Their works include Richard Dawkins, *The God Delusion* (London: Transworld Publishers, 2016); Christopher Hitchens, *god is not Great: How Religion Poisons Everything* (New York and Boston: Twelve, 2007).

2. The wisdom of Gamaliel (Acts 5:35–39) was superior to that of today's skeptics.

3. See note 1 to the Introduction.

4. The Hebrew of 2 Samuel 12:25 suggests that it was either Nathan or the Lord who gave the name Jedidiah to Solomon. So NIV and HCSB (less clear in the ESV). Curiously the God-given name does not appear again. Perhaps it was a rather private sign for David and Bathsheba.

5. This is contrary to a number of commentators who are inclined to be suspicious of Nathan's motives and methods. While Nathan himself can make mistakes (as in 2 Samuel 7:3ff.), I find it difficult to see any justification for the negative assumptions about his motives in 1 Kings 1 on which these suspicions rest. For example, one commentator has as a heading for verses 11–14: "Nathan Conspires to Make Solomon King" and goes on to say, "Here, where he is embroiled in a sordid palace intrigue with no apparent divine mandate, the narrative insistently—and ironically—reminds us at almost every opportunity that this schemer is 'the prophet.'" Jerome T. Walsh, *1 Kings*, Berit Olam: Studies in Hebrew Narrative & Poetry (Collegeville, MN: The Liturgical Press, 1996), p. 10. Another titles verses 11–31 "Nathan and Bathsheba organize a *coup d'état.*" Gwilym H. Jones, *1 and 2 Kings*, 2 volumes, New Century Bible Commentary (Grand Rapids, MI and London: Eerdmans and Marshall, Morgan & Scott, 1984), p. 93. Similarly: "Nathan proposes a way to manipulate the situation to his and Bathsheba's own advantage . . ." Burke O. Long, *1 Kings with an Introduction to Historical Literature*, The Forms of Old Testament Literature, Vol. 9 (Grand Rapids, MI: Eerdmans, 1984), p. 37. Such interpretations are only possible because the narrator has withheld certain information from us. This I understand to be deliberate. The reader, like many in Jerusalem that day, must make a decision without knowing everything. As we proceed, my reasons for thinking positively of Nathan will emerge. This should not be a matter of each reader making his or her own subjective judgment of characters and events, but each reader seeking to understand the perspective the narrator (with whatever subtlety) intends. Davis rightly rejects what he calls the "hermeneutics-of-suspicion approach" here. Dale Ralph Davis, *The Wisdom and the Folly: An Exposition of the Book of First Kings* (Fearn, Ross-shire, UK: Christian Focus, 2002), p. 19, note 6.

6. Matthew Henry says, "he knew God's mind." Matthew Henry, *Matthew Henry's Commentary on the Whole Bible*, Vol. 2 (Old Tappan, NJ: Fleming H. Revell Company, no date), p. 579.

7. Nathan "acted tactfully and judiciously, just as he had done when he reprimanded David for his sin with Bathsheba and Uriah." Richard D. Patterson and Hermann J. Austel, "1, 2 Kings," in *The Expositor's Bible Commentary*, Revised Edition, ed. Tremper Longman III and David E. Garland, Vol. 3 (Grand Rapids, MI: Zondervan, 2009), p. 644.

8. For a brief discussion of what we should make of David having several wives, see John Woodhouse, *2 Samuel: Your Kingdom Come*, Preaching the Word (Wheaton, IL: Crossway, 2015), pp. 100, 101.

9. Admittedly Nathan does not here explicitly connect Adonijah's investiture with the En-rogel feast. However, the reader may be expected to make that connection from the proximity (in the text and in narrative time) of Nathan's words to Bathsheba in Jerusalem and the feast at En-rogel. The feast was going on as Nathan was speaking (see v. 41). Nathan will confirm the connection in verse 25.

10. It seems to me to be more natural by far to assume that Nathan ("the prophet," remember!) was telling Bathsheba the truth than that he was making this up.

The idea that he was manipulating her for his own political ends and that he did not really know that Adonijah's banquet was an investiture of him as king strikes me as an unreasonably cynical reading. For an interpretation along these lines, see Tomoo Ishida, "Solomon's Succession to the Throne of David—A Political Analysis," in Tomoo Ishida, ed., *Studies in the Period of David and Solomon and Other Essays* (Winona Lake, IN: Eisenbrauns, 1982), pp. 178, 179.

11. The phrases "Absalom is king" in 2 Samuel 15:10 and "Adonijah . . . has become king" in 1 Kings 1:11 are identical in Hebrew except for the personal names.

12. The Hebrew clearly marks Nathan's words as a question (as the sense requires).

13. This point should not be overstated since Adonijah is referred to as "the son of Haggith" a number of times where nothing pointed seems intended (2 Samuel 3:4; 1 Kings 1:5; 2:13; cf. 1 Chronicles 3:2).

14. This literal rendering attempts to reflect the similarity of the sentences in Hebrew.

15. Similarly Iain W. Provan, *1 & 2 Kings*, Understanding the Bible Commentary Series (Grand Rapids, MI: Baker Books, 1995), pp. 28, 29.

16. In Hebrew "you" and "my lord the king" are emphatic: "Was it not *you, my lord the king,* who swore . . . ?"

17. Again in Hebrew "Solomon your son" is emphatic, implying "and no one else." Walsh, *1 Kings*, p. 11.

18. In Hebrew "he" is emphasized: "*he* is the one who shall sit on my throne."

19. "[T]his is probably a case of auto-suggestion, Nathan exploiting the dotage of the king." John Gray, *I & II Kings: A Commentary*, Third, Fully Revised, Edition (London: SCM, 1977), p. 88. "Many points in the narrative suggest that the oath is completely fabricated by Nathan, who was taking advantage of David's senility." Jones, *Kings*, p. 93. "[W]e suspect that Nathan is pulling a deception on the senile king, although the narrator cannily keeps us in the dark about this . . ." Richard D. Nelson, *First and Second Kings*, Interpretation: A Bible Commentary for Teaching and Preaching (Louisville: John Knox Press, 1987), p. 20. ". . . the dishonest manipulations by the unscrupulous Nathan." Volkmar Fritz, *1 & 2 Kings: A Continental Commentary* (Minneapolis: Fortress Press, 2003), p. 19, quoting Ernst Würthwein. Similarly Martin J. Mulder, *1 Kings: Volume 1: 1 Kings 1–11*, Historical Commentary on the Old Testament (Leuven, Belgium: Peeters, 1998), pp. 54, 55; Choon-Leong Seow, "The First and Second Book of Kings," in *The New Interpreter's Bible*, ed. Leander E. Keck, *et al*, Vol. 3 (Nashville: Abingdon Press, 1999), p. 19; Walter Brueggemann, *1 & 2 Kings*, Smyth & Helwys Bible Commentary (Macon, GA: Smyth & Helwys, 2000), p. 14; Ishida, "Solomon's Succession," p. 179. More reasonably: "We simply do not know if Nathan's words, repeated by Bathsheba, recall an actual event. Neither do we know if David, in v. 30, genuinely recalls a pronouncement once made by him or simply succumbs to the strong, suggestive pressure applied by wife and prophet." J. P. Fokkelman, *Narrative Art and Poetry in the Books of Samuel: A Full Interpretation Based on Stylistic and Structural Analyses, Volume 1: King David (II Sam. 9–20 & I Kings 1–2)* (The Netherlands: Van Gorcum, Assen, 1981), p. 354; similarly Walsh, *1 Kings*, p. 12. However, I consider that the previous narrative has given us good reasons to be much more positive about the words of "Nathan the prophet." Similarly, Fokkelman, *David*, p. 354, note 12; Simon J. DeVries, *1 Kings*, Word Biblical

Commentary, Vol. 12 (Waco, TX: Word Books, 1985), p. 15; Russell H. Dilday, *1, 2 Kings*, The Communicator's Commentary (Waco, TX: Word Books, 1987), p. 40; Peter J. Leithart, *1 & 2 Kings*, Brazos Theological Commentary on the Bible (Grand Rapids, MI: Brazos Press, 2006), p. 31.

20. "Undoubtedly, our narrator knew that Solomon had actually usurped the throne of David by a court intrigue, though he described it with ingenious obscurity." Ishida, "Solomon's Succession," p. 180.

21. The Hebrew imperfect tense is not as unambiguously future in its sense as the English future tense, but the inference drawn here is a reasonable understanding of the context. Similarly David G. Firth, *1 & 2 Samuel*, Apollos Old Testament Commentary 8 (Nottingham and Downers Grove, IL: Apollos and InterVarsity Press, 2009), p. 385.

22. I do not therefore go along with John Olley's assertion that "there has been not even a hint as to [David's] successor." John W. Olley, *The Message of Kings: God Is Present*, The Bible Speaks Today (Nottingham, UK: Inter-Varsity Press, 2011), p. 40.

23. Contra Gray who expresses surprise that Nathan's sympathies were not with Adonijah, given Nathan's involvement in rebuking David in 2 Samuel 12. Gray, *Kings*, p. 87. Likewise Jones, *Kings*, p. 93. This fails to give adequate weight to Nathan's involvement in declaring the Lord's continued grace toward David, and more particularly his love for Solomon (2 Samuel 12:13, 24, 25).

24. In Hebrew there is an evocative wordplay in verse 13 between "my lord the king" (*adoni hammelek*) and "Adonijah [is] king" (*adoniyahu malak*). The striking similarity of the phrases suggests the struggle is between David and Adonijah. Who is really king? My lord (*adoni*) or Adonijah (*adoniyahu*)? Similarly Walsh, *1 Kings*, p. 11.

25. "The responsibility which David, as father, has avoided for so long now strikes back in the contention for the throne. Here, as in the Absalom affair, an unmistakable friction has arisen between David's sub-personalities as father and king." Fokkelman, *David*, p. 355.

26. ". . . forced to deal with state affairs in his private quarters." Fokkelman, *David*, p. 355.

27. Jones, *Kings*, p. 95. Contra Cogan who prefers to think that we are being told that "Bathsheba entered the chamber, even though the king was intimately in bed with Abishag, and no one was allowed to enter without permission, except her, for she was his wife." Mordechai Cogan, *1 Kings: A New Translation with Introduction, Notes & Commentary*, The Anchor Bible, Vol. 10 (New York: Doubleday, 2001), p. 160, citing David Qimhi. This interpreter's imagination has been allowed to get away from him, don't you think? Less colorfully Wiseman assumes that Abishag "was not dismissed when Bathsheba and Nathan were present." Donald J. Wiseman, *1 and 2 Kings*, Tyndale Old Testament Commentaries (Leicester, UK: Inter-Varsity Press, 1993), p. 68. Similarly Paul R. House, *1, 2 Kings*, The New American Commentary, Vol. 8 (Nashville: Broadman & Holman, 1995), p. 91; Martin J. Mulder, *1 Kings 1–11*, p. 56.

28. The reader or hearer of this in Hebrew may notice an echo of a key word of the whole episode. *Ma-lak* ("What for-you?") is very close to *malak* ("has become/is king," vv. 11, 13, 18). Fokkelman, *David*, p. 355; also Walsh, *1 Kings*, p. 12.

29. This whole episode is a fine example of how Biblical narratives employ repetition as a powerful literary technique. Much of what we read in verses 15–27 repeats what Nathan had said in his advice to Bathsheba in verse 11–14. The repetitions emphasize that Nathan's advice was being followed. But it was not followed exactly, and the differences between what Nathan proposed and what was actually said to the king add life to the narrative. For a discussion of this literary technique in 1 Kings 1, see Robert Alter, *The Art of Biblical Narrative* (New York: Basic Books, 1981), pp. 97–100.

30. Some who see Nathan and Bathsheba as conspirators duping the old king read too much into Bathsheba's assertion in place of Nathan's question. "The question has become a fact. The ruthless mother generates new political reality. The alleged oath of David to Bathsheba now becomes the premise for the rest of the story." Brueggemann, *Kings*, p. 15.

31. Some Hebrew manuscripts have (literally rendered), "and now my lord the king . . . ," perhaps expressing "the energy with which Bathsheba speaks." C. F. Keil, "1 and 2 Kings," in C. F. Keil and F. Delitzsch, *Commentary on the Old Testament*, Vol. 3 (Peabody, MA: Hendrickson Publishers, 1996), p. 16. Other Hebrew manuscripts and ancient versions have, "and you, my lord the king, . . . ," perhaps striking an accusatory note. So Gray, *Kings*, p. 85; Lissa M. Wray Beal, *1 & 2 Kings*, Apollos Old Testament Commentary, Vol. 9 (Nottingham, UK and Downers Grove, IL: Apollos, 2014), p. 66.

32. The play on words we noted in verse 13 reappears here: "Adonijah is king" (*adoniyah malak*)/"my lord the king" (*adoni hammelek*). See note 24.

33. "Behold" represents a Hebrew idiom that emphasizes "the immediate presence of an object or a fact." *IBH*, p. 150, also pp. 168–170. Here it contributes to the vividness of Bathsheba's presentation of the fact of Adonijah's investiture, which she will fill out with some detail in verse 19.

34. "Bathsheba dares to confront David squarely with his impotence." Fokkelman, *David*, p. 356. Also Walsh, *1 Kings*, p. 13.

35. In Hebrew "oxen, fattened cattle, and sheep" in verse 19 differs from "sheep, oxen, and fattened cattle" in 1:9 in the vocabulary used as well as in the order of the words.

36. "All the sons of the king" certainly should remind the readers of this text of the events of 2 Samuel 13, where exactly the same Hebrew phrase was almost a refrain (esv, "all the king's sons," 2 Samuel 13:23, 27, 29, 30, 33).

37. The presence of Joab and Abiathar had not been mentioned in 1:9 (although reasonably deduced from 1:7).

38. Some Hebrew manuscripts have "And now . . ." So Gray, *Kings*, p. 85. Others have "And you . . ." giving added emphasis to the person of the king to whom all Israel was now looking. So Keil, *Kings*, p. 16; Walsh, *1 Kings*, p. 14; Mulder, *1 Kings 1–11*, p. 58.

39. "Lies down with his fathers" closely echoes "lie down with your fathers" in 2 Samuel 7:12.

40. Although the Hebrew word is often translated "sinners" (see 1 Samuel 15:18), its basic meaning is commonly supposed to be "those who have missed the mark." So Gray, *Kings*, p. 89, who cites Judges 20:16; see also Job 5:24; Proverbs 8:36; 19:2. In the present context the word seems to have a relational and political

sense, "to be on the wrong side." DeVries, *1 Kings*, p. 15; Fokkelman, *David*, p. 357, note 14. Furthermore strictly speaking the Hebrew does not say that they will be "counted" on the wrong side; they will *be* on the wrong side! Mulder, *1 Kings 1–11*, pp. 58, 59. Contra K. Koch, *"chata',"* *TDOT* 4, p. 311, who doubts that there was ever a "concrete basic meaning" and regards the religious usage as fundamental to all occurrences.

41. Fokkelman is unfair to her: "Although Bathsheba probably says nothing which is factually incorrect, her address at the same time consists of total and refined manipulation." Fokkelman, *David*, p. 358.

42. There are slight variations in the descriptions of Bathsheba's and Nathan's bowing down before the king in verses 16, 23, and 31, but these do not appear to be significant.

43. "Where Bathsheba's speech was personal and emotional, Nathan's is formal and concerned about political policy." Walsh, *1 Kings*, p. 16.

44. Once again interpreters who see dubious motives in Nathan's "conspiracy" are too harsh: "He mixes insinuating questions (vv. 24, 27) with what seems to be an outright lie (v. 25)." Nelson, *Kings*, p. 20. However, we have seen such careful cunning in Nathan's dealings with David before, and it was just what was needed (2 Samuel 12:1–12).

45. Italics reflect emphases in the Hebrew. Similarly DeVries, *1 Kings*, p. 15; Jones, *Kings*, p. 96; Walsh, *1 Kings*, p. 16. Contra Cogan, *1 Kings*, p. 160 and Mulder, *1 Kings 1–11*, p. 60, who regard verse 24 as a question.

46. "For" has its full logical force here. These are the facts that force Nathan to the conclusion expressed (or implied) in verse 24. Fokkelman, *David*, p. 362.

47. "The commanders of the army" is a little surprising, as previously we have heard only of "Joab the commander of the army" (v. 19), and the Septuagint seems to have smoothed over any difficulty by conforming verse 25 to verse 19 at this point. Since none of the lists of Adonijah's invited guests is exhaustive there is no real problem with the ESV, which follows the Hebrew here.

48. Walsh, *1 Kings*, p. 16. The immediacy of the situation described is further emphasized by the use of "behold" (see note 33) and the (present) participles "eating" and "drinking."

49. Once again I find myself disagreeing with the conspiracy theorists. One calls this "Nathan's questionable assertion." Nelson, *Kings*, p. 18.

50. Similarly Walsh, *1 Kings*, p. 17.

51. The Hebrew behind "me" is strikingly emphatic.

52. The Hebrew syntax of this question is unusual. See GKC §§ 150i, 150f; Gray, *Kings*, p. 89. It could be "a conditional statement, not a question . . . he simply and somewhat diffidently expresses his surprise and disappointment that David has acted without consulting his loyal retainers." Walsh, *1 Kings*, p. 17.

53. "Servants" follows the consonants of the Hebrew text (so NIV, REB; also DeVries, *1 Kings*, p. 16), while the vowels suggest the singular, "your servant," that is, Nathan himself (so HCSB; also Beal, *Kings*, p. 66). Either way, Nathan's complaint sounds personal. *How could you authorize such a thing without telling me (and perhaps other servants of the king)?*

54. Fokkelman argues (perhaps more ingeniously than convincingly) that this section stands at the structural center of 1:5—53, in *David*, p. 365. A simpler and

(to my mind) more persuasive argument along the same lines is found in Long, *1 Kings*, p. 38.

55. Similarly Fokkelman, *David*, p. 363.

56. Similarly Walsh, *1 Kings*, p. 19.

57. "He" is emphatic in the Hebrew: "*he* is the one who shall sit . . ."

58. "After me/him" in verses 13, 17, 20, and 30 point to the time after David's death (see v. 21 and 2 Samuel 7:12). "In my place" in verses 30, 35 refers to a co-regency.

59. "This day" in verse 30 is King David's response to "this day" in verse 25, the Hebrew expression in verse 30 being more emphatically "*this* day" than the phrase in verse 25.

60. Note the identical expression in 2 Samuel 4:9.

61. "Invited" in verse 26 and "Call" in verse 32 represent the same Hebrew verb (*qara'*).

62. The Hebrew text could be rendered "the servants of your lords," which could mean those who assisted all the senior figures in David's circle. "The servants of your lord" recognizes that the grammatical plural of *'adon* frequently has a singular meaning (so the Septuagint).

63. It was as though he was "to be seen in the king's limo, like arriving on 'Air Force One.'" Brueggemann, *Kings*, p. 16.

64. Perhaps "a horse is the symbol of war, a donkey the symbol of peace. Adonijah prepared for war but Solomon did not allow himself to be intimidated by this." Mulder, *1 Kings 1–11*, p. 65.

65. James A. Montgomery, *A Critical and Exegetical Commentary on the Books of Kings*, The International Critical Commentary (Edinburgh: T. & T. Clark, 1951), p. 77.

66. See Map 5–9 in Currid, *Atlas*, p. 126.

67. The fact that the location of Adonijah's gathering is not mentioned in the reported words spoken to David is hardly relevant (contra Walsh, *1 Kings*, p. 21). No narrative records *everything*.

68. The Hebrew verb "anoint" is singular, suggesting that Zadok is the main subject, who is joined by Nathan. See verse 39.

69. For a helpful brief discussion of the act of anointing in the Bible see Brueggemann, *Kings*, p. 17.

70. Better, "ram's horn." The ram's horn was used to signal a number of important occasions. See 1 Samuel 13:3; 2 Samuel 2:28; 6:15; 15:10; 18:16; 20:1; 20:22.

71. The Hebrew expression appears in various contexts: with Saul (1 Samuel 10:24), Absalom (2 Samuel 16:16), and Joash (2 Kings 11:12).

72. Similarly Walsh, *1 Kings*, p. 23.

73. In the Hebrew "he" is emphatic: "*he* is the one who . . ."

74. Similarly DeVries, *1 Kings*, p. 17. The same word (translated "prince" in the ESV) was used in this non-royal sense of Saul (1 Samuel 9:16; 10:1) and of David (1 Samuel 13:14; 25:30; 2 Samuel 5:2; 6:21; 7:8). See John Woodhouse, *1 Samuel: Looking for a Leader*, Preaching the Word (Wheaton, IL: Crossway, 2008), p. 162.

75. I have argued that the heart of the tension between "Israel" and "Judah" lies in the historic rejection (by "Israel") and acceptance (by "Judah") of David as king in 2 Samuel 2. See Woodhouse, *2 Samuel*, pp. 81 and 569, note 45.

76. "Amen" is a direct transliteration of a Hebrew word that expresses a confirming response to something said before. It indicates a stronger commitment than English usage suggests. It is an expression of trust. Walsh, *1 Kings*, p. 24; Cogan, *1 Kings*, p. 162. A suggested paraphrase of the sense of "Amen!" in 1 Kings 1:36 is: "Precisely! I feel the same way about it, may God do it!" Alfred Jepsen, *"aman,"* *TDOT* 1, p. 320. The practice of transliterating, rather than attempting to translate the word, finds a parallel in the New Testament where a Greek transliteration of the Hebrew word appears frequently. For a survey, see Bruce Chilton, "Amen," *ABD* 1, pp. 184–86.

77. The Hebrew of Benaiah's remarkable speech could be understood as confident assertions rather than a prayer: "The LORD, the God of my lord the king, will say so . . . he will be with Solomon and make his throne greater . . ." Similarly Fokkelman, *David*, p. 370; Beal, *Kings*, p. 66.

78. "May the LORD, the God of my lord the king, say so" could be translated: "Thus the LORD, the God of my lord the king, says."

79. "This is the language of his faith in that promise of God on which Solomon's government was founded." Henry, *Commentary*, p. 582. The excessively cynical interpreters fail to see this: "In the circumstances the wish . . . seems tactless." Jones, *Kings*, p. 102. "The military man dares to expect that Yahweh will 'ordain' what palace intrigue has evoked and what the duped David has enacted." Brueggemann, *Kings*, p. 17. Walsh judges Benaiah to be a "yes man." Walsh, *1 Kings*, p. 24.

80. On the Cherethites and the Pelethites see our earlier discussion of 1:8.

81. Cf. 1 Samuel 10:1; 16:13.

82. "From the tent" is probably best understood as indicating where the oil *had* come from, "the tent" being either the tabernacle (now located at Gibeon [3:15; 2 Chronicles 1:3]) or the tent David had pitched in Jerusalem for the ark (2 Samuel 6:17; 7:2).

Chapter Four: Sooner or Later . . .

1. We have noted that a careful reading of 2 Samuel 7:12 ("who *shall* come from your body") suggests someone other than Adonijah, but that is hardly enough to exclude Adonijah from the minds of those who may have simply heard about the promise.

2. Most English translations have the hearing occur *as* the feast was finishing (so ESV, NIV). I take the Hebrew to mean that it was the hearing that put an end to the feasting, a possibility noted by Gwilym H. Jones, *1 and 2 Kings*, 2 volumes, New Century Bible Commentary (Grand Rapids, MI and London: Eerdmans and Marshall, Morgan & Scott, 1984), p. 104 and Mordechai Cogan, *1 Kings: A New Translation with Introduction, Notes & Commentary*, The Anchor Bible, Vol. 10 (New York: Doubleday, 2001), p. 163, with reference to E. F. Sutcliffe, "Simultaneity in Hebrew: A Note on 1 Kings i.41," *Journal of Semitic Studies* 3 (1958), pp. 80, 81.

3. The Hebrew may be represented quite literally: "And Adonijah heard [singular verb], and all the called ones who were with him. And they finished eating."

4. "With" in 1:8 and 1:41 is translated from two different Hebrew words, but in these contexts they appear essentially synonymous.

5. Jerome T. Walsh, *1 Kings*, Berit Olam: Studies in Hebrew Narrative & Poetry (Collegeville, MN: The Liturgical Press, 1996), p. 27.

6. The Hebrew word (*qiryah*) translated "city" is unusual. Almost all occurrences are in poetic texts, and the precise nuance here is difficult to determine. One suggestion is that "it properly means a walled fortress, a citadel rather than a city." John Gray, *I & II Kings: A Commentary*, Third, Fully Revised, Edition (London: SCM, 1977), p. 95. Here it may then refer to the part of the city where the king resided. So Jones, *Kings*, p. 104. If so we may wonder what made Joab think that the sound he heard came so precisely from there? What did the cunning old warrior suspect? Another suggestion is that here it refers "particularly to the populace within the walls of Jerusalem." M. J. Mulder, "*qiryah*," *TDOT* 13, p. 166. This perhaps makes better sense.

7. Compare the similar question asked by Eli when the news of a terrible defeat caused an uproar in Shiloh: "What is the sound of this uproar?" (1 Samuel 4:14, literal translation).

8. The Hebrew sentences at 1:22 and 1:42a are almost identical except, of course, for the personal names. This suggests a comparison of the roles of Nathan and Jonathan in the two scenes. Similarly Walsh, *1 Kings*, p. 27. Indeed the names invite comparison: Nathan and Jo-Nathan! Ibid., p. 29. Shortly we may even see a subtle irony in the fact that Jonathan's name means "Yahweh has given," perhaps a "testimony to the fact that Solomon's kingship is a gift from God." So J. P. Fokkelman, *Narrative Art and Poetry in the Books of Samuel: A Full Interpretation Based on Stylistic and Structural Analyses, Volume 1: King David (II Sam. 9–20 & I Kings 1–2)* (The Netherlands: Van Gorcum, Assen, 1981), p. 376.

9. More than "a good chap" as suggested by Fokkelman, *David*, p. 372. Rather the phrase here "suggests reliability and trust in adverse circumstances." Cogan, *1 Kings*, p. 163.

10. For further discussion of this gospel language, see John Woodhouse, *1 Samuel: Looking for a Leader*, Preaching the Word (Wheaton, IL: Crossway, 2008), p. 551; John Woodhouse, *2 Samuel: Your Kingdom Come*, Preaching the Word (Wheaton, IL: Crossway, 2015), pp. 447, 646, notes 20, 21.

11. "Far from it" (REB); "Unfortunately not" (HCSB); "Not at all" (NIV). Similarly "On the contrary." Fokkelman, *David*, p. 374; Cogan, *1 Kings*, p. 163. Wiseman calls it "a strong adversative." Donald J. Wiseman, *1 and 2 Kings*, Tyndale Old Testament Commentaries (Leicester, UK: Inter-Varsity Press, 1993), p. 73.

12. The old standard lexicon maintains that in older Hebrew (including 1 Kings 1:43) this term has "an asseverative force, **verily, of a truth**," while in late Hebrew it is a "decided adversative, **howbeit, but**" (citing Daniel, Ezra and 2 Chronicles). BDB, p. 6. The Hebrew word (*'abal*) occurs only eleven times in the Old Testament, with striking variations in the English renderings, as the following table illustrates:

	RV	JB	REB	HCSB	ESV	NIV
Genesis 17:19	Nay, but	No, but	No, but	No, but	No, but	Yes, but
Genesis 42:21	Verily	Truly	No doubt	It is plain	In truth	Surely
1 Kings 1:43	Verily	Yes	Far from it	Unfortunately not	No	Not at all

13. So Martin J. Mulder, *1 Kings: Volume 1: 1 Kings 1–11*, Historical Commentary on the Old Testament (Leuven, Belgium: Peeters, 1998), p. 75.

14. "At the time this scene was probably written, the word conveys strong agreement: 'Yes, indeed!'" Walsh, *1 Kings*, p. 28. Keil has a bet each way: "'Yea, but' . . . an expression of assurance with a slight doubt." C. F. Keil, "1 and 2 Kings," in C. F. Keil and F. Delitzsch, *Commentary on the Old Testament*, Vol. 3 (Peabody, MA: Hendrickson Publishers, 1996), p. 19.

15. The ironic play on words we noted earlier in the conversations with David appears again in verse 43: "Jonathan answered Adonijah (*adoniyah*), '. . . our lord (*adoneynu*) King David . . .'" Who is lord (*adon*) here?

16. As suggested by Walsh, *1 Kings*, p. 28. Similarly: "He possesses a youthful frankness and trustfulness which are disarming but must be called politically naïve." Fokkelman, *David*, p. 376.

17. In retrospect Nathan's earlier words to David lend support to this understanding. Nathan presented an almost credible argument that King David must have supported Adonijah's elevation to the kingship (see 1:24–27). Should we now see that Nathan was giving voice to a rather widespread perception among those who were supporting Adonijah?

18. "You" here is plural, referring to the whole crowd at Adonijah's feast.

19. The repetition is not conveyed in the ESV, which omits "And also" from verse 46, has "Moreover" in verse 47, and breaks up the phrase "And . . . also" in verse 48. A breathless messenger blurting out his news with "and also . . . and also . . ." was heard on an earlier occasion (see 1 Samuel 4:17: "Israel has fled before the Philistines, *and* there has *also* been a great defeat among the people. Your two sons *also*, Hophni and Phinehas, are dead, and the ark of God has been captured").

20. I am not at all persuaded by those who think there is some problem with Jonathan appearing so quickly in En-rogel if he had witnessed the events and words that had taken place in Jerusalem. So Cogan, *1 Kings*, p. 163. A swift runner like Jonathan would not have taken long to cover the (downhill) distance from the city to En-rogel.

21. This point is obscured by the English translations rendering "the throne of the kingdom" as "the royal throne" (JB, REB, HCSB, ESV, NIV).

22. See, for example, 1 Samuel 10:16, 25 (ESV, "kingship"); 11:14 and the discussions in Woodhouse, *1 Samuel*, pp. 179, 187, 188, 206, 207.

23. Note the phrase "the throne of his kingdom" in 2 Samuel 7:13 (also in Deuteronomy 17:18). The whole 2 Samuel 7 passage uses a slightly different word for "kingdom" from the one Jonathan used in 1 Kings 1:46, but this does not seem significant. On the essentially synonymous (and similar sounding) Hebrew words for "kingdom," see Woodhouse, *2 Samuel*, pp. 597, 598, note 21.

24. Or "bless," meaning "invoke the blessing of God upon David in his son Solomon." Gray, *Kings*, p. 95.

25. The same Hebrew verb is used in each of these three verses.

26. Notice the three significant occurrences of the phrase "the God of Israel" in 2 Samuel: in David's response to the Lord's kingdom promise (2 Samuel 7:27), Nathan's reminder to David of the Lord's purposes for him (2 Samuel 12:7), and David's recollection of God's promise to him (2 Samuel 23:3).

27. The Septuagint has "one of my offspring" in place of "someone," making an even stronger link to 2 Samuel 7.

28. This is in contrast to "how fickle the crowd can be." Russell H. Dilday, *1, 2 Kings*, The Communicator's Commentary (Waco, TX: Word Books, 1987), p. 46.

29. Similarly Fokkelman, *David*, p. 378.

30. The reaction of the guests strongly suggests that Nathan's report (1:11, 25; repeated by Bathsheba, 1:18) that Adonijah had been declared king at En-rogel was no fabrication ("Nathan's questionable assertion" according to Richard D. Nelson, *First and Second Kings*, Interpretation: A Bible Commentary for Teaching and Preaching [Louisville: John Knox Press, 1987], p. 18). If nothing of the kind had happened at En-rogel, why would the guests now tremble?

31. The Hebrew emphasizes the focus now on Adonijah: "But as for Adonijah, he feared . . ." Walsh, *1 Kings*, p. 30.

32. Over-literally: "Adonijah feared from the face of Solomon."

33. Some think that the altar was in the tent that David had pitched in Jerusalem for the ark of the covenant (2 Samuel 6:17; 7:2) rather than in the tabernacle. So Keil, *Kings*, p. 19; Gray, *Kings*, p. 96; Richard D. Patterson, and Hermann J. Austel, "1, 2 Kings," in *The Expositor's Bible Commentary*, Revised Edition, ed. Tremper Longman III and David E. Garland, Vol. 3 (Grand Rapids, MI: Zondervan, 2009), p. 649. However, it seems more likely that the altar referred to here was at Gibeon where the tabernacle (without the ark) was now located. There was certainly an altar there (see 3:4; 2 Chronicles 1:3).

34. In Amos 3:14 the Lord announces that "the horns of the altar shall be cut off and fall to the ground." This probably means that "all Israel has become guilty of such grave crimes that Yahweh himself destroys the place of refuge." Hans Walter Wolff, *Joel and Amos*, Hermeneia (Philadelphia: Fortress Press, 1977), p. 201.

35. "It is a great change with him; he that, in the morning, was grasping at a crown, is, before night, begging for his life." Matthew Henry, *Matthew Henry's Commentary on the Whole Bible*, Vol. 2 (Old Tappan, NJ: Fleming H. Revell Company, no date), p. 584.

36. The Hebrew has the word "day" here (NIV, "today"), which reminds us that everything since Adonijah began his feast at En-rogel (1:9) had taken place on that same day ("this day" in 1:25, 30, 48).

37. Note the fourfold "King Solomon" in verses 51, 53.

38. Compare Saul (1 Samuel 11:12, 13) and David (2 Samuel 2:4–7), who both began their reigns showing mercy to people who could be enemies.

39. ". . . on condition that he behave like a gentleman." James A. Montgomery, *A Critical and Exegetical Commentary on the Books of Kings*, The International Critical Commentary (Edinburgh: T. & T. Clark, 1951), p. 81.

40. The Hebrew phrases differ slightly, literally "man of worth" (1:42) and "son of worth" (1:52).

41. The Hebrew (literally, "from upon the altar") may suggest that Adonijah had climbed up onto the altar and had to be brought down.

42. Compare David's treatment of the rebellious Absalom in 2 Samuel 14:24.

Chapter Five: Good Government—What Would It Be Like?

1. Compare NIV, "he gave a charge to Solomon his son." Similar language is used of Jacob in Genesis 49:29 and of Hezekiah in 2 Kings 20:1 (where the ESV's "Set your house in order" is more literally "Command your house").

2. There are traditions that Solomon was twelve (some manuscripts of the Septuagint) or fourteen (rabbinic tradition and Josephus) at the time of David's death. Martin J. Mulder, *1 Kings: Volume 1: 1 Kings 1–11*, Historical Commentary on the Old Testament (Leuven, Belgium: Peeters, 1998), p. 105.

3. The Bible gives particular prominence to the last words of a number of key individuals in its history. Compare Jacob's words in Genesis 49, Moses' in Deuteronomy 33, Joshua's in Joshua 23, 24 (not to mention the words of Jesus in John 14–17). Note that the words recorded in 2 Samuel 23:1–7 are described as "the last words of David." They were probably actually uttered earlier than the words we are about to hear. However, both utterances expressed David's consciousness of God's promise. See John Woodhouse, *2 Samuel: Your Kingdom Come*, Preaching the Word (Wheaton, IL: Crossway, 2015), pp. 517–26.

4. Psalm 72, the superscription of which may be translated "For Solomon" (REB) rather than "Of Solomon" (ESV), has been understood by some older commentators to be David's prayer, near the end of his life, for Solomon. So John Calvin, *Commentary on the Book of Psalms*, Vol. 2 (Grand Rapids, MI: Baker Book House, 1989), pp. 99, 100; Matthew Henry, *Matthew Henry's Commentary on the Whole Bible*, Vol. 3 (Old Tappan, NJ: Fleming H. Revell Company, no date), p. 505; similarly C. H. Spurgeon, *The Treasury of David*, Vol. 3 (London, Edinburgh and New York: Marshall Brothers, Ltd, no date.), p. 226. Note that the last line of the psalm says, "The prayers of David, the son of Jesse, are ended," which is at least consistent with the suggestion that Psalm 72 is a prayer from the last days of David's life (although later in the Book of Psalms other prayers of David are included [see Psalms 138—145]). If we accept this (and I am inclined to), then Psalm 72 is the *prayer* that expressed King David's vision of the promised king and kingdom, just as 1 Kings 2:1–9 is the *charge* that conveyed the same vision. John Calvin's judgment is insightful: "David in this psalm prays to God, in the name of the whole Church, for the continual prosperity of the kingdom which was promised him, and teaches us at the same time, that the true happiness of the godly consists in their being placed under the government of a king who was raised to the throne by the appointment of heaven." Calvin, *Psalms*, 2, pp. 99, 100. Most modern commentators do not accept this understanding of the psalm's origin. For example, A. A. Anderson, *Psalms: Volume 1*, New Century Bible (London: Oliphants, 1972), p. 518. F. Delitzsch thought that the psalm was composed by Solomon as a prayer for the people to pray for their king. F. Delitzsch, "Psalms," in C. F. Keil and F. Delitzsch, *Commentary on the Old Testament*, Vol. 5 (Peabody, MA: Hendrickson Publishers, 1996), p. 479.

5. The Hebrew rendered "Take courage, and be men" in the ESV of 1 Samuel 4:9 is the plural of exactly the same expression as "Be strong, and show yourself a man" in 1 Kings 2:2. Similar (but not identical) expressions are found in Deuteronomy 31:23; Joshua 1:6, 8, 9, 18.

6. "[K]eeping that which God wishes to have kept." J. P. Fokkelman, *Narrative Art and Poetry in the Books of Samuel: A Full Interpretation Based on Stylistic and Structural Analyses, Volume 1: King David (II Sam. 9–20 & I Kings 1–2)* (The Netherlands: Van Gorcum, Assen, 1981), p. 385. The peculiar Hebrew expression

(over-literally, "Keep the keeping of the LORD") appears in Genesis 26:5; Leviticus 8:35; 18:30; 22:9; Numbers 9:19, 23; Deuteronomy 11:1; Joshua 22:3.

7. Four of the Hebrew terms used for God's laws in 1 Kings 2:3 appear in Psalm 19 (ESV, "commandment," "rules," "testimony," and "law").

8. "Law" is an unfortunate rendering particularly because the Hebrew *torah* is not always identical to the Greek *nomos* in the Apostle Paul's very important teaching about "law." Choon-Leong Seow, "The First and Second Book of Kings," in *The New Interpreter's Bible*, ed. Leander E. Keck, et al, Vol. 3 (Nashville: Abingdon, 1999), p. 26, note 12.

9. The Hebrew conjunction (*lema'an*) rendered "that" ("*that* you may prosper . . ." [v. 3] and "*that* the LORD may establish . . ." [v. 4]) usually expresses purpose ("in order that"), but sometimes result ("so that"). *CHALOT*, p. 207.

10. The word (*skl* hiphil) translated "prosper" in the ESV here (HCSB, "have success") is used widely in the Old Testament to mean, on the one hand, having insight, wisdom, and understanding of God and his ways and, on the other hand, the "success" in life that derives from such wisdom. ". . . that thou mayest act wisely and execute well." C. F. Keil, "1 and 2 Kings," in C. F. Keil and F. Delitzsch, *Commentary on the Old Testament*, Vol. 3 (Peabody, MA: Hendrickson Publishers, 1996), p. 22. See K. Koenen, "*sakal*," *TDOT* 14, pp. 112–28, especially pp. 122–24.

11. All verses cited in this paragraph use the verb discussed in the previous note.

12. Unless, of course, we were to assume that the words of 1 Kings 2:4b had been spoken to David at some time, but not recorded in the narrative before this point. That, I think, is unlikely.

13. This is closely related to the relationship between human responsibility and divine sovereignty. For very helpful discussions of the important issues involved, see D. Broughton Knox, *The Everlasting God* (Welwyn, Hertfordshire, UK: Evangelical Press, 1982), pp. 27–48; J. I. Packer, *Evangelism and the Sovereignty of God* (London: Inter-Varsity Fellowship, 1961); A. W. Pink, *The Sovereignty of God* (London: The Banner of Truth Trust, 1961).

14. See how both sides of this are expressed in 1 Kings 11:11–13, 31–39.

15. One writer says of verses 5–9, "We cannot but draw the conclusion that it is chiefly the dark side of David's life and personality which is made visible here . . . he is, above all, filled with the desire for revenge and his successor is consequently given a heavy work-load . . . the vulgar settling of two old accounts." Fokkelman, *David*, p. 386. Another sees in the two parts of David's speech "a combination of sincere piety and pragmatic calculating politics." John W. Olley, *The Message of Kings: God Is Present,* The Bible Speaks Today (Nottingham, UK: Inter-Varsity Press, 2011), p. 49. Similarly: "Here [verses 5–9] the issue seems to be not Torah requirements, but political prudence." Walter Brueggemann, *1 & 2 Kings*, Smyth & Helwys Bible Commentary (Macon, GA: Smyth & Helwys, 2000), p. 27. Some consider that the problem is a fictional creation of the writer of this account; by attributing verses 5–9 to David he "has exonerated Solomon of bloodshed and made David himself fully responsible for the measures taken." Gwilym H. Jones, *1 and 2 Kings*, 2 volumes, New Century Bible Commentary (Grand Rapids, MI and London: Eerdmans and Marshall, Morgan & Scott, 1984), p. 106. I find all of these views thoroughly unconvincing. I hope you do too!

16. Literally "And also . . ." This may suggest that David means verses 5–9 as a sequel to verses 1–4. "Keeping the sevenfold Torah to establish the four corners of the world *as a king* means employing the sword against evildoers." Peter J. Leithart, *1 & 2 Kings*, Brazos Theological Commentary on the Bible (Grand Rapids, MI: Brazos Press, 2006), p. 37.

17. ". . . avenging in time of peace for blood that had been shed in war" refers to the murder of Abner, killed by Joab after he had made "peace" with David (2 Samuel 3:21–23), because of Abner's earlier action in the battle at Gibeon (2 Samuel 3:30; 2:23).

18. The Septuagint has "my waist . . . my feet," which would graphically emphasize the sense in which David saw the acts as done "to me." This reading is favored by a number of commentators including James A. Montgomery, *A Critical and Exegetical Commentary on the Books of Kings*, The International Critical Commentary (Edinburgh: T. & T. Clark, 1951), p. 89; John Gray, *I & II Kings: A Commentary*, Third, Fully Revised, Edition (London: SCM, 1977), p. 98, note d; Jones, *Kings*, pp. 107, 108; Simon J. DeVries, *1 Kings*, Word Biblical Commentary, Vol. 12 (Waco, TX: Word, 1985), p. 26; Richard D. Nelson, *First and Second Kings*, Interpretation: A Bible Commentary for Teaching and Preaching (Louisville, Kentucky: John Knox Press, 1987), p. 24; Lissa M. Wray Beal, *1 & 2 Kings*, Apollos Old Testament Commentary, Vol. 9 (Nottingham, UK and Downers Grove, IL: Apollos, 2014), p. 67. The Hebrew text (followed by the ESV) is defended by Donald J. Wiseman, *1 and 2 Kings*, Tyndale Old Testament Commentaries (Leicester, UK: Inter-Varsity Press, 1993), p. 76.

19. So Keil: "David ought to have punished these two crimes." Keil, *Kings*, p. 23.

20. So Woodhouse, *2 Samuel*, p. 125. This would be consistent with David's attitude in other contexts (see especially 1 Samuel 24:12, 13, 15; 25:33; 26:10, 23).

21. "Sheol" is a Hebrew word for the place of the dead. "The meaning of Sheol moves between the ideas of the grave, the underworld and the state of death." D. K. Innes, "Sheol," *IBD* 3, p. 1436.

22. Explicitly Joab murdered Abner after he had "gone in peace" from David (see 2 Samuel 3:21–23). David had made "peace" with Absalom (2 Samuel 15:9) and no doubt was longing to make peace again when Joab killed him (see 2 Samuel 18:5). Although the word is not used, it is clear that David's appointment of Amasa as his commander was part of his peace deal with those who had risen against him (2 Samuel 19:13).

23. The following examples could be multiplied. "David was wrong in passing on responsibility to Solomon to execute the judgment he himself should have ordered at the time. This was to cause his son and successors much trouble and feuding." Wiseman, *1 and 2 Kings*, p. 77. "The true reason for his unfathomable bitterness and rancor is very personal. . . . The reason lies in the direct David-Joab relationship and nowhere else. It is Joab's insufferably cruel treatment of his monarch during the latter's first mourning for Absalom and the equally insufferable deed immediately prior to and inseparable from the slaying of Absalom. David has never forgiven his general for either of these two facts, especially because his satisfaction derived from Joab's dismissal was all too brief, having been cut short by the general's annulment of the measure in an acme of high-handedness." Fokkel-

man, *David*, p. 388. "David's measures against Joab are then simply the last step in a relationship which has degenerated to the level of a vendetta." Ibid., p. 386, note 5. "David uses the old grievance to cover the political exigency of Joab's death." Beal, *Kings*, p. 75.

24. ". . . there is no doubt that [Joab's] death was owing to the part he took with Adonijah against Solomon." Gray, *Kings*, p. 101. Since the text does not say this, there *is* doubt in my mind.

25. In the context of the story of Solomon, this first mention of his "wisdom" should not be reduced to some kind of politically motivated pragmatism, as do a number of commentators. "The punishment of so powerful a man as Joab the commander-in-chief was, required great wisdom, to avoid occasioning a rebellion in the army, which was devoted to him." Keil, *Kings*, p. 23. "According to your wisdom" means "find some specious pretext" according to Montgomery, *Kings*, p. 89, or "the practical and even unprincipled path to success" according to Gray, *Kings*, p. 102. "It is a chilling first appearance of the word 'wisdom' in the narrative, for it is a wisdom that contextualizes politically expedient murder in torah obedience (vv. 2–4)." Beal, *Kings*, p. 75.

26. To eat at the king's table was "the equivalent of having a pension, the beneficiary receiving a regular royal allowance of food and clothing, with a house and land to support him and his family (*cf.* 2 Sa. 9:7; 1 Ki. 18:19; 2 Ki. 25:29–30)." Wiseman, *1 and 2 Kings*, p. 77.

27. ". . . the verb means 'to be neighbourly.'" Montgomery, *Kings*, p. 90. The plural verb indicates that Barzillai's sons had joined their father in his support for David at Mahanaim, which had not been previously mentioned.

28. See 1 Samuel 20:8; 2 Samuel 2:5, 6; 7:15; 9:1, 3, 7; 10:2; 15:20; 22:51. The ESV has various renderings: "loyalty," "loyally," "steadfast love," "kindness." The word usually refers to exceptional acts of kindness, beyond any obligation, shown to one in need by one with the power to help. See discussions of the term in John Woodhouse, *1 Samuel: Looking for a Leader*, Preaching the Word (Wheaton, IL: Crossway, 2008), p. 611, note 14; Woodhouse, *2 Samuel*, pp. 76, 77, 104, 257–59, 269, 568 note 28.

29. See the discussion of 2 Samuel 2:6 and 9:3 in Woodhouse, *2 Samuel*, pp. 78, 259.

30. The Hebrew has an emphasis that could be rendered, "*He* was the one who cursed me . . ."

31. There is the tantalizing possibility that this Shimei is the one who was mentioned in 1:8. So Iain W. Provan, *1 & 2 Kings*, Understanding the Bible Commentary Series (Grand Rapids, MI: Baker Books, 1995), p. 28; Olley, *Kings*, p. 53; Beal, *Kings*, p. 75. This suggestion is given a little more plausibility by the descriptions of the Shimei of 1:8 as "not *with* Adonijah" and the Shimei of 2:8 as "*with* you [Solomon]." However, the absence of the words "the son of Gera" in 1:8 raises a doubt about the identification. Further uncertainty is introduced by a reference to a "Shimei the son of Ela" among Solomon's officials in 4:18. It seems more likely that this was the Shimei in 1:8 and that the two occurrences of "with" in 1:8 and 2:8 are coincidental.

32. It is interesting that the case of Shimei had this connection with the case of Joab—the trouble David had with the sons of Zeruiah (see 2 Samuel 16:10; 19:22).

33. "Grievous" represents a quite rare Hebrew word (*mrts* niphal) (appearing also in Micah 2:10; possibly Job 6:25 and Job 16:3). Suggested renderings include "bitter" (NIV), "malicious" (HCSB), "crippling" (Gray, *Kings*, p. 103), "sickening" or "painful" (Jones, *Kings*, p. 109), "offensive" (Mulder, *1 Kings 1–11*, p. 99).

34. Therefore I do not agree that "the way David rewords his oath" was "deceptive." Jerome T. Walsh, *1 Kings*, Berit Olam: Studies in Hebrew Narrative & Poetry (Collegeville, MN: The Liturgical Press, 1996), p. 42.

35. David's charge to Solomon "did not spring from personal revenge, but was the duty of the king as judge and administrator of the divine right." Keil, *Kings*, p. 24. Contra, for example, Provan, *Kings*, p. 32.

36. In 2 Samuel 3:28 the word rendered "guiltless" is the adjective from the same root as the verb "hold him guiltless" in 1 Kings 2:9. See the discussion of this term in Woodhouse, *2 Samuel*, p. 575, 576, note 13.

37. A number of modern commentators are, in my opinion, unduly suspicious of this (and the previous) reference to Solomon's wisdom. "The hint is that Solomon by some subtlety should find some legal pretext on which to eliminate Shimei." Gray, *Kings*, p. 104. ". . . a cynical ring this time as well, partly due to the fact that the evasion of an oath is now called for." Fokkelman, *David*, p. 389.

38. Provan argues that David's motive was primarily political in his orders regarding Joab, Barzillai, and Shimei, intending to enhance the possibility of a united kingdom. Provan, *Kings*, pp. 33, 34.

39. There is also more to Shimei's story than punishment. "Shimei is and remains rather a proof of David's magnanimity than of vengeance. It was not a little thing to tolerate the miscreant in his immediate neighbourhood for his whole life long (not even banishment being thought of). And if under the following reign also he had been allowed to end his days in peace (which had never been promised him), this would have been a kindness which would have furnished an example of unpunished crimes that might easily have been abused." J. J. Hess, quoted by Keil, *Kings*, p. 24, note 1.

40. On the city of David see discussion of 3:1d.

41. The ESV obscures the verbal similarity of these two verses by translating the same Hebrew verb (*shakab*) "slept" and "lie down." The expression "he slept with his fathers" becomes a standard expression in the books of Kings and Chronicles for the death of a king (for example, 11:43; 14:20, 31; 15:8, 24; 16:6, 28; 22:40, 50). Sometimes (although not here in David's case) the expression may indicate that the king was buried in his ancestors' tomb (see 14:31; 15:24; 22:50).

42. Strictly speaking David only reigned over "Israel" (the whole nation) for his thirty-three years in Jerusalem.

43. About 1000–961 B.C.

44. There is some debate about the appropriate divisions of the text, particularly whether to take verse 12 with what follows (Keil, *Kings*, p. 22; DeVries, *1 Kings*, p. 28; Richard D. Patterson, and Hermann J. Austel, "1, 2 Kings," in *The Expositor's Bible Commentary*, Revised Edition, ed. Tremper Longman III and David E. Garland, Vol. 3 [Grand Rapids, MI: Zondervan, 2009], p. 651) or with what precedes it (Gray, *Kings*, p. 104). Arguments are finely balanced, and it is perhaps best to see verse 12 as transitional, concluding 2:1–12 and announcing the theme of 2:12–46.

Chapter Six: The Bible's Disturbing News

1. For example, in the episodes before us Brueggemann sees "the utter ruthlessness and uncompromising resolve of Solomon on his way to power." Walter Brueggemann, *1 & 2 Kings*, Smyth & Helwys Bible Commentary (Macon, GA: Smyth & Helwys, 2000), p. 30. Similarly: "For readers today, the account provides a mirror to human behavior in complex situations of power and leadership, with examples of questionable 'wisdom'. No direct answers are given, but we are helped to see below the surface and consider human motives and rationalizations, to the ease with which God's words can be used to serve human ends." John W. Olley, *The Message of Kings: God Is Present*, The Bible Speaks Today (Nottingham, UK: Inter-Varsity Press, 2011), p. 58. "Whatever hopes one held that David's son would attain heights of greatness untainted by sin are immediately dashed in these opening chapters. The progress of Solomon's narrative similarly presents him as flawed in the midst of greatness: one is presented with a wise, blessed and lauded king who nevertheless falls short." Lissa M. Wray Beal, *1 & 2 Kings*, Apollos Old Testament Commentary, Vol. 9 (Nottingham, UK and Downers Grove, IL: Apollos, 2014), p. 81.

2. I have suggested previously that verse 12 is transitional: it both concludes 2:1–12 and announces the theme of 2:12–46.

3. "Kingdom" in verses 12 and 46 represents two slightly different Hebrew words (*malkuth* and *mamlakah* respectively). *Mamlakah* is the word for "kingdom" in 2 Samuel 7. Walsh suggests that *malkuth* "has a stronger nuance of power." Jerome T. Walsh, *1 Kings*, Berit Olam: Studies in Hebrew Narrative & Poetry (Collegeville, MN: The Liturgical Press, 1996), p. 46. The terms are, however, essentially synonymous. See John Woodhouse, *2 Samuel: Your Kingdom Come*, Preaching the Word (Wheaton, IL: Crossway, 2015), pp. 597, 598, note 21.

4. Literally "And . . ." The Hebrew does not indicate when Adonijah took the fatal steps about to be described.

5. While there is no explicit evidence of rivalry between Bathsheba and Haggith (we do not even know whether Haggith was still alive), the Old Testament typically portrays the tension implicit in polygamous marriages. Note how Peninnah is called Hannah's "rival" in 1 Samuel 1:6 (cf. Leviticus 18:18). See also Deuteronomy 21:15–17.

6. On the importance of the queen mother, see Brueggemann, *Kings*, p. 32.

7. The Septuagint adds a reference to Adonijah bowing. Someone noticed that he should have! See Martin J. Mulder, *1 Kings: Volume 1: 1 Kings 1–11*, Historical Commentary on the Old Testament (Leuven, Belgium: Peeters, 1998), p. 106.

8. The unease Bathsheba must have felt at Adonijah's approach may be suggested by another occasion on which precisely the same question was asked many years earlier. The elders in Bethlehem trembled as they asked Samuel, "Do you come peaceably?" (1 Samuel 16:4).

9. It is probably significant that the Hebrew word Adonijah used for the "kingdom" (*melukah*) is different from the words used by the narrator in verses 12 and 46. Adonijah's word means the position or rank of king. It was the trappings that Adonijah had longed for (see 1:5). Similarly Walsh, *1 Kings*, p. 49.

10. In the Hebrew there is an emphasis on "You," suggesting that Bathsheba was particularly in a position to know these things. There is also an emphasis on

"mine" and "me." "He is far from having unlearned the habit of 'self-promotion' (1:5)." Mulder, *1 Kings 1–11*, p. 107.

11. "You" here is masculine singular in the Hebrew, but such anomalous usage is not unusual. GKC, §135o.

12. The English translation smooths over awkward expressions in the Hebrew sentence that probably reflects Adonijah's "almost incoherent" nervousness. Walsh, *1 Kings*, p. 50.

13. The Hebrew could mean "about you." So Walsh: "She does not comment on his request or even say that she will speak to Solomon about it. She will speak about *him*." Walsh, *1 Kings*, p. 51. However the ESV makes better sense in view of what Bathsheba in fact said to Solomon in verse 21.

14. It has been suggested that there may have been more to Bathsheba's acquiescence than at first appears. Was she "naive, vindictive or opportunistic against the Adonijah party . . ."? Remember that Joab was her first husband's murderer. So Beal, *Kings*, p. 76. Perhaps she could see where all this would lead? In my judgment such suggestions are speculative and do not accord with the tone of the narrative.

15. Similarly Olley, *Kings*, p. 55; Beal, *Kings*, p. 76. However, Fokkelman (who is far from kind to Adonijah) seems to think he was just naïve: "Abishag has had no intercourse with the old king—and so Adonijah is under the illusion that he may ask for her." J. P. Fokkelman, *Narrative Art and Poetry in the Books of Samuel: A Full Interpretation Based on Stylistic and Structural Analyses, Volume 1: King David (II Sam. 9–20 & I Kings 1–2)* (The Netherlands: Van Gorcum, Assen, 1981), p. 394. But did Adonijah know the intimacies of the old king's bedroom? I doubt it.

16. Indeed what it would mean to be "strictly speaking" a concubine is far from clear. On concubines in the Old Testament see Woodhouse, *2 Samuel*, pp. 102, 103.

17. On the political dimensions to sexual relations with wives or concubines of a king, see also 2 Samuel 12:8.

18. "Throne" and "seat" in this sentence represent a repetition of the same Hebrew word, which should probably be translated "throne" in each case. So RV, REB, HCSB, NIV.

19. This is part of the evidence that the queen mother in the Davidic kingdom had a recognized position of prestige. See our discussion of 15:13.

20. "I will not refuse you" sounds more emphatic in English than the Hebrew idiom, literally "I will not cause your face to return." This polite courtly language does not really amount to an absolute promise to do whatever is asked, which Solomon would be about to break. Similarly Mulder, *1 Kings 1–11*, p. 110.

21. On the masculine verb form in the Hebrew see GKC, §121a, b.

22. Plenty of commentators take a contrary view. ". . . Solomon is partly characterized by his own preoccupation with the safety of his throne. His display of power is . . . a sign of inner insecurity and weakness . . . simply practical and tactical intelligence, cleverness." Fokkelman, *David*, p. 408. ". . . the request supplies Solomon with a convenient excuse to eliminate a rival he still perceives as a danger." Walsh, *1 Kings*, p. 67. However, in my judgment these comments reflect more the sensitivities of the commentators than the implications of the text.

23. A number of commentators are clearly (and understandably) discomforted by this speech by Solomon: ". . . these venomous words of Solomon." Mulder,

1 Kings 1–11, p. 111; "The self-righteous, self-serving decree of vv. 23–24 . . ." Brueggemann, *Kings*, p. 34. I share their unease, but not their evaluation.

24. "House" is certainly to be understood in terms of the 2 Samuel 7 promise, where it is a key word. It is also possible that there is a reference to the fact that Solomon had, by this time, a son who would have been about a year old. See 11:42; 14:21. So C. F. Keil, "1 and 2 Kings," in C. F. Keil and F. Delitzsch, *Commentary on the Old Testament*, Vol. 3 (Peabody, MA: Hendrickson Publishers, 1996), p. 25.

25. So, among others, Olley, *Kings*, p. 56. Cf. Fokkelman, *David*, p. 396; Walsh, *1 Kings*, p. 67.

26. The key words "established," "throne," and "David my father" in verse 24 echo these words in verses 12 and 46. The additional allusions to the 2 Samuel 7 promise in verse 24 ("house," "as he promised") strengthen the impression that Solomon's words are endorsed by the narrative framework in which they are set.

27. "The king was perfectly just in doing this. For since Adonijah, even after his first attempt to seize the throne had been forgiven by Solomon, endeavoured to secure his end by fresh machinations, duty to God, who had exalted Solomon to the throne, demanded that the rebel should be punished with all the severity of the law, without regard to blood relationship." Keil, *Kings*, pp. 25, 26.

28. "Thus the ruin of the enemies of Christ's kingdom is as sure as the stability of his kingdom, and both as sure as the being and life of God, the Founder of it." Matthew Henry, *Matthew Henry's Commentary on the Whole Bible*, Vol. 2 (Old Tappan, NJ: Fleming H. Revell Company, no date), p. 588.

29. "[H]e was certainly eighty years old already." Keil, *Kings*, p. 26, note 2.

30. The text in 2 Samuel 7:22, 25 is uncertain. See Woodhouse, *2 Samuel*, p. 599, note 7.

31. For a fuller discussion of this striking phrase, see Woodhouse, *2 Samuel*, p. 224.

32. Literally, "a man of death you [are]," an unusual expression in the Old Testament, but similar to "son of death" found in 1 Samuel 20:31; 26:16; 2 Samuel 12:5.

33. For example, "The only possible reading is that anyone Solomon perceives as opposed to him deserves death." Walsh, *1 Kings*, p. 67.

34. The Hebrew is awkward (literally, "Anathoth! Go!"), possibly an expression of the king's anger. So Beal, *Kings*, p. 77. If so, however, the king's anger was tempered with surprising mercy.

35. Literally "fields."

36. Mulder, *1 Kings 1–11*, p. 113. Note that Abiathar and Eli were descendants of Aaron's fourth son Ithamar, while Zadok was descended from Aaron's third son Eleazar. See 1 Samuel 14:3; 22:20; 1 Chronicles 6:3–8; 24:3.

37. So John Bright, *Jeremiah: A New Translation with Introduction, Notes & Commentary*, The Anchor Bible, Vol. 21 (New York: Doubleday, 1965), pp. LXXXVII, LXXXVIII. See also John Woodhouse, *1 Samuel: Looking for a Leader*, Preaching the Word (Wheaton, IL: Crossway, 2008), p. 563, note 5. Some see irony in this: "Centuries later a priestly prophet will return to Jerusalem from Anathoth, bringing Yahweh's decree condemning the throne of David and the Temple that Solomon himself built and announcing the coming exile of God's unfaithful people (Jer. 1:1–3)." Walsh, *1 Kings*, p. 56. See also Jeremiah 32:6–15. Also Brueggemann, *Kings*, pp. 35, 41.

38. It is true that the king only promised to spare Abiathar "at this time" (literally, "on this day," v. 26). However, this did not mean that Solomon planned to execute him on some other day, but simply that the mercy shown applied to his past acts of treason, not necessarily to anything similar in the future.

39. On this much-disputed text, see Woodhouse, *2 Samuel*, pp. 252, 606, note 28.

40. The only certain reference to Abiathar carrying the ark in the preceding history is 2 Samuel 15:29 (and in a possible reading of 2 Samuel 15:24 reflected in the ESV; see Woodhouse, *2 Samuel*, p. 639, note 26). However, we have no reason to suppose that Abiathar was absent from the famous occasion in 2 Samuel 6 when the ark was brought from Baale-Judah to Jerusalem. There may have been other unrecorded occasions when Abiathar "carried the ark of the Lord GOD before David." Therefore, suggestions that "ark" should be emended (without textual support) to "ephod" are unnecessary. See Keil, *Kings*, p. 26, note 1; John Gray, *I & II Kings: A Commentary*, Third, Fully Revised, Edition (London: SCM, 1977), pp. 108, 109.

41. For more about the ark, see Woodhouse, *2 Samuel*, pp. 176–78.

42. See, for example, the superscriptions to Psalms 3, 18, 52, 54, 56, 57, 59, 63, 142.

43. See this major New Testament theme reflected, for example in Acts 5:41; 9:16; Romans 8:17; 2 Corinthians 1:5; Philippians 1:29; 3:10; Colossians 1:24; 2 Timothy 1:8; 2:3; 1 Peter 2:21; 4:13, 16.

44. The surprising mention of Abiathar in 4:4 suggests that although Solomon had banished him from an active role as priest, he retained the dignity of that title. So Keil, *Kings*, p. 34.

45. Abiathar was the son of Ahimelech, grandson of Ahitub, great-grandson of Phinehas, and great-great-grandson of Eli (1 Samuel 14:3; 22:20). See Woodhouse, *1 Samuel*, p. 612, note 2.

46. For a review of these matters see our discussion of 1:7 and 2:5.

47. Some ancient versions have "Solomon" here, but the Hebrew, followed by the ESV, is probably correct. Keil, *Kings*, p. 26, note 3; James A. Montgomery, *A Critical and Exegetical Commentary on the Books of Kings*, The International Critical Commentary (Edinburgh: T. & T. Clark, 1951), p. 49; Gray, *Kings*, p. 107, note b.

48. Similarly Fokkelman, *David*, p. 400.

49. Walsh surely misreads this: "Any animosity Solomon bears [Joab] is based on personal affront, not on true treason." Walsh, *1 Kings*, p. 57.

50. On the significance of this action see our discussion of 1:50.

51. See the more detailed discussion of this in our comments on 2:5, 6.

52. Of course, there is irony here if we recall another death that occurred at Joab's hand. In *obedience* to King David he had murdered Uriah the Hittite (2 Samuel 11:14–17). Olley, *Kings*, pp. 57, 58. However, the stain of that crime had been removed by God's remarkable grace (2 Samuel 12:13).

53. The ESV correctly interprets the Hebrew (literally, "his blood") as a reference not to Joab's own blood, but to the blood Joab had shed.

54. The accounts of Joab's bloody deeds in 2 Samuel make clear that David was not a party to these crimes (see especially 2 Samuel 3:26b, 28, 37–39).

55. Literally "seed." The same Hebrew word is rendered "offspring" in 2 Samuel 7:12.

56. This was probably the wilderness of Judah, since Joab had family links with David and may therefore have lived in the vicinity of Bethlehem, where Joab's brother, Asahel, was buried (2 Samuel 2:32).

57. On Benaiah and Zadok, see our discussion of 1:8.

58. Unless "with you" in 2:8 indicated a temporary presence of Shimei in Jerusalem, in which case Solomon would probably be summoning him from Bahurim (see 2 Samuel 16:5).

59. It seems from 1 Samuel 25:10 that runaway servants were not uncommon.

60. Gray thinks that the Achish of 1 Kings 2:39 was probably the son of the Achish of David's day. Gray, *Kings*, p. 112. The evidence suggests, however, that either it was the same Achish (who would by now be an old man), whose father's name "Maacah" was a variant spelling of "Maoch" (1 Samuel 27:2) or Achish, the son of Maoch, the king with whom David had dealings, was succeeded by Maacah, whose son Achish II was the king in 1 Kings 2:39. The historical question is less interesting than the literary fact that "Achish, king of Gath" is well known to readers of this history.

61. See Map 5–10 in Currid, *Atlas*, p. 128.

62. I suspect that Shimei returned as quickly as possible to Jerusalem hoping that his brief departure would not be noticed by Solomon. Contra Walsh: "His departure has no political agenda, nor is it an attempt to escape Solomon's control. It violates the letter of Solomon's prohibitions but not their spirit." Walsh, *1 Kings*, p. 62. Furthermore Achish's implied return of the servants to Shimei was against at least the spirit of God's Law. See Deuteronomy 23:15, 16.

63. It is not uncommon in Biblical narratives for details of events to be held back and dropped into the story at a later point for dramatic effect. Failure to appreciate this technique has led some to judge Solomon's speech here unfairly, as though he was misquoting the earlier speech to suit his present purpose. For example, Walsh, *1 Kings*, pp. 62, 63.

64. Contra Walsh: "Given the falsity of Solomon's claims, it is not surprising that he does not allow his victim a chance to respond." Walsh, *1 Kings*, p. 63.

65. So Keil, *Kings*, p. 28.

Chapter Seven: It's Complicated

1. At the time of writing the most recent of these was a number of attacks in Paris on Friday evening, November 13, 2015, in which 129 people were killed. Prior to this a Russian passenger plane was brought down by a bomb killing all passengers, and horrendous attacks have recently been perpetrated in Beirut and Baghdad.

2. I am not suggesting for one moment that Christians should not be involved in politics, even party politics. On the contrary. My point is simply that Christians, of all people, should understand that in this fallen world all human politics will be marred by foolishness, wickedness, and weakness. Uncritical endorsement of a political party (right, left, or center) is likely to be as inappropriate for a Christian as the uncritical rejection of all that another party stands for.

3. The Hebrew is quite stark, with "Solomon" as subject and "Pharaoh king of Egypt" as object of a verb. The verb itself (*khtn* hitpael) does not necessarily carry the formal connotations suggested in the ESV's "made a marriage alliance with" (although this may be implied by the context). The verb is derived from a noun (*khatan*)

that means "son-in-law" (as in 1 Samuel 18:18; 22:14; 2 Kings 8:27). Literally, "Solomon became son-in-law of Pharaoh king of Egypt." See 1 Samuel 18:21, 22, 23, 26, 27. E. Kutsch, "*khtn*," *TDOT* 5, pp. 270–77.

4. The verb in verse 1a (and the corresponding noun, "son-in-law") occurs in 1 Samuel 18:18, 21, 22, 23, 26, 27; 22:14, but nowhere else in the books of Samuel and Kings except 2 Kings 8:27.

5. David also had at least one wife who was the daughter of a foreign king (2 Samuel 3:3). This marriage, no doubt, had a political dimension. See John Woodhouse, *2 Samuel: Your Kingdom Come*, Preaching the Word (Wheaton, IL: Crossway, 2015), p. 101. However, it does not have anything like the prominence given to Solomon's marriage to the daughter of Pharaoh, and indeed the marriage itself is not explicitly mentioned, certainly not with the vocabulary "became son-in-law of."

6. "Intermarry" in the ESV of Deuteronomy 7:3 and "make marriages with" in Joshua 23:12 represent the same Hebrew verb as "made a marriage alliance with" in 1 Kings 3:1.

7. "Solomon, right at the beginning of his reign, carried with him the seeds of his own destruction." Iain Provan, V. Philips Long, and Tremper Longman III, *A Biblical History of Israel* (Louisville: Westminster/John Knox, 2003), p. 247.

8. Plenty of modern commentators see this marriage in entirely negative terms. For example, "The marriage to the daughter of pharaoh is a signal for engagement with Egypt, an engagement that led Solomon into the political 'big time,' but conversely, also led Solomon away from old Mosaic roots." "Solomon has allied himself with Pharaoh, the antithesis of everything Israelite. . . . The marriage signals Solomon's deliberate departure from what traditional Israel treasured most." Walter Brueggemann, *1 & 2 Kings*, Smyth & Helwys Bible Commentary (Macon, GA: Smyth & Helwys, 2000), pp. 43, 45. Similarly Iain W. Provan, *1 & 2 Kings*, Understanding the Bible Commentary Series (Grand Rapids, MI: Baker Books, 1995), p. 44; Jerome T. Walsh, *1 Kings*, Berit Olam: Studies in Hebrew Narrative & Poetry (Collegeville, MN: The Liturgical Press, 1996), pp. 70, 71; Lissa M. Wray Beal, *1 & 2 Kings*, Apollos Old Testament Commentary, Vol. 9 (Nottingham, UK and Downers Grove, IL: Apollos, 2014), p. 85.

9. So Abraham Malamat, "A Political Look at the Kingdom of David and Solomon and Its Relations with Egypt," in Ishida, ed., *Studies in the Period of David and Solomon and Other Essays*, p. 197. Malamat notes, "From ancient Near Eastern records in general . . . it is now clear that Egyptian kings rarely, if ever, married off their daughters to foreign potentates, whom they apparently regarded as inferior," p. 198.

10. While there is an understandable historical interest in identifying the particular Pharaoh who became Solomon's father-in-law, Brueggemann is correct: "It is, however, crucial that he is not named, for in his anonymity he is emotionally connected to the ancient pharaoh of the Exodus narrative, also left unnamed (Exod 1:8)." Brueggemann, *1 & 2 Kings*, p. 45. Those preoccupied with the questions of historians can misunderstand badly. For example: "The full significance of Solomon's marriage with Pharaoh's daughter eluded the biblical historiographer, who failed even to mention the name of the Pharaoh, let alone that of the bride." Malamat, "A Political Look," p. 198.

11. Indeed Solomon is the active subject of all three verbs in verse 1a, b. In David's case the initiative had been Saul's ("Saul *gave* [David] his daughter Michal . . . ," 1 Samuel 18:27).

12. Malamat, "A Political Look," p. 200.

13. "Marriage with an Egyptian princess was not a transgression of the law, as it was only marriages with Canaanitish women that were expressly prohibited (Ex. 34:16; Deut. 7:3), whereas it was allowable to marry even foreign women taken in war (Deut. 21:10ff.). At the same time it was only when the foreign wives renounced idolatry and confessed their faith in Jehovah, that such marriages were in accordance with the spirit of the law. And we may assume that this was the case even with Pharaoh's daughter; because Solomon adhered so faithfully to the Lord during the first years of his reign, that he would not have tolerated any idolatry in his neighbourhood, and we cannot find any trace of Egyptian idolatry in Israel in the time of Solomon. . . ." C. F. Keil, "1 and 2 Kings," in C. F. Keil and F. Delitzsch, *Commentary on the Old Testament*, Vol. 3 (Peabody, MA: Hendrickson Publishers, 1996), p. 29.

14. Ibid.

15. Contra Beal, *Kings*, p. 85.

16. For another positive assessment of Solomon becoming Pharaoh's son-in-law, see Peter J. Leithart, *1 & 2 Kings*, Brazos Theological Commentary on the Bible (Grand Rapids, MI: Brazos Press, 2006), pp. 43, 44, who goes so far as to say, "Solomon's marriage to Pharaoh's daughter points to Jesus, who, like Solomon, covenants with a bride from the nations, but who, unlike Solomon, remains faithful to his Father."

17. We should note that very little attention was given to this "house" in the promise of 2 Samuel 7—just four words in the Hebrew text. See Woodhouse, *2 Samuel*, p. 216.

18. The word in question (*hekal*) is used for the "main hall" (NIV; ESV, "nave") of the house in 6:3, 5, 17, 33; 7:50, but not for the house itself, although English versions can be a little confusing on this point. This observation, but without the interpretation offered here, is made by M. Ottosson, "*hekal*," *TDOT* 3, p. 383. Only much later in this history, when this house had fallen on hard times, is the word *hekal* possibly used with reference to the house of the Lord itself, although even then it may still be a reference to the main hall of the house (2 Kings 18:16; 23:4; 24:13). (My comment in Woodhouse, *2 Samuel*, p. 594, note 11 was mistaken on this point.)

19. See, for example, 1 Samuel 9:16 and the discussion in John Woodhouse, *1 Samuel: Looking for a Leader*, Preaching the Word (Wheaton, IL: Crossway, 2008), p. 162.

20. See the discussion of this point in Woodhouse, *2 Samuel*, p. 200.

21. So Walsh, *1 Kings*, p. 71. Similarly Beal, *Kings*, pp. 83, 85. However, I do not think that this point stands up to a careful reading of chapters 6 and 7, as we will see.

22. BDB, p. 956.

23. The meaning of the Hebrew terms *bamah* (singular) and *bamoth* (plural) is uncertain. The translation "high place(s)" is based on the Septuagint and Vulgate renderings of these terms. For a fuller discussion see D. L. Petter, "High Places," *DOTHB*, pp. 413–18.

24. The people of Israel had "high places" that the Lord threatened to destroy *if* they became idol worshippers (Leviticus 26:30). These high places "seem to be regarded as legitimate." Gordon J. Wenham, *The Book of Leviticus*, The New International Commentary on the Old Testament (Grand Rapids, MI: Eerdmans, 1979), p. 332, note 11.

25. Without doubt King David had loved the Lord (see Psalm 18:1, with a different word for "love"), and all of God's people are called to "love" the Lord (Deuteronomy 6:5; 7:9; 10:12; 11:1, 13; 30:6).

26. In this context therefore I cannot agree with Walsh that "walk in the statutes of" a human (rather than God) is always *unrighteous* behavior." Walsh, *1 Kings*, p. 73, note 1.

27. In the books of Samuel the "love" most often mentioned was various people's love for David (1 Samuel 16:21; 18:1, 3, 16, 20, 22, 28; 20:17; 2 Samuel 1:26; cf. 1 Kings 5:1). See the discussion of what "love" means in this context in Woodhouse, *1 Samuel*, pp. 345–55.

28. See note 42 to Chapter 20.

Chapter Eight: What a Complicated World Needs

1. I differ from those who consider the experience at Gibeon in 3:4–15 to be "the legitimization of the succession of Solomon after his anomalous elevation to the throne without obvious aptitude for leadership, such as the people had recognized by spontaneous acclaim in the case of the judges, and without the covenant, such as David had made with the people of Israel at Hebron. Hence the claim of Solomon was given a new basis, the covenant of Yahweh with David and his house." John Gray, *I & II Kings: A Commentary*, Third, Fully Revised, Edition (London: SCM, 1977), pp. 120, 121. I have argued that the legitimacy of Solomon's succession has never been in doubt from the narrator's point of view, based on the 2 Samuel 7 promise and the Lord's particular "love" for Solomon (2 Samuel 12:24, 25), known by Nathan, David, and Bathsheba (and possibly others).

2. The Hebrew word for "thousand" (*'elep*) appears to have also been used for a military unit of unspecified size. We might say that Solomon used to offer a "legion" or "battalion" of burnt offerings. See John W. Wenham, "Large Numbers in the Old Testament," *TB* 18 (1967), pp. 19–53. Furthermore the text does not indicate the time period over which Solomon offered these sacrifices. Did he perhaps offer a "thousand" burnt offerings each year?

3. Gordon J. Wenham, *The Book of Leviticus*, The New International Commentary on the Old Testament (Grand Rapids, MI: Eerdmans, 1979), p. 58.

4. In the Hebrew "appeared" is a passive form of the verb "see."

5. See John Woodhouse, *2 Samuel: Your Kingdom Come*, Preaching the Word (Wheaton, IL: Crossway, 2015), p. 222.

6. "Ask" and "make" in the ESV of Psalm 2:8 represent the same Hebrew verbs as "ask" (*sha'al*) and "give" (*nathan*) in 1 Kings 3:5.

7. The Hebrew conjunction (*ka'asher*) here indicates a general correspondence between David's faithfulness, righteousness, and uprightness on the one hand and God's great kindness to him on the other. However, the correspondence is not necessarily causal ("because"). The awkward English of the RV is more accurate in pre-

serving the ambiguity at this point: ". . . great kindness, *according as* he walked before thee in truth . . ." (emphasis added).

8. On the Hebrew word (*khesed*), see our discussion of 2:7 and note 28 in Chapter 5.

9. See Woodhouse, *2 Samuel*, p. 594, note 17.

10. Solomon here "reflects a common distortion" according to John W. Olley, *The Message of Kings: God Is Present*, The Bible Speaks Today (Nottingham, UK: Inter-Varsity Press, 2011), p. 64. Similarly Walter Brueggemann, *1 & 2 Kings*, Smyth & Helwys Bible Commentary (Macon, GA: Smyth & Helwys, 2000), p. 47. Walsh is even skeptical about Solomon's claim that the Lord's hand was in his coming to the throne. "It is noteworthy that this claim is made several times in these chapters (see also 1:37, 48; 2:15, 24), but it is always made by Solomon himself or by some other character. Neither Yahweh nor the narrator ever confirms the claim . . . the narrator's silence leaves open the possibility that God approved Solomon's kingship only *post factum*, after Nathan and Bathsheba succeeded in gaining him the throne." Jerome T. Walsh, *1 Kings*, Berit Olam: Studies in Hebrew Narrative & Poetry (Collegeville, MN: The Liturgical Press, 1996), p. 77. This is (in my opinion) unreasonable skepticism. The narrator has told us the Lord set his love on Solomon from birth and that the Lord himself sent Nathan the prophet with a message to that effect (2 Samuel 12:24, 25). To fail to see any connection between those *pre factum* statements and Solomon's accession to the throne is far from satisfactory.

11. Note the key word "righteousness" in 1 Kings 3:6 and 2 Samuel 22:21, 25. See Woodhouse, *2 Samuel*, pp. 511–13.

12. The words "before you" and "toward you" in verse 6 are therefore weighty. However wicked David may have appeared to others, *before the Lord* he was washed clean.

13. The Hebrew conjunction (*ka'asher*) rendered "because" in verse 6 does not necessarily have the *causal* sense of the English and should probably be translated "as." See note 7.

14. So C. F. Keil, "1 and 2 Kings," in C. F. Keil and F. Delitzsch, *Commentary on the Old Testament*, Vol. 3 (Peabody, MA: Hendrickson Publishers, 1996), p. 31.

15. The ESV "child" renders a Hebrew word (*na'ar*) that is often translated "young man" (as, for example, in 2 Samuel 1:5, 13, 15; 2:14, 21; 4:12). For further discussion of the term, see John Woodhouse, *1 Samuel: Looking for a Leader*, Preaching the Word (Wheaton, IL: Crossway, 2008), p. 557, note 15.

16. This is a theme of the exposition of 2 Samuel 7 in Woodhouse, *2 Samuel*, pp. 197–232.

17. "Great" here means "many" and should not be related (directly at least) to the "great nation" of Genesis 12:2, where a different word for "great" suggests status and reputation (as in 2 Samuel 7:9).

18. Walsh seems to miss the point when he dismisses Solomon's description of the people as "too many to be numbered" as "an exaggeration" because David had taken a census of the nation less than a generation earlier (2 Samuel 24). Walsh, *1 Kings*, p. 75.

19. English translations generally fall short of the richness of this Hebrew idiom: "an understanding heart" (RV); "a heart to understand" (JB); "a heart with

skill to listen" (REB); "an obedient heart" (HCSB); "a discerning heart" (NIV). A fine paraphrase is supplied by Eugene H. Peterson, *The Message: The Bible in Contemporary Language* (Colorado Springs: NavPress, 2002), p. 568: "a God-listening heart."

20. This expression is borrowed from the title of Francis Schaeffer's classic *He Is There and He Is Not Silent* (Wheaton, IL: Crossway, 1982).

21. Some understand "a hearing heart" as simply the ability to be a good listener to other people. It "implies patience to hear a case and understand it fully," according to Gray, *Kings*, p. 126. Likewise: "the gift of being open and able to listen to others is to be highly prized in leadership." Olley, *Kings*, p. 64. In my opinion this seriously misses the point.

22. See Woodhouse, *1 Samuel*, p. 260.

23. The history of Israel will eventually reach the point when the whole nation will fail as Saul failed. Their hearts will stubbornly turn away, they will no longer be willing to listen, they will serve other gods (Deuteronomy 30:17; Ezekiel 3:7).

24. The Hebrew term (*mishpat*) rendered "justice" here is cognate with the verb in question.

25. "Great" here represents a Hebrew word similar to the word for "glory." I am inclined to suggest that the "glory" (*kabod*) that departed from Israel according to 1 Samuel 4:21, 22 had now returned to this "great" (*kabed*) people. ("Great" [*rab*] in verse 8 means "numerous.")

26. In the Hebrew the two statements are strikingly parallel, as the literal translations attempt to show.

27. Literally, "many days."

28. The Hebrew contains repetitions that emphasize what Solomon did *not ask*: "you have not asked for yourself many days, and you have not asked for yourself riches, and you have not asked for the life of your enemies."

29. Exactly the same Hebrew word is used for "understanding" in verse 11 and "discern" in verse 9.

30. On this important word, see Woodhouse, *2 Samuel*, pp. 250, 251.

31. The words "as your father David walked" introduce the striking idea of David's integrity for the second time in 1 Kings. See our discussions of 3:6 and 15:5.

32. Compare the identical phrasing concerning Pharaoh's experience in Genesis 41:7.

33. "Solomon becomes the first man in the Old Testament to *stand* before the ark." Peter J. Leithart, *1 & 2 Kings*, Brazos Theological Commentary on the Bible (Grand Rapids, MI: Brazos Press, 2006), p. 44. Contrast Joshua 7:6.

Chapter Nine: The Wisdom of God to Do Justice

1. See note 4 to Chapter 5.

2. "Then" suggests a close connection (not necessarily only temporal) to the preceding scene at Gibeon.

3. As Walsh observes, the narrator "names none of the characters: we are to concentrate on them as types, 'king' and 'prostitutes,' not as individuals." Jerome T. Walsh, *1 Kings*, Berit Olam: Studies in Hebrew Narrative & Poetry (Collegeville, MN: The Liturgical Press, 1996), p. 78.

4. The Hebrew phrase (literally, "two women, prostitutes") may suggest the distortion of womanhood: two women who were not wives but prostitutes. Prostitutes are quite often referred to in this way (so Leviticus 21:7; Joshua 2:1; 6:22; Judges 11:1; 16:1; Jeremiah 3:3; Ezekiel 16:30; 23:44; Proverbs 6:26).

5. This reference has been understood to apply to "cult prostitution," thought to be part of Canaanite religious practices. There are no grounds for thinking that this supposed practice had anything to do with the story of the two prostitutes before King Solomon. Indeed the existence of "cult prostitution" in the world of the Old Testament is doubtful. See our discussion of 14:24a.

6. Perhaps for this reason the Targum uses the word for "innkeeper" in the text before us (3:16), avoiding the embarrassment of the whole subject of prostitution in Israel. James A. Montgomery, *A Critical and Exegetical Commentary on the Books of Kings*, The International Critical Commentary (Edinburgh: T. & T. Clark, 1951), p. 109.

7. The Hebrew for "prostitute" in 1 Kings 3:16 is a participle of the verb rendered "whore" in the ESV of these texts. The verb can refer to any and all sex between a man and a woman outside marriage.

8. In view of the material in this paragraph, I cannot agree with Gray's comment: "Harlots . . . were a regular institution of the ancient Near East, about which the Hebrews had apparently no inhibitions." John Gray, *I & II Kings: A Commentary*, Third, Fully Revised, Edition (London: SCM, 1977), p. 128. Similarly Walsh underestimates the evidence: "This sort of prostitution was not considered morally wrong, though it certainly was not a very respectable profession." Walsh, *1 Kings*, p. 79.

9. For a fuller discussion of prostitutes in the Old Testament, see S. Erlandsson, *"zanah," TDOT* 4, pp. 99–104; Elaine Adler Goodfriend, "Prostitution," *ABD* 5, pp. 505–10; Richard M. Davidson, *Flame of Yahweh: Sexuality in the Old Testament* (Peabody, MA: Hendrickson, 2007), pp. 302–15.

10. Walsh is half-right: "The identification of the women as prostitutes, then, is not intended to cast them as sinful and to depict the king's dilemma as how to do justice in a fundamentally immoral situation. It is intended rather to cast them as among the lowest and most disadvantaged members of society, and to depict the king as attending to justice even in a case involving the least important of his people." Walsh, *1 Kings*, p. 80. However, he is half-wrong. The very mention of "two prostitutes" immediately raises moral questions for the reader, even if these questions are (surprisingly) not the issue of concern in what follows.

11. The woman's address to the king begins with a word (*biy*) (ESV, "Oh"; HCSB, "Please") used to introduce an entreaty expressed by a socially inferior and dependent person to a superior. It is always followed by "my lord." BDB, p. 106.

12. This is not indicated in verses 17, 18, but see "son" in verses 19, 20. Also the six occurrences of "child" in verses 21, 22 should more literally be rendered "son."

13. "Looked at him closely" renders an intensive form of the verb rendered "discern," "discerning" in 3:9, 11, 12. It suggests "how the mother made her sad discovery: back and forth, turning the baby this way and that!" Martin J. Mulder, *1 Kings: Volume 1: 1 Kings 1–11*, Historical Commentary on the Old Testament (Leuven, Belgium: Peeters, 1998), p. 157.

14. "Far from a factual or even an eyewitness account, it has all been a reconstruction without a shred of supporting evidence; and worse, it soon transpires, one affirmed by an interested party and denied outright by her opponent. As such, it turns out worthless." Meir Sternberg, *The Poetics of Biblical Narrative: Ideological Reading and the Drama of Reading*, IN Studies in Biblical Literature (Bloomington, IN: IN University Press, 1987), p. 168.

15. A number of commentators *are* persuaded! "We are not told what proof this woman had for her assertion, but in the framework of the story this is in no way important." Mulder, *1 Kings 1–11*, p. 156. "We should probably understand this as her reconstruction of events, though not an unlikely one, since she would surely know the identity of her own baby (v. 21) and so be able to hypothesize events." Dale Ralph Davis, *The Wisdom and the Folly: An Exposition of the Book of First Kings* (Fearn, Ross-shire, UK: Christian Focus, 2002), p. 39, note 8.

16. Notice how the women's status as "prostitutes" has given way to their identity as mothers. After verse 16 they are simply referred to as one or the other "woman."

17. This is not the place to defend the view that the attribution of much of the Book of Proverbs to Solomon (see Proverbs 1:1; 10:1; 25:1) is credible. See 1 Kings 4:32. For a brief discussion of this matter, see Derek Kidner, *Proverbs*, Tyndale Old Testament Commentaries (Leicester, UK and Downers Grove, IL: Inter-varsity Press, 1964), pp. 21–27.

18. The Hebrew *lo' kiy* ("No, but . . .") "conveys an emotional denial." Mulder, *1 Kings 1–11*, p. 157.

19. Notice "yours" twice in verse 22, indicating the women turning on each other.

20. The verb "said" in verse 22b is a participle, suggesting simultaneous speaking, as in a squabble. Similarly Walsh, *1 Kings*, p. 81.

21. Contra Walsh who thinks that the king here was speaking to himself, which is "relatively unusual in biblical Hebrew narrative" Walsh, *1 Kings*, p. 82.

22. "Solomon does not cross-examine the complainant regarding the glaring inconsistencies in her testimony," nor pursue an examination to see whether the baby was two or five days old. Stuart Lasine, "The Riddle of Solomon's Judgment and the Riddle of Human Nature in the Hebrew Bible," *JSOT* 45 (1989), pp. 64, 79, note 4. But the point of the story is that here was a king, like the promised king of Isaiah 11:1–9, who did not judge merely by what he saw with his eyes and heard with his ears.

23. The words Solomon attributed to the two women are exactly parallel, so that it makes no difference which woman was "the one" or "the other":

	A	B		C	D
"This is	my son	that is alive,	and	your son	is dead"
	C'	D'		A'	B'
"No; but	your son	is dead,	and	my son	is the living one"

24. "Solomon is challenged to distinguish between the two, in spite of the fact that the women remain indistinguishable in terms of name, profession, dwelling, reason for pregnancy, and, except for the three-day discrepancy, conditions of giving birth." Lasine, "Riddle," p. 64.

25. In the whole episode from verse 16 through verse 27 this is the only action described. Everything else is words spoken by the women and the king. Notice "before [the king]" in verses 16 (the two prostitutes), 22 (their bickering), and here (a sword).

26. "Divide" is a plural verb form.

27. In the Hebrew each reference to the babies in verses 19–23 uses the word for "son" (*ben*) ("child" in the ESV of verses 21, 22 obscures this). The king's words in verse 25 introduce the word "child" (*yeled*).

28. This aspect of the story is examined in detail by Lasine, "Riddle," pp. 66–69.

29. The Hebrew term refers to "the abdomen as womb," thought of as the seat of deep emotions. Hans Walter Wolff, *Anthropology of the Old Testament* (London: SCM, 1974), pp. 63, 64. See Genesis 43:14 (ESV, "mercy"), 30 (ESV, "compassion"). Similarly Walsh, *1 Kings*, pp. 82, 83.

30. Like the Scottish "bairn." The particular word (*yalud*, passive participle of *yalad*, "to bear [a child]") suggests the mother-baby relationship (see Job 14:1; 15:14; 25:4). Walsh suggests "baby" may capture the poignancy and intimacy. Walsh, *1 Kings*, p. 83.

31. The verb form used for "said" (identical to the form in verse 22 suggesting the simultaneous quarreling) suggests that she spoke these words *at the same time* as the true mother was speaking.

32. By interpreting "her" with the words "the first woman" the ESV (also HCSB, NIV) removes an ambiguity but also misleads us to think that the text tells us that the first woman to speak (in verse 17) was the mother. This is exactly what we are *not* told. For a helpful study highlighting what the narrator has chosen not to reveal, see Sternberg, *Poetics*, pp. 167–69; also Lasine, "Riddle," p. 66.

33. Walsh argues that the narrator leaves this interpretation open. Walsh, *1 Kings*, p. 83. Similarly Iain W. Provan, *1 and 2 Kings*, Understanding the Bible Commentary Series (Grand Rapids, MI: Baker Books, 1995), pp. 51, 52 is cited but refuted (rather too thoroughly, I think) by Davis, *Wisdom*, p. 39, note 9.

34. Mulder attempts to resolve this by emending the text, so that he makes the king say: "She (who said) 'Give her the living baby; don't kill him,' she is the mother." Mulder, *1 Kings 1–11*, p. 159. Much less interesting!

35. There is a slight variation. The woman used a negative particle (*'al*) that was somewhat more emphatic than the word the king used (*lo'*). The king's words, of course, carried the king's authority and did not need the added emphasis.

36. See John Woodhouse, *2 Samuel: Your Kingdom Come*, Preaching the Word (Wheaton, IL: Crossway, 2015), pp. 249–51.

37. Contra Walsh, who finds the response of fear a "troubling element" of the story. Walsh, *1 Kings*, p. 84.

Chapter Ten: What a Kingdom!

1. In 1 Kings 1—11 this is consistently the sense (although 5:13 is disputed). Contrast 12:1, 16, etc. In the book of Deuteronomy the nation as a whole is often referred to as "all Israel" (see, for example, Deuteronomy 1:1; 5:1; 13:11; 21:21; 31:7, 11; 32:45; 34:12). See Lissa M. Wray Beal, *1 & 2 Kings*, Apollos Old Testament Commentary, Vol. 9 (Nottingham, UK and Downers Grove, IL: Apollos, 2014), p. 94.

2. The expressions "was king [Hebrew, *melek*]" (1 Kings 4:1) and "reigned [the verb *malak*]" (2 Samuel 8:15) are even more obviously synonymous in Hebrew than in English.

3. See John Woodhouse, *2 Samuel: Your Kingdom Come*, Preaching the Word (Wheaton, IL: Crossway, 2015), pp. 478–80.

4. This is the general tone found in Jerome T. Walsh, *1 Kings*, Berit Olam: Studies in Hebrew Narrative & Poetry (Collegeville, MN: The Liturgical Press, 1996), pp. 78–92 and Walter Brueggemann, *1 & 2 Kings*, Smyth & Helwys Bible Commentary (Macon, GA: Smyth & Helwys, 2000), pp. 57–72. Davis has a better sense (in my opinion) of the text's mood: "Far from being the trademark of an oppressive regime, I propose that 1 Kings 3—4 want us to see the organization of Solomon's kingdom as a reflection of wisdom from God." Dale Ralph Davis, *The Wisdom and the Folly: An Exposition of the Book of First Kings* (Fearn, Ross-shire, UK: Christian Focus, 2002), p. 46.

5. The Hebrew term (*sar*) translated "high officials" is a word that can refer to a number of positions of leadership or responsibility under the king. For a comprehensive survey of the use of the term, see H. Niehr, "*sar*," *TDOT* 14, pp. 196–98. See also Roland de Vaux, *Ancient Israel: Its Life and Institutions*, trans. John McHugh (London: Darton, Longman & Todd, 1973), pp. 69, 70. Interestingly all uses of the term in the books of Samuel and up to this point in 1 Kings have referred to military or military-like "commanders" at various levels (1 Samuel 8:12; 12:9; 14:50; 17:18, 55; 18:13, 30; 22:2, 7; 26:5; 29:3, 4, 9; 2 Samuel 2:8; 3:38; 4:2; 10:3, 16, 18; 18:1, 5; 19:6, 13; 23:19; 24:2, 4; 1 Kings 1:19, 25; 2:5, 32). In Solomon's kingdom, however, "commanders" had a wider range of more peaceful roles.

6. See the comparison of these two lists in Woodhouse, *2 Samuel*, pp. 479, 480.

7. It is reasonable to assume that this is the same Zadok who has been mentioned numerous times in chapters 1 and 2, most importantly in 2:35, particularly as that Zadok is consistently referred to as "Zadok *the priest*" and now his son is named as "the priest."

8. See de Vaux, *Ancient Israel*, p. 131.

9. I agree with Brueggemann's comment that this "suggests that this was a 'writing government' of a formal kind with many records and statistics." Brueggemann, *Kings*, p. 58. But I do not think that this was necessarily a bad thing.

10. So de Vaux, *Ancient Israel*, p. 132.

11. "Solomon had deprived him of the *arche*, i.e., of the priest's office, but not of the *hierosune* or priestly dignity, because this was hereditary." C. F. Keil, "1 and 2 Kings," in C. F. Keil and F. Delitzsch, *Commentary on the Old Testament*, Vol. 3 (Peabody, MA: Hendrickson Publishers, 1996), p. 34. Alternatively, and more simply, Abiathar may be mentioned here because he was priest at the very beginning of Solomon's reign until his expulsion (see 2:22, 26).

12. So Beal, *Kings*, p. 95; contra Keil, *Kings*, p. 34. I would expect "Nathan, the son of David" if it was not the Nathan who has played such a prominent role in recent events. It could, of course, have been another Nathan altogether.

13. So Keil, *Kings*, p. 34.

14. On the honor of being a "friend" of the king, see Woodhouse, *2 Samuel*, p. 414.

15. See Woodhouse, *2 Samuel*, pp. 253, 607, note 33.

16. As Brueggemann seems to do: "The memory of emancipation makes Israel endlessly resistant and vigilant against such exploitative practice. Solomon, however, seems not to notice." Brueggemann, *Kings*, p. 59.

17. The last sentence probably refers to Azariah, the son of Nathan who was the "one governor" over all of the twelve officers (v. 5a). The NIV makes the sentence refer to Geber, which makes less sense. Similarly Keil, *Kings*, p. 37. Others think that "the land" is Judah. So the Septuagint and John Gray, *I & II Kings: A Commentary*, Third, Fully Revised, Edition (London: SCM, 1977), p. 140; Beal, *Kings*, p. 93; Walsh, *1 Kings*. p. 87. I prefer to see "the land" in verse 19 corresponding to "all Israel" in verse 7, thus neatly rounding off the paragraph.

18. "Solomon's grandiose schemes must have evoked immense hostility from those who paid for them." Brueggemann, *Kings*, p. 61.

19. It is interesting to note that Brueggemann maintains his thoroughly negative assessment of Solomon's regime by suggesting that 1 Kings 4 is "an ironically critical comment, exposing the hazardous political commitments of Solomon." Brueggemann, *Kings*, pp. 58, 59. In my judgment the irony here is entirely in the eye of the beholder. There is no hint of it in the text.

20. So James A. Montgomery, *A Critical and Exegetical Commentary on the Books of Kings*, The International Critical Commentary (Edinburgh: T. & T. Clark, 1951), p. 120; Gray, *Kings*, p. 134, note b. Others have suggested that these officers filled hereditary posts and are named with reference to the first officeholder. So de Vaux, *Ancient Israel*, p. 133. Neither hypothesis is particularly persuasive. We simply do not know why most of these officers were called Ben.

21. There are a number of individuals named Hur in the Old Testament (Exodus 17:10; 31:2; Numbers 31:8; Joshua 13:21). It is unclear whether there is any relationship here with any of them.

22. This Iddo is generally thought to be unrelated to any of the other persons of the same name in the Old Testament (1 Chronicles 6:21; 27:21; 2 Chronicles 9:29; Zechariah 1:1). The situation is complicated by the fact that the English "Iddo" conceals some variations in Hebrew spelling.

23. Mulder thinks that this identification is "extremely uncertain," but does not say why. Martin J. Mulder, *1 Kings: Volume 1: 1 Kings 1–11*, Historical Commentary on the Old Testament (Leuven, Belgium: Peeters, 1998), p. 184.

24. This observation seems to me much more in tune with the text before us than cynical observations about nepotism or elites: "This list [verses 1–6, but implicitly also verses 7–19] clearly reflects 'the next generation' of elites after David, the heirs of the founding generation of David's company who continue to be the privileged and powerful into the next generation." Brueggemann, *Kings*, p. 57.

25. So G. E. Wright, cited by Mulder, *1 Kings 1–11*, p. 171.

26. Proposals that differ in detail can be found in Donald J. Wiseman, *1 and 2 Kings*, Tyndale Old Testament Commentaries (Leicester, UK: Inter-Varsity Press, 1993), p. 91; Mulder, *1 Kings 1–11*, p. 170; Brueggemann, *Kings*, p. 60; and Map 5–14 in Currid, *Atlas*, p. 132.

27. Once again we find commentators who are critical of Solomon's supposed disregard for the old tribal arrangement in the interests of his taxation scheme. Indeed it has been suggested that "the new tax districts deliberately cut across old tribal lines in order to nullify what might have been tribal resistance to the new arrangement."

Brueggemann, *Kings*, p. 59; contra Beal, *Kings*, p. 96. Again I feel that modern cynicism (not to mention modern political theory) has distorted judgments. We need to take seriously the statement that immediately follows verses 7–19, to which we will come shortly: "Judah and Israel . . . were *happy*" (v. 20).

28. Jones has suggested that verse 19a may not be the twelfth district (as most understand it), but a footnote to verse 13 referring to pre-Solomonic times, and verse 19b identifies Judah as the twelfth district. Gwilym H. Jones, *1 and 2 Kings*, 2 volumes, New Century Bible Commentary (Grand Rapids, MI and London: Eerdmans and Marshall, Morgan & Scott, 1984), p. 144; also Beal, *Kings*, p. 96. This seems to me a tortuous reading of the text as it stands.

29. Seeing verse 20 as a summary conclusion to verses 1–19 (so also Keil, *Kings*, p. 37) is supported by the Hebrew text, which closes chapter 4 with verse 20 (4:21 in English is 5:1 in the Hebrew). Although the chapter division should not be regarded as definitive, in this particular case it makes good sense. Verses 1 and 20 provide a significant frame around verses 2–19. ESV, NIV, HCSB, REB make the very positive verse 20 the beginning of a new section or paragraph, perhaps influenced (wrongly in my opinion) by a negative understanding of verses 7–19. The chapter division in English versions goes back at least to the Vulgate and Septuagint, although these versions contain a number of other deviations from the order of the Hebrew text. For details see Mulder, *1 Kings 1–11*, p. 161. For a brief discussion of the origin and significance of chapter divisions in the Old Testament, see John Woodhouse, *1 Samuel: Looking for a Leader*, Preaching the Word (Wheaton, IL: Crossway, 2008), pp. 572, 573, note 3.

30. This is the first time in 1 Kings that "Israel" (meaning the northern tribes) has been distinguished from "Judah" in the south, with the one exception of 2:32, which was looking back to the days of civil war. Sadly the history will soon be dominated by the historic split of Israel from Judah (beginning at 1 Kings 12).

31. Better, "were eating and drinking." This was an ongoing situation.

32. The history of Israel in the Old Testament is sprinkled with echoes of God's promise to Abraham, repeatedly indicating that this is the history of God's faithfulness to his promise. The image of sand by the sea is just one way in which that promise was expressed. See Joshua 11:4 and the ironic 2 Samuel 17:11.

33. As so often, Matthew Henry captured this brilliantly: "Go where you would [in Solomon's kingdom], you might see all the marks of plenty, peace, and satisfaction. The spiritual peace, joy, and holy security, of all the faithful subjects of the Lord Jesus, were typified by this. *The kingdom of God is not*, as Solomon's was, *meat and drink*, but, what is infinitely better, *righteousness, and peace, and joy in the Holy Ghost*." Matthew Henry, *Matthew Henry's Commentary on the Whole Bible*, Vol. 2 (Old Tappan, NJ: Fleming H. Revell Company, no date), p. 600.

34. As often, the Hebrew has simply "the river." The context leads to the identification of "the river" as the Euphrates. See also verse 24 (twice); 14:15.

35. The Hebrew text begins chapter 5 with this verse and therefore ties the broader description of the significance of Solomon's kingdom in the English 4:21–34 (Hebrew, 5:1–14) more closely to the preparations for building the house in the English 5:1–18 (Hebrew, 5:15–32).

36. See note 4 to Chapter 5.

37. "Served" in verse 21b does not suggest the negative connotations of "forced labor" (v. 6). Contra Mulder, *1 Kings 1–11*, p. 189.

38. "Tribute" here is the usual word for "grain offering" (Genesis 4:3; Leviticus 2:1, 3) and also means "present" (Genesis 32:13, 18, 20, 21). Again I find Brueggemann seems to work against the tone of the text: "Thus the *coercive taxation* of colonies in v. 21 permits the *affluence* at home in v. 20. . . . A more informed reading may take this text with some irony, already recognizing that the appearance of well-being is mostly appearance, while the seeds of destruction that come with self-indulgence are already sown. They are not voiced in the text because they are not yet visible in the community." Brueggemann, *Kings*, p. 62 (emphasis his). No. They are not voiced in the text because that is not yet the point being made.

39. A "cor" is a large measure of volume applied to both dry and liquid substances, but its exact size is uncertain. See de Vaux, *Ancient Israel*, pp. 199–203.

40. See Keil, *Kings*, p. 38; Mulder, *1 Kings 1–11*, p. 190.

41. Montgomery, *Kings*, p. 128.

42. Henry, *Commentary*, p. 600. Henry is much closer to the sense of the text than Brueggemann: "The picture of the royal household is one of extravagance and self-indulgence." Brueggemann, *Kings*, p. 62.

43. I am giving full force to "For" at the beginning of verse 24.

44. The Hebrew emphasizes "he": "*he* is the one who had dominion . . ."

45. Literally, "beyond" (twice in this verse), probably indicating that the author was located east of the river, perhaps during or after the exile. So Keil, *Kings*, p. 39; Mulder, *1 Kings 1–11*, p. 192.

46. John H. Hull Jr., "Tiphsah," *ABD* 6, p. 571.

47. See Map 5–16 in Currid, *Atlas*, p. 137.

48. It occurs twenty-two times in the Old Testament, only seven times prior to this in Genesis to Kings (Genesis 1:26, 28; Leviticus 25:43, 46, 53; 26:17; Numbers 24:19).

49. Similarly Brueggemann, *Kings*, p. 65.

50. Again, Davis reads the mood of the text well: "this text is ecstatic over the fidelity of Yahweh, which should stir our joy, for this interim fulfillment under Solomon provides a sample of Yahweh's dependability for all his yet-to-be-fufilled promises." Davis, *Wisdom*, pp. 48, 49.

51. "From Dan [north of Lake Galilee] even to Beersheba [in the far south]" was a way of describing the full extent of Israel's land, from one end to the other, so to speak (see Judges 20:1; 1 Samuel 3:20; 2 Samuel 3:10; 17:11; 24:2, 15).

52. "All the days of Solomon," like the similar phrase in verse 21, should not be taken as underlining the temporariness of the situation, even if it will turn out to be such. Contra Walsh, *1 Kings*. p. 89.

53. It was "a set phrase in Israel to refer to an adequate, secure economic existence in a peaceful environment." Brueggemann, *Kings*, p. 66. See also 2 Kings 18:31, 32; Isaiah 36:16; Hosea 2:12; Habakkuk 3:17, 18; Joel 1:12; Haggai 2:19. ". . . when the prophets mourn the withering of the vine and the fig tree they are lamenting Israel's fall from the glories of Solomon (Isa. 34:4; Jer. 5:17; 8:13; cf. the ironic temptation of Isa. 36:16)." Peter J. Leithart, *1 & 2 Kings*, Brazos Theological Commentary on the Bible (Grand Rapids, MI: Brazos Press, 2006), p. 51.

54. Some suggest that 40,000 may be a copyist's error for 4,000, Cf. 10:26 and 2 Chronicles 1:14; 9:25. See Keil, *Kings*, p. 39; Gray, *Kings*, p. 141, note f.; Mulder, *1 Kings 1–11*, p. 193. Alternatively we should note that the Hebrew word for "thousand" may be very far from precise. See note 2 to Chapter 8.

55. There is disagreement as to whether the translation of the Hebrew *parashiym* here should be "horsemen" (so ESV; Mulder, *1 Kings 1–11*, p. 195) or "horses" (so NIV; Walsh, *1 Kings*. p. 88). Certainly "horses" in verse 28 is a different Hebrew word (*susiym*). See note 14 to Chapter 2.

56. A comparison with the descriptions of the Philistine military might in 1 Samuel 13:5 and the Syrians in 2 Samuel 10:18 suggests that Solomon's forces were modest for such a realm.

57. See further note 16 to Chapter 2.

58. Similarly Graeme Goldsworthy, *Gospel and Wisdom: Israel's Wisdom Literature in the Christian Life* (Exeter, Devon, UK: The Paternoster Press, 1987), p. 63.

59. The four names here appear again in 1 Chronicles 2:6 (with "Dara" for "Darda") as "sons of Zerah," the son of Judah by Tamar. In the present verse it is possible that "Ezrahite" is a variation on "Zera," and "sons of Mahol" may be a title referring to a role in the temple: "sons of the dance." So Keil, *Kings*, pp. 40, 41. "Ethan the Ezrahite" is mentioned in the superscription to Psalm 89 and "Heman the Ezrahite" in the superscription to Psalm 88. A suggestion that "Ezrahite" means "native," that is, Canaanite, seems to me less likely. On the reputation of these men for wisdom we know nothing more than the assertion of 1 Kings 4:31 that Solomon was wiser.

60. I suspect that most Australians who use this phrase have no idea who Solomon was!

61. Of the vocabulary in verse 33, "trees," "beasts," "birds," "reptiles" [or "creeping things"], and "fish" occur repeatedly and prominently in Genesis 1 (see Genesis 1:11, 12, 20, 21, 22, 24, 25, 26, 28, 30).

62. "This exuberant affirmation of the king would suggest that he is represented and celebrated as the true, judicious, all-knowing manager of all creation. That is, the king is understood as 'the true Adam,' the *real* human being. And he is treated so in later Israelite development which attributes to him the wisdom materials of Proverbs, Ecclesiastes, and Song of Solomon." Brueggemann, *Kings*, p. 68. (Unfortunately Brueggemann seriously qualifies this fine statement on page 69.)

63. This subject is important and deserves to be explored at greater length than is possible in this exposition of 1 Kings 4. I warmly recommend the book-length treatment by Goldsworthy, *Gospel and Wisdom*.

64. "All nations" and "all the kings of the earth" should not be pressed literally. The sense is "all *known* nations" and "all the *known* kings of the earth," and even then we should allow for the fact that the language deliberately echoes God's promise to Abraham (see Genesis 18:18; 22:18; 26:4).

Chapter Eleven: A Chosen and Precious Stone

1. We have noted previously that 4:21—5:18 in English Bibles is chapter 5 in the Hebrew text. Readers of the ESV and other modern translations need to be aware that the headings placed above sections of the text are not part of the Biblical text. They have been added by modern translators.

2. The Hebrew flows smoothly: literally, "And Hiram king of Tyre sent his servants . . ."

3. "Him" is emphasized in the Hebrew: "*he* was the one they had anointed . . ."

4. See especially Isaiah 23; Ezekiel 26:1—28:19. Cf. Luke 10:13, 14.

5. What Hiram "heard" is a repeated note in this chapter (vv. 1, 7, 8).

6. More literally, "Hiram was loving to David all his days."

7. See John Woodhouse, *1 Samuel: Looking for a Leader*, Preaching the Word (Wheaton, IL: Crossway, 2008), p. 349.

8. As Matthew Henry thought likely. Matthew Henry, *Matthew Henry's Commentary on the Whole Bible*, Vol. 2 (Old Tappan, NJ: Fleming H. Revell Company, no date), p. 602.

9. "The house of the LORD" in 2 Samuel 12:20 was not this house.

10. In contrast to the absence of references to the promised "house for the name of the LORD" since 2 Samuel 7, the other "house" promised to David (that is, his dynasty) has been mentioned a number of times (2 Samuel 12:10, 11; 23:5; 1 Kings 2:24, 31, 33).

11. The terms of the promise in 2 Samuel 7 here briefly summarized are explored in some detail in John Woodhouse, *2 Samuel: Your Kingdom Come*, Preaching the Word (Wheaton, IL: Crossway, 2015), pp. 197–220.

12. Contra Gray who thinks that in Nathan's oracle in 2 Samuel 7 "no mention is made of war as the prevention of David's building the Temple." John Gray, *I & II Kings: A Commentary*, Third, Fully Revised, Edition (London: SCM, 1977), p. 151.

13. "The allusion is to the gesture of the victor setting his foot on the neck of his prostrate enemy." Gray, *Kings*, p. 151.

14. Psalm 110:1 is an important text in the New Testament's teaching about Jesus Christ. See the citations and allusions in Matthew 22:44; 26:64; Mark 12:36; Luke 20:42, 43; Acts 2:34, 35; 1 Corinthians 15:25; Ephesians 1:20, 22; Colossians 3:1; Hebrews 1:3, 13; 2:8; 8:1; 10:12, 13; 12:2; 1 Peter 3:22.

15. The Hebrew word *hekal* (often translated "temple," although the same word can mean "palace") is used only sparingly in 1 Kings, and then only for part of the building (ESV, "nave" in 6:3, 5, 17, 33; also 7:21, 50). See our earlier discussion of 3:1d. I will follow the lead of our writer and avoid calling the building a "temple."

16. The Hebrew term *satan* is the name given to the great adversary, Satan. Matthew Henry shrewdly comments: "Satan does all he can to hinder temple-work, 1 Thess. ii. 18. Zech. iii. 1. but when he is bound (Rev. xx. 2.) we should be busy. . . . When the churches have rest, let them be edified, Acts ix. 31." Henry, *Commentary*, p. 602.

17. In due course we will hear twice that the Lord raised up an "adversary" (again the Hebrew is *satan*) against Solomon (11:14, 23). However, at the time of 5:4 Solomon had no knowledge of this tragic development. See our discussion of 11:14 and note 17 to Chapter 23.

18. The verbal form (*paga'*) of the Hebrew noun (*pega'*) is translated "strike down" or "attack" in 2:25, 29, 31, 32, 34, 46 in connection with the executions of Adonijah, Joab, and Shimei. "Evil" (sometimes translated "harmful," as in 1 Samuel 16:14, 15) does not necessarily carry moral connotations.

19. The Hebrew emphasizes the subject of the verb: *"he* is the one who shall build ..."

20. Literally, "And now," the usual introduction to the substance of a letter or message after introductory preliminaries. Cf. 2 Kings 5:6; 10:2 where the same expression is used. Gray, *Kings*, p. 152.

21. Literally "the Lebanon" (from a root meaning "to be white," perhaps a reference to the mountains of this region when covered with snow). "The Lebanon" referred to a geographical region rather than a country with defined borders. It was at the northern extremity of the land God promised to the people of Israel in Deuteronomy 11:24; Joshua 1:4. Solomon's dominion reached the Lebanon according to 1 Kings 9:19. Robert Houston Smith, "Lebanon," *ABD* 4, pp. 269, 270.

22. "Sidonians" means Phoenicians. Sidon, along with Tyre, was a leading city of Phoenicia.

23. Contra Beal, who seems to have mistaken "command" in verse 6 as a reference to Solomon's words. Lissa Wray M. Beal, *1 & 2 Kings*, Apollos Old Testament Commentary, Vol. 9 (Nottingham, UK and Downers Grove, IL: Apollos, 2014), p. 106.

24. "It must have been a matter of great importance to the king of Tyre to remain on good terms with Israel, because the land of Israel was a granary for the Phoenicians, and friendship with such a neighbour would necessarily tend greatly to promote the interests of Phoenician commerce." C. F. Keil, "1 and 2 Kings," in C. F. Keil and F. Delitzsch, *Commentary on the Old Testament*, Vol. 3 (Peabody, MA: Hendrickson Publishers, 1996), p. 44.

25. See Woodhouse, *2 Samuel*, p. 599, note 6.

26. The cynical reading found in some modern commentators is (in my opinion) a serious misreading. For example: "It is plausible to read Hiram's remark in verse 7 as an ironic comment on the reports he has heard about Solomon's wisdom (4:34): he rejoices not only that relations between their kingdoms will remain peaceful but also that this reputedly 'wise' son of David is offering him such an opportunity to profit from the prosperity of 'this great people.'" Jerome T. Walsh, *1 Kings*, Berit Olam: Studies in Hebrew Narrative & Poetry (Collegeville, MN: The Liturgical Press, 1996), p. 98.

27. Other foreigners who will similarly and gladly acknowledge the Lord include the queen of Sheba (10:9) and the widow of Zarephath (17:12, 24).

28. These verses all have words for rejoicing cognate with the word (*shamakh*) used for Hiram's joy in verse 7.

29. There is some uncertainty about the precise type of timber referred to here. It may be juniper wood. So *CHALOT*, p. 47; also Martin J. Mulder, *1 Kings: Volume 1: 1 Kings 1–11*, Historical Commentary on the Old Testament (Leuven, Belgium: Peeters, 1998), pp. 214, 215.

30. "Hiram rejects Solomon's proposal that Israelites should be employed in the Lebanon, and undertakes all responsibility for felling and transport of the timber to the coast and to Palestine." Gray, *Kings*, p. 153. "Under the guise of agreement ('I will fulfill all your needs'; literally, 'I shall do whatever you want'), Hiram in fact rejects Solomon's terms completely and renegotiates them in his own favor. . . . *His* workers will do all the logging and deliver the timber by sea to wherever (presumably in Israel) Solomon specifies. That way Tyrian income is maximized, there is

no infiltration of Hiram's territory by foreigners, and no industrial secrets are lost." Walsh, *1 Kings*, pp. 96, 97. Leithart has the measure of this kind of reading: "Walsh's interpretation is overly subtle. . . . It is simpler to conclude that Hiram's terms are never so radically opposed to Solomon's as Walsh imagines. . . . Hiram's response to Solomon suggests some changes in the specifics of Solomon's proposal, but all of them are advantageous to Solomon. . . . This is underhanded only to the cynical, for to the cynical all things are cynical." Peter J. Leithart, *1 & 2 Kings*, Brazos Theological Commentary on the Bible (Grand Rapids, MI: Brazos Press, 2006), p. 52, note 3.

31. "Beaten oil" was "the finest kind of oil, which was obtained from the olives when not quite ripe by pounding them in mortars, and which had not only a whiter colour, but also a purer flavour than the common oil obtained by pressing from the ripe olives." Keil, *Kings*, p. 45. See Exodus 27:20; 29:40; Leviticus 24:2; Numbers 28:5.

32. Walsh, *1 Kings*, p. 99.

33. Similarly Gray, *Kings*, p. 154.

34. Similarly Beal, *Kings*, p. 108. One study of the Hebrew term (*mas*) and its use in the Old Testament concludes: "What emerges is thus a general biblical view that work is good in and of itself and a necessary component of human life, even when it is 'mobilized by force' for worthy, although not private purposes: here the danger of misuse arises, which must be countered." R. North, "*mas*," *TDOT* 8, p. 430.

35. Whether those complaints were entirely honest is a moot point. "The basis for some of the Solomon-bashing (e.g. his harsh, repressive measures) comes from the complaint of his former subjects in 12:3–4. And scholars gullibly swallow this complaint as though it were the gospel truth, apparently not realizing that it comes from a politically motivated opposition and is therefore likely to have as much propaganda as truth in it." Dale Ralph Davis, *The Wisdom and the Folly: An Exposition of the Book of First Kings* (Fearn, Ross-shire, UK: Christian Focus, 2002), p. 57, note 10.

36. This is the consistent sense of "all Israel" in 1 Kings 1—11. Similarly Keil, *Kings*, p. 45; Beal, *Kings*, p. 108.

37. So Walsh, *1 Kings*, p. 100.

38. For an analysis of the numbers in verses 13–16 and an argument that they seem realistic, see K. A. Kitchen, *The Bible in Its World: Archaeology and the Bible Today* (Exeter, UK: The Paternoster Press, 1977), pp. 103–6.

39. So Walsh, *1 Kings*, p. 100; similarly Beal, *Kings*, p. 108. Provan understands "his house" as Solomon's palace. Iain W. Provan, *1 & 2 Kings*, Understanding the Bible Commentary Series (Grand Rapids, MI: Baker Books, 1995), p. 65.

40. Keil, *Kings*, p. 46.

41. Gebal was a Phoenecian seaport north of Tyre, closer to the Lebanon forests. See Map 5–16 in Currid, *Atlas*, p. 137.

Chapter Twelve: A True Perspective on the History of the Whole World

1. A glance at the notes in the margin of the ESV gives some idea of the problems the translators have faced.

2. Consider, for example, the long description of the plan for and the construction of the tabernacle in Exodus 26, 27, 35—40. A careful reader will pick up a sense

of wonder through these chapters that should dispel boredom! Likewise the detailed description of the distribution of the land to the Israelite tribes in Joshua 13—21: the text is bursting with the excitement at what God had done in faithfulness to his promise to Abraham (see Joshua 21:43–45). Perhaps the most striking example is the long genealogy that stands at the very beginning of the New Testament (Matthew 1:1–17). The list of names is no less than a demonstration that the historic events about to be told in the Gospel According to Matthew are the point to which all preceding history has been moving.

3. Similarly John W. Olley, *The Message of Kings: God Is Present*, The Bible Speaks Today (Nottingham, UK: Inter-Varsity Press, 2011), p. 79.

4. A literal understanding is argued by C. F Keil, "1 and 2 Kings," in C. F. Keil and F. Delitzsch, *Commentary on the Old Testament*, Vol. 3 (Peabody, MA: Hendrickson Publishers, 1996), p. 50, note 1; Richard D. Patterson and Herman J. Austel, "1, 2 Kings," in *The Expositor's Bible Commentary*, Revised Edition, ed. Tremper Longman III and David E. Garland, Vol. 3 (Grand Rapids, MI: Zondervan, 2009), p. 682. There have been various suggestions of how the 480 years (literally understood) may have been computed. For example: 40 years in the wilderness with Moses + 40 years (presumed) under Joshua + 296 in the period of the judges + 40 years under Eli (1 Samuel 4:18) + 20 of the ark's residence at Kiriath-jearim (1 Samuel 7:2) + 40 years under David (1 Kings 2:11) + 4 years of Solomon (1 Kings 6:1) = 480 years. Cited by Lissa M. Wray Beal, *1 & 2 Kings*, Apollos Old Testament Commentary, Vol. 9 (Nottingham, England and Downers Grove, IL: Apollos, 2014), p. 119.

5. So, for example, Beal, *Kings*, p. 118. Some take the figure as indicating "the mid-point of the historian's overview from the Exodus to the Exile." Donald J. Wiseman, *1 and 2 Kings*, Tyndale Old Testament Commentaries (Leicester, UK: Inter-Varsity Press, 1993), p. 104. Similarly Gwilym H. Jones, *1 and 2 Kings*, 2 volumes, New Century Bible Commentary (Grand Rapids, MI and London: Eerdmans and Marshall, Morgan & Scott, 1984), p. 163; Walter Brueggemann, *1 & 2 Kings*, Smyth & Helwys Bible Commentary (Macon, GA: Smyth & Helwys, 2000), pp. 83, 84. For other possible symbolic understandings of "480 years" see John Gray, *I & II Kings: A Commentary*, Third, Fully Revised, Edition (London: SCM, 1977), p. 159. Opinions about the literalness or otherwise of the 480 years in 1 Kings 6:1 have featured in discussions of the date of the exodus, since the fourth year of Solomon's reign is generally agreed to have been about 966 B.C. A literal understanding of our verse yields a date of about 1446 B.C. for the exodus, while the symbolic understanding would be consistent with a date in the thirteenth century B.C. Sometimes convictions about the exodus date have colored the interpretation of our verse. For example, K. A. Kitchen, who is persuaded that the most likely date for the exodus is mid-thirteenth century B.C., dismisses a literal reading of 1 Kings 6:1 as the "lazy man's solution." K. A. Kitchen, "Exodus, The," *ABD* 2, p. 702. For a judicious argument that neither position should be held dogmatically, see Iain W. Provan, V. Philips Long, and Tremper Longman III, *A Biblical History of Israel* (Louisville: Westminster John Knox Press, 2003), pp. 131, 132.

6. The presentation of historical information in a schematized way in order to show the *significance* of the period on view is well illustrated by Matthew 1:1–17, which is certainly not a complete genealogy, nor can the three periods

of "fourteen generations" in verse 17 be understood literally. See D. Davies and Dale C. Allison Jr., *A Critical and Exegetical Commentary on the Gospel According to Saint Matthew*, Vol. 1 ((London and New York: T & T Clark, 1988), pp. 161–65, 185, 186.

7. So Martin Noth, *Exodus: A Commentary*, Old Testament Library (London and Philadelphia: SCM Press, 1962), p. 125.

8. About 966 B.C. This was probably the fourth year after the death of David (2:10) rather than after Solomon's acclamation as king in 1:39.

9. Possibly meaning "brilliancy, splendour, probably so called from the splendour of the flowers." Keil, *Kings*, p. 50.

10. "House" occurs twenty-four times in 1 Kings 6.

11. Importantly, as we noted previously, even the Hebrew word often translated "temple" (*hekal*) is not in itself a religious term. It can equally be applied to a king's "palace" without religious connotations (21:1). The word occurs four times in 1 Kings 6 (ESV, "nave"; NIV, "main hall"), referring to the main hall of the building, but never for the whole building, nor even of the most important part of the building behind the main hall, the Most Holy Place. See our discussion of 3:1d.

12. "House" occurs fifteen times in 2 Samuel 7, twice referring to David's palace, nine times to the dynasty promised to David, and four times to a building such as Solomon built according to 1 Kings 6.

13. A fine example of such an attempt can be found in Currid, *Atlas*, pp. 134, 135.

14. Contra Martin J. Mulder, *1 Kings: Volume 1: 1 Kings 1–11*, Historical Commentary on the Old Testament (Leuven, Belgium: Peeters, 1998), p. 232: "it is most natural to think of outside measurements."

15. The Hebrew term *'ammah* has the basic meaning, "forearm."

16. For more information about the cubit measure of length, see Marvin A. Powell, "Weights and Measures," *ABD* 6, pp. 899, 900.

17. Like the Hebrew word translated "temple," the Hebrew for "tabernacle" is not itself a "religious" word. It is the ordinary word for a "dwelling-place" or "home." The context, rather than the word itself, shapes the particular significance of the structure in question.

18. The details given in Exodus 26 for the tabernacle require some interpretation to deduce the length and width. The height of the tabernacle (10 cubits) was just one third of the height of Solomon's structure. The evidence does not support the idea that Solomon was building a scaled-up "model" of the tabernacle, although similarities to the tabernacle are unmistakable. For more details see Richard Elliot Friedman, "Tabernacle," *ABD* 6, pp. 295–297.

19. The Hebrew term here appears to be a technical architectural term for a hall. In 7:6–8 the term occurs six times (ESV, "hall" or "porch") in the description of Solomon's palace.

20. On the Hebrew term (*hekal*) see our discussion of 3:1d and note 18 to Chapter 7. Here it refers to the large space inside the building further described in verse 17. It seems confusing to use a term drawn from medieval church architecture ("nave") for a part of the house Solomon was building.

21. See ESV margin. The precise meaning of the Hebrew expression is unclear. For some possibilities, see Gray, *Kings*, p. 164.

22. See the helpful diagram of this structure in Wiseman, *1 and 2 Kings*, p. 108.

23. Earlier prohibitions on the use of iron tools in the construction of stone altars may have influenced the building process. See Exodus 20:25; Deuteronomy 27:5; Joshua 8:31.

24. The ESV follows the Septuagint and Targum here. The Hebrew has "middle." The versions may have "corrected" the Hebrew, which is difficult to understand. How could an external door give access to the "middle" level? Were there unmentioned external stairs?

25. A rare Hebrew word here may mean "trap-doors." So Gray, *Kings*, p. 166.

26. For a thorough discussion of the verse yielding a different understanding, see Mulder, *1 Kings 1–11*, pp. 245–48.

27. So Keil, *Kings*, p. 53.

28. Perhaps the ceiling served as the roof. So Gray, *Kings*, p. 166.

29. The Hebrew verb "to build" is used in the creation narrative at Genesis 2:22 (ESV, "made").

30. While there is a different Hebrew word (*shbt*) for "rested" in Genesis 2:2 from that rendered "rest" (*nwkh*) in 1 Kings 5:4, they are essentially synonymous in these contexts, as the use of the latter in Exodus 20:11 shows.

31. This seems to be the sense. So Keil, *Kings*, p. 53. If the three floors were five cubits high in total, each room would be only a couple of feet high.

32. In the narrative of the books of Samuel and Kings this is the first time since 2 Samuel 7 that we read "the word of the LORD came" to someone (with the exception of 2 Samuel 24:11 in the epilogue to the books of Samuel). It will soon become a frequently recurring refrain (13:20; 16:1, 7; 17:2; etc.) for reasons we will need to consider. On the phrase, see our introduction to Chapter 27. Since we are told in 3:5 that "the LORD appeared to Solomon" and in 9:2 that "the LORD appeared to Solomon *a second time*" (see also 11:9), "the word of the LORD" coming to Solomon in 6:11 must be different. Perhaps on this occasion a prophet was involved (as in 2 Samuel 7:4; 24:11).

33. All four occurrences of "you"/"your" in verse 12 are singular and refer to Solomon.

34. See our discussion of 2:4 on the complex relationship between human obedience and divine grace.

35. The Hebrew verb in 1 Kings 6:13 (*shaken*) is cognate with *mishkan* ("tabernacle") and is rendered in Greek by the verb we find in John 1:14 (*skenoo*, "to dwell in a tent").

36. "Walls of the ceiling" is an awkward expression, which may mean or be a copyist's error for "beams of the ceiling." Keil, *Kings*, p. 55.

37. *CHALOT*, p. 66. The Hebrew word is similar to the word for "speak." Older translations therefore rendered it "an oracle" (RV), meaning "the place where the speaking takes place." So Keil, *Kings*, p. 55. James Barr took this as an example of seriously flawed reasoning, persuasively arguing that the word in question simply means "back room." James Barr, *The Semantics of Biblical Language* (Oxford: Oxford University Press, 1961), pp. 129–37.

38. The dimensions of the tabernacle's Most Holy Place are deduced from data in the Exodus description. J. P. Hyatt, *Exodus*, New Century Bible (London: Marshall, Morgan & Scott, 1971), p. 275.

39. The Hebrew term (*peqaʻiym*) is understood to refer to a cucumber-like plant (cf. 2 Kings 4:39).

40. See note 33 to Chapter 4 and our discussion of 3:4.

41. As shown in the attempt to draw the building in Currid, *Atlas*, pp. 114, 115.

42. Possibly mentioned in 2 Chronicles 3:9. Of course, the Most Holy Place may have been both somewhat elevated from the floor and also lower than the ceiling.

43. Gray, *Kings*, p. 170.

44. So Keil, *Kings*, pp. 56, 57. There is some uncertainty about the location of the altar of incense. Hebrews 9:4 seems to understand that it was inside the Most Holy Place, although there is some ambiguity. See Peter T. O'Brien, *The Letter to the Hebrews*, The Pillar New Testament Commentary (Grand Rapids, MI and Cambridge, UK: Eerdmans, 2010), pp. 308, 309.

45. The statement about chains is obscure. One reasonable suggestion is: "the doors into the Most Holy Place . . . were closed and fastened with gold chains, which were stretched across the whole breadth of the door and stood out against the wall." Keil, *Kings*, p. 57.

46. What "it" refers to is unclear, but that matters little since just about everything was overlaid with gold.

47. So Brueggemann, *Kings*, p. 91. "Finished" is a different Hebrew word from the term in verses 9, 14, and 38. In certain contexts this word has a moral sense ("blameless" in 2 Samuel 22:26; Psalm 19:13).

48. Keil, *Kings*, p. 57.

49. "Cherubim" is a transliteration of the Hebrew, "-im" representing the masculine plural ending. Translators have resisted calling them "cherubs," no doubt to avoid the associations of the English word with cute chubby-faced, winged babies. The cherubim of the Bible were not cute or cuddly.

50. The remarkable feature of a gold-plated floor is considered "impractical" and "unlikely" by Gray, *Kings*, pp. 172, 173. I am not sure that "practical" and "likely" should be the criteria for credibility here!

51. The Hebrew of this clause is obscure, and variously interpreted: ". . . the lintel *and* door posts were a fifth part *of the wall*" (RV); ". . . and five-sided door jambs" (JB); ". . . the pilasters and the doorposts were pentagonal" (REB); ". . . doors out of olive wood that were one fifth of the width of the sanctuary" (NIV).

52. Again the Hebrew is unclear. It may indicate that the framework for the door occupied a fourth of the breadth of the wall, that is, five cubits: "for the entrance to the main hall he made doorframes out of olive wood that were one fourth of the width of the hall" (NIV). So also Keil, *Kings*, p. 59.

53. Keil argues that the doors were probably divided halfway up "so that the lower half could be opened without the upper." Ibid., p. 60.

54. Ibid.

55. "Bul" means "moisture" and refers to the rain month in the fall. Gray, *Kings*, p. 176; Mulder, *1 Kings 1–11*, p. 283.

56. See John Woodhouse, *2 Samuel: Your Kingdom Come*, Preaching the Word (Wheaton, IL: Crossway, 2015), pp. 249–51.

Chapter Thirteen: The King Who Will Build

1. This astute observation was made by *Matthew Henry's Commentary on the Whole Bible*, Vol. 2 (Old Tappan, NJ: Fleming H. Revell Company, no date) p. 608.

2. In due course, when the behavior of the kings became offensive to God, the close proximity of the king's house and the Lord's house became objectionable. It then defiled God's holy name (see Ezekiel 43:7, 8). However, it was the wickedness of these kings that made the arrangement of palace and temple unacceptable, not the arrangement itself.

3. The Christological point could be explored richly through Jesus' prayer in John 17 (see vv. 1, 5). "The objection that Solomon's glory challenges Yahweh's assumes a false doctrine of God. God's glory does not compete with human glory, nor does God glorify himself by siphoning glory from his people. He glorifies himself by freely and abundantly bestowing glory, just as the Father glorifies himself in the Son through the Spirit, and the Son in the Father through the same Spirit. Yahweh gives Solomon glory, but this makes the name of Yahweh glorious among the Gentiles, precisely because it makes the name of Solomon glorious." Peter J. Leithart, *1 & 2 Kings*, Brazos Theological Commentary on the Bible (Grand Rapids, MI: Brazos Press, 2006), p. 60.

4. ". . . the juxtaposition of 6:38 and 7:1 invites us to infer that the governmental buildings are far more important to Solomon than the religious one. In view of the ruinous annual tariff Solomon is paying Hiram, it is quite clear which project brings Solomon to the brink of bankruptcy." Jerome T. Walsh, *1 Kings*, Berit Olam: Studies in Hebrew Narrative & Poetry (Collegeville, MN: The Liturgical Press, 1996), p. 106. Similarly Lissa M. Wray Beal, *1 & 2 Kings*, Apollos Old Testament Commentary, Vol. 9 (Nottingham, UK and Downers Grove, IL: Apollos, 2014), p. 122. This view is cogently refuted by Dale Ralph Davis, *The Wisdom and the Folly: An Exposition of the Book of First Kings* (Fearn, Ross-shire, UK: Christian Focus, 2002), p. 71, note 2.

5. "The relative proportions of the Temple and the rest of the buildings . . . would make seven years and 13 respectively appropriate." John Gray, *I & II Kings: A Commentary*, Third, Fully Revised, Edition (London: SCM, 1977), p. 177.

6. The Jewish historian Josephus argued that the palace was not built with the same zeal as the temple. Martin J. Mulder, *1 Kings: Volume 1: 1 Kings 1–11*, Historical Commentary on the Old Testament (Leuven, Belgium: Peeters, 1998), p. 285. Matthew Henry suggested that the thirteen years on his own house indicated "not that he was more exact, but less eager and intent, in building his own house than in building God's; he was in no haste for his own palace, but impatient till the temple was finished, and fit for use; thus we ought to prefer God's honour before our own ease and satisfaction." Henry, *Commentary*, p. 609.

7. So C. F. Keil, "1 and 2 Kings," in C. F. Keil and F. Delitzsch, *Commentary on the Old Testament*, Vol. 3 (Peabody, MA: Hendrickson Publishers, 1996), p. 65 and most more recent commentators. Some older writers thought this was a summer house for the king, located in Lebanon. So Henry, *Commentary*, p. 609. This seems less plausible than the explanation followed here.

8. The Hebrew term (*tsela'*) rendered "chambers" is unclear. It is used for "side chambers" in 6:5, "story" in 6:8, "boards" in 6:15, 16, and "leaves" in 6:34. Mulder, *1 Kings 1–11*, pp. 240ff. argues for a consistent meaning in these chapters: "buttress." In other contexts it can mean "rib" (Genesis 2:21) or "side" (2 Samuel 16:13).

9. Similarly Keil, *Kings*, p. 66; Gray, *Kings*, p. 178.

10. The word for "window" (*mekhezah*) in the expression "window opposite window" (vv. 4, 5) occurs only here in the Old Testament. It is related to the verb "see" and is similar to a word meaning "vision."

11. So Keil, *Kings*, p. 67. For a diagram suggesting a possible layout of the complex of buildings described in 1 Kings 6, 7 see Currid, *Atlas*, p. 136.

12. "Vestibule" in 6:3 represents the same Hebrew term (*'ulam*) as "Hall" and "porch" in 7:6. This term recurs in 7:7, 8 ("hall") and 7:12 ("vestibule").

13. Walsh offers an analysis of the structure of 7:1–12 that has verse 7 at the center of the whole section. Walsh, *1 Kings*, p. 105.

14. The Hebrew has, literally, "floor to floor," which may mean "from one floor to the other," that is, "from the lower floor to the upper, inasmuch as there were rooms built over the throne-room, just as in the case of the house of the forest of Lebanon." Keil, *Kings*, p. 68.

15. So Walter Brueggemann, *1 & 2 Kings*, Smyth & Helwys Bible Commentary (Macon, GA: Smyth & Helwys, 2000), p. 93.

16. This completes the account without indicating when the house for Pharaoh's daughter was built. It was after work on the wall around Jerusalem (3:1; see 9:15). Its completion is noted in 9:24.

17. Gray, *Kings*, p. 181.

18. Similarly Leithart, *Kings*, p. 61.

19. It is important to note carefully that the word "church" in English translations of the New Testament represents the Greek *ekklesia*, which means "gathering," "assembly." The word often refers to a local gathering of Christian believers. It can also refer to the spiritual "gathering" of all believers under the Lord Jesus Christ. See D. W. B. Robinson, "Church," in J. D. Douglas, ed., *The Illustrated Bible Dictionary*, Part 1 (Leicester, UK and Wheaton, IL: Inter-Varsity Press and Tyndale House, 1980), pp. 283–86; John Woodhouse, *Colossians and Philemon: So Walk in Him*, Focus on the Bible (Fearn, Ross-shire, UK: Christian Focus, 2011), pp. 61–63, 82.

Chapter Fourteen: The Truth about Everything

1. This passage includes unusual technical terms whose meaning is now unclear as well as a number of places where the text is uncertain. The marginal notes in the ESV indicate some of the issues. A comparison of different English translations will show how some details have been variously understood. This exposition will generally follow the ESV and will refrain from technical discussions of disputed details since the important message of this chapter does not really depend on those disputes.

2. Since 2 Chronicles 2:13 indicates that Solomon sent for this man at the very beginning of the building work, "had sent" may be more accurate here. However, my intention is to follow the presentation of events as we find it in 1 Kings, generally independent of the parallel history in the books of Chronicles. It is probable that the author(s) of the later books of Chronicles assumed that readers would be familiar with 1 and 2 Kings. Therefore it is more appropriate to draw on the books of Kings as we read Chronicles than vice versa. Of course, there is a place for doing both.

3. In the Hebrew text this Hiram's name is given as Hiram in 7:13, 45, Hirom in 7:40, and Huram-abi in 2 Chronicles 2:13; 4:16. There is a similar variation in the

form of the name of the king of Tyre: he is called Hiram in 1 Kings and Huram in 2 Chronicles.

4. In view of 2 Chronicles 2:14, it seems likely that the mother belonged to the tribe of Dan by birth, but married into the tribe of Naphtali. C. F. Keil, "1 and 2 Kings," in C. F. Keil and F. Delitzsch, *Commentary on the Old Testament*, Vol. 3 (Peabody, MA: Hendrickson Publishers, 1996), p. 70.

5. For more detail about the history of bronze, see F. V. Winnett, "Bronze," *IDB* 1, p. 467.

6. The Hebrew verb is a passive form, suggesting that he had been filled with wisdom, etc., *by the Lord*.

7. The explicit reference to the Spirit (or breath) of God in Exodus 31:3 is lacking in 1 Kings 7:14, but is perhaps implied by the passive verb there. See previous note.

8. I have translated Exodus 31:3, 4 to reflect the vocabulary in the Hebrew that is identical to 1 Kings 7:14 (the words in italics). This is not evident in the ESV.

9. The ESV follows some of the ancient versions here. The Hebrew lacks "It was hollow, and its thickness was four fingers" and has some other difficulties. Compare Jeremiah 52:21.

10. The latter part of this sentence is obscure. See discussion in Keil, *Kings*, pp. 71, 72.

11. The "rounded projection" (literally "belly") must refer to the bowl shape of the capital. See verses 41, 42.

12. "Temple" is misleading here if the vocabulary is consistent (which I think it is). The Hebrew word (*hekal*) refers to what the ESV has called the "nave," that is, the main hall of the house of the Lord in 6:3, 5, 17, 33. See our discussion of 3:1d and note 18 to Chapter 7.

13. On the interpretation of the significance of Jachin and Boaz, see the fuller discussions in R. B. Y. Scott, "Jachin and Boaz," *IDB* 2, pp. 780, 781; Carol Meyers, "Jachin and Boaz," *ABD* 3, pp. 597, 598.

14. While these measurements are not intended to be precise, they are accurate within a reasonable margin. A circle with a diameter of 10 cubits would have a circumference of just over 31.4 cubits.

15. So NIV. This seems to make more sense, implying that the gourds were a little over two inches in diameter. So Keil, *Kings*, p. 74.

16. So Keil, *Kings*, p. 75.

17. Gray correctly describes verses 27–39 as "this highly technical passage, which betrays a specialist's interest in a fine piece of craftsmanship . . . there are many obscurities, chiefly resulting from *hapax legomena*." John Gray, *I & II Kings: A Commentary*, Third, Fully Revised, Edition (London: SCM, 1977), pp. 191, 192.

18. These may have included the "basins" of verse 38 (same Hebrew word), but since the same word is used of a cooking pan in 1 Samuel 2:14, we may suppose that there were many such objects with various unspecified uses.

19. Shovels were no doubt used in connection with burnt offerings, in the removal of ashes (Exodus 27:3).

20. "Basins" translates one of several Hebrew words for bowls, pots, or basins. This one has not been used earlier in the chapter. The precise distinctions between different terms are not clear.

21. The verbal echoes are indicated in italics.

22. See Maps 5–14 and 6–2 in Currid, *Atlas*, pp. 132, 142.

23. "So" is misleading. Verses 48–50 describe *additional* work, not related to what precedes. See NIV.

24. The Hebrew expressions for "pure gold" in Exodus 25:31 and 1 Kings 7:49 are different and may reflect differences in the technology used.

25. See note 12.

26. I am not counting 7:7 where "finished" (ESV) has the sense "covered" (so NIV). The Hebrew word here is rendered "made" in 6:9 and "covered" in 7:3. It does not have the sense "completed."

Chapter Fifteen: King Solomon's "Church"

1. The Greek word (*ekklesia*) translated "church" in the New Testament means "assembly" or "gathering." It is unfortunate (to say the least) that this sense, which is present in all occurrences of the Greek word in the New Testament, is lost in the English translation. This was understood by William Tyndale in his famous English translation of the New Testament, first published in 1526, in which he consistently rendered *ekklesia* as "congregation," thus conveying the sense of the original better than any subsequent English translation. *William Tyndale's New Testament*, Wordsworth Classics of World Literature (Ware, Hertfordshire, UK: Wordsworth Editions Limited, 2002). See the important study by D. W. B. Robinson, "Church," *IBD* 1, pp. 283–86.

2. The understanding of "church" reflected in these comments is more thoroughly explored in the important work of D. B. Knox and Donald Robinson. See Kirsten Birkett, ed., *D. Broughton Knox: Selected Works, Volume 2: Church and Ministry* (Kingsford, N.S.W., Australia: Matthias Media, 2003), pp. 9–106; Peter G. Bolt and Mark D. Thompson, eds., *Donald Robinson: Selected Works, Volume 1: Assembling God's People* (Camperdown, N.S.W., Australia: Australian Church Record, 2008), pp. 195–336.

3. See the excellent study of the theme of God gathering through the Bible by Christopher Ash, *Remaking a Broken World: The Heart of the Bible Story* (Milton Keynes, UK: Authentic Media Limited, 2010).

4. The Hebrew is *qahal*; the Greek is *ekklesia*. Here is a further problem with the use of "church" for *ekklesia* in the New Testament. It obscures the connections with the Old Testament assemblies, which (inexplicably) our English versions never call "church."

5. It is the Hebrew verb *qahal*, corresponding to the noun mentioned in the previous note.

6. This remark is contrary to some Biblical studies that read a great deal of theological weight into the Hebrew word *qahal*, "assembly" (as well as the Greek equivalent *ekklesia*). There is much good sense in the response to such tendencies in James Barr, *The Semantics of Biblical Language* (Oxford: Oxford University Press, 1961), pp. 119–29.

7. The Hebrew does not have "and" here. It is better omitted and replaced with a comma. "The elders" and "the heads" are not two different groups, but two ways of referring to the same people.

8. Years earlier still "the elders of Israel" had defiantly demanded that Samuel give them a king "like all the nations" (1 Samuel 8:4, 5). That did not work out well.

9. The ark did feature in more recent events when David fled from Jerusalem (2 Samuel 15:24–29), but the upshot of that was that the ark was sent back into Jerusalem to stay there pending David's return. In 1 Kings the ark has been mentioned in 2:26; 3:15; 6:19.

10. On "Zion" see John Woodhouse, *2 Samuel: Your Kingdom Come*, Preaching the Word (Wheaton, IL: Crossway, 2015), p. 157.

11. See the clear and detailed map in Currid, *Atlas*, pp. 296, 297 (also p. 131). The higher ground was in fact Mount Moriah (2 Chronicles 3:1), which is where Abraham had (almost) offered up his son Isaac as a sacrifice in obedience to the Lord (Genesis 22:2). Since the place is not named in 1 Kings, these connections are not part of our exposition of this text.

12. So C. F. Keil, "1 and 2 Kings," in C. F. Keil and F. Delitzsch, *Commentary on the Old Testament*, Vol. 3 (Peabody, MA: Hendrickson Publishers, 1996), p. 84. This is explicitly said in the Septuagint, which has the wording of 9:10 reproduced here. John Gray, *I & II Kings: A Commentary*, Third, Fully Revised, Edition (London: SCM, 1977), p. 204, note a.

13. "Ethanim" means "ever-flowing" and probably applied to the seventh month because then only the permanent streams were still flowing. *CHALOT*, p. 14.

14. "The temple marks a moment in the history of the Gentiles, not merely in the history of Israel." Peter J. Leithart, *1 & 2 Kings*, Brazos Theological Commentary on the Bible (Grand Rapids, MI: Brazos Press, 2006), p. 68.

15. This discussion of the Feast of Booths/Tabernacles has drawn on a similar presentation in Lissa M. Wray Beal, *1 & 2 Kings*, Apollos Old Testament Commentary, Vol. 9 (Nottingham, UK and Downers Grove, IL: Apollos, 2014), pp. 134, 135. Leithart also sees significance in the Feast of Tabernacles as the timing of these things: "In this, it contrasts with the Sinai covenant, established at Pentecost in the third month. In agricultural terms, Pentecost was a firstfruits festival, the beginning of the harvest, but not yet the end of the harvest. The temple completes the process of maturation begun at Sinai. With the Mosaic covenant came the firstfruits, but with Solomon the full corn appears." Leithart, *Kings*, p. 68.

16. The tabernacle is frequently called "the tent of meeting" in Exodus, Leviticus, and Numbers. The most recent reference in this history was 1 Samuel 2:22.

17. The relationship between priests (descended from Aaron) and Levites (other members of the tribe of Aaron's ancestor Levi) is complicated. A helpful outline of the issues is given by D. A. Hubbard, "Priests and Levites," *IBD* 3, pp. 1266–273.

18. Our historian can be infuriating. He omits many things the curious Bible student would love to know. The history of the tabernacle is one of the puzzles created by lack of information. The tent in which David had placed the ark in the city of David (2 Samuel 6:17) was *not* the tabernacle (see 2 Chronicles 1:3–5). In the days of Samuel's youth the tabernacle had stood in Shiloh for many years (Joshua 18:1; 19:51; 22:19, 29; 1 Samuel 1:3, 7, 9; 2:22). Some time after the destruction of Shiloh and the capture of the ark by the Philistines (1 Samuel 4; cf. Jeremiah 7:12, 14; 26:6, 9), it seems that the ark was separated from the tabernacle (1 Samuel 7:1, 2) and was never placed in the tabernacle again. The tabernacle (or a reconstructed tabernacle if the Philistines had destroyed the original) was apparently subsequently located at Nob (1 Samuel 21:1, 6). A later historian informs us that the tabernacle had most re-

cently been at Gibeon (2 Chronicles 1:3, 5; cf. 1 Kings 3:4). The tabernacle featured in our story (as we have understood it) as recently as 1:50, 51; 2:28–30.

19. On the seventy years, see Woodhouse, *2 Samuel*, p. 587, note 2.

20. If David brought up the ark to the city of David in about his tenth year as king, then it was another thirty years before David died (2 Samuel 5:5). To this we need to add the number of years since Solomon became king (more than twenty if we have been correct about the date of this assembly). While it is not possible to be precise, it was more than a hundred years from the capture of the ark by the Philistines in 1 Samuel 4 to the ark and the tabernacle being brought into the house of the Lord by Solomon.

21. See Woodhouse, *2 Samuel*, pp. 187, 188.

22. The participle "sacrificing" in verse 5 may suggest the continuous offering of sacrifices as the ark was approaching its destination. So Gray, *Kings*, p. 209.

23. We might be reminded of the terrified Philistines who wanted to send the ark back to "its own place" (1 Samuel 5:11; 6:2).

24. The verb here (*sakak*) has the same root as the noun translated "booths" (*sukkah*) in connection with the feast (Leviticus 23:34; etc.).

25. Perhaps this influenced the alternative rendering in the RV margin: "And they drew out the staves." This is not a natural reading of the Hebrew. See Keil, *Kings*, p. 86.

26. "To this day" is curious, for by the time this history was compiled, the poles were certainly no longer there. See 2 Kings 25. It is probably best to understand "to this day" as a reference to the day of the writer of a source document (perhaps the Book of the Acts of Solomon, 11:41) from which the historian has drawn the present material.

27. This is perhaps "more correctly rendered in the present tense as part of the narrator's aside to his contemporary reader: 'There *is* nothing in the ark . . .'" Jerome T. Walsh, *1 Kings*, Berit Olam: Studies in Hebrew Narrative & Poetry (Collegeville, MN: The Liturgical Press, 1996), p. 110, note 7.

28. "Except" represents the small Hebrew word (*raq*) we noted in 3:2 (ESV, "however") and 3:3 (ESV, "only"), signaling that what follows is some kind of contrast or limitation to what has just been said.

29. Other objects that had been associated with the ark, namely Aaron's rod and the sample of the wilderness manna, as well as the copy of the Book of the Law, were not placed *in* the ark but *before* or *by* it; Exodus 16:33, 34; Numbers 17:10; Deuteronomy 31:26. Keil, *Kings*, p. 87, note 1.

30. The Hebrew text does not actually have the word for "covenant" in verse 9, but the verb (literally "cut") is the word frequently used for the making of a covenant. Similarly 1 Samuel 20:16; 22:8.

31. This is the last mention of the ark in the books of Kings (apart from the back reference in 8:21). At some stage, apparently before the Babylonians sacked Jerusalem and destroyed the house of the Lord, the ark was either destroyed or taken. Jeremiah insisted that it was not to be made again (Jeremiah 3:16). For a discussion of various possibilities of what may have happened to the ark, see Choon-Leong Seow, "Ark of the Covenant," *ABD* 1, pp. 386–93, particularly 390, 391.

32. The literal translation, "*the* cloud," exactly as in Exodus 40:34, probably implies the *same* cloud as then.

Chapter Sixteen: Excited about Church?

1. In context Jesus' words, "Where two or three are gathered in my name" (Matthew 18:20) indicate what he meant by "the church" (Matthew 18:17). Subsequent institutional understandings of "church" distort this.

2. Verse 12, like 8:1, begins with "Then," clearly connecting what follows with what precedes. The words we are about to hear from Solomon are in the context of what we have seen, especially in 8:10–11.

3. It is just possible, following the Septuagint, that verse 12 should read: "Then Solomon said, 'The LORD has set the sun in the heavens, but he has said . . .'" See ESV margin. As well as identifying the Lord as the Creator, Solomon would then be contrasting God's creation of the sun with his promise to dwell in "thick darkness," as well as, perhaps, repudiating sun worship. So Samuel Terrien, *The Elusive Presence: Toward a New Biblical Theology*, Religious Perspectives, Vol. 26 (New York, Hagerstown, San Francisco, London: Harper & Row, 1978), pp. 193, 194. Solomon's brief speech in verses 12, 13 could then be seen as four lines of poetry. So REB; cf. HCSB. For details see John Gray, *I & II Kings: A Commentary*, Third, Fully Revised, Edition (London: SCM, 1977), pp. 211, 212.

4. On the important subject of God's promise and the nature of faith in connection with the promise God made to David, see John Woodhouse, *2 Samuel: Your Kingdom Come*, Preaching the Word (Wheaton, IL: Crossway, 2015), pp. 207–9.

5. The ESV (also HCSB) lacks "the," but the Hebrew text has the definite article here, which contributes to the sense that Solomon was speaking about *the* thick darkness of the cloud before him as well as alluding to "the (famous) thick darkness" at Mount Sinai.

6. The closest is, "I will appear in the cloud . . ." (Leviticus 16:2), which Solomon could well have had in mind.

7. Apart from verse 12 and the parallel text in 2 Chronicles 6:1, "*the* thick darkness" (with the definite article) occurs only in Exodus 20:21 and Deuteronomy 5:22, referring to the experience at Mount Sinai.

8. As Walsh: "it is, most of all, the hiddenness of his mystery." Jerome T. Walsh, *1 Kings*, Berit Olam: Studies in Hebrew Narrative & Poetry (Collegeville, MN: The Liturgical Press, 1996), p. 111. "He is '*mysterium tremendum et fascinans.*'" Gray, *Kings*, p. 212.

9. Perhaps "a royal house." So Gray, *Kings*, p. 212.

10. In the Bible "A blessed B" is primarily about the positive and good relationship between A and B. See Kent Harold Richards, "Bless/Blessing," *ABD* 1, pp. 753–55. However, in this case the king "blessing" the people was a consequence of the Lord blessing them both, as we will hear in verses 15–21.

11. Note the word "blessed" in verse 14 (with the assembly as the object) and in verse 15 (with God as the object).

12. When God is the object of the verb "bless," the meaning is close to "praise." Richards, "Bless," p. 754. "Blessed be the LORD" is frequently heard in the Psalms (28:6; 31:21; 41:13; etc.).

13. Since God's words to David in verse 16 are not, strictly speaking, a promise, a more literal rendering of the Hebrew is preferable.

14. The Hebrew of verse 15b emphasizes actions that match words. Literally: ". . . who spoke by his mouth with David my father, and by his hand has fulfilled . . ."

15. I do not believe there is any problem in the fact that the wording of verse 16 does not exactly reproduce the words found in 2 Samuel 7. We have no reason to think that the 2 Samuel 7 passage records everything that was said that night. Solomon probably learned about God's word to his father from David himself (or possibly from Nathan). He may have been told more than the historian reported in 2 Samuel 7. Furthermore, it is possible for God's word (message) to be faithfully reported in different words. That is why the Bible can and should be translated. This is an important difference from the Muslim understanding of the Qur'an, which is *in principle* untranslatable.

16. "Nevertheless" represents the Hebrew particle (*raq*) we noted in 3:2 ("however"), 3 ("only"), and 8:9 ("except"), signaling that what follows is some kind of contrast or limitation to what has just been said.

17. "You" is emphatic: "*You* are not the one who shall build . . ."

18. The Hebrew emphasizes "your son" and an additional pronoun "he": "your son . . . *he* is the one who shall build . . ."

19. This is the last mention of the ark in 1 and 2 Kings. It was apparently lost at some subsequent point in history, perhaps before the destruction of Jerusalem by Nebuchadnezzar, because it is not included in the inventory of furnishings taken by him (2 Kings 25:13–17). The absence of any mention of the ark after its installation in the house of the Lord, and particularly the Bible's silence about its loss, strongly suggests that its role was superseded by the house itself. See Jeremiah 3:16–17. "The ark serves as the transportable throne of Yahweh until he takes his rest in the temple, but once there the temple itself is seen as the 'throne' of Yahweh." Peter J. Leithart, *1 & 2 Kings*, Brazos Theological Commentary on the Bible (Grand Rapids, MI: Brazos Press, 2006), p. 67.

Chapter Seventeen: "Whatever You Ask in My Name"

1. Jesus did insist that his adult hearers needed to "become like children" (Matthew 18:3; cf. 19:14; Mark 10:15; Luke 18:17).

2. "All the assembly [Hebrew, *qahal*] of Israel" repeats the phase that we heard twice in 8:14.

3. He could hardly have been standing "in the presence of all the assembly" if he was positioned before the smaller altar inside the house (6:20, 22).

4. The Hebrew is *khesed*. See our discussion of 2:7 and note 28 to Chapter 5.

5. "Your servants" includes David ("your servant" in vv. 25, 26) and Solomon (v. 28) as well as later descendants of David if they are obedient (v. 25).

6. On the theological and factual paradox of the words "who walk before you with all their heart," particularly when applied to David, see our discussion of 3:6.

7. The Hebrew phrase (literally, "And now") is frequently used to draw a conclusion, especially a practical one, from what has been stated. BDB, p. 774.

8. The main difference is that in place of the words "in faithfulness with all their heart and with all their soul" in 2:4, 8:25 has "as you [David] have walked before me." Cf. Psalm 132:11, 12.

9. See our discussion of 6:12, 13.

10. See our fuller discussion of these issues in our treatment of 2:4.

11. Matthew Henry, *Matthew Henry's Commentary on the Whole Bible*, Vol. 2 (Old Tappan, NJ: Fleming H. Revell Company, no date), p. 618.

12. Literally, "the heavens and the heavens of the heavens"; in other words, the entirety of the heavens. In Hebrew (as in English) "the heavens" can refer to the vast space above us: the sky (as the NIV renders "heavens" in Genesis 1:8, 9, etc.). Solomon's words here probably do not refer to a spiritual place where God dwells. He may be saying (in modern idiom), "The entire universe cannot contain you." "Why, the cosmos itself isn't large enough to give you breathing room." Eugene Peterson, *The Message: The Bible in Contemporary Language* (Colorado Springs: NavPress, 2002), p. 579.

13. "Jesus cleansed the temple . . . he also replaced it, fulfilling its purpose." D. A. Carson, *The Gospel According to John* (Leicester, UK and Grand Rapids, MI: Inter-Varsity Press and Eerdmans, 1991), p. 182. For a book-length treatment of this important subject, see Nicholas Perrin, *Jesus the Temple* (London and Grand Rapids, MI: SPCK and Baker Academic, 2010). While some of the argument is (in my opinion) excessively dependent on hypothetical historical reconstructions, the emphasis on Jesus himself and the community of believers being the promised new temple is important. See also the important study by G. K. Beale, *The Temple and the Church's Mission: A Biblical Theology of the Dwelling Place of God*, New Studies in Biblical Theology 17 (Downers Grove, IL and Leicester, UK: InterVarsity Press and Apollos, 2004).

14. However, the ESV correctly sees the imperative ("keep") and jussive ("let your word be confirmed") verb forms in verses 25, 26, lending an imperatival sense to the imperfect verb forms in the following verses.

15. John Gray, *I & II Kings: A Commentary*, Third, Fully Revised, Edition (London: SCM, 1977), p. 221.

16. Again "when you hear, forgive" could be rendered "you will hear, and you will forgive."

17. ". . . seven as a sacred or covenant number was more appropriate than any other to embrace all prayers addressed to God." C. F. Keil, "1 and 2 Kings," in C. F. Keil and F. Delitzsch, *Commentary on the Old Testament*, Vol. 3 (Peabody, MA: Hendrickson Publishers, 1996), p. 93, note 1.

18. "Likewise" (ESV; more literally, "And also") should not be understood as suggesting that the following situation is like the previous ones. The similarity lies in the possibility of prayer in these very different situations, as we will see.

19. Notice the use of the number "seven" in Leviticus 26:18, 21, 24, 28. On Situation 2, see Leviticus 26:17; Deuteronomy 28:25; on Situation 3, see Leviticus 26:19, 20; Deuteronomy 28:23, 24; on Situation 4, see Leviticus 26:25; Deuteronomy 28:21, 22, 38, 59–61; on Situation 5, see Deuteronomy 28:10; on Situation 6, see perhaps Leviticus 26:7, 8; Deuteronomy 28:7; on Situation 7, see Leviticus 26:33–39; Deuteronomy 28:36, 37, 64, 65, 68.

20. The vocabulary of "sin" can have a wider reference than an immoral action, as in 1:21 where Bathsheba envisages herself and her son Solomon being considered "sinners" (ESV, "offenders") if Adonijah became king. See note 40 to Chapter 3.

21. It is natural to understand the repeated "because they have sinned against you" in verses 33 and 35 to be implied in verse 37. This is supported by the allusions to Leviticus 26 and Deuteronomy 28 and is confirmed by "forgive" in verse 39, echoing verses 34 and 36.

22. Again Solomon's prayer may be influenced by reflections on his reading of his copy of the book of the Law. See Leviticus 26:14, 15, 21, 23, 27; Deuteronomy 28:15, 45, 58. These texts fill out what Solomon meant by "sin."

23. Once again Solomon's prayer may have been influenced here by his reading of Leviticus 26:40–41.

24. There are technical textual difficulties with the Hebrew behind "made to take an oath" and "comes and swears his oath." See Martin J. Mulder, *1 Kings: Volume 1: 1 Kings 1–11*, Historical Commentary on the Old Testament (Leuven, Belgium: Peeters, 1998), pp. 420–24.

25. A comparable case of a woman accused of adultery, whose guilt or innocence was to be determined through a process involving an oath, is outlined in Numbers 5:11–31. It was probably a perversion of this practice of making oaths that Jesus condemned in Matthew 23:16–22.

26. In all these verses "hear in heaven" could be translated, "you will hear in heaven." In five cases "you" is emphasized in the Hebrew: "*you* are the one who will hear . . ."

27. Although not directly relevant here, in the Old Testament God's vindication of "the righteous" may involve forgiveness, as David had experienced. That is, a person may be "righteous" not because he or she had done nothing wrong in fact, but because his or her sin had been forgiven and therefore was no longer taken into account. See 2 Samuel 22:21, 25 and the discussion in John Woodhouse, *2 Samuel: Your Kingdom Come*, Preaching the Word (Wheaton, IL: Crossway, 2015), pp. 511–13.

28. "Vindicating" in verse 32 represents the Hebrew equivalent (*tsdq* hiphil) of the Greek verb *dikaioo*, rendered "justify" in key New Testament texts such as Romans 2:13; 3:20, 24, 26, 28.

29. See Romans 4:5–8, citing the example of David in Psalm 32:1, 2. See also the magnificent exposition in Romans 3:21–26.

30. In this context, where the people's sin against God is clear (see especially v. 46), it may sound strange to describe God's merciful forgiveness as rendering to each "according to all his ways." The Bible is not quite as neat as some systems of theology. While sinners can never claim that their repentance *deserves* forgiveness, only the truly repentant can expect forgiveness. There *is* a correspondence between our "ways" and God's forgiveness. Jesus taught us to pray for forgiveness "as we also have forgiven our debtors" (Matthew 6:12).

31. "These are not primarily 'righteous' acts, but 'right' acts which are 'proper' to, and vindicate, the nature and purpose of Yahweh revealed to and through his chosen people. They are acts which vindicate his chosen people, but always with reference to the divine purpose for which they are chosen." Gray, *Kings*, p. 227.

32. "Your servant" is Solomon himself, as in verse 28.

33. "Lord GOD" (literally, "my Lord Yahweh") is a form of God's name that occurs only here and in 2:26 in the books of Kings. It is striking because this is the form of God's name that David used seven (or perhaps eight) times in his prayer responding to God's great promise to him in 2 Samuel 7, although it occurs nowhere else in the books of Samuel. It is the form of God's name Abraham used in response to God's promise (Genesis 15:2, 8), but it is found nowhere else in the book of Genesis. Woodhouse, *2 Samuel*, p. 224.

34. Jesus spoke of the fulfillment he brought in similar terms in his conversation with the woman of Samaria in John 4:20–24.

35. Some of the wonderful implications of this statement are explored in a profound and hugely helpful way by Christopher Ash, under the heading "How to pray the Psalms in Christ." Christopher Ash, *Teaching Psalms*, From Text to Message, Vol. 1 (Fearn, Ross-shire, UK: Christian Focus, 2017), pp. 19–104.

36. We will not here explore the wonder of Jesus' speaking of requests that could be addressed to Jesus himself (John 14:14) or to his Father (John 15:16). This is an aspect of his claim, "I and the Father are one" (John 10:30).

37. Again we will not discuss further the fact that the granting of such a request can be described by Jesus as "this *I* will do" (John 14:13) or "*the Father* . . . will give it to you" (John 16:23).

Chapter Eighteen: The Joy of God's Blessing

1. Something like this is noted by several commentators. "The narrative account of 1 Kings 8 seems clearly to be the interpretive center of the long history of Joshua, Judges, Samuel, and Kings. From here on it is all downhill." Walter Brueggemann, *1 & 2 Kings*, Smyth & Helwys Bible Commentary (Macon, GA: Smyth & Helwys, 2000), p. 119.

2. The shift is marked grammatically. In 8:23–66 Solomon's words are addressed to God in the grammatical second person singular; in verses 56–61 God is referred to consistently in the third person singular, with second person plural reference to the people ("your heart") in verse 61.

3. The essential unity of God's promise to Abraham, Moses, and David is an important caution to systems of Biblical interpretation that emphasize the differences between the Abrahamic, Mosaic, and Davidic "covenants."

4. The Hebrew verb in 5:4 ("given me rest") and the noun in 8:56 ("rest") have the same root (*nwkh*). With reference to the promised "rest" of the people these terms appear only in these two places in the books of Kings. In the books of Samuel the verb occurs importantly in 2 Samuel 7:1, 11.

5. In these contexts there are two Hebrew words meaning "rest." While *shbt* (Sabbath) seems to convey the idea of rest from work and *nwkh* often means rest from the threats of enemies, both terms appear as virtual synonyms in Exodus 20:8–11.

6. In verses 57–61 the verbs are jussives: "*May* the LORD our God be with us," "*May* he not . . . ," and so on. However, these are wishes that conform to Solomon's understanding of God's promise. This is much more than wishful thinking.

7. The ESV "incline" in 8:58 and "turn away" in 11:2, 4, 9 represent the same Hebrew verb.

8. This expression (literally, "the thing of a day in its day") emphasizes the *daily* need of the people for God to hear, forgive, and act to put things right for them. It may remind us of the daily provision of manna in the wilderness (the same expression is rendered "a day's portion every day" in Exodus 16:4) and perhaps the petition in the Lord's Prayer, "Give us this day our daily bread" (Matthew 6:11). The Hebrew idiom appears in Exodus 5:13; 2 Kings 25:30; Daniel 1:5.

9. C. J. H. Wright has described verse 60 (along with 8:41–43) as "most remarkable of all the passages with a universal vision in the historical books." "The missional hope . . . is turned into a missional challenge to the people that they must

be as committed to God's law as God is committed to such a worldwide goal." Cited in John W. Olley, *The Message of Kings: God Is Present*, The Bible Speaks Today (Nottingham, UK: Inter-Varsity Press, 2011), p. 100.

10. "Your" is plural referring to the people; "heart" is singular suggesting that the people are together in this.

11. "Wholly true" renders a Hebrew adjective (*shalem*) that in various contexts, can mean "whole, undivided," "peaceably inclined," or "well-meaning, upright." There may be a deliberate resonance with Solomon's name and the word *shalom*, "peace." K. J. Illman, *"shalem," TDOT* 15, pp. 97–105.

12. The wording of 11:4 exactly echoes 8:61, clearly signaling the enormity of Solomon's failure.

13. For a cogent argument that the number of animals mentioned in verse 63 is credible and that this many sacrifices could be made in the time indicated, see C. F. Keil, "1 and 2 Kings," in C. F. Keil and F. Delitzsch, *Commentary on the Old Testament*, Vol. 3 (Peabody, MA: Hendrickson Publishers, 1996), pp. 95, 96. Some insist that the numbers are an "exaggeration." So Martin J. Mulder, *1 Kings: Volume 1: 1 Kings 1–11*, Historical Commentary on the Old Testament (Leuven, Belgium: Peeters, 1998), p. 451.

14. The verb in question (*khanak*) appears only four times in the Old Testament. Second Chronicles 7:5 parallels the present verse. In Deuteronomy 20:5 "has not dedicated it" probably means has "not yet begun to live in it" (NIV). In Proverbs 22:6 the NIV again captures the sense well: "Start children off on the way they should go . . ." The corresponding noun (*hanukkah*) is more common and probably came to refer to acts of "dedication" (so perhaps Numbers 7:10, 11, 84, 88; Daniel 3:2, 3). At a later time this became the name of the Feast of *Hanukkah* celebrating the rededication of the temple in the days of Judas the Maccabee (1 Maccabees 4:59). W. Dommershausen, *"khanak," TDOT* 5, pp. 19–21.

15. "Consecrate" or "make holy" means to set apart for God. See 1 Samuel 7:1; 16:5; 2 Samuel 8:11 (ESV, "dedicated").

16. The Hebrew text (followed here) is probably correct, although a little awkward. This seems to be supported by 2 Chronicles 7:9. So Keil, *Kings*, p. 97; also Lissa M. Wray Beal, *1 & 2 Kings*, Apollos Old Testament Commentary, Vol. 9 (Nottingham, UK and Downers Grove, IL: Apollos, 2014), p. 140.

17. Toi, king of Hamath, had paid tribute to King David (2 Samuel 8:9, 10). Lebo-Hamath may mean "the Hamath approaches" (so John Gray, *I & II Kings: A Commentary*, Third, Fully Revised, Edition [London: SCM, 1977], p. 235) or "the entrance to Hamath," meaning where the river on which Hamath stood (the Orontes) empties into the Mediterranean Sea (so Mulder, *1 Kings 1–11*, pp. 456, 457). For other possibilities, see Tom F. Wei, "Hamath, Entrance of," *ABD* 3, pp. 36, 37.

18. The precise location of "the Brook of Egypt" is uncertain. See M. Görg, "Egypt, Brook of," *ABD* 2, p. 321.

19. See Maps 4–12 and 5–1 in Currid, *Atlas*, pp. 106, 120.

20. Literally, "tents." Perhaps this was the temporary accommodation of those who had traveled to Jerusalem from all over the land. So Gray, *Kings*, p. 235.

Chapter Nineteen: What Could Possibly Go Wrong?

1. "As soon as" sounds rather more precise than the Hebrew. The NIV has "When Solomon had finished . . ." The event about to be recounted occurred after

the twenty years of building work had been completed (6:38; 7:1; 9:10). See our discussion of 8:2.

2. These texts have the verb form (*khashaq*) of the noun (*khesheq*) in verse 1. The noun is quite rare, appearing only in the context of Solomon's completed buildings (9:1, 19; 2 Chronicles 8:6) and Isaiah 21:4.

3. Contra John W. Olley, *The Message of Kings: God Is Present*, The Bible Speaks Today (Nottingham, UK: Inter-Varsity Press, 2011), p. 105: "Solomon's 'desire' is not toward God and his ways but on increasing material wealth, evidenced in buildings. Solomon needs the warning."

4. Gray overstates a good point: "The schematization does not visualize any other activity or interest in the early part of Solomon's reign than the building of the Temple, despite the statement that the hostile activities of Hadad of Edom and Rezon of Damascus began early in Solomon's reign (11.21, 25)." John Gray, *I & II Kings: A Commentary*, Third, Fully Revised, Edition (London: SCM, 1977), p. 237. The account does focus on Solomon's building work, but not only on the so-called temple.

5. It would be a mistake to think that the house of the Lord itself was only about religion (narrowly conceived). See the dismissal of "such narrow and anachronistically modern views of the temple" in Nicholas Perrin, *Jesus the Temple* (London and Grand Rapids, MI: SPCK and Baker Academic, 2010), p. 7. While Perrin has the temple of first-century Judaism in mind, his comments are relevant to the significance of the house of the Lord from the beginning.

6. "You" and "your" and the corresponding verbs in verses 3–5 are all singular; in verse 6 they are plural. In verses 7–9 Israel is spoken of in the third person.

7. This is the only reference in the books of Kings to God's heart. In the books of Samuel, however, God's heart had a lot to do with David, the man on whom God set his heart (1 Samuel 13:14; 16:7; 2 Samuel 7:21). See John Woodhouse, *1 Samuel: Looking for a Leader*, Preaching the Word (Wheaton, IL: Crossway, 2008), pp. 235, 286, 287; John Woodhouse, *2 Samuel: Your Kingdom Come*, Preaching the Word (Wheaton, IL: Crossway, 2015), p. 601, note 15.

8. On the reference to David as the model for Solomon to follow, see our discussion of 3:6.

9. If there is anyone left who reads the older translations, here is one distinct advantage. The RV of verses 3–5 has "thou," "thee," and "thy"; verses 6–9 have "ye," "you," and "your."

10. In the Hebrew "turn aside" has an added emphasis that is difficult to express in English. Beal suggests, "if you ever turn aside." Lissa M. Wray Beal, *1 & 2 Kings*, Apollos Old Testament Commentary, Vol. 9 (Nottingham, UK and Downers Grove, IL: Apollos, 2014), p. 149.

11. The plural "you" and "your" make it natural to understand this in terms of succeeding generations of the people rather than the king and his successors.

12. The Hebrew word translated "worship" refers to the physical action of bowing down and by implication the recognition and honor given by this act to the one before whom it is done, whether another human (1 Samuel 20:41; 24:8; 25:23, 41; 28:14; 2 Samuel 1:2; 9:6, 8; 14:4, 22, 33; 15:5; 16:4; 18:21, 28; 24:20; 1 Kings 1:16, 23, 31, 53; 2:19) or God (1 Samuel 1:3, 19, 28; 15:25, 30, 31; 2 Samuel 12:20; 15:32; 1 Kings 1:47[?]). To perform such an action before an idol or "other gods"

was an expression of apostasy (Exodus 20:5; 23:24; 34:14; Leviticus 26:1; Deuteronomy 5:9; 30:17; 1 Kings 11:33; 16:31; 22:53; Psalm 81:9).

13. Matthew Henry, *Matthew Henry's Commentary on the Whole Bible*, Vol. 2 (Old Tappan, NJ: Fleming H. Revell Company, no date), p. 624.

14. The point is not so much that "the experience of Israel would be an example and an admonition to others." Gray, *Kings*, p. 238. In Hebrew "byword" (or, "object of ridicule," NIV) is related to the verb "to sharpen." It refers to "taunts which aggravate the discomfiture of the sufferer in the psalms of lamentation," as in Psalm 64:3; 140:3. Ibid.

15. The ESV here follows some ancient versions because the Hebrew is difficult: literally, "And this house will be exalted." The point may be the contrast between the exalted state of the house of the Lord prior to the disaster and its subsequent destruction (SO RV, JB, HCSB).

16. To "hiss" (or "whistle") is an expression of malicious gloating or amazed derision over the destruction of a city, land, people, or, as here, the house of the Lord; 2 Chronicles 29:8; Job 27:23; Jeremiah 18:16; 19:8; 25:9, 18; 49:17; 50:13; 51:37; Lamentations 2:15, 16; Ezekiel 27:36; Micah 6:16; Zephaniah 2:15; cf. Lamentations 2:15, 16; Micah 6:16.

17. See the careful discussion of the warnings in Hebrews in Peter T. O'Brien, *God Has Spoken in His Son: A Biblical Theology of Hebrews*, New Studies in Biblical Theology 39 (Downers Grove, IL and London: InterVarsity Press and Apollos, 2016), pp. 159–207.

Chapter Twenty: Are We There Yet?

1. In particular Galatians, Colossians, and Hebrews seem to be written to believers who underestimated the enormity of what it means to be in Christ. This is sometimes referred to as "under-realized eschatology": a failure to appreciate that in Jesus Christ the new age really has dawned, "the last days" are here.

2. The believers in Corinth seem to have had an "over-realized eschatology," so filled with their present experience that they denied their future resurrection (1 Corinthians 15:12). Their present spiritual experience was the only "resurrection" that mattered to them (cf. 2 Timothy 2:18).

3. Strictly speaking the Hebrew rendered "desired" in verse 11 echoes the word I have translated "delighted" in 9:1.

4. "Then" is omitted in the ESV, but probably indicates that Solomon's surprising gift to Hiram was consequent on Hiram's provision just described: "*Thereupon* King Solomon . . ." So Martin J. Mulder, *1 Kings: Volume 1: 1 Kings 1–11*, Historical Commentary on the Old Testament (Leuven, Belgium: Peeters, 1998), p. 474. Cf. NIV, which makes the same point by inverting the two parts of the verse: "King Solomon gave twenty towns in Galilee to Hiram king of Tyre, *because* Hiram had supplied him with all the cedar and juniper and gold he wanted."

5. The Hebrew imperfect form of the verb here is puzzling. DeVries says it is "modal," which could be rendered, "the king would give to Hiram . . . ," but what does that mean? Simon J. DeVries, *1 Kings*, Word Biblical Commentary, Vol. 12 (Waco, TX: Word Books, 1985), p. 130. Without further explanation, Gray simply says that it "may be the preterite tense." John Gray, *I & II Kings: A Commentary*, Third, Fully Revised, Edition (London: SCM, 1977), p. 239, note a.

6. Donald J. Wiseman, *1 and 2 Kings*, Tyndale Old Testament Commentaries (Leicester, UK: Inter-Varsity Press, 1993), p. 126.

7. Gray, *Kings*, p. 240.

8. Keil attempts to address the obvious problem here by arguing that the villages concerned "certainly belonged . . . to the cities of the Canaanites mentioned in 2 Sam. 24:7; that is to say, they were cities occupied chiefly by a heathen population, and in all probability they were in a very bad condition." C. F. Keil, "1 and 2 Kings," in C. F. Keil and F. Delitzsch, *Commentary on the Old Testament*, Vol. 3 (Peabody, MA: Hendrickson Publishers, 1996), p. 99. I think that this may be special pleading.

9. See Map 5–13 in Currid, *Atlas*, p. 130.

10. It certainly looks inconsistent with Deuteronomy 19:14; 27:17; Proverbs 22:28; 23:10.

11. The Hebrew noun rendered "uprightness" is cognate with the verb "to be right."

12. "Hiram judges that Solomon is not dealing straight with him." Peter J. Leithart, *1 & 2 Kings*, Brazos Theological Commentary on the Bible (Grand Rapids, MI: Brazos Press, 2006), p. 75.

13. Literally, "What are these cities . . . ?"

14. Gray, *Kings*, p. 241.

15. Similarly Keil, *Kings*, p. 100. Some deduce from 2 Chronicles 8:2 that Hiram returned these cities to Solomon. So ibid. They may have been returned because of Hiram's displeasure with them or because they were only collateral for the loan of verse 14 and were returned when the loan was repaid. It is not certain, however, that the "cities" of 2 Chronicles 8:2 were the same as the "cities" of 1 Kings 9:11. So Cyril J. Barber, *2 Chronicles: God's Blessing of His Faithful People*, Focus on the Bible (Fearn, Ross-shire, UK: Christian Focus Publications, 2004), p. 64.

16. The expression "to this day" occurs a number of times in the books of Kings. It sometimes seems to refer to a time when the kingdom of Judah was intact and therefore before the writing of the books that tell of the destruction of that kingdom. See Keil, *Kings*, pp. 10, 11. See 8:8; 9:21; 10:12; 12:19; 2 Kings 2:22; 8:22; 10:27; 14:7; 16:6; 17:23, 34, 41; cf. 1 Samuel 5:5; 6:18; 27:6; 30:25; 2 Samuel 4:3; 6:8; 18:18.

17. See Wiseman, *1 and 2 Kings*, p.126; Gwilym H. Jones, *1 and 2 Kings*, 2 volumes, New Century Bible Commentary (Grand Rapids, MI and London: Eerdmans and Marshall, Morgan & Scott, 1984), p. 214.

18. "Instead of extending the conquest, Solomon reverses it, and a portion of the land falls back into the hands of the Gentiles—Canaanites no less." Leithart, *Kings*, p. 75, note 4. Historian John Bright has made the observation: "In any event, when a state begins to sell off its territory, it is evident that its financial situation is parlous indeed." John Bright, *A History of Israel*, Third Edition (London: SCM, 1980), p. 223.

19. See the photograph of a structure that may have been "the Millo" in Currid, *Atlas*, p. 129. It is possible that the reference to the "Millo" in 2 Samuel 5:9 means simply that David built from where the Millo later stood. So Gray, *Kings*, p. 243.

20. Gray, *Kings*, p. 244, 245. See Map 5–14 in Currid, *Atlas*, p. 132.

21. On Hazor, see Judges 4:2, 17; on Megiddo, see Judges 1:27; on Gezer, see Judges 1:29.

22. In this case "Canaanites" in verse 16 denotes a culture rather than a race. So Gray, *Kings*, p. 247.

23. Wiseman, *1 and 2 Kings*, p. 127.

24. Some manuscripts have "Tadmor" (cf. 2 Chronicles 8:4). Since the list of place names in verses 15–18 moves from north to south, and Tadmor was in the far north (see Map 5–16 in Currid, *Atlas*, p. 137), Tamar (in the south, see Map 5–14 in Currid, *Atlas*, p. 132) seems to be the correct reading.

25. The Hebrew lacks "of Judah" (cf. NIV). The simple reference to "the land" is similar to 4:19 and is perhaps a suitable closure to a list of the land's defenses. See note 17 to Chapter 10. Compare other references to "the land" in 8:34, 37, 40; 9:7, 19, 21.

26. See note 14 to Chapter 2.

27. Before the reign of Solomon Exodus 1:11 is the only occurrence of this expression. It is also found in 2 Chronicles 8:4, 6; 17:12; 16:4.

28. The wording in the Hebrew of 9:1 and 9:19 is very similar, but subtly different. There is a greater emphasis in verse 19 on "desire" and a more explicit reference to "building."

29. Walter Brueggemann, *1 & 2 Kings*, Smyth & Helwys Bible Commentary (Macon, GA: Smyth & Helwys, 2000), p. 124.

30. Leithart, *Kings*, p. 76.

31. "The Amorites, the Hittites, the Perizzites, the Hivites, and the Jebusites" is typical of many lists of the inhabitants of the land that God had promised to give to the people of Israel. See Exodus 3:8, 17; cf. Joshua 12:7, 8; 24:11. God had promised to drive these peoples out of the land he was giving to the Israelites. See Exodus 23:23; 33:2; 34:11; Deuteronomy 7:1; Joshua 3:10; cf. Joshua 9:1; 11:3. These were the peoples that God had commanded the Israelites to "devote . . . to complete destruction." See Deuteronomy 20:17. The fact that the people of Israel now lived among these peoples (see Judges 3:5) was connected to Israel's disobedience. See Judges 2:20–23.

32. It is difficult not to sympathize with modern readers who see this as a "crude, fanatical practice." However, this is a profound misunderstanding of the Bible's presentation. See the fuller discussion of this phenomenon in John Woodhouse, *1 Samuel: Looking for a Leader*, Preaching the Word (Wheaton, IL: Crossway, 2008), p. 261.

33. I am not suggesting that Solomon ought to have destroyed these people. The Bible writer does not say or imply that. The time for such judgment may well have passed. The point is simply that the continued presence of these peoples was an ongoing reminder of the failure of the earlier generation of Israelites to do as they had been commanded by God. "Thus Israel's earlier disobedience is compounded by Solomonic administrative practice." Lissa M. Wray Beal, *1 & 2 Kings*, Apollos Old Testament Commentary, Vol. 9 (Nottingham, UK and Downers Grove, IL: Apollos, 2014), p. 151.

34. Also Genesis 49:15 ("a servant at forced labor") and Joshua 16:10 ("forced labor"). See note 34 to Chapter 11.

35. "To this day" could be a reference not to the time of the writer of 1 Kings, but to the days of the author of a document from which he was citing, an account of Solomon's labor force (see v. 15).

36. The Hebrew word (*'ebed*) translated "slaves" here must be understood as shorthand for the longer phrase (*mas 'obed*) rendered "slaves" in verse 21. Israelites were not made "slaves" or "servants" in the same sense as the foreigners. Curiously the same word (*'ebed*) appears in the next clause, translated "officials." Israelites could still be "servants," but their service was of a different kind.

37. The Hebrew links the two sentences of verse 22 with a conjunction (*kiy*) that has the sense "because."

38. Who could forget two foreign soldiers who served King David faithfully: Ittai the Gittite (a Philistine, 2 Samuel 15:19, 22; 18:2) and Uriah the Hittite (2 Samuel 11:3, 6, 17, 21, 24; 12:9, 10; 23:39)?

39. Since 550 and 3,300 are multiples of 11, some have suggested that each tribe (except Levi, or perhaps Judah?) was equally represented in the two groups of "chief officers." So Wiseman, *1 and 2 Kings*, p. 127.

40. Brueggemann, *Kings*, pp. 124, 125. Brueggemann makes a point of his own by adding ". . . without reference to human treatment."

41. The force of "But" is unclear. The Hebrew particle (*'ak*, often rendered "only") generally introduces a "restrictive clause." GKC, §153. Perhaps the sense is that "Only then," that is, at the end of the twenty years mentioned in verse 10, did Solomon bring his Egyptian wife to her own house. Cf. Gray, *Kings*, p. 252, note a.

42. The Hebrew has a "technical expression here [*qtr* hiphil] for the burning of the portions of the sacrificial flesh upon the altar, as in Ex. 29:18, Lev. 1:9, etc." Keil, *Kings*, p. 103. It "describes the act of burning the sacrificial portions on the altar—the fat portions in the case of animals, the aromatic portions in the case of grain offerings." R. E. Clements, "*qtr*," *TDOT* 13, p. 12. The term also occurs in 3:3; 11:8; 12:33; 13:1, 2; 22:43, mostly of improper sacrifices.

43. I prefer "completed" because the Hebrew verb here (*slm*, a word play on Solomon's name) is different from the word rendered "finished" (*klh*) in the similar and very significant statement in 9:1. The verb in verse 25 is elsewhere translated "reward" (1 Samuel 24:19), "repay" (2 Samuel 3:39), "restore" (2 Samuel 12:6), and "pay a vow" (2 Samuel 15:7). It seems improbable to me that the word here means "finished (or completed) the building work." More probably we are to understand that the building was "completed" by being put to its proper use. Only then had the building become what it was intended to be. The NIV approaches a sense along the lines: "and so fulfilled the temple obligations."

44. Or "Sea of Reeds." Depending on the context, this term (*yam sup*) seems to be used in the Old Testament with reference to marshland in the region of the Bitter Lakes, the Gulf of Aqaba (as here), the Gulf of Suez, and the Red Sea more generally.

45. See Map 5–16 in Currid, *Atlas*, p. 137. On the archaeological search for Ezion-geber, see Meir Lubetski, "Ezion-geber," *ABD* 2, pp. 723–26.

46. "Solomon collects gold from Ophir as a greater Adam, moving out from the garden to collect the resources of the outlying lands and bringing them back to adorn the house of the Lord." Leithart, *Kings*, p. 73.

Chapter Twenty-One: "All the Treasures of Wisdom"

1. The Sheba mentioned in 1 Kings 10 has nothing to do with another Sheba mentioned in Joshua 19:2 (perhaps related to Beersheba), located in the territory of the Israelite tribe of Simeon.

2. Sheba may be connected to the Sabeans (Isaiah 45:14; Joel 3:8; Job 1:15; cf. 6:19). Sheba was apparently famous for gold (Psalm 72:15), frankincense (Isaiah 60:6; Jeremiah 6:20), and also spices and precious stones (Ezekiel 27:22), products for which Southern Arabia was known. The story before us was probably an important source for the later fame of Sheba. Stephen Ricks, "Sheba, Queen of," *ABD* 5, pp. 1170, 1171.

3. Apart from two references in the New Testament (Matthew 12:42; Luke 11:31), the queen of Sheba is mentioned extensively in Jewish, Ethiopian, and Muslim traditions, always with some connection to her visit to Solomon. Ibid., p. 1171.

4. As suggested by Map 5–16 in Currid, *Atlas*, p. 137.

5. More literally, "And the queen of Sheba was hearing what was being heard of Solomon . . ." The participle ("was hearing") suggests that she "kept hearing over and over of Solomon's fame." Martin J. Mulder, *1 Kings: Volume 1: 1 Kings 1–11*, Historical Commentary on the Old Testament (Leuven, Belgium: Peeters, 1998), p. 510.

6. In my opinion "baptizing them in the name" in Matthew 28:19 is much more important than a reference to the Christian ceremony known as "baptism." The sense is better conveyed if we translate rather than transliterate the Greek verb *baptizo*, which, depending on context, can mean "engulf," "overwhelm," "dip," or "wash." As people from all nations become disciples of the Lord Jesus, the "name" of God overwhelms them "as the waters cover the sea" (Isaiah 11:9). In a similar way the queen of Sheba found her experience breathtaking (v. 5). For a brief discussion of how "baptism" vocabulary may often be better translated than transliterated, see my exposition of Colossians 2:11, 12 in John Woodhouse, *Colossians and Philemon: So Walk in Him*, Focus on the Bible (Fearn, Ross-shire, UK: Christian Focus, 2011), pp. 132–37. For a more thorough examination, see the illuminating work by Barry Newman, *The Gospel, Freedom and the Sacraments: Did the Reformers Go Far Enough?* (Eugene, OR: Resource Publications, 2015), particularly pp. 55–138.

7. Unfortunately we cannot here explore the wonder that because of Jesus Christ "the name of the LORD" associated with King Solomon becomes "the name of the Father and of the Son and of the Holy Spirit."

8. God "tested" Abraham (Genesis 22:1; cf. Exodus 20:20), and the Israelites "test[ed]" the Lord (Exodus 17:2).

9. The Hebrew word (*khiydoth*) rendered "hard questions" can mean "riddles" (see Judges 14:12–20). It is close in meaning to the word for "proverbs" in 1 Kings 4:32 (both words appear in Psalm 49:4; 78:2; Proverbs 1:6; Ezekiel 17:2; Habakkuk 2:6).

10. This could have been a military escort. So John Gray, *I & II Kings: A Commentary*, Third, Fully Revised, Edition (London: SCM, 1977), pp. 257 note d, 260. However, the peaceful tone of the visit (as well as the Hebrew syntax) suggests that the "very great retinue" consisted of the camels and their valuable cargo.

11. The Hebrew word can refer to the balsam shrub, balsam oil, or (as probably here) perfume in general.

12. On Psalm 72 as David's prayer for Solomon, see note 4 to Chapter 5.

13. So Gray, *Kings*, p. 260.

14. The Hebrew translated here "his burnt offerings that he offered at the house of the LORD" has been taken to mean "his ascent by which he was accustomed to go up into the house of the LORD." So C. F. Keil, "1 and 2 Kings," in C. F. Keil and F. Delitzsch, *Commentary on the Old Testament*, Vol. 3 (Peabody, MA: Hendrickson Publishers, 1996), p. 112. This could refer to "the pomp and circumstance with which he headed the procession from the city of David to the new Temple." Gray, *Kings*, p. 258, note c. The significance would be the same. The queen was impressed with the way in which King Solomon honored the Lord.

15. The Hebrew word *ruakh* ("breath") is often rendered "spirit." See, for example, the similar expressions in Joshua 2:11; 5:1.

16. "True" is emphatic in the Hebrew word order.

17. Possibly in the sense "people." So NIV; Mulder, *1 Kings 1–11*, p. 518. Brueggemann is mistaken to say, "The populace is nowhere on the queen's screen of perception as it was not on the king's monitor either. . . . This is royal, hegemonic thinking at its most seductive and dangerous." Walter Brueggemann, *1 & 2 Kings*, Smyth & Helwys Bible Commentary (Macon, GA: Smyth & Helwys, 2000), pp. 133, 134.

18. The Hebrew word translated "Happy" means "How fortunate!" The corresponding Greek word appears in Jesus' sermon on the Mount: "Blessed . . ." (Matthew 5:3ff.).

19. See 2 Samuel 12:24, 25.

20. The words in italics find a precise echo in the verse before us (obscured in many English versions).

21. See 2 Samuel 8 and the discussion of "justice and righteousness" in John Woodhouse, *2 Samuel: Your Kingdom Come*, Preaching the Word (Wheaton, IL: Crossway, 2015), pp. 249–51.

22. See also our discussion of 7:7.

23. On "to this day," see note 16 to Chapter 20.

24. Suggestions have ranged from a red sandalwood, indigenous to India and Ceylon, to coral (considered to be petrified wood). J. C. Trever, "Almug," *IDB* 1, p. 88; Mulder, *1 Kings 1–11*, p. 520.

25. The Hebrew word occurs only here and is probably a technical architectural term. Suggested meanings include "steps" (HCSB), "stools" (REB), "railings," and "paneling."

26. It has sometimes been suggested that verse 13a alludes to a sexual relationship between the queen and Solomon. For details see Gwilym H. Jones, *1 and 2 Kings*, 2 volumes, New Century Bible Commentary (Grand Rapids, MI and London: Eerdmans and Marshall, Morgan & Scott, 1984), p. 225. Others have understood "all that she desired" as something like a trade agreement. See Brueggemann, *Kings*, p. 135. These suggestions reflect the imagination of the interpreters more than the text before us. The Hebrew expression for "desire" has been used five times in our narrative related in various ways to Solomon's desire to build the house of the Lord (5:8, 9, 10; 9:1, 11) and most recently of the Lord's "delight" in Solomon (10:9). The context of 10:13 suggests that "all that she desired" had to do with Solomon's wisdom and the Lord's name.

27. "Sheba is no neutral international observer. She is a convert, won by Solomon's sapiential evangelism. In this, Solomon typifies his successor, Jesus, who is the

full embodiment of the wisdom and word of the Father, who is wisdom made tangible, visible, and audible (1 John 1:1–5), who attracts the nations through the wisdom manifested within his kingdom." Peter J. Leithart, *1 & 2 Kings*, Brazos Theological Commentary on the Bible (Grand Rapids, MI: Brazos Press, 2006), pp. 78, 79.

28. "[P]robably the tradesmen or smaller dealers who travelled about the country" Keil, *Kings*, p. 113.

29. Probably the wholesale dealers. Ibid.

30. Probably a reference to the northern part of the Arabian territory that borders on Israel. Mulder, *1 Kings 1–11*, p. 527.

31. Probably the officers of 4:7–19.

32. Large rectangular body-sized shields.

33. About 3.5 kilograms.

34. Smaller handheld shields.

35. About 1.5 kilograms.

36. This may account for the precision of the number 666. In any case it seems unlikely that this number should be regarded as ominous because of its later use in Revelation 13:18, nor does it seem likely that the later use had any connection with this text.

37. The alternative reading in the ESV margin ("and at the back of the throne was a calf's head") follows the Septuagint, but is less likely. Mulder, *1 Kings 1–11*, p. 532.

38. Gray, *Kings*, p. 265.

39. The Hebrew words translated "apes" and "peacocks" occur only here and in 2 Chronicles 9:21. Their meanings are uncertain.

40. This is the first mention of Tarshish (the place) in the Old Testament (cf. Genesis 10:4). It is mentioned about twenty more times. See David W. Baker, "Tarshish (Place)," *ABD* 6, pp. 331–33.

41. Gray, *Kings*, p. 267.

42. See note 14 to Chapter 2.

43. Curiously the number of chariots (1,400) falls far short of the number of stalls for them according to 4:26 (40,000?). Too much should not be made of this as the Hebrew word translated "thousand" is notoriously inexact, and there are doubts about the number 40,000 in the text of 4:26. See note 2 to Chapter 8.

44. See note 16 to Chapter 2.

45. Mentioned only here in the Old Testament (and the parallel text in 2 Chronicles 1:16). See Map 5–16 in Currid, *Atlas*, p. 137. There is no evidence for a Kue that was "a place for the collection of customs upon the frontier of Egypt." Contra Keil, *Kings*, p. 116.

46. The Hebrew *aram* ("Aram" in JB, REB, NIV, HCSB, but represented as "Syria" in some English versions, including ESV) in various contexts is a term that seems to refer to a broad geographical area north and northeast of Israel, covering modern Syria, Lebanon, and upper Mesopotamia. Sometimes greater precision is provided with a qualifying term as in "Aram of Damascus" (2 Samuel 8:6). The ESV's "Syria" should not, of course, be directly identified with the modern nation of that name. To avoid confusion the simple transliteration is preferred. See further Woodhouse, *2 Samuel*, p. 603, note 15.

47. Brueggemann, *Kings*, p. 137.

Chapter Twenty-Two: The Failure of King Solomon

1. These two paragraphs therefore form a bracket around the account of Solomon's reign in 3:1—11:8. Similarly Lissa M. Wray Beal, *1 & 2 Kings*, Apollos Old Testament Commentary, Vol. 9 (Nottingham, UK and Downers Grove, IL: Apollos, 2014), p. 168.

2. The close semantic connection between the Hebrew terms for "love" (*'hb*) and "desire" (or "delight") (*khpts*) can be seen, for example, in 1 Samuel 18:22; 1 Kings 10:9; Psalm 34:12; 109:17.

3. The Hebrew syntax is disjunctive, and the change of tone at this point in the narrative is better expressed by "But . . ." Henry rightly observed that it is "as melancholy a *but* as almost any we find in all the Bible." Matthew Henry, *Matthew Henry's Commentary on the Whole Bible*, Vol. 2 (Old Tappan, NJ: Fleming H. Revell Company, no date), p. 631.

4. Walter Brueggemann, *1 & 2 Kings*, Smyth & Helwys Bible Commentary (Macon, GA: Smyth & Helwys, 2000), p. 141.

5. The record of David's wives and concubines may well *implicitly* suggest that all was not well. See the discussions in John Woodhouse, *2 Samuel: Your Kingdom Come*, Preaching the Word (Wheaton, IL: Crossway, 2015), pp. 100, 162.

6. Note that 8:41, in effect, provides a definition of the word translated "foreigner" in this context: one "who is not of your people Israel."

7. It is worth noting that a "foreigner" who comes to know and fear the Lord seems to be regarded no longer as a "foreigner" in the full sense. Generally "foreigners" who joined the people of Israel were no longer called "foreigners" but "sojourners." See, for example, Deuteronomy 5:14; 10:18, 19; 29:11; 31:12; Joshua 20:9; 2 Samuel 4:3 (some English versions, such as NIV and HCSB, obscure this). David had described Ittai as a "foreigner" perhaps precisely because he was trying to persuade him *not* to stay with him (2 Samuel 15:19).

8. See J. A. Thompson, "The Significance of the Verb *LOVE* in the David-Jonathan Narratives in 1 Samuel," *VT* 24(1974), pp. 334–38; William L. Moran, "The Ancient Near Eastern Background of the Love of God in Deuteronomy," *CBQ* 25 (1963), pp. 77–87; and the discussion of "love" for David in 1 Samuel 18 in John Woodhouse, *1 Samuel: Looking for a Leader*, Preaching the Word (Wheaton, IL: Crossway, 2008), pp. 345–55.

9. Hebrew has one word translated "women" in verse 1 and "wives" in verses 3, 4, 8. In particular the Hebrew behind "foreign women" in verse 1 is identical to "foreign wives" in verse 8.

10. "She is thereby distinguished from the foreign wives who turned away Solomon's heart from the Lord, so that the blame pronounced upon those marriages does not apply to his marriage to the Egyptian princess." C. F. Keil, "1 and 2 Kings," in C. F. Keil and F. Delitzsch, *Commentary on the Old Testament*, Vol. 3 (Peabody, MA: Hendrickson Publishers, 1996), p. 118. Contra Jerome T. Walsh, *1 Kings*, Berit Olam: Studies in Hebrew Narrative & Poetry (Collegeville, MN: The Liturgical Press, 1996), p. 135; Martin J. Mulder, *1 Kings: Volume 1: 1 Kings 1–11*, Historical Commentary on the Old Testament (Leuven, Belgium: Peeters, 1998), p. 549.

11. Similarly Walsh, *1 Kings*, p. 134.

12. On Moabites, see 1 Samuel 22:3; 2 Samuel 8:2 and Woodhouse, *2 Samuel*, pp. 236–38. On Ammonites, see 1 Samuel 11; 2 Samuel 10; 17:27 and Woodhouse, *1 Samuel*, p. 194. On Edomites, see 1 Samuel 21:7; 2 Samuel 8:13, 14 and

Woodhouse, *1 Samuel*, p. 412; Woodhouse, *2 Samuel*, pp. 248, 249. On all three see 1 Samuel 14:47 and Map 5–1 in Currid, *Atlas*, p. 120.

13. On Hittites see Woodhouse, *2 Samuel*, p. 617, note 19.

14. See Map 5–16 in Currid, *Atlas*, p. 137.

15. Gray calls them "political marriages." John Gray, *I & II Kings: A Commentary*, Third, Fully Revised, Edition (London: SCM, 1977), pp. 271, 272.

16. "Enter into marriage with them" is more literally, "come into them." Likewise, "neither shall they with you" is, "they shall not come into you." This is a direct reference to sexual relations with these peoples. The same idiom is found, for example, in Genesis 16:2, 4; Deuteronomy 22:13; Joshua 23:12; Judges 16:1; Ezekiel 23:44. Similarly Beal, *Kings*, p. 170.

17. There are two potential problems here that need not detain us. The first is that the words quoted are not an actual citation of any recorded earlier word from God, although God had certainly said things like this (see Exodus 34:16; Deuteronomy 7:3, 4; cf. Joshua 23:12). The writer tells us *what God had said*, but puts it into his own words. The second potential problem is that people groups listed in verse 1 had not, as such, been specified in God's earlier prohibitions (except the Hittites, Exodus 34:11; Deuteronomy 7:1). The writer is telling us that God's prohibition nonetheless applied to the peoples mentioned.

18. "Surely" in verse 2 represents an emphatic asseverative word (*'aken*) in the Hebrew text.

19. The verb (*dabaq*) will appear with other disturbing meanings in 2 Kings 3:3; 5:27.

20. The grammatical point should not be pressed. Grammatical gender is not always strictly consistent. See GKC, §145p. The text is pointedly ambiguous.

21. Probably not meaning "wives of royal birth" (NIV; Mulder, *1 Kings 1–11*, p. 551). "Princesses" more probably refers to their status after they became Solomon's wives, as distinct from the concubines who did not receive this recognition. So Gray, *Kings*, p. 274; Walsh, *1 Kings*, p. 134, note 3.

22. On concubines, see Woodhouse, *2 Samuel*, pp. 102, 103.

23. Even such a conservative commentator as Keil considers the possibility that there has been an error in the numbers. Keil, *Kings*, p. 119, note 1. However, apart from the reader's incredulity, there is no evidence for such.

24. The Hebrew does not have a causal conjunction here; simply "And . . ."

25. "When Solomon clings to foreign women, and foreign gods, in love, he ceases to be Solomon because he ceases to be Solomon-with-Yahweh." Peter J. Leithart, *1 & 2 Kings*, Brazos Theological Commentary on the Bible (Grand Rapids, MI: Brazos Press, 2006), p. 85.

26. The positive view of David here and elsewhere in the books of Kings is not adequately accounted for by saying that he "had indeed grievously sinned, but had not fallen into idolatry." Keil, *Kings*, p. 119. See our discussion of 3:6.

27. Again (as in verse 4) the Hebrew is more literally rendered, "And . . ."

28. The phrase "went after" "is to be understood primarily as a literal 'going after (in procession),' but figuratively means something like 'following and serving cultically and religiously.'" Mulder, *1 Kings 1–11*, p. 553.

29. John Day, "Ashtoreth," *ABD* 1, pp. 491–94. A similar linguistic put-down can be seen in various names that originally included the word *ba'al*, where this

element of the name is replaced with *bosheth* ("shame") as in Ish-*bosheth* (2 Samuel 2:8); Mephi*bosheth* (2 Samuel 4:4). See Woodhouse, *2 Samuel*, p. 80, 577, note 13.

30. The plural probably refers to the multiplicity of idols representing this god. The singular form is found only here, 11:33, and 2 Kings 23:13.

31. Barry G. Webb, *The Book of Judges*, The International Commentary on the Old Testament (Grand Rapids, MI and Cambridge, UK: Eerdmans, 2012), p. 143.

32. Malcam is sometimes translated "their king" in English versions (for example, Amos 1:15), but in a number of contexts is probably a variant spelling of Milcom and Molech. So Jeremiah 49:1, 3 (where ESV has "Milcom"). However, it is possible (though less likely in my opinion) that these names represent distinct and different deities. So Beal, *Kings*, p. 171.

33. There is some uncertainty about the meaning of "Molech" and therefore the interpretation of texts in which this term appears. However, the traditional approach represented here remains compelling. For more details see George C. Heider, "Molech," *ABD* 4, pp. 895–98.

34. See Deuteronomy 7:26. The term (*shiqquts*) is applied to various pagan gods (2 Kings 23:13; also the plural "detestable things," "abominations" in Hosea 9:10; Jeremiah 4:1; 7:30; 16:18; 32:34).

35. Henry, *Commentary*, p. 633.

Chapter Twenty-Three: There Are Consequences

1. That is not to say that these three texts are the only references to God's anger in the history, only that these three texts are linked by the use of the same vocabulary for God's anger (*'np*). We will note other occasions of God's anger shortly.

2. Helpful and important studies of the subject of God's wrath include R. V. G. Tasker, *The Biblical Doctrine of the Wrath of God* (London: Tyndale Press, 1951); Leon Morris, *The Apostolic Preaching of the Cross: A Study of the Significance of Some New Testament Terms* (London: Tyndale, 1965), pp. 179–84; and J. I. Packer, *Knowing God* (London, Sydney, Auckland and Toronto: Hodder and Stoughton, 1973), pp. 134–42.

3. In addition the word of the Lord had come to Solomon (perhaps by a prophet this time, and therefore not counted as an "appearance") in connection with the building of the house of the Lord (6:11–13).

4. It may have been Ahijah (see 11:29). So C. F. Keil, "1 and 2 Kings," in C. F. Keil and F. Delitzsch, *Commentary on the Old Testament*, Vol. 3 (Peabody, MA: Hendrickson Publishers, 1996), p. 120.

5. "This has been your practice" represents a Hebrew phrase (literally, "this has been with you") denoting set purpose, as in Job 10:13; "a psychological process that is hidden from others." John Gray, *I & II Kings: A Commentary*, Third, Fully Revised, Edition (London: SCM, 1977), p. 280. Similarly Martin J. Mulder, *1 Kings: Volume 1: 1 Kings 1–11*, Historical Commentary on the Old Testament (Leuven, Belgium: Peeters, 1998), p. 560.

6. Of the various essentially synonymous words for "kingdom," the term here (*mamlakah*) is the same as in 2:46; 9:5. See John Woodhouse, *2 Samuel: Your Kingdom Come*, Preaching the Word (Wheaton, IL: Crossway, 2015), pp. 597, 598, note 21.

7. "Surely tear" represents a double use of the Hebrew verb, making its appearance here more striking.

8. "The parallel rhetoric is surely deliberate." Walter Brueggemann, *1 & 2 Kings*, Smyth & Helwys Bible Commentary (Macon, GA: Smyth & Helwys, 2000), p. 143.

9. Note that David, speaking to Saul, had called himself "your servant" (1 Samuel 17:32, 34, 36). "Your servant" is therefore not derogatory, but does refer to a subordinate. Contra Gray, *Kings*, pp. 279, 280.

10. The Hebrew particle (*'ak*) here (as in 9:1) generally introduces a restrictive phrase. See note 41 to Chapter 20.

11. It is true that Saul did not actually lose the kingdom immediately upon his disobedience either. However, the departure of the Spirit of the Lord from him (1 Samuel 16:14), his tormented relationship with David (1 Samuel 18:8), and the manner of his tragic death (1 Samuel 31) were not paralleled in Solomon's experience. The delay in Solomon's case was an act of grace; not so for Saul.

12. Here we find the Hebrew particle (*raq*) we noted in 3:2, 3; 8:9, 19 signaling that what follows is some kind of contrast or limitation to what has just been said.

13. Exactly what was meant by "one tribe" will be discussed when we get to 11:32.

14. "Upon this message, which God graciously sent to Solomon, to awaken his conscience, and bring him to repentance, we have reason to hope that he humbled himself before God, confessed his sin, begged pardon, and returned to his duty; that he then published his repentance in the book of Ecclesiastes, where he bitterly laments his own folly and madness, *ch.* vii. 25, 26, and warns others to take heed of the like evil courses, and to *fear God*, and *keep his commandments*, in consideration of *the judgment to come*, which, it is likely, had made him tremble, as it did Felix; that penitential sermon was as true an indication of a heart broken for sin, and turned from it, as David's penitential psalms, though of another nature." Matthew Henry, *Matthew Henry's Commentary on the Whole Bible*, Vol. 2 (Old Tappan, NJ: Fleming H. Revell Company, no date), p. 634. Cf. Keil, *Kings*, p. 127. The restoration of Solomon in his latter days may be hinted at in a later historian's reference to "the way of David *and Solomon*" (2 Chronicles 11:17).

15. "The grammatical form makes this statement the consequence of what precedes it, thus implying that this story begins the punishment God decreed in 11:9–13, even though nothing was said there about external enemies." Jerome T. Walsh, *1 Kings*, Berit Olam: Studies in Hebrew Narrative & Poetry (Collegeville, MN: The Liturgical Press, 1996), p. 139. More importantly, and paradoxically, the *consequence* turns out to begin years *before* the events concerned.

16. See Woodhouse, *2 Samuel*, p. 325.

17. The use of the term here (as in 1 Samuel 29:4; 2 Samuel 19:22) contributes to our understanding of the word when it is used as the title Satan (1 Chronicles 21:1; Job 1:6; Zechariah 3:1, 2; and more than thirty times in the New Testament). Cf. Psalm 109:20, 29 (esv, "accusers").

18. This should not be taken as undermining Solomon's positive appreciation of what God had done for him and his people at that earlier time. Contra Walsh: "We realize only here at the end of the story of Solomon that early in his reign [at 5:4] the king was either ignorant of or cavalier toward serious external danger." Walsh,

1 Kings, p. 141. Not so. Solomon was right to appreciate the fullness of the Lord's blessing in 5:4. His error was his turning from the Lord in his old age, the consequences of which, although prepared by the Lord at an earlier time, were not seen by Solomon at that time.

19. Briefly outlined in John Woodhouse, *1 Samuel: Looking for a Leader*, Preaching the Word (Wheaton, IL: Crossway, 2008), p. 412.

20. Walter A. Maier III, "Hadad (Deity)," *ABD* 3, p. 11. Also Gray, *Kings*, p. 283.

21. Literally, "from the seed of the king who was in Edom." We find some details of the royal line in Edom before the monarchy in Israel, including a Hadad and a Hadar, in Genesis 36:31–43. This Hadar is called Hadad in 1 Chronicles 1:50.

22. On which see Woodhouse, *2 Samuel*, pp. 247–49. It is possible that this was another event altogether, not mentioned elsewhere in the Biblical record. So Gray, *Kings*, p. 284.

23. Alternatively Keil suggests that they were those who had been slain when the Edomites had previously invaded Israel. Joab then defeated the Edomites in the Valley of Salt, after which he remained in Edom for six months to cut off every Edomite male. Keil, *Kings*, p. 121.

24. The parallel is noted by several commentators. See Walsh, *1 Kings*, p. 140; Brueggemann, *Kings*, p. 145.

25. The Hebrew has a slightly different spelling of Hadad's name here.

26. Similarly Gray, *Kings*, p. 284. See the same expression in 3:7 and note 15 to Chapter 8.

27. Similarly Walsh, *1 Kings*, p. 139.

28. See Map 6–1 in Currid, *Atlas*, p. 141. In this history Paran has been mentioned most recently in 1 Samuel 25:1.

29. No more is known of this wife of Pharaoh than we learn from this passage.

30. The Hebrew word (*gebiyrah*) rendered "queen" is "the title of the senior lady of the royal harem, the queen-mother or the mother of the heir-apparent" according to Gray, *Kings*, p. 285. Similarly Keil, *Kings*, p. 122. The term is translated "queen mother" in 15:13 (see our discussion); 2 Kings 10:13; "mistress" in 2 Kings 5:3.

31. No more is known of Hadad's son Genubath.

32. Similarly Brueggemann, *Kings*, p. 145.

33. The parallels with David are noted by Walsh, *1 Kings*, p. 140. Also Peter J. Leithart, *1 & 2 Kings*, Brazos Theological Commentary on the Bible (Grand Rapids, MI: Brazos Press, 2006), pp. 87, 88.

34. There is evidence suggesting that this occurred quite late in Solomon's reign. Second Chronicles 8:4 suggests that twenty years into Solomon's reign he still held sway as far north as Tadmor, well beyond Damascus. See Map 5–16 in Currid, *Atlas*, p. 137. This is not conclusive and is interpreted rather differently by Keil, *Kings*, pp. 123, 124.

35. The Hebrew is "an abbreviated expression." Keil, *Kings*, p. 123. Literally: "and the evil which Hadad."

36. See note 46 to Chapter 21.

37. For the force of the Hebrew word (*qwts*) represented here by "loathed," see Genesis 27:46 ("loathe"); Exodus 1:12 ("were in dread"); Leviticus 20:23

("detested"); Numbers 21:5 ("loathe"); 22:3 ("was overcome with fear"); Proverbs 3:11 ("be weary of"); Isaiah 7:16 ("dread").

38. The details of hostilities between Rezon and Solomon are not provided. Olley suggests "some kind of guerilla warfare that would have threatened at least the shipping trade based at Ezion Geber (9:26)." John W. Olley, *The Message of Kings: God Is Present*, The Bible Speaks Today (Nottingham, UK: Inter-Varsity Press, 2011), p. 122.

Chapter Twenty-Four: What Hope Can There Possibly Be?

1. While "Ephrathite" in verse 26 probably means "Ephraimite" (so ESV, as in Judges 12:5, where the ESV also has "Ephraimite"), it is a pity to obscure the literary parallel to David, who was "the son of an Ephrathite" (1 Samuel 17:12), as was Samuel (1 Samuel 1:1). In the case of David, and probably Samuel too, "Ephrathite" means a person from the area inhabited by the clan of Ephrathah, near Bethlehem. See John Woodhouse, *1 Samuel: Looking for a Leader*, Preaching the Word (Wheaton, IL: Crossway, 2008), p. 556, note 1. Further Lamontte M. Luker, "Ephrathah (Place)," *ABD* 2, pp. 557, 558.

2. "Zeredah" may be an alternative spelling for Zarethan (7:46), as in 2 Chronicles 4:17. So C. F. Keil, "1 and 2 Kings," in C. F. Keil and F. Delitzsch, *Commentary on the Old Testament*, Vol. 3 (Peabody, MA: Hendrickson Publishers, 1996), p. 124; rejected by James A. Montgomery, *A Critical and Exegetical Commentary on the Books of Kings*, The International Critical Commentary (Edinburgh: T. & T. Clark, 1951), p. 242. Alternatively Wiseman locates Zeredah northwest of Bethel. Donald J. Wiseman, *1 and 2 Kings*, Tyndale Old Testament Commentaries (Leicester, UK: Inter-Varsity Press, 1993), p. 138; likewise Currid, *Atlas*, p. 287.

3. In the Hebrew this phrase stands as the last item in the list of details about Jeroboam, enhancing the rhetorical impact. In the light of verse 11 Walsh calls it "an explosive phrase." Jerome T. Walsh, *1 Kings*, Berit Olam: Studies in Hebrew Narrative & Poetry (Collegeville, MN: The Liturgical Press, 1996), p. 143.

4. Similarly Walsh, *1 Kings*, pp. 142, 143; Lissa M. Wray Beal, *1 & 2 Kings*, Apollos Old Testament Commentary, Vol. 9 (Nottingham, UK and Downers Grove, IL: Apollos, 2014), p. 172.

5. Similarly John Gray, *I & II Kings: A Commentary*, Third, Fully Revised, Edition (London: SCM, 1977), p. 290, note a; contra Mordechai Cogan, *1 Kings: A New Translation with Introduction, Notes & Commentary*, The Anchor Bible, Vol. 10 (New York: Doubleday, 2001), p. 337.

6. It has been suggested that both Jeroboam and Rehoboam ("May the People Expand") may have been throne names, the former being a deliberate parallel to the latter. So B. T. Dahlberg, "Jeroboam," *IDB* 2, p. 840.

7. For the sense of the idiom "to lift up one's hand against" compare the similar expressions in 2 Samuel 18:28; 20:21.

8. The Hebrew (*dabar*) (ESV, "reason") also means "word." The "word" concerning Jeroboam's rebellion will be the "word" of God we are about to hear in verses 31–39. Similarly Walsh, *1 Kings*, p. 143. In 9:15 the same phrase is rendered, "And this is the account . . ."

9. Similarly JB, REB.

10. The Hebrew (*sebel*) is different from the word for "forced labor" (*mas*) in 4:6; 5:13; 9:15; 12:18. It is "a general word for the labor of bearing burdens."

D. Kellermann, *sabal*, *TDOT* 10, p. 143. The cognate word (*sabal*) is rendered "burden-bearers" in 5:15 and apparently distinguished from the "forced labor" in 5:13.

11. Probably "the ravine which separated Zion from Moriah and Ophel . . . through the closing of which the temple mountain was brought within the city wall, and the fortification of the city of David was completed." Keil, *Kings*, p. 124.

12. "Very able" (*gibbor khayil*) is more literally, "mighty of strength." It seems less likely that the phrase here means that he was a man of property because he "had succeeded to the property of his father, who had died early, since his mother is designated as a widow." Gray, *Kings*, pp. 293, 294; cf. NIV, "a man of standing." Mulder suggests that he was "a man endowed with striking qualities which would make him an able administrator." Martin J. Mulder, *1 Kings: Volume 1: 1 Kings 1–11*, Historical Commentary on the Old Testament (Leuven, Belgium: Peeters, 1998), p. 584.

13. Only after the establishment of the northern kingdom did the expression "house of Joseph" come to mean all of the northern tribes. So Gray, *Kings*, p. 294.

14. So Carl D. Evans, "Jeroboam (Person)," *ABD* 3, p. 742; Mulder, *1 Kings 1–11*, pp. 584, 585.

15. So Evans, "Jeroboam," p. 742, who also mentions the possibility that Solomon's giving of twenty northern villages to Hiram (9:11) may have been the "last straw."

16. There have been others with the same name: a priest in Shiloh descended from Eli (1 Samuel 14:3) and a secretary in Solomon's bureaucracy (1 Kings 4:3).

17. "Found" (*matsa'*) "can mean 'to light upon by chance' as well as 'to find' as a result of a search." Gray, *Kings*, p. 294. In this context the latter seems to be implied.

18. The Hebrew has "And he . . ." allowing for the possibility that it was Jeroboam who was wearing the new garment. So Beal, *Kings*, p. 173. This seems unlikely, particularly in the light of the obvious parallel with Samuel's robe in 1 Samuel 15:27, 28 (where there is a similar ambiguity). See Woodhouse, *1 Samuel*, p. 595, notes 18, 19. Similarly Keil, *Kings*, pp. 124, 125 and most modern English versions.

19. So Keil, *Kings*, p. 125.

20. "When Ahijah tears the *slmh* into twelve pieces, it is symbolically the destruction of *slmh* himself." Walsh, *1 Kings*, p. 144.

21. ". . . the still young and vigorous condition, of the kingdom." Keil, *Kings*, p. 125.

22. This symbolism of "twelve" is not dependent on a particular counting of the twelve tribes. Genealogically the people of Israel were the descendants of the twelve sons of Jacob (Genesis 35:22–26; 49:28). The number twelve was retained when Joshua allocated tribal territories (even though the tribe of Levi did not receive a territory as such) by the descendants of Joseph being treated as two tribes, Ephraim and Manasseh (Joshua 13—21). There are further complications and variations in the lists of Israel's tribes, but the number "twelve" retains its symbolic force. For a helpful summary of the issues, see R. S. Hess, "Tribes of Israel and Land Allotments/Borders," *DOTHB*, pp. 967–71.

23. The two parts of the speech are strikingly similar in content. I am indebted to the detailed analysis in Walsh, *1 Kings*, pp. 144, 145.

24. "[T]he numbers are intended to be understood symbolically and not arithmetically. *Ten* as the number of completeness and totality is placed in contrast with *one*, to indicate that all Israel was to be torn away from the house of David, as is

stated in 12:20 . . . and only one single fragment was to be left to the house of Solomon out of divine compassion." Keil, *Kings*, p. 125.

25. The actual division of the kingdom was probably more complicated than this. See discussions in Keil, *Kings*, pp. 125, 126; Gray, *Kings*, p. 296; Walsh, *1 Kings*, p. 169; Beal, *Kings*, p. 173. See further 12:20, 21.

26. Several ancient versions have "he has" twice in the verse (ESV margin). The plural in the Hebrew is to be preferred. See Keil, *Kings*, p. 126.

27. See particularly our discussion of 3:6 and 11:4b.

28. "Ruler" (rather than "king") may suggest a diminution of Solomon's status. So Walsh, *1 Kings*, p. 146.

29. See Woodhouse, *1 Samuel*, p. 76.

30. There are two similar Hebrew words for "lamp" (*ner* and *niyr*) in the texts referred to in this paragraph.

31. The words in the two texts are identical despite a slight variation in the ESV. Admittedly the promise to David was spoken not by God, but by Abner. No doubt Abner spoke more truly than he knew. The exact echo of the words spoken to David count against seeing the expression here as a criticism of Jeroboam's aspiration to grasp the throne. Contra Keil, *Kings*, p. 126; cf. Gray, *Kings*, p. 297.

32. This time the words are not quite identical, and the speaker to David was Saul.

33. We have discussed the relationship between the unconditional promise of God and the condition of obedience in several places. See particularly the discussion of 2:4. Furthermore on "as David my servant did," cf. 11:4, 6, 33, 34 and our discussion of 3:6.

34. "But" (*'ak*) introduces a "restrictive clause." See note 41 to Chapter 20.

35. This "not forever" will become a prophetic theme as the promise of a reunited people of God takes shape. See Isaiah 11:12, 13; Jeremiah 3:18; 33:25, 26; 50:4; Ezekiel 37:15–28; Hosea 1:11; 3:5; Zechariah 10:6. For the gospel fulfillment of these promises (and more), see John 10:16; 17:20–23; Ephesians 1:10; 2:15.

36. The ESV inserts "therefore" here, suggesting that Solomon's action was motivated either by the word Ahijah spoke to Jeroboam (how would Solomon have heard about that?) or the rebellion of Jeroboam referred to in verses 26, 27 (whenever that occurred). However, the Hebrew syntax indicates a sequence of events without the implications of "therefore." This makes Solomon's action sound more like Saul's against David, lacking any stated justification.

37. Cf. Walsh, *1 Kings*, p. 147.

38. Beal goes further: "Solomon's action against Jeroboam seeks to forestall or prevent the prophetic word of YHWH." Beal, *Kings*, p. 172. I am less sure that this was Solomon's conscious intention.

39. Shishak (in English usually spelled Sheshonk) is known from extra-Biblical sources. He came to the Egyptian throne quite late in Solomon's reign and ruled from about 931–910 B.C. He was probably the successor to the Pharaoh who became Solomon's father-in-law (3:1). For a brief statement of what is known about him, see Donald B. Redford, "Shishak," *ABD* 5, pp. 1221, 1222.

40. In the history from here a formal notice like this will be given summarizing the reigns of various kings (14:19, 20, 29–31; 15:7, 8; etc.).

41. About 961–922 B.C.

42. We do not know precisely how long it was after David's death that Solomon commenced his building work, but 5:1 suggests that it was not very long.

Chapter Twenty-Five: Power in Unworthy Hands

1. Consider the sons of Eli (1 Samuel 2:12) and Samuel (1 Samuel 8:3), Saul's son Ish-bosheth (2 Samuel 2:10), and David's oldest sons Amnon and Absalom (2 Samuel 13). The exception to this pattern was Saul's eldest son Jonathan, who surrendered his claims to David (1 Samuel 18:4).

2. Even in the terrible story of Abimelech, who became king (in Shechem!) by murdering his brothers, he was "made king" by the leaders of Shechem (Judges 9:1–6).

3. Up to this point in 1 Kings "all Israel" has meant the whole nation (see 1:20; 2:15; 3:28; 4:1, 7; 5:13; 8:62, 65; 11:16, 42). So Lissa M. Wray Beal, *1 & 2 Kings*, Apollos Old Testament Commentary, Vol. 9 (Nottingham, UK and Downers Grove, IL: Apollos, 2014), p. 180, although (as we have seen) there is some debate about 4:7 and 5:13. See note 1 to Chapter 10.

4. So, among others, John Gray, *I & II Kings: A Commentary*, Third, Fully Revised, Edition (London: SCM, 1977), p. 304; Jerome T. Walsh, *1 Kings*, Berit Olam: Studies in Hebrew Narrative & Poetry (Collegeville, MN: The Liturgical Press, 1996), p. 160. The northern tribes (excluding Judah) have been called "Israel" in 1:35; 2:32; 4:20, 25. Furthermore in verse 6 we will learn that Rehoboam was already "*King* Rehoboam," presumably among the southerners.

5. From this point in 1 Kings "all Israel" will refer to the northern tribes (12:16, 18, 20; 14:13, 18; 15:27, 33; 16:16, 17; 18:19; 22:17).

6. Shechem was located about forty miles north of Jerusalem, between Mount Gerizim and Mount Ebal, at the juncture of the main north-south and east-west routes. See Map 6–2 in Currid, *Atlas*, p. 142.

7. So RV, REB, NIV, HCSB.

8. "Remained in" follows the Hebrew (similarly RV, REB, HCSB; see ESV margin). The Hebrew text is defended by C. F. Keil, "1 and 2 Kings," in C. F. Keil and F. Delitzsch, *Commentary on the Old Testament*, Vol. 3 (Peabody, MA: Hendrickson Publishers, 1996), p. 135, note 2. Following several of the ancient versions (and 2 Chronicles 10:2) ESV has "returned from" (similarly JB, NIV). The latter is supported by Gray, *Kings*, p. 301, note a.

9. This rendering of verse 2 is close to Beal, *Kings*, p. 176 and to the same effect as Walsh, *1 Kings*, p. 161.

10. Similarly Beal, *Kings*, p. 181.

11. The "yoke" can be a symbol of servitude as in Genesis 27:40; Leviticus 26:13; Deuteronomy 28:48; Isaiah 9:4; 10:27; 14:25; 58:6; Jeremiah 2:20; Ezekiel 34:27. It can also represent government without necessary negative connotations. See Jeremiah 27:8, 11, 12; 28:14; Lamentations 3:27; Hosea 10:11; 11:4. For the literal sense, see Numbers 19:2; Deuteronomy 21:3; 1 Samuel 6:7; 11:7; 1 Kings 19:19, 21; Job 1:3; 42:12.

12. Similarly Peter J. Leithart, *1 & 2 Kings*, Brazos Theological Commentary on the Bible (Grand Rapids, MI: Brazos Press, 2006), p. 91; John W. Olley, *The Message of Kings: God Is Present*, The Bible Speaks Today (Nottingham, UK: InterVarsity Press, 2011), p. 132.

13. Probably "as courtiers or counsellors." Gray, *Kings*, p. 305.

14. In Hebrew "you" is emphasized. "How do *you* advise me?" Shortly he will seek advice from others.

15. Walsh, *1 Kings*, p. 162.

16. I am not at all persuaded by Walsh's clever suggestion that the Hebrew consonants of the word "answer" are ambiguous and can mean "afflict." Walsh, *1 Kings*, pp. 162, 163.

17. The word order here (slightly different from the ESV) reflects the Hebrew, which has "today" at the beginning and "all the days" (ESV, "forever") at the end of the sentence.

18. Gray finds this puzzling and suggests that it might mean that the king should be a servant *of God* for the people. He then omits "and serve them." Gray, *Kings*, p. 305. Walsh is more cynical: "Their recommendation is to dissemble. If Rehoboam pretends to appease the Israelites now ('be servant today, and say good things to them'), they will make him king. He will then have their allegiance for 'all days.'" Walsh, *1 Kings*, p. 162. On this occasion I believe Brueggemann has the better sense: "This is the proper relation of people and their rulers. Rulers exist in order to enhance the realm and those who occupy it. In Ezek. 34, however, one can observe the process of governance by which the ruled come to exist for the rulers, so that political power exists only to enhance those already powerful. It is unmistakably clear that such a theory of governance now dominates the U. S. political scene." Walter Brueggemann, *1 & 2 Kings*, Smyth & Helwys Bible Commentary (Macon, GA: Smyth & Helwys, 2000), p. 156. In this the U. S. is hardly alone.

19. So Walsh, *1 Kings*, p. 162. The word *yeled* often means "child" and here has a clearly derogatory sense. So Gray, *Kings*, p. 305.

20. Brueggemann, *Kings*, p. 156.

21. As in verse 6, "you" is emphatic. In Hebrew the contrast between the two groups of advisers is underlined.

22. Similarly Walsh, *1 Kings*, p. 168; also Dale Ralph Davis, *The Wisdom and the Folly: An Exposition of the Book of First Kings* (Fearn, Ross-shire, UK: Christian Focus, 2002), p. 128. It "suggests a pre-commitment to their advice." Beal, *Kings*, p. 182. Note that Hebrew did not have a "royal 'we.'"

23. Similarly Walsh, *1 Kings*, p. 163; Beal, *Kings*, p. 182.

24. So Gwilym H. Jones, *1 and 2 Kings*, 2 volumes, New Century Bible Commentary (Grand Rapids, MI and London: Eerdmans and Marshall, Morgan & Scott, 1984), p. 252 (citing Martin Noth); Walsh, *1 Kings*, p. 164; Davis, *Wisdom*, p. 129, note 2; Beal, *Kings*, p. 182. See *CHALOT*, p. 316. Leithart suggests the implication of this vulgar expression: "If Israel feels 'raped' by Solomon, Rehoboam plans to give them more of the same." Leithart, *Kings*, p. 92.

25. Leithart, *Kings*, p. 92.

26. Keil, *Kings*, p. 137. ". . . a sadistic elaboration of lashes loaded with leather bags stuffed with sand and armed with spikes." Gray, *Kings*, p. 306.

27. So Olley, *Kings*, p. 132, note 5. See Deuteronomy 8:15.

28. If "came" is singular in the Hebrew, it suggests that Jeroboam was the leader of the delegation: "Jeroboam came, and all the people." Contra Beal, *Kings*, p. 178 who outlines the textual issues.

29. Similarly Walsh, *1 Kings*, p. 164; Beal, *Kings*, p. 182.

30. Behind "harshly" in verse 13 and "hard" in verse 4 is the same Hebrew word (*qashah*). Walsh, *1 Kings*, p. 164.

31. Matthew Henry, *Matthew Henry's Commentary on the Whole Bible*, Vol. 2 (Old Tappan, NJ: Fleming H. Revell Company, no date), p. 640.

32. Beal, *Kings*, p. 182.

33. The Hebrew word here (*sibbah*, "turn of affairs") is rare and probably derived from the verb "to turn about" (*sbb*).

34. "God serves his own wise and righteous purposes by the imprudences and iniquities of men, and snares sinners in the work of their own hands. They that lose the kingdom of heaven, throw it away, as Rehoboam did his, by their own willfulness and folly." Henry, *Commentary*, p. 641. Further, if less spectacular, examples of this principle are seen in 2 Samuel 16:11, 12; 17:1–14.

35. So Gray, *Kings*, p. 306.

36. Similarly Walsh, *1 Kings*, p. 165.

37. See Map 4–13 in Currid, *Atlas*, p. 107.

38. So Walsh, *1 Kings*, p. 165; Beal, *Kings*, p. 182.

39. Keil is more generous than I: "the king was no doubt serious in his wish to meet the demands of the people." Keil, *Kings*, p. 138. Gray suggests that "Adoram was sent to explain the distinction between the occasional corvée which might be levied on Israel, and the perpetual liability of the non-Israelite subjects [see 5:13; 9:21, 22]." Gray, *Kings*, p. 307.

40. On "to this day," see note 16 to Chapter 20.

41. "All Israel" now refers to all the people, not just the representatives who had met in Shechem as in verse 1.

42. "Assembly" in verse 20 is the Hebrew word *'edah* (only here and 8:5 ["congregation"] in the books of Kings), not *qahal* as in verse 3.

43. The year was about 922 B.C.

44. In my opinion Walsh finds verse 21 rather too helpful. "This resolves the loose end left over from Ahijah's oracle in chapter 11: the twelfth piece of Ahijah's garment is Benjamin, whose loyalties are probably with the north while its territory belongs in large part to Rehoboam." Walsh, *1 Kings*, p. 169. That would not account for Simeon. The numbers ten, two, and one in Ahijah's prophecy are better treated as symbolic than mathematically precise.

45. Such as Walsh, *1 Kings*, p. 169.

46. Some regard the figure of 180,000 as "utterly unrealistic." So Walsh, *1 Kings*, p. 169; also Jones, *Kings*, p. 255. It is defended by reference to 2 Samuel 24:9 by Keil, *Kings*, p. 138. However see note 2 to Chapter 8.

47. See John Woodhouse, *1 Samuel: Looking for a Leader*, Preaching the Word (Wheaton, IL: Crossway, 2008), p. 562, note 1.

48. That is, in the books of Kings. He appears in a later incident in Rehoboam's reign recorded in 2 Chronicles 12.

49. Similarly Walsh, *1 Kings*, p. 170.

50. Beal notes that Rehoboam "is not specifically noted in the acquiescence. This is a subtle jab at his inability to lead his people wisely." Beal, *Kings*, p. 183; cf. Walsh, *1 Kings*, p. 170.

Chapter Twenty-Six: The Terrifying Prospect of Actually Trusting God

1. See Map 6–2 in Currid, *Atlas*, p. 142.

2. The exact location is not known for certain, but it was on the south bank of the Jabbok River, between Succoth and Mahanaim (see Judges 8:8, 9, 17). See Map 2–5 in Currid, *Atlas*, p. 73.

3. So C. F. Keil, "1 and 2 Kings," in C. F. Keil and F. Delitzsch, *Commentary on the Old Testament*, Vol. 3 (Peabody, MA: Hendrickson Publishers, 1996), p. 138.

4. My more literal rendering preserves the wordplay in this verse between "house of David" and "house of the LORD," as well as the consistency of our text's use of "house" for the building concerned. This and verse 31 are the only places in 1 Kings where the ESV has rendered *bayith* as "temple(s)" rather than "house(s)." See further our discussion of 3:1.

5. The Hebrew word rendered "lord" is grammatically plural, possibly referring not just to Rehoboam but to the dynasty he represented. Similarly John Gray, *I & II Kings: A Commentary*, Third, Fully Revised, Edition (London: SCM, 1977), p. 313, note b. Readers of English translations should be aware that "LORD" and "lord" in verse 27 represent distinctly different Hebrew words.

6. Contra Walsh: "Jeroboam's fears strike us as unrealistic," although I agree that they "reinforce our impression that he does not trust in Yahweh's continuing favor." Jerome T. Walsh, *1 Kings*, Berit Olam: Studies in Hebrew Narrative & Poetry (Collegeville, MN: The Liturgical Press, 1996), p. 172.

7. Iain W. Provan, *1 & 2 Kings*, Understanding the Bible Commentary Series (Grand Rapids, MI: Baker Books, 1995), p. 109, where I think "the only king of Judah" should read "only the king of Judah."

8. H. Ringgren, "*'egel*," *TDOT* 10, p. 446. The bulls may have been carved from wood and then covered with gold overlay. So Van Dam, "Golden Calf," *DOTP*, p. 370. However, the evidence for how the images were made is complicated. See John R. Spencer, "Golden Calf," *ABD* 2, p. 1067.

9. The unmistakable reminder of the calamitous incident in Exodus 32 does not depend on precise verbal echoes. The Hebrew word rendered "calves" in our verse 28 is the plural of "calf" (*'egel*) in Exodus 32:4, but "golden" in the latter verse (ESV) has been supplied by the translator from the context. On this point the NIV rendering of Exodus 32:4 is more literal than the ESV, although the verse has a number of difficulties. See C. Van Dam, "Golden Calf," pp. 369, 370.

10. It is astonishing to read Brueggemann's presentation of Jeroboam's action as "a creative step presented, in the first instance, with no hint of censure (12:28, 29). . . . Read in this way, the two calves are unexceptional and unobjectionable." Walter Brueggemann, *1 & 2 Kings*, Smyth & Helwys Bible Commentary (Macon, GA: Smyth & Helwys, 2000), pp. 160, 161. This could surely be the case only for a reader unfamiliar with the book of Exodus. Who would such a reader be? Brueggemann's reading is, in my opinion, distorted by the hypothesis entertained by much modern critical scholarship that Exodus 32 was written long *after* 1 Kings 12 as a polemical attack on Jeroboam's action. This is an outstanding example of a scholarly theory that is more confusing than illuminating, using a proposed *history* of the text of Scripture to overturn the received *form* of the text. On the theory, see Ringgren, "*'egel*," pp. 448, 449; Van Dam, "Golden Calf," p. 371.

11. This view is favored by Van Dam, "Golden Calf," pp. 369, 370.

12. For a fuller discussion of the possibilities see Spencer, "Golden Calf," pp. 1068, 1069. Some suggest that the golden bulls may not have been intended to represent God or gods directly, but were thought of as pedestals for the deity/deities, as the ark of the covenant was the Lord's "footstool" (1 Chronicles 28:2; cf. Psalm 99:5; 132:7). Ringgren, "*'egel*," p. 449. Such nuances do not seem to be of any

interest to the account before us, nor (we can guess) were they part of Jeroboam's thinking, such as it was.

13. Or "It is too much for you to go up to Jerusalem" (NIV); "Going to Jerusalem is too difficult for you" (HCSB).

14. See HCSB. The grammatically plural *'elohim* (literally, "gods") is the usual Hebrew word for "God." See GKC, §124g. The rendering "gods" here may be supported by the plural form of the verb "brought." When *'elohim* means "God" it usually has a singular verb, although there are exceptions (for example, Genesis 20:13; 31:53; 35:7; 2 Samuel 7:23). Cf. John Woodhouse, *2 Samuel: Your Kingdom Come*, Preaching the Word (Wheaton, IL: Crossway, 2015), p. 601, note 19. See GKC, §145i.

15. Alternatively Keil suggests that what Jeroboam *meant* to say by these words was, "this is no new religion, but this was the form of worship which our fathers used in the desert, with Aaron himself leading the way." Keil, *Kings*, p. 139. This assumes that Aaron's action was remembered, but its consequences had been forgotten. That, I think, is unlikely.

16. Brueggemann makes a similar observation that, despite his explicit channeling of Karl Marx, is worth hearing: "The combination of *virility* and *money* may be taken as emblematic of the powers of free market aggressiveness and acquisitiveness nowhere more clearly enacted than in professional sports that knows no restraints concerning money and macho, seconded by all sorts of gross hints of sexuality. Professional sports in our society, moreover, have become a metaphor for free market aggressiveness in which neighborly questions disappear and human issues become invisible." Brueggemann, *Kings*, p. 164.

17. See Map 6–2 in Currid, *Atlas*, p. 142.

18. Ibid.

19. "Jeroboam's action was entirely in keeping with Dan's earlier history and confirmed its status as a shrine famous for its idolatry. It was idolatrous from its inception." Barry G. Webb, *The Book of Judges*, The International Commentary on the Old Testament (Grand Rapids, MI and Cambridge, U.K.: Eerdmans, 2012), p. 449.

20. The Septuagint makes this assumption explicit: ". . . for the people went to the one at Bethel and to the other as far as Dan" (ESV margin; similarly NIV). The Hebrew (reflected in the ESV) may be defended as the (slightly) more difficult reading. Similarly Lissa M. Wray Beal, *1 & 2 Kings*, Apollos Old Testament Commentary, Apollos Old Testament Commentary, Vol. 9 (Nottingham, UK and Downers Grove, IL: Apollos, 2014), p. 178; contra Gray, *Kings*, p. 313, note h.

21. So K. Koch, *"khata',"* *TDOT* 4, p. 312. Examples of "sin" (same word) to this point in the books of Samuel and 1 Kings include the reprehensible behavior of Eli's sons, the repeated rebellion of the people of Israel culminating in their demand for a king, (ironically) the behavior of Jonathan in Saul's eyes, divination, Saul's disobedience, David's acts of adultery and murder that the Lord "put away," the sin of the people that Solomon prayed the Lord would forgive (1 Samuel 2:17; 12:19; 14:38; 15:23, 25; 2 Samuel 12:13; 1 Kings 8:34–36). See further the cognate word discussed in note 40 to Chapter 3.

22. See note 4. The Hebrew has, literally, "a house of high places," probably meaning "a house for each of the high places."

23. More literally, "from the ends [or edges or extremities] of the people." This has been variously understood: *"from the extremest parts of the people*, that is, some

out of every corner of the country." Matthew Henry, *Matthew Henry's Commentary on the Whole Bible*, Vol. 2 (Old Tappan, NJ: Fleming H. Revell Company, no date), p. 644. Also "from the whole of the people any one without distinction even to the very last." Keil, *Kings*, p. 140; also "from every class of the people" (REB; HCSB); "from ordinary families" (JB); "from all sorts of people" (NIV). The KJV ("of the lowest of the people") has generally been rejected. So, explicitly, Gray, *Kings*, p. 317.

24. On Levites see 1 Samuel 6:15; 2 Samuel 15:24; 1 Kings 8:4. These are the only other references to Levites in the books of Samuel and Kings.

25. Similarly D. A. Hubbard, "Priests and Levites," *IBD* 3, p. 1268.

26. The Hebrew uses the verb *'asah* ("make" or "do") eight times in verses 31–33 (ESV, "made," "appointed," "did," "instituted"). It is almost as though he is mocking Jeroboam, suggesting that he was *making* all this up. Similarly Dale Ralph Davis, *The Wisdom and the Folly: An Exposition of the Book of First Kings* (Fearn, Ross-shire, UK: Christian Focus, 2002), p. 144; Beal, *Kings*, p. 180.

27. A pretext covering his true motives for the later feast in the north could have been corn ripening a month later in the north. So Keil, *Kings*, p. 140.

28. Walsh, *1 Kings*, p. 175, note 2.

29. On the particular term rendered "make offerings," see note 42 to Chapter 20. Jeroboam was attempting to do what Solomon had done (3:3; 9:25; but see also 11:8).

30. The Hebrew may be read as "from his own heart" (ESV, following the vocalization) or "on his own" (HCSB, following the consonantal text). The former reading fits well with what Jeroboam said "in his heart" at the beginning of this episode (v. 26). "Devised" represents a Hebrew word that occurs only here and Nehemiah 6:8 (ESV, "inventing"; NIV, "just making it up").

Chapter Twenty-Seven: The Word of the Lord versus Human Religion

1. Walter Brueggemann, *1 & 2 Kings*, Smyth & Helwys Bible Commentary (Macon, GA: Smyth & Helwys, 2000), p. 175. It is "one of the strangest narrative passages in the Old Testament and deserves a monograph to itself." Peter J. Leithart, *1 & 2 Kings*, Brazos Theological Commentary on the Bible (Grand Rapids, MI: Brazos Press, 2006), p. 98.

2. The theological importance of 1 Kings 13 was appreciated by Karl Barth, who devoted seventeen pages (of small print!) to a remarkable exposition of this story. Karl Barth, *Church Dogmatics*, Vol., II Part 2 (Edinburgh: T. & T. Clark, 1957), pp. 393–409. He observes that 1 Kings 13 "constitutes a kind of heading, not only for the whole ensuing history of the two separated kingdoms of Israel, but at the same time for the history of the conflict which now begins between professional and original prophets on the one hand, and false and true prophets on the other. All that follows is already announced and prefigured in this story." Ibid., p. 403.

3. On the chapter divisions in the Old Testament, see John Woodhouse, *1 Samuel: Looking for a Leader*, Preaching the Word (Wheaton, IL: Crossway, 2008), pp. 572, 573, note 3. The chapter division here encourages the reader to see the coming of the word of the Lord into the situation (the theme of 1 Kings 13) as a new and important development, as indeed it is.

4. I am writing these words a few days after the election of Donald Trump to be President of the United States of America, fully aware that the debates among

Christians about this development are far from simple or straightforward. You may be reading these words years after that event and will have the wisdom of hindsight.

5. Similarly Jerome T. Walsh, *1 Kings*, Berit Olam: Studies in Hebrew Narrative & Poetry (Collegeville, MN: The Liturgical Press, 1996), p. 177; John W. Olley, *The Message of Kings: God Is Present*, The Bible Speaks Today (Nottingham, UK: Inter-Varsity Press, 2011), p. 138. I have not counted a slightly different Hebrew expression rendered "the word of the LORD" in the ESV of verses 21 and 26 (literally "the mouth of the LORD"; also found in Numbers 3:16, 51; 24:13; 36:5; Deuteronomy 34:5). However, "the word that the LORD spoke to him" in verse 26 is, literally, "*the word of the LORD* that he spoke to him."

6. Not counting the two occurrences of the slightly different expression in 13:21, 26. See previous note. The expression "the word of the LORD" appears much more frequently in the books of Kings than in preceding books. It is found twice in each of Genesis, Exodus, and Joshua; once in Deuteronomy and in Numbers; six times in 1 Samuel; three times in 2 Samuel; and not at all in Leviticus or Judges. Again this is not counting the variant phrase mentioned in note 5 and another in 2 Samuel 22:31.

7. Gerhard von Rad made this important observation, with a similar interpretation. "It is very significant that the phrase always appears with the definite article, '*the* word of Jahweh,' and never in the indefinite form, '*a* word of Jahweh,' as a superficial glance at the extremely large number of such 'word-events' might have led one to expect. The latter would however have shown a radical misunderstanding of the process, for however brief and concise the word might be, it was intended as *the* word of Jahweh for the man who received it and for his situation. The word that came on each occasion is not to be set alongside the rest of the words of Jahweh, so that it is only in the synthesis that it yields something like the message the prophet has to announce; on the contrary, for the person concerned it is the complete word of God, and has no need of tacit supplementation by the other words which the prophet had already spoken on other occasions. At different times and to different people the prophet takes different ways of saying the same thing. Paradoxical as it may seem, in principle the prophet says the same thing to everyone; he plays variations upon it only to meet differences in the condition of his audience." Gerhard von Rad, *Old Testament Theology. Volume II: The Theology of Israel's Prophetic Traditions* (London: SCM Press Ltd, 1965), pp. 87, 88. See also the insightful study by Andrew G. Shead, *A Mouth Full of Fire: The Word of God in the Words of Jeremiah*, New Studies in Biblical Theology 29 (Downers Grove, IL: InterVarsity Press, 2012), particularly pp. 107–9.

8. These reflections on "the word of the LORD" provide a vital background to the opening words of the Gospel according to John: "In the beginning was *the Word*, and *the Word* was with God, and *the Word* was God. . . . All things were made through him, and without him was not any thing made that was made. . . . And *the Word* became flesh and dwelt among us . . ." (John 1:1, 3, 14).

9. See John Woodhouse, *2 Samuel: Your Kingdom Come*, Preaching the Word (Wheaton, IL: Crossway, 2015), pp. 207, 208.

10. I have attempted to draw out the connections between the promise as given to David and to Abraham in my exposition of 2 Samuel 7:8–16. Woodhouse, *2 Samuel*, pp. 207–20.

11. "From Judah" is preferred simply because exactly the same Hebrew expression is rendered this way through the chapter (13:12, 14, 21), and (as we will see in our next chapter) the repetitions are important.

12. "To make offerings" is the technical term we have seen in 3:3; 9:25; 11:8; 12:33. See note 42 to Chapter 20.

13. "Behold" represents a Hebrew idiom that emphasizes the immediate presence of whatever is then described. The approaching man of God was immediately present *to Jeroboam*. See Woodhouse, *2 Samuel*, p. 555, note 3.

14. The Hebrew verb [ESV, "came"] may be understood as a participle. So Walsh, *1 Kings*, p. 176.

15. In the story that extends through the rest of 1 Kings 13 the otherwise essentially synonymous terms "man of God" and "prophet" are used to distinguish two unnamed prophets. See 13:11. Olley, *Kings*, p. 139, note 25.

16. See further Woodhouse, *1 Samuel*, p. 562, note 1.

17. "The disruption [that is, the separation of the northern tribes from Judah] did not mean that the north was released and expelled from the sphere of the Word of God, and therefore from the scope of His grace. The disruption was hardly completed before salvation began to appear more than ever in the place where grace had been repudiated—and from that place where it had been received as grace, from the Jews." Barth, *Church Dogmatics*, II/2, p. 404.

18. Cf. Amos 7:15. There are a number of parallels between this man of God and Amos about 200 years later. Both were from Judah; both brought the word of God to the northern kingdom, and to Bethel in particular; both denounced a king named Jeroboam; for both the title "prophet" seems to have been avoided. See Amos 1:2; 3:14; 4:4, 5; 7:10–17; cf. Hosea 10:15.

19. Elsewhere it is found only in 1 Samuel 3:21; 1 Kings 20:35; 2 Chronicles 30:12; Psalm 33:6; Jeremiah 8:9.

20. Similarly C. F. Keil, "1 and 2 Kings," in C. F. Keil and F. Delitzsch, *Commentary on the Old Testament*, Vol. 3 (Peabody, MA: Hendrickson Publishers, 1996), p. 142. Brueggemann puzzlingly says, "We are not told that he is commissioned by Yahweh. We only know he is 'out of Judah.'" Brueggemann, *Kings*, p. 167. He seems to have disregarded "by the word of the LORD."

21. On Bethel see our discussion of 12:29.

22. "Nowhere else in Hebrew narrative does someone address words to an inanimate object. . . . We must picture the king standing on the altar platform in full ceremonial regalia and the man of God ignoring him completely to speak to the stones on which the king is standing. Even before the man of God delivers his oracle, his snub to the royal presence heralds Yahweh's anger at Jeroboam." Walsh, *1 Kings*, p. 177.

23. "Thus the LORD has said" (as in the ESV of 1 Samuel 2:27) is generally (in my opinion) a preferable rendering of the Hebrew phrase often translated "thus says the LORD." The speaker is reporting the word of the Lord that had come to him earlier. See Woodhouse, *1 Samuel*, pp. 64, 562, note 2.

24. See note 13.

25. Here I have in mind particularly the *books* of the prophets (Isaiah to Malachi) in the Old Testament canon, the earliest of which (probably Amos) comes about 200 years after the events of 1 Kings 13. See most famously Isaiah 9:6, 7; 11:1–10;

also Jeremiah 23:5; 33:15, 20–22; Ezekiel 34:23, 24; 37:24, 25; Hosea 3:5; Amos 9:11; Zechariah 12:7, 8, 10; 13:1.

26. The obvious parallel is the naming of Cyrus in Isaiah 44:28; 45:1. If these words were spoken by the prophet Isaiah sometime around 700 B.C., it was about a century and a half before Cyrus. Barry G. Webb, *The Message of Isaiah: On Eagles' Wings*, The Bible Speaks Today (Leicester, UK: Inter-Varsity Press, 1996), p. 182, note 75. However, if my suggestion here is followed, the parallel is much less relevant.

27. There are other possibilities that, I think, are less likely. Keil suggests that the name Josiah "occurs primarily according to its appellative meaning, viz., 'he whom Yahweh supports,' . . . and expresses this thought: there will be born a son to the house of David, whom Jehovah will support or establish, so that he shall execute judgment upon the priests of the high places at Bethel. This prophecy was then afterwards so fulfilled by the special arrangement of God, that the king who executed this judgment bore the name *Joshiyahu* as his proper name." Keil, *Kings*, p. 143. The ambiguity should caution against using the specific detail of Josiah's name here as evidence for the supernatural nature of prophecy.

28. The Hebrew word (*zabakh*) rendered "sacrificed" (also in 1:9, 19, 25; 3:2, 3, 4; 8:5, 62, 63; 11:8; 12:32) can refer to a religious ritual act or slaughter in a more mundane sense. See note 32 to Chapter 2.

29. "It is inconceivable that there could be a harsher denial of the legality of the worship practiced at Bethel, a harsher threat regarding its future, a harsher expression of the irreconcilability of what takes place there with the cult at Jerusalem, a harsher emphasis on the fact that cleansing and vengeance will come from Jerusalem because God is there and not here, and says Yes there and No here, a more complete exclusiveness in favour of David's kingdom as opposed to the separated North, than are expressed in this divine utterance." Barth, *Church Dogmatics*, II/2, pp. 393, 394.

30. The same Hebrew verb appears in 12:33; 13:1. Similarly Walsh, *1 Kings*, p. 178. See note 12.

31. Most commentaries (with the ESV) see a smooth chronological movement through the narrative from verse 1 to verse 10, the altar being torn down (v. 5) between the king's paralysis (v. 4) and his request (v. 6). So, for example, John Gray, *I & II Kings: A Commentary*, Third, Fully Revised, Edition (London: SCM, 1977), p. 326; Iain W. Provan, *1 & 2 Kings*, Understanding the Bible Commentary Series (Grand Rapids, MI: Baker Books, 1995), p. 113; Brueggemann, *Kings*, p. 168; Dale Ralph Davis, *The Wisdom and the Folly: An Exposition of the Book of First Kings* (Fearn, Ross-shire, UK: Christian Focus, 2002), p. 151. Walsh perceptively notes that the Hebrew has a number of uneven elements that suggest verses 3 and 5 should be understood as parenthetical, in effect asides to the reader that break the chronological flow. Walsh, *1 Kings*, pp. 176–79. This makes good sense once we put aside the initial impression we might get from the English translation that the destruction of the altar was a sign for the contemporary audience to prove that the prophet was speaking from God. I think the Hebrew is better understood to mean that *the words that the Lord had spoken* were the "sign" that the altar would be destroyed. In other words, verse 3 is essentially a reiteration of verse 2 rather than an addition to it. This is an unusual but certainly not impossible use of the word "sign." Cf. S. Wagner, "*mopet*," *TDOT* 8, p. 179.

32. Walsh cogently argues that the "unnecessary" introductory words and the unexpected Hebrew grammatical form of "And he gave" mean that the statement in

verse 3 should not be understood as the continuation of the oracle in verse 2. It is, in his view, an aside heard by us, but not by Jeroboam. Walsh, *1 Kings*, p. 178.

33. The ESV could be understood to mean: "This is the sign *indicating that* the LORD has spoken." However, the Hebrew means: "This is the sign *that* the LORD has spoken."

34. Similarly Davis, *Wisdom*, p. 152; Leithart, p. 98.

35. Similarly Walsh, *1 Kings*, p. 178. This makes better sense of the text than the idea that the altar was torn down at the time of these events, only to be rebuilt by Jeroboam (or someone else?). There is no suggestion of a rebuilding of the altar, surely something that would have been important for this historian.

36. The Hebrew for "dried up" or "withered" typically refers to bodies of water being dried up (Genesis 8:7; Joshua 2:10; 1 Kings 17:7) or plants withering (Isaiah 15:6; 40:7, 8). Metaphorically it is used to describe the frailty of human life (Psalm 22:15; 102:11; Proverbs 17:22; Isaiah 40:7, 8, 24; cf. Ezekiel 37:11) and for paralysis in parts of the body (Lamentations 4:8; Zechariah 11:17).

37. The ESV adds "also," but the Hebrew does not require this.

38. So Walsh, *1 Kings*, p. 179.

39. Walsh, *1 Kings*, p. 179.

40. His words are therefore explicitly his *response* either to the words of verse 2 or to the paralysis in his hand or, probably, both.

41. "Entreat the favor" represents a difficult Hebrew idiom whose precise meaning is uncertain. The problem is the verb, which in other contexts refers to becoming sick or weak. The noun literally means "face." Suggested meanings include "Make the face weak" (as opposed to hard or stern); "make the face sweet, or pleasant." See Gray, *Kings*, pp. 324, note d, 327. The idiom is also found in Exodus 32:11; 1 Samuel 13:12; 2 Chronicles 33:12; Job 11:19; Psalm 45:12; 119:58; Proverbs 19:6; Jeremiah 26:19; Daniel 9:13; Malachi 1:9; Zechariah 7:2; 8:21, 22. "The expression designates a gesture of respect, of worship, and of submission, performed with the purpose of seeking favor." K. Seybold, *"challah," TDOT* 4, p. 409.

42. The Hebrew has a small word (*na'*) that "softens the imperative to a request." Walsh, *1 Kings*, p. 179.

43. "Jeroboam is *Saul redivivus*, and the people who adhere to him are by this very fact the people who have rejected God as their king—and therefore the house of David." Barth, *Church Dogmatics*, II/2, p. 400.

44. To these obvious parallels with Saul's story we may add the appearance in 1 Samuel 13:12 of the somewhat unusual idiom discussed in note 41 and the significant use of the word "tear (down)" in the context (1 Samuel 15:27, 28).

45. "Come home with me" sounds like an invitation to Shechem (12:25). That seems unlikely. The most obvious "house" in the context is the house of the high place in Bethel (see 12:32). Similarly Gray, *Kings*, p. 327.

46. "What Jeroboam would like is reconciliation, tolerance, amicable compromise between himself and the divinely commissioned bearer of the word from Judah. For his own part he sees no reason why they could not shake hands, or why Jerusalem and Bethel could not settle down alongside one another. It is precisely that which the man of God refuses to concede by refusing the invitation." Barth, *Church Dogmatics*, II/2, p. 394.

47. Similarly Provan, *Kings*, p. 114.

48. "This place" is best understood as the "house" in Bethel, Jeroboam's alternative to the "place" of the house of the Lord in Jerusalem (8:13, 21, 29).

49. In view of what happens next (13:11ff.) I think this is preferable to Provan's suggestion: "he is to vary his route so that he cannot easily be found and prevented from completing his mission (cf. Matt. 2:12)." Provan, *Kings*, p. 114.

50. There is no chapter of the Old Testament in which this term appears more often (although there are also sixteen occurrences in Jeremiah 3). Olley, *Kings*, p. 143, note 36.

Chapter Twenty-Eight: The Word of the Lord versus Human Lies

1. Part of that damage is that in the world now distorted by the devil's lie, there may be circumstances in which lying is necessary. On this see John Woodhouse, *1 Samuel: Looking for a Leader*, Preaching the Word (Wheaton, IL: Crossway, 2008), pp. 377, 378.

2. It is put well by Leithart: "One effect of this technique [main characters unnamed] is to highlight geography. By virtue of his designation, the man of God becomes representative of Judah, while the old prophet stands for Bethel and Israel, suggesting that the whole history of Israel and Judah is somehow foreshadowed in this chapter." Peter J. Leithart, *1 & 2 Kings*, Brazos Theological Commentary on the Bible (Grand Rapids, MI: Brazos Press, 2006), p. 99.

3. I would not go so far as Gray who says that "prophet" here could be "a derogatory term." John Gray, *I & II Kings: A Commentary*, Third, Fully Revised, Edition (London: SCM, 1977), p. 329. It is an ambiguous term.

4. I am therefore more dubious than Beal who thinks that "there is no a priori reason for the prophet not being Yahwistic." Lissa M. Wray Beal, *1 & 2 Kings*, Apollos Old Testament Commentary, Vol. 9 (Nottingham, UK and Downers Grove, IL: Apollos, 2014), p. 193. Matthew Henry was closer to the mark in my opinion: "I cannot but call him a false prophet and a bad man. . . . If he had been a good prophet, he would have reproved Jeroboam's idolatry, and not have suffered his sons to attend his altars, as, it should seem, they did." Matthew Henry, *Matthew Henry's Commentary on the Whole Bible*, Vol. 2 (Old Tappan, NJ: Fleming H. Revell Company, no date), p. 647. There is an alternative (but I think unpersuasive) argument for a positive view of the old prophet in C. F. Keil, "1 and 2 Kings," in C. F. Keil and F. Delitzsch, *Commentary on the Old Testament*, Vol. 3 (Peabody, MA: Hendrickson Publishers, 1996), p. 145.

5. See ESV margin. The Hebrew suggests that one "son" was the initial spokesman and then others ("They") joined in. Likewise Keil, *Kings*, p. 144; Beal, *Kings*, p. 189.

6. Groups of prophets have been mentioned in 1 Samuel 10:5; 19:20. Elsewhere such groups are known as "sons of the prophets" (1 Kings 20:35; 2 Kings 2:3, 5, 7, 15; 4:1, 38; 5:22; 6:1; 9:1; cf. Amos 7:14). See further Woodhouse, *1 Samuel*, p. 172.

7. The word in question (*derek*) is rendered "way" or "road" and occurs in verses 12 (twice), 17, 24 (twice), 25, 26, 28, 33.

8. "From Judah" is another phrase that is highlighted through the chapter by its repetition (vv. 1, 12, 14, 21).

9. The definite article in the Hebrew perhaps suggests "the tree well known from that event." Keil, *Kings*, p. 144.

10. "Come with me to the house" closely echoes the words of the king in 13:7, although a different Hebrew verb is used, probably because of the different context. In 13:7 the speakers were close to the "house" (the verb used can mean "enter"); now they were some distance from the "house" (the verb suggests *going* to the house).

11. "... he has perceived the importance of the refusal given to Jeroboam in vv. 6–10, and ... he is determined to reverse it at any price." Karl Barth, *Church Dogmatics*, II, 2 (Edinburgh: T. & T. Clark, 1957), p. 395.

12. The Hebrew word (*'eth*) rendered "with" in the speech to the old prophet suggests a closer association than the corresponding word (*'im*) in the speech to the king. I am reminded of the story of Ittai ("With Me") in 2 Samuel 15:19, 20, where *'eth* was used with a similar sense of intimacy. John Woodhouse, *2 Samuel: Your Kingdom Come*, Preaching the Word (Wheaton, IL: Crossway, 2015), pp. 398, 399. On the difference between the two Hebrew prepositions see BDB, p. 87.

13. Barth called this "the wholly devilish temptation to accept the Israelite form of Canaanitism ('I am a prophet also as thou art') as the Israelite way of life, as a possible and legitimate form—within the divine covenant—of the life of the one people of God." Barth, *Church Dogmatics*, II/2, p. 401.

14. "With you" in verse 18c is the expression explained in note 12.

15. In the Hebrew "But he lied to him" is two words, unconnected with the surrounding text, "inserted as it were parenthetically, simply as an explanation." Keil, *Kings*, p. 144.

16. "Always, the church's greatest tests come not from kings who call for imprisonment and torture; Christians relish martyrdom. The great tests arise from lying prophets, from wolfish bishops and priests, pastors and preachers." Leithart, *Kings*, p. 100.

17. Again "with him" echoes the expression explained in note 12, underlining that the man of God did precisely what he had refused to do in verse 16, even if in a different "place."

18. "All Jerusalem and all Judah will do as this man of Judah has done. . . . They will become tolerant and then disobedient." Barth, *Church Dogmatics*, II/2, p. 399.

19. "The evil and ungrateful man, addressed by the Word of God, becomes himself its bearer and messenger. This is not, of course, because he has any merit or worth. It is apart from and even against his own intention. It is simply because God is always God, because He has not cast away His people, His whole people Israel." Barth, *Church Dogmatics*, II/2, p. 407.

20. Of course, this phrase can be used falsely (as did the false prophet Hananiah in Jeremiah 28:2). Here, however, the narrator has assured us that the word of the Lord *did* come to this prophet.

21. The idiom of "rebelling" against God's "mouth" is also used of Israel's disobedience in Numbers 20:24; 27:14; Lamentations 1:18 (cf. Joshua 1:18; Isaiah 1:20). The same verb is used in a number of other phrases depicting Israel's rebelliousness. For a concise survey, see L. Schwienhorst, "*mara*," *TDOT* 9, pp. 5–10.

22. HCSB has "corpse." The Hebrew word (*nebelah*, also in vv. 24 [twice], 25 [twice], 28 [three times], 29, 30) is frequently used of the dead carcass of an animal (Leviticus 5:2; 11:8, 11, 24, 25, 27, 28, 35–40; Deuteronomy 14:8) and also

of the dead body of an executed person (Deuteronomy 21:23; 28:26; Joshua 8:29; 2 Kings 9:37).

23. There is some ambiguity in the Hebrew syntax, so that "the prophet" could still refer to the one from Bethel: "the prophet who had brought him back saddled his donkey for him" (NIV; similarly REB); "he saddled the ass for him, the one belonging to the prophet who had brought him back" (Simon DeVries, *1 Kings*, Word Biblical Commentary, Vol. 12 [Waco, Texas: Word Books, 1985)]). Similarly Beal, *Kings*, p. 189. RV, ESV, and HCSB understand "the prophet" here to mean the man from Judah, and on balance I think that is right.

Chapter Twenty-Nine: The Word of the Lord and Human Hope

1. In the Hebrew the use of participles in verse 25 ("passed by," "thrown," "standing," as well as "lived," all Hebrew participles) evokes the continuing state of affairs we are being invited to witness. Cf. GKC, §116a.

2. See note 22 to Chapter 28.

3. Along with slight variants as in 2:27.

4. Walsh sets out clearly the parallels (perhaps slightly overstated) between 13:11–24 and 13:25–32. Jerome T. Walsh, *1 Kings*, Berit Olam: Studies in Hebrew Narrative & Poetry (Collegeville, MN: The Liturgical Press, 1996), pp. 182, 183.

5. "The beast, unlike the man, is obedient to Yahweh." Walsh, *1 Kings*, p. 187. "The lion is an illustration of what the prophet should have done." Lissa M. Wray Beal, *1 & 2 Kings*, Apollos Old Testament Commentary, Vol. 9 (Nottingham, UK and Downers Grove, IL: Apollos, 2014), p. 194.

6. Since the Hebrew for "body" here is grammatically feminine and the pronoun is masculine, the latter appears to refer to the man of God himself ("him"), not just his body ("it") (twice in this verse). So also Walsh, *1 Kings*, p. 187.

7. This translation follows the slightly awkward Hebrew (see ESV margin) rather than the easier Septuagint, on the principle of textual criticism that, all things being equal, the more difficult reading is to be preferred. Here the difference between the two readings does not appear significant.

8. These are all the previous occurrences in Samuel and Kings of the verb (*sapad*) rendered "mourn" in verses 29, 30. It occurs twice more in 1 Kings 14:13, 18.

9. "The man is buried, then, not in his ancestor's tomb but in a tomb nonetheless belonging to his 'family.'" Walsh, *1 Kings*, p. 188.

10. The Hebrew word is typically found in laments for the dead. H. J. Zobel, "*hoy*," *TDOT* 3, p. 361.

11. We should not suppose that the old prophet himself anticipated the term "Samaria." The historian translates his words, so to speak, into the language of his own time. So C. F. Keil, "1 and 2 Kings," in C. F. Keil and F. Delitzsch, *Commentary on the Old Testament*, Vol. 3 (Peabody, MA: Hendrickson Publishers, 1996), p. 145.

12. Karl Barth, *Church Dogmatics*, II/2 (Edinburgh: T. & T. Clark, 1957), p. 402.

13. In verse 34 the Hebrew has literally, "*in* this thing," expressing "the idea of being and persisting in a thing." Keil, *Kings*, p. 147.

14. "Sin" could be rendered "failure." Cf. 1:21. See note 40 to Chapter 3. Also John Gray, *I & II Kings: A Commentary*, Third, Fully Revised, Edition (London: SCM, 1977), p. 333.

15. "To cut off" is more literally "to make disappear," hence "to destroy." See H. Eising, "*kkhd*," *TDOT* 7, p. 130.

16. See the very similar words of Amos in Amos 9:8, also with reference to the northern kingdom, but about a century and a half after our King Jeroboam. The Hebrew verb (*shmd* hiphil) rendered "destroy" is particularly forceful and refers to an action after which nothing is left. The action may be actual annihilation or something like banishment. The verb occurs frequently in Deuteronomy, referring either to the annihilation of the original inhabitants of the land of Canaan (Deuteronomy 7:23, 24; 9:3; 12:30; 31:3, 4; 33:27) or to the possibility of the people of Israel being "destroyed" (Deuteronomy 1:27; 4:3, 26; 6:15; 7:4; 9:8, 14, 19, 25; 28:20, 24, 45, 48, 51, 61, 63; cf. Genesis 34:30). In the books of Samuel and Kings the verb is used of the (possible) destruction (in various senses) of royal dynasties (see 1 Samuel 24:21; 2 Samuel 14:7, 11, 16; 1 Kings 13:34; 15:29; 16:12; 2 Kings 10:17, 28 [ESV, "wiped out"]). See N. Lohfink, "*smd*," *TDOT* 15, pp. 177–98.

Chapter Thirty: Deceiving God

1. See Joshua 12:24. For the probable location of Tirzah, see Map 6–2 in Currid, *Atlas*, p. 142. It is suggested that the probable site "would have been a strategic location in Jeroboam's attempt to establish and maintain control of the fledgling kingdom." Dale W. Manor, "Tirzah (Place)," *ABD* 6, p. 574.

2. The precise chronology is notoriously difficult, but here I am taking as my guide John Bright who proposes 901 B.C. for the death of Jeroboam and 876 B.C. for the accession of Omri. John Bright, *A History of Israel*, Third Edition (London: SCM, 1980), p. 470.

3. Walsh argues (I think unconvincingly) that the phrase may mean "There came a time when. . . ." Jerome T. Walsh, *1 Kings*, Berit Olam: Studies in Hebrew Narrative & Poetry (Collegeville, MN: The Liturgical Press, 1996), p. 193. This is based on the view that because Ahijah was old (as we will see in verse 4) and relations between the prophet and the king seem strained, this must have been late in Jeroboam's reign. But we do not know how old Ahijah was at the beginning of Jeroboam's reign, nor how soon there may have been a falling out. It is difficult to imagine that Ahijah was pleased with Jeroboam's innovations (early in his reign) at Dan and Bethel.

4. On this point I agree with Walsh. Ibid.

5. The Hebrew word (*khalah*, "fell sick") can refer to relatively minor illness (1 Samuel 30:13; 2 Samuel 13:2; 1 Kings 15:23), even feigned sickness (1 Samuel 19:14; 2 Samuel 13:5, 6), as well as fatal (or potentially so) disease (1 Kings 17:17; 2 Kings 1:2; 8:7, 29; 13:14; 20:1, 12).

6. Although this supposition is not explicitly confirmed in the text, the various hints in this direction include the extent of national mourning when the child died (v. 18).

7. On Yahweh, see our discussion of 5:7b.

8. The Hebrew has a particle here (*na'*) that softens the imperative to sound more like a request than a command. Since the speaker was the king and her husband, the politeness may have been more formal than real.

9. The verb (*shnh* hitpael) translated "disguise" appears in this form only here in the Old Testament. Another form of the verb occurs, tellingly, in 1 Samuel 21:13

where David "changed" his behavior in order to deceive his Philistine enemies. It is not entirely unfair to suggest that Jeroboam was dealing with God (as we will see) after the manner of David's behavior toward the Philistines!

10. For a discussion of several stories of kings and disguises in the Old Testament and their theological importance see Richard Coggins, "On Kings and Disguises," *JSOT* 50 (1991), pp. 55–62.

11. On Shiloh's earlier history, see John Woodhouse, *1 Samuel: Looking for a Leader*, Preaching the Word (Wheaton, IL: Crossway, 2008), p. 26.

12. The Hebrew word (*na'ar*) can refer to a young child, but also to a mature young man. At this time Jeroboam's son may not have been a child. On the Hebrew word, see note 15 to Chapter 8.

13. Matthew Henry, *Matthew Henry's Commentary on the Whole Bible*, Vol. 2 (Old Tappan, NJ: Fleming H. Revell Company, no date), p. 651.

14. Verse 4 repeats words and phrases from these earlier references.

15. Such conjectures are not certainties. It is possible to imagine motives for the disguise, even if Jeroboam knew about Ahijah's blindness. However, what the narrator chooses to tell us, and not tell us, seems to me to lead his readers to think along the lines I have indicated.

16. The Hebrew syntax is disjunctive. *IBH*, p. 162. So NIV, HCSB.

17. In the Hebrew sentence "the LORD" is emphatic. The actions of all other characters fade in significance, because "*the LORD* had said . . ."

18. More literally, "to seek a word from you toward her son." This suggests that she was seeking a word that would be directed toward the boy, effecting his healing.

19. In this sentence I have followed the Hebrew quite literally (similarly NIV, HCSB; also Walsh, *1 Kings*, p. 195; Lissa M. Wray Beal, *1 & 2 Kings*, Apollos Old Testament Commentary, Vol. 9 [Nottingham, UK and Downers Grove, IL: Apollos, 2014], p. 197). The ESV ends the Lord's speech before this sentence and then makes the sentence in question a comment by the narrator: "When she came, she pretended to be another woman." This involves revocalizing the Hebrew, following the Septuagint. So also John Gray, *I & II Kings: A Commentary*, Third, Fully Revised, Edition (London: SCM, 1977), p. 334. The Hebrew, though a little awkward, makes better sense. It explains how the blind Ahijah knew that Jeroboam's wife was in disguise, even before she entered the house (v. 6).

20. The English convention of quotation marks could mislead us into thinking that the Lord actually said, "Thus and thus." Hebrew does not mark quotations in the same way and "Thus and thus" are the narrator's way of keeping us in suspense as to precisely what Ahijah will say. I have suggested a similar intrusion of the narrator's words ("Josiah by name") into the quotation in 13:2.

21. The Hebrew syntax is conjunctive. *IBH*, p. 162.

22. Ahijah used exactly the same word that he had heard from the Lord at the end of verse 5.

23. "I" is emphatic. "*I* am the one being sent."

24. The force of the word I have rendered "hard" (*qashah*) can be seen in 12:4 ("heavy"), 13 ("harshly").

25. Previously in 1 Kings the title "God of Israel" has resonated with God's kindness to his people in keeping the promise to David concerning his son's king-

dom (1:30, 48) and the building of the house for his name (8:15, 17, 20, 23, 25, 26). The seriousness of Solomon's apostasy is that he turned from "the LORD, the God of Israel" (11:9). It was "the LORD, the God of Israel" who had given Jeroboam the ten tribes (11:31). See also note 26 to Chapter 4.

26. The term (*nagiyd*, "leader") sometimes seems to be used as a deliberate alternative to "king," avoiding some of the connotations of the latter. See our discussion of the same word (ESV, "ruler") in 1:35c.

27. Now "Israel" clearly has its narrower sense, the northern kingdom.

28. We should by now be familiar with this remarkably positive view of David. See 3:6, 14; 9:4; 11:4, 6, 33, 34, 38 and particularly our discussion of 3:6.

29. So Gray, *Kings*, p. 337.

30. Concerning Israel, see 14:15; 15:30; 16:2, 7, 13, 26, 33; 21:22; 22:53; 2 Kings 17:11, 17; 23:19. Concerning Judah, see 2 Kings 21:6, 15; 22:17; 23:26.

31. Similarly N. Lohfink, "*ka'as*," *TDOT* 7, pp. 286, 287.

32. There are a number of Hebrew words for anger. The much more common word (*'anaph*) was used in 8:46; 11:9. My comments here apply to the particular word (verbal and noun forms of *k's*) found in 14:9. See Jan Bergman and Bo Johnson, "*'anap*," *TDOT* 1, pp. 351–56.

33. The particular vocabulary here for the Lord's anger had been used once in the book of Judges when the people of Israel "abandoned the LORD, the God of their fathers, who had brought them out of the land of Egypt" and "went after other gods, from among the gods of the peoples who were around them, and bowed down to them" (Judges 2:12). Just like Jeroboam! It had appeared six times in Deuteronomy, anticipating the apostasy that Jeroboam had now introduced (Deuteronomy 4:25; 31:29; 32:16, 19, 21 [twice]), and once with reference to the earlier version of what Jeroboam did, when Aaron made a golden bull (Deuteronomy 9:18).

34. "Therefore behold" "introduces a prophetic threat in the imminent future, as regularly in the prophetic books." Gray, *Kings*, p. 337.

35. The Hebrew has a participle here, expressing a vivid present tense: "Therefore, here I come bringing evil upon the house of Jeroboam!" Walsh, *1 Kings*, p. 197.

36. "Harm" is a good rendering because what God will do is not, of course, morally "evil." However, the English obscures a word play on the "evil" that Jeroboam had done (v. 9).

37. On the expression itself see Woodhouse, *1 Samuel*, p. 619, note 18.

38. See Gray, *Kings*, pp. 337, 338.

39. Walsh compares English phrases like "man and boy" or "young and old." Walsh, *1 Kings*, p. 197. Provan suggests that "it is their nature as sources of 'power' and 'help' to the king that is in view." Iain W. Provan, *1 & 2 Kings*, Understanding the Bible Commentary Series (Grand Rapids, MI: Baker Books, 1995), p. 119.

40. "The dogs, excluded from dwelling-houses . . . were the scavengers of the ancient East. Never regularly fed, they were ready at all times to devour any edible thing exposed in the streets." Gray, *Kings*, p. 338.

41. The bitter poignancy of the moment is underlined by the word the prophet used (*yeled*, "child"), which is cognate with the verb *yalad*, "to give birth," thus alluding to the mother-child relationship. See our discussion of this word in 3:25. The word does not necessarily refer to a young child.

42. "Today" is awkward and should probably be taken with the following words at the end of verse 14 (ESV, "And henceforth . . ."). The whole phase is hardly translatable (literally, "this is the day and what? even now"). Attempts to convey the sense include: "This first; and what next?" (REB); "This is the day, yes, even today!" (HCSB); "This is the day! What? Yes, even now" (1984 NIV); "Even now this is beginning to happen" (NIV); "This is the day! What more can there be now?" (Provan, *Kings*, p. 120); "This today—then what indeed is next?" (Beal, *Kings*, p. 197). Walsh suggests that we read the words "as an alien voice . . . speaking to us from the days of the downfall of Jeroboam or perhaps of the northern kingdom: 'This is happening! Now, what next?'" Walsh, *1 Kings*, p. 198.

43. See note 34 to Chapter 10.

44. The force of this part of Ahijah's speech is captured well by Leithart: "One day, Israel's clock will be turned back, and Israel's history will unravel like a movie in reverse. The people who came through the sea of reeds will be shaken like a reed in the water; the people whom God planted as his vine and as his oak will be uprooted and scattered; and the people who long ago left Gentile Egypt, the land of the Nile, to settle in the promised land will one day return to another Gentile nation, beyond the River Euphrates." Peter J. Leithart, *1 & 2 Kings*, Brazos Theological Commentary on the Bible (Grand Rapids, MI: Brazos Press, 2006), p. 106.

45. John Day, "Asherah (Deity)," *ABD* 1, p. 483.

46. On "the word of the LORD," see the introduction to Chapter 27.

47. "Chronicles" (NIV, "annals"; HCSB, "Historical Record") renders exactly the same Hebrew term (*debariym*) as "acts" earlier in the verse, which is the common Hebrew word for "words" or "things." In this context it seems to be a technical term for historical records of some kind.

48. For various suggestions about these books, see Duane L. Christensen, "Chronicles of the Kings (Israel/Judah), Book of the," *ABD* 1, pp. 991, 992.

49. The years of Jeroboam's reign were about 922–901 B.C.

Chapter Thirty-One: Do You Dare to Hope?

1. The years of Rehoboam's reign were about 922–915 B.C.

2. This calculation assumes that the forty years of Solomon's reign dates from David's death (that is, beginning at 2:12) and does not include the period of co-regency that began with his anointing and acclamation in 1:39. This is the position reflected in John Bright's chronology. John Bright, *A History of Israel*, Third Edition (London: SCM, 1980), p. 469. If Solomon's forty years includes the co-regency, then Rehoboam would have been born, say, two or three years before David's death. This is reflected in the chronology presented by Mordecai Cogan, "Chronology, Hebrew Bible," *ABD* 1, p. 1010. See further our discussion of 15:1, 2a.

3. On the significance of Jerusalem for those who believe the promises of God, see the exposition of 2 Samuel 5:4–16 in John Woodhouse, *2 Samuel: Your Kingdom Come*, Preaching the Word (Wheaton, IL: Crossway, 2015), pp. 153–63. Gray makes the observation that "the situation of Jerusalem as the capital of Judah was precarious, and only its sacral significance and its status as a crown possession on which the Davidic dynasty based its authority may have prevented Jerusalem being superseded at this time by either Bethlehem or Hebron." John Gray, *I & II Kings: A Commentary*, Third, Fully Revised, Edition (London: SCM, 1977), p. 352.

4. The Hebrew has a striking alliteration that seems to highlight the two "names" in these sentences: ". . . to put (*shum*) his name (*shemo*) there (*sham*). And the name (*shem*) of his mother. . . ."

5. On Ammonites, see our discussion of 11:1 and note 12 to Chapter 22.

6. There are incidental references to the mothers of just three of the northern kings: Jeroboam (1 Kings 11:26), Ahaziah (1 Kings 22:52), and Joram (2 Kings 9:22). In contrast, the formal notices of almost all of the southern kings include the mother's name (1 Kings 14:21; 15:2, 10; 22:42; 2 Kings 8:26; 12:1; 14:2; 15:2, 33; 18:2; 21:1, 19; 22:1; 23:31, 36; 24:8, 18). The exceptions are Jehoram and Ahaz (2 Kings 8:17; 16:2). "The omission of any such notice in the case of the kings of Israel may indicate that affairs in Israel were peripheral to the interest of the Judean editor. With the new significance of the hereditary principle the mother of the heir-apparent had a distinctive status. Perhaps the omission of any reference to the queen-mother in Northern Israel reflects the fact that the hereditary monarchy was never freely accepted there." Gray, *Kings*, p. 342.

7. Was Naamah perhaps related to the Shobi, the son of Nahash the Ammonite, with whom David seems to have had good relations (see 2 Samuel 10:2; 17:27)?

8. The Hebrew words for "anger" (*k's*) in 14:9, 15 and "jealousy" (*qn'*) in 14:22 are used as near synonyms in Deuteronomy 32:16, 21; Ezekiel 16:42; and especially Psalm 78:58.

9. E. Reuter, "*qn'*," *TDOT* 13, p. 49.

10. The ESV's "they also" suggests that building high places, pillars and Asherim, etc., was additional to the "sins" of verse 22. The alternative, "they themselves," suggests these things are an enumeration of those "sins."

11. J. Gamberoni, "*masseba*," *TDOT* 8, p. 485.

12. "[T]hey may well have been phallic symbols." Iain Provan, *1 & 2 Kings*, Understanding the Bible Commentary Series (Grand Rapids, MI: Baker Books, 1995), p. 122. ". . . as a specifically or emphatically masculine symbol." Gamberoni, "*masseba*," *TDOT* 8, p. 493.

13. "Judah has abandoned its first lover for others and made him 'jealous.'" Provan, *1 & 2 Kings*, p. 123.

14. Cult prostitution is understood as sexual intercourse with worshippers at a sacred place, in the belief that this would encourage the gods and goddesses to do likewise, resulting in the increased fertility of the land and the people. This traditional understanding is probably influenced by the context of the expression in Hosea 4:14. This is the view presented in O. J. Baab, "Prostitution," *IDB* 3, pp. 931–34. More recently the evidence for such a belief and practice has been questioned. The possibility (prohibited!) of the house of the Lord receiving the fees of a prostitute (Deuteronomy 23:18) is noted, but evidence (in the Old Testament or elsewhere) for cult prostitution is not convincing. So Karel van der Toorn, "Cultic Prostitution," *ABD* 5, pp. 510–13; W. Kornfeld and H. Ringgren, "*qds*," *TDOT* 12, pp. 542, 543. Davis notes that he is "not convinced" by these more recent arguments. Dale Ralph Davis, *The Wisdom and the Folly: An Exposition of the Book of First Kings* (Fearn, Ross-shire, UK: Christian Focus, 2002), p. 235, note 11.

15. The Hebrew term (*to'ebah*) here seems to refer to a range of practices abhorrent to the Lord. It is rendered "despicable practices" in 2 Kings 16:3; 21:2; "abominations" in 2 Kings 21:11. It is different from the term (*shiqquts*) translated

"abomination" in 1 Kings 11:5, 7, but both words are found as synonyms in 2 Kings 23:13.

16. See note 39 to Chapter 24.

17. See Bright, *History*, pp. 233, 234; K. A. Kitchen, *The Bible in Its World: Archaeology and the Bible Today* (Exeter: The Paternoster Press, 1977), pp. 109, 110.

18. A fuller account, also indicating that there was much more to this Egyptian campaign than we are told in 1 Kings 14, is found in 2 Chronicles 12:1–12. Our primary task here is to listen to what the writer of 1 Kings chooses to tell us.

19. The Hebrew emphasizes "everything."

20. Provan, *Kings*, p. 123.

21. In the list of 154 conquered places in Shishak's inscription, Jerusalem is conspicuously absent. Donald B. Redford, "Shishak," *ABD* 5, p. 1222.

22. Similarly Peter J. Leithart, *1 & 2 Kings*, Brazos Theological Commentary on the Bible (Grand Rapids, MI: Brazos Press, 2006), p. 108, note 5.

23. On bronze, see our discussion of 7:14.

24. "[T]he king is forced to 'fake it' with bronze decorations instead of gold, and even they must be kept under lock and key." Walter Brueggemann, *1 & 2 Kings*, Smyth & Helwys Bible Commentary (Macon, GA: Smyth & Helwys, 2000), p. 182.

25. Gray, *Kings*, p. 349. Similarly C. F. Keil, "1 and 2 Kings," in C. F. Keil and F. Delitzsch, *Commentary on the Old Testament*, Vol. 3 (Peabody, MA: Hendrickson Publishers, 1996), p. 152.

26. Issues arising from the forms of Abijam's name are discussed in Keith W. Whitelam, "Abijah, King of Judah," *ABD* 1, p. 18. Some consider that the form in 1 Kings (Abijam) is a scribal error. So Gray, *Kings*, p. 347, note c. Others think that the form in 2 Chronicles (Abijah) is "an ideologically motivated change," since *yam/ jam* ("Sea") is the name of a pagan god. So Lissa M. Wray Beal, *1 & 2 Kings*, Apollos Old Testament Commentary, Vol. 9 (Nottingham, UK and Downers Grove, IL: Apollos, 2014), p. 210.

27. Similarly Provan, *Kings*, p. 122.

Chapter Thirty-Two: Where Is the Promise?

1. Brueggemann's stimulating commentary on 1 and 2 Kings is an outstanding example of this approach. He frequently moves from the political situation of Israel or Judah to what he regards as comparable circumstances in the United States of America today. Walter Brueggemann, *1 & 2 Kings* Smyth & Helwys Bible Commentary (Macon, GA: Smyth & Helwys, 2000).

2. The years of Abijam's reign were about 915–913 B.C.

3. A later historian has provided a more detailed account of Abijam's reign, with a significantly different evaluation of him (2 Chronicles 13). Here our interest will focus on the 1 Kings account. As Davis helpfully notes, "the writers of Chronicles and Kings are making two different points. Chronicles implies Abijah was reasonably orthodox when compared to Jeroboam; Kings says he is covenantally defective when compared to David." Dale Ralph Davis, *The Wisdom and the Folly: An Exposition of the Book of First Kings* (Fearn, Ross-shire, UK: Christian Focus, 2002), p. 173, note 5.

4. For a clear and concise presentation of the issues from which my presentation here has drawn, see Mordecai Cogan, "Chronology, Hebrew Bible," *ABD* 1, pp. 1006–7. Also Simon J. DeVries, "Chronology, OT," *IDBSup*, pp. 161–166.

5. So C. F. Keil, "1 and 2 Kings," in C. F. Keil and F. Delitzsch, *Commentary on the Old Testament*, Vol. 3 (Peabody, MA: Hendrickson Publishers, 1996), p. 153; John Gray, *I & II Kings: A Commentary*, Third, Fully Revised, Edition (London: SCM, 1977), pp. 347, 348, note g. Beal rejects this understanding. Lissa M. Wray Beal, *1 & 2 Kings*, Apollos Old Testament Commentary, Vol. 9 (Nottingham, UK and Downers Grove, IL: Apollos, 2014), p. 210. Even if this Abishalom was not David's son Absalom (which I think is unlikely), the name is enough to remind readers of the treacherous prince. The literary effect does not depend entirely on the sure identification of Abishalom. Cf. Jerome T. Walsh, *1 Kings*, Berit Olam: Studies in Hebrew Narrative & Poetry (Collegeville, MN: The Liturgical Press, 1996), p. 210.

6. It seems that Absalom's three sons (2 Samuel 14:27) died young (see 2 Samuel 18:18). Josephus claims that Maacah was the daughter of Tamar who was fifty when Solomon died. See Keil, *Kings*, p. 153. It is just possible that Maacah was another daughter of Absalom, but then she would have been a lot older than Rehoboam who was born a considerable time after Absalom's death.

7. See note 11 to Chapter 18.

8. See our discussion of 3:6.

9. It is possible to read verse 4 as a reference to Solomon's kingdom: "Nevertheless, for David's sake the Lord his God *had given* him [that is, David] a lamp in Jerusalem, setting up his son [that is, Solomon] after him, and establishing Jerusalem [cf. 2:46b]." This would mean that the writer was pointing to the glory of Solomon's kingdom as a sign of God's faithfulness to his promise to David. I think that the context, including the reference to David as Abijam's "father" at the end of verse 3, makes it more natural to understand "his son" here as Abijam.

10. The Hebrew verb (*'md* hiphil) rendered "establishing" means "to cause to stand firm" as in 2 Samuel 22:34 (ESV, "set [me] secure"). It is the opposite of "overthrow." BDB, p. 764.

11. The Hebrew conjunction (*'asher*) here indicates a connection between what precedes and what follows, but that connection is not necessarily *causal* as "because" suggests.

12. "Except" represents the Hebrew particle (*raq*) we have noted a number of times, signaling that what follows is some kind of contrast or limitation to what has just been said. See 3:2, 3; 8:9, 19; 11:13.

13. In addition to our discussion of 3:6, see John Woodhouse, *2 Samuel: Your Kingdom Come*, Preaching the Word (Wheaton, IL: Crossway, 2015), pp. 510–13.

14. See our discussion of 14:19.

15. See note 3.

16. Once again there is a much longer account of Asa's reign in 2 Chronicles 14—16 in which we hear complexities not mentioned by the writer of 1 Kings. See note 3.

17. The years of Asa's reign were about 913–873 B.C.

18. Provan regards this as a possibility "certainly not beyond imagining (cf. Lev. 18:6ff.)." Iain W. Provan, *1 & 2 Kings*, Understanding the Bible Commentary Series (Grand Rapids, MI: Baker Books, 1995), p. 126. Leithart regards it as a fact. "Abijam is a true 'son of Absalom,' who takes his father's wife (2 Sam. 16:20–23)."

Peter J. Leithart, *1 & 2 Kings*, Brazos Theological Commentary on the Bible (Grand Rapids, MI: Brazos Press, 2006), p. 111.

19. The argument against this understanding is that in identical contexts (14:21, 31; 22:42; 2 Kings 8:26; 12:1; 14:2; 15:2, 33; 18:2; 21:1, 19; 22:1; 23:31, 36; 24:8, 18; we could add 1 Kings 11:26) "mother" seems to always mean mother. Provan, *Kings*, p. 126. My response is that this is not an identical context since Maacah *was* Asa's grandmother, a factor not present in the other settings.

20. This also suggests the "right" that the people had not done under old Solomon according to 11:33 and the "right" God required Jeroboam to do in 11:38.

21. In due course we will hear of seven more kings in Judah who did what was "right," as Asa did. They were Jehoshaphat (Asa's son), Jehoash, Amaziah, Azariah (Uzziah), Jotham, Hezekiah, and Josiah (22:43; 2 Kings 12:2; 14:3; 15:3, 34; 18:3; 22:2). Cf. Jehu in 2 Kings 10:30.

22. As we expound 1 Kings, I am deliberately not drawing on additional information provided by a later writer in 2 Chronicles 14—16. See note 3.

23. See our discussion of 14:24a.

24. The verb (*'br* hiphil) appears quite frequently with various meanings. The two occurrences noted here may not therefore be particularly striking.

25. By "previously" I mean at an earlier point in the canonical narrative that runs from Genesis to 2 Kings. It assumes nothing about when the material was written.

26. The term (*gillulim*) occurs in 21:26; 2 Kings 17:12; 21:11, 21; 23:24. It is strikingly common (thirty-nine times) in the book of Ezekiel. See H. D. Preuss, "*gillulim*," *TDOT* 3, pp. 1–5.

27. The Hebrew term (*gebirah*) represented by "queen mother" (which does not have the word for "queen" or "mother") appears to be a title that "implied a certain dignity and special powers." See the thorough discussion in Roland de Vaux, *Ancient Israel: Its Life and Institutions*, trans. John McHugh (London: Darton, Longman & Todd, 1973), pp. 117–19. De Vaux prefers to render the title "Great Lady."

28. See Gray, *Kings*, p. 350.

29. See Woodhouse, *2 Samuel*, p. 393.

30. "[T]he intransitive verb is used to spare the kings censure in the Deuteronomistic appraisal of them." Gray, *Kings*, p. 349, note a, citing Martin Noth.

31. So Keil, *Kings*, p. 154.

32. Again (as in v. 5) the Hebrew particle (*raq*) signals that what follows is some kind of contrast or limitation to what has just been said.

33. We are given no more details about where these "sacred gifts" came from. The same Hebrew word (*qodesh*) was used in the very similar context of 7:51 (ESV, "the things . . . dedicated"), adding to the impression that Asa was acting to restore the former glory of the house of the Lord.

34. There are several places named Ramah (see Joshua 19:8 ["Ramah of the Negeb"], 29, 36; also 1 Samuel 30:27 ["Ramoth of the Negeb"]). See John Woodhouse, *1 Samuel: Looking for a Leader*, Preaching the Word (Wheaton, IL: Crossway, 2008), p. 555, note 5. In identifying this Ramah with Samuel's hometown I am following Patrick M. Arnold, "Ramah," *ABD* 5, p. 614. Gray rejects the identification. Gray, *Kings*, p. 352.

35. See Map 6–11 in Currid, *Atlas*, p. 150.

36. Contra Beal who states that Ramah was "controlled by Israel since the secession," mistakenly citing Arnold, who actually says, "Ramah was left inside Judah very near to the N border with Israel after the division of the kingdom." Arnold, "Ramah," p. 614; Beal, *Kings*, p. 212.

37. So Davis, *Wisdom*, p. 175.

38. See note 46 to Chapter 21.

39. The Hebrew is ambiguous. Asa could be referring to an existing covenant ("There is . . ."). So RV; HCSB; Gray, *Kings*, p. 352. Or he may be proposing one ("Let there be . . ."). So REB; ESV; NIV; Beal, *Kings*, p. 209. The reference to the fathers of Asa and Ben-hadad suggests that the covenant already existed. Curiously the ESV translates precisely the same wording in the parallel passage as I am proposing here: "There is a covenant between me and you, as there was between my father and your father" (2 Chronicles 16:3).

40. On the various Ben-hadads, see note 1 to Chapter 42.

41. On Hadad, see our discussion of 11:14.

42. Rimmon was a god who appears in 2 Kings 5:18 and may have been another name for Hadad (as suggested by the compound name "Hadad-rimmon" in Zechariah 12:11). Pauline A. Viviano, "Tabrimmon (Person)," *ABD* 6, p. 305.

43. So Gray, *Kings*, p. 353.

44. Contra Gray, *Kings*, p. 352.

45. This discomfort is confirmed by the more detailed account in 2 Chronicles (see 2 Chronicles 16:7). However, I am suggesting that the 1 Kings account itself is troubling to a thoughtful reader.

46. See also 2 Kings 16:8. The connotations of the word (*shokhad*) in question may be seen in a wide range of texts, where it is usually translated "bribe." See Exodus 23:8; Deuteronomy 16:19; 27:25; 1 Samuel 8:3; Job 15:34; Psalm 15:5; 26:10; Proverbs 17:8, 23; 21:14; Isaiah 1:23; 5:23; 33:15; Ezekiel 22:12; Micah 3:11. These texts are generally about *taking* bribes. One of the Lord's distinctive qualities is that he "takes no bribe" (Deuteronomy 10:17; 2 Chronicles 19:7). The problem with bribes is that justice is corrupted. Either the person accepting the bribe only does what is right when bribed or is prepared to act unjustly for a fee. The person who *pays* a bribe is obviously acting wrongly when the gift secures unjust actions. The moral dilemma of a person who is forced to pay a bribe in order to get a just outcome is not directly addressed in the Old Testament, although of course the person requiring the bribe would be condemned. See K. M. Beyse, "*sahad*," *TDOT* 14, pp. 555–58.

47. It is apparently coincidental that the name of Asa's disgraced grandmother, Maacah, is also part of this place name. The town featured in the story of King David (2 Samuel 20:14, 15). See Woodhouse, *2 Samuel*, p. 476.

48. See Map 6–11 in Currid, *Atlas*, p. 150.

49. See Map 4–13 in Currid, *Atlas*, p. 107.

50. See Map 6–11 in Currid, *Atlas*, p. 150. "Mizpah" means "a lookout post," and "Geba" means "a hill," and these terms are applied to several places in the Old Testament. Gray, *Kings*, p. 355.

51. On the Hebrew particle (*raq*), see verses 5, 14 and our discussion of "however" in 3:2 and "only" in 3:3.

52. Second Chronicles 16:12 has a little more to say about this, but it is not directly relevant to our exposition of 1 Kings.

Chapter Thirty-Three: Power Politics in Perspective

1. There will be a brief glance at the southern kingdom in 22:41–50 to notice the reign of Asa's son Jehoshaphat and in 2 Kings 8:16–24 to see Jehoshaphat's son Jehoram and grandson Ahaziah. Otherwise sustained attention will not return to the southern kingdom until 2 Kings 11.

2. A number of commentators focus on this repetitious pattern and discuss at some length the tedious nature of sin and idolatry. So Dale Ralph Davis, *The Wisdom and the Folly: An Exposition of the Book of First Kings* (Fearn, Ross-shire, UK: Christian Focus, 2002), pp. 181, 182; Peter J. Leithart, *1 & 2 Kings*, Brazos Theological Commentary on the Bible (Grand Rapids, MI: Brazos Press, 2006), pp. 110–16; Lissa M. Wray Beal, *1 & 2 Kings*, Apollos Old Testament Commentary, Vol. 9 (Nottingham, UK and Downers Grove, IL: Apollos, 2014), pp. 215–17.

3. Nadab's reign was about 900–901 B.C.

4. The full text of this paragraph looks forward to a yet future time when the people will be carried away to the land of the enemy. However, the prayer can be applied in principle to the days of Nadab.

5. "Ahijah of Issachar may have sired Baasha, but Ahijah of Shiloh is his father in the spirit." Jerome T. Walsh, *1 Kings*, Berit Olam: Studies in Hebrew Narrative & Poetry (Collegeville, MN: The Liturgical Press, 1996), p. 213; similarly Leithart, *Kings*, p. 114.

6. See Map 4–13 in Currid, *Atlas*, p. 107.

7. Walter Brueggemann, *1 & 2 Kings*, Smyth & Helwys Bible Commentary (Macon, GA: Smyth & Helwys, 2000), pp. 192, 193.

8. See Map 6–11 in Currid, *Atlas*, p. 150.

9. The Hebrew term (*qashar*) has a basic meaning, "to bind," and frequently refers to people bound in a conspiracy. J. Conrad, "*qashar*," *TDOT* 13, p. 199.

10. In the northern kingdom there will be six plots ("conspiracies") led by individuals to take hold of the throne: Baasha against Nadab (15:27); Zimri against Elah (16:9, 16, 20); Jehu against Joram (2 Kings 9:14; 10:9); Shallum against Zechariah (2 Kings 15:10, 15); Pekah against Pekahiah (2 Kings 15:25); and Hoshea against Pekah (2 Kings 15:30). In the southern kingdom there will be three schemes by groups resulting in the reigning king being replaced by another son of David: Amaziah for Joash (2 Kings 12:20, 21); Azariah for Amaziah (2 Kings 14:19, 21); Josiah for Amon (2 Kings 21:23, 26). See also 2 Kings 11:14 (ESV, "Treason!"); 17:4 ("treachery").

11. On "the word of the LORD," see the introduction to Chapter 27.

12. "Herein he was barbarous, but God was righteous." Matthew Henry, *Matthew Henry's Commentary on the Whole Bible*, Vol. 2 (Old Tappan, NJ: Fleming H. Revell Company, no date), p. 659.

13. The years of Baasha's reign were about 900–877 B.C.

14. Similarly John Gray, *I & II Kings: A Commentary*, Third, Fully Revised, Edition (London: SCM, 1977), p. 358, note a; also Beal, *Kings*, p. 219.

15. He makes an appearance many (perhaps fifty?) years later in 2 Chronicles 19:2, which suggests that he was quite a young man in the days of Baasha and that

his appearance here was late in Baasha's reign. He was apparently something of an historian, being responsible for a record of Jehoshaphat's reign (2 Chronicles 20:34).

16. So Brueggemann, *Kings*, p. 197.

17. See note 26 to Chapter 30.

18. Brueggemann, *Kings*, p. 198.

19. The Hebrew preposition (*'el*) usually means "to" or "towards." So Walsh, *1 Kings*, p. 214. Leithart argues for "against." Leithart, *Kings*, p. 115, note 7.

20. The Hebrew behind "and also because he destroyed it" is a little difficult, but the ESV is almost certainly right. Similarly JB; REB; NIV; HCSB; Davis, *Wisdom*, p. 184, note 5; Beal, *Kings*, p. 219. Some seem to misunderstand or underestimate the profound theological truth represented in these words and insist that since the destruction of the house of Jeroboam was according to the word of the Lord, it could not also be a reason for Baasha's condemnation. So Gray renders the phrase, "in spite of the fact that he had struck it down." Gray, *Kings*, pp. 359, 361, following James A. Montgomery, *A Critical and Exegetical Commentary on the Books of Kings*, The International Critical Commentary (Edinburgh: T. & T. Clark, 1951), pp. 282, 289. Walsh finds that the phrase (as rendered in the ESV) "has the shocking effect of finding Baasha blameworthy for actions that in fact fulfilled a prophecy." Walsh, *1 Kings*, p. 214. Precisely.

21. Elah's reign was about 877–876 B.C.

22. The Hebrew behind this sentence may be taken slightly differently. A more literal translation is: "He did not leave for him a male or his relatives or his friend." It is just possibly that "his friend" was a particular person, like David's friend Hushai (2 Samuel 15:37; 16:16, 17) and "the king's friend" among Solomon's officials (1 Kings 4:5).

23. See John Woodhouse, *2 Samuel: Your Kingdom Come*, Preaching the Word (Wheaton, IL: Crossway, 2015), p. 366. More generally the term refers to "a man's brother, uncle, cousin, or some other kinsman who is responsible for standing up for him and maintaining his rights." H. Ringgren, "*ga'al*," *TDOT* 2, p. 351.

24. The word (*hebel*) is found most frequently in Ecclesiastes (ESV, "vanity"). In 1 Kings it occurs only here and 16:26. However, it is important in the climactic statement in 2 Kings 17:15 (ESV, "false idols," "became false"). K. Seybold, "*hebel*," *TDOT* 3, p. 317.

25. The year was about 876 B.C.

26. Walsh doubts that the males of Elah's family, relatives, and friends could have been tracked down in just seven days. Walsh, *1 Kings*, p. 216, note 6. I suspect that it was accomplished with a great deal of preplanning.

27. "All Israel" indicates that the troops took on the role of the representative assembly of Israel, as, in other contexts, the elders sometimes do. See 8:1, 2; 12:1, 3; also 2 Samuel 5:3.

28. Some have concluded, from the lack of further information about Omri, that he may not have been an Israelite, but may have been a foreigner who had joined himself to the people of Israel (like Uriah the Hittite and Ittai the Gittite in David's day, both also military men, 2 Samuel 23:39; 18:2). If that is so, Omri's thorough acceptance of his new identity in Israel is evidenced by the name given to

his (grand)daughter (Athaliah, a "Yahweh" name, 2 Kings 8:26). Winfried Thiel, "Omri (Person)," *ABD* 5, p. 17.

29. Again "all Israel" refers to the army, considered here as representing the whole nation.

30. "The citadel of the king's house" probably refers to the royal residence in the palace complex. Gray, *Kings*, p. 363, note a.

31. We cannot even be sure that Ginath was his father. It may be the name of his hometown. So Gray, *Kings*, p. 365.

32. The ESV may be taken to suggest that Omri's gaining the upper hand led to ("So") Tibni's death. I suspect that it was the other way around.

33. The years of Omri's reign were about 876–869 B.C.

34. The Hebrew is plural.

35. Beal, *Kings*, p. 224.

36. See Map 6–11 in Currid, *Atlas*, p. 150. "[Omri] saw the wisdom of exchanging an eastward-facing fairly low hilltop for a westward-facing, high and isolated eminence. For strategic location, Samaria can hardly be praised too much. It stands entirely alone, with rich fields on every side. It can be reached directly from Shechem on the east, but looks out over the westernmost Manassite hills toward the coastal highway." Simon J. DeVries, *1 Kings*, Word Biblical Commentary, Vol. 12 (Waco, TX: Word Books, 1985), p. 202.

37. So Gray, *Kings*, p. 367.

38. "The purchase price exceeds the value of barren land," according to Beal, *Kings*, p. 224, who goes on to point out that archaeological evidence suggests that a Canaanite village had earlier stood on the site.

39. These parallels are highlighted by Leithart, *Kings*, p. 119.

40. "On the basis of indirect references and extrabiblical sources, however, one can see that Omri must have been one of Israel's greatest, most energetic, and most foresighted kings." Thiel, "Omri," pp. 18, 19.

41. In the Hebrew "Ahab the son of Omri" stands at the beginning of the verse, emphasizing the name of this notorious king. Indeed the threefold repetition of "Ahab the son of Omri" in verses 29, 30 add to this emphasis. We are going to hear a lot more about this king.

42. The years of Ahab's reign were about 869–850 B.C.

43. The Hebrew lacks "in" and, in effect, identifies the "altar" and the "house": "an altar for Baal, the house of Baal."

44. This information is now known from the Jewish historian Josephus who draws from the historian Menander. For details, see Pauline A. Viviano, "Ethbaal (Person)," *ABD* 2, p. 645. Jezebel "was therefore, as tyrant and murderess of the prophets, a worthy daughter of her father, the idolatrous priest and regicide." C. F. Keil, "1 and 2 Kings," in C. F. Keil and F. Delitzsch, *Commentary on the Old Testament*, Vol. 3 (Peabody, MA: Hendrickson Publishers, 1996), p. 161.

45. See map 6–3 in Currid, *Atlas*, p. 144.

46. Cf. 2 Kings 9:37 (although with a different word for "dung"). So Gale A. Yee, "Jezebel (Person)," *ABD* 3, pp. 848, 849, followed by Beal, *Kings*, p. 225.

47. See John Day, "Baal (Deity)," *ABD* 1, pp. 545–49.

48. Asherah and Baal appear together in several Old Testament texts (Judges 3:7; 6:25–30; 1 Kings 18:19; 2 Kings 17:16; 21:3; 23:4).

49. So Gray, *Kings*, p. 371.

50. "Instead of destroying Canaanites, Ahab busies himself in restoring their cities." Leithart, *Kings*, p. 120.

51. Precisely what happened to Hiel's sons is a matter of some speculation. "At the cost of" is an interpretation of the Hebrew preposition *be* ("in"). Some have suggested a pagan practice of "foundation sacrifice," where (it is supposed) a child was sacrificed and buried in the foundation of a new building to ensure the success and safety of the structure. So DeVries, *1 Kings*, p. 205; followed by Paul House, *1, 2 Kings*, The New American Commentary, Vol. 8, (Nashville: Broadman & Holman Publishers, 1995), p. 204; cf. Montgomery, *Kings*, pp. 287, 288. However, evidence for this practice is far from certain. We simply do not know how these boys died. The more important fact is that their deaths were the fulfillment of the word of the Lord spoken by Joshua. So Donald J. Wiseman, *1 and 2 Kings*, Tyndale Old Testament Commentaries (Leicester, UK: Inter-Varsity Press, 1993), p. 163; Davis, *Wisdom*, p. 200, note 6.

Chapter Thirty-Four: Does Your God Rule the Rain?

1. For a summary of what is known about belief in Baal from the Old Testament and other texts, see John Day, "Baal (Deity)," *ABD* 1, pp. 545–49.

2. By "our Old Testament" I am referring to the arrangement of books in the English versions, which is based on the Septuagint. While the Hebrew Bible is arranged differently, Malachi is still the last of the books of the Prophets.

3. So D. A. Carson, *The Gospel According to John* (Leicester, UK: Inter-Varsity Press and Grand Rapids, MI: Eerdmans, 1991), p. 143.

4. The ESV margin has "of the settlers," following the Hebrew. Similarly John Gray, *1 & II Kings: A Commentary*, Third, Fully Revised, Edition (London: SCM, 1977), p. 377, note a; Jerome T. Walsh, *1 Kings*, Berit Olam: Studies in Hebrew Narrative & Poetry (Collegeville, MN: The Liturgical Press, 1996), p. 226; Dale Ralph Davis, *The Wisdom and the Folly: An Exposition of the Book of First Kings* (Fearn, Ross-shire, UK: Christian Focus, 2002), p .203; Lissa M. Wray Beal, *1 & 2 Kings*, Apollos Old Testament Commentary, Vol. 9 (Nottingham, UK and Downers Grove, IL: Apollos, 2014), p. 228. The ESV main text ("of Tishbe") follows the Septuagint and reflects the fact that the Hebrew word (*toshab*) at this point has the same consonants as the preceding "Tishbite" (*tishbiy*). However, in other contexts *toshab* is rendered in the ESV "foreigner" (Genesis 23:4; Exodus 12:45), "foreign guest" (Leviticus 22:10), "sojourner" (Leviticus 25:6, 23, 35, 40, 47; Numbers 35:15; 1 Chronicles 29:15), "strangers" (Leviticus 25:45), and "guest" (Psalm 39:12).

5. On Yahweh, see our discussion of 5:7b.

6. An alternative is that "Tishbite" was an otherwise unknown category of persons. Walsh, *1 Kings*, p. 225.

7. See Map 6–9 in Currid, *Atlas*, p. 148.

8. ". . . one who lived away from his home and tribal relations in the territory of a different tribe." C. F. Keil, "1 and 2 Kings," in C. F. Keil and F. Delitzsch, *Commentary on the Old Testament*, Vol. 3 (Peabody, MA: Hendrickson Publishers, 1996), p. 165.

9. Gray, *Kings*, pp. 377, 378.

10. The Hebrew for "word" (*dabar*) appears in verses 1, 2, 5, 8, 13 (literally "according to your word"), 15 ("according to the word of Elijah"), 16, 24.

11. On "the word of the LORD," see the introduction to Chapter 27. Compare the most recent mention of "the word of the LORD" in 16:34.

12. Literally "upon the face of the Jordan," which could mean "before" or "toward" the Jordan, not necessarily "east."

13. For one suggested location, see Map 6–3 in Currid, *Atlas*, p. 144.

14. So Iain W. Provan, *1 & 2 Kings*, Understanding the Bible Commentary Series (Grand Rapids, MI: Baker Books, 1995), p. 132; Walsh, *1 Kings*, p. 227; John W. Olley, *The Message of Kings*, The Bible Speaks Today (Nottingham, UK: Inter-Varsity Press, 2011), p. 166.

15. Peter J. Leithart, *1 & 2 Kings*, Brazos Theological Commentary on the Bible (Grand Rapids, MI: Brazos Press, 2006), p. 126.

16. The Hebrew gives emphasis to the surprising object of God's command: "*the ravens* I have commanded . . ." A small emendation of the Hebrew for "ravens" turns them into "Arabs"! Although there is no support for this change in Hebrew manuscripts or ancient versions, Gray argues that this would fit with the theme of Elijah being fed by a foreigner in 17:9. Gray, *Kings*, p. 378, note d.

Chapter Thirty-Five: Is Your God Too Small?

1. J. B. Phillips, *Your God Is Too Small* (New York, London, Toronto, and Sydney: Simon & Schuster, 2004 [first published 1952]), p. 7.

2. Walsh points out that the Jordan's "spring-fed flow is permanent." Jerome T. Walsh, *1 Kings*, Berit Olam: Studies in Hebrew Narrative & Poetry (Collegeville, MN: The Liturgical Press, 1996), p. 233.

3. The small difference in the ESV ("And" in verse 2; "Then" in verse 8) slightly obscures the identical wording of the Hebrew.

4. Ray L. Roth, "Zarephath (Place)," *ABD* 6, p. 1041. See Map 6–3 in Currid, *Atlas*, p. 144.

5. The Hebrew has a double expression here that we could render "widow-woman." So John Gray, *I & II Kings: A Commentary*, Third, Fully Revised, Edition (London: SCM, 1977), p. 379. The two terms reinforce the sense of powerlessness and disadvantage.

6. Verse 8 clearly echoes 17:4 with the exact repetition of "I have commanded," "there," and "to feed you."

7. Similarly Walsh, *1 Kings*, p. 229.

8. The plural of this word is translated "crumbs" in Psalm 147:17 (ESV)!

9. So C. F. Keil, "1 and 2 Kings," in C. F. Keil and F. Delitzsch, *Commentary on the Old Testament*, Vol. 3 (Peabody, MA: Hendrickson Publishers, 1996), p. 167.

10. So Walsh, *1 Kings*, p. 229; Dale Ralph Davis, *The Wisdom and the Folly: An Exposition of the Book of First Kings* (Fearn, Ross-shire, UK: Christian Focus, 2002), p. 213, note 12.

11. This is similar in significance to other foreigners acknowledging the Lord, such as Hiram in 5:7 and the queen of Sheba in 10:9.

12. He appears to be a small bundle in the sad scene in 17:19 and is repeatedly referred to as a "child" in 17:21–23.

13. Gray, *Kings*, p. 380.

14. The Hebrew word (*ma'og*) occurs only twice on the Old Testament (here and Psalm 35:16 [ESV, "feast"]) and seems to be related to another rare word understood to mean "bake" in Ezekiel 4:12.

15. Beal reads too much into the woman's speech: "Her hesitancy expresses her uncertainty of YHWH's power of life." Lissa M. Wray Beal, *1 & 2 Kings*, Apollos Old Testament Commentary, Vol. 9 (Nottingham, UK and Downers Grove, IL: Apollos, 2014), p. 233. The way in which her hesitancy evaporates (v. 15) as soon as she hears the Lord's promise (v. 14) suggests a more positive view of her.

16. The Hebrew word (*'ak*) rendered "But" can make a big difference. See 9:24 ("But"), 11:12 ("Yet"), 11:39 ("but"), and note 41 to Chapter 20.

17. The words "cake" here and "oil" in verse 12 are seen by Walsh as another allusion to the story of Moses (Numbers 11:8, where both words occur). Walsh, *1 Kings*, p. 285.

18. Walsh notes that the best Hebrew manuscripts have "he and she," echoing Elijah's "But first . . ." in verse 13. Walsh, *1 Kings*, p. 230.

19. We will hear more about "her household" in 17:17.

20. Too much should not be read into "many." The Hebrew simply has "days."

21. It is clear that the narrator is reporting what we would call a miracle. Attempts to explain away the miraculous aspect of the story are fundamentally misguided. For example: "The factual basis may be that the generosity of the widow touched the conscience of her better-provided neighbours." Gray, *Kings*, p. 381. For a sensible response, see Davis, *Wisdom*, p. 216, note 17.

22. Tannehill suggests that "the rest of the Lukan story (Acts as well as Luke) should be read in light of this scene." Robert C. Tannehill, *Luke*, Abingdon New Testament Commentaries (Nashville: Abingdon Press, 1996), p. 91.

Chapter Thirty-Six: Can Your God Beat Death?

1. It is possible that some Old Testament texts in which "death" is personified may be polemical and/or poetical reflections of these Canaanite myths. Possible examples include Job 18:13; Psalm 49:14; Isaiah 28:15, 18; Hosea 13:14; Habakkuk 2:5; see also Isaiah 25:8. I am indebted here to an informative article by Theodore J. Lewis, "Mot (Deity)," *ABD* 4, pp. 922–24.

2. The wording of 14:1 and 17:17 is similar. In particular "fell sick" (14:1) and "became ill" (17:17) represent exactly the same Hebrew word.

3. "[T]he narrative rather carefully avoids the bald statement that he was 'dead.'" Walter Brueggemann, *1 & 2 Kings*, Smyth & Helwys Bible Commentary (Macon, GA: Smyth & Helwys, 2000), p. 212.

4. So Hans Walter Wolff, *Anthropology of the Old Testament* (London: SCM, 1974), p. 59. Contra John Gray, *I & II Kings: A Commentary*, Third, Fully Revised, Edition (London: SCM, 1977), p. 382 who thinks the lad may not have been "actually dead." For those with a keen memory, note that there is a difference between the expression here where "breath" is the Hebrew *neshamah* (as in Genesis 2:7; 7:22) and 10:5 where the queen with "no more breath (*ruakh*) in her" was very much alive.

5. The Hebrew idiom here (literally, "What to me and to you?") is rendered "What have I to do with you?" in 2 Samuel 16:10; 2 Kings 3:13 and "What have we to do with each other?" in 2 Chronicles 35:21. The expression is reflected in "What have you to do with us?" in Mark 1:24.

6. The woman's second sentence is either her answer to the question of the first sentence (so RV, REB, ESV) or a further question elaborating the first one (so RV margin, JB, NIV, HCSB). I think the latter is more likely.

7. "Man of God" must remind us of 1 Kings 13 where this title occurs no less than fifteen times.

8. The Hebrew does not indicate whose remembrance she meant, but since she seems to be saying that the remembering of her sin has resulted in her son's death, I understand her to mean *God's* remembrance. So Iain W. Provan, *1 & 2 Kings*, Understanding the Bible Commentary Series (Grand Rapids, MI: Baker Books, 1995), p. 135; contra HCSB, NIV.

9. "He lodged" is literally "he was dwelling there," in exact obedience to the word of the Lord in 17:9 ("dwell there").

10. This paragraph is indebted to Gray, *Kings*, p. 381. Less probably he suggests: "The removal of the invalid to the airy upper chamber, clean of the household debris, was a matter of simple hygiene, and may have been the factual basis of the tradition of the healing of the lad . . ." Ibid., p. 382.

11. Perhaps referring to "other calamities occasioned by the drought." C. F. Keil, "1 and 2 Kings," in C. F. Keil and F. Delitzsch, *Commentary on the Old Testament*, Vol. 3 (Peabody, MA: Hendrickson Publishers, 1996), p. 168.

12. Indeed the Hebrew for "by killing her son" exactly matches "to cause the death of my son" in verse 18.

13. See John Woodhouse, *2 Samuel: Your Kingdom Come*, Preaching the Word (Wheaton, IL: Crossway, 2015), pp. 48, 560, note 8.

14. Cf. Jerome T. Walsh, *1 Kings*, Berit Olam: Studies in Hebrew Narrative & Poetry (Collegeville, MN: The Liturgical Press, 1996), p. 285.

15. "Child" (*yeled*) adds to the impression that the boy was young.

16. Gray, *Kings*, p. 382. The context is a most powerful rejection of paganism.

17. Walsh, *1 Kings*, p. 232.

18. Simon J. DeVries, *1 Kings*, Word Biblical Commentary, Vol. 12 (Waco, TX: Word Books, 1985), p. 222; endorsed by Dale Ralph Davis, *The Wisdom and the Folly: An Exposition of the Book of First Kings* (Fearn, Ross-shire, UK: Christian Focus, 2002), p. 223, note 3. Keil, *Kings*, p. 169, note 1 suggests that Elijah's action was similar in significance to other cases of miracle where there was an imposition of the hand.

19. Similarly Peter J. Leithart, *1 & 2 Kings*, Brazos Theological Commentary on the Bible (Grand Rapids, MI: Brazos Press, 2006), p. 129.

20. The Hebrew *nephesh* here refers to the "breath" (*neshamah*) that was no longer "in him" (v. 17). Wolff, *Anthropology*, p. 13. Similarly Gray, *Kings*, p. 383. As in verse 17 "breath" represents life.

21. So Walsh, *1 Kings*, p. 232.

22. The wording of verse 22b is even closer to verse 21b in the Hebrew than in English.

23. See the introduction to Chapter 27.

Chapter Thirty-Seven: The Troubler

1. For example, Christopher Hitchens, *god is not Great: How Religion Poisons Everything* (New York and Boston: Twelve, 2007).

2. So C. F. Keil, "1 and 2 Kings," in C. F. Keil and F. Delitzsch, *Commentary on the Old Testament*, Vol. 3 (Peabody, MA: Hendrickson Publishers, 1996), p. 170; contra Lissa M. Wray Beal, *1 & 2 Kings*, Apollos Old Testament Commentary, Vol. 9 (Nottingham, UK and Downers Grove, IL: Apollos, 2014), p. 241 who understands "the third year" to be the third year of the drought.

3. Compare the three-year famine in the days of David in 2 Samuel 21:1 and the threat of the same in 2 Samuel 24:13.

4. Similarly John Gray, *I & II Kings: A Commentary*, Third, Fully Revised, Edition (London: SCM, 1977), p. 386; Jerome T. Walsh, *1 Kings*, Berit Olam: Studies in Hebrew Narrative & Poetry (Collegeville, MN: The Liturgical Press, 1996), p. 237; Beal, *Kings*, p. 242. On the syntactical point see *IBH*, p. 119.

5. On my translation "you will hear" and "will forgive," see note 26 to Chapter 17.

6. In the Hebrew "send rain" in 18:1 exactly echoes "grant rain" in 8:36.

7. This was "a technical term, referring to a chief officer of the royal court, sometimes called the 'chief steward' or 'majordomo.' [The office] . . . eventually became second only to the king." Walsh, *1 Kings*, p. 238. See Isaiah 22:15–24; 2 Kings 15:5.

8. So Beal, *Kings*, p. 242. Ahishar held this office for King Solomon (4:6 where the Hebrew expression behind "in charge of the palace" is the same as "over the household" here). See also Arza for King Elah (16:9) and Eliakim for King Hezekiah (2 Kings 18:18, 37; 19:2). Cf. 2 Kings 10:5; 15:5.

9. Interestingly Obadiah is the first person since Samuel's momentous speech in 1 Samuel 12 who is said to "fear the Lord." Much later we will see that to "fear the Lord" came to mean (in some circles) something more ambiguous (see 2 Kings 17:33).

10. Hebrew *krt* hiphil. *CHALOT*, p. 165. Cf. 1 Samuel 2:33; 24:21; 28:9; 2 Samuel 7:9; 1 Kings 11:16; 14:10, 14.

11. See note 6 to Chapter 28.

12. "By fifties in a cave" is an attempt to makes sense of a difficult Hebrew phrase. Alternatives include "in two caves, fifty in each" (NIV); "50 men to a cave" (HCSB); "by fives in the caves" (Gray, *Kings*, p. 386, note a).

13. The Hebrew syntax indicates a continuous provision of food: "and he was feeding them." The Hebrew word rendered "fed" (*cwl* pilpel) in verse 4 appeared in 17:4, 9 ("to feed"). Obadiah was doing just what the ravens and the widow had done at the Lord's command.

14. Similarly Walsh, *1 Kings*, p. 239; Dale Ralph Davis, T*he Wisdom and the Folly: An Exposition of the Book of First Kings* (Fearn, Ross-shire, UK: Christian Focus, 2002), p. 231, note 3; Beal, *Kings*, p. 242.

15. Similarly Walsh, *1 Kings*, p. 239; Beal, *Kings*, p. 242. Here we might be reminded of the use of the key word "way" in 1 Kings 13. See our discussion of 13:12, 33.

16. Similarly Walsh, *1 Kings*, p. 239.

17. I am not persuaded that Elijah's "your lord" means "Obadiah's 'lord' is either Elijah and the God he represents, or Ahab and the god he follows: it cannot be both." Walsh, *1 Kings*, p. 240. The narrator has already shown Obadiah as a supremely faithful servant of Yahweh while also serving the king. We may suppose that he had in fact taken advantage of his position in Ahab's household to achieve his secret protection of the prophets.

18. Contra Walsh, *1 Kings*, p. 240.

19. There may be an intensification of the language from verse 9 where the verb means "cause to die" (Hebrew, *mwt* hiphil), while in verses 12 and 14 the verb refers, perhaps with a more violent sense, to the act of killing (Hebrew, *hrg* qal).

20. On "breath"/"spirit" and "word" as parallel ideas, see Psalm 33:6; 147:18; Proverbs 1:23; Isaiah 59:21; Zechariah 7:12. For a brief discussion of the relationship between the Spirit (breath) and Word of God, see John Woodhouse, *God of Word: The Word, the Spirit and How God Speaks to Us*, Brief Books (Sydney and Youngstown: Matthias Media, 2015), particularly pp. 31–45. In some other contexts the breath or wind (*ruakh*; ESV, Spirit) of the Lord appears to physically transport a person from one place to another (see 2 Kings 2:16; Ezekiel 8:3).

21. The context, therefore, discourages reading too much into Obadiah's words "*your* God" in verse 10. Contrast 13:6 and our discussion there. Obadiah's deference to Elijah confirms that Elijah's God is Obadiah's God.

22. Similarly Meir Sternberg, *The Poetics of Biblical Narrative: ideological reading and the drama of reading*, IN Studies in Biblical Literature (Bloomington: IN University Press, 1987). p. 418.

23. "The LORD of hosts" or "the LORD, the God of hosts" appears in 1 Samuel 4:4; 15:2; 17:45; 2 Samuel 5:10; 6:2, 18; 7:8, 26, 27; 1 Kings 18:15; 19:10, 14; (cf. 22:19); 2 Kings 3:14. See John Woodhouse, *1 Samuel: Looking for a Leader*, Preaching the Word (Wheaton, IL: Crossway, 2008), pp. 556, 557, note 3.

24. See R. Mosis, "*'akar*," *TDOT* 11, pp. 67–71.

25. For further illustrations of the sense of the term "trouble," see Genesis 34:30; Judges 11:35; Proverbs 15:27.

26. The plural "Baals" refers to various local representations (idols) of the god Baal. Gray, *Kings*, p. 393.

27. No doubt "all Israel" would be some kind of representative gathering rather than literally every single Israelite. See our discussion of 8:1a.

28. It is possible that these 400 "prophets" survived to serve Ahab in days to come. See 22:6.

29. The text is not clear whether the prophets of Baal were also maintained by the queen. They may well have been.

30. See Map 6–3 in Currid, *Atlas*, p. 144.

31. Similarly Gray, *Kings*, p. 395.

Chapter Thirty-Eight: Religion for Dummies

1. Similarly Jerome T. Walsh, *1 Kings*, Berit Olam: Studies in Hebrew Narrative & Poetry (Collegeville, MN: The Liturgical Press, 1996), p. 244.

2. See Map 6–3 in Currid, *Atlas*, p. 144.

3. This is asserted as fact by Lissa M. Wray Beal, *1 & 2 Kings*, Apollos Old Testament Commentary, Vol. 9 (Nottingham, UK and Downers Grove, IL: Apollos, 2014), p. 243.

4. In this paragraph I have drawn on Henry O. Thompson, "Carmel, Mount (Place)," *ABD* 1, pp. 874, 875.

5. So E. Otto, "*pasha*," *TDOT* 12, p. 5. See 2 Samuel 4:4 where the ESV translates the passive form, "became lame."

6. So John Gray, *I & II Kings: A Commentary*, Third, Fully Revised, Edition (London: SCM, 1977), p. 396, following Fohrer. Also Walsh, *1 Kings*, p. 245.

7. Iain W. Provan, *1 & 2 Kings*, Understanding the Bible Commentary Series (Grand Rapids, MI: Baker Books, 1995), pp. 140, 141. The main difficulty here is that the Hebrew word (*se'ippiym*) rendered "different opinions" occurs only here in the Old Testament. It may be related to *se'appah* meaning "branch" (hence "crutches") or *se'ep* meaning "divided" (hence "different opinions" or "cross-roads").

8. This is the first time that the term "prophet" has been applied to Elijah, and it is a self-designation. Soon the narrator will confirm his claim (see v. 36), although no one who has read 1 Kings 17 could doubt its truth. However, it is striking that Elijah is only rarely called a "prophet" (apart from the two times in this chapter only 2 Chronicles 21:12; Malachi 4:5). Cf. "Nathan the prophet" eighteen times in 1 Kings 1! Was this because the designation had been somewhat debased by the "prophets" of Baal? Or perhaps Elijah's importance was such that the Bible writers thought of him as "more than a prophet" (cf. Matthew 11:9).

9. Mount Carmel has a number of limestone caves with evidence of habitation from prehistoric times, thousands of years before the time of Elijah. Thompson, "Carmel," p. 874.

10. My more literal rendering here emphasizes that Elijah was giving Baal's prophets every advantage. The obvious antecedent to "them" is "Baal's prophets" in verse 22.

11. Walsh observes, "there is nothing to prevent them from providing one worthy and one unworthy animal and leaving the imperfect one to Elijah." Walsh, *1 Kings*, p. 246. Gray notes that "they will have no excuse that [their] victim was less fit for sacrifice." Gray, *Kings*, pp. 396, 397.

12. Similarly Walsh, *1 Kings*, p. 246, although he does not see the ambiguity in "your god."

13. See Chapter 17 of this book.

14. In Israel's history there was a precedent for Elijah's expectation. See Leviticus 9, particularly verse 24. But see also Leviticus 10:2; Numbers 16:35.

15. The fire by itself could not decide the ultimate question. See Revelation 13:13.

16. Similarly Walsh, *1 Kings*, p. 246.

17. My literal rendering does not contradict the fact that the prophets were given the opportunity to choose both the pair of bulls and the one bull for themselves. It simply emphasizes that Elijah was in charge of the whole procedure. Contra Walsh, *1 Kings*, p. 247.

18. The ESV ("and no one answered") does not quite convey the absence of anyone to answer, which seems to be the sense of the Hebrew.

19. Walsh, *1 Kings*, p. 248.

20. "Limped" is an intensified form (*pskh* piel) of the verb used (*pskh* qal) in verse 21 ("limping").

21. The Hebrew verb (*htl* piel) occurs only here in the Old Testament (cf. the related noun in Job 17:2). It is thought to be a variant on a similar verb that is rendered "mock" in Judges 16:10, 13, 15. BDB, p. 1068.

22. The Hebrew has a series of four bitterly ironic phrases, but a fair translation of the first two is difficult. The first phrase (Hebrew, *kiy siyach*) suggests that Baal is "occupied with something" (ESV, "he is musing"), often thought to be a euphemism for relieving himself. The second phrase (*kiy siyg lo*) has been understood to mean,

rather crudely, "he has a bowel movement," encouraging the euphemistic understanding of the previous clause. *CHALOT*, pp. 350, 351. It is also possible that the euphemism is more in the mind of the interpreter than in Elijah's intention. See, for example, JB, RB, NIV, HCSB.

23. There may be further irony here. "Custom" (*mishpat*) can refer to God's Law ("rules" in 11:33) or "justice" (10:9). Just look at what their *mishpat* produced! Cf. John Woodhouse, *1 Samuel: Looking for a Leader*, Preaching the Word (Wheaton, IL: Crossway, 2008), p. 148.

24. It is what Saul did when the harmful spirit rushed on him (1 Samuel 18:10). Cf. Jeremiah 29:26. The verb (in this form) can have a positive sense, as in 1 Samuel 10:10.

25. Literally "between the evenings," meaning between sunset and dark.

26. This offering was accompanied by a *minkhah* (ESV, "grain offering," Exodus 29:41), the word rendered "oblation" in the present verse.

27. The phrase rendered in the ESV "the offering of the oblation" occurs only here, verse 36, and 2 Kings 3:20 (ESV, "offering the sacrifice") in the Old Testament.

28. In the hiphil, a causative form ("cause to go up"), it is frequently the word for "offering" sacrifices (as in 3:4, 15; 9:25; 10:5; 12:32). The basic qal form is fitting here precisely because (as we will see) no one will "offer" this sacrifice. It will just "go up" (see 18:38)!

29. The Hebrew *minkhah* can refer to "tribute" or gifts paid by foreign powers to a great king (as in 4:21; 10:25; 2 Samuel 8:2, 6; similarly 1 Samuel 10:27). It can refer to the "grain offering" that accompanied burnt offerings at the house of the Lord (8:64). It can also be a more general word for sacrifices and offerings of all kinds (1 Samuel 2:17).

30. "[S]ince all sacrifice tended to establish good relations between God and man, every sacrifice had some expiatory value." Roland de Vaux, *Ancient Israel: Its Life and Institutions*, trans. John McHugh (London: Darton, Longman & Todd, 1973), p. 453.

31. These verses all have the verb (*qshb*) cognate with the noun (*qesheb*) I have translated "attentiveness."

Chapter Thirty-Nine: Decision Time

1. Since the Baal prophets raved on "until the time of the offering of the oblation" (18:29), and that time is not reached until verse 36, it is clear that the prophets were carrying on with their antics in the background of verses 30–35.

2. Since this is a flashback (see previous note) "Then" is misleading.

3. Cf. Jerome T. Walsh, *1 Kings*, Berit Olam: Studies in Hebrew Narrative & Poetry (Collegeville, MN: The Liturgical Press, 1996), p. 286.

4. The trench was large. That is all we need to know. The expression "as great as would contain two seahs of seed" is difficult to interpret more precisely. See John Gray, *1 & II Kings: A Commentary*, Third, Fully Revised, Edition (London: SCM, 1977), p. 400; Walsh, *1 Kings*, p. 251 note 6.

5. An extended discussion of the meaning of "to make atonement" is beyond our purpose here, except to note that it had to do with dealing with sin and uncleanness. Furthermore I am not suggesting that atonement was all that the sacrificial system entailed. But it was fundamental. See Gordon J. Wenham, *The Book of Le-*

viticus, The New International Commentary on the Old Testament (Grand Rapids, MI: Eerdmans, 1979), p. 28.

6. I do not think we should be distracted by questions about where all this water came from on the drought-ravaged heights of Mount Carmel. If it mattered the narrator would have told us. Those who worry about such things may be comforted by suggestions that it could have been sea water (Mount Carmel was not far from the sea, see 18:43, 44) or perhaps there was a spring nearby that had not dried up. C. F. Keil, "1 and 2 Kings," in C. F. Keil and F. Delitzsch, *Commentary on the Old Testament*, Vol. 3 (Peabody, MA: Hendrickson Publishers, 1996), p. 175, note 2; Iain W. Provan, *1 & 2 Kings*, Understanding the Bible Commentary Series (Grand Rapids, MI: Baker Books, 1995), p. 142.

7. One difficulty with this common interpretation is that it would put Elijah's prayer rather late in the day (about sunset). A lot more seems to have happened that day, apparently before dark (see 18:40–46). Cf. Roland de Vaux, *Ancient Israel: Its Life and Institutions*, trans. John McHugh (London: Darton, Longman & Todd, 1973), p. 469.

8. This impression does not rest on the repetition of the word "offering" in the ESV that does not exactly reflect the Hebrew. However, as we have noted, the Hebrew, *'olah* (ESV, "burnt offering") in verses 33 and 38 echoes *'aloth* (ESV, "offering") in 18:29, 36. Furthermore the ESV "oblation" (*minkhah*), while often referring to the "grain offering" that accompanied a "burnt offering" (Exodus 40:29; Leviticus 9:17; Numbers 7:87; etc.), can be a general word for any sacrifice. See de Vaux, *Ancient Israel*, pp. 430, 431, 452.

9. "You" here and in the next clause is emphatic: "*you* are the one who is . . ."; "*you* are the one who has . . ."

10. While the Hebrew for "come near" (*nagash*) is an ordinary word with a simple literal meaning, it is part of the vocabulary of the tabernacle, priesthood, and other contexts where people approach God. See Exodus 19:22; 20:21; 24:2; cf. James 4:8. For a detailed discussion, see H. Ringgren, "*nagash*," *TDOT* 9, pp. 215–17.

11. Similarly Walsh, *1 Kings*, p. 256.

12. Cf. Walsh, *1 Kings*, p. 286.

13. Montgomery argued that Elijah wanted the people to know that it was Yahweh who had turned their hearts "backwards" to Baal. That is, they were to learn that Baal could not even take the credit for seducing the people in the first place. It had been like the hardening of Pharaoh in Egypt. James A. Montgomery, *A Critical and Exegetical Commentary on the Books of Kings*, The International Critical Commentary (Edinburgh: T. & T. Clark, 1951), p. 305. Few commentators have followed this line, but among those who do is Walsh, *1 Kings*, p. 253. Montgomery's argument is based on what he calls the "past tense of the verb" and the meaning of the adverb "back." He puts too much weight on a temporal understanding of the Hebrew perfect tense, but in any case fails to notice that the turning of the people's hearts had well and truly begun, as we have seen. His argument about the rare adverb (*'akhoranniyth*, only here and Genesis 9:23; 1 Samuel 4:18; 2 Kings 20:10, 11; Isaiah 38:8) is particularly weak.

14. The Kishon flows along the valley north of the Mount Carmel range to the Mediterranean Sea. See Map 6–3 in Currid, *Atlas*, p. 144.

15. So, rightly, Dale Ralph Davis, *The Wisdom and the Folly: An Exposition of the Book of First Kings* (Fearn, Ross-shire, UK: Christian Focus, 2002), pp. 243, 244.

16. I recall hearing this striking way of putting the issue in a recording of a sermon on this passage preached by Peter Marshall in 1944. From memory I was less comfortable with the close analogy he drew between Elijah's Israel and the United States of America.

Chapter Forty: The God Who Answers

1. So C. F. Keil, "1 and 2 Kings," in C. F. Keil and F. Delitzsch, *Commentary on the Old Testament*, Vol. 3 (Peabody, MA: Hendrickson Publishers, 1996), p. 176; contra John Gray, *I & II Kings: A Commentary*, Third, Fully Revised, Edition (London: SCM, 1977), p. 403.

2. Gray, *Kings*, p. 403.

3. So Iain W. Provan, *1 & 2 Kings*, Understanding the Bible Commentary Series (Grand Rapids, MI: Baker Books, 1995), p. 139; Jerome T. Walsh, *1 Kings*, Berit Olam: Studies in Hebrew Narrative & Poetry (Collegeville, MN: The Liturgical Press, 1996), p. 286; Peter J. Leithart, *1 & 2 Kings*, Brazos Theological Commentary on the Bible (Grand Rapids, MI: Brazos Press, 2006), p. 137; Lissa M. Wray Beal, *1 & 2 Kings*, Apollos Old Testament Commentary, Vol. 9 (Nottingham, UK and Downers Grove, IL: Apollos, 2014), p. 245. Davis is not convinced of this oft-cited parallel, and I am inclined to agree that it is reading a lot into "eat and drink." Dale Ralph Davis, *The Wisdom and the Folly: An Exposition of the Book of First Kings* (Fearn, Ross-shire, UK: Christian Focus, 2002), p. 247, note 1.

4. "Rushing" renders a Hebrew word (*hamon*) that suggests a tumultuous sound. See 1 Samuel 4:14 ("uproar"); 14:19 ("tumult"); 2 Samuel 18:29 ("commotion").

5. The clear sky implied in verse 43 makes Gray's suggestion improbable, namely that it was "perhaps the sound of the rising west wind, which was the herald of the storm." Gray, *Kings*, p. 403.

6. We might have expected, "So Ahab went up *and* ate *and* drank." Since the meal itself is not the focus of the writer's interest, we do not hear about the actual meal. But Ahab went up "*to* eat and *to* drink." We assume that he carried out his intentions, just as Elijah did when he "went *to* show himself to Ahab" (18:2).

7. "Elijah" is emphatic in the Hebrew, perhaps indicating that Elijah (but not Ahab) went up to the top of the mountain. Alternatively the Hebrew could imply "that after their encounter [in the Kishon valley] Ahab and Elijah climb Carmel at the same time, though to different places." Walsh, *1 Kings*, p. 257.

8. So Gray, *Kings*, p. 403.

9. The description of Elijah's posture here is not found anywhere else in the Old Testament. The verb (*gahar*, "bowed himself down") occurs only here and in the story of Elisha (2 Kings 4:34, 35, "stretched himself").

10. This is the first we have heard of Elijah's "servant" (or "lad"). On the word (*na'ar*), see note 15 to Chapter 8.

11. "Now" represents a Hebrew word (*na'*) that softens the command, a little like adding "please" in English.

12. In the up and down movements on the mountain this "Go up" probably just means "Get up," since Ahab seems to have been lower on the mountain than Elijah's prayer spot (v. 42).

13. The Hebrew does not mention a chariot. The ESV's "Prepare your chariot" paraphrases a verb ('asar) that here seems to mean "to harness" (horses). They may have been harnessed to a chariot or (perhaps more probable on the mountainside) Ahab may have been on horseback. On Ahab's love of horses, see 18:5.

14. So NIV; Gray, Kings, p. 404. The Hebrew phrase (literally, "until thus and until thus") occurs only here and is difficult to interpret. Perhaps the sense is "between one moment and the next." The point "is almost certainly the immediacy of the rain. In other words this was no natural rainstorm." Walsh, 1 Kings, p. 257.

15. So Walter Brueggemann, 1 & 2 Kings, Smyth & Helwys Bible Commentary (Macon, GA: Smyth & Helwys, 2000), p. 227.

16. Ibid., p. 228.

17. Melvin Hunt, "Jezreel (Place)," ABD 3, p. 850.

18. See Map 6–3 in Currid, Atlas, p. 144.

19. This is the first occurrence in the Old Testament of this particular sense of "the hand of the LORD." Frequently the phrase has referred to God's power in judgment (Exodus 9:3; 16:3; Deuteronomy 2:15; Judges 2:15; 1 Samuel 5:6, 9; 7:13; 12:15; 2 Samuel 24:14). The prophet Ezekiel frequently experienced "the hand of the LORD," often associated with the word of the Lord coming to him (Ezekiel 1:3; 3:14, 22; 8:1; etc.; cf. 2 Kings 3:15, 16).

20. Gray notes that "it is not impossible for a man to outstrip a horse over this distance, especially since the man runs cross country in a straight line and the horse and chariot must pass slowly over rough ground and make certain detours." Gray, Kings, p. 404. This may be true, even without a chariot.

21. Davis, Wisdom, p. 255; also Leithart, Kings, p. 136. Contrary to Provan who sees this as a race that Elijah won: "[Ahab] is as impotent as the god he worships. Elijah's 'win' over him is as comprehensive as his 'win' over the prophets of Baal." Provan, Kings, p. 139.

22. The image of Elijah running "before Ahab" is highly suggestive as the following two reflections illustrate. "This act of Elijah, whom Ahab had hitherto only known as a stern, imperious, and powerful prophet, was admirably adapted to touch the heart of the king, and produce the conviction that it was not from any personal dislike to him, but only in the service of the Lord, that the prophet was angry at his idolatry, and that he was not trying to effect his ruin, but rather his conversion and the salvation of his soul." Keil, Kings, p. 177. "[H]aving won Ahab's sympathy in his triumph on Carmel, he now sought to exploit the situation in face of Jezebel's opposition in Jezreel, well knowing the support that Ahab needed against that dominant lady." Gray, Kings, p. 405.

23. The passage in James's letter is much discussed in some circles. I understand the flow of the passage (illuminated by the 1 Kings account of Elijah) along the following lines:

And the prayer of faith will save [in the full sense of James 1:21; 2:14; 5:20] the one who is sick, and the Lord will raise him up [that is, on the last day]. And if he has committed sins, he will be forgiven [that is, the salvation we are talking about]. Therefore, confess your sins to one another and pray for one another, that you may be healed [in the full sense, that is, forgiven]. The prayer of a righteous person has great power as it is working [what could be more powerful than sins being forgiven?]. Elijah was a man with a nature like ours [as we will see more plainly in 1 Kings 19], and he prayed fervently that it might not rain, and for three years and six months it did not rain on the earth [because of the sins of the people]. Then he prayed again, and heaven gave rain, and the earth bore its fruit [the great display in Israel's history of *sins forgiven*!]. (James 5:15–18)

Chapter Forty-One: There Is No Plan B

1. In the Hebrew the word "all" is used three times in verse 1 (only two of which are translated), emphasizing the fullness of Ahab's account to Jezebel. Similarly Jerome T. Walsh, *1 Kings*, Berit Olam: Studies in Hebrew Narrative & Poetry (Collegeville, MN: The Liturgical Press, 1996), p. 265.

2. The Hebrew word (*nephesh*) occurs seven times in this chapter (verses 2 [twice], 3, 4 [twice], 10, 14).

3. So C. F. Keil, "1 and 2 Kings," in C. F. Keil and F. Delitzsch, *Commentary on the Old Testament*, Vol. 3 (Peabody, MA: Hendrickson Publishers, 1996), p. 178; Walsh, *1 Kings*, p. 266.

4. The issue is a subtle textual uncertainty. The standard Hebrew text has "And he saw." However, the same consonants can be vocalized differently to mean "And he was afraid." A few Hebrew manuscripts and ancient versions have taken the latter meaning. For a sensible defense of the standard Hebrew text, see Dale Ralph Davis, *The Wisdom and the Folly: An Exposition of the Book of First Kings* (Fearn, Ross-shire, UK: Christian Focus, 2002), p. 261. Also Keil, *Kings*, p. 178; contra John Gray, *I & II Kings: A Commentary*, Third, Fully Revised, Edition (London: SCM, 1977), p. 406, note c ; Lissa M. Wray Beal, *1 & 2 Kings*, Apollos Old Testament Commentary, Vol. 9 (Nottingham, UK and Downers Grove, IL: Apollos, 2014), p. 249.

5. Most English translations give the impression the Elijah was fleeing in terror. The Hebrew is rather calmer and is conveyed well by the RV: "And when he saw that, he arose, and went . . ." Even the expression "went for his life" is not equivalent to the English idiom, which suggests extreme haste. Certainly Elijah's departure meant that he took his "life" (*nephesh*) out of Jezebel's reach. But there was more going on than "running for his life." Similarly Keil, *Kings*, pp. 178, 179; Peter J. Leithart, *1 & 2 Kings*, Brazos Theological Commentary on the Bible (Grand Rapids, MI: Brazos Press, 2006), p. 140; contra Beal, *Kings*, p. 252.

6. See Map 6–3 in Currid, *Atlas*, p. 144.

7. See the vigorous criticism of the many attempts to diagnose Elijah's troubled state of mind in this chapter in Davis, *Wisdom*, pp. 257–75, largely followed by Leithart, *Kings*, p. 140.

8. On the Hebrew term (*na'ar*) see note 15 to Chapter 8.

9. Walsh interprets the whole story along these lines: "The dramatic line, then, is the question of what happens when a prophet attempts to resign from his office. How will Yahweh respond? And what will happen to the prophet?" Walsh, *1 Kings*, p. 265. Cf. Iain W. Provan, *1 & 2 Kings*, Understanding the Bible Commentary Series (Grand Rapids, MI: Baker Books, 1995), p. 144.

10. The key word *nephesh* ("life") appears again here. Literally, "he asked for his life to die."

11. The single syllable in Hebrew (*rab*) is stark. Jeroboam had said that he had had "enough" (*rab*) of the people going up to Jerusalem (12:28).

12. Commentators who overlook the theological dimension to Elijah's distress are (in my opinion) far from the mark. For example, this was much more than "the self-loathing of the high achiever who thinks he has failed." Provan, *Kings*, p. 148.

13. See John Woodhouse, *2 Samuel: Your Kingdom Come*, Preaching the Word (Wheaton, IL: Crossway, 2015), p. 369.

14. The location of Mount Horeb/Sinai is disputed. The 200 miles mentioned here assumes the traditional site in the south of the Sinai Peninsula. See Map 3–2 in Currid, *Atlas*, p. 85.

15. Beal, *Kings*, p. 252. Beal thinks that the journey of verse 7 was meant to be to Damascus (v. 15). Ibid., p. 253.

16. Similarly Provan, *Kings*, p. 145; Davis, *Wisdom*, p. 263; contra Walsh, *1 Kings*, p. 270.

17. "Such parallels suggest that at the very least we may be dealing with matters of redemptive-historical moment and not merely with a whining prophet." Davis, *Wisdom*, p. 263.

18. So Keil, *Kings*, p. 180; Gray, *Kings*, p. 409; Beal, *Kings*, p. 253. Elijah's experience in this "cave" will be very different from some other prophets we have recently heard of who were hidden in a "cave" (same word in 18:4, 13).

19. So Walsh, *1 Kings*, p. 272; contra Keil, *Kings*, p. 180.

20. "What is your business here, Elijah?" Gray, *Kings*, p. 406.

21. Apart from its repetition in verse 14, the only other occurrence of the title "the LORD, the God of hosts" in Genesis through 2 Kings is 2 Samuel 5:10. It is a majestic title, an expansion of the more common "LORD of hosts." See our discussion of 18:15.

22. See further our discussion of 14:22.

23. Walter Brueggemann, *1 & 2 Kings*, Smyth & Helwys Bible Commentary (Macon, GA: Smyth & Helwys, 2000), p. 241.

24. Walsh, *1 Kings*, pp. 273, 274.

25. Provan, *Kings*, p. 145.

26. Walsh, *1 Kings*, p. 273.

27. The NIV includes the words, "for the LORD is about to pass by" in the Lord's speech. Walsh argues that the Lord's speech continues to the end of verse 12. Walsh, *1 Kings*, p. 275. This yields an awkward reading with the repeated third-person references to the Lord, particularly the threefold "but the LORD was not in . . ." In my opinion the ESV punctuation makes best sense.

28. I notice that the RV retained this old (and much loved?) rendering, while noting in the margin that the Hebrew really means "a sound of gentle stillness."

29. I have tried to briefly outline the Bible's teaching about how we experience God today, particularly how we hear his voice, in the booklet *God of Word: The Word, the Spirit and How God Speaks to Us*, Brief Books (Sydney and Youngstown: Matthias Media, 2015).

30. In the Hebrew phrase (*qol demamah daqah*) the first word is a noun in the construct state meaning "sound of" or "voice of." The third word is an adjective meaning "thin" or "fine" and qualifying the critical second word. The second word is a noun that occurs only three times in the Old Testament (here; Job 4:16; Psalm 107:29). It refers to stillness or silence. From its etymology (always an uncertain line of argument) it has been suggested that it means a profound, meaningful

silence, such as following a catastrophe or accompanying a great expectation. "[I]t is a silence caused by the powerful impress of an impending or actual calamity or by the expectation of coming salvation, and this is what gives it its specific nuance." A. Baumann, "*damah* II," *TDOT* 1, p. 264. In my judgment the best rendering of the Hebrew phrase is "a sound of thin silence." So also Gray, *Kings*, p. 406.

31. Walsh makes much of the supposed incompleteness of Elijah's obedience. Walsh, *1 Kings*, p. 276. However, we have no reason to think that standing at the cave entrance did not count as standing "on the mount before the LORD" (v. 11).

32. This "voice" (Hebrew, *qol*) is not the "sound" (*qol*) of the silence (or even "the still small voice") of verse 12, otherwise it would be "*the* voice." So Walsh, *1 Kings*, p. 276; contra Davis, *Wisdom*, p. 269.

33. The wilderness of Damascus (a phrase found only here in the Old Testament) "probably refers to the desert region bordering the large oasis of Damascus, capital of Aram." Walsh, *1 Kings*, p. 277.

34. See note 46 to Chapter 21.

35. Brueggemann, *Kings*, p. 237.

36. Similarly Keil, *Kings*, p. 183. In support of this understanding there is no instance of a prophet in the Old Testament being "anointed." Priests and kings were "anointed," but not prophets. So Gray, *Kings*, p. 411.

37. Although the number should not be taken as precise, it is substantially more than Elijah had imagined (namely one). At the same time it is a small fraction of the nation's population. "Seven" may be a "conventional indefinite number." Gray, *Kings*, p. 412. On "thousand," see note 2 to Chapter 8.

38. The Hebrew verb translated "I will leave" (*sh'r*, hiphil) is related to one of the main words for "remnant" (*she'ar*), as in Isaiah 10:19–22; 11:11; etc. We could translate this: "I will provide a remnant . . ." So Brueggemann, *Kings*, p. 241.

39. Abel-meholah was mentioned in the description of King Solomon's tax system (4:12) and featured in the story of Gideon (Judges 7:22). The precise location is uncertain, but see Map 6–3 in Currid, *Atlas*, p. 144.

40. Similarly Walsh, *1 Kings*, p. 279, although Gray explains this as a community rather than a family activity. Gray, *Kings*, p. 413.

41. The word "kiss" occurs only in these two verses in the books of Kings.

42. "Sacrificed" can simply mean "slaughtered." So Gray, *Kings*, p. 407. See note 32 to Chapter 2.

Chapter Forty-Two: King Ahab Did Not Destroy the Enemy

1. Ben-hadad ("son-of-[the god] Hadad") may have been a throne name for kings of Aram. On the god Hadad, see our discussion of 11:14. The books of Kings mention three kings of Aram with the name or title Ben-hadad: Ben-hadad I in 15:18–20; Ben-hadad II in 20:1–34; 2 Kings 6:24; 8:7–15; and Ben-hadad III in 2 Kings 13:3, 24, 25. There are historical issues here that we will not pursue. See K. A. Kitchen, "Ben-hadad," *IBD* 1, pp. 184, 185. It has been argued that Ben-hadad II and Ben-hadad III were the same person, but this is not possible without attributing unsubstantiated "mistakes" to the Biblical account. For the (unpersuasive) argument, see Wayne T. Pitard, "Ben-Hadad (Person), *ABD* 1, pp. 663–65. I share Davis's disapproval of the reasoning involved. Dale Ralph Davis, *The Wisdom and the Folly: An Exposition of the Book of First Kings* (Fearn, Ross-shire, UK: Christian Focus, 2002), p. 287 note 2.

2. Throughout this chapter (as elsewhere) I prefer to render the Hebrew *aram* as "Aram." See note 46 to Chapter 21.

3. This will be sorted out in 2 Kings 8:7–15.

4. The "kings of Aram" were mentioned in 10:29 (ESV, "Syria"). Compare the "kings" of various cities in, for example, Joshua 10:5.

5. See our discussion of 10:26–29.

6. Cf. note 23 to Chapter 27.

7. The Hebrew has a particle (*kiy*) here that may be adversative ("No! I sent to you . . ."). So John Gray, *I & II Kings: A Commentary*, Third, Fully Revised, Edition (London: SCM, 1977), p. 419, note b. Alternatively it may be emphatic ("See here! I sent to you . . ."). So Jerome T. Walsh, *1 Kings*, Berit Olam: Studies in Hebrew Narrative & Poetry (Collegeville, MN: The Liturgical Press, 1996), p. 296.

8. The Hebrew expression here (*kiy 'im*) is probably emphatic. What follows is not a different action from the demand of verse 5 (as "Nevertheless" implies), but the means by which he intended to enforce that demand. Similarly Walsh, *1 Kings*, p. 296.

9. Some commentators (from modern liberal democracies!) look favorably on Ahab at this point. "Ahab is the kind of king who is aware of his subjects and attentive to their voice." He mentions "family before his silver and gold," showing a better value system than Ben-hadad. Walsh, *1 Kings*, p. 297. Also Lissa M. Wray Beal, *1 & 2 Kings*, Apollos Old Testament Commentary, Vol. 9 (Nottingham, UK and Downers Grove, IL: Apollos, 2014), p. 264. I think that is much too kind. This weak king needed his people to make the decision for him that he should have made from the beginning: "Do not listen and do *not* consent" (v, 8).

10. "Now" represents a Hebrew particle (*na'*) that generally softens imperatives, giving them a tone of politeness. Here it seems to me to make the king's words to the elders sound rather pathetic. *Please understand what a bully he is. Help me!* Cf. 13:6.

11. Contra Beal who thinks Ahab "shows considerable pluck." Beal, *Kings*, p. 264.

12. However, "booths" (*sukkoth*) could be the place name "Succoth" (also in 2 Samuel 11:11). So Gray, *Kings*, p. 423; considered possible by Walsh, *1 Kings*, p. 298, note 4; Beal, *Kings*, p. 260. If so, Ben-hadad's base camp was a good thirty or forty miles east of Samaria. See Map 6–2 in Currid, *Atlas*, p. 142. The arguments for "booths" or "Succoth" seem to me to be finely balanced, although Davis thinks it unlikely that the hostilities would be directed from such a distance. Davis, *Wisdom*, p. 287, note 3. He has a point since in verse 17 news of the Israelites' movements out of Samaria seems to reach Ben-hadad "in the booths" rather too quickly for him to be miles away in Succoth. For further details, see John Woodhouse, *2 Samuel: Your Kingdom Come*, Preaching the Word (Wheaton, IL: Crossway, 2015), p. 619, note 13.

13. The designation, literally "one prophet," makes this prophet anonymous, and therefore different from the well-known (to us and to Ahab) Elijah.

14. The Hebrew often refers to a loud noise: "uproar" (1 Samuel 4:14), "tumult" (1 Samuel 14:19), "commotion" (2 Samuel 18:29), "rushing" (1 Kings 18:41). Perhaps here there is "a wry overtone: Ben-hadad's troops (like Ben-hadad himself) are noisy, but it is all bluster." Walsh, *1 Kings*, p. 299.

15. The Hebrew word rendered "districts" (*mediynah*) has not appeared before this in the Old Testament text, but could refer to whatever remained in Ahab's day of King Solomon's administrative system outlined in 4:7–19. "Governor(s)" is a common enough word (*sar*) with various meanings in different contexts ("commander[s]" in 1:19, 25; 2:5, 32; 9:22; 11:15, 21; 15:20; 16:9, 16; "high officials" in 4:2; "chief officers" in 5:16; 9:23; "leader" in 11:24; "officers" in 14:27).

16. On the Hebrew word (*na'ar*, "lads"; ESV, "servants"), see note 15 to Chapter 8.

17. Keil calls it "a small and weak host." C. F. Keil, "1 and 2 Kings," in C. F. Keil and F. Delitzsch, *Commentary on the Old Testament*, Vol. 3 (Peabody, MA: Hendrickson Publishers, 1996), p. 186. Similarly Iain W. Provan, *1 & 2 Kings*, Understanding the Bible Commentary Series (Grand Rapids, MI: Baker Books, 1995), p. 155. Contra Gray who calls them "a picked body of striking troops." Gray, *Kings*, pp. 424, 425. Also Walsh: "a select group of commandos." Walsh, *1 Kings*, p. 300. The term *na'ar* can refer to young soldiers (2 Samuel 2:14), perhaps "cadets." Roland de Vaux, *Ancient Israel: Its Life and Institutions*, trans. John McHugh (London: Darton, Longman & Todd, 1973), pp. 220, 221. However, it is also used for young men in various roles. For example, Jeroboam in 11:28 and Jeroboam's sick son in 14:3, 17.

18. Provan, *Kings*, p. 155.

19. Keil, *Kings*, p. 186.

20. Gray, *Kings*, p. 425.

21. Davis, *Wisdom*, p. 289.

22. See note 2 to Chapter 8.

23. "Seven thousand" is a verbal reminder of the promise, but does not, of course, mean that the army should be identified with the remnant.

24. Walsh helpfully shows how verses 16–19 brilliantly manage to describe the developments taking place simultaneously in two places. Walsh, *1 Kings*, pp. 300, 301.

25. Ben-Hadad showed "apparent inability to utter coherent or sensible instructions." Provan, *Kings*, p. 152.

26. Walsh, *1 Kings*, p. 301.

27. Similarly Walsh, *1 Kings*, p. 302.

28. So Keil, *Kings*, p. 187; Provan, *Kings*, p. 152.

29. Gray, *Kings*, p. 420; similarly Walsh, *1 Kings*, p. 303. See the same expression in 2 Samuel 11:1 and the discussion in Woodhouse, *2 Samuel*, p. 283.

30. "Know and see" is an exact echo of the same words in verse 7 (ESV, "Mark . . . and see").

31. The Hebrew syntax of this sentence suggests that a contrast is being made between the advice given to the two kings. Similarly Walsh, *1 Kings*, p. 303.

32. The Hebrew for "gods" is identical to the usual word for the "God" of Israel. The clause could be translated, "Their God is a God of the hills."

33. "Commander" (*pekhah*) is "a rather vague title," but not strictly a military one. *CHALOT*, p. 291. It is rendered "governors" in 10:15, the only other occurrence of the Hebrew word in 1 Kings. "It is apparently centralization of power that is in view here—the replacement of vassal kings with officials directly accountable to Ben-Hadad. The royal advisors seek greater military cohesion through a greater degree of political control." Provan, *Kings*, p. 156.

34. The Hebrew syntax suggests a contrast between the active muster of the Arameans (by Ben-hadad) and the passive experience ("were mustered") of the Israelites, implying the agency of God. Similarly Walsh, *1 Kings*, p. 304.

35. This Aphek may have been to the east of the Sea of Galilee, just inside Aram (this is consistent with verse 30, where the Aramean survivors flee into the city of Aphek). See Map 6–4 in Currid, *Atlas*, p. 145. The Aphek in 1 Samuel was further west, close to (or within) Philistine territory. On five possible Biblical sites called Aphek (perhaps meaning "Valley Bed"), see Rafael Frankel, "Aphek (Place)," *ABD* 1, pp. 275–77.

36. The Hebrew word (*khaship*) rendered "little flocks" appears only here in the Old Testament, and the meaning is not certain. "Little flocks" has support from the ancient versions. BDB, p. 362. REB has "a pair of new-born goats," apparently taking a clue from supposed etymology.

37. The Hebrew expression is definite (*'iysh ha'elohiym*, "*the* man of God"), as in 12:22; 13:4, 5, 6, 7, 8, 11, 12, 14, 21, 26, 29, 31; not the indefinite expression (*'iysh 'elohiym*, "*a* man of God") as in 13:1; 17:24.

38. Possibly "entered the city, from one room to another." Keil, *Kings*, p. 188; similarly Gray, *Kings*, p. 426. He "scurries to find a safe hiding place." Walsh, *1 Kings*, p. 306.

39. The word is *khesed*. See our discussion of 2:7 and note 28 to Chapter 5.

40. So Gray, *Kings*, p. 430; Beal, *Kings*, p. 263.

41. The Hebrew does not have "And Ahab said" (ESV) at this point, leaving open the possibility that the following words were the continuation of Ben-hadad's speech. They could then mean, "And I shall release you from your vassal treaty," possibly meaning Ahab's agreement to be Ben-hadad's vassal in verse 4. Similarly Gray, *Kings*, p. 427; cf. JB. The matter at hand, however, is the release of Ben-hadad. It would sound rather absurd that the defeated king would be releasing the victor— but perhaps not impossible for an arrogant man like the king of Aram.

42. See note 6 to Chapter 28.

43. See our discussion of 13:1.

44. Strangely our text not only echoes the word "found" from 13:24, but also has, literally, "*the* lion." I doubt that is was actually the *same* lion all these years later, but the definite article does suggest that this lion was playing a familiar role.

45. The word is a reflexive form (hitpael) of the verb "to search" (*khps*, as in v. 6), suggesting the idea "to let oneself be searched for," that is, "to disguise oneself." *CHALOT*, p. 113. Cf. Saul "disguising himself" in 1 Samuel 28:8 and Ahab in 1 Kings 22:30 where the same quite rare form is used. See also Richard Coggins, "On Kings and Disguises," *JSOT* 50 (1991), pp. 55–62.

46. That is, "turned aside" as in, for example, Exodus 3:3; 1 Samuel 6:12; 12:20, 21; 1 Kings 15:5.

47. The word (*milkhamah*) has recurred through this chapter in verses 14 ("battle"), 18 ("war"), 26 ("to fight"), 29 ("battle").

48. Gray, *Kings*, p. 432. A talent (about 30 kilograms) was 3,000 shekels (a shekel was about 10 grams).

49. "Hurried" (*mhr*, piel) echoes the same word in verse 33 (ESV, "quickly"), adding to the verbal links tying together the accounts of the enacted story and the earlier experience of Ahab.

50. Other suggestions include the unlikely possibility that prophets had marks on themselves, perhaps tattoos (a practice prohibited by the Law, Leviticus 19:28). So Gray, *Kings*, p. 433. It is possible, of course, that Ahab just happened to know this particular prophet.

51. John Woodhouse, *1 Samuel: Looking for a Leader*, Preaching the Word (Wheaton, IL: Crossway, 2008), p. 261.

52. Walsh, *1 Kings*, p. 313. The description is based on the meaning of the cognate verb *sarar*, "to be stubborn."

53. Ibid., based again on the meaning of the cognate verb *za'ap*, "to rage."

Chapter Forty-Three: King Ahab Did Not Put Things Right

1. The Septuagint has the chapters in a different order. The present chapter 21 follows chapter 19 (thus grouping together the stories involving Elijah that began with chapter 17), and chapter 22 then directly follows chapter 20 (bringing together the account of the conflicts with Aram in which Elijah does not appear). The arrangement in our English versions corresponds to the Hebrew and sets the present story in the context of the series of stories that show the failure of Ahab.

2. In the Hebrew the chapter begins with the words "And it was after these things . . . ," that is, after the events of chapter 20. The ESV moves this introductory phrase to verse 2 ("And after this . . .") because the action of the story begins in verse 2.

3. Here the Hebrew word *hekal*, which was used of the "main hall" of the house of the Lord built by Solomon (ESV, "nave" or "temple") in 6:3, 5, 17, 33; 7:21, 50, appears for the first time in the Old Testament with the meaning "palace" (see also 2 Kings 20:18, the only similar use of the word in Genesis to 2 Kings). Regarding this word, see note 18 to Chapter 7.

4. There is no reason to think that "the Jezreelite" suggests that Naboth was "a representative figure, the head of an influential local family." Contra John Gray, *1 & II Kings: A Commentary*, Third, Fully Revised, Edition (London: SCM, 1977), p. 440.

5. So C. F. Keil, "1 and 2 Kings," in C. F. Keil and F. Delitzsch, *Commentary on the Old Testament*, Vol. 3 (Peabody, MA: Hendrickson Publishers, 1996), p. 191.

6. So Gray, *Kings*, p. 439.

7. Gray speculates that Jezreel "may have been the ancestral home of the Omrids, with whose collapse the place sank into insignificance." Gray, *Kings*, p. 439.

8. In the Hebrew "And after this" comes at the beginning of verse 1, making clear that "this" refers to the events of chapter 20. Cf. NIV, HCSB. See note 2.

9. Iain W. Provan, *1 & 2 Kings*, Understanding the Bible Commentary Series (Grand Rapids, MI: Baker Books, 1995), pp. 157, 158. Similarly Lissa M. Wray Beal, *1 & 2 Kings*, Apollos Old Testament Commentary, Vol. 9 (Nottingham, UK and Downers Grove, IL: Apollos, 2014), p. 274. Cf. our discussions of the same tendency in King Solomon in 9:19, 24; 10:28.

10. "The LORD forbid" represents a strong Hebrew expression that means something like, "May it be (my) profanation (in the eyes of God) if I break my oath." W. Dommershausen, "*khalal*," *TDOT* 4, p. 417.

11. Brueggemann speaks of "conflicting theories of land ownership." "Ahab has wrongly seen the land as a tradable commodity, and made an offer that must on

principle be refused." Walter Brueggemann, *1 & 2 Kings*, Smyth & Helwys Bible Commentary (Macon, GA: Smyth & Helwys, 2000), p. 257.

12. I agree with Walsh in this more literal translation, which most naturally has Ahab as the subject here. The sulking king was muttering his own version of what Naboth had said. Walsh offers the following rendering of the verse: "Resentful and sullen over what Naboth the Jezreelite had said to him, Ahab went home, muttering, 'I will not give you my ancestral inheritance.'"

Jerome T. Walsh, *1 Kings*, Berit Olam: Studies in Hebrew Narrative & Poetry (Collegeville, MN: The Liturgical Press, 1996), p. 319.

13. So, for example, Keil, *Kings*, p. 191; Provan, *Kings*, p. 158; Walsh, *1 Kings*, p. 319, note 5.

14. Similarly Walsh, *1 Kings*, p. 319, note 6.

15. Similarly Walsh, *1 Kings*, p. 319.

16. Beal suggests that "Ahab's passive pout is really masterful manipulation." Beal, *Kings*, p. 274.

17. These changes are noted similarly by Walsh, *1 Kings*, p. 320; Dale Ralph Davis, *The Wisdom and the Folly: An Exposition of the Book of First Kings* (Fearn, Ross-shire, UK: Christian Focus, 2002). p. 303, note 3.

18. See note 9 to Chapter 6.

19. See our discussions of 10:26, 29.

20. The process itself was not unusual. "Letters were usually written by a scribe or amanuensis in the name of a correspondent, who is usually depicted as speaking in the third person, and sealed in clay or wax with the seal of the sender." Gray, *Kings*, p. 440. It is the context that makes Jezebel's action significant.

21. "Elders" and "leaders" are probably two designations for the same group of people. So Walsh, *1 Kings*, p. 322. The second term (*khor*) occurs here for the first time in the Old Testament and may have the sense "freeborn." *CHALOT*, p. 115.

22. So Keil, *Kings*, p. 192.

23. So Gray, *Kings*, p. 441; Walsh, *1 Kings*, p. 322.

24. See John Woodhouse, *1 Samuel: Looking for a Leader*, Preaching the Word (Wheaton, IL: Crossway, 2008), pp. 53, 54.

25. Cf. our discussion of "Josiah by name" in 13:2.

26. This basic principle of justice was reiterated by Jesus (Matthew 18:16; John 8:17) and Paul (2 Corinthians 13:1; 1 Timothy 5:19; cf. Hebrews 10:28).

27. A curiosity of Hebrew is that the word (*brk*) that normally means "bless" can carry the opposite meaning (as here and in Job 1:5, 11; 2:5, 9; Psalm 10:3).

28. The most natural antecedent for "they" in verse 13 (and also 14) is "the worthless men." Similarly Walsh, *1 Kings*, p. 324.

29. Similarly Walsh, *1 Kings*, p. 324.

30. So Provan, *Kings*, p. 160; cf. Walsh, *1 Kings*, p. 326, note 10. Contra Beal, *Kings*, p. 275, citing 2 Samuel 16:4; Ezra 10:8; cf. Ezekiel 45:8; 46:18. These texts are not close parallels to the situation here.

31. On "the Tishbite," see our discussion of 17:1.

32. In the Old Testament "go down" usually reflects the geography accurately. Jezreel is only about 375 feet above sea level. Samaria is almost 1,340 feet above sea level. Gray, *Kings*, p. 442. However, we are not told where Elijah was when he received this word.

33. This is not the first time we have been reminded of the episode in David's life when he killed and took. He, too, was confronted by a prophet with a devastating question. See 2 Samuel 12:9. Brueggemann, *Kings*, p. 260.

34. The words "kill" (*rtskh*) and "take possession" (*yrsh*) are given their nuance and weight by the context. In other contexts these words can refer to less offensive, even innocent acts.

35. Ahab did not in fact die in the same *place* as Naboth. I take it that this was a consequence of the mitigation of the punishment we will see in verse 29. It is therefore unnecessary to attempt a harmonization of 21:19 and 22:38, although that is possible. Provan manages it by translating the relevant words of verse 19: "Instead of dogs licking up Naboth's blood, dogs will lick up your blood—yes, yours!" Provan, *Kings*, p. 160. See our discussion of 22:38b and note 26 to Chapter 46.

36. This form of this verb (*mkr* hitpael) occurs only four times (Deuteronomy 28:68; 1 Kings 21:20, 25; 2 Kings 17:17).

37. In verses 21, 22 "I" becomes the Lord.

38. "Disaster" avoids the suggestion that what God will do is morally "evil," but obscures the verbal echo of the "evil" in verse 20.

39. Contra Brueggemann: "Elijah takes liberties to offer a much more insistent and unflinching statement than the one given by Yahweh." Brueggemann, *Kings*, p. 260. See our discussion of "the word of the LORD" in the introduction to Chapter 27. Brueggemann could learn a thing or two from the widow of Zarephath: "you [Elijah] are a man of God, and . . . the word of the LORD in your mouth is truth" (17:24).

40. See our discussion of 14:10, particularly the coarse expression softened in the ESV to "every male."

41. On "the anger to which you have provoked me" see our discussion of "provoking me to anger" in 14:9.

42. My more literal translation here attempts to convey the emphasis of the Hebrew. Similarly Walsh, *1 Kings*, p. 332.

43. Here "Amorites" is a general term for the pre-Israelite population of Canaan as in Genesis 15:16; Joshua 24:15; 1 Samuel 7:14; 2 Samuel 21:2. Keil, *Kings*, p. 193.

44. The verb "dispossessed" is a form of the verb (*yrsh*) that has appeared in verses 15, 16, 18, 19 to describe what Ahab did to Naboth's vineyard.

45. Keil, *Kings*, p. 193.

Chapter Forty-Four: King Ahab Hated the Truth

1. See note 46 to Chapter 21. Again we will represent the Hebrew *aram* as Aram through this chapter.

2. This would have been toward the end of the 850s B.C. In Hebrew the verse consists of two sentences. Literally: "And they dwelt for three years. There was no war between Aram and Israel." The second sentence explains the first in terms that clearly mark a return to the international scene of 1 Kings 20.

3. See the introduction to Chapter 33.

4. There is a problem here with John Bright's chronological scheme (which we have been generally following). He has Jehoshaphat's reign beginning in 873 B.C., which is about four years *before* his date for the beginning of Ahab's reign (869 B.C.). Since there seem to be problems with every chronological scheme, I am happy to

retain Bright's table as a reasonable guide, which is, after all, more than we need for our purpose of expounding the text before us. See our discussion of 15:1, 2a.

5. "It is conventional in Hebrew to treat Jerusalem as the highest point in the land." Jerome T. Walsh, *1 Kings*, Berit Olam: Studies in Hebrew Narrative & Poetry (Collegeville, MN: The Liturgical Press, 1996), p. 343.

6. Athaliah is called "the daughter of Ahab" in 2 Kings 8:18 (therefore possibly a daughter of Jezebel) and "the daughter [ESV, granddaughter] of Omri" in 2 Kings 8:26. The harmonization in the ESV is possible, but it has also been argued that Athaliah was actually Omri's daughter and Ahab's sister. So Winfried Thiel, "Athaliah (Person)," *ABD* 1, p. 511.

7. Walter Brueggemann, *1 & 2 Kings*, Smyth & Helwys Bible Commentary (Macon, GA: Smyth & Helwys, 2000), p. 268.

8. These "servants" were the king's advisers as in 20:23 (to Ahab), 20:31 (to Ben-hadad).

9. Walsh, *1 Kings*, p. 343. Brueggemann suggests that the disputed territory is disputed still: it is the Golan Heights. Brueggemann, *Kings*, p. 267. Of course, the text before us has no direct relevance to the contemporary dispute.

10. The precise location is uncertain, but see the proposal of Map 6–4 in Currid, *Atlas*, p. 145.

11. See note 1 to Chapter 42.

12. According to Gray, it was "a key fortress dominating the approach to the heart of Israel by the eastern end of the Plain of Jezreel." John Gray, *I & II Kings: A Commentary*, Third, Fully Revised, Edition (London: SCM, 1977), p. 448.

13. "Keep quiet" in verse 3 represents a Hebrew participle suggesting an ongoing state of inactivity. The verb (*khshh* hiphil) suggests silent acquiescence or perhaps simply "doing nothing" as in Judges 18:9.

14. "[T]he stylistic polish is untranslatable. Literally, Jehoshaphat says: 'Like me, like you; like my people, like your people; like my horses, like your horses.'" Walsh, *1 Kings*, p. 343.

15. Contra Gray, *Kings*, p. 449; Walsh, *1 Kings*, p. 344.

16. The Hebrew has a particle (*na'*) here that makes this sound like a polite request rather than a command or demand.

17. Yes, this is confusing. The Hebrew word here (*'adonay*), literally "my lord," can certainly refer to Israel's God (as in 2:26; 3:10, 15; 8:53; etc.), but can also refer to any other lord and master (as in 1:2, 11, 13, 17, 18; etc.). It is not to be confused with the unambiguous name of Israel's God, Yahweh (*yhwh*), usually represented in English versions as "the LORD." The present text is further complicated by the fact that some Hebrew manuscripts do have *yhwh* at this point. However, this is probably the result of a scribe's misguided desire to make these prophets say what they should have said. Similarly Walsh, *1 Kings*, p. 345, note 3; Lissa M. Wray Beal, *1 & 2 Kings*, Apollos Old Testament Commentary, Vol. 9 (Nottingham, UK and Downers Grove, IL: Apollos, 2014), p. 281. Contra Gray, *Kings*, p. 445, note c.

18. The ambiguities of the prophets' message are noted by Walsh, *1 Kings*, p. 345; Beal, *Kings*, p. 281. Brueggemann misses this and evaluates the matter differently: "The prophets voice no more than conventional jingoistic support for royal policy. They have no critical distance from the king, and therefore they offer no serious second opinion." Brueggemann, *Kings*, p. 269.

19. The ESV implies that Jehoshaphat regarded the 400 prophets as prophets of Yahweh but wanted to hear one more such voice. The Hebrew suggests otherwise.

20. Beal seems to favor this idea, while noting the ambiguity. Beal, *Kings*, p. 284.

21. C. F. Keil, "1 and 2 Kings," in C. F. Keil and F. Delitzsch, *Commentary on the Old Testament*, Vol. 3 (Peabody, MA: Hendrickson Publishers, 1996), p. 194. Followed by Dale Ralph Davis, *The Wisdom and the Folly: An Exposition of the Book of First Kings* (Fearn, Ross-shire, UK: Christian Focus, 2002), p. 320.

22. Walsh suggests that Ahab may be "being petty in not calling him a 'prophet.'" Walsh, *1 Kings*, p. 346.

23. I have changed the word order in the ESV to reflect the Hebrew where Micaiah's name comes only at the very end of Ahab's speech.

24. Walsh thinks that "hate" is too severe, and prefers "reject." Walsh, *1 Kings*, p. 346. I see no basis, in the use of the verb (*sana'*) elsewhere or the context here, to soften the usual meaning, "hate." Other examples illustrating this include Genesis 37:4, 5, 8; 2 Samuel 13:15, 22.

25. The groundless suggestion (made by Josephus) that Micaiah was the unnamed prophet of 20:35 is rightly rejected by Keil, *Kings*, p. 194.

26. Micaiah does appear in the parallel account of the same occasion in 2 Chronicles 18.

27. Hence Gray's skepticism is unjustified: "If this incident had really concerned Ahab, Elijah, who outlived him, would surely have been introduced at this point." Gray, *Kings*, p. 449.

28. Walsh, *1 Kings*, p. 346.

29. "Threshing floor" (*goren*) may just mean an open public space. So Gray, *Kings*, p. 450.

30. The two Hebrew words are almost identical (*kena'anah* and *kena'an*). H. H. Guthrie, "Chenaanah," *IDB* 1, p. 556.

31. See note 23 to Chapter 27.

32. This was part of Moses' blessing of the people of Israel before his death. These lines applied to the tribes of Joseph, Ephraim, and Manasseh, now a large part of Ahab's kingdom.

33. "You" in verse 11 is masculine singular, presumably meaning Ahab, the initiator of this matter.

34. There was still no explicit object to the verb "will give," but naming Ramoth-gilead and predicting "triumph" takes away the ambiguity.

35. The Hebrew syntax signals that the two scenes in verses 11, 12 and 13, 14 were simultaneous. Walsh, *1 Kings*, p. 348.

36. Each sentence has a Hebrew particle (*na'*) that softens the imperative.

37. The Hebrew tense indicates that the Lord had not yet said to him what the prophet would in due course speak. Contrast the claim of "Thus the LORD has said" in verse 11. Similarly Gray, *Kings*, p. 451.

38. The italics are an attempt to reflect the emphasis in the Hebrew.

Chapter Forty-Five: King Ahab Did Not Have a Listening Heart

1. This was early in Solomon's reign that began about 961 B.C. We are now near the end of Ahab's life. He died about 850 B.C.

2. Similarly Jerome T. Walsh, *1 Kings*, Berit Olam: Studies in Hebrew Narrative & Poetry (Collegeville, MN: The Liturgical Press, 1996), p. 348.

3. The only difference is that Micaiah omitted the words "to Ramoth-gilead" from the reply in 22:12 since those words were already in Ahab's question.

4. Davis makes this point persuasively, pointing out that the verb ("make you swear") is a participle. He offers the translation: "How many times must I keep putting you on oath . . . ?" Dale Ralph Davis, *The Wisdom and the Folly: An Exposition of the Book of First Kings* (Fearn, Ross-shire, UK: Christian Focus, 2002), p. 325.

5. I must say that Gray seems insensitive to the tone of the text when he writes, "It is to the credit of the king, however, that he did not remain satisfied with this response, but looked for something deeper 'in the name' (i.e. with the authority) of Yahweh." John Gray, *I & II Kings: A Commentary*, Third, Fully Revised, Edition (London: SCM, 1977), p. 451. The narrator (in my opinion) is giving Ahab no "credit" at all.

6. Gray and others correctly recognize that Micaiah spoke (as prophets often did) in poetic verse. Gray, *Kings*, pp. 446, 451. See HCSB.

7. The image could imply the deaths of both Ahab and Jehoshaphat, but the way in which Micaiah focused his response on Ahab in verse 15b suggests that this vision was really about him.

8. The Hebrew for "master" (*'adoniym*) is grammatically plural. Again (see previous note) this could imply the deaths of both Ahab and Jehoshaphat ("These have no masters"), but the plural form of this noun is very often used when the referent is one master or lord (as in 22:6, ESV, "the Lord").

9. Similarly Davis, *Wisdom*, p. 325.

10. The Hebrew does not have Micaiah's name, but simply, "And he said." This is taken by Walsh to strengthen his impression (not mine) that this was the continuation of Micaiah's speech from verse 17, verse 18 being "merely a parenthetical interruption." Walsh, *1 Kings*, p. 350.

11. This is close to Walsh's understanding. See previous note.

12. Keil understands the text along these lines. C. F. Keil, "1 and 2 Kings," in C. F. Keil and F. Delitzsch, *Commentary on the Old Testament*, Vol. 3 (Peabody, MA: Hendrickson Publishers, 1996), p. 196.

13. See the introduction to Chapter 27.

14. "The host of heaven" "refers to heavenly beings as an organized force or army under Yahweh." Gray, *Kings*, p. 452. Cf. 18:15; 19:10; and note 23 to Chapter 37.

15. The expression behind "fall at" (*napal be*) can also mean "fall upon," that is, attack (so, for example, Joshua 11:7). There may be a deliberate double meaning here. Ahab will be fooled into attacking Ramoth-gilead and so will die. Gray, *Kings*, p. 452; Walsh, *1 Kings*, p. 351.

16. That is, to "make a 'fool' out of the king, making him incapable of seeing and doing what is necessary to avoid defeat." R. Mosis, "*pth*," *TDOT* 12, pp. 169, 170. Cf. the same verb in 2 Samuel 3:25 (ESV, "deceive"); Judges 16:5 (ESV, "seduce").

17. "I" is emphasized in the Hebrew, answering the Lord's question, "Who?" The volunteer does not just have something to *say* (like the others in verse 20). He will himself be the agent of the Lord's will. *He* will do it.

18. Contra Walsh, *1 Kings*, p. 351; Lissa M. Wray Beal, *1 & 2 Kings*, Apollos Old Testament Commentary, Vol. 9 (Nottingham, UK and Downers Grove, IL: Apollos, 2014), p. 285.

19. Gray, in my opinion, overthinks this: "This was an emanation, or extension, of the divine personality, and so may be personified. We may see here a germ of the conception of the Holy Spirit as a person of the Godhead, though at a very primitive level." Gray, *Kings*, pp. 452, 453.

20. Cf. note 20 to Chapter 37.

21. That "spirit" is explicitly distinguished from "the Spirit of the LORD" in 1 Samuel 16:14. See further John Woodhouse, *1 Samuel: Looking for a Leader*, Preaching the Word (Wheaton, IL: Crossway, 2008), pp. 294, 295, 598, note 14.

22. "Yahweh cannot be charged with deception when he clearly tells Ahab about the deception by which he is deceiving him!" Davis, *Wisdom*, p. 327.

23. The question is more difficult to understand in Hebrew than any one English translation. The NIV has, "Which way did the spirit from the LORD go when he went from me to speak to you?" (implying that Zedekiah was referring to the "spirit" Micaiah had mentioned in verse 23).

24. If you want to be more precise, Davis is helpful, taking Zedekiah's remark "as an implicit claim that he himself spoke by 'the Spirit of Yahweh' and cannot fathom how Yahweh's Spirit who moved his prophecy could so quickly leave him and inspire Micaiah with a directly opposing word." Davis, *Wisdom*, p. 328, note 10.

25. Possibly "when you go from one room to another." So Keil, *Kings*, p. 197; Gray, *Kings*, p. 446. The same phrase was used of Ben-hadad in 20:30. Cf. note 38 to Chapter 42.

26. "The explanation may be that this officer was perhaps chosen originally from among the king's sons." Roland de Vaux, *Ancient Israel: Its Life and Institutions*, trans. John McHugh (London: Darton, Longman & Todd, 1973), p. 120. De Vaux cites 2 Chronicles 28:7; Jeremiah 36:26; 38:6 as other examples of this office, which he suggests was a "police officer." Similarly Gray, *Kings*, p. 453.

27. The Hebrew is forceful: "If you indeed return . . ."

28. Contra HCSB and NIV who have "people" rather than "peoples." The Hebrew is *'ammiym* ("peoples"), the plural of *'am* ("a people").

29. Despite the slight variations in the English translation, the Hebrew sentences of Micah and Micaiah are identical.

30. I am unimpressed by commentators who dismiss the last sentence of 1 Kings 22:28 as, for example, "obviously a gloss by a late hand which wrongly considered the son of Impah identical with the prophet Micah." Gray, *Kings*, p. 447, note b. Similarly Walsh, *1 Kings*, p. 352. What is "obvious" to Gray is less so to me, particularly as the words immediately preceding the words in Micah 1:2 make it abundantly clear that Micah was not Micaiah.

31. "This invites us (at the very least) to consider the book of Micah and this story in 1 Kgs. 22 in relation to each other. It is, indeed, an interesting book to read against the background of the whole Ahab story. It looks forward to the destruction of Samaria because of idolatry and prostitution (1:2–7) and it condemns both social injustice (2:1–5) and false prophecy (2:6–11; 3:1–12)." Iain W. Provan, *1 & 2 Kings*, Understanding the Bible Commentary Series (Grand Rapids, MI: Baker Books, 1995), p. 166.

Chapter Forty-Six: King Ahab Died

1. This message was not necessarily a death sentence at the time (cf. 20:39), but in the light of the later words must now be understood as such.

2. Going up to Ramoth-gilead was not a *consequence* ("So . . .") of what preceded. It was more *despite* what had gone before.

3. A later historian will tell us that after the battle, when he returned to Jerusalem, Jehoshaphat received a stern rebuke from the prophet Jehu for helping Ahab (2 Chronicles 19:2).

4. The two verbs ("disguise" and "go") are infinitives in Hebrew and convey a certain vagueness. The sense is "To disguise oneself and to go into battle." Walsh suggests that it is "as if Ahab is mulling over his plans before turning to direct Jehoshaphat." Jerome T. Walsh, *1 Kings*, Berit Olam: Studies in Hebrew Narrative & Poetry (Collegeville, MN: The Liturgical Press, 1996), p. 354. Beal considers that it "suggests some level of unease." Lissa M. Wray Beal, *1 & 2 Kings*, Apollos Old Testament Commentary, Vol. 9 (Nottingham, UK and Downers Grove, IL: Apollos, 2014), p. 286. Similarly Keil: "probably employed here to express the anxiety that impelled Ahab to take so much trouble to ensure his own safety." C. F. Keil, "1 and 2 Kings," in C. F. Keil and F. Delitzsch, *Commentary on the Old Testament*, Vol. 3 (Peabody, MA: Hendrickson Publishers, 1996), p. 197.

5. Walsh proposes this as a possibility at this stage of the story. Walsh, *1 Kings*, p. 354.

6. See note 10 to Chapter 30.

7. Curiously the Septuagint suggests a more sinister motive in Ahab's thinking. It has "but you wear *my* robes." This reading is followed by John Gray, *I & II Kings: A Commentary*, Third, Fully Revised, Edition (London: SCM, 1977), p. 447, note d.

8. See note 46 to Chapter 21.

9. The ESV is right with "*had* commanded," suggesting that the king of Aram's command was at about the same time that Ahab proposed his disguise. The two strategies are set side by side.

10. Similarly Walsh, *1 Kings*, p. 355.

11. The Hebrew has "a man," which is even more vague than "a certain man." So Walsh, *1 Kings*, p. 356.

12. Cf. the identical expression in 2 Samuel 15:11 (ESV, "in their innocence").

13. Similarly Walsh, *1 Kings*, p. 356, note 8.

14. The Hebrew word (*makhaneh*) usually means "camp," but the context indicates that he was referring to the fighting. Walsh reads more into this, namely that Ahab was so disoriented by the shock of his wound that he did not know where he was. Walsh, *1 Kings*, p. 356.

15. So Keil, *Kings*, p. 198.

16. "Ahab stayed in his chariot, propped up because he would not quit." Walter Brueggemann, *1 & 2 Kings*, Smyth & Helwys Bible Commentary (Macon, GA: Smyth & Helwys, 2000), p. 275.

17. So Walsh, *1 Kings*, p. 356; similarly Gray, *Kings*, p. 455. Contra Keil: "that he might not dishearten his soldiers." Keil, *Kings*, p. 198.

18. As it seems in Psalm 17:1; 61:1; 88:2; 106:44; 119:169; 142:6; Jeremiah 7:16; 11:14; 14:12.

19. This sense can be seen in the ESV renderings of *rinnah*: "sing" or "sing-ing" in 2 Chronicles 20:22; Psalm 105:43; Isaiah 14:7; 35:10; 44:23; 49:13; 51:11; 54:1; 55:12; Zephaniah 3:17; "rejoice" in Isaiah 43:14; "shout(s) of joy" in Isaiah 48:20; Psalm 126:2, 5, 6; "joy" in Psalm 30:5; 47:1; "glad shouts" in Psalm 42:4; "songs of joy" in Psalm 107:22; "glad songs" in Psalm 118:15; and "shouts of glad-ness" in Proverbs 11:10. See J. Hausmann, "*ranan*," *TDOT* 13, pp. 515–22.

20. Similarly Walsh, *1 Kings*, p. 357.

21. Literally, "he," probably the chariot driver mentioned in verse 34.

22. The Hebrew does not say that the prostitutes washed *in Ahab's blood* (as the ESV might suggest), but (in a circumstantial clause) simply notes that they "washed" or "bathed" (Hebrew *rakhats*, as in Exodus 2:5; 2 Samuel 11:2, 8), presumably in the pool where the chariot was being rinsed off (Hebrew *shatap*, as in Leviticus 6:28; 15:12). Similarly Keil, *Kings*, p. 199. Contra Gwilym H. Jones, *1 and 2 Kings*, Vol. 2, New Century Bible Commentary (Grand Rapids, MI and London: Eerdmans and Marshall, Morgan & Scott, 1984), p. 372.

23. W. L. Reed, "Pool," *IDB* 3, pp. 842, 843. It is "likely to have been some catchment area used for washing clothes and watering of animals outside of the wall of the citadel." Gray, *Kings*, pp. 455, 456.

24. Keil, *Kings*, p. 199.

25. On prostitutes in the Bible, see our discussion of 3:16.

26. Therefore Davis's attempt at harmonizing seems to me unnecessary: "If . . . the pool of Samaria was outside that city . . . , we could understand the 'place' of 21:19 as indicating not a precise but a generic location. That is, dogs would also lick up Ahab's blood outside of town (not necessarily Jezreel)." Dale Ralph Davis, *The Wisdom and the Folly: An Exposition of the Book of First Kings* (Fearn, Ross-shire, UK: Christian Focus, 2002), p. 332. Walsh seems to think (mistakenly in my opinion) that every detail of the fulfillment must have been included in the word of prophecy: "Somewhere, the narrator tells us, there was a prophetic word spoken against Ahab about prostitutes bathing in his blood, even though we have not heard the story." Walsh, *1 Kings*, p. 358. See also note 35 to Chapter 43.

27. So Gray, *Kings*, p. 456.

28. The year was about 850 B.C.

Chapter Forty-Seven: The Hope of the World and the Legacy of King Ahab

1. In the Hebrew Bible the eleven books from Genesis to 2 Kings present an ob-viously continuous and coherent narrative. (Ruth is placed in another section of the Hebrew canon.) The beginning of each book takes up where the previous one ended. At the same time each book has its own character, usually with an obvious and sig-nificant beginning and end. This is more subtle in the last four books (1 Samuel to 2 Kings), but in my opinion there is significance in 1 Samuel ending with the death of Saul, 2 Samuel ending with the carefully crafted epilogue of chapters 21—24, and 1 Kings ending with the death of Ahab and the passage before us now.

2. Jehoshaphat's reign was about 873–849 B.C. according to John Bright's scheme, although there are problems with lining up Bright's dates for Jehoshaphat and Ahab (869–850 B.C.) with the Biblical statements. See our discussion of 15:1, 2a and note 1 to the Introduction; also note 4 to Chapter 44.

3. See also our discussion of 14:21b.

4. See our discussion of 15:2b and 15:13 and note 27 to Chapter 32.

5. Hebrew *'ak*; see note 41 to Chapter 20.

6. A later historian will tell of the prophetic rebuke Jehoshaphat received for his friendly dealings with Ahab (see 2 Chronicles 19:2) and also with his son Ahaziah (2 Chronicles 20:37). See further our discussion of 22:2.

7. See our discussion of 14:24a and note 14 to Chapter 31.

8. Hebrew, *ntsb* niphal participle.

9. So Iain W. Provan, *1 & 2 Kings*, Understanding the Bible Commentary Series (Grand Rapids, MI: Baker Books, 1995), pp. 169, 170.

10. So Jerome T. Walsh, *1 Kings*, Berit Olam: Studies in Hebrew Narrative & Poetry (Collegeville, MN: The Liturgical Press, 1996), p. 366.

11. Similarly Dale Ralph Davis, *The Wisdom and the Folly: An Exposition of the Book of First Kings* (Fearn, Ross-shire, UK: Christian Focus, 2002), p. 337; Lissa M. Wray Beal, *1 & 2 Kings*, Apollos Old Testament Commentary, Vol. 9 (Nottingham, UK and Downers Grove, IL: Apollos, 2014), p. 287. Note that the later historian records the words of a prophet who made it clear that the involvement of Ahaziah was the reason that the Lord destroyed Jehoshaphat's ships (2 Chronicles 20:37).

12. The years of Ahaziah's reign were about 850–849 B.C.

Scripture Index

1 Kings

2 Kings

Proverbs

Ecclesiastes

Lamentations

Ezekiel

General Index

Index of Sermon
Illustrations

The violence of power politics is exemplified during Asa's reign in the northern kingdom. Comparing Asa's reign and the violence during his tenure can give us a crucial perspective on the politics of power in our contemporary world, 441–43

Prayer

The Apostle Paul on the difficulty of praying: We may have doubts about God answering prayer or our difficulty may be due to our own uncertainty, weak faith, or unbelief, 245–46

The power of prayer exists because God is all powerful and answers prayer. The common misunderstanding we make is to think that prayer is a way to *have my will done*. But the perfect prayer of faith is "Your will be done . . . not as I will, but as you will," 525–26

Problems Facing Our World Today

Although the problems facing the world today are complicated and distressing (terrorism, the financial crisis, global warming and climate change), Christians can be positive about the future because faith brings confidence, 111–12, 123

The Bible presents a clear perspective on the disintegration and extraordinary confusion of our contemporary times, 177

Religion

Religion cannot be man-made nor used for political gain. The example of Jeroboam's attempt at modifying religion to make it useful to him and the nation was a natural inclination, but we are deceived if we do not follow the Word of the Lord in the practice of our faith, 367–70

Questions concerning religion we must address include "Is religion good for society as a whole"? "Is religion simply a matter of taste or an aspect of culture?" "How is religion viewed in multicultural societies," 507–8

There exists a foolishness and empty reality concerning religion. This was on display at

Mount Carmel when Elijah challenged the prophets of Baal. The events at Mount Carmel can teach us much about the ridiculousness of religion in some instances, 517

The Seriousness of Life

Young persons are often impulsive and do not take life seriously. But the failures of Solomon remind us that older persons often do the same. We must remember that not taking life seriously may have serious consequences, 319–20, 553

Trust

To trust we must see Jesus as he truly is with all his riches, wisdom, and goodness just as the Queen of Sheba's saw the riches of Solomon's kingdom and his personal goodness and wisdom, 295

Truth

The Bible teaches us not every truth about everything but rather the essential and most important truths about everything, 205–6

We live in the so-called "post-truth" world but a world in which we still often profoundly disagree about what is true and of the means wherein we can discern the truth. We view the world through the distortion of our sinfulness which twists and distorts the truth. We must turn to the Bible for guidance for the truth about God and Jesus, 589–90

Who Is God?

Every society in every age has developed answers to this question including atheists and theoretical physicists. Contemporary theories to answer this question are enticing, but we must turn to the Bible for accurate answers, 465–66

In *Your God Is Too Small*, J. B. Phillips raises that exact question. The answer is not that God is too small but that our understanding of God, confidence in him, and love for him may not be "big enough for modern needs," 473–74

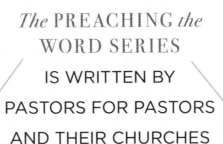

The PREACHING *the*
WORD SERIES

IS WRITTEN BY

PASTORS FOR PASTORS

AND THEIR CHURCHES